It Came From God

Commentary on
The Doctrine and Covenants

Volume 2

by

Monte S. Nyman

Distributed by:

Granite Publishing and Distribution, LLC
868 North 1430 West • Orem, Utah 84057
(801) 229-9023 • Toll Free (800) 574-5779 • Fax (801) 229-1924
www.granitepublishing.biz

Page Layout & Design by Myrna Varga
Cover Design by Steve Gray

ISBN: 978-1-59936-039-3
Library of Congress Control Number: 2009921728

Printed in the United States of America
First Printing, June 2009
1 3 5 7 9 10 8 6 4 2

It Came From God

Commentary on
The Doctrine and Covenants

Contents

Introduction 1

Explanation of the Format 2

Chapter

1 Proclaim My Gospel
   Sections 71; 72:1-8; 73; 75 5

2 The Plainest Book Written
   Sections 74; 77; 91; 130:4-11 21

3 Six Visions of Eternity
   Section 76 37

4 More on the Law of Consecration
   Sections 72:9–26; 78; 82; 83, 92 75

5 The Oath and Covenant of the Priesthood
   Section 84 95

6 Ye Are of Israel
   Sections 85–86 127

7 Wars Upon All Nations
   Sections 87; 88:87-116; 130:12–13 139

8 The Olive Leaf
   Section 88:1-86; 117-141 157

9 The Weakest of All Saints
   Section 89 191

10 The First Presidency
   Sections 81; 90 203

11 Know How and What You Worship
    Section 93 217

12 Zion Shall Be Great and Terrible
    Sections 94–97 237

13 Concerning the Laws of the Land
    Sections 98; 99; 134 257

14 The Lord's Jewels
    Sections 100–101 281

15 The Constitution of the High Council
    Sections 102; 107:76, 81-84 309

16 When Will Zion Be Redeemed?
    Sections 103; 105 325

17 The Law of Tithing
    Sections 104; 119–120 351

18 Even A Great Revelation
    Section 106–108 371

19 The Keys of This Dispensation
    Section 109–110 401

20 Truth Will Prevail
    Section 112; 114; 118 421

21 The Destinies of All Nations
    Sections 111; 115–117 435

22 Prayer and Prophecies
    Sections 121–123 453

23 Proclamation to the World
    Sections 124–126 475

24 Baptisms For the Dead
    Sections 127–130 507

25 The New and Everlasting Covenant of Marriage
    Sections 131–132 529

26 The Appendix
    Section 133 561

27 Praise to the Man
   Sections 113; 135 583

28 Brigham Young Colonizer
   Section 126; Official Declaration—1 & 2 595

29 The Life Beyond
   Sections 137– 138 609

Epilogue 631

Abbreviations used in this Book 635

Scripture Index 637

Topical Index 663

Introduction

Volume 1, *More Precious Than Gold*, covered sections 1–70 of the Doctrine and Covenants. The title of volume 2, this work, covering sections 71–138, is *It Came From God*. The title is taken from a statement of the Prophet Joseph Smith after recording what is known as "The Vision," Doctrine and Covenants 76:

> Nothing could be more pleasing to the Saints upon the order of the kingdom of the Lord, than the light which burst upon the world through the foregoing vision. Every law, every commandment, every promise, every truth, and every point touching the destiny of man, from Genesis to Revelation, where the purity of the scriptures remain unsullied by the folly of men, go to show thee perfection of the theory (of different degrees of glory in the future life) and witness the fact that the document is a transcript from the record of the eternal world. The sublimity of the ideas; the purity of the language; the scope for action; the continued duration for completion, in order that the heirs of salvation may confess the Lord and bow the knee; the rewards of for faithfulness, and the punishments for sins, are so much beyond the narrow-mindedness of men, that every man is constrained to exclaim; *"It came from God."* [*History of the Church*, 1:252–253 (February 1832)]

Since many other revelations in the Doctrine and Covenants could draw the same exclamation, for perhaps other reasons, it seemed a fitting title for the entire book. Coincidentally, this title is supported from the description of the book from the fifteenth President and Prophet of the Church, Gordon B. Hinckley:

> The Doctrine and Covenants is unique among our books of scripture. It is the constitution of the Church. While the Doctrine and Covenants includes writings and statements of various origins, it is primarily a book of revelation given through the Prophet of this dispensation [It came from God].

> These revelations open with a thundering declaration of the encom-

passing purposes of God in the restoration of His great latter-day work: (quotes D&C 1:1–2)

From that majestic opening there unfolds a wondrous doctrinal panorama that comes from the fountain of eternal truth. Some is direct revelation, with the Lord dictating to His Prophet. Some is the language of Joseph Smith, written or spoken as he was moved upon by the Holy Ghost. Also included is the narrative of events that occurred in various circumstances. All brought together, they constitute in very substantial measure the doctrine and the practices of The Church of Jesus Christ of Latter-day Saints.

I look with wonder at the farm boy of Palmyra. He had very little of schoolboy education. He knew little of the classroom. His opportunity for reading was severely restricted. But as an instrument in the hands of the Almighty, he spoke words that have become the law and the testimony of this great, vital work. The Doctrine and Covenants is a conduit for the expressions of the Lord to His people [It came from God]. *Teachings of Gordon B. Hinckley* (1997), 163–164]

EXPLANATION OF THE FORMAT

The same format is followed for each chapter of the book. The historical setting of when the revelation was received is given in the beginning paragraphs for each of the sections discussed therein. This brief synopsis is taken primarily from Prophet Joseph Smith's *History of the Church*, abbreviated as *HC*.

The next section, the "Introduction," is designed to be a starting point for the reader as he or she begins to study the chapter. For a teacher, it is an attention getter to focus the students on the subject for that class period.

The third section, an outline of the revelations, is intended to give a framework for a deeper study. Some readers may wish to skip, or skim, this section of the chapter, but it seems helpful for many to get the full content of the revelation. Too often we just pick out a few verses and use as a topical point without seeing the context of those verses, and the overall message of the revelation.

In the "Notes and Commentary" section, segments of the text of the revelation are quoted, and followed by comments, cross references, and explanations for a better understanding of the message of those verses.

The last section is a selection of quotations from various presidents of the Church, Apostles and other General Authorities. These quotations are not all inclusive, but were selected to verify and clarify the concepts and teachings referred to within the chapter. There is some duplication of quotations, other materials, and references in the chapters that follow.

This duplication is because the material also applies to other sections of the Doctrine and Covenants, and also so that the reader will not have to turn back to previous pages while reading.

Chapter One

Proclaim My Gospel

D&C 71; 72:1–8; 73, 75, 79, 80

DOCTRINE AND COVENANTS 71

*H*istorical Setting: "After Oliver Cowdery and John Whitmer had departed for Jackson County, Missouri, I resumed the translation of the Scriptures, and continued to labor in this branch of my calling with Elder Sidney Rigdon as my scribe, until I received [Doctrine and Covenants 71]" (*HC*, 1:238).

The translation work "was temporarily laid aside so as to enable them to fulfil the instructions given [therein]. The brethren were to go forth to preach in order to allay the unfriendly feelings that had developed against the Church as a result of the publication of some newspaper articles by Ezra Boothe, who had apostatized" (D&C 71, heading).

SECTION 71 • OUTLINE

➤ 71:1–6 It is necessary for Joseph and Sidney to proclaim the gospel and expound the mysteries out of the scriptures as the spirit is given.

    a. Proclaim unto the regions round about and in the Church also (v. 2).

    b. This is a mission for a season to prepare for the command-ments and revelations that are to come (vv. 3–4).

    c. It is wisdom for those who read to understand that they may receive more abundantly (vv. 5–6).

➤ 71:7–11   Confound your enemies, call on them to meet you in public and in private.

    a. Let them bring forth their strong reasons against the Lord (v. 8).

    b. No weapon that is formed against you shall prosper (v. 9).

    c. Any man who lifts his voice against you shall be confounded in the Lord's due time (v. 10).

    d. Keep my commandments, they are true and faithful (v. 11).

Introduction

President Ezra Taft Benson declared: "Not all truths are of equal value, nor are all scriptures of the same worth" (Conference Report, October 1984, 6). President Benson was speaking of the greater value of the Book of Mormon, but the sections we are studying in this first chapter also could relate to his remarks. Some of the greatest revelations of the Restoration are in future revelations (i.e., 76, 84, 88, 132, and others); the revelations studied here are paled by those great ones. However, every revelation was important at the time it was given. To appreciate the value of each revelation, one must understand the conditions that brought it forth. That is why the historical background of each revelation is given in this book.

TEXT AND COMMENTARY

71:1–6 • Expound the Scriptures

1 Behold, thus saith the Lord unto you my servants Joseph Smith, Jun., and Sidney Rigdon, that the time has verily come that it is necessary and expedient in me that you should open your mouths in proclaiming my gospel, the things of the kingdom, expounding the mysteries thereof out of the scriptures, according to that portion of Spirit and power which shall be given unto you, even as I will.

2 Verily I say unto you, proclaim unto the world in the regions round about, and in the church also, for the space of a season, even until it shall be made known unto you.

3 Verily this is a mission for a season, which I give unto you.

4 Wherefore, labor ye in my vineyard. Call upon the inhabitants of

the earth, and bear record, and prepare the way for the commandments and revelations which are to come.

5 Now, behold this is wisdom; whoso readeth, let him understand and receive also;

6 For unto him that receiveth it shall be given more abundantly, even power.

Lisa Johnson, wife of John Johnson from Hiram, Ohio went with Ezra Boothe (their minister) and his wife, and some other citizens of Hiram, to visit Joseph Smith at Kirtland.

> Mrs. Johnson had been afflicted for some time with a lame arm, and was not at the time of the visit able to lift her arm above her head. . . . Some one said, 'Here is Mrs. Johnson with a lame arm; has God given any power to men now on earth to cure her?' A few minutes later, when the conversation had turned in another direction, Smith rose, and walking across the room, taking Mrs. Johnson by the hand said in the most solemn and impressive manner: 'Woman, in the name of the Lord Jesus Christ I command thee to be whole,' and immediately left the room. . . . Mrs Johnson at once lifted it up with ease, and on her return the next day she was able to do her washing without difficulty or pain. [*HC,* 1:215–216; footnote; taken from *Hayden's History of the Disciples* (a Campbellite work), 250–251]

> [Ezra Boothe] had been a Methodist minister for some time previous to his embracing the fulness of the gospel. . . . He turned away . . . became an apostate, and wrote a series of letters, which, by their coloring, falsity, and vain calculations to overthrow the work of the Lord, exposed his weakness, wickedness and folly, and left him a monument of his own shame, for the world to wonder at. [*HC,* 1:215–217]

Joseph and Sidney's mission at this time (D&C 71:3) was to counter the effects of the letters. Ezra Boothe was not the first apostate of the Church, but was the first to publish against the Church. At that time, it was apparently critical to respond to these letters. Today such things would probably be ignored since the Church is now firmly established. Some of those promised revelation—for which the mission was to prepare the people to receive (v. 4)—would be the great ones mentioned above. However, there are still many promised revelations yet to come forth. The sealed portion of the Book of Mormon plates (see 2 Nephi 27:8, 10–11), other Book of Mormon records (see 3 Nephi 26:9), and a more complete record of the Revelation of John the Beloved (see Ether 4:16) are three of many records promised. Mormon was told that when his abridged record was believed, "then shall the greater things be made manifest" (3 Nephi 26:9). Obviously, we are not yet using the Book of Mormon as extensively as we should.

71:7–11 • No Weapon Shall Prosper

7 Wherefore, confound your enemies; call upon them to meet you both in public and in private; and inasmuch as ye are faithful their shame shall be made manifest.

8 Wherefore, let them bring forth their strong reasons against the Lord.

9 Verily, thus saith the Lord unto you—there is no weapon that is formed against you shall prosper;

10 And if any man lift his voice against you he shall be confounded in mine own due time.

11 Wherefore, keep my commandments; they are true and faithful. Even so. Amen.

The current policy of the Church is to not engage in public debates as Joseph and Sidney were called to do (v. 7). However, we do point out the correct position of the Church when it is necessary, as determined by the leaders of the Church (see Elder Dallin H. Oaks in "General Authority Quotes," end of chapter). When it is expedient to counter an attack upon the Church, the Lord has told us to expound the mysteries thereof "out of the scriptures" (D&C 71:1).

As the Lord points out in this revelation, those who attack the Church are really attacking him (v. 8). He then repeats what he told the Old Testament prophet Isaiah: "no weapon that is formed against you will prosper" (v. 9; Isaiah 54:17; 3 Nephi 22:17). The Lord sometimes waits for a time to allow justice and judgment to come upon the wicked (see Alma 60:13). Thus, the "due time" of the Lord will come (D&C 71:10).

DOCTRINE AND COVENANTS 72

Historical Setting: "Knowing now the mind of the Lord, that the time had come that the Gospel should be proclaimed in power and demonstration to the world, from the Scriptures, reasoning with men as in days of old, I took a journey to Kirtland [from Hiram], in company with Elder Sidney Rigdon on the 3rd day of December [1831], to fulfill the above revelation [D&C 71]. On the 4th several of the Elders and members assembled together to learn their duty, and for edification, and after some time had been spent in conversing about our temporal and spiritual welfare, I received [Doctrine and Covenants 72]" (*HC,* 1:239)

SECTION 72 • OUTLINE

➤ 72:1–8   Listen to the voice of the Lord, the high priests of the church assembled, to whom have the kingdom and the power been given.

      a.   It is expedient for a bishop to be appointed in this part of the vineyard (v. 2).

      b.   Every steward is required to account for his stewardship both in time and in eternity (v. 3).

      c.   The faithful and wise in time is accounted worthy to inherit the mansions prepared by the Father (v. 4).

      d.   The elders shall render an account of their stewardship to the bishop (v. 5).

      e.   These records shall be handed over to the bishop in Zion (v. 6).

      f.   The bishop's duties shall be known by commandment and the voice of the conference (v. 7).

      g.   Newel K. Whitney shall be appointed and ordained unto this power (v. 8).

Note: ➤ 72:9–26 The duties of the bishop are discussed in chapter 4 of this work.

TEXT AND COMMENTARY

D&C 72:1–8 • Expedient for a Bishop to be Appointed

1 Hearken, and listen to the voice of the Lord, O ye who have assembled yourselves together, who are the high priests of my church, to whom the kingdom and power have been given.

2 For verily thus saith the Lord, it is expedient in me for a bishop to be appointed unto you, or of you, unto the church in this part of the Lord's vineyard.

3 And verily in this thing ye have done wisely, for it is required of the Lord, at the hand of every steward, to render an account of his stewardship, both in time and in eternity.

4 For he who is faithful and wise in time is accounted worthy to inherit the mansions prepared for him of my Father.

5 Verily I say unto you, the elders of the church in this part of my vineyard shall render an account of their stewardship unto the bishop, who shall be appointed of me in this part of my vineyard.

6 These things shall be had on record, to be handed over unto the bishop in Zion.

7 And the duty of the bishop shall be made known by the commandments which have been given, and the voice of the conference.

8 And now, verily I say unto you, my servant Newel K. Whitney is the man who shall be appointed and ordained unto this power. This is the will of the Lord your God, your Redeemer. Even so. Amen.

In accordance with the revelation given a few days earlier (see D&C 71), Joseph is given another revelation directing him to appoint a bishop in Kirtland (see D&C 72:2). This appointment was also in accordance with a previous revelation. In November 1831, the Lord had told four elders, through the Prophet Joseph, that "in the due time of the Lord, other bishops [are] to be set apart unto the church" (D&C 68:14). The requirement for every steward to "render an account" (D&C 72:3) in time was to be given unto the bishop (v. 5). The account given in eternity would be unto the Lord (v. 3). The faithful and wise stewards in time would inherit a mansion in eternity prepared by the Father for him (v. 4). This promise was also given previously (see D&C 59:2; see also John 14:2). The bishop in Kirtland was to be accountable to the bishop in Zion (see D&C 72:6), according to the directions he was given in the revelations and in the conferences (v. 7). Newel K. Whitney was to be appointed and ordained to the office of bishop in Kirtland (v. 8).

DOCTRINE AND COVENANTS 73

*H*istorical Setting:

From this time until the 8th or 10th of January, 1832, myself and Elder Rigdon continued to preach in Shalersville, Ravenna, and other places, setting forth the truth, vindicating the cause of our Redeemer; showing that the day of vengeance was coming upon this generation like a thief in the night. And that prejudice, blindness and darkness filled the minds of many, and caused them to persecute the true Church, and reject the true light; by which means we did much towards allaying the excited feelings which were growing out of the scandalous letters then being published in the *Ohio Star,* at Ravenna, by the afore-mentioned apostate, Ezra Boothe [D&C 71]. On the 10th of January, I received [Doctrine and Covenants 73] making known the will of the Lord concerning the elders of the Church until the convening of the next conference. [*HC,* 1:241]

SECTION 73 • OUTLINE

➤ 73:1–6   It is expedient for the elders to continue to preach until the next conference when their several missions shall be made known.

     a.   Joseph and Sidney are to translate again, and preach as it is practicable (vv. 3–4).

     b.   Let this be a pattern to the elders until further knowledge is given (vv. 5–6).

TEXT AND COMMENTARY

D&C 73:1–6 • Continue to Preach and Exhort the Church

1 FOR verily, thus saith the Lord, it is expedient in me that they should continue preaching the gospel, and in exhortation to the churches in the regions round about, until conference;

2 And then, behold, it shall be made known unto them, by the voice of the conference, their several missions.

3 Now, verily I say unto you my servants, Joseph Smith, Jun., and Sidney Rigdon, saith the Lord, it is expedient to translate again;

4 And, inasmuch as it is practicable, to preach in the regions round about until conference; and after that it is expedient to continue the work of translation until it be finished.

5 And let this be a pattern unto the elders until further knowledge, even as it is written.

6 Now I give no more unto you at this time. Gird up your loins and be sober. Even so. Amen.

These verses are self-explanatory. The next conference was to be held on January 25, 1832, so the instructions herein were for the next two weeks. The Lord seems anxious to get the translation of the Bible to His Saints.

DOCTRINE AND COVENANTS 75

*H*istorical Setting:

A few days before the conference was to commence in Amherst, Lorain County, I started with the Elders that lived in my own vicinity, and arrived in good time. At this conference much harmony prevailed, and considerable business was done to advance the kingdom, and promulgate the Gospel to the inhabitants of the surrounding country. The Elders seemed anxious for me to inquire of the Lord that they might know His will, or learn what would be most pleasing to Him for them to do, in order to bring men to a sense of their condition; for, as it was written, all men have gone out of the way, so that none doeth good, no, not one. I inquired and received [D&C 75]. Footnote. The chief item of interest connected with the Amherst conference held on the 25th of January, 1832, is the fact that it was here that the Prophet Joseph was sustained and ordained as President of the High Priesthood. [*HC*, 1:242–243]

SECTION 75 • OUTLINE

➤ 75:1–5   Alpha and Omega speaks to those who have given their names to proclaim my gospel and prune my vineyard.

a. Do not tarry or be idle but labor with your might (v. 3).

b. Proclaim the truth according to the revelations and commandments (v. 4).

c.   The faithful will be crowned with glory, and immortality and eternal life (v. 5).

➤ 75:6–12   William E. McLellin and Luke Johnson are to go into the south countries.

a.   Brother McLellin is chastened and forgiven for murmuring in his heart (vv. 7–8).

b.   They are to call on the Lord's name for the Comforter, and pray that the Lord will be with them (vv. 10–11).

➤ 75:13–17   Orson Hyde and Samuel Smith are to go into the eastern countries and proclaim these things. If faithful, the Lord will be with them.

a.   Lyman Johnson and Orson Pratt are to go to the eastern countries (v. 14).

b.   Asa Dodds and Calves Wilson are to go to the western countries (vv. 15–16).

c.   Major Ashley and Burr Riggs are to go into the south country (v. 17).

➤ 75:18–22   All are to go from house to house, from village to village, and from city to city.

a.   Whatever house that receives you leave a blessing (v. 19).

b.   Whatever house receives you not, shake off the dust of your feet, as a testimony against them (v. 20).

c.   In the day of judgment, you shall judge those houses and condemn them, and it shall be more tolerable for the heathen than for them (vv. 21–22).

d.   Be faithful, you shall overcome all things and be lifted up at the last day (v. 22).

➤ 75:23–36   It is the duty of the church to assist the families of those called to proclaim the gospel to the world.

a.   The elders are to obtain places for their families (v. 25).

b.   Those who can obtain places and support, do fail to go into the world (v. 26).

c.   Ask and receive, knock and the Comforter will make known where to go (v. 27).

    d.   He who provides for his own family shall in nowise lose his crown (v. 28).

    e.   Be diligent in all things, the idler shall not have place in the church (v. 29).

    f.   Fourteen other elders are called to be united in the ministry (vv. 30–36).

TEXT AND COMMENTARY

D&C 75:1–5 • Lift Up Your Voices as the Sound of a Trump

1 Verily, verily, I say unto you, I who speak even by the voice of my Spirit, even Alpha and Omega, your Lord and your God—

2 Hearken, O ye who have given your names to go forth to proclaim my gospel, and to prune my vineyard.

3 Behold, I say unto you that it is my will that you should go forth and not tarry, neither be idle but labor with your might—

4 Lifting up your voices as with the sound of a trump, proclaiming the truth according to the revelations and commandments which I have given you.

5 And thus, if ye are faithful ye shall be laden with many sheaves, and crowned with honor, and glory, and immortality, and eternal life.

The Lord expects his missionaries to work. He had previously commanded that they not be idle (v. 2; see also D&C 60:13). He had also instructed them to teach what he had revealed (v. 4; see D&C 49:4). The promised blessings were also stated before (v. 5; see D&C 31:3; 33:9; 66:12).

D&C 75:12 • Murmurings of the Heart

6 Therefore, verily I say unto my servant William E. McLellin, I revoke the commission which I gave unto him to go unto the eastern countries;

7 And I give unto him a new commission and a new commandment, in the which I, the Lord, chasten him for the murmurings of his heart;

8 And he sinned; nevertheless, I forgive him and say unto him again, Go ye into the south countries.

9 And let my servant Luke Johnson go with him, and proclaim the

things which I have commanded them—

10 Calling on the name of the Lord for the Comforter, which shall teach them all things that are expedient for them—

11 Praying always that they faint not; and inasmuch as they do this, I will be with them even unto the end.

12 Behold, this is the will of the Lord your God concerning you. Even so. Amen.

As he previously said: "I the Lord command and revoke" (D&C 56:4; 75:6). Brother McLellin had been murmuring in his heart over his previous call to the eastern countries (v. 6). He had apparently been tarrying as well (see D&C 75:3). His call was on November the 12th and he had not gone yet, and so the Lord changed his call to the south countries (v. 8; see D&C 68:7). The Lord did chasten him because He loved him (v. 7; see D&C 95:1; Hebrews 12:6), and He forgave him and gave him another opportunity to serve (v. 8). To be successful, He reminded him of the basic formula for missionaries; obtain the Spirit, and pray for the Lord to be with you (vv. 10–11).

D&C 75:13–22 • Go from House to House

13 And again, verily thus saith the Lord, let my servant Orson Hyde and my servant Samuel H. Smith take their journey into the eastern countries, and proclaim the things which I have commanded them; and inasmuch as they are faithful, lo, I will be with them even unto the end.

14 And again, verily I say unto my servant Lyman Johnson, and unto my servant Orson Pratt, they shall also take their journey into the eastern countries; and behold, and lo, I am with them also, even unto the end.

15 And again, I say unto my servant Asa Dodds, and unto my servant Calves Wilson, that they also shall take their journey unto the western countries, and proclaim my gospel, even as I have commanded them.

16 And he who is faithful shall overcome all things, and shall be lifted up at the last day.

17 And again, I say unto my servant Major N. Ashley, and my servant Burr Riggs, let them take their journey also into the south country.

18 Yea, let all those take their journey, as I have commanded them, going from house to house, and from village to village, and from city to city.

19 And in whatsoever house ye enter, and they receive you, leave your blessing upon that house.

20 And in whatsoever house ye enter, and they receive you not, ye shall depart speedily from that house, and shake off the dust of your feet as a testimony against them.

21 And you shall be filled with joy and gladness; and know this, that in the day of judgment you shall be judges of that house, and condemn them;

22 And it shall be more tolerable for the heathen in the day of judgment, than for that house; therefore, gird up your loins and be faithful, and ye shall overcome all things, and be lifted up at the last day. Even so. Amen.

The instructions given to the eight missionaries are verified in the New Testament. They were called to go two by two, and from house to house, and city to city (vv. 13–18; compare Luke 8:1; 10:1; Acts 20:20).[1] Dusting off of the feet as a testimony against those who reject them, and it being more tolerable for the heathen in the day of judgment (D&C 75:19–20, 22), was given to the Jerusalem Twelve (Matthew 10:14–15). However, the missionaries must use caution, and remember that this is symbolic, and not do it as a vengeance against the people. It was done after they had left, and to be done speedily. This suggests that the action was in secret, and was more in the context of moving on to the next house. As in all missionary acts, it would only be done when moved upon by the Spirit. The door should be left open for future missionaries to call when the house may be more receptive. The promise of being filled with joy and gladness suggests that the missionaries will be consoled by knowing they have done as the Lord wanted, to give every house an opportunity to hear the message of the Restoration. A successful mission is based on how hard you have worked, not on the number of baptisms. The missionaries being judges of that house should not be interpreted to mean they will give a sentence, but will stand as witnesses that they did give that house an opportunity to receive the gospel (D&C 75:21). The Lord "employeth no servant" at the judgment bar, but will have his witnesses to confirm his sentence to a glory (see 2 Nephi 9:41; Mormon 3:18–21;

---

[1] Although Luke 10:7 says; "go not from house to house," the beginning of the verse says: "In the same house remain, eating" . . . instructing them to keep instructing that house as long as they are receptive. See also Matthew 10:11.

D&C 29:12). Those who are faithful witnesses, or missionaries, will be judged with the same degree of righteousness as they have judged (see JST, Matthew 7:2).

D&C 75:23–29 • Support those Who Proclaim the Gospel

23 And again, thus saith the Lord unto you, O ye elders of my church, who have given your names that you might know his will concerning you—

24 Behold, I say unto you, that it is the duty of the church to assist in supporting the families of those, and also to support the families of those who are called and must needs be sent unto the world to proclaim the gospel unto the world.

25 Wherefore, I, the Lord, give unto you this commandment, that ye obtain places for your families, inasmuch as your brethren are willing to open their hearts.

26 And let all such as can obtain places for their families, and support of the church for them, not fail to go into the world, whether to the east or to the west, or to the north, or to the south.

27 Let them ask and they shall receive, knock and it shall be opened unto them, and be made known from on high, even by the Comforter, whither they shall go.

28 And again, verily I say unto you, that every man who is obliged to provide for his own family, let him provide, and he shall in nowise lose his crown; and let him labor in the church.

29 Let every man be diligent in all things. And the idler shall not have place in the church, except he repent and mend his ways.

"He who is appointed to administer spiritual things [a missionary], the same is worthy of his hire" (D&C 70:12). Therefore, the duty of the Church is to assist the families of those who go out to proclaim the gospel (D&C 75:24). However, the individual is expected to do all he can to obtain comfort and support for the family before leaving (v. 25). A person should not make arrangements for assistance, and then not go (v. 26). As they go, the Lord will bless His missionaries both in this life and in the world to come. He will guide them by the Comforter in their mission if they will ask, and will bless them temporally to provide for their family. They will "in nowise lose their eternal crown" as they labor in the church

(vv. 27–28). Again the Lord warns that the idler "shall not have place in the church, except he repent" (v. 29).

Note: The fourteen missionaries who are called to be united in the ministry (D&C 75:30–36) need no commentary. The text will not be quoted here, and their names can be seen in the Doctrine and Covenants.

Doctrine and Covenants 79 calls Jared Carter to proclaim the gospel, and gives basically the same promises as D&C 75:27–28. The text will not be included here.

Doctrine and Covenants 80 calls Stephen Burnett and Eden Smith to preach the gospel and declare the things they know to be true. The text will not be included here.

General Authority Quotes

—President Joseph Fielding Smith • D&C 71:7–11

> Quite generally the Lord counsels his servants not to engage in debates and arguments. But to preach in power the fundamental principles of the Gospel. This was a condition that required some action of this kind, and the Spirit of the Lord directed these brethren to go forth and confound their enemies which they proceeded immediately to do, as their enemies were unable to substantiate their falsehoods and were surprised by this sudden challenge so boldly given. Much of the prejudice was allayed and some friends were made through this action. [*Church History and Modern Revelation* (1946),1:269]

—President Harold B. Lee • D&C 71:7–11

> What he is trying to have us understand is that he will take care of our enemies if we continue to keep the commandments. So, you Saints of the Most High God, when these things come, and they will come—this has been prophesied—you just say,
>
> "No weapon formed against the work of the Lord will ever prosper, but all glory and majesty of this work that the Lord gave will long be remembered after those who have tried to befoul the name of the Church and those of its leaders will be forgotten, and their works will follow after them."
>
> We feel sorry for them when we see these things happen. [CR, October 1973, 167]

—Elder Boyd K. Packer • D&C 71:7–11

Not many days ago, in a moment of great concern over a rapid series of events that demonstrated the challenge of those within the Church who have that feeling of criticism and challenge and apostasy, I had an impression, as revelations are. It was strong and it was clear, because lingering in my mind was 'why, why? When we needed so much to be united.' And there came the answer: 'It is permitted to be so now that the sifting might take place, and it will have negligible effect upon the Church. [CES Religious Educators Symposium, August 10, 1993, 2]

—Elder Dallin H. Oaks • D&C 71:7–11

The Church does have a responsibility to point out what is the voice of the Church and what is not. This is especially necessary when some alternate voice, deliberately or inadvertently, communicates a message that in a way implies Church sponsorship or acquiescence. . . .

Church leaders are sometimes invited to state the Church's position at a debate or symposium about some doctrine, ordinance, or practice of the Church. This kind of presentation gives an audience the benefit of whatever illumination results from the adversarial clash of opposing viewpoints. . . . But the Church is directed to avoid disputation and contention. Moreover, if a representative of the Church participated in such an event, this could have the unwanted effect of encouraging Church members to look to the sponsors of alternative voices to bring them information on the positions of the Church.

Members of the Church are free to participate or to listen to any alternate voices they choose, but the Church leaders should avoid official involvement, directly or indirectly.

There are disadvantages to official nonparticipation in events where Church doctrines, ordinances, or practices are discussed. In some instances, the overall presentation will be decidedly inaccurate or unfair because the position of the Church and the knowledge of its leaders are not presented. In other instances, a volunteer will step forward to present what he or she considers to be the Church's position. Sometimes these volunteers are well-informed and capable, and they contribute to a well balanced presentation. Sometimes they are not, and their contribution makes matters worse. When attacked by error, truth is better served by silence than by a bad argument.

In any case, volunteers do not speak for the Church. As long as Church leaders feel they should not participate in an event where the

Church or its doctrines are discussed, the overall presentation will be incomplete and unbalanced. In such circumstances, no one should think that the Church's silence constitutes an admission of facts asserted in that setting. [CR, April 1989, 35–36]

—Elder Loren C. Dunn • D&C 75:28

Certainly well-planned and well-scheduled meetings are as much a blessing to the families of the fathers of the Church as they are to those fathers who attend the meetings.

. . . the Lord expects us to take care of our families and to also attend to our duties in the Church.

It may not be true that a heavy load of church responsibility is the reason a father does not draw close to his family. . . .

If we can express sincere interest in them and let them know that we know what is going on, even if we have to do it on the run sometimes, this seems to be far more important than a parent who has more time but somehow does not convey this interest. [CR, October 1, 1971, 18–19]

Chapter Two

The Plainest Book Written

D&C 74; 77; 91; 130:4–11

DOCTRINE AND COVENANTS 74

*H*istorical Setting: "Upon the reception of the foregoing word of the Lord [Doctrine and Covenants 73, January 10, 1832], I recommenced the translation of the Scriptures, and labored diligently until just before the conference, which was to convene on the 25th of January. During this period, I also received [Doctrine and Covenants 74] as an explanation of the First Epistle to the Corinthians, 7th chapter, 14th verse" (*HC,* 1:242).

The Apostle Peter acknowledged that in the Apostle Paul's writings "are some things hard to be understood" (2 Peter 3:15–16). Apparently Joseph Smith was finding it difficult to interpret Paul as he was translating, and the Lord gave him a detailed explanation of this verse: 1 Corinthians 7:14 (quoted in D&C 74:1).

TEXT AND COMMENTARY

74:1–7 • Little Children Are Holy through the Atonement

1 FOR the unbelieving husband is sanctified by the wife, and the unbelieving wife is sanctified by the husband; else were your children unclean, but now are they holy.

2 Now, in the days of the apostles the law of circumcision was had among all the Jews who believed not the gospel of Jesus Christ.

3 And it came to pass that there arose a great contention among the people concerning the law of circumcision, for the unbelieving husband was desirous that his children should be circumcised and become subject to the law of Moses, which law was fulfilled.

4 And it came to pass that the children, being brought up in subjection to the law of Moses, gave heed to the traditions of their fathers and believed not the gospel of Christ, wherein they became unholy.

5 Wherefore, for this cause the apostle wrote unto the church, giving unto them a commandment, not of the Lord, but of himself, that a believer should not be united to an unbeliever; except the law of Moses should be done away among them,

6 That their children might remain without circumcision; and that the tradition might be done away, which saith that little children are unholy; for it was had among the Jews;

7 But little children are holy, being sanctified through the atonement of Jesus Christ; and this is what the scriptures mean.

Circumcision is first mentioned in the Bible when God commanded Abraham to circumcise every male child when he was eight days old (see Genesis 17:10–12). However, as Joseph had translated this Genesis chapter, he was given much more information concerning the meaning of the original text.[2]

11 *And I will establish a covenant of circumcision with thee, and it shall be* my covenant between me and thee, and thy seed after thee, in their generations; *that thou mayest know for ever that children are not accountable before me until they are eight years old.*

12 *And thou shalt observe to keep all my covenants wherein I covenanted with thy fathers; and thou shalt keep the commandments which I have given thee with mine own mouth, and I will be a God unto thee and thy seed after thee.* [JST, Genesis 17:11–12; italics show additions to the text]

The controversy among the Jewish people, at the time of the New Testament Apostles (D&C 74:3–4), is further evidence of the apostate condition they were in. The tradition that little children were unholy (v. 6) was a part of the infant baptism doctrine that later crept into the Christian apostasy that followed, and is still prevalent today. It was the

---

[2] For further background on the practice of circumcision in ancient times, see the Bible Dictionary, 626.

same false doctrine that led God to give the above revelation to Abraham (see JST, Genesis 17:1–9). The same false doctrine led Mormon to write his missionary son, Moroni, concerning the mockery of baptizing little children because little children were alive in Christ (see Moroni 8). The revelation to Joseph validates Mormon's epistle.

Another tradition in the Christian world is that the ordinance of baptism replaced circumcision when the law of Moses was fulfilled. The Prophet Joseph refuted this concept: "Circumcision is not baptism, neither was baptism instituted in the place of circumcision. Baptism is for the remission of sins. Children have no sins. Jesus blessed them and said, 'Do what you have seen me do.' Children are made alive in Christ, and those of riper years through faith and repentance" (*TPJS*, 314).

The Apostle Paul knew he could not speak for the whole Church (see D&C 74:5), but as one of the Twelve Apostles he could write "by wisdom" (D&C 28:5). Thus he advised against uniting in marriage with an unbeliever unless the law of Moses was done away; or they agreed that their children would not be considered unholy and be circumcised under the law of Moses (D&C 74:6). Wherefore, we have three witnesses that little children are not to be baptized until they are accountable: the JST (Genesis 17), the Book of Mormon (Moroni 8), and the Doctrine and Covenants (68:25; 74:6–7). With these additional witnesses we can understand what Paul was writing to the Corinthian Saints.

DOCTRINE AND COVENANTS 77

*H*istorical Setting: "About the first of March, in conjunction with the translation of the Scriptures, I received the [Doctrine and Covenants 77] explanation of the Revelation of St. John" (*HC*, 1:253).

Introduction

The Prophet Joseph Smith declared: "The book of Revelation is one of the plainest books God ever caused to be written" (*TPJS*, 290). Unfortunately, many people confuse the word plainest with easiest. Joseph was making a comparison between the Old Testament prophets and the writings of John the Revelator. The prophets wrote in symbolic terms or imagery, while John told exactly what he saw in heaven. The prophet's imagery represented things on earth. John was shown what was in heaven and recorded it plainly, or described literally what he saw. Therefore, we should read it as it is written (see *TPJS,* 290–292). The Book of Mormon promises its readers that John's revelations will "be unfolded in the eyes of all people" after the Book of Mormon has come forth" (Ether 4:16). In the meantime, the revelation given to Joseph Smith (D&C 77) gives us several keys to open the door and help us understand what John actually saw and wrote about.

The format of the revelation (D&C 77) is a question by Joseph, and the answer from Jesus Christ. The fifteen questions are from Revelation chapters four through eleven, and will be treated in sequence. The verse from the book of Revelation that brought about the question is printed before the question for the readers convenience.

TEXT AND COMMENTARY

The Key to Understanding the Imagery

Revelation 4:6 • And before the throne *there was* a sea of glass like u.. crystal: and in the midst of the throne, and round about the throne, *were* four beasts full of eyes before and behind.

1 Q. What is the sea of glass spoken of by John, 4th chapter, and 6th verse of the Revelation?

A. It is the earth, in its sanctified, immortal, and eternal state.

The earth upon which we now live will become the eternal home for those inhabitants who attain the celestial kingdom (see D&C 88:17–20). The Prophet Joseph later further described the celestial earth, and what will be given to the inhabitants:

9 This earth, in its sanctified and immortal state, will be made like unto crystal and will be a Urim and Thummim to the inhabitants who dwell thereon, whereby all things pertaining to an inferior kingdom, or all kingdoms of a lower order, will be manifest to those who dwell on it; and this earth will be Christ's.

10 Then the white stone mentioned in Revelation 2:17, will become a Urim and Thummim to each individual who receives one, whereby things pertaining to a higher order of kingdoms will be made known;

11 And a white stone is given to each of those who come into the celestial kingdom, whereon is a new name written, which no man knoweth save he that receiveth it. The new name is the key word. [D&C 130:9–11]

The earth, in its present condition is a telestial earth where telestial people can live. When angels minister to this earth, they belong to it, but come from the presence of God, who resides on another celestial earth. Their time frame is reckoned with God's time.

4 In answer to the question—Is not the reckoning of God's time, angel's time, prophet's time, and man's time, according to the planet on which they reside?

5 I answer, Yes. But there are no angels who minister to this earth but those who do belong or have belonged to it.

6 The angels do not reside on a planet like this earth;

7 But they reside in the presence of God, on a globe like a sea of glass and fire, where all things for their glory are manifest, past, present, and future, and are continually before the Lord.

8 The place where God resides is a great Urim and Thummim. [D&C 130:4–8]

The earth being a Urim and Thummin explains God's foreknowledge and omniscience, or all knowledge. His Son Jesus Christ also lives with Him and belongs to this earth. He is the great Jehovah, and "the past, the present, and the future were and are, with Him, one eternal 'now'" (*TPJS*, 220).

2 Q. What are we to understand by the four beasts, spoken of in the same verse?

A. They are figurative expressions, used by the Revelator, John, in describing heaven, the paradise of God, the happiness of man, and of beasts, and of creeping things, and of the fowls of the air; that which is spiritual being in the likeness of that which is temporal; and that which is temporal in the likeness of that which is spiritual; the spirit of man in the likeness of his person, as also the spirit of the beast, and every other creature which God has created.

The description of heaven, paradise, and things on the earth is apparently to show that their creation was a step to their happiness, or "that they might have joy" (2 Nephi 2:25). The Prophet Joseph declared: "The great principle of happiness consists in having a body" (*TPJS*, 181).

All beasts, creeping things, and fowls that live on this earth have spirits within their earthly or temporal bodies. These spirits are in the likeness of their bodies. God created "man in our image, after our likeness" (Genesis 1:26; see also v. 27; Moses 1:26–27; Abraham 1:26–27). The brother of Jared saw the spirit body of Jesus the Christ and was told: "Behold, this body, which ye now behold, is the body of my spirit; and man have I created after the body of my spirit; and even as I appear unto thee to be in the spirit will I appear unto my people in the flesh" (Ether 3:16).

> Revelation 4:7 • And the first beast was like a lion, and the second beast like a calf, and the third beast had a face as a man, and the fourth beast was like a flying eagle.
>
> 3 Q. Are the four beasts limited to individual beasts, or do they represent classes or orders?
>
> A. They are limited to four individual beasts, which were shown to John, to represent the glory of the classes of beings in their destined order or sphere of creation, in the enjoyment of their eternal felicity.

The four individual beasts seem to show that the beasts have a purpose in their creation; and will have a place in eternity and be happy. It may be comforting to those who had personal pets or other animals to know they will be in heaven, and we will have association with them.

> Revelation 4:8 • And the four beasts had each of them six wings about him; and they were full of eyes within: and they rest not day and night, saying, Holy, holy, holy, Lord God Almighty, which was, and is, and is to come.
>
> 9 And when those beasts give glory and honor and thanks to him that sits on the throne, who liveth forever and ever,
>
> 4 Q. What are we to understand by the eyes and wings, which the beasts had?
>
> A. Their eyes are a representation of light and knowledge, that is, they are full of knowledge; and their wings are a representation of power, to move, to act, etc.

Six wings suggest that they have more ability to move in heaven than they did on earth. "They were full of knowledge within" also indicates that they have much more knowledge than they had on earth. In their eternal state they need no rest as when on the earth, but they also recognize the Lord Jesus Christ and His having brought about their eternal condition, something not usually considered on earth.

> **Revelation 4:10** • The four and twenty elders fall down before him that sat on the throne, and worship him that liveth forever and ever, and cast their crowns before the throne, saying,
>
> 11 Thou art worthy, O Lord, to receive glory and honor and power; for thou hast created all things, and for thy pleasure they are and were created.
>
> 5 Q. What are we to understand by the four and twenty elders, spoken of by John?
>
> A. We are to understand that these elders whom John saw, were elders who had been faithful in the work of the ministry and were dead; who belonged to the seven churches, and were then in the paradise of God.

At the time of John's vision, the seven churches were the only branches of the Church that were still acceptable to God. These elders had not been corrupted by the apostasy that was underway while they were on the earth. Were these elders leaders in the branches while on earth? Were they the only ones who were saved? Is the number twenty-four significant? These answers will have to come later. That they were with the righteous in paradise, and had received a crown of eternal life, is all that we now know.

The Key to History

> **Revelation 5:1** • AND I saw in the right hand of him that sat on the throne a book written within and on the backside, sealed with seven seals.
>
> 6 Q. What are we to understand by the book which John saw, which was sealed on the back with seven seals?
>
> A. We are to understand that it contains the revealed will, mysteries, and the works of God; the hidden things of his economy concerning this earth during the seven thousand years of its continuance, or its temporal existence.

The seven thousand years are four thousand years of the Old Testament, two thousand years of the New Testament, and the thousand-

year Millennium. During the Millennium, the earth will become a terrestrial planet instead of a telestial one, as it now is. It will still be a
temporal earth until it becomes a celestial, and a spiritual and eternal
planet. Since we are into the seventh thousand years, assuming our dating
is accurate, it may be that we are in the silence period of "about the space
of half hour" (Revelation 8:1).

The mysteries, works, and hidden things of the seven thousand years
are the things recorded on the sealed portion of the plates delivered to
Joseph that were never translated (see 2 Nephi 27:7–8; 10–11).

> **Revelation 5:2** • 2 And I saw a strong angel proclaiming with a loud
> voice, Who is worthy to open the book, and to loose the seals thereof?
>
> 3 And no man in heaven, nor in earth, neither under the earth, was
> able to open the book, neither to look thereon.
>
> 4 And I wept much, because no man was found worthy to open and
> to read the book, neither to look thereon.
>
> 5 And one of the elders saith unto me, Weep not: behold, the Lion
> of the tribe of Juda, the Root of David, hath prevailed to open the book,
> and to loose the seven seals thereof.
>
> 7 Q. What are we to understand by the seven seals with which it was
> sealed?
>
> A. We are to understand that the first seal contains the things of the
> first thousand years, and the second also of the second thousand years,
> and so on until the seventh.

The words of the book with seven seals, covering the end from the
beginning, "shall be read upon the house tops . . . by the power of Christ"
(2 Nephi 27:10–11). This reading will no doubt be done in the Millennium.[3] Christ is "the Lion of the tribe Judah, the root of David (Revelation 5:5; see Revelation 22:16). The power of Christ will apparently be
given to angels, who will sound their trump and reveal the secret acts of
each of the seven thousand years (see D&C 88:108–110).

Key to the Second Coming

> **Revelation 7:1** • And after these things I saw four angels standing

---

[3] The 2 Nephi 27 verses quoted above are taken from Isaiah 29 before the plain
and precious parts were taken away (see JST, Isaiah 29).

on the four corners of the earth, holding the four winds of the earth, that the wind should not blow on the earth, nor on the sea, nor on any tree

8 Q. What are we to understand by the four angels, spoken of in the 7th chapter and 1st verse of Revelation?

A. We are to understand that they are four angels sent forth from God, to whom is given power over the four parts of the earth, to save life and to destroy; these are they who have the everlasting gospel to commit to every nation, kindred, tongue, and people; having power to shut up the heavens, to seal up unto life, or to cast down to the regions of darkness.

The four angels having the everlasting gospel to commit to all people immediately remind us of the oft quoted: "And I saw another angel fly in the midst of heaven, having the everlasting gospel to preach unto them that dwell on the earth, and to every nation, and kindred, and tongue, and people" (Revelation 14:6). There are four major writers and abridgers of the record of the Book of Mormon: Nephi, Jacob, Mormon, and Moroni. It seems very plausible that these four men are the angels who hold that power spoken of in the answer to Revelation 7:1. Who else would fit this description, and are better qualified to fulfill this role? They "do belong or have belonged to" this earth, and thus "minister to it" (D&C 130:5). Furthermore, all four of these men testify in the Book of Mormon that they will see us at the judgment bar of Christ (see 2 Nephi 33:15, Jacob 4:13; Mormon 3:16–22; Moroni 19:34). Their testimony will witness for or against us, and be instrumental in sealing us up unto life or casting us down into darkness. If we reject their testimony, we reject the Book of Mormon, which is "Another Testament of Jesus Christ."

Revelation 7:2 • And I saw another angel ascending from the east, having the seal of the living God: and he cried with a loud voice to the four angels, to whom it was given to hurt the earth and the sea,

9 Q. What are we to understand by the angel ascending from the east, Revelation 7th chapter and 2nd verse?

A. We are to understand that the angel ascending from the east is he to whom is given the seal of the living God over the twelve tribes of Israel; wherefore, he crieth unto the four angels having the everlasting gospel, saying: Hurt not the earth, neither the sea, nor the trees, till we have sealed the servants of our God in their foreheads. And, if you will receive it, this is Elias which was to come to gather together the tribes of Israel and restore all things.

The Elias spoken of here is obviously Noah, the one who was given power to restore all things after the flood, and again in the last days. This conclusion is based on: "Then the disciples understood that he spake unto them of John the Baptist, and *also of another who should come and restore all things, as it is written by the prophets*" (JST, Matthew 17:14; italics added). Elias, Noah, and Gabriel are all the same person, or title. The Prophet Joseph declared: ". . . Noah, who is Gabriel, he stands next in authority to Adam in the priesthood; he was called of God to this office, and was the father of all living in this day, and to him was given the dominion. These men held keys first on earth and then in heaven" (*TPJS,* 157). It was Gabriel, or Noah, who appeared to Zacharias, the father of John the Baptist, and announced that his son, John, would go before Christ "in the spirit and power of Elias" to prepare the way of the Lord (Luke 1:17, 19). Elias, or Noah, or Gabriel, who appeared to Zacharias, and will attend the great sacrament meeting conducted by Christ prior to His Second Coming (see D&C 27:6–7). It was Elias, or Noah, or Gabriel who brought the keys of the gospel of Abraham to Joseph Smith and Oliver Cowdery in the Kirtland Temple (see D&C 110:12). Abraham was the great grandfather of the twelve tribes to whom Elias would restore all things after they are gathered. With all this evidence, it is evident that Noah is the Elias spoken of in Revelation 7:2.

10 Q. What time are the things spoken of in this chapter to be accomplished?

A. They are to be accomplished in the sixth thousand years, or the opening of the sixth seal.

The sixth seal is the earth's existence from A.D. 1000 to 2000, assuming again that our dating system is accurate. It was A.D. 1830 that the Church was brought out of the wilderness, and other ordinances, principles, and keys of the gospel were periodically restored. Remember that the things that happened during this time were to be *verified* by the power of Christ, when the seal was opened, not to be restored when it was opened, as some may interpret it.

11 Q. What are we to understand by sealing the one hundred and forty-four thousand, out of all the tribes of Israel—twelve thousand out of every tribe?

A. We are to understand that those who are sealed are high priests, ordained unto the holy order of God, to administer the everlasting gospel; for they are they who are ordained out of every nation, kindred, tongue, and people, by the angels to whom is given power over the nations of the earth, to bring as many as will come to the church of the Firstborn.

Note: The question is almost a verbatim quote of Revelation 7:4, and is therefore not quoted here. Verses five through eight name each of the twelve tribes from whom the twelve thousand will be taken.

The Prophet Joseph, in February 1844, "made some remarks respecting the hundred and forty-four thousand mentioned by John the Revelator, showing that the selection of persons to form that number had already commenced" (*HC,* 6:196). Unfortunately a more complete record of what he said was not taken. In May 1844, three months later, he said: "It is not only necessary that you should be baptized for your dead, but you will have to go through all the ordinances for them, the same that you have gone through for yourselves. There will be 144,000 saviors on Mount Zion, and with them an innumerable host that no man can number. Oh! I beseech you to go forward, go forward and make your calling and your election sure" (*HC,* 6:365). This suggests that the sealing in their foreheads (Revelation 7:3) is their calling and election made sure which will give them membership in the Church of the Firstborn, the eternal church (see also D&C 131:5–6).

Key to the Millennial Reign

Revelation 8:2 • And I saw the seven angels which stood before God; and to them were given seven trumpets.

12 Q. What are we to understand by the sounding of the trumpets, mentioned in the 8th chapter of Revelation?

A. We are to understand that as God made the world in six days, and on the seventh day he finished his work, and sanctified it, and also formed man out of the dust of the earth, even so, in the beginning of the seventh thousand years will the Lord God sanctify the earth, and complete the salvation of man, and judge all things, and shall redeem all things, except that which he hath not put into his power, when he shall have sealed all things, unto the end of all things; and the sounding of the trumpets of the seven angels are the preparing and finishing of his work, in the beginning of the seventh thousand years—the preparing of the way before the time of his coming.

The sounding of the seven trumps, by the seven angels, and their messages is recorded in Revelation 8–10. A summary of the trumps is given in Doctrine and Covenants 88:92–107. We will leave commentary on these messages to a study of the book of Revelation, but will discuss the summary in section 88 in chapter 9 of this work.

> **13 Q.** When are the things to be accomplished, which are written in the 9th chapter of Revelation?
>
> **A.** They are to be accomplished after the opening of the seventh seal, before the coming of Christ.

Although the ninth chapter of Revelation speaks of the fifth and sixth angels sounding their trumps, the events John saw were the things happening after the seventh angel had sounded his trump, but before the Second Coming. Again we will leave a discussion of Revelation 9 to another time. As mentioned above, when the seventh seal was opened, there was silence for half an hour. The Lord's time equals one day to a thousand years of earth time (see Abraham 5:3; 2 Peter 3:8; Psalm 90:4). One half hour, a forty-eighth of one day, is approximately twenty-one years. This shows the Second Coming to be a few years into the twenty-first century. The events described in Revelation 9 are not the peaceful era of the Millennium, but the beginning of the destruction of the wicked.

Key to the Gathering of Israel

> **Revelation 10:8** • And the voice which I heard from heaven spake unto me again, and said, Go [and] take the little book which is open in the hand of the angel which standeth upon the sea and upon the earth.
>
> 9 And I went unto the angel, and said unto him, Give me the little book. And he said unto me, Take [it], and eat it up; and it shall make thy belly bitter, but it shall be in thy mouth sweet as honey.
>
> 10 And I took the little book out of the angel's hand, and ate it up; and it was in my mouth sweet as honey: and as soon as I had eaten it, my belly was bitter.
>
> 11 And he said unto me, Thou must prophesy again before many peoples, and nations, and tongues, and kings.

14 Q. What are we to understand by the little book which was eaten by John, as mentioned in the 10th chapter of Revelation?

A. We are to understand that it was a mission, and an ordinance, for him to gather the tribes of Israel; behold, this is Elias, who, as it is written, must come and restore all things.

"The spirit of Elias is to prepare the way for a greater revelation of God, which is the Priesthood of Elias, or the Priesthood that Aaron was ordained unto. And when God sends a man into the world to prepare for a greater work, holding the keys of the power of Elias, it was called the doctrine of Elias, even from the early ages of the world" (*TPJS*, 335–36).

According to John Whitmer's *History of the Church* (chapter 5): "The Spirit of the Lord fell upon Joseph in an unusual manner, and he prophesied that John the Revelator was then among the ten tribes of Israel who had been led away by Shalmaneser, king of Assyria, to prepare them for their return from their long dispersion, to again possess the land of their fathers" (*HC*, 1:176; footnote).

John the Revelator, acting in the spirit of Elias in June of 1831, is consistent with the answer given in Doctrine and Covenants 77:14. It is also consistent with the Prophet Joseph's later teachings quoted above. It may also relate with the book of Revelation saying he "must prophesy again among before many peoples, and nations, and tongues, and kings" (Revelation 10:11). Now, over one hundred and seventy years later, we may see the results of John's preparation. Although there are many theories about the return of the ten tribes, the keys of "the leading of the ten tribes from the land of the north" were delivered to Joseph Smith and Oliver Cowdery on April 3, 1836 in the Kirtland Temple (D&C 110:11). The ten tribes' return fall into the category of what Nephi said about Isaiah: "In the days that the prophecies of Isaiah shall be fulfilled, men shall know of a surety, at the time when they come to pass" (2 Nephi 25:7).

Revelation 11:7 • And when they shall have finished their testimony, the beast that ascendeth out of the bottomless pit shall make war against them, and shall overcome them, and kill them.

8 And their dead bodies [shall lie] in the street of the great city, which spiritually is called Sodom and Egypt, where also our Lord was crucified.

9 And they of the people and kindreds and tongues and nations shall see their dead bodies three days and an half, and shall not suffer their dead bodies to be put in graves.

10 And they that dwell upon the earth shall rejoice over them, and make merry, and shall send gifts one to another; because these two prophets tormented them that dwelt on the earth.

11 And after three days and an half the Spirit of life from God entered into them, and they stood upon their feet; and great fear fell upon them which saw them.

15 Q. What is to be understood by the two witnesses, in the eleventh chapter of Revelation?

A. They are two prophets that are to be raised up to the Jewish nation in the last days, at the time of the restoration, and to prophesy to the Jews after they are gathered and have built the city of Jerusalem in the land of their fathers [see Revelation 11:3].

2 Nephi 8:19 • These two sons are come unto thee, who shall be sorry for thee—thy desolation and destruction, and the famine and the sword—and by whom shall I comfort thee?

20 Thy sons have fainted, save these two; they lie at the head of all the streets; as a wild bull in a net, they are full of the fury of the Lord, the rebuke of thy God. [See also Isaiah 51:19–20; note the italicized words, compare JST, Isaiah 51:19–20]

The prophecy of Isaiah and John's prophecy are yet to be fulfilled, but will undoubtedly come to pass in a relatively short time (see also Zechariah 4:14; Revelation 11:4). Again, we will know more about these prophecies when they come to pass.

THE APOCRYPHA

Historical Setting: "Having come to that portion of [translating] the ancient writings called the Apocrypha, I received [Doctrine and Covenants 91]" (*HC*, 1:331)

TEXT AND COMMENTARY

91:1 Verily, thus saith the Lord unto you concerning the Apocry-

pha—There are many things contained therein that are true, and it is mostly translated correctly;

2 There are many things contained therein that are not true, which are interpolations by the hands of men.

3 Verily, I say unto you, that it is not needful that the Apocrypha should be translated.

4 Therefore, whoso readeth it, let him understand, for the Spirit manifesteth truth;

5 And whoso is enlightened by the Spirit shall obtain benefit therefrom;

6 And whoso receiveth not by the Spirit, cannot be benefited. Therefore it is not needful that it should be translated. Amen.

Apocrypha

"Secret or hidden." By this word is generally meant those sacred books of the Jewish people which were not included in the Hebrew Bible (see Canon). They are valuable as forming a link connecting the Old and New Testaments, . . . although not all of the books are of equal value [A synopsis of some seventeen of the books of special value follows]" (Bible Dictionary, 610–612).

Unfortunately, the revelation does not identify any books, or doctrines, that are true or not true. The Lord left it to each reader to determine the truths by the Spirit (vv. 4–5). It is this writer's opinion that few members of the Church ever read it at all. One reason is that the Apocrypha is not included in the King James Version of the Bible, which is the official Bible used by the Church, and was not included in the Latter-day Saint edition of the King James Version. Another reason is that the members hear or read that there are things in it that are not true, so they forget all about it. It should not be forgotten that there are many things in it that are true as well. May we read it by the Spirit, as we are told, and we will be benefited (v. 5). The link between the Testaments is very helpful, and there are other benefits; however, we will not enlarge upon those benefits here.

General Authority Quotes

—*The Prophet Joseph Smith* • D&C 77:3–4

John saw curios beasts in heaven; he saw every creature that was in heaven—all the beasts, fowls and fish in heaven—actually there, giving glory to God. How do you prove it? (quotes Revelation 5:13).

I suppose John saw beings there of a thousand forms, that had been saved from ten thousand times ten thousand earths like this—strange beasts of which we have no conception; all might be seen in heaven. The grand secret was to show John what there was in heaven. John learned that God glorified Himself by saving all that His hands had made, whether beasts, fowls, fish or men; and He will glorify Himself with them.

Says one, "I cannot believe in the salvation of beasts." Any man who would tell you that this cannot be, would tell you that the revelations are not true. John heard the words of the beasts giving glory to god, and understood them. God who made the beasts could understand every language spoken by them. The four beasts were four of the noble animals that had filled the measure of their creation, and had been saved from other worlds, because they were perfect; they were like angels in their sphere. We are not told where they came from, and I do not know; but they were seen and heard by John praising and glorifying God. [*TPJS,* 291–92]

—*President Joseph Fielding Smith*: D&C 77:9, 14

Elias came and restored the gospel of Abraham. Who was Elias? Well, Elias was Noah, who came and restored his keys (quotes *DHC,* 3:385–86 [*TPJS,* 157 quoted above]) It was Gabriel who appeared to Zacharias and promised him a son, and who appeared to Mary and announced the coming of the Son of God as recorded in Luke. It was also Gabriel as an Elias who is mentioned in Doctrine and Covenants 27:7. It was Gabriel or Noah, who stands next to Michael or Adam in the priesthood. [CR, April 1960, 72]

Chapter Three

Six Visions of Eternity

D&C 76

DOCTRINE AND COVENANTS 76

*H*istorical Setting: The most comprehensive vision of this dispensation, and perhaps others as well, was given to Joseph Smith Jr. and Sidney Rigdon on February 16, 1832 at Hiram, Ohio in the upper story of the Johnson home. Other people were in the room but did not see the vision according to Philo Dibble, one of those present (see section heading taken from *HC*, 1:245).

> The vision which is recorded in the book of Doctrine and Covenants was given at the house of "Father Johnson," in Hyrum [sic], Ohio, and during the time that Joseph and Sidney were in the spirit and saw the heavens open, there were other men in the room, perhaps twelve, among whom I was one during a part of the time—probably two-thirds of the time,—I saw the glory and felt the power, but did not see the vision.

> The events and conversation, while they were seeing what is written (and many things were seen and related that are not written,) I will relate as minutely as is necessary.

> Joseph would, at intervals, say: "What do I see?" as one might say while looking out the window and beholding what all in the room could not see. Then he would relate what he had seen or what he was looking at. Then Sidney replied, "I see the same." Presently Sidney would say, "What do I see?" and would repeat what he had seen or was seeing, and Joseph would reply, "I see the same."

> This manner of conversation was repeated at short intervals to the end of the vision, and during the whole time not a word was spoken by

any other person. Not a sound nor motion made by anyone but Joseph and Sidney, and it seemed to me that they never moved a joint or limb during the time I was there, which I think was over an hour, and to the end of the vision.

Joseph sat firmly and calmly all the time in the midst of a magnificent glory, but Sidney sat limp and pale, apparently as limber as a rag, observing which, Joseph remarked smilingly, "Sidney is not used to it as I am."[4]

Introduction

The vision apparently lasted somewhere around two hours, a lengthy time in light of a later statement by the Prophet, "Could you gaze into heaven five minutes, you would know more than you would by reading all that was ever written on the subject."[5]

Joseph and Sidney were certainly qualified to tell us about "the Saints' eternal home," including "more kingdoms than one" (see section heading). Perhaps others have seen the same or a similar vision as did Joseph and Sidney, but there are only two other men recorded in our present-day scriptures to whom this great revelation was revealed: Jacob, the father of the twelve tribes of Israel (Genesis 28:10–12), and Paul, the Apostle to the Gentiles (2 Corinthians 12:1–7). And even our knowledge of these two men having seen such a vision is dependent upon a statement of the Prophet Joseph Smith: "Paul ascended into the third heavens, and he could understand the three principal rounds of Jacob's ladder—the telestial, the terrestrial, and the celestial glories or kingdoms, where Paul saw and heard things which were not lawful for him to utter."[6]

While several men have seen a vision of the beginning of the world to the end thereof (for example, see 1 Nephi 14:26), Joseph Smith's vision went beyond the scope of this world and into the eternal worlds of varying degrees of glory. It is also possible that Joseph Smith was the one privileged to record this vision for the inhabitants of this telestial world, just as John the Revelator was the one ordained to record the vision to the end of the world (see 1 Nephi 14:25, 27).

---

[4] *Juvenile Instructor*, May 15, 1892, vol. 27, 303–304.

[5] *TPJS*, 324.

[6] *TPJS*, 304–305.

Although the Brother of Jared also recorded his vision of the beginning of the world to the end thereof (2 Nephi 27:6–11), his record is apparently reserved for the Millennium when only those of a terrestrial or celestial nature will be living on the earth. Even though Jacob saw a vision of the degrees of glory, the biblical text provides only this meager account: "And he dreamed, and behold a ladder set up on the earth, and the top of it reached to heaven: and behold the angels of God ascending and descending on it" (Genesis 28:12). Paul's account is not much fuller, and although it sounds as if he is speaking of someone else, a careful reading of verses 5–7 reveals this man to be himself:

"And I knew such a man, (whether in the body, or out of the body, I cannot tell: God knoweth;) How that he was caught up into paradise, and heard unspeakable words, which it is not lawful for a man to utter" (2 Corinthians 12:3–4). Although Paul mentions a third heaven, the Prophet Joseph's explanation does much to clarify what he intended. Paul's treatise of the three different types of resurrection, recorded in 1 Corinthians chapter 15, was undoubtedly based on his vision. Note also that Paul was forbidden to reveal his revelation.

A section outline is not included, but is shown in the sequence of quoting the parts of the text.

TEXT AND COMMENTARY

D&C 76:1–10

1 Hear, O ye heavens, and give ear, O earth, and rejoice ye inhabitants thereof, for the Lord is God, and beside him there is no Savior.

2 Great is his wisdom, marvelous are his ways, and the extent of his doings none can find out.

3 His purposes fail not, neither are there any who can stay his hand.

4 From eternity to eternity he is the same, and his years never fail.

5 For thus saith the Lord—I, the Lord, am merciful and gracious unto those who fear me, and delight to honor those who serve me in righteousness and in truth unto the end.

6 Great shall be their reward and eternal shall be their glory.

7 And to them will I reveal all mysteries, yea, all the hidden mysteries of my kingdom from days of old, and for ages to come, will I make

known unto them the good pleasure of my will concerning all things pertaining to my kingdom.

8 Yea, even the wonders of eternity shall they know, and things to come will I show them, even the things of many generations.

9 And their wisdom shall be great, and their understanding reach to heaven; and before them the wisdom of the wise shall perish, and the understanding of the prudent shall come to naught.

10 For by my Spirit will I enlighten them, and by my power will I make known unto them the secrets of my will—yea, even those things which eye has not seen, nor ear heard, nor yet entered into the heart of man.

In almost the identical language of Isaiah's opening sentence (see Isaiah 1:2), the Lord addresses the inhabitants of the heavens as well as of the earth. As to why the inhabitants of the heavens are included one can only speculate; however, inasmuch as they are invited to rejoice, it seems the Lord may be making them aware that he is revealing information to the earth's inhabitants that has long been withheld from them. Certainly those in the heavens are desirous that the earth's inhabitants know "the term 'Heaven,' . . . must include more kingdoms than one" (D&C 76, the preface to the revelation).

Another reason for including the heavens is implied by the Lord's statement that he honors those who serve him, and will reward those who do so by revealing the mysteries of the kingdom to them (vv. 5–7). If the heavens, as used herein, refers to beings who have once lived on this earth and now serve the Lord as his messengers, but have not yet received their eternal status or blessings, it may be that they are also being shown and enlightened by the power of the Lord's spirit (v. 10).

D&C 76:11–18

11 We, Joseph Smith, Jun., and Sidney Rigdon, being in the Spirit on the sixteenth day of February, in the year of our Lord one thousand eight hundred and thirty-two—

12 By the power of the Spirit our eyes were opened and our understandings were enlightened, so as to see and understand the things of God—

13 Even those things which were from the beginning before the world

was, which were ordained of the Father, through his Only Begotten Son, who was in the bosom of the Father, even from the beginning;

14 Of whom we bear record; and the record which we bear is the fulness of the gospel of Jesus Christ, who is the Son, whom we saw and with whom we conversed in the heavenly vision.

15 For while we were doing the work of translation, which the Lord had appointed unto us, we came to the twenty-ninth verse of the fifth chapter of John, which was given unto us as follows—

16 Speaking of the resurrection of the dead, concerning those who shall hear the voice of the Son of Man:

17 And shall come forth; they who have done good, in the resurrection of the just; and they who have done evil, in the resurrection of the unjust.

18 Now this caused us to marvel, for it was given unto us of the Spirit.

Since Joseph and Sidney were working on "the translation of the Scriptures" when this vision was given (v. 15), this knowledge could have once been in the Bible and was being restored through Joseph (see the preface to section 76). Whether Joseph was the only one who recorded it, or if he was restoring knowledge which had previously been recorded, the fact remains that he is the one who has given this generation the knowledge of the varying degrees of glory.

Of course, all of the above evidence of there being more kingdoms than one in the heavens above is further sustained by Jesus' declaration to his disciples: "In my Father's house are many mansions: if it were not so, I would have told you. I go to prepare a place for you" (John 14:2). Regarding this text, Joseph Smith said: "It should be—'In my Father's kingdom are many kingdoms' . . . there are mansions for those who obey a celestial law, and there are other mansions for those who come short of the law every man in his order" (*TPJS,* 366). As the Prophet said earlier, and is recorded in the section 76 heading, "If God rewarded every one according to the deeds done in the body, the term 'Heaven,' as intended for the Saints' eternal home, must include more kingdoms than one." An analysis of the revelation given to sustain the Prophet Joseph's thesis follows.

Before further analyzing the recorded portion of this vision, it should be noted that Joseph and Sidney actually wrote very little of what they actually saw and heard. Over eleven years later, May 1843, the Prophet said: "I could explain a hundred fold more than I ever have of the glories of the kingdom manifested to me in the vision, were I permitted, and were the people prepared to receive them"(*TPJS,* 305). Importantly, some parts of the vision were recorded while yet in the Spirit (see vv. 28, 80, and 113) and under the command of the Lord (v. 15), while other parts were not recorded, again by direction of the Lord's command (v. 115). That which was not recorded was either unlawful for man to utter, or men were incapable to make them known; such things are only seen and understood by the power of the Holy Spirit (see vv. 115–116). Rather than worrying about what *was not* recorded, we should carefully ponder what *is* recorded. Are the inhabitants of the earth, and particularly the members of the Church, prepared to receive what is recorded? What some people today may esteem as deep doctrine that should not be discussed was considered by the Lord to be basic doctrine necessary to prepare the people for some of the actual deeper doctrines of the gospel of Jesus Christ. These deeper doctrines the Lord would readily reveal if the people were prepared to receive them. The more basic doctrines will be analyzed in this work.

The interpretation of these basic doctrines may also need to be clarified. What one may consider to be a fundamental basic doctrine taught in the revelation, another may consider an erroneous interpretation of doctrine. Correct interpretations can be ascertained by appealing to the other revelations in the Doctrine and Covenants, the other standard works, and modern-day Apostles and prophets. In addition to these sources, there is another primary source from which one may confirm interpretation. In a reply to a poem written by W. W. Phelps, the Prophet Joseph dictated a poetic answer upon the revelation of the three degrees of glory (see *HC,* 5:288), which is published at the end of this chapter. The wording of this poem often confirms or dictates the interpretation that should be given to the revelation. With this background, an analysis of the vision may be undertaken.

D&C 76:19–24 • First Vision—the Throne of God

19 And while we meditated upon these things, the Lord touched the eyes of our understandings and they were opened, and the glory of the Lord shone round about.

20 And we beheld the glory of the Son, on the right hand of the Father, and received of his fulness;

21 And saw the holy angels, and them who are sanctified before his throne, worshiping God, and the Lamb, who worship him forever and ever.

22 And now, after the many testimonies which have been given of him, this is the testimony, last of all, which we give of him: That he lives!

23 For we saw him, even on the right hand of God; and we heard the voice bearing record that he is the Only Begotten of the Father—

24 That by him, and through him, and of him, the worlds are and were created, and the inhabitants thereof are begotten sons and daughters unto God.

As indicated in the title of this chapter, the "vision" is really a series of six visions. The first vision is of the glory of the Son on the right hand of the Father. Very little is said about what they saw; the emphasis is upon what they heard. What they saw, however, is important. They "received of his fulness" (v. 20). From the poetic version we learn that this meant that they saw the Son was "in a fulness of glory and holy applause," not that Joseph and Sidney received of the fulness. Secondly, they saw holy angels and those who were sanctified worshipping God and the Lamb (v. 21). While this may sound like Hebrew parallelism, the poetic version qualifies that these are two separate groups: holy angels (implying those who were assigned to this world), and "sanctified beings from worlds that have been." This is the first indication of the vision including other worlds. What Joseph and Sidney heard further enlightens us on this concept. They testify that through the Only Begotten, other worlds were created and the inhabitants of those worlds were also saved (vv. 22–24). The poetic version is even more descriptive:

> By him, of him, and through him, the worlds were all made,
> Even all that careen in the heavens so broad.
> Whose inhabitants, too, from the first to the last,
> Are sav'd by the very same Savior of ours;
> And, of course, are begotten Gods daughters and sons
> By the very same truths and the very same powers.

The fact that other worlds were created by Jesus Christ, under the

Father's direction, is a prevalent New Testament teaching, although it is often not recognized (see John 1:3, 10; Colossians 1:16–17; Hebrews 1:1–2). This doctrine is also confirmed in the Pearl of Great Price (Moses 1:33), which source also reminds us that "only an account of this world and the inhabitants thereof, give I [the Lord] unto you" (Moses 1:35). Perhaps this is why nothing is said in the New Testament about the Atonement covering the inhabitants of other worlds. On the other hand, perhaps it did originally, but was lost with many other "plain and precious things" (see 1 Nephi 13:24–29).

The Doctrine and Covenants later confirms that Jesus Christ atoned for other worlds as well. In speaking of the many kingdoms and the inhabitants thereof existing in the universe, the Lord likened them unto a man having a field and sending his servants into the field, and promising to visit each man in his own hour and in his own order (see D&C 88:37, 51–61). After quoting these verses in section 88, President John Taylor wrote: "That is, each kingdom or planet, and the inhabitants thereof, were blessed with the visits and presence of their Creator, in their several times and seasons."[7] Also, in the 1879 edition of the Doctrine and Covenants, Elder Orson Pratt wrote the following footnotes to verses 51 and 61: "Each planetary kingdom is visited by its Creator in its time and season" (v. 51), and "the inhabitants of each planet [are] blessed with the presence and visits of their Creator" (v. 61). Therefore, just as the Nephite prophets had their prophecies and sign of Christ's birth and Atonement verified by the Savior's visit among them, it seems logical that the other planets or kingdoms that were created and covered by the Savior and His Atonement received a verification of the Atonement when He visited them. The Lord has, through this vision, enlarged our understanding of the Savior's mission.

D&C 76:25–29 • Second Vision—the Fall of Satan

25 And this we saw also, and bear record, that an angel of God who was in authority in the presence of God, who rebelled against the Only Begotten Son whom the Father loved and who was in the bosom of the Father, was thrust down from the presence of God and the Son,

---

[7] *Mediation and Atonement* [1950], 77.

26 And was called Perdition, for the heavens wept over him—he was Lucifer, a son of the morning.

27 And we beheld, and lo, he is fallen! is fallen, even a son of the morning!

28 And while we were yet in the Spirit, the Lord commanded us that we should write the vision; for we beheld Satan, that old serpent, even the devil, who rebelled against God, and sought to take the kingdom of our God and his Christ—

29 Wherefore, he maketh war with the saints of God, and encompasseth them round about.

Joseph and Sidney next beheld the fall of Lucifer from the presence of God (v. 25). Although this fall is documented in the Bible (see Isaiah 14:12 and Revelation 12:7–9) and in the Pearl of Great Price (Moses 4:1–4 and Abraham 3:27–28), there are many additional insights about Satan and the fall revealed in section 76. That he was in a position of authority in the beginning is amplified in the poetic version by the descriptive "authority great." The titles given him in section 76 are revealing. That he was called "Perdition" explains why the heavens wept over him. According to the dictionary, the word means to destroy, utter destruction, ruin, loss, eternal damnation, hell. According to President Joseph Fielding Smith, Lucifer means a torch bearer.[8] As Isaiah also said, "he was Lucifer, a son of the morning" (Isaiah 14:12). A "son of the morning" is usually interpreted to mean he was one of the early born of the spirit children of Elohim. Thus, as one of the older of the children of God and being in a position of authority, the title of Lucifer implies he was not only rebelling against God but was leading others to do likewise; therefore, he is designated a torch bearer or crusader against God. In fact, as both Isaiah (see 14:13–14) and this section teach, "he sought to take the kingdom of our God and his Christ." To do this "he maketh war with the saints of God, and encompasseth them round about" (v. 29). In other words, his primary function on the earth is to oppose the work of the Church and its members. He spends considerable time and effort upon the Church members. Therefore, we may be assured that whenever there are members of the Church individually or collectively assembled to further their own spiritual progress or that of the Church, the devil

---

[8] *Church History and Modern Revelation* [1946], 1:281.

will be there in opposition. In the words of the Prophet Joseph Smith, "In relation to the kingdom of God, the devil always sets up his kingdom at the very same time in opposition to God" (*TPJS*, 365).

D&C 76:30–49 • Third Vision—the Sons of Perdition

30 And we saw a vision of the sufferings of those with whom he made war and overcame, for thus came the voice of the Lord unto us:

31 Thus saith the Lord concerning all those who know my power, and have been made partakers thereof, and suffered themselves through the power of the devil to be overcome, and to deny the truth and defy my power—

32 They are they who are the sons of perdition, of whom I say that it had been better for them never to have been born;

33 For they are vessels of wrath, doomed to suffer the wrath of God, with the devil and his angels in eternity;

34 Concerning whom I have said there is no forgiveness in this world nor in the world to come—

35 Having denied the Holy Spirit after having received it, and having denied the Only Begotten Son of the Father, having crucified him unto themselves and put him to an open shame.

36 These are they who shall go away into the lake of fire and brimstone, with the devil and his angels—

37 And the only ones on whom the second death shall have any power;

38 Yea, verily, the only ones who shall not be redeemed in the due time of the Lord, after the sufferings of his wrath.

39 For all the rest shall be brought forth by the resurrection of the dead, through the triumph and the glory of the Lamb, who was slain, who was in the bosom of the Father before the worlds were made.

40 And this is the gospel, the glad tidings, which the voice out of the heavens bore record unto us—

41 That he came into the world, even Jesus, to be crucified for the world, and to bear the sins of the world, and to sanctify the world, and to cleanse it from all unrighteousness;

42 That through him all might be saved whom the Father had put into his power and made by him;

43 Who glorifies the Father, and saves all the works of his hands,

except those sons of perdition who deny the Son after the Father has revealed him.

44 Wherefore, he saves all except them—they shall go away into everlasting punishment, which is endless punishment, which is eternal punishment, to reign with the devil and his angels in eternity, where their worm dieth not, and the fire is not quenched, which is their torment—

45 And the end thereof, neither the place thereof, nor their torment, no man knows;

46 Neither was it revealed, neither is, neither will be revealed unto man, except to them who are made partakers thereof;

47 Nevertheless, I, the Lord, show it by vision unto many, but straightway shut it up again;

48 Wherefore, the end, the width, the height, the depth, and the misery thereof, they understand not, neither any man except those who are ordained unto this condemnation.

49 And we heard the voice, saying: Write the vision, for lo, this is the end of the vision of the sufferings of the ungodly.

Having seen the glory of God and the fall of Satan, Joseph and Sidney were now shown the eternal destinies of the earth's inhabitants in a series of four visions. The order of the next four visions is interesting. As members of the Church, we usually speak of the various kingdoms in the descending order of celestial, terrestrial, telestial, and those who qualify for none of the above, the sons of perdition. In this revelation, the sons of perdition are treated first and then the celestial, terrestrial, and telestial kingdoms. While this may have been merely for contrast, there may be another purpose for this order. The sons of perdition had known and experienced the principles of exaltation necessary for the celestial kingdom and then had rejected them, choosing to follow Satan. Therefore, laws designed for exalting God's children will result in one becoming a son of perdition if he meets the requirements for exaltation and then commits the unpardonable sin.[9] This concept is supported by there being a

---

[9] President Brigham Young taught: "How much does it take to prepare a man, or woman, or any being, to become angels to the devil, to suffer with him to all eternity? Just as much as it does to prepare a man to go into the celestial kingdom, into the presence of the Father and the Son, and to be made an heir to His Kingdom, and all

(continued...)

definition of the gospel (see vv. 40–43) inserted within the description of the vision, concerning the sons of perdition. By comparison, the division of the terrestrial and telestial peoples is caused by their following or failing to follow lesser portions of the laws that are given to make men honorable, but not like unto God.

What was seen in the vision of those who were overcome by Satan (sons of perdition) was not recorded. However, what the Lord said about the vision was recorded (v. 30). From the Lord's description, we learn that those who were overcome had not only come to a *knowledge* of the power of the Lord but had *experienced* that power in their lives. The Lord also explained that these people had *chosen* to follow Satan, they had suffered (allowed) themselves to be overcome. The poetic version says they were guilty of "despising [Christ's] name." Having had such a spiritual experience, their rebellion means they "deny the truth and defy my power." This further substantiates their willful disobedience.

Many years after he had seen this vision, the Prophet Joseph commented:

> The contention in heaven was—Jesus said there would be certain souls that would not be saved; and the devil said he could save them all, and laid his plans before the grand council, who gave their vote in favor of Jesus Christ. So the devil rose up in rebellion against God, and was cast down, with all who put up their heads for him.

> All sins shall be forgiven, except the sin against the Holy Ghost; for Jesus will save all except the sons of perdition. What must a man do to commit the unpardonable sin? He must receive the Holy Ghost, have the heavens opened unto him, and know God, and then sin against Him. After a man has sinned against the Holy Ghost, there is no repentance for him. He has got to say that the sun does not shine while he sees it; he has got to deny Jesus Christ when the heavens have been opened unto him, and to deny the plan of salvation with his eyes open to the truth of it; and from that time he begins to be an enemy. This is the case with many apostates of the Church of Jesus Christ of Latter-day Saints.

> When a man begins to be an enemy to this work, he hunts me, he seeks to kill me, and never ceases to thirst for my blood. He gets the spirit of the devil—the same spirit that they who had crucified the Lord of

---

[9] (...continued)
His glory, and be crowned with crowns of glory, immortality, and eternal lives" (*Journal of Discourses,* 3:93).

Life—the same spirit that sins against the Holy Ghost. You cannot save such persons; you cannot bring them to repentance; they make open war, like the devil, and awful is the consequences. [*TPJS,* 357–58]

In describing the fate of the sons of perdition, the Lord uses several New Testament phrases (see Matthew 26:24; 12:32; Hebrews 6:6; Revelation 19:20), and concludes with the declaration that these are "the only ones on whom the second death shall have any power; yea, verily the only ones who shall not be redeemed. . . ." (vv. 37–38). Some conclude from this declaration that the sons of Perdition will not be resurrected, basing their conclusion on "all the rest shall be brought forth by the resurrection of the dead" (v. 39). A careful reading of section 88 shows that redemption, as used here, refers to receiving a degree of glory after the Resurrection and not the Resurrection, *per se* (see D&C 88:25–32). The New Testament and Book of Mormon also repeatedly teach a universal resurrection, and modern-day prophets have confirmed that sons of perdition will be resurrected.[10]

The Lord concluded his remarks about what Joseph and Sidney had seen concerning the sons of perdition by declaring that only those "who are made partakers thereof," or "are ordained to this condemnation," will ever know the torment, the misery, and the end of such punishment (D&C 76:46–49). Over a year later, June 1833, in a letter to W. W. Phelps and others in Zion, the Prophet and his counselors reaffirmed what the Lord had stated in the Revelation: "Say to the brothers Hulet and to all others, that the Lord never authorized them to say that the devil, his angels, or the sons of perdition, should ever be restored; for their state of destiny was not revealed to man, is not revealed, nor ever shall be revealed, save to those who are made partakers thereof: consequently those who teach this doctrine have not received it of the Spirit of the Lord. Truly Brother Oliver declared it to be the doctrine of devils. We, therefore, command that this doctrine be taught no more in Zion. We sanction the decision of the Bishop and his council, in relation to this doctrine being a bar to communion" (*TPJS,* 24).

Therefore, we should not speculate concerning these things. Our goal is to achieve the celestial kingdom, and we would profit more by seeking

---

[10] Joseph Fielding Smith, *Answers to Gospel Questions,* comp. Joseph Fielding Smith Jr., 5 vols. [1957–66], 2:39.

understanding of how to attain his goal than by speculating about the sons of perdition. Those who are striving for this celestial goal will naturally avoid the pitfalls that lead to becoming a son of perdition.

Although a candidate for the celestial kingdom is also a candidate for becoming a son of perdition (if he rebels and defies God), as long as he seeks knowledge and gives heed to the commandments, he will attain salvation. Joseph Smith described it this way:

> A man cannot commit the unpardonable sin after the dissolution of the body, and there is a way possible for escape. Knowledge saves a man; and in the world of spirits no man can be exalted but by knowledge. So long as a man will not give heed to the commandments, he must abide without salvation. If a man has knowledge, he can be saved; although, if he has been guilty of great sins, he will be punished for them. But when he consents to obey the Gospel, whether here or in the world of spirits, he is saved.

> A man is his own tormenter and his own condemner. Hence the saying, They shall go into the lake that burns with fire and brimstone. The torment of disappointment in the mind of man is as exquisite as a lake burning with fire and brimstone. I say, so is the torment of man.

> I know the Scriptures and understand them. I said, no man can commit the unpardonable sin after the dissolution of the body, nor in this life, until he receives the Holy Ghost; but they must do it in this world. Hence the salvation of Jesus Christ was wrought out for all men, in order to triumph over the devil; for if it did not catch him in one place, it would in another; for he stood up as a Savior. All will suffer until they obey Christ himself. [*TPJS,* 357]

D&C 76:50–70 • Fourth Vision—the Celestial Kingdom

> 50 And again we bear record—for we saw and heard, and this is the testimony of the gospel of Christ concerning them who shall come forth in the resurrection of the just—

> 51 They are they who received the testimony of Jesus, and believed on his name and were baptized after the manner of his burial, being buried in the water in his name, and this according to the commandment which he has given—

> 52 That by keeping the commandments they might be washed and cleansed from all their sins, and receive the Holy Spirit by the laying on of the hands of him who is ordained and sealed unto this power;

53 And who overcome by faith, and are sealed by the Holy Spirit of promise, which the Father sheds forth upon all those who are just and true.

54 They are they who are the church of the Firstborn.

55 They are they into whose hands the Father has given all things—

56 They are they who are priests and kings, who have received of his fulness, and of his glory;

57 And are priests of the Most High, after the order of Melchizedek, which was after the order of Enoch, which was after the order of the Only Begotten Son.

58 Wherefore, as it is written, they are gods, even the sons of God—

59 Wherefore, all things are theirs, whether life or death, or things present, or things to come, all are theirs and they are Christ's, and Christ is God's.

60 And they shall overcome all things.

61 Wherefore, let no man glory in man, but rather let him glory in God, who shall subdue all enemies under his feet.

62 These shall dwell in the presence of God and his Christ forever and ever.

63 These are they whom he shall bring with him, when he shall come in the clouds of heaven to reign on the earth over his people.

64 These are they who shall have part in the first resurrection.

65 These are they who shall come forth in the resurrection of the just.

66 These are they who are come unto Mount Zion, and unto the city of the living God, the heavenly place, the holiest of all.

67 These are they who have come to an innumerable company of angels, to the general assembly and church of Enoch, and of the Firstborn.

68 These are they whose names are written in heaven, where God and Christ are the judge of all.

69 These are they who are just men made perfect through Jesus the mediator of the new covenant, who wrought out this perfect atonement through the shedding of his own blood.

70 These are they whose bodies are celestial, whose glory is that of the sun, even the glory of God, the highest of all, whose glory the sun of the firmament is written of as being typical.

The knowledge and heed which a person must achieve to receive a celestial glory was shown in the fourth vision, concerning them "who shall come forth in the resurrection of the just," or as stated in the poetic version "in the first resurrection of Christ." The description of these people is based upon what Joseph and Sidney saw and heard. Twelve descriptions, or requirements, or blessings, for people who will be in the celestial kingdom are recorded, each introduced with the introductory phrase "they are they" or "these are they." We know from other revelations that there are three heavens or degrees within the celestial glory (see D&C 131:1–4). Some of these descriptions are undoubtedly requirements for the various "heavens or degrees," but we are not informed which are required for which. For example, the priests and kings after the orders of Melchizedek, Enoch, and the Only Begotten Son, and who are gods, might well be describing the highest degree. The revelation also says that these are "priests and kings who have received of his fulness, and of his glory" (v. 56). Their blessing is given further enlightenment by the poetic version, which declares that "they hold the keys of the kingdom of heav'n, and reign with the Savior, as priests and kings." These statements certainly imply more than ministering angels.

The first requirement for the celestial kingdom is receiving the testimony of Jesus and following the principles of the gospel (vv. 51–52). An acceptance of the principles of the gospel means more than receiving the ordinances. Through the guidance of the Holy Ghost they must overcome all sin and eventually be sealed unto eternal life. In the words of President Harold B. Lee: "Conversion must mean more than just being a "card carrying" member of the Church with a tithing receipt, a membership card, a temple recommend, etc. It means to overcome the tendencies to criticize and to strive continually to improve inward weaknesses and not merely the outward appearances."[11] The poetic version stresses the trials that have been faced and overcome:

> For these overcome, by their faith and their works
>> Being tried in their life-time, as purified gold.
> And seal'd by the spirit of promise to life,
>> By men called of God, as was Aaron of old.

---

[11] Harold B. Lee, CR, April 1971, 92.

Their being sealed by the Holy Spirit of Promise (v. 53) is to be sealed to eternal life as shown in a later revelation (May 17th, 1843). "The more sure word of prophecy means a man's knowing that he is sealed up unto eternal life, by revelation and the spirit of prophecy, through the power of the Holy Priesthood" (D&C 131:5). Therefore, those people who attain the celestial glory are those who fully live the gospel after receiving it and endure to the end.

The blessing of being in the Church of the Firstborn (v. 54) is a second description of the celestial people, which is the heavenly Church of Jesus Christ (see Hebrews 12:23; D&C 93:22). The third and fourth blessings are their being given all things, and are priests and kings who dwell in presence of God and His Christ (vv. 55–62). Their bodies, after being resurrected, are celestial and are typical of the sun, the twelfth description (v. 70; see 1 Corinthians 15:40–41). We will not comment on the other characteristics, numbers five through eleven, they seem self-explanatory (vv. 63–69).

D&C 76:92–96 • More on the Fourth Vision—Celestial

92 And thus we saw the glory of the celestial, which excels in all things—where God, even the Father, reigns upon his throne forever and ever;

93 Before whose throne all things bow in humble reverence, and give him glory forever and ever.

94 They who dwell in his presence are the church of the Firstborn; and they see as they are seen, and know as they are known, having received of his fulness and of his grace;

95 And he makes them equal in power, and in might, and in dominion.

96 And the glory of the celestial is one, even as the glory of the sun is one.

The Church of the Firstborn (vv. 54–94) is the heavenly Church of Jesus Christ (see Hebrews 12:23; D&C 93:22), and are given all things and dwell in the presence of God and His Christ (vv. 54–62, 94). They are equal in all things with those who dwell there (v. 95). Their bodies, after being resurrected, are celestial and are typical of the sun (v. 70, 96;

1 Corinthians 15:40–41). We will not comment on the other characteristics.

D&C 76:71–80, 91, 97 • Fifth Vision—the Terrestrial Kingdom

71 And again, we saw the terrestrial world, and behold and lo, these are they who are of the terrestrial, whose glory differs from that of the church of the Firstborn who have received the fulness of the Father, even as that of the moon differs from the sun in the firmament.

72 Behold, these are they who died without law;

73 And also they who are the spirits of men kept in prison, whom the Son visited, and preached the gospel unto them, that they might be judged according to men in the flesh;

74 Who received not the testimony of Jesus in the flesh, but afterwards received it.

75 These are they who are honorable men of the earth, who were blinded by the craftiness of men.

76 These are they who receive of his glory, but not of his fulness.

77 These are they who receive of the presence of the Son, but not of the fulness of the Father.

78 Wherefore, they are bodies terrestrial, and not bodies celestial, and differ in glory as the moon differs from the sun.

79 These are they who are not valiant in the testimony of Jesus; wherefore, they obtain not the crown over the kingdom of our God.

80 And now this is the end of the vision which we saw of the terrestrial, that the Lord commanded us to write while we were yet in the Spirit.

The fifth vision shown to Joseph and Sidney was the terrestrial world. The description of these beings is much shorter and mention is made only of seeing, not of hearing. Only six descriptions of terrestrial beings are enumerated or recorded, although there may be more. These are likewise introduced with the phrase "these are they who." Only two of these categories will receive some comment here.

The first description, those who "died without law," is further described in the poetic version as "The heathen of ages that never had hope." Thus the law must refer to the law of Christ, and those described in this category are those who were never exposed to that law or the gospel while living upon the earth. This group included those who were visited in the spirit prison where the gospel was preached to them to give them the opportunity they had missed on the earth. They "received not the testimony of Jesus in the flesh, but afterwards received it" (v. 74). Some have erroneously interpreted this verse as saying that those who were preached to in the spirit world could attain no higher than the terrestrial kingdom. However, a careful reaching will show that these people did not accept the gospel in the spirit world, but only received the testimony of Jesus. A person may receive a testimony of Jesus, but reject the principles and ordinances of His gospel. Those in the celestial kingdom accepted both (vv. 51–53). Note also that those in the telestial kingdom are described as receiving not the gospel neither the testimony of Jesus (v. 82). In other words, the celestial kingdom requires a testimony of Jesus *and* an acceptance of the gospel, while all that is required for the terrestrial order is to receive a testimony of Jesus, either in this life or in the spirit world. Those who reject both the gospel and the testimony of Jesus will be in the telestial kingdom. It is only logical that those who receive both the testimony of Jesus and the gospel in the spirit world will be able to enter the celestial kingdom when the vicarious work is done for them. The summary of each kingdom's requirements are:

Celestial	Terrestrial	Telestial
1. Testimony of Jesus	1. Testimony of Jesus	1. Not the testimony of Jesus
2. Gospel of Christ		2. Neither the gospel of Christ
D&C 76:50–53	D&C 76:74	D&C 76:82

The other description which seems to need some explanation is the last—those "who are not valiant in the testimony of Jesus" (v. 79). This may sound like those who are not keeping the commandments. But those who do not keep the commandments are candidates for the telestial kingdom, not the terrestrial, unless they repent. The word *valiant* means to be of worth, to be strong, to be courageous. Those who are valiant were seen in President Joseph F. Smith's vision of the spirit world: "And there were gathered together in one place an innumerable company of the spirits of the just, who had been faithful in the testimony of Jesus while they lived in mortality; And who had offered sacrifice in the similitude of the great sacrifice of the Son of God, and had suffered tribulation in their Redeemer's name" (D&C 138:12–13). Therefore, it is probably not what they do but what they don't do. In the words of Elder Bruce R. McConkie: "Members of the Church who have testimonies and who live clean and upright lives, but who are not courageous and valiant, do not gain the celestial kingdom. Theirs is a terrestrial inheritance" (CR, October 1974, 44).

The two summary statements that follow in the revelation need no comment:

D&C 76:91, 97 • Additional on the Terrestrial Kingdom

91 And thus we saw the glory of the terrestrial which excels in all things the glory of the telestial, even in glory, and in power, and in might, and in dominion.

97 And the glory of the terrestrial is one, even as the glory of the moon is one.

D&C 76:81–90, 98–113 • Sixth Vision—the Telestial Kingdom

81 And again, we saw the glory of the telestial, which glory is that of the lesser, even as the glory of the stars differs from that of the glory of the moon in the firmament.

82 These are they who received not the gospel of Christ, neither the testimony of Jesus.

83 These are they who deny not the Holy Spirit.

84 These are they who are thrust down to hell.

85 These are they who shall not be redeemed from the devil until the last resurrection, until the Lord, even Christ the Lamb, shall have finished his work.

86 These are they who receive not of his fulness in the eternal world, but of the Holy Spirit through the ministration of the terrestrial;

87 And the terrestrial through the ministration of the celestial.

88 And also the telestial receive it of the administering of angels who are appointed to minister for them, or who are appointed to be ministering spirits for them; for they shall be heirs of salvation.

89 And thus we saw, in the heavenly vision, the glory of the telestial, which surpasses all understanding;

90 And no man knows it except him to whom God has revealed it.

The sixth and final vision shown to Joseph and Sidney was of the glory of the telestial kingdom. The description of what they saw is written in twelve descriptions of people who will be in the telestial kingdom. These are introduced again with the phrase "These are they who." That these rejected both the gospel and the testimony of Jesus has already been emphasized. The other eleven descriptions are easily understood and not controversial.

D&C 76:98–113 • Additional on the Telestial Kingdom

98 And the glory of the telestial is one, even as the glory of the stars is one; for as one star differs from another star in glory, even so differs one from another in glory in the telestial world;

99 For these are they who are of Paul, and of Apollos, and of Cephas.

100 These are they who say they are some of one and some of another—some of Christ and some of John, and some of Moses, and some of Elias, and some of Esaias, and some of Isaiah, and some of Enoch;

101 But received not the gospel, neither the testimony of Jesus, neither the prophets, neither the everlasting covenant.

102 Last of all, these all are they who will not be gathered with the saints, to be caught up unto the church of the Firstborn, and received into the cloud.

103 These are they who are liars, and sorcerers, and adulterers, and whoremongers, and whosoever loves and makes a lie.

104 These are they who suffer the wrath of God on earth.

105 These are they who suffer the vengeance of eternal fire.

106 These are they who are cast down to hell and suffer the wrath of Almighty God, until the fulness of times, when Christ shall have subdued all enemies under his feet, and shall have perfected his work;

107 When he shall deliver up the kingdom, and present it unto the Father, spotless, saying: I have overcome and have trodden the wine-press alone, even the wine-press of the fierceness of the wrath of Almighty God.

108 Then shall he be crowned with the crown of his glory, to sit on

the throne of his power to reign forever and ever.

109 But behold, and lo, we saw the glory and the inhabitants of the telestial world, that they were as innumerable as the stars in the firmament of heaven, or as the sand upon the seashore;

110 And heard the voice of the Lord saying: These all shall bow the knee, and every tongue shall confess to him who sits upon the throne forever and ever;

111 For they shall be judged according to their works, and every man shall receive according to his own works, his own dominion, in the mansions which are prepared;

112 And they shall be servants of the Most High; but where God and Christ dwell they cannot come, worlds without end.

113 This is the end of the vision which we saw, which we were commanded to write while we were yet in the Spirit.

There are some interesting additions to the poetic version. Those who say they are of various men—Paul, Apollos, Cephas (v. 99) and others, must be in a different category than the honorable men spoken of in the terrestrial world. In the poetic version, there are some additional names of men whom they followed, i.e., "For Luther and Calvin, and even the Pope." These telestial men were apparently justifying their actions through what they claimed Paul or others had taught. This is implied in both the scriptural and the poetic version. The poetic version states: "They went their way, and have their reward." These were obviously not honorable men.

The scriptural account again confirms that they received not the gospel, nor the testimony of Jesus, and adds "neither the prophets, neither the everlasting covenant" (v. 101). The poetic version also repeats that they rejected the gospel and the prophetic spirit of the Lord (the testimony of Jesus). It also qualifies the everlasting covenant as that "which Jacob once had."

The great number of people who will be in this degree of glory is "as innumerable as the stars in the heaven, or as the sand upon the seashore" (v.109). While these will all eventually acknowledge the Savior, and have to go through the judgments of God for one thousand years, they will yet receive the glory of the telestial kingdom. But even this glory surpasses all understanding by earth standards, and can only be known by revelation

(vv. 89–90) "in a world vain as this" (poetic version). The poetic version also gives an interesting comparison of the kingdoms:

The glory celestial is one like the sun; The glory terrestrial is one like the moon; The glory telestial is one like the stars, And all harmonize like the parts of a tune.	As the stars are all different in luster and size, So the telestial region is mingled in bliss; From the least unto greatest, and greatest to least The reward is exactly as promised in this.

The vision of the telestial concludes with a declaration that these will "be servants of the Most High; but where God and Christ dwell they cannot come, worlds without end" (v. 112). This seems to say that there is no progression from one kingdom to another, at least from the telestial. And if there is no progression from the telestial, it is only logical that the same is true from other kingdoms. Jesus taught the Nephites that: ". . . he that endureth not unto the end, the same is he that is also hewn down and cast into the fire, from whence they can no more return, because of the justice of the Father" (3 Nephi 27:17). To "no more return" strongly supports no progression from kingdom to kingdom.

In September of 1830, over a year and a half before section 76 was revealed, the Lord declared that the wicked at that day of judgment would be told to depart from Him and go into "everlasting fire, prepared for the devil and his angels" (D&C 29:27–28). He then declared: "And now, behold, I say unto you, never at any time have I declared from mine own mouth that they should return, for where I am they cannot come, for they have no power" (D&C 29:29). This also supports no progression after the final judgment.

Modern scriptures lend further support to there being no progression after the final judgment. Section 88 describes a qualitative resurrection for the earth's inhabitants. Those who attain the celestial kingdom are quickened by a celestial glory to bring about their resurrection. Those who attain either of the lesser kingdoms are quickened by the glory which they attain. This enables them to abide in that kingdom in which they are resurrected. Their spirits and the elements of their bodies are thus inseparably connected (D&C 93:33), "they can die no more; their spirits uniting with their bodies, never to be divided; thus the whole becoming spiritual and immortal" (Alma 11:45). This implies a permanent status, and while it could be suggested that a higher glory could infuse the already permanent body, there is no scriptural evidence to substantiate this. Until further information is revealed by the power of the Holy Spirit to those who are granted the "privilege of seeing and knowing for themselves" (vv. 116–117 below), the concept of no progression from kingdom to kingdom is more scriptural. But first we must grasp that great amount of knowledge recorded about these visions which Joseph was permitted to record.

D&C 76:114–119 • The Mysteries of the Kingdom

114 But great and marvelous are the works of the Lord, and the mysteries of his kingdom which he showed unto us, which surpass all understanding in glory, and in might, and in dominion;

115 Which he commanded us we should not write while we were yet in the Spirit, and are not lawful for man to utter;

116 Neither is man capable to make them known, for they are only to be seen and understood by the power of the Holy Spirit, which God bestows on those who love him, and purify themselves before him;

117 To whom he grants this privilege of seeing and knowing for themselves;

118 That through the power and manifestation of the Spirit, while in the flesh, they may be able to bear his presence in the world of glory.

119 And to God and the Lamb be glory, and honor, and dominion forever and ever. Amen.

The end of the revelation concerning the visions which they had seen is a proclamation of the greatness and glory of the Lord. Joseph Smith provided a fitting conclusion, recorded following the recording of this revelation:

Nothing could be more pleasing to the Saints upon the order of the kingdom of the Lord, than the light which burst upon the world through the foregoing vision. Every law, every commandment, every promise, every truth, and every point touching the destiny of man, from Genesis to Revelation, where the purity of the Scriptures remains unsullied by the folly of men, go to show the perfection of the theory (of different degrees of glory in the future life) and witness the fact that the document is a transcript from the record of the eternal world. The sublimity of the ideas; the purity of the language; the scope for action; the continued duration for completion, in order that the heirs of salvation may confess the Lord and bow the knee; the rewards for faithfulness, and the punishments for sins, are so much beyond the narrow-mindedness of men, that every man is constrained to exclaim: *"It came from God."*[12]

General Authority Quotes

—Elder Wilford Woodruff • D&C 76 (October 1874)

I consider that the Doctrine and Covenants, our Testament, contains a code of the most solemn, the most Godlike proclamations ever made to the human family. I will refer to the "vision" alone, as a revelation which gives more light, more truth, than any revelation contained in any other book we ever read. It makes plain to our understanding our present condition, where we came from, why we are here, and where we are going to. Any man may know through that revelation what his part and condition will be. For all men know what laws they keep, and the laws which men keep here will determine their positions hereafter; they will be preserved by those laws and receive the blessings which belong to them.[*Journal of Discourses* (1875), 17:250]

—President John Taylor • D&C 76:52

We may say . . . if any man or woman expects to enter into the celestial kingdom of our god without being tested to the very uttermost, they have not understood the gospel. If there is a weak spot in our nature, or if there is a fiber that can be made to quiver or to shrink, we may rest assured that it will be tested. Our own weaknesses will be brought fully to light, and in seeking for help, the strength of our God will also be made manifest to us. [*in Messages of the First Presidency*, 3:27–28]

—President George Albert Smith • D&C 76:112

When the time comes for the resurrection, if we are worthy, . . . we will be quickened celestial bodies, and from then on, we will dwell in the celestial kingdom, the highest of all kingdoms. But the Lord has taught us also that there are other places where we may go. If we don't go to the celestial kingdom, by being less careful and particular about keeping the commandments of God, we may go into the terrestrial kingdom, and if we are still more careless, we may find our way into the telestial kingdom, which is the least of the kingdoms of glory.

There are some people who have supposed that if we are quickened

---

[12] *HC,* 1:252-253; February 1832.

telestial bodied that eventually, throughout the ages of eternity, we will continue to progress until we find our place in the celestial kingdom, but the scriptures and revelations of God have said that those who are quickened telestial cannot come where God and Christ dwell, worlds without end. [CR, October 1945, 172]

—President Spencer W. Kimball • D&C 76:112

After a person has been assigned to his place in the kingdom, either in the telestial, the terrestrial, or the celestial, or to his exaltation, he will never advance from his assigned glory to another glory. That is eternal! That is why we must make our decisions early in life and why it is imperative that such decisions be right. [*The Teachings of Spencer W. Kimball*, ed. Edward L. Kimball (1982), 50]

The Vision
from Joseph Smith to W. W. Phelps, Esq.
A Vision[13]

I will go, I will go, to the home of the Saints,
    Where the virtue's the value, and life the reward;
But before I return to my former estate,
    I must fulfil the mission I had from the Lord

    (76:1)[14]
    Wherefore, hear O ye heavens, and give ear O ye earth,
        And rejoice, ye inhabitants, truly again;
    For the Lord he is God, and his life never ends,
        And besides him there ne'er was a Savior of men.

(76:2–4)
His ways are a wonder, his wisdom is great;
    The extent of his doings there's none can unveil;
His purposes fail not; from age unto age
    He still is the same, and his years never fail.

---

[13] First published in the *Times and Seasons*, Nauvoo, Illinois, February 1843, 4:82–85.

[14] Bold references are the verses in section 76 upon which the poem is based. Adapted from Lawrence R. Flake's arrangement of the poetry and the scripture.

His throne is the heavens—his life-time is all
    Of eternity *now*, and eternity *then*;
His union is power, and none stays his hand,
    The Alpha, Omega, for ever. Amen.

(76:5)
For thus saith the Lord, in the spirit of truth,
    I am merciful, gracious, and good unto those
That fear me, and live for the life that's to come:
    My delight is to honour the Saints with repose,

    (76:6–7)
    That serve me in righteousness true to the end;
        Eternal's their glory and great their reward.
    I'll surely reveal all my myst'ries to them—
        The great hidden myst'ries in my kingdom stor'd;

(76:8)
From the council in Kolob, to time on the earth,
    And for ages to come unto them I will show
My pleasure and will, what the kingdom will do:
    Eternity's wonders they truly shall know.

    (76:9–10)
    Great things of the future I'll show unto them,
        Yea, things of the vast generations to rise;
    For their wisdom and glory shall be very great,
        And their pure understanding extend to the skies.

And before them the wisdom of wise men shall cease,
    And the nice understanding of prudent ones fail!
For the light of my spirit shall light mine elect,
    And the truth is so mighty 'twill ever prevail.

    And the secrets and plans of my will I'll reveal,
        The sanctifi'd pleasures when earth is renew'd;
    What the eye hath not seen, nor the ear hath yet heard,
        Nor the heart of the natural man ever view'd.

(76:12)

I, Joseph, the prophet, in spirit beheld,
    And the eyes of the inner man truly did see
Eternity sketch'd in a vision from God,
    Of what was, and now is, and yet is to be.

        (76:13)

    Those things which the Father ordained of old,
        Before the world was or a system had run;
    Through Jesus, the Maker and Savior of all—
        The only begotten (Messiah) his son.

(76:14)

Of whom I bear record, as all prophets have,
    And the record I bear is the fulness—yea, even
The truth of the gospel of Jesus—*the Christ*,
    With whom I convers'd in the vision of heav'n.

        (76:15)

    For while in the act of translating his word,
        Which the Lord in his grace had appointed to me,
    I came to the gospel recorded by John,
        Chapter fifth, and the twenty-ninth verse which you'll see.

(76:18–20)

I marvell'd at these resurrections, indeed,
    For it came unto me by the spirit direct:
And while I did meditate what it all meant,
    The Lord touch'd the eyes of my own intellect.

        Hosanna, for ever! They open'd anon,
        And the glory of God shone around where I was;
    And there was the Son at the Father's right hand,
        In a fulness of glory and holy applause.

(76:21)

I beheld round the throne holy angels and hosts,
    And sanctified beings from worlds that have been,
In holiness worshipping God and the Lamb,
    For ever and ever. Amen and amen.

(76:22–24)
And now after all of the proofs made of him,
   By witnesses truly, by whom he was known,
This is mine, last of all, that he lives; yea, he lives!
   And sits at the right hand of God on his throne.

And I heard a great voice bearing record from heav'n,
   He's the Saviour and only begotten of God;
By him, of him, and through him, the worlds were all made,
   Even all that career in the heavens so broad.

   Whose inhabitants, too, from the first to the last,
      Are sav'd by the very same Saviour of ours;
   And, of course, are begotten God's daughters and sons
      By the very same truths and the very same powers.

(76:25–27)
And I saw and bear record of warfare in heaven;
   For an angel of light, in authority great,
Rebell'd against Jesus and sought for his power,
   But was thrust down to woe from his glorified state.

   And the heavens all wept, and the tears dropp'd like dew.
      That Lucifer, son of the morning, had fell!
   Yea, is fallen! Is fallen and become, oh alas!
      The son of perdition, the devil of hell!

(76:28–29)
And while I was yet in the spirit of truth,
   The commandment was—"Write ye the vision all out,
For Satan, old serpent, the devil's for war,
   And yet will encompass the Saints round about."

   (76:30)
   And I saw, too, the suff'ring and misery of those
      (Overcome by the devil, in warfare and fight,)
   In hell-fire and vengeance—the doom of the damn'd;
      For the Lord said the vision is further, so write:

(76:31–33)
For thus saith the Lord, now concerning all those,
    Who know of my power and partake of the same;
And suffer themselves that they be overcome
    By the power of Satan, despising my name—

    Defying my power, and denying the truth:
        They are they of the world, or of men most forlorn
    The sons of perdition, of whom, ah! I say,
        'Twere better for them had they never been born.

They're the vessels of wrath, and dishonour to God,
    Doom'd to suffer his wrath in the regions of woe,
Through all the long night of eternity's round,
    With the devil and all of his angels below.

    (76:34–35)
    Of whom it is said no forgiveness is found,
        In this world, alas! Nor the world that's to come
    For they have deny'd the spirit of God,
        After having receiv'd it, and mis'ry's their doom.

And denying the only begotten of God,
    And crucify him to themselves, as they do,
And openly put him to shame in their flesh,
    By gospel they cannot repentance renew.

    (76:36–39)
    They are they who go to the great lake of fire,
        Which burneth with brimstone, yet never consumes,
    And dwell with the devil, and angels of his,
        While eternity goes and eternity comes.

They are they who must groan through the great second death,
    And are not redeemed in the time of the Lord;
While all the rest are, through the triumph of Christ,
    Made partakers of grace, by the power of his word.

(76:40)

The myst'ry of godliness truly is great;
    The past, and the present, and what is to be;
And this is the gospel—glad tidings to all,
    Which the voice from the heavens bore record to me.

(76:41)

That he came to the world in the middle of time,
    To lay down his life for his friends and his foes,
And bear away sin as a mission of love,
    And sanctify earth for a blessed repose.

(76:42)

'Tis decreed that he'll save all the work of his hands,
    And sanctify them by his own precious blood;
And purify earth for the Sabbath of rest,
    By the agent of fire as it was by the flood.

(76:43)

The Saviour will save all his Father did give,
    Even all that he gave in the regions abroad,
Save the sons of perdition—they are lost, ever lost!
    And can never return to the presence of God.

(76:44)

They are they who must reign with the devil in hell,
    In eternity now, and eternity then!
Where the worm dieth not, and the fire is not quench'd,
    And the punishment still is eternal. Amen.

(76:46–48)

And which is the torment apostates receive,
    But the end or the place where the torment began,
Save to them who are made to partake of the same,
    Was never, nor will be revealed unto man.

Yet God, by a vision, shows a glimpse of their fate,
    And straightway he closes the scene that was shown;
So the width, or the depth, or the misery thereof,
    Save to those that partake, is forever unknown.

(76:49)

And while I was pondering, the vision was closed,
    And the voice said to me, write the vision; for, lo!
'Tis the end of the scene of the sufferings of those,
    Who remain filthy still in their anguish and woe.

    (76:50)

    And again I bear record of heavenly things,
       Where virtue's the value above all that is priz'd,
    Of the truth of the gospel concerning the just,
       That rise in the first resurrection of Christ.

(76:51–52)

Who receiv'd, and believ'd, and repented likewise,
    And then were baptiz'd as a man always was,
Who ask'd and receiv'd a remission of sin,
    And honoured the kingdom by keeping its laws.

    Being buried in water, as Jesus had been,
       And keeping the whole of his holy commands,
    They received the gift of the spirit of truth,
       By the ordinance truly of laying on hands.

(76:53–56)

For these overcome, by their faith and their works,
    Being tried in their life-time, as purified gold,
And seal'd by the spirit of promise to life,
    By men called of God, as was Aaron of old.

    They are they, of the church of the first-born of God,
       And unto whose hands he committeth all things;
    For they hold the keys of the kingdom of heav'n,
       And reign with the Saviour, as priests and as kings.

(76:57–58)

They're priests of the order of Melchizedek,
    Like Jesus (from whom is this highest reward),
Receiving a fulness of glory and light;
    As written—they're Gods even sons of the Lord.

(76:59–60)

So all things are theirs; yea, of life or of death;
   Yea, whether things now, or to come, all are theirs,
And they are the Saviour's, and he is the Lord's,
   Having overcome all, as eternity's heirs.

(76:61)

'Tis wisdom that man never glory in man,
   But give God the glory for all that he hath;
For the righteous will walk in the presence of God,
   While the wicked are trod under foot in his wrath.

(76:62–63)

Yea, the righteous shall dwell in the presence of God,
   And of Jesus, forever, from earth's second birth—
For when he comes down in the splendour of heav'n,
   All those he'll bring with him to reign on the earth.

(76:64)

These are they that arise in their bodies of flesh,
   When the trump of the first resurrection shall sound;
These are they that come up to Mount Zion, in life,
   Where the blessings and gifts of the spirit abound.

(76:65–66)

These are they that have come to the heavenly place;
   To the numberless courses of angels above:
To the city of God, e'en the holiest of all,
   And the home of the blessed, the fountain of love;

(76:67–68)

To the church of old Enoch, and of the first-born:
   And gen'ral assembly of ancient renown'd,
Whose names are all kept in the archives of heav'n,
   As chosen and faithful, and fit to be crown'd.

(76:69–70)

These are they that are perfect through Jesus' own blood,
   Whose bodies celestial are mention'd by Paul,
Where the sun is the typical glory thereof,
   And God, and his Christ, are the true judge of all.

(76:71)
Again, I beheld the terrestrial world,
    In the order and glory of Jesus go on;
'Twas not as the church of the first-born of God;
    But shone in its place, as the moon to the sun,

(76:72–74)
Behold, these are they that have died without law;
    The heathen of ages that never had hope,
And those of the region and shadow of death,
    The spirits in prison, that light has brought up.

To spirits in prison the Saviour once preach'd,
    And taught them the gospel, with powers afresh;
And then were the living baptiz'd for their dead,
    That they might be judg'd as if men in the flesh.

(76:75)
These are they that are hon'rable men of the earth;
    Who were blinded and dup'd by the cunning of men;
They receiv'd not the truth of the Saviour at first;
    But did, when they heard it in prison again.

(76:76–79, not in sequence)
Not valiant for truth, they obtain'd not the crown,
    But are of that glory that's typ'd by the moon:
They are they, that come into the presence of Christ,
    But not to the fulness of God on his throne.

(76:81)
Again, I beheld the telestial, as third,
    The lesser, or starry world, next in its place,
For the leaven must leaven three measures of meal,
    And every knee bow that is subject to grace.

(76:82)
These are they that receiv'd not the gospel of Christ,
    Or evidence, either, that he ever was;
As the stars are all diffrent in glory and light,
    So differs the glory of these by the laws.

(76:83–85)
These are they that deny not the spirit of God,
    But are thrust down to hell, with the devil, for sins,
As hypocrites, liars, whoremongers and thieves,
    And stay 'till the last resurrection begins.

'Till the Lamb shall have finish'd the work he begun;
    Shall have trodden the winepress in fury alone,
And overcome all by the pow'r of his might:
    He conquers to conquer, and saves all his own.

(76:86–87)
These are they that receive not a fulness of light,
    From Christ, in eternity's world, where they are,
The terrestrial sends them the Comforter, though,
    And minist'ring angels, to happify there.

And so the telestial is minister'd to,
    By ministers from the terrestrial one,
As terrestrial is, from the celestial throne;
    And the great, greater, greatest, seem's stars, moon, and sun.

(76:89–90)
And thus I beheld, in the vision of heav'n,
    The telestial glory, dominion and bliss,
Surpassing the great understanding of men,—
    Unknown, save reveal'd, in a world vain as this.

(76:91)
And lo! I beheld the terrestrial, too,
    Which excels the telestial in glory and light,
In splendour and knowledge, and wisdom and joy,
    In blessings and graces, dominion and might.

(76:92–93)
I beheld the celestial, in glory sublime;
    Which is the most excellent kingdom that is,
Where God, e'en the Father, in harmony reigns;
    Almighty, supreme, and eternal in bliss.

(76:94–95)
Where the church of the first-born in union reside,
    And they see as they're seen, and they know as they're known
Being equal in power, dominion and might,
    With a fulness of glory and grace round his throne.

(76:96–98, 95)
    The glory celestial is one like the sun;
        The glory terrestrial is one like the moon;
    The glory telestial is one like the stars,
        And all harmonize like the parts of a tune.

As the stars are all different in lustre and size,
    So the telestial region is mingled in bliss;
From the least unto greatest, and greatest to least,
    The reward is exactly as promised in this.

(76:99–100)
    These are they that came out for Apollos and Paul;
        For Cephas and Jesus, in all kinds of hope;
    For Enoch and Moses, and Peter and John;
        For Luther and Calvin, and even the Pope.

(76:101)
For they never received the gospel of Christ
    Nor the prophetic spirit that came from the Lord;
Nor the covenant neither, which Jacob once had;
    They went their own way, and they have their reward.

(76:102)
    By the order of God, last of all, these are they,
        That will not be gather'd with saints here below,
    To be caught up to Jesus, and meet in the cloud;
        In darkness they worshipp'd; to darkness they go.

(76:103–104)
These are they that are sinful, the wicked at large,
    That glutted their passion by meanness or worth;
All liars, adulterers, sorcerers, and proud,
    And suffer as promis'd, God's wrath on the earth.

(76:105, 107–108)
These are they that must suffer the vengeance of hell,
'Till Christ shall have trodden all enemies down,
And perfected his work, in the fulness of time,
And is crowned on his throne with his glorious crown.

(76:109–110)
The vast multitude of the telestial world—
As the stars of the skies, or the sands of the sea;
The voice of Jehovah echo'd far and wide,
Every tongue shall confess and they all bow the knee.

(76:111–112)
Ev'ry man shall be judg'd by the works of his life,
And receive a reward in the mansions prepar'd;
For his judgments are just, and his works never end,
As his prophets and servants have always declar'd.

(76:114–117)
But the great things of God, which he show'd unto me,
Unlawful to utter, I dare not declare;
They surpass all the wisdom and greatness of men,
And only are seen, as has Paul where they are.

I will go, I will go, while the secret of life,
Is blooming in heaven, and blasting in hell;
Is leaving on earth, and a-budding in space:
I will go, I will go, with you, brother, farewell.

[First published in the *Times and Seasons,* Nauvoo, Illinois, February 1843, 4:82–85]

Chapter Four

More on the Law of Consecration

D&C 72:9–26; 78; 82; 83; 92

I ntroduction: The ninth article of faith states: "We believe all that God has revealed, all that He does now reveal, and we believe that He will yet reveal many great and important things pertaining to the Kingdom of God."

God had revealed that the Saints were to move from New York to the Ohio in December of 1830 (D&C 37). On January 2, 1831 He promised the Saints that "there I will give unto you my law" (D&C 38:32). The law of the Church was given to them in Kirtland, Ohio on February 9, 1831, and included the law of consecration (D&C 42:29–73). He gave several other revelations concerning the law of consecration periodically in the next year—Doctrine and Covenants 48, 51, 53, 55, and 70 (see chapter 21 of *More Precious Than Gold*, volume 1 of this work).

He now gives several other revelations regarding the law of consecration which we will discuss in this chapter. There were other revelations pertaining to this law that followed before Joseph the Prophet was martyred. We will discuss these revelations later in this book, which will show why it was discontinued.

There are yet other revelations to be given that will show when the Saints will have the opportunity and privilege to live the law again. The first revelation discussed here is Doctrine and Covenants 72:9–26.

DOCTRINE AND COVENANTS 72

*H*istorical Setting: See the section heading, or chapter 1 of this work.

SECTION 72 • OUTLINE

➤ 72:9–16   The duty of the ordained bishop in this part of the vineyard [Kirtland].

     a.   Keep the Lord's storehouse, and receive the funds of the church (v. 10).

     b.   Take an account of the elders, and administer to their needs, who shall pay for what they receive if they can (v. 11).

     c.   What is received may be consecrated to the poor and needy (v. 12).

     d.   Pay the debts from the accounts received for those not able to pay (v. 13).

     e.   Pay the faithful who labor in spiritual things with funds from the bishop in Zion (v. 14).

     f.   Every man that comes to Zion shall lay all things before the bishop (v. 16).

➤ 72:17–19   Every elder in this part of the vineyard must give an account of his stewardship unto the bishop here.

     a.   The bishop gives a certificate to the bishop in Zion rendering every man acceptable for an inheritance in Zion as a wise and faithful member (vv. 17–18).

     b.   The elder may render himself and his accounts approved in all things (v. 19).

➤ 72:20–23   The stewards over literary concerns have claim for assistance from the bishop.

     a.   The revelations may be published and go to the ends of the earth, and obtain funds to benefit the church (v. 21).

     b.   The stewards may consider themselves worthy in all things (v. 22).

    c.   This process is an ensample to all branches of the church (v. 23).

72:24–26   The members appointed by the Holy Spirit are privileged to go up to Zion.

    a.   Let them carry a certificate from the bishop or from three elders (v. 25).

    b.   Otherwise, they will not be accounted as a wise steward (v. 26).

TEXT AND COMMENTARY

72:9–16 • The Duty of the Bishop in Kirtland

9 The word of the Lord, in addition to the law which has been given, making known the duty of the bishop who has been ordained unto the church in this part of the vineyard, which is verily this—

10 To keep the Lord's storehouse; to receive the funds of the church in this part of the vineyard;

11 To take an account of the elders as before has been commanded; and to administer to their wants, who shall pay for that which they receive, inasmuch as they have wherewith to pay;

12 That this also may be consecrated to the good of the church, to the poor and needy.

13 And he who hath not wherewith to pay, an account shall be taken and handed over to the bishop of Zion, who shall pay the debt out of that which the Lord shall put into his hands.

14 And the labors of the faithful who labor in spiritual things, in administering the gospel and the things of the kingdom unto the church, and unto the world, shall answer the debt unto the bishop in Zion;

15 Thus it cometh out of the church, for according to the law every man that cometh up to Zion must lay all things before the bishop in Zion.

16 And now, verily I say unto you, that as every elder in this part of the vineyard must give an account of his stewardship unto the bishop in this part of the vineyard—

The duties of the bishop that had been previously given were in Doctrine and Covenants 42:31–35, 71–73, 82; 48:6; 51:5, 12–13; 53:4;

57:15; 58:35, 51, 55; 64:40; and 70:11. We will not repeat these duties here, but add to the ones already revealed. There will be some repetition, but an expansion of the previous duties. The law of consecration revolves around the bishop as illustrated in the references cited above.

The bishops' storehouse was where the surplus commodities, produced through individual stewardships, were kept (see D&C 42:34), including the funds or monies that were contributed (v. 10). It was possible for elders, as they managed their stewardships, to obtain things from the storehouse to supplement their wants. These items were to be paid for unless their circumstances were such that they could not afford it (v. 11). This procedure was similar to our modern welfare program. What the elders paid for would be consecrated to the poor and needy of the Church (v. 12), a major purpose of the storehouse. If more was needed than the Kirtland bishop had at his disposal, he could draw from the bishop in Zion (v. 13), another similarity to today's welfare program. A ward bishop may draw upon the general Church funds. Those whose stewardships were to labor in spiritual things, the bishop himself and others (see D&C 42:71–73), were to draw their living needs from the storehouse (v. 14). The funding for the bishop in Zion was to come from the elders laying "all things before the bishop" as they came to Zion and entered the Zion society (v. 15). Every elder was accountable to the bishop for how he operated his personal stewardship (v. 16).

D&C 72:17–19 • A Certificate of Acceptability

17 A certificate from the judge or bishop in this part of the vineyard, unto the bishop in Zion, rendereth every man acceptable, and answereth all things, for an inheritance, and to be received as a wise steward and as a faithful laborer;

18 Otherwise he shall not be accepted of the bishop of Zion.

19 And now, verily I say unto you, let every elder who shall give an account unto the bishop of the church in this part of the vineyard be recommended by the church or churches, in which he labors, that he may render himself and his accounts approved in all things.

The certificate affirming they were accountable, and wise and faithful stewards, would have served the same purpose as our temple recommends today, or as the letter certifying they were regular members as required

when the Church was organized (D&C 20:84). The Lord does not want His members to cast pearls before swine (Matthew 7:6) or share sacred things with those who do not understand or cannot be trusted.

D&C 72:20–23 • Funding for the Benefit of the Church

20 And again, let my servants who are appointed as stewards over the literary concerns of my church have claim for assistance upon the bishop or bishops in all things—

21 That the revelations may be published, and go forth unto the ends of the earth; that they also may obtain funds which shall benefit the church in all things;

22 That they also may render themselves approved in all things, and be accounted as wise stewards.

23 And now, behold, this shall be an ensample for all the extensive branches of my church, in whatsoever land they shall be established. And now I make an end of my sayings. Amen.

Even though the Saints were basically an agriculture community, there were other stewardships needed in a Zion society. One of these stewardships was the printing committee headed by William W. Phelps (D&C 55). This was a full time calling, and was to be supported by the bishops' storehouse (D&C 72:20). The committee would possibly earn a profit, and were accountable to the bishop (vv. 21–22). These profits were to go into the storehouse for other benefits of the Church. The ensample (example) has been followed (v. 23). The Church has and does engage in many business endeavors where it is a benefit to the Church.

D&C 72:24–26 • Appointed to Go Up to Zion

24 A few words in addition to the laws of the kingdom, respecting the members of the church—they that are appointed by the Holy Spirit to go up unto Zion, and they who are privileged to go up unto Zion—

25 Let them carry up unto the bishop a certificate from three elders of the church, or a certificate from the bishop;

26 Otherwise he who shall go up unto the land of Zion shall not be accounted as a wise steward. This is also an ensample. Amen.

The building up of Zion was to be a gradual process, even in the early days of the Church. Kirtland was to be a stronghold for five years (see D&C 64:21). However, those who were directed to go to Zion by the Holy Spirit were to have that privilege (v. 24). The bishop's certificate was probably a second witness that they had been directed by the Spirit, and not just following their own whims or desires. Under circumstances where the bishop was not available, for some reason, to obtain the certificate of being accountable, three elders could give the departing family a written statement (v. 25). The law of witnesses was again honored (v. 26, see Matthew 18:16). There is security in the affirmation of three honorable men.

DOCTRINE AND COVENANTS 78

H *istorical Setting:* "Besides the work of translating, previous to the 20th of March [1832], I received the four following revelations: [78; 79 and 80 covered in chapter 1 of this work; and 81 covered in chapter 10]" (*HC,* 1:255; see the section heading for an explanation of the code-names appearing in the text of the previous editions).

SECTION 78 • OUTLINE

➤ 78:1–7   The Lord speaks to those who are ordained to the high priesthood, and invites them to listen to the counsel of him who ordained them.

    a.   He speaks the words of wisdom that they may have salvation (v. 2).

    b.   There must be an organization to regulate and establish the affairs of the storehouse in Ohio and Zion (v. 3).

    c.   It is to be a permanent and everlasting establishment that the people may be equal in earthly things for obtaining heavenly things (vv. 4–5).

    d.   If you are not equal in earthly things, you cannot be equal in obtaining heavenly things, and a place in the celestial world (vv. 6–7).

➤ 78:8–16   It is expedient for all joined in this order to do all things unto Christ's glory.

   a.   Newel K. Whitney, Joseph Smith Jun., and Sidney Rigdon are to sit in council with the saints in Zion (v. 9).

   b.   Satan seeks to turn their hearts from the truth, and not understand what is prepared for them (v. 10).

   c.   They are commanded to bind themselves with an everlasting covenant that cannot be broken (v. 11).

   d.   He that breaks the covenant shall lose his office and standing in the church, and be delivered to the buffetings of Satan until the day of redemption (v. 12).

   e.   The preparation, foundation, ensample, and tribulation that will come, will enable the church to stand independent above all creatures (vv. 13–14).

   f.   You may be crowned and made ruler over many kingdoms says He who laid the foundation of Adam-ondi-Ahman (v. 15).

   g.   Michael your prince has been established and given the keys of salvation under the Holy One (v. 16).

78:17–22   You little children have not understood the blessings the Father has for you.

   a.   You cannot bear all things now, but the kingdom, blessings, and riches of the earth are yours (v. 18).

   b.   Those who receive all things with thankfulness shall be glorious, and have all things added unto him a hundred fold (v. 19).

   c.   Do all things commanded saith your Redeemer, the Son of Ahman (v. 20).

   d.   Ye are the Church of the Firstborn, and he will take you up in a cloud and appoint every man his portion (v. 21).

   e.   He that is a faithful and wise servant shall inherit all things (v. 22).

TEXT AND COMMENTARY

D&C 78:1–7 • Equal in Earthly Things

1 THE Lord spake unto Joseph Smith, Jun., saying: Hearken unto me, saith the Lord your God, who are ordained unto the high priesthood of my church, who have assembled yourselves together;

2 And listen to the counsel of him who has ordained you from on high, who shall speak in your ears the words of wisdom, that salvation may be unto you in that thing which you have presented before me, saith the Lord God.

3 For verily I say unto you, the time has come, and is now at hand; and behold, and lo, it must needs be that there be an organization of my people, in regulating and establishing the affairs of the storehouse for the poor of my people, both in this place and in the land of Zion—

4 For a permanent and everlasting establishment and order unto my church, to advance the cause, which ye have espoused, to the salvation of man, and to the glory of your Father who is in heaven;

5 That you may be equal in the bonds of heavenly things, yea, and earthly things also, for the obtaining of heavenly things.

6 For if ye are not equal in earthly things ye cannot be equal in obtaining heavenly things;

7 For if you will that I give unto you a place in the celestial world, you must prepare yourselves by doing the things which I have commanded you and required of you.

In March of 1832, thirteen months after the law of consecration was first given, the Lord revealed that it was time to regulate and establish "the affairs of the storehouse for the poor of my people" in Kirtland as well as in the land of Zion [Missouri] (v. 3). In this later revelation, the Lord gives a further cause of the bishops' storehouse. In addition to the care of the poor, it was to bring about "the salvation of man, and to glorify your father in Heaven (v. 4). The Father glorifies himself by bringing others to "immortality and eternal life" (Moses 1:39; D&C 132:31). The Prophet Joseph explained Jesus' example: "My Father worked out his kingdom with fear and trembling, and I must do the same; and when I get my kingdom, I shall present it to my Father, so that he may obtain kingdom upon kingdom, and it will exalt him in glory. He will then take a higher exaltation, and I will take his place, and thereby become exalted myself. So that Jesus treads in the tracks of his Father, and inherits what his Father did before; and God is thus glorified and exalted in the salvation of all his children" (*TPJS*, 347–48; see also Isaiah 53:12; Luke 22:29).

Through the storehouse, the Lord brings about the equality of man, a requirement for "the celestial world" (D&C 78:5–7). The Lord's definition of equality is not one of exact physical possessions, but of being

"liberal to all, both old and young, both bond and free, both male and female, whether out of the church or in the church, having no respect to persons as to those who stood in need" (Alma 1:30).

D&C 78:8–16 • The Church Stands Independent

8 And now, verily thus saith the Lord, it is expedient that all things be done unto my glory, by you who are joined together in this order;

9 Or, in other words, let my servant Newel K. Whitney and my servant Joseph Smith, Jun., and my servant Sidney Rigdon sit in council with the saints which are in Zion;

10 Otherwise Satan seeketh to turn their hearts away from the truth, that they become blinded and understand not the things which are prepared for them.

11 Wherefore, a commandment I give unto you, to prepare and organize yourselves by a bond or everlasting covenant that cannot be broken.

12 And he who breaketh it shall lose his office and standing in the church, and shall be delivered over to the buffetings of Satan until the day of redemption.

13 Behold, this is the preparation wherewith I prepare you, and the foundation, and the ensample which I give unto you, whereby you may accomplish the commandments which are given you;

14 That through my providence, notwithstanding the tribulation which shall descend upon you, that the church may stand independent above all other creatures beneath the celestial world;

15 That you may come up unto the crown prepared for you, and be made rulers over many kingdoms, saith the Lord God, the Holy One of Zion, who hath established the foundations of Adam-ondi-Ahman;

16 Who hath appointed Michael your prince, and established his feet, and set him upon high, and given unto him the keys of salvation under the counsel and direction of the Holy One, who is without beginning of days or end of life.

The Church leaders were to "sit in council with the saints" in Zion that they might understand why and how the law of consecration was extended into Ohio (v. 9). Whenever the kingdom is set up, "the devil always sets up his kingdom in opposition to it" (*TPJS*, 365). Satan would be there to turn their hearts from the truth (v. 10).

The law in Ohio was also entered into with "a bond or covenant that cannot be broken (v. 11; see D&C 42:30). Those who broke their covenant would lose their office and standing in the Church. Furthermore, the Atonement would not cover their sin in this case because, having been taught and brought to understanding, they would have to suffer for their sins through experiencing "the buffetings of Satan until the day of redemption," or until they had "paid the uttermost farthing" (D&C 78:12; see Matthew 5:26; 3 Nephi 12:26). "For if we sin wilfully after that we have received the knowledge of the truth, there remaineth no more sacrifice for sins" (Hebrews 10:26).

Through the keeping of the covenant through the tribulations that the Lord knew would come, the Church and its members would be able to "stand independent above all other creatures beneath the celestial world" (D&C 78:13–14). In the eternal sense, those who kept the covenants would receive "the crown prepared for them, and be made rulers over many kingdoms" (v. 15). This is the first mention of Adam-ondi-Ahman, and Michael (v. 16), our prince. Note that Jesus is the God of that special place on earth, and Michael is tied closely with it as well.

D&C 78:17–22 • The Riches of Eternity Are Yours

17 Verily, verily, I say unto you, ye are little children, and ye have not as yet understood how great blessings the Father hath in his own hands and prepared for you;

18 And ye cannot bear all things now; nevertheless, be of good cheer, for I will lead you along. The kingdom is yours and the blessings thereof are yours, and the riches of eternity are yours.

19 And he who receiveth all things with thankfulness shall be made glorious; and the things of this earth shall be added unto him, even an hundred fold, yea, more.

20 Wherefore, do the things which I have commanded you, saith your Redeemer, even the Son Ahman, who prepareth all things before he taketh you;

21 For ye are the church of the Firstborn, and he will take you up in a cloud, and appoint every man his portion.

22 And he that is a faithful and wise steward shall inherit all things. Amen.

Again we are reminded of the ninth article of faith. The Lord will continue to teach His Saints and further declare the blessings He has in store for them (v. 17). The general promise of the kingdom, "and the riches of eternity" were sufficient for the time being (v. 18). A hundred fold being added of the "things of this earth" are staggering to say the least (v. 19). We will also wait to comment on "Son Ahman," when he so identifies himself again (D&C 95:17).

The Church of the Firstborn is mentioned in the New Testament epistle to the Hebrews (12:23). It is the heavenly Church (D&C 76:67). Its members receive the fulness of the Father (76:71), and dwell in His presence (76:94). Being taken up in the cloud is the promise repeated in Hebrews 12 and section 76 above. In summation, the Lord promises all things to the faithful and wise steward of the law of consecration (v. 22). There is still much more to be revealed about the law of consecration.

◔◍◔

DOCTRINE AND COVENANTS 82

*H*istorical Setting: "On the 26th, I called a general council of the Church, and was acknowledged as the president of the High Priesthood, according to a previous ordination at a conference of High Priests, Elders and members, held at Amherst, Ohio; on the 25th of January, 1832. The right hand of fellowship was given to me by the Bishop, Edward Partridge, in behalf of the Church. The scene was solemn, impressive and delightful. During the intermission, a difficulty or hardness that had existed between Bishop Partridge and Elder Rigdon was amicably settled, and when we came together in the afternoon, all hearts seemed to rejoice and I received [Doctrine and Covenants 82]" (*HC,* 1:267).

SECTION 82 • OUTLINE

➤ 82:1–4   Inasmuch as the Lord's people had forgiven one another, he forgives them.

         a.   Those among them had sinned exceedingly, all had sinned; repent lest sore judgments fall on you (v. 2).

b. Unto whom much is given much is required, and whoso sins against the greater light receives greater condemnation (v. 3).

c. You ask for revelation and I give it, as ye keep not my sayings, justice and judgments are the penalty affixed to my law (v. 4).

➤ 82:5–10   The Lord says unto all: Watch, for the adversary spreads his dominions, and darkness reigns.

a. The Lord's anger kindles against the earth's inhabitants; none do good, all have gone astray (v. 6).

b. Go your way and sin no more, but that soul that sins shall the former sins return (v. 7).

c. I give a new commandment; you may act and turn it to your salvation (vv. 8–9).

d. I the Lord am bound when you do what I say, but when you do not ye have no promise (v. 10).

➤ 82:11–14   It is expedient that my servant be bound by a covenant that cannot be broken by transgression except judgment follows in both Kirtland and Zion.

a. Kirtland is consecrated in time to benefit the saints as a stake in Zion (v. 13).

b. Zion must increase in beauty, in holiness, her borders enlarged, her stakes strengthened, and arise and put on her beautiful garments (v. 14).

➤ 82:15–21   I give a commandment to bind yourselves by covenant according to my laws.

a. It is wisdom that you have equal claim on the properties to manage your stewardships according to your just wants and needs (vv. 16–17).

b. It is the benefit of the church for every man to improve his talents and gain other talents to cast into the storehouse to benefit the whole church (v. 18).

c. Every man seeking the interest of his neighbor, and doing all things with an eye single to the glory of God (v. 29).

d. An everlasting order unto you and your successors, if you sin not (v. 20).

e. The soul that sins against this order is to be dealt with according to the laws of my church, and be delivered to the buffetings of Satan until redemption (v. 21).

➤ 82:22–24 Make friends with the mammon of unrighteousness, and be not destroyed.

  a. Leave judgment to me and I will repay. My peace and blessings continue (v. 23).

  b. The kingdom is yours and shall be forever (v. 24).

TEXT AND COMMENTARY

D&C 82:1–4 • Much Given—Much Required

1 Verily, verily, I say unto you, my servants, that inasmuch as you have forgiven one another your trespasses, even so I, the Lord, forgive you.

2 Nevertheless, there are those among you who have sinned exceedingly; yea, even all of you have sinned; but verily I say unto you, beware from henceforth, and refrain from sin, lest sore judgments fall upon your heads.

3 For of him unto whom much is given much is required; and he who sins against the greater light shall receive the greater condemnation.

4 Ye call upon my name for revelations, and I give them unto you; and inasmuch as ye keep not my sayings, which I give unto you, ye become transgressors; and justice and judgment are the penalty which is affixed unto my law.

In the Lord's Prayer, it says "to forgive us our debts as we forgive our debtors (Matthew 6:11; 3 Nephi 13:11). The Lord requires us "to forgive all men" (D&C 64:10). The blessing of forgiving others brings our own forgiveness (v. 1). After being forgiven, one must be even more careful for more is required, and judgment is more severe (vv. 2–3). The Lord taught this principle to His disciples during His mortal ministry. "For unto whomsoever much is given, of him shall much be required; and to whom *the Lord* has committed much, of him will men ask the more" (JST, Luke 12:57 italics show differences between Luke 12:48). The Saints, having received more revelations, are subject to penalties for not observing these revelations. Other people are not accountable (v. 4).

D&C 82:5–10 • The Former Sins Return

5 Therefore, what I say unto one I say unto all: Watch, for the adversary spreadeth his dominions, and darkness reigneth;

6 And the anger of God kindleth against the inhabitants of the earth; and none doeth good, for all have gone out of the way.

7 And now, verily I say unto you, I, the Lord, will not lay any sin to your charge; go your ways and sin no more; but unto that soul who sinneth shall the former sins return, saith the Lord your God.

8 And again, I say unto you, I give unto you a new commandment, that you may understand my will concerning you;

9 Or, in other words, I give unto you directions how you may act before me, that it may turn to you for your salvation.

10 I, the Lord, am bound when ye do what I say; but when ye do not what I say, ye have no promise.

"All have gone out of the way" (v. 6) may be the Lord's recognition of the apostasy, or it may be speaking of all people living in a fallen world, and are subject to Satan, and make mistakes (v. 5). The latter is taught in the Old Testament: "For there is not a just man upon earth, that doeth good, and sinneth not (Ecclesiastes 7:20). It is also taught in the New Testament: "For all have sinned, and come short of the glory of God" (Romans 3:23). The Lord again warns that those who sin, after being forgiven, will be accountable for those sins for which they were forgiven (v. 7). Occasionally it is taught that if a person can remember their sin they have not been forgiven. They quote D&C 58:42: "I, the Lord, remember them no more," to justify their conclusion. How can the Lord bring back our former sins if He cannot remember what we did? What the Lord is saying, in this passage, is that He puts the sins in the back of His mind, and will not hold us accountable for them unless we repeat the same sin again.

The new commandment the Lord gives them (v. 8) is the law of consecration (see v. 11 and D&C 42:30). Its purpose was to show them how to act that it may bring them salvation (D&C 82:9). All of God's commandments are for the same purpose overall. There are blessings attached to each one, but they are conditional upon our keeping them (v. 10). The Prophet Joseph taught this principle years later: "There is

a law, irrevocably decreed in heaven before the foundations of this world, upon which all blessings are predicated—and when we obtain any blessing from God, it is by obedience to that law upon which it is predicated" (D&C 130:20–21). The Lord always keeps His part of the covenant, but we often do not keep our part.

D&C 82:11–14 • Zion Arise and Put On Her Garments

11 Therefore, verily I say unto you, that it is expedient for my servants Edward Partridge and Newel K. Whitney, A. Sidney Gilbert and Sidney Rigdon, and my servant Joseph Smith, and John Whitmer and Oliver Cowdery, and W. W. Phelps and Martin Harris to be bound together by a bond and covenant that cannot be broken by transgression, except judgment shall immediately follow, in your several stewardships—

12 To manage the affairs of the poor, and all things pertaining to the bishopric both in the land of Zion and in the land of Kirtland;

13 For I have consecrated the land of Kirtland in mine own due time for the benefit of the saints of the Most High, and for a stake to Zion.

14 For Zion must increase in beauty, and in holiness; her borders must be enlarged; her stakes must be strengthened; yea, verily I say unto you, Zion must arise and put on her beautiful garments.

The bond and the covenant that the Lord's servants were to enter into (vv. 11–12) was again the law of consecration. Each person was appointed a stewardship (see D&C 42:32), and one of the overall purposes was to care for the poor (see D&C 42:30). It is the law of the celestial kingdom (see D&C 105:5).

Both Zion [Kirtland] and Zion [Missouri] were a part of the Lord's plan to begin fulfilling the words of the Prophet Isaiah, for Zion to "put on thy beautiful garments" (v. 14; Isaiah 52:1; 2 Nephi 8:24). Kirtland was the first stake to enlarge the borders of Zion, a stake to help set up the tent of Israel (v. 13). There would be many other stakes established in order to raise the tent (see Isaiah 54:2; 3 Nephi 22:2). All of these stakes would be for the benefit of the Saints of the Most High (D&C 82:13).

D&C 82:15–21 • Every Man May Improve His Talents

15 Therefore, I give unto you this commandment, that ye bind

yourselves by this covenant, and it shall be done according to the laws of the Lord.

16 Behold, here is wisdom also in me for your good.

17 And you are to be equal, or in other words, you are to have equal claims on the properties, for the benefit of managing the concerns of your stewardships, every man according to his wants and his needs, inasmuch as his wants are just—

18 And all this for the benefit of the church of the living God, that every man may improve upon his talent, that every man may gain other talents, yea, even an hundred fold, to be cast into the Lord's storehouse, to become the common property of the whole church—

19 Every man seeking the interest of his neighbor, and doing all things with an eye single to the glory of God.

20 This order I have appointed to be an everlasting order unto you, and unto your successors, inasmuch as you sin not.

21 And the soul that sins against this covenant, and hardeneth his heart against it, shall be dealt with according to the laws of my church, and shall be delivered over to the buffetings of Satan until the day of redemption.

In the wisdom of the Lord, the same principles were to govern the Kirtland Stake as had been revealed to govern the center place of Zion, and were for their good (vv. 15–16). The major good it would do was to bring equality among its members, according to their just wants and needs (v. 17; see D&C 51:3). Again, the equality was not the exact sameness of physical possessions, but the same respect of persons and their agency to choose (see D&C 78:5–7 and comments above). This kind of equality allows people in the order to draw on the Lord's storehouse to improve upon their talents, or to gain new talents, even a hundred fold (v. 18). It also fulfills the two commandments of all the law and the prophets: to love God, by having an eye single to the glory of God; and to love your neighbor as yourself, by seeking their interest (v. 19; see Matthew 22:36–40).

The order revealed to the Church leaders at this time was an everlasting order, or an eternal order of the celestial world, and to their successors as long as they did not sin (v. 20). However, those who did sin against the covenant they had made were to be disciplined by the laws of Christ's

Church, and turned over to the buffetings of Satan as stated above (v. 21; see 78:12 above).

D&C 82:22–24 • Friends of the Mammon of Unrighteousness

22 And now, verily I say unto you, and this is wisdom, make unto yourselves friends with the mammon of unrighteousness, and they will not destroy you.

23 Leave judgment alone with me, for it is mine and I will repay. Peace be with you; my blessings continue with you.

24 For even yet the kingdom is yours, and shall be forever, if you fall not from your steadfastness. Even so. Amen.

To be friends of the mammon of unrighteousness (v. 22) is to "be in the world, but not of the world." Jesus prayed for His disciples: "I pray not that thou shouldest take them out of the world, but that thou shouldest keep them from the evil. They are not of the world, even as I am not of the world. Sanctify them through thy truth: thy word is truth. As thou hast sent me into the world, even so have I also sent them into the world. And for their sakes I sanctify myself, that they also might be sanctified through the truth" (John 17:15–19). The Father has "committed all judgment unto the Son" (John 5:22). Jesus judges by eternal law (see Alma 42:18–26). We should leave the judgment of others unto him, and justice and mercy will be properly balanced. We will all receive the blessings or punishments for what we have chosen to do. We should concentrate on obtaining the peace, blessings, and the kingdom that shall be ours forever (D&C 82:23–24).

DOCTRINE AND COVENANTS 83

*H*istorical Setting:

On the 27th [March 1832], we transacted considerable business for the salvation of the Saints, who were settling among a ferocious set of robbers, like lambs among wolves. It was my endeavor to so organize the church, that the brethren might eventually be independent of every incumbrance beneath the celestial kingdom, by bonds and covenants of mutual friendship and mutual love.

On the 28th and 29th, I visited the brethren above Big Blue River, in Kaw township, a few miles west of Independence, and received a welcome only known by brethren and sisters united as one in the same faith, and by the same baptism, and supported by the same Lord. The Colesville branch, in particular, rejoiced as the ancient Saints did with Paul. It is good to rejoice with the people of God. On the 30th, I returned to Independence, and again set in council with the brethren, and received [Doctrine and Covenants 83]. [*HC,* 1:269]

TEXT AND COMMENTARY

D&C 83:1–6 • Claims of Widows and Children

1 Verily, thus saith the Lord, in addition to the laws of the church concerning women and children, those who belong to the church, who have lost their husbands or fathers:

2 Women have claim on their husbands for their maintenance, until their husbands are taken; and if they are not found transgressors they shall have fellowship in the church.

3 And if they are not faithful they shall not have fellowship in the church; yet they may remain upon their inheritances according to the laws of the land.

4 All children have claim upon their parents for their maintenance until they are of age.

5 And after that, they have claim upon the church, or in other words upon the Lord's storehouse, if their parents have not wherewith to give them inheritances.

6 And the storehouse shall be kept by the consecrations of the church; and widows and orphans shall be provided for, as also the poor. Amen.

Four days after the previous revelation (D&C 82), the Lord further revealed the law concerning the improvement of talents for women and children, who belong to the Church, and had lost their husbands or fathers (v. 1). The faithful women maintained their claims on the storehouse of the Church for their needs. If they were not faithful, they still had ownership of their husband's stewardship that had been legally deeded to them (vv. 2–3). However, they would have to work their stewardship for their own maintenance. All children, regardless of their parent's faithfulness, had claim on the storehouse until they were of age

(v. 4). Even then they could receive help from the storehouse if the parents could not provide inheritances for them (vv. 5–6). The age was not stated, but is assumed to be according to the law of the land, at that time being twenty-one years old. Therefore, the law of consecration provided for all children to develop their talents, and become a contributing member of the Zion society. There was no reason for there being any poor among them, just as it was among Enoch's people (see Moses 7:18), or the Nephites after Christ's visit to them, and they were all converted (see 4 Nephi 1:2–18).

DOCTRINE AND COVENANTS 92

H istorical Setting: This revelation was given to Frederick G. Williams, who had recently been appointed a counselor in the First Presidency (see section heading). No comments are given in the *History of the Church*.

TEXT AND COMMENTARY

D&C 92:1–2 • A Lively Member of the Order

1 Verily, thus saith the Lord, I give unto the united order, organized agreeable to the commandment previously given, a revelation and commandment concerning my servant Frederick G. Williams, that ye shall receive him into the order. What I say unto one I say unto all.

2 And again, I say unto you my servant Frederick G. Williams, you shall be a lively member in this order; and inasmuch as you are faithful in keeping all former commandments you shall be blessed forever. Amen.

As a member of the First Presidency, Frederick G. Williams would join the brethren named in Doctrine and Covenants 82:11 as leaders in order of the law of consecration. The text is self-explanatory.

General Authority Quotes
—*President J. Reuben Clark Jr.* • D&C 78; 82; 83

The fundamental principle of this system was the private ownership of property. Each man owned his portion, or inheritance, or stewardship, with an absolute title, which he could alienate, or hypothecate or otherwise treat as his own. The Church did not own all of the property, and the life under the United Order was not a communal life, as the Prophet Joseph, himself said. (*HC*, 3:28. The United Order is an individualistic system, not a communal system. [*J Reuben Clark, Selected Papers*, ed. David H. Yarn, Jr. (1984), 3: 39]

—*President Ezra Taft Benson* • D&C 78:7

Until one abides by the laws of obedience, sacrifice, the gospel, and chastity, he cannot abide the law of consecration, which is the law pertaining to the celestial kingdom. "For if you will that I give you place in the celestial world, you must prepare yourselves by doing the things which I have commanded you and required of you" (D&C 78:7). [Ezra Taft Benson, *The Teachings of Ezra Taft Benson* (1988), 121]

—*Elder Harold B. Lee* • D&C 78:14

Now, keep in mind with all the crowding in of the socialistic reform programs that are threatening the very foundation of the Church, we must never forget what the Lord said, "that the church must stand independent above all other creatures beneath the celestial world" (D&C 78:14). Whenever we allow ourselves to become entangled and have to be subsidized from government sources—and we think that it's the expedient way to do business in this day—or when we yield to such pressures, I warn you that government subsidies are not the Lord's way; and if we begin to accept, we are on our way to become subsidized politically as well as financially. [*The Teachings of Harold B. Lee,* ed. Clyde J. Williams (1996), 314–315]

—*Elder Harold B. Lee* • D&C 82:14–19

While the world today is groping for a solution (and some of our people, I am afraid, have the mistaken notion that they must look to some development of the philosophies of men in this nation or copied from nations abroad to solve present problems), the Latter-day Saints should never lose sight of the fact that for over one hundred years the Lord has given us the way and the plan by which might come the solution of all the economic problems of this day [quotes D&C 82:14–19]. [*The Teachings of Harold B. Lee,* 316]

Note: See also quotes in volume 1, *More Precious Than Gold*, chapter 21.

Chapter Five

The Oath and Covenant of the Priesthood

D&C 84

DOCTRINE AND COVENANTS 84

Historical Setting: "The Elders during the month of September began to return from their missions to the Eastern States, and present the histories of their several stewardships in the Lord's vineyard; and while together in these seasons of joy, I inquired of the Lord, and received on the 22ⁿᵈ and 23ʳᵈ of September, the [Doctrine and Covenants 84] revelation on the Priesthood" (*HC,* 1:286–87).

SECTION 84 • OUTLINE

➤ 84:1–5   The Church was established to gather the Saints to the New Jerusalem.

    a.   To begin at the temple reared in this generation (vv. 4–5).

    b.   A cloud shall rest upon it, the glory of the Lord (v. 5).

➤ 84:6–18   Moses received the holy priesthood from Jethro, his father-in-law.

    a.   The authority line from Jethro back to Esaias (vv. 7–13).

    b.   Abraham received the priesthood from Melchizedek, back to Adam (vv. 14–16).

    c.   The priesthood continued in the Church in all generations, and is without beginning of days or end of years (v. 17).

    d.   A priesthood was also confirmed upon Aaron throughout all generations (v. 18).

➤ 84:19–25   The greater priesthood administers the gospel and holds the keys of the mysteries of God, even to see the face of God and live.

    a.   Moses taught this to Israel, but they hardened their hearts and could not enter into his rest (vv. 23–24).

    b.   The Lord took Moses and the holy priesthood out of their midst (v. 25).

➤ 84:26–32   The lesser priesthood holds the keys of the ministering of angels and the preparatory gospel.

    a.   The preparatory gospel continued from Aaron to John (v. 27).

    b.   John was ordained by an angel to prepare the way before the Lord (v. 28).

    c.   The offices of elder and bishop are appendages to the High Priesthood (v. 29).

    d.   Offices of deacon and teacher are appendages to the lesser priesthood (v. 30).

    e.   Moses' and Aaron's sons will make an offering in the Lord's house (v. 31–32).

➤ 84:33–62   The oath and covenant of the priesthood. (Details in the Text and Commentary.)

➤ 84:63–98   The Apostles' instructions, same as to the New Testament Apostles.

➤ 84:99–102   The new song to be sung about Zion.

➤ 84:103–108   The way the Apostles built up the church in ancient days.

➤ 84:109–120   Let every man stand in his own office and calling.

    a.   The high priests, elders, and lesser priests shall travel, but not others (v. 111).

    b.   The bishop should travel about the Church seeking after the poor (vv. 112–113).

    c.   Warn New York, Albany, and Boston of rejecting these things (vv. 114–116).

    d.   The rest of the servants go forth as circumstances permit (v. 117).

    e.   The Lord will exert the powers of heaven, and reign with them (vv. 118–120).

Introduction

Although the Prophet designates the revelation as being on the subject of the priesthood, it begins with a declaration concerning the Church gathering to the New Jerusalem and building a temple. Why are these verses an appropriate beginning to a revelation on the priesthood? Joseph later, April 28, 1842, answers this question: ". . . the Church is not fully organized, in its proper order, and cannot be, until the temple is completed, where places will be provided for the administration of the ordinances of the Priesthood" (*TPJS,* 224). The temple must be built in Zion, the city of the New Jerusalem, before the Second Coming.

D&C 84:1–5 • The Temple in the New Jerusalem

1 A revelation of Jesus Christ unto his servant Joseph Smith, Jun., and six elders, as they united their hearts and lifted their voices on high.

2 Yea, the word of the Lord concerning his church, established in the last days for the restoration of his people, as he has spoken by the mouth of his prophets, and for the gathering of his saints to stand upon Mount Zion, which shall be the city of New Jerusalem.

3 Which city shall be built, beginning at the temple lot, which is appointed by the finger of the Lord, in the western boundaries of the State of Missouri, and dedicated by the hand of Joseph Smith, Jun., and others with whom the Lord was well pleased.

4 Verily this is the word of the Lord, that the city New Jerusalem shall be built by the gathering of the saints, beginning at this place, even the place of the temple, which temple shall be reared in this generation.

5 For verily this generation shall not pass away until an house shall be built unto the Lord, and a cloud shall rest upon it, which cloud shall be even the glory of the Lord, which shall fill the house.

According to the *revelation* there were six elders present, and "as they united their hearts and lifted their voices on high," he received the revelation (v. 1). The names of these six elders are not specifically given. Thus, the Lord seems to be reminding the elders and the Saints of the importance of the gathering and the building of the temple as he reveals further principles for the magnifying of the priesthood.

An oft-raised question regarding the building of the New Jerusalem temple should be considered. Why was the temple not built in "this generation" as the Lord stated? (v. 2). The answer usually given to this question is from other revelations in the Doctrine and Covenants. As the Prophet and other members of the Church arrived in the land of Missouri, and the place for the temple was designated by revelation (D&C 57:3), the Lord gave further direction concerning the land of Zion (D&C 58:34). Prefacing these directions he declared: "Who am I, saith the Lord, that have promised and have not fulfilled? I command and men obey not; I revoke and they receive not the blessing" (D&C 58:31). Therefore, it is concluded, the Lord revoked his commandment to build the temple at that time. However, it was not because the Saints had not obeyed. Later, the Lord revealed why he had revoked the commandment to build the temple in Jackson County, Missouri:

> Verily, verily, I say unto you, that when I give a commandment to any of the sons of men to do a work unto my name, and those sons of men go with all their might and with all they have to perform that work, and cease not their diligence, and their enemies come upon them and hinder them from performing that work, behold, it behooveth me to require that work no more at the hands of those sons of men, but to accept their offering.
>
> And the iniquity and transgression of my holy laws and commandments I will visit upon the heads of those who hindered my work, unto the third and fourth generation, so long as they repent not, and hate me, saith the Lord God. [D&C 124:49–50]

The Lord then commanded them to build a house to him, but in Nauvoo (see D&C 124:55).

In a broader sense, the Lord has not revoked the building of the temple in Jackson County "in this generation" as revealed in section 84. The word generation has variant meanings in the scriptures. A generation sometimes is considered to be from a father to a child, or approximately twenty years. The judgment upon the "heads of those who hindered my work, unto the third and fourth generation," (v. 49) is an example of this meaning of the word. The Book of Mormon gives a second meaning. It sometimes uses a generation as a period of one hundred years (see Helaman 13:8–11). The Lord, on other occasions, uses yet another period of time as a generation. He speaks of the time period prior to the Second Coming of Christ as the "crooked and perverse" or "wicked generation" (D&C 33:2; 34:6; 88:75), or as "the times of the Gentiles" (D&C 45:28–30; JST, Luke 21:24–32; 3 Nephi 16:7–10). The period following "the times of the Gentiles" is designated as the time of the fulfilling of the covenant made to Israel, or the times of Israel (3 Nephi 16:11; 20:12). Joseph Smith was called to give the word of the Lord (the Book of Mormon) to "this unbelieving and stiffnecked [Gentiles] generation" (D&C 5:8–10). The time for the fulfilling of the covenant to Israel would follow that wicked generation. The Lord had made a covenant with Jacob, the father of the twelve tribes of Israel, that he would establish His people in the land of America, and they would build the New Jerusalem (3 Nephi 21:21–23). The Savior taught the Nephites, during His visit to them, that the Gentiles who accepted the gospel would assist His people in building the New Jerusalem (3 Nephi 21:22–23). Therefore, the temple in Jackson County could still be built before "this generation," the generation that "shall not all pass away until an house shall be built unto the Lord" (D&C 84:4–5). In that generation, a cloud "shall rest upon it, which cloud shall be even the glory of the Lord, which shall fill the house" (D&C 84:5). The cloud resting upon the temple will fulfill the prophecy of Isaiah (Isaiah 4:5). This prophecy, therefore, is a good example of that which the Lord "has spoken by the mouth of his prophets" (D&C 84:2).

D&C 84:6–18 • The Priesthood Authority

6 And the sons of Moses, according to the Holy Priesthood which he received under the hand of his father-in-law, Jethro;

7 And Jethro received it under the hand of Caleb;

8 And Caleb received it under the hand of Elihu;

9 And Elihu under the hand of Jeremy;

10 And Jeremy under the hand of Gad;

11 And Gad under the hand of Esaias;

12 And Esaias received it under the hand of God.

13 Esaias also lived in the days of Abraham, and was blessed of him—

14 Which Abraham received the priesthood from Melchizedek, who received it through the lineage of his fathers, even till Noah;

15 And from Noah till Enoch, through the lineage of their fathers;

16 And from Enoch to Abel, who was slain by the conspiracy of his brother, who received the priesthood by the commandments of God, by the hand of his father Adam, who was the first man—

17 Which priesthood continueth in the church of God in all generations, and is without beginning of days or end of years.

18 And the Lord confirmed a priesthood also upon Aaron and his seed, throughout all their generations, which priesthood also continueth and abideth forever with the priesthood which is after the holiest order of God.

Having established the relationship of the priesthood to the gathering and the building of the temple, the Lord traced the authority of the priesthood given to Moses by "his father-in-law, Jethro," back to "Adam who was the first man" (D&C 84:6–16). There are a dozen individual ordinations revealed, most of which we know little about. A few of these deserve some commentary.

Caleb, from whom Jethro received the priesthood (D&C 84:7), is not the Caleb who was one of the twelve spies sent by Moses to search out the land of Canaan (Numbers 13:6). Since the Caleb who ordained Moses was obviously a righteous man, perhaps the spy Caleb was a descendant of or named after him. The earlier Caleb was ordained by Elihu, but we do not know anything definite about him (D&C 84:8). There is an Elihu that comes on the scene in the book of Job (Job 32:2). If the Elihu is the same one who ordained Caleb, it would certainly help in dating the time period of Job, a very controversial topic among Bible scholars.

Esaias, who received the priesthood "under the hand of God" (D&C 84:12) seems to designate an apostasy prior to his lifetime. However, since he lived in the time of Abraham (v. 13), perhaps he was given the priesthood after Abraham had left "the land of the Chaldeans" (Abraham 2:3–4), or it was given him in another part of the ancient lands. The

Doctrine and Covenants text merely says that he lived in the day of Abraham, but does not tell us where.[15]

There has been much discussion about verse 14 of this revelation: "Which Abraham received the priesthood from Melchizedek, who received it through the lineage of his fathers, even till Noah" (D&C 84:14). Some have reasoned that Melchizedek could not have been Shem, as some traditions state, because Melchizedek received the priesthood "through the lineage of his fathers, even till Noah," indicating more than one family generation, and Shem was the son of Noah. Others, however, point out that the term "through the lineage of his fathers" is a common Hebrew expression that does not designate generation plurality. The argument regarding Shem and Melchizedek is thus not solved through this Doctrine and Covenants revelation.[16]

Adam being "the first man" is confirmed in all of the four standard works.[17] The Lord established His word in the mouth of two or three witnesses (Deuteronomy 19:15; Matthew 18:16). In our dispensation, His word is firmly established.

The authority of the priesthood is eternal, but is delegated to man in mortality in all generations. The two priesthoods spoken of (vv. 17–18) are compared in various aspects in the revelation, but will be spoken of separately here.

D&C 84:19–25 • Melchizedek—the Eternal Priesthood

> 19 And this greater priesthood administereth the gospel and holdeth the key of the mysteries of the kingdom, even the key of the knowledge of God.

---

[15] Abraham is dated around 2000 B.C.; Isaiah is dated at about 740 B.C.; it is also noted that Esaias is the New Testament translation of the prophet Isaiah (see Luke 4:16–20) and compare Isaiah 61:1–2), but the Old Testament prophet Isaiah did not live in the days of Abraham.

[16] This argument will not be discussed here since it is irrelevant to an understanding of this revelation.

[17] In addition to D&C 84:16, see Moses 1:34, the Pearl of Great Price; 1 Nephi 5:11; 2 Nephi 2:19–20, 25; 9:21, the Book of Mormon; Genesis 5:1–2, the Old Testament; JST, Luke 3:38; 1 Corinthians 15:45, the New Testament.

20 Therefore, in the ordinances thereof, the power of godliness is manifest.

21 And without the ordinances thereof, and the authority of the Priesthood, the power of godliness is not manifest unto men in the flesh;

22 For without this no man can see the face of God, even the father, and live.

23 Now this Moses plainly taught to the children of Israel in the wilderness, and sought diligently to sanctify his people that they might behold the face of God;

24 But they hardened their hearts and could not endure his presence; therefore, the Lord in his wrath, for his anger was kindled against them, swore that they should not enter into his rest while in the wilderness, which rest is the fulness of his glory.

25 Therefore, he took Moses out of their midst, and the Holy Priesthood also;

The Lord described above the priesthood that had been in the Church of God in all generations[18] as being "without beginning of days or end of years" (v. 18). Alma gave a similar description of the priesthood in the Book of Mormon. "This high priesthood being after the order of his Son, which order was from the foundation of the world; or in other words, being without beginning of days or end of years, being prepared from eternity to all eternity, according to his foreknowledge of all things" (Alma 13:7). Paul, in writing to the Hebrews, also recognized the eternal nature of the Melchizedek Priesthood. "For this Melchizedek was ordained a priest after the order of the Son of God, which order was without father, without mother, without descent, having neither beginning of days, nor end of life. And all those who are ordained unto this priesthood are made like unto the Son of God, abiding a priest continually" (JST, Hebrews 7:3). In other words, the Melchizedek Priesthood is an eternal priesthood, not just an earthly authority.

The primary purpose of the higher priesthood is to administer the

---

[18] It must be remembered that the Melchizedek Priesthood was had among the children of Israel even after Moses was taken from their midst (D&C 84:25). Although the lay people of the Church had only the Aaronic Priesthood, Joseph Smith taught that "all the prophets had the Melchizedek Priesthood and were ordained by God himself" (*TPJS*, 181). More will be said of this ordination later.

principles of the gospel through the various offices of this priesthood (v. 19), as is revealed in Doctrine and Covenants 107. The ultimate purpose, however, is to bring people to the knowledge of God. This knowledge is to come as personal knowledge of His existence, not just factual knowledge about Him. As Jesus taught during his mortal ministry in what is called "the great intercessory prayer" or the "high priestly prayer," "this is life eternal, that they might know thee the only true God, and Jesus Christ, whom thou hast sent" (John 17:3). To know God is to come unto Him through receiving the ordinances of the Melchizedek Priesthood, administered by the authority of that priesthood. It does not come automatically through receiving the ordinances, but is dependent upon one's individual preparations and diligence. The Lord had earlier declared:

> And again, verily I say unto you that it is your privilege, and a promise I give unto you that have been ordained unto this ministry, that inasmuch as you strip yourselves from jealousies and fears, and humble yourselves before me, for ye are not sufficiently humble, the veil shall be rent and you shall see me and know that I am—not with the carnal neither natural mind, but with the spiritual.
>
> For no man has seen God at any time in the flesh, except quickened by the Spirit of God.
>
> Neither can any natural man abide the presence of God, neither after the carnal mind. [D&C 67:10–12]

The Lord was more specific in a later revelation: "Verily, thus saith the Lord: It shall come to pass that every soul who forsaketh his sins and cometh unto me, and calleth on my name, and obeyeth my voice, and keepeth my commandments, shall see my face and know that I am" (D&C 93:1). The forsaking of sins is based on the principle of repentance. To come unto Christ is to receive the ordinance of baptism (see 3 Nephi 21:6; 27:20). Those who call on the name of Christ are prayerful and seek the guidance of the Lord. To obey the Lord's voice is to receive by revelation the answers to prayer. Those who keep His commandments are aware of and follow the written commandments contained in the scriptures. When a person comes face to face with Christ, he or she will certainly know Him, and thus be qualified for eternal life. He or she will be able to see the face of God in the flesh and live (D&C 82:22). The persons will have their calling and election made sure, as will be further discussed in section 88.

As revealed in the revelation on eternal marriage, man and wife will attain eternal lives. "This is eternal lives—to know the only wise and true God, and Jesus Christ, whom he hath sent. I am he. Receive ye, therefore, my law" (D&C 132:24)[19] Through eternal marriage, the family will be brought into the fulness of the Lord's glory. Thus the gospel is not a "do it yourself" plan but a joint effort of the family.

The principle of the Melchizedek Priesthood manifesting the power of godliness was plainly taught by Moses to the children of Israel, but they rejected them and the Lord "took Moses out of their midst, and the Holy Priesthood also" (D&C 84:23–25). However, as will be discussed in section 107, the office of high priest, which seems to have been an office of the Melchizedek Priesthood, remained, and also the prophets were given the Melchizedek Priesthood. The Prophet Joseph declared, "All the prophets had the Melchizedek Priesthood and were ordained by God himself" (TPJS, 181), and from other statements, it is concluded that God took away the Melchizedek Priesthood as a lay priesthood, but specified certain individuals to hold the higher priesthood. Since all ordinances are earthly ordinances, being ordained by God himself, suggests that God designated who was to be ordained, but others actually performed the ordination or at least followed His ordination with an earthly ordination.[20]

D&C 84:26–32 • The Aaronic Priesthood

26 And the lesser priesthood continued, which priesthood holdeth the key of the ministering of angels and the preparatory gospel;

27 Which gospel is the gospel of repentance and of baptism, and the remission of sins, and the law of carnal commandments, which the Lord in his wrath caused to continue with the house of Aaron among the children of Israel until John, whom God raised up, being filled with the Holy Ghost from his mother's womb.

28 For he was baptized while he was yet in his childhood, and was

---

[19] The concept of eternal marriage is discussed more fully in chapter 25.

[20] After John the Baptist conferred the Aaronic Priesthood upon Joseph Smith and Oliver Cowdery, they ordained each other. This is the basis of the doctrinal assumption that all ordinations must be earthly ordinations (JS—H 1:69–71).

ordained by the angel of God at the time he was eight days old unto this power, to overthrow the kingdom of the Jews, and to make straight the way of the Lord before the face of his people, to prepare them for the coming of the Lord, in whose hand is given all power.

29 And again, the offices of elder and bishop are necessary appendages belonging unto the high priesthood.

30 And again, the offices of teacher and deacon are necessary appendages belonging to the lesser priesthood, which priesthood was confirmed upon Aaron and his sons.

31 Therefore, as I said concerning the sons of Moses—for the sons of Moses and also the sons of Aaron shall offer an acceptable offering and sacrifice in the house of the Lord, which house shall be built unto the Lord in this generation, upon the consecrated spot as I have appointed—

32 And the sons of Moses and of Aaron shall be filled with the glory of the Lord, upon Mount Zion in the Lord's house, whose sons are ye; and also many whom I have called and sent forth to build up my church.

The priesthood given to Aaron and his sons was not a substitute for the Melchizedek Priesthood that was taken away, but one which "also continueth and abideth forever with the priesthood which is after the holiest order [the Melchizedek] of God" (D&C 84:18). This companion priesthood to the Melchizedek Priesthood, that was to continue with the house of Israel, "holdeth the key of the ministering of angels and the preparatory gospel" (v. 26). Wherefore, those who hold the keys of this priesthood have the right to be ministered to by the angels. Through the ordinances of this priesthood, others may be so ministered to, depending upon their worthiness. About ten months earlier, the Lord in a special conference of the Church had said (part of which was quoted earlier), "Ye are not able to abide the presence of God now, neither the ministering of angels; wherefore, continue in patience until ye are perfected. Let not your minds turn back; and when ye are worthy, in mine own due time, ye shall see and know that which was conferred upon you by the hands of my servant Joseph Smith, Jun. Amen" (D&C 67:13–14).

The preparatory gospel was defined as "the gospel of repentance and of baptism, and the remission of sins, and the law of carnal commandments" (D&C 84:27). It is probably called the preparatory gospel because it is to prepare a person to receive the Melchizedek Priesthood. This priesthood also has the authority to administer the ordinances that will bring a remission of sins. While the ordinance of water baptism does not in itself bring a remission of sins, it prepares a person to receive the cleansing power of the Holy Ghost (see 2 Nephi 31:17; Moroni 6:4; 8:25–26; *TPJS*, 314). The preparatory gospel was given to Aaron and continued with his house "among the children of Israel until John, whom God raised up, being filled with the Holy Ghost from his mother's womb" (D&C 84:27, compare Luke 1:39–41).

The mission of John (who is called John the Baptist in the New Testament, see section 13 heading) was to overthrow the kingdom of the Jews and to prepare the way for the earthly ministry of Jesus Christ (D&C 84:28). Being baptized in his childhood does not refer to infant baptism, but undoubtedly to when he was eight years of age. The age of eight is an eternal principle. A male child was circumcised at eight days of age in the days of Abraham as a covenant to teach "that children are not accountable before me until they are eight years old" (JST, Genesis 17:11; compare D&C 68:25). However, an angel of God did ordain John at the time he was eight days old to fulfill his foretold mission (v. 28).

The Prophet Joseph enlightened us further on the ordination of John the Baptist:

> As touching the Gospel and baptism that John preached, I would say that John came preaching the Gospel for the remission of sins; he had his authority from God, and the oracles of God were with him, and the kingdom of God for a season seemed to rest with John alone. The Lord promised Zacharias that he should have a son who was a descendant of Aaron, the Lord having promised that the priesthood should continue with Aaron and his seed throughout their generations. Let no man take this honor upon himself, except he be called of God, as was Aaron; and Aaron received his call by revelation. An angel of God also appeared unto Zacharias while in the Temple, and told him that he should have a son, whose name should be John, and he should be filled with the Holy Ghost. Zacharias was a priest of God, and officiating in the Temple, and John was a priest after his father, and held the keys of the Aaronic priesthood, and was called of God to preach the Gospel of the kingdom of God. The Jews, as a nation, having departed from the law of God and the Gospel of the Lord, prepared the way for transferring it to the Gentiles. [*TPJS*, 272–273]

Regarding the angel ordaining John, the Prophet Joseph stated further:

Here is a little of law which must be fulfilled. The Levitical Priesthood is forever hereditary—fixed on the head of Aaron and his sons forever, and was in active operation down to Zacharias the father of John. Zacharias would have had no child had not God given him a son. He sent his angel to declare unto Zacharias that his wife Elizabeth should bear him a son, whose name was to be called John.

The keys of the Aaronic Priesthood were committed unto him, and he was as the voice of one crying in the wilderness, saying: "Prepare ye the way of the Lord and make his paths straight."

The Kingdom of heaven suffereth violence, etc.

The kingdom of heaven continueth in authority until John.

The authority taketh it by absolute power.

John having the power took the Kingdom by authority.

How have you obtained all this great knowledge? By the gift of the Holy Ghost. [*TPJS,* 319]

We certainly should accept and appreciate what Joseph learned by the Holy Ghost.

Through the restoration of the Aaronic and the Melchizedek Priesthood, the way was prepared for the sons of Moses and Aaron to officiate in the temple that the Lord commanded to be built, and be filled with the glory of the Lord (D&C 84:31–32). At the dedication of the Kirtland Temple, there was an outpouring of the Lord's Spirit (*HC,* 4:428) as the Lord promised. The promise was not limited to the Kirtland Temple, but whenever "my people build a house unto me in the name of the Lord" (D&C 97:15). Furthermore, the Lord promised that "all the pure in heart that shall come into it shall see God" (v. 16). This is a promise attained through the ordinances of the Melchizedek Priesthood, as noted earlier (see D&C 84:20–22). Therefore, it seems to be a specific blessing of the priesthood covenant. The priesthood and the temple are inseparably connected.

D&C 84:33–39 • The Lord's Oath to the Priesthood

33 For whoso is faithful unto the obtaining these two priesthoods of which I have spoken, and the magnifying their calling, are sanctified by the Spirit unto the renewing of their bodies.

34 They become the sons of Moses and of Aaron and the seed of

Abraham, and the church and kingdom, and the elect of God.

35 And also all they who receive this priesthood receive me, saith the Lord;

36 For he that receiveth my servants receiveth me;

37 And he that receiveth me receiveth my Father;

38 And he that receiveth my Father receiveth my Father's kingdom; therefore all that my Father hath shall be given unto him.

39 And this is according to the oath and covenant which belongeth to the priesthood.

One must be "faithful unto the obtaining these two priesthoods of which I [the Lord] have spoken" (v. 33). The sons of Moses and of Aaron were promised several blessings as they officiated in the temple (vv. 34–38). These blessings also imply that the temple is where a man gets "the fulness of the priesthood." (*TPJS,* 308). The Lord then declared, "And this is according to the oath and covenant which belongeth to the priesthood" (D&C 84:39). Later the Prophet further qualified that the Levitical Priesthood was "made without an oath; but the Melchizedek Priesthood is by an oath and covenant." (*TPJS,* 323). It requires two parties to enter into a covenant agreement. In the case of the Melchizedek Priesthood, God gives an oath that He will pour out certain blessings upon a man if he will keep the prescribed conditions of the covenant. The lesser priesthood was given as a "preparatory gospel," or as suggested before, a priesthood that would prepare them to receive the higher priesthood. Later in this great revelation on priesthood, the Lord instructed:

> If any man among you be strong in the Spirit, let him take with him him that is weak, that he may be edified in all meekness, that he may become strong also.
>
> Therefore, take with you those who are ordained unto the lesser priesthood, and send them before you to make appointments, and to prepare the way, and to fill appointments that you yourselves are not able to fill.
>
> Behold, this is the way that mine apostles, in ancient days, built up my church unto me. [D&C 84:106–108]

The Lord designated the Prophet Joseph and the six elders assembled as the sons of Moses and of Aaron, as well as many "whom I have called and sent forth to build up my church" (D&C 84:32). The same designation of sons of Moses and Aaron are applicable to those who receive the two priesthoods (Aaronic and Melchizedek) today.

The first promised blessing of the Lord to those "magnifying their calling" in the priesthood is to be "sanctified by the Spirit unto the renewing of their bodies" (v. 33). The blessing is two-fold; spiritual, and physical. To be sanctified is to become pure and holy. It comes by the Spirit that accompanies those who fulfill their priesthood assignments (see Alma 5:54). It is the "purifying and the sanctification of their hearts, which sanctification cometh because of their yielding their hearts unto God" (Helaman 3:35). At the same time, the body is physically renewed to enable the priesthood holder to carry out his assignments. Many of the General Authorities of the Church are examples of the renewing of their bodies physically to enable them to fulfill their heavy responsibilities in the Church. The majority of the Quorum of the Twelve Apostles and the First Presidency are well beyond the normal retirement age of our day, but still carry on a schedule of daily activities that often would not be attempted by younger men.

The Book of Mormon also confirms a fulfillment of the promise of sanctification to priesthood holders. Alma bore record that the High Priesthood holders who worked righteousness:

> . . . were called after this holy order, and were sanctified, and their garments were washed white through the blood of their Lamb.
>
> Now they, after being sanctified by the Holy Ghost, having their garments made white, being pure and spotless before God, could not look upon sin save it were with abhorrence; and there were many, exceedingly great many, who were made pure and entered into the rest of the Lord their God. [Alma 13:11–12]

Their entering into the rest of the Lord was accomplished through the ordinances of the Melchizedek Priesthood, as Moses had taught his people (D&C 84:23–24). Therefore, Alma cited Melchizedek as an example of one who magnified his priesthood to this end (see Alma 13:14–10).

Those priesthood holders who magnify their callings will: "become the sons of Moses and of Aaron and the seed of Abraham, and the church and kingdom, and the elect of God" (D&C 84:34). This is the second promise of the covenant made by the Lord. Many of these brethren are already of the lineage of Abraham (see D&C 103:17), and thus, "lawful heirs, according to the flesh" (D&C 86:8–9). Abraham was promised that his seed "shall bear this ministry and Priesthood unto all nations." He was further promised that the right of the priesthood would continue in the literal seed of the body to bless all the families of the earth, "even with the blessings of the Gospel, which are the blessings of salvation, even of life eternal" (Abraham 2:9, 11). Nevertheless, they too must magnify their priesthood to eternally inherit their lineage blessing. As Paul taught the Romans: "They are not all Israel, which are of Israel" (Romans 9:6). Those who are not literal offspring of Abraham and "receive this Gospel shall be called after [Abraham's] name, and shall be accounted [Abraham's] seed, and shall rise up and bless thee, as their father" (Abraham 2:10). They become adopted sons and are a part of the Church and kingdom that is again restored upon the earth. Wherefore they are accounted "the elect of God" (v. 34). The "elect according to the covenant" (of Abraham) who have magnified their callings will be given the guidance and power to not be deceived by the false Christs and false prophets who will attempt to deceive them in the last days (see JS—Matthew 1:21–23). The value of this blessing will be appreciated more and more as the false Christs and false prophets intensify their efforts against the Church and kingdom.

The third blessing promised to those who magnify their calling is progressive or sequential. The blessing is introduced with: "And also all they who receive this priesthood receive me" (D&C 84:35). The prerequisite for receiving the Lord is then outlined. "For he that receiveth my servants receiveth me" (v. 36). The Lord speaks to mankind through His servants, and "Surely the Lord God will do nothing *until* he revealeth *the* secret unto his servants the prophets" (JST, Amos 3:7; italics added). The Old Testament principle of speaking through the prophets was reaffirmed in the preface to the Doctrine and Covenants: "Search these commandments, for they are true and faithful, and the prophecies and promises which are in them shall all be fulfilled. What I the Lord have spoken, I have spoken, and I excuse not myself, and though the heavens and the earth pass away, my word shall not pass away, but shall all be fulfilled, whether by mine voice or by the voice of my servants, it is the same" (D&C 1:37–38).

As we search the commandments and prophecies, the Spirit will bear record of their truthfulness, and we will qualify ourselves to receive Jesus Christ Himself. As we qualify ourselves to receive the Lord, we also become qualified to receive the Father, for the Lord has promised that: "he that receiveth me receiveth my father" (D&C 84:37). The appearance of the Son and the Father to those who have met the prerequisites were promised by the Savior to His disciples following the last supper: "He that hath my commandments, and keepeth them, he it is that loveth me; and he that loveth me shall be loved of my Father, and I will love him, and will manifest myself to him. Jesus answered and said unto him, If a man love me, he will keep my words; and my Father will love him, and we will come unto him, and make our abode with him" (John 14:21, 23).

The Prophet Joseph Smith commented on these and previous verses from John, promising what Jesus called "another Comforter" (John 14:16):

> Now what is this other Comforter? Is it no more nor less than the Lord Jesus Christ Himself; and this is the sum and substance of the whole matter; that when any man obtains this last Comforter, he will have the personage of Jesus Christ to attend him, or appear unto him from time to time, and even He will manifest the Father unto him, and they will take up their abode with him, and the visions of the heavens will be opened unto him, and the Lord will teach him face to face, and he may have a perfect knowledge of the mysteries of the Kingdom of God; and this is the state and place the ancient Saints arrived at when they had such glorious visions—Isaiah, Ezekiel, John upon the Isles of Patmos, St. Paul in the three heavens, and all the Saints who held communion with the general assembly and Church of the Firstborn. [*TPJS,* 150–151]

Thus, through the ordinances and "the authority of the priesthood, the power of Godliness is . . . manifest . . . in the flesh" and men "can see the face of God, even the Father and live" (D&C 84:20–22).

But there is more than just the appearance of the Father and the Son. The blessings continue: "And he that receiveth my Father receiveth my Father's kingdom; therefore all that my Father hath shall be given unto him" (D&C 84:38). The extent of these promised blessings are incomprehensible to man. President Wilford Woodruff, reflecting upon the promises concerning the priesthood asked:

> I often reflect upon the promises made concerning the priesthood.
> . . . Now, I sometimes ask myself the question, Do we comprehend these

things? Do we comprehend that if we abide the laws of the priesthood we shall become heirs of God and joint-heirs with Jesus Christ? Who in the name of the Lord can apprehend such language as this? Who can comprehend that, by obeying the celestial law, all that our Father has shall be given unto us—exaltation, thrones, principalities, power, dominion—who can comprehend it? Nevertheless it is here stated.[21]

D&C 84:40–42 • The Father Cannot Break

40 Therefore, all those who receive the priesthood, receive this oath and covenant of my Father, which he cannot break, neither can it be moved.

41 But whoso breaketh this covenant after he hath received it, and altogether turneth therefrom, shall not have forgiveness of sins in this world nor in the world to come.

42 And wo unto all those who come not unto this priesthood which ye have received, which I now confirm upon you who are present this day, by mine own voice out of the heavens; and even I have given the heavenly hosts and mine angels charge concerning you.

All of the above incomprehensible blessings are available to those who receive the Melchizedek Priesthood. It is an unbreakable oath of the Father that guarantees it (v. 40). However, man has his agency and may break his covenant. The seriousness of doing so is also revealed in the revelation (v. 41). All men have weaknesses and shortcomings and through constant repentance can gain forgiveness, but if some "altogether" turn from the covenants of the Melchizedek Priesthood, they will be committing unforgivable sins. The Atonement of Christ will not pay for these sins; instead, these men will "be delivered over to the buffetings of Satan until the day of redemption" (D&C 78:12; 82:21; Hebrews 10:26).

Since the oath and covenant of the Melchizedek Priesthood has such serious consequences, some may choose to not enter into such an agreement. However, the Lord contemplated such decisions and gave a solemn warning to them, and also a few words of comfort to those who received the priesthood at the time of this revelation (v. 42). Those who will receive the priesthood by covenant will also receive the assistance of the heavenly hosts and angels to help them keep their agreement.

---

[21] *The Discourses of Wilford Woodruff,* comp. G. Homer Durham, 79–80.

D&C 84:43–48 • The Covenant of the Priesthood Holder

43 And I now give unto you a commandment to beware concerning yourselves, to give diligent heed to the words of eternal life.

44 For you shall live by every word that proceedeth forth from the mouth of God.

45 For the word of the Lord is truth, and whatsoever is truth is light, and whatsoever is light is Spirit, even the Spirit of Jesus Christ.

46 And the Spirit giveth light to every man that cometh into the world; and the Spirit enlighteneth every man through the world, that hearkeneth to the voice of the Spirit.

47 And every one that hearkeneth to the voice of the Spirit cometh unto God, even the Father.

48 And the Father teacheth him of the covenant which he has renewed and confirmed upon you, which is confirmed upon you for your sakes, and not for your sakes only, but for the sake of the whole world.

Having revealed the blessings that are attached to the reception of the priesthood, the Lord now outlines his expectations for those who enter into the covenant. He has already spoken of the first requirement—"the magnifying their calling" (v. 33) in the priesthood as they administer the gospel and the ordinances of the Church. The magnifying of one's priesthood is further defined in the scriptures. Jacob, brother of Nephi, recorded that he and his brother Joseph: " . . . did magnify our office unto the Lord, taking upon us the responsibility, answering the sins of the people upon our own heads if we did not teach them the word of God with all diligence; wherefore, by laboring with our might their blood might not come upon our garments; otherwise their blood would come upon our garments, and we would not be found spotless at the last days" (Jacob 1:19; see also 2 Nephi 9:44 and Ezekiel 33:1–9).

As a servant of the Lord, to magnify one's calling is to fulfill the second great commandment to "love thy neighbor as thyself" (Matthew 22:29). As the Lord later recorded, the priesthood holder must "learn his duty, and to act in the office in which he is appointed, in all diligence" (D&C 107:99).

The Lord revealed the second requirement of the covenant: "I now give unto you a commandment to beware concerning yourselves, to give diligent heed to the words of eternal life. For you shall live by every word that proceedeth forth from the mouth of God" (D&C 84:43–44). To "live by every word" tells us we cannot be selective in keeping the commandments, but must "serve [the Lord] and keep all [His] commandments" (D&C 42:29). We must "keep the whole law (James 2:10). The Prophet Joseph Smith declared: "Any person who is exalted to the highest mansion has to abide a celestial law, and the whole law too" (*TPJS*, 331). In this revelation the Lord lists three sources of the words of eternal life.

The first source of truth is the Light of Christ. Every person is born into the world with the Spirit of Christ (John 1:9). The purpose of that light is to judge between good and evil (see Moroni 7:16). By following that light, a person is led to the Father: "Every one that hearkeneth to the voice of the Spirit cometh unto God, even the Father" (D&C 84:47). They are also led to the waters of baptism (3 Nephi 12:3; 21:6; 27:20) where they will receive the second source of the words of eternal life, the Holy Ghost (see D&C 84:64).

After receiving the Holy Ghost, we are taught more regarding the covenant of baptism into which we have entered (see D&C 84:48). As the Prophet Joseph taught, "The Holy Ghost is God's messenger to administer in all [the] priesthoods" (*TPJS*, 323). The Holy Ghost will not only benefit those who receive him, but will benefit the whole world by revealing truths that have been lost from the world through apostasy. The apostasy has been universal.

D&C 84:49–53 • The Whole World Lies in Sin

49 And the whole world lieth in sin, and groaneth under darkness and under the bondage of sin.

50 And by this you may know they are under the bondage of sin, because they come not unto me.

51 For whoso cometh not unto me is under the bondage of sin.

52 For whoso receiveth not my voice is not acquainted with my voice, and is not of me.

53 And by this you may know the righteous from the wicked, and that the whole world groaneth under sin and darkness even now.

In order to overcome the bondage of sin that is upon the whole world,

the inhabitants must come unto Christ through the waters of baptism. The Light of Christ will lead them to those waters, and then the Holy Ghost will teach those who have come unto Christ. Thus the whole world is benefited. Wherefore, the righteous and the wicked are separated.

D&C 84:54–59 • The Whole Church Under Condemnation

54 And your minds in times past have been darkened because of unbelief, and because you have treated lightly the things you have received—

55 Which vanity and unbelief have brought the whole church under condemnation.

56 And this condemnation resteth upon the children of Zion, even all.

57 And they shall remain under this condemnation until they repent and remember the new covenant, even the Book of Mormon and the former commandments which I have given them, not only to say, but to do according to that which I have written—

58 That they may bring forth fruit meet for their Father's kingdom; otherwise there remaineth a scourge and judgment to be poured out upon the children of Zion.

59 For shall the children of the kingdom pollute my holy land? Verily, I say unto you, Nay.

The third source of the words of eternal life are the scriptures, both ancient and latter-day. Although the Book of Mormon had been available to the latter-day Church members for about two and one-half years, they had not been using the book or previous revelations as they should (v. 54), so the Lord gave them a warning. The condemnation was upon the Church collectively, although certainly there were many individuals who were not guilty of "vanity and unbelief" (see D&C 1:30). The solution to remove the condemnation was then given: ". . . they repent and remember the new covenant, even the Book of Mormon and the former commandments" (v. 57).

Elder Dallin H. Oaks interpreted the former commandments to have reference to both the Bible and to the revelations given to the Church since 1820.[22] Both are accepted as part of the standard works of the Church (A of F 1:8). The important point to consider is that we must not just give lip service, but "live by [these words] that proceeded forth from the mouth of God" (v. 44). King Benjamin gave a similar admonition:

> Believe in God; believe that he is, and that he created all things, both in heaven and in earth; believe that he has all wisdom, and all power, both in heaven and in earth; believe that man doth not comprehend all the things which the Lord can comprehend.
>
> And again, believe that ye must repent of your sins and forsake them, and humble yourselves before God; and ask in sincerity of heart that he would forgive you; and now, if you believe all these things see that ye do them. [Mosiah 4:9–10]

However, the Church did not "do" as the Book of Mormon and the former revelations taught. Hence, the Saints were driven from the Lord's holy land, although not permanently (see D&C 101:1–11; 105:1–9). Nor has the Church today fully grasped the teachings of the Book of Mormon and the former commandments. President Ezra Taft Benson was obviously raised up to bring the Church from the scourge and judgment that still rested upon the Church in the 1980s because of not using the Book of Mormon and the former commandments as they should.[23]

A fourth source of the words of eternal life is the words of the Lord's servants. As stated above, those who receive the Lord must receive the Lord's servants (D&C 84:36). The Lord gives His words to the Church through those He has called and ordained to His work (D&C 1:38). These servants exemplify the ninth article of faith.

D&C 84:60–76 • Bear Testimony to All the World

60 Verily, verily, I say unto you who now hear my words, which are my voice, blessed are ye inasmuch as you receive these things;

---

[22] See Dallin H. Oaks, "Another Testament of Jesus Christ," CES Fireside for College-Age Young Adults, 6 June 1993, Brigham Young University, Provo, Utah, 4.

[23] See Ezra Taft Benson, CR, April 1986, 100; the scourge seems to be the Gentile influence upon the Church instead of the Saints following the revelations of God (see D&C 113:10).

61 For I will forgive you of your sins with this commandment—that you remain steadfast in your minds in solemnity and the spirit of prayer, in bearing testimony to all the world of those things which are communicated unto you.

62 Therefore, go ye into all the world; and unto whatsoever place ye cannot go ye shall send, that the testimony may go from you into all the world unto every creature.

63 And as I said unto mine apostles, even so I say unto you, for you are mine apostles, even God's high priests; ye are they whom my Father hath given me; ye are my friends;

64 Therefore, as I said unto mine apostles I say unto you again, that every soul who believeth on your words, and is baptized by water for the remission of sins, shall receive the Holy Ghost.

65 And these signs shall follow them that believe—

66 In my name they shall do many wonderful works;

67 In my name they shall cast out devils;

68 In my name they shall heal the sick;

69 In my name they shall open the eyes of the blind, and unstop the ears of the deaf;

70 And the tongue of the dumb shall speak;

71 And if any man shall administer poison unto them it shall not hurt them;

72 And the poison of a serpent shall not have power to harm them.

73 But a commandment I give unto them, that they shall not boast themselves of these things, neither speak them before the world; for these things are given unto you for your profit and for salvation.

74 Verily, verily, I say unto you, they who believe not on your words, and are not baptized in water in my name, for the remission of their sins, that they may receive the Holy Ghost, shall be damned, and shall not come into my Father's kingdom where my Father and I am.

75 And this revelation unto you, and commandment, is in force from this very hour upon all the world, and the gospel is unto all who have not received it.

76 But, verily I say unto all those to whom the kingdom has been given—from you it must be preached unto them, that they shall repent of their former evil works; for they are to be upbraided for their evil

hearts of unbelief, and your brethren in Zion for their rebellion against you at the time I sent you.

A third requirement of the Church members, under the covenant of the Melchizedek Priesthood, was to bear "testimony to all the world of those things which are communicated unto you" (v. 61). Again the Lord quoted, or paraphrased, biblical passages to confirm the requirement. The first passage so referred to contains the instructions given to the eleven apostles in Jerusalem just prior to the Savior's Ascension into heaven, as recorded in the Gospel of Mark (16:14–19; compare Doctrine and Covenants 84:62–74). Although quoted with some variation, the contents are sufficiently well known and understandable to proceed without comment. The Lord puts the revelation and commandments to preach these principles to the Church members in force from that very hour (vv. 75–76).

D&C 84:77–86 • The Lord's Friends

77 And again I say unto you, my friends, for from henceforth I shall call you friends, it is expedient that I give unto you this commandment, that ye become even as my friends in days when I was with them, traveling to preach the gospel in my power;

78 For I suffered them not to have purse or scrip, neither two coats.

79 Behold, I send you out to prove the world, and the laborer is worthy of his hire.

80 And any man that shall go and preach this gospel of the kingdom, and fail not to continue faithful in all things, shall not be weary in mind, neither darkened, neither in body, limb, nor joint; and a hair of his head shall not fall to the ground unnoticed. And they shall not go hungry, neither athirst.

81 Therefore, take ye no thought for the morrow, for what ye shall eat, or what ye shall drink, or wherewithal ye shall be clothed.

82 For, consider the lilies of the field, how they grow, they toil not, neither do they spin; and the kingdoms of the world, in all their glory, are not arrayed like one of these.

83 For your Father, who is in heaven, knoweth that you have need of all these things.

84 Therefore, let the morrow take thought for the things of itself.

85 Neither take ye thought beforehand what ye shall say; but treasure up in your minds continually the words of life, and it shall be given you in the very hour that portion that shall be meted unto every man.

86 Therefore, let no man among you, for this commandment is unto all the faithful who are called of God in the church unto the ministry, from this hour take purse or scrip, that goeth forth to proclaim this gospel of the kingdom.

Other instructions to the missionaries of the latter days will be only briefly summarized because they are also quotes and paraphrases from the Bible. The Lord again calls Joseph Smith and the six elders his friends, reminiscent of His calling the Apostles friends during His earthly ministry (v. 77; see v. 63 and John 15:13–14). He then repeats instructions given to the newly called Jerusalem Twelve Apostles as He sent them on their first missionary journey (see D&C 84:78–86; compare Matthew 10:5–39). The Matthew account of instructions to the Twelve concludes with promises similar to those given in God's oath regarding the Melchizedek Priesthood (see Matthew 10:40–41). Matthew's conclusion suggests that He had also taught the Jerusalem Twelve of the oath and covenant of the priesthood.

Twice in these verses the Lord instructs them not to take purse or scrip (vv. 78, 86; read all of the latter verse to see it is commanding them not to take them). A scrip is a small bag for a change of clothing that could be compared to our overnight bag. The question might be raised concerning why our missionaries do not go without purse or scrip today? The answer is because of the current culture. In Joseph Smith's day it was common for people to travel and ask to stay with someone, who would provide a place to sleep and give them a meal. Today thousands of homeless are traveling about the country, and apparently the Lord doesn't want His missionaries being associated with that group in the minds of the people, because He caused His modern day servants to change the policy. In the New Testament, those traveling were told to not take purse or scrip (Matthew 10:9–10), and in their later ministry were told to take purse and scrip (Luke 22:35–36).

D&C 84:87–98 • Know My Disciples

87 Behold, I send you out to reprove the world of all their unrighteous deeds, and to teach them of a judgment which is to come.

88 And whoso receiveth you, there I will be also, for I will go before your face. I will be on your right hand and on your left, and my Spirit shall be in your hearts, and mine angels round about you, to bear you up.

89 Whoso receiveth you receiveth me; and the same will feed you, and clothe you, and give you money.

90 And he who feeds you, or clothes you, or gives you money, shall in nowise lose his reward.

91 And he that doeth not these things is not my disciple; by this you may know my disciples.

92 He that receiveth you not, go away from him alone by yourselves, and cleanse your feet even with water, pure water, whether in heat or in cold, and bear testimony of it unto your Father which is in heaven, and return not again unto that man.

93 And in whatsoever village or city ye enter, do likewise.

94 Nevertheless, search diligently and spare not; and wo unto that house, or that village or city that rejecteth you, or your words, or your testimony concerning me.

95 Wo, I say again, unto that house, or that village or city that rejecteth you, or your words, or your testimony of me;

96 For I, the Almighty, have laid my hands upon the nations, to scourge them for their wickedness.

97 And plagues shall go forth, and they shall not be taken from the earth until I have completed my work, which shall be cut short in righteousness—

98 Until all shall know me, who remain, even from the least unto the greatest, and shall be filled with the knowledge of the Lord, and shall see eye to eye, and shall lift up their voice, and with the voice together sing this new song, saying:

Those sent out by the Lord do not go alone; He, His Spirit, and His angels are with them (vv. 87–88). An earlier revelation had defined a disciple as "He that receiveth my law [of the Church] and doeth it" (D&C 41:3). That definition is enlarged here (vv. 89–91). The cleansing of the feet (vv. 92–94) was discussed in chapter 1 of this work (see D&C 75:20–21). Those who reject the Lord's servants were to be warned of the plagues that will go forth until the Lord has "completed my work, which will be cut short in righteousness (D&C 84:97; compare Matthew

24:22). The Lord's work of destroying the wickedness of the earth will be cut short by the gospel being preached and those under the bondage of sin coming to Christ (D&C 84:49–51). The righteous will come to know the Lord and sing a new song (D&C 84:98).

D&C 84:99–102 • The New Song in Zion

99 The Lord hath brought again Zion;

The Lord hath redeemed his people, Israel,

According to the election of grace,

Which was brought to pass by the faith

And covenant of their fathers.

100 The Lord hath redeemed his people;

And Satan is bound and time is no longer.

The Lord hath gathered all things in one.

The Lord hath brought down Zion from above.

The Lord hath brought up Zion from beneath.

101 The earth hath travailed and brought forth her strength;

And truth is established in her bowels;

And the heavens have smiled upon her;

And she is clothed with the glory of her God;

For he stands in the midst of his people.

102 Glory, and honor, and power, and might,

Be ascribed to our God; for he is full of mercy,

Justice, grace and truth, and peace,

Forever and ever, Amen.

The singing of this new song was foretold by the prophet Isaiah. The prophecy is connected with the preaching of the gospel just as it is in this revelation:

7 How beautiful upon the mountains are the feet of him that bringeth good tidings, that publisheth peace; that bringeth good tidings of good, that publisheth salvation; that saith unto Zion, Thy God reigneth!

8 Thy watchmen shall lift up the voice; with the voice together shall they sing: for they shall see eye to eye, when the LORD shall bring again Zion. [Isaiah 52:7–8]

D&C 84:103–105 • Money Consecrated to Building Zion

103 And again, verily, verily, I say unto you, it is expedient that every man who goes forth to proclaim mine everlasting gospel, that inasmuch as they have families, and receive money by gift, that they should send it unto them or make use of it for their benefit, as the Lord shall direct them, for thus it seemeth me good.

104 And let all those who have not families, who receive money, send it up unto the bishop in Zion, or unto the bishop in Ohio, that it may be consecrated for the bringing forth of the revelations and the printing thereof, and for establishing Zion.

105 And if any man shall give unto any of you a coat, or a suit, take the old and cast it unto the poor, and go on your way rejoicing.

Instructions are given regarding money and gifts for the publishing of the revelations, and establishing Zion (vv. 103–104). Giving the old coat to the poor (v. 105) is similar to the admonition of John the Baptist in Luke 3:11. Verses 106–108 were discussed above with Doctrine and Covenants 84:33–39.

D&C 84:109–111 • Every Man in His Own Office

109 Therefore, let every man stand in his own office, and labor in his own calling; and let not the head say unto the feet it hath no need of the feet; for without the feet how shall the body be able to stand?

110 Also the body hath need of every member, that all may be edified together, that the system may be kept perfect.

111 And behold, the high priests should travel, and also the elders, and also the lesser priests; but the deacons and teachers should be appointed to watch over the church, to be standing ministers unto the church.

The comparison of the priesthood offices with the body having need of every member (D&C 84:109–110) was taught more extensively by Paul to the Corinthians (1 Corinthians 12:14–16). We will not compare them here. No comment seems necessary on verse eleven.

D&C 84:112–116 • The Poor and the Rich

112 And the bishop, Newel K. Whitney, also should travel round about and among all the churches, searching after the poor to administer to their wants by humbling the rich and the proud.

113 He should also employ an agent to take charge and to do his secular business as he shall direct.

114 Nevertheless, let the bishop go unto the city of New York, also to the city of Albany, and also to the city of Boston, and warn the people of those cities with the sound of the gospel, with a loud voice, of the desolation and utter abolishment which await them if they do reject these things.

115 For if they do reject these things the hour of their judgment is nigh, and their house shall be left unto them desolate.

116 Let him trust in me and he shall not be confounded; and a hair of his head shall not fall to the ground unnoticed.

The traveling of Bishop Whitney to care for the poor was later given in the same words as the Lord's purpose "to provide for my saints (vv. 112–113; D&C 104:15–16). We will leave the warning to the three cities in the category of Nephi's analysis of Isaiah's writings: "in the days that the prophecies of Isaiah shall be fulfilled men shall know of a surety, at the times when they shall come to pass" (2 Nephi 25:7).

D&C 84:117–120 • The Missionary Companions

117 And verily I say unto you, the rest of my servants, go ye forth as your circumstances shall permit, in your several callings, unto the great and notable cities and villages, reproving the world in righteousness of all their unrighteous and ungodly deeds, setting forth clearly and understandingly the desolation of abomination in the last days.

118 For, with you saith the Lord Almighty, I will rend their kingdoms; I will not only shake the earth, but the starry heavens shall tremble.

119 For I, the Lord, have put forth my hand to exert the powers of heaven; ye cannot see it now, yet a little while and ye shall see it, and know that I am, and that I will come and reign with my people.

120 I am Alpha and Omega, the beginning and the end. Amen.

The Lord's final words are a reassurance that the Lord will control the future from the heavens. The Church will do its part, but the Lord will have the final say. He is "Alpha and Omega, the beginning and the end" (D&C 84:118–120). Thus, a great revelation was given as a reward to the returning missionaries, and for their guidance for the coming months. These words are applicable to all faithful members of the Church.

General Authority Quotes

—President Joseph Fielding Smith • D&C 84:33–62

There is no exaltation in the kingdom of God without the fullness of the priesthood, and every who receives the Melchizedek Priesthood does so with an oath and a covenant that he shall be exalted.

The covenant on man's part is that he will magnify his calling in the priesthood, and that he will live by every word that proceedeth forth from the mouth of God, and that he will keep the commandments.

The covenant on the Lord's part is that if man does as he promises, then all that the Father hath shall be given unto him; and this is such a solemn and important promise that the Lord swears with an oath that it shall come to pass. [CR, April 1970, 58–59]

—Elder Marion G. Romney • D&C 84:33–34, 38

A covenant is an agreement between two or more parties. An oath is a sworn attestation to the inviolability of the promises to the agreement. In the covenant of the priesthood the parties are the Father and the receivers of the priesthood. Each party to the covenant undertakes certain obligations. The receiver undertakes to magnify his calling in the priesthood. The Father, by oath and covenant, promises the receiver that if he does so magnify his priesthood he will be sanctified by the Spirit unto the renewing of his body; (see D&C 84:33) that he will become a member of ". . . the church and kingdom, and the elect of God," (D&C 84:34) and receive the ". . . Father's kingdom; therefore" said the Savior, "all that my Father hath shall be given unto him" (D&C 84:38). [CR, April 1962, 17]

—Elder Bruce R. McConkie • D&C 84:33–40

Salvation, eternal life, exaltation—these three are all one. In the true sense they are identically the same thing and consist of an inheritance in the highest heaven of the celestial world, where alone the family unit continues. Those who so obtain gain the fullness of the glory of the Father and become like him in all things. The whole purpose and end of the Melchizedek Priesthood is to enable men to gain this exalted state in which they will be as their God is. . . .

When we receive the Melchizedek Priesthood, we enter into a covenant with the Lord. It is the covenant of exaltation. [reviews the commitments and blessings] . . .

. . . That there neither is nor can be a covenant more wondrous and great is self evident. This Covenant, made when the priesthood is received, is renewed when the recipient enters the order of eternal marriage.

It takes two parties to make a covenant, but any person alone can swear an oath. Man and Deity enter into the covenant of the priesthood, but only the Lord, meaning the Father, swears the oath. . . . [*A New Witness for the Articles of Faith* (1985), 312–313]

—President Spencer W. Kimball • D&C 84:41

One breaks the priesthood by transgressing commandments—but also by leaving undone his duties. Accordingly, to break this covenant one needs only to do nothing. [*The Teachings of Spencer W. Kimball*, 497]

Chapter Six

Ye Are of Israel

D&C 85–86

DOCTRINE AND COVENANTS 85

Historical Setting: "In answer to letters received from the brethren in Missouri, I [Joseph] wrote as follows" (*HC,* 1:297):

"Part of the . . . letter . . . was accepted afterwards as the word of the Lord, that is, as a revelation upon the matters treated therein, and appears in the Doctrine and Covenants as section [85]" (*HC,* 1:298; footnote).

SECTION 85 • OUTLINE

➤ 5:1–5   It is the duty of the Lord's clerk to keep a history and general record of what transpires in Zion, and who consecrates property and receives inheritances legally.

     a. Also their faith and works, and apostates who received an inheritance (v. 2).

     b. It is contrary to God that those who receive not an inheritance to be tithed and have their names with the people of God (v. 3).

     c. Their genealogy is not to be found on the records of the Church (v. 4).

     d. Their names, the names of their fathers and children, are not to be written in the book of the law of God (v. 5).

➤ 85:6–12 The still small voice which whispers and pierces all things, manifests and says:

    a.   The Lord will send one mighty to set in order the house of God, and arrange the inheritances of saints who are in the book of the law of God (v. 7).

    b.   The man called of God who tries to steady God's ark shall fall by death (v. 8).

    c.   Those not found in the book of remembrance shall find no inheritance, and be among those wailing and gnashing their teeth (v. 9).

    d.   As the Lord speaketh, he will also fulfill (v. 10).

    e.   Those of the high priesthood, lesser priesthood, or members whose names are not written in the book shall not have an inheritance among the saints (v. 11).

    f.   It shall be done to them as the children of the priest as written in Ezra 2:61–62.

Introduction

The two revelations considered in this chapter were received within nine days of each other. The second one was about the parable of the wheat and the tares (Matthew 13:34–43), which Joseph was apparently reviewing and editing. The first one illustrates the tares being among the wheat, the apostates and those who had been cut off from the Church. Was this coincidental? Regardless, the two revelations relate to each other.

TEXT AND COMMENTARY

D&C 85:1–5 • The Book of the Law of God

1 IT is the duty of the Lord's clerk, whom he has appointed, to keep a history, and a general church record of all things that transpire in Zion, and of all those who consecrate properties, and receive inheritances legally from the bishop;

2 And also their manner of life, their faith, and works; and also of the apostates who apostatize after receiving their inheritances.

3 It is contrary to the will and commandment of God that those who receive not their inheritance by consecration, agreeable to his law, which he has given, that he may tithe his people, to prepare them against the

day of vengeance and burning, should have their names enrolled with the people of God.

4 Neither is their genealogy to be kept, or to be had where it may be found on any of the records or history of the church.

5 Their names shall not be found, neither the names of the fathers, nor the names of the children written in the book of the law of God, saith the Lord of Hosts.

All those who receive inheritances legally (v. 1), suggests that some were receiving them illegally, or not through the bishop. Such would be an example of a tare (weed) among the wheat. A second example of a tare was the apostates who had received an inheritance (v. 2). These apostates would lose the promised blessing of tithing: "he that is tithed shall not be burned at his coming" (D&C 64:23). This promise being withdrawn answers another doctrinal point of the law of consecration. Tithing was a part of the law, but when the law was discontinued, the tithing principle continued (v. 3). The Old Testament prophet Malachi, who prophesied of the burning at the Second Coming, said "it shall leave them neither root nor branch" (Malachi 4:1). The genealogy of the apostates not being kept (v. 4) confirms his prophecy. "The names of the fathers [root], nor the names of the children [branches]," were not to be "written in the book of the law of God" (v. 5).

D&C 85:6–12 • The Still Small Voice

6 Yea, thus saith the still small voice, which whispereth through and pierceth all things, and often times it maketh my bones to quake while it maketh manifest, saying:

7 And it shall come to pass that I, the Lord God, will send one mighty and strong, holding the scepter of power in his hand, clothed with light for a covering, whose mouth shall utter words, eternal words; while his bowels shall be a fountain of truth, to set in order the house of God, and to arrange by lot the inheritances of the saints whose names are found, and the names of their fathers, and of their children, enrolled in the book of the law of God;

8 While that man, who was called of God and appointed, that putteth forth his hand to steady the ark of God, shall fall by the shaft of death, like as a tree that is smitten by the vivid shaft of lightning.

9 And all they who are not found written in the book of remembrance

shall find none inheritance in that day, but they shall be cut asunder, and their portion shall be appointed them among unbelievers, where are wailing and gnashing of teeth.

10 These things I say not of myself; therefore, as the Lord speaketh, he will also fulfil.

11 And they who are of the High Priesthood, whose names are not found written in the book of the law, or that are found to have apostatized, or to have been cut off from the church, as well as the lesser priesthood, or the members, in that day shall not find an inheritance among the saints of the Most High;

12 Therefore, it shall be done unto them as unto the children of the priest, as will be found recorded in the second chapter and sixty-first and second verses of Ezra.

The still small voice that "pierceth all things" is the voice of revelation (v. 6). It was a still small voice that came to Elijah in "Horeb, the mount of God" (1 Kings 19:8, 12). It was the still small voice that spoke to the Lamanites when Nephi and Lehi were imprisoned and the walls were shaken (see Helaman 5:21–30). It was the still small voice that spoke to the Nephite multitude when Christ appeared to them after his Resurrection (see 3 Nephi 11:3). It is that voice which at times brings the emotions of tears, or other physical feelings, to our hearts and bodies as written by the Prophet Joseph (v. 6).

There have been many speculations and false claims as to whom the "one mighty and strong" to set in order the house of God and arrange the inheritances was referring (v. 7). According to the First Presidency, it was referring to Bishop Edward Partridge at that time, and a future bishop "called and appointed of God as Aaron of old, as was Edward Partridge.[24] Those who put "forth [their hands] to steady the ark of God" (v. 8) was referring to those who attempt to give directions to God about His work, or go contrary to His word. Concerning the tabernacle carried in the wilderness with Moses and his people, the Lord had instructed: "And when the tabernacle setteth forward, the Levites shall take it down: and when the tabernacle is to be pitched, the Levites shall set it up: and the stranger that cometh nigh shall be put to death" (Numbers 1:51). The

---

[24] Letter of the First Presidency, November 13, 1905, Joseph F. Smith, John R. Winder, Anthon H. L. *Messages of the First Presidency of The Church of Jesus Christ of Latter-day Saints*, comp. James R. Clark, 6 vols. [1970], 4:107–120.

sons of Aaron, had been told further; "the sons of Kohath shall come to bear [it]: but they shall not touch [any] holy thing, lest they die" (Numbers 4:15). An Old Testament incident is the source of the wording used by the Lord in this revelation. "And when they came to Nachon's threshingfloor, Uzzah put forth his hand to the ark of God, and took hold of it; for the oxen shook it. And the anger of the LORD was kindled against Uzzah; and God smote him there for his error; and there he died by the ark of God" (2 Samuel 6:6–7). The commandment not to touch the Ark was probably because of the glory of the Lord that attended the sacred items in the Ark (see Hebrews 9:4–5), which was a part of the tabernacle. Natural man could not endure that glory (see Mosiah 8:13). Another similar incident took place with the Ark when the Philistines returned it to the Israelites because of the plagues that came upon them (see 1 Samuel 5 & 6). These incidents are a similitude of the tares among the wheat.

Those who were not found written in the book of remembrance, or in the book of the law of God, and were cut asunder, or cut off from the Church (vv. 9, 11), are others in the similitude of the tares among the wheat. Whether these books were kept on earth or in heaven, or both, is not stated. The Lord makes a distinction of records kept in heaven and on earth in D&C 128:7, but does not include these two books in either category. The Lord supports His actions of cutting asunder the apostates by again using an example from the Old Testament. "And of the children of the priests: the children of Habaiah, the children of Koz, the children of Barzillai; which took a wife of the daughters of Barzillai the Gileadite, and was called after their name: these sought their register [among] those that were reckoned by genealogy, but they were not found: therefore were they, as polluted, put from the priesthood" (Ezra 2:61–62). The Lord does fulfill His word (see D&C 85:10). Paul further qualified who the house of Israel were: "Not as though the word of God hath taken none effect. For they are not all Israel, which are of Israel: neither, because they are the seed of Abraham, are they all children: but, In Isaac shall thy seed be called. That is, They which are the children of the flesh, these are not the children of God: but the children of the promise are counted for the seed" (Romans 9:6–8). Only those in the covenant line are Israel, but the covenant line must keep that covenant or be cut off.

DOCTRINE AND COVENANTS 86

*H*istorical Setting: "On the 6th of December, 1832, I [Joseph Smith] received [D&C 86] explaining the parable of the wheat and tares" (*HC,* 1:300).

SECTION 86 • OUTLINE

➤ 86:1–7   The Lord explains the parable of the wheat and the tares.

       a.   The field was the world, and the apostles the sowers of the seed (v. 2).

       b.   After the apostles fall asleep, the persecutor of the church, Satan, sows the tares, and drives the church into the wilderness (v. 3).

       c.   In the last days, the Lord is bringing the word, and the blade is yet tender (v. 4).

       d.   The angels are crying to the Lord day and night to reap down the fields (v. 5).

       e.   The Lord says: pluck not the tares lest you destroy the wheat (v. 6).

       f.   Let the wheat and tares grow together until ripe, first gather the wheat, then bind the tares to be burned (v. 7).

➤ 86:8–11   The Lord speaks to the priesthood who have continued through your fathers.

       a.   Ye are lawful heirs, according to the flesh, and have been hid from the world with Christ in God (v. 9).

       b.   Your priesthood must remain until the restoration of all things, as foretold by the prophets (v. 10).

       c.   Blessed are ye if ye continue to be a light to the Gentiles, and a savior to Israel (v. 11).

TEXT AND COMMENTARY

D&C 86:1–7 • Let the Wheat and Tares Grow Together

1 Verily, thus saith the Lord unto you my servants, concerning the parable of the wheat and of the tares:

2 Behold, verily I say, the field was the world, and the apostles were the sowers of the seed;

Matthew 13:36 • Then Jesus sent the multitude away, and went into the house: and his disciples came unto him, saying, Declare unto us the parable of the tares of the field.

37 He answered and said unto them, He that soweth the good seed is the Son of man;

38 The field is the world; the good seed are the children of the kingdom; but the tares are the children of the wicked one;

39 The enemy that sowed them is the devil;

The slight differences between the Doctrine and Covenants and the New Testament account are insignificant. While Matthew said that the Son of Man sowed the good seed (Matthew 13:37), the modern revelation says the Apostles sowed the good seed (D&C 86:2). Jesus obviously began the sowing, but his Apostles helped Him and carried out the work after His death. Their work lasted much longer and so the later account refers to those who did the majority of the work. Matthew identifies the good seed as the children of the kingdom, and the tares as the children of the wicked one (Matthew 13:38). The modern revelation only enlarges upon Matthew's account:

3 And after they have fallen asleep the great persecutor of the church, the apostate, the whore, even Babylon, that maketh all nations to drink of her cup, in whose hearts the enemy, even Satan, sitteth to reign—behold he soweth the tares; wherefore, the tares choke the wheat and drive the church into the wilderness.

After the Apostles had fallen asleep refers to after they had been killed, or their death. Babylon, that made "all nations to drink of her cup," is taken from Revelation 14:8, and is enlarged upon in Revelation 17:2–5. The Church being driven into the wilderness was also seen by John the Revelator (see Revelation 12:6 or JST, Revelation 12:5). The Doctrine and Covenants testifies repeatedly that the Church has been brought out of the wilderness (see D&C 1:30; 5:14; 33:5; 109:73). This brings us to the last days to which the modern revelation now refers.

4 But behold, in the last days, even now while the Lord is beginning to bring forth the word, and the blade is springing up and is yet tender—

> 5 Behold, verily I say unto you, the angels are crying unto the Lord day and night, who are ready and waiting to be sent forth to reap down the fields;

The angels crying to reap down the field shows their knowledge of the work as they view the wickedness of the world (v. 5). The Lord told the Prophet Joseph of their waiting for His command in January of 1831 (see D&C 38:12), but the time was not yet, nor is it now.

> 6 But the Lord saith unto them, pluck not up the tares while the blade is yet tender (for verily your faith is weak), lest you destroy the wheat also.

> 7 Therefore, let the wheat and the tares grow together until the harvest is fully ripe; then ye shall first gather out the wheat from among the tares, and after the gathering of the wheat, behold and lo, the tares are bound in bundles, and the field remaineth to be burned.

> **Matthew 13:39** • . . . the harvest is the end of the world; and the reapers are the angels.

> 40 As therefore the tares are gathered and burned in the fire; so shall it be in the end of this world.

> 41 The Son of man shall send forth his angels, and they shall gather out of his kingdom all things that offend, and them which do iniquity;

> 42 And shall cast them into a furnace of fire: there shall be wailing and gnashing of teeth.

> 43 Then shall the righteous shine forth as the sun in the kingdom of their Father. Who hath ears to hear, let him hear.

Matthew places the burning at the end of the world (Matthew 13:39–40). Modern revelation states to gather the wheat first, and then burn the tares when the harvest is fully ripe (D&C 86:7). Both accounts are speaking of the same time. Matthew says the angels will gather all the things that offend and do iniquity (Matthew 13:41–42). This gathering could not be done until the wheat had been gathered, so there is no contradiction, just a difference in the description.

86:8–11 • Lawful Heirs of the Priesthood

> 8 Therefore, thus saith the Lord unto you, with whom the priesthood hath continued through the lineage of your fathers—

9 For ye are lawful heirs, according to the flesh, and have been hid from the world with Christ in God—

10 Therefore your life and the priesthood have remained, and must needs remain through you and your lineage until the restoration of all things spoken by the mouths of all the holy prophets since the world began.

11 Therefore, blessed are ye if ye continue in my goodness, a light unto the Gentiles, and through this priesthood, a savior unto my people Israel. The Lord hath said it. Amen.

The Lord addresses those who hold the priesthood as those who have "continued through the lineage of their fathers" (v. 8). Since He is speaking to first generation members of the Church, the fathers would not be their immediate fathers, but would logically refer to Abraham, Isaac, and Jacob, the priesthood covenant holders of past generations. The Lord further defines them as "lawful heirs according to the flesh" (v. 9). This reminds us of the covenant made to our father Abraham:

> And I will bless them that bless thee, and curse them that curse thee; and in thee (that is, in thy Priesthood) and in thy seed (that is, thy Priesthood), for I give unto thee a promise that this right shall continue in thee, and in thy seed after thee (that is to say, the literal seed, or the seed of the body) shall all the families of the earth be blessed, even with the blessings of the Gospel, which are the blessings of salvation, even of life eternal. [Abraham 2:11]

The descendants of Abraham, Isaac, and Jacob were sifted among all nations: "Behold, the eyes of the Lord GOD are upon the sinful kingdom, and I will destroy it from off the face of the earth; saving that I will not utterly destroy the house of Jacob, saith the LORD. For, lo, I will command, and I will sift the house of Israel among all nations, like as corn is sifted in a sieve, yet shall not the least grain fall upon the earth" (Amos 9:8–9). The word corn is interchangeable with wheat in the scriptures (see the Bible Dictionary, 650). Does not Amos' prophecy fit into the parable of the wheat and the tares?

The remnant of Israel, the literal seed of the body, is now being gathered out from among the Gentiles and other nations as Amos also prophesied. "And I will bring again the captivity of my people of Israel, and they shall build the waste cities, and inhabit them; and they shall plant vineyards, and drink the wine thereof; they shall also make gardens, and eat the fruit of them. And I will plant them upon their land, and they shall no more be pulled up out of their land which I have given them, saith the LORD thy God" (Amos 9:14–15). They "have been hid from the world with Christ in God" (D&C 86:9), or as Isaiah said: ". . . in the shadow of his hand hath he hid me [Israel]" (Isaiah 49:2). The Lord knew where they were, but the world did not know. The gathering began with those of scattered Ephraim, the birthright holder (see Jeremiah 31:6–14; 1 Chronicles 5:1). As President Joseph F. Smith said: "A striking peculiarity of the Saints gathered from all parts of the earth is that they are almost universally of the blood of Israel."[25] After Ephraim is gathered, and the mother trunk of the tree is established, the other branches of Israel will be grafted back into the tree. The last one scattered [Nephites] will be grafted first, and the first one scattered [lost tribes] will be grafted last (see Jacob 5:54–63).

The Lord continued the latter-day revelation with a declaration that His priesthood would continue through the lineage of the first-generation Church members "until the restoration of all things spoken by the mouths of all the prophets since the world began" (D&C 86:10). This is the end of the world as used in the parable of the wheat and the tares (see Matthew 13:40 above). He promised further that that if they continued in the Lord's goodness, they would be "a light to the gentiles, and through this priesthood, a savior unto my people Israel" (D&C 86:11). From the above scriptures it seems evident that the parable of the wheat and the tares, as explained to the Prophet Joseph, teaches that the wheat pertains to scattered Israel who have been gathered from among the tares who are the Gentiles. This interpretation is sustained in a later revelation (D&C 101:64–66) that will be discussed in chapter 14. The tenth article of faith declares that "We believe in the literal gathering of Israel." There are many other revelations in the Doctrine and Covenants that sustain this declaration, and we will continue to point them out as we study the following sections of the book.

General Authority Quotes

—*Elder Boyd K. Packer* • D&C 85:6

---

[25] Joseph F. Smith, *Gospel Doctrine* [1959], 115.

Answers to prayers come in a quiet way. The scriptures describe that voice of inspiration as a still small voice.

If you really try, you can learn to respond to that voice. [CR, October 1979, 28]

—*The Prophet Joseph Smith* • D&C 86:7 (quoting Matthew 13:37–39)

. . . The harvest is the end of the world. (let them carefully mark this expression—the end of the world) and the reapers are the angels.

Now men cannot have any possible grounds to say that this is figurative, or that it does not mean what it says: for He is now explaining what He had previously spoken in parables; and according to this language, the end of the world is the destruction of the wicked, the harvest and the end of the world have an allusion to the human family in the last days, instead of the earth, as many have imagined; and that which shall precede the coming of the Son of Man, and the restitution of all things spoken of by the mouth of all the holy prophets since the world began; and the angels are to have something to do in this great work, for they are the reapers. As, therefore, the tares are gathered and burned in the fire, so shall it be in the end of the world; that is, as the servants of God go forth warning the nations, both priests and people, and as they harden their hearts and reject the light of truth, these first being delivered over to the buffetings of Satan, and the law and the testimony being closed up, as it was in the case of the Jews, they are left in darkness, and delivered over unto the day of burning: thus being bound by their creeds, and their bands being made strong by their priests, are prepared for the saying of the Savior—[quotes Matthew 13:41–43]. [*TPJS,* 100–101]

—*President Brigham Young* • D&C 86:8–9

Israel is dispersed among all the nations of the earth; the blood of Ephraim is mixed with the blood of all the earth. Abraham's seed is mingled with the rebellious seed through the whole world of mankind.

The elders who have risen in this Church and Kingdom are actually of Israel.

Those Islanders and the natives of this country are of the house of Israel—of the seed of Abraham, and to them pertain the promise, and every soul of them, sooner or later, will be saved in the kingdom of God, or be destroyed root and branch.

Again, if a pure Gentile firmly believes the gospel of Jesus Christ, and yields obedience to it, in such a case I will give you the words of the

Prophet Joseph: "The effect of the Holy Ghost upon a Gentile is to purge out the old blood, and make him actually of the seed of Abraham [see Joseph's statement below]. [*Discourses of Brigham Young*, arr. by John A. Widtsoe (1951), 436]

—The Prophet Joseph Smith • D&C 86:8–9

This first Comforter or Holy Ghost has no other effect than pure intelligence. It is more powerful in expanding the mind, enlightening the understanding, and storing the intellect with present knowledge; of a man who is of the literal seed of Abraham, than one that is a Gentile, though it may not have half as much visible effect upon the body; for as the Holy Ghost falls upon one of the literal seed of Abraham, it is calm and serene; and his whole soul and body are only exercised by the pure spirit of intelligence; while the effect of the Holy Ghost upon a Gentile, is to purge out the old blood, and make him actually of the seed of Abraham. That man that has none of the blood of Abraham (naturally) must have a new creation by the Holy Ghost. In such a case, there may be more of a powerful effect upon the body, and visible to the body, than upon an Israelite, while the Israelite at first might be far before the Gentile in pure intelligence. [*TPJS*, 148–49]

—President Joseph Fielding Smith • D&C 86:8–9

In scattering Ephraim the Lord had two purposes in mind: (1) The scattering was to be a punishment to a rebellious people; (2) It was the purpose of blessing the people of other nations with the blood of Israel among whom Ephraim mixed himself. The scattering of other Israelites answered the same purpose.

We have very good reason to believe, however, that it was the tribe of Ephraim, rebellious, proud, and headstrong, which was scattered *more* than any other among the people of other nations. In these last days the Lord said that Ephraim should not be rebellious as he was formerly, and that now, the rebellious were not of Ephraim and should be "plucked out" (D&C 64:35–36).

It is essential in this dispensation that Ephraim stand in his place at the head, exercising the birthright in Israel which was given to him by direct revelation. Therefore *Ephraim must be gathered first to prepare the way*, through the gospel and the priesthood, for the rest of the tribes of Israel when the time comes for them to be gathered to Zion. The great majority of those who have come into the Church are Ephraimites. It is the exception, to find one of any other tribe, unless it is of Mannasseh. [Joseph Fielding Smith, *Doctrines of Salvation,* comp. Bruce R. McConkie, 3 vols. (1954–56), 3:252]

Chapter Seven

Wars Upon All Nations

D&C 87; 88:87–116; 130:12–13

DOCTRINE AND COVENANTS 87

*H*istorical Setting: "The people of South Carolina, in convention assembled (in November); passed ordinances, declaring their state a free and independent nation; and appointed Thursday, the 31st of January, 1833, as a day of humiliation and prayer, to implore Almighty God to vouchsafe His blessings, and restore liberty and happiness within their borders. President Jackson issued his proclamation against this rebellion, called out a force sufficient to quell it, and implored the blessings of God to assist the nation to extricate itself from the horrors of the approaching and solemn crisis.

"On Christmas day [1832], I received [Doctrine and Covenants 87] revelation and prophecy on war" (*HC*, 1:301).

SECTION 87 • OUTLINE

➤ 87:1–3   Wars will shortly come, beginning at the rebellion of South Carolina, and eventually terminate in the destruction and misery of many souls.

    a. Wars will be poured out on all nations, beginning at this place (v. 2).

    b. The Southern States will divide against the Northern States, the South will call on Great Britain, who will call other nations, and thus war on all nations (v. 3).

➤ 87:4–8   After many days, slaves shall rise against their masters who are ready for war.

    a.   The remnants of the land shall have a sore vexation upon the Gentiles (v. 5).

    b.   The earth's inhabitants shall mourn over the famine, plague, and earthquake as they feel the indignation of God until the end of all nations (v. 6).

    c.   Then shall the cry and blood of the saints cease to come to the Lord (v. 7).

    d.   Stand in holy places until the day of the Lord come (v. 8).

Introduction

21 And if thou say in thine heart, How shall we know the word which the LORD hath not spoken?

22 When a prophet speaketh in the name of the LORD, if the thing follow not, nor come to pass, that [is] the thing which the LORD hath not spoken, [but] the prophet hath spoken it presumptuously: thou shalt not be afraid of him. [Deuteronomy 18:21–22]

While some point to section 87 as evidence of Joseph being a prophet, based on the Deuteronomy criteria of it happened as Joseph foretold, others argue that Joseph was well aware of the South Carolina conflict (see Historical Setting above) and so it was not a prophecy. However, it should be kept in mind that the Civil War did not begin until about twenty-eight years after the revelation was given, and section 87 is about more than the Civil War. It foretells of wars that will follow and are still being fought, or yet to be fought. Joseph had no background to predict these wars, as will be shown from an analysis of the section.

TEXT AND COMMENTARY

D&C 87:1–3 • War Upon All Nations

1 Verily, thus saith the Lord concerning the wars that will shortly come to pass, beginning at the rebellion of South Carolina, which will eventually terminate in the death and misery of many souls;

2 And the time will come that war will be poured out upon all nations, beginning at this place.

3 For behold, the Southern States shall be divided against the Northern States, and the Southern States will call on other nations, even the nation of Great Britain, as it is called, and they shall also call upon other nations, in order to defend themselves against other nations; and then war shall be poured out upon all nations. [D&C 87:1–3]

That the war would begin in South Carolina (v. 1) was made known to Joseph by revelation, and was verified by him over ten years later, April 2, 1843, still eighteen years before the war began: "I prophesy, in the name of the Lord God, that the commencement of the difficulties which will cause much bloodshed previous to the coming of the Son of Man will be in South Carolina. It may probably arise through the slave question. This a voice declared to me, while I was praying earnestly on the subject, December 25th, 1832" (D&C 130:12–13). The death and misery of many souls has been verified also: "The civil war took a grisly toll in gore, about as much as all of America's subsequent wars combined. Over six hundred thousand men died in action or disease, and in all over a million were killed or seriously wounded. To its lasting hurt, the nation lost the cream of its young manhood and potential leadership. In addition, tens of thousands of babies went unborn because potential fathers were at the front."[26]

The Civil War, beginning at South Carolina, started a period of war that involved all nations: A noted scholar wrote of the frequency of wars:

The war index shows a slow upward trend from the twelfth to the seventeenth century, with an especially sharp rise in the latter century.... Accordingly the war indicator registers a unique upswing, for only one quarter of [last of the nineteenth century] the figures exceed those of all the preceding twenty-five centuries with the exception of the third century B.C. in Rome. But the Roman indicator (63) is for the whole century; the twentieth century index is only twenty-five years—from 1900 to 1925. If to the European wars of 1900 to 1925 we add all the subsequent wars up to the present time, the figures will eclipse even those for the third century B.C. If, further we add the wars that will doubtless occur from 1940 to 2000, the twentieth century will unquestionably

---

[26] Thomas A. Bailey, *The American Pageant,* ed. David M. Kennedy [1994], 1:483.

prove the bloodiest and most belligerent of all the twenty-five centuries under consideration.[27]

The division of the southern states and the northern states, the south calling upon Great Britain, who called on the other nations (v. 3), are well known facts of the Civil War that need no documentation. "Thus war shall be poured out all nations" (v. 3) is somewhat controversial. Some want to say that this statement refers to the Civil War, and that all nations were involved in the war either directly or indirectly. Others interpret it to refer to a sequential occurrence; that war will be poured out upon all nations after the Civil War. Both positions seem to be correct in their context. Except as evidenced above, the wars are still going on, and the following verses strongly indicate they are still going on, and will continue until the Second Coming.

D&C 87:4–8 • A Full End of All Nations

4 And it shall come to pass, after many days, slaves shall rise up against their masters, who shall be marshaled and disciplined for war.

5 And it shall come to pass also that the remnants who are left of the land will marshal themselves, and shall become exceedingly angry, and shall vex the Gentiles with a sore vexation.

6 And thus, with the sword and by bloodshed the inhabitants of the earth shall mourn; and with famine, and plague, and earthquake, and the thunder of heaven, and the fierce and vivid lightning also, shall the inhabitants of the earth be made to feel the wrath, and indignation, and chastening hand of an Almighty God, until the consumption decreed hath made a full end of all nations;

7 That the cry of the saints, and of the blood of the saints, shall cease to come up into the ears of the Lord of Sabaoth, from the earth, to be avenged of their enemies.

8 Wherefore, stand ye in holy places, and be not moved, until the day of the Lord come; for behold, it cometh quickly, saith the Lord. Amen.

There are more slaves in the world than the African-American ones that were a dominant factor in the Civil War. Most wars were and are over the lack of freedom for one group or another. To "destroy the agency

---

[27] Pitirim Sorokin, *The Crisis of Our Age,* 216.

of man" is the plan of Satan (Moses 4:3). Many of the Nephite wars were fought for "their liberty, yea, their freedom from bondage" (Alma 43: 28–29; 51:6; 58:40; 61:21; Helaman 1:8; 3 Nephi 2:12). The wars against terrorism today are fighting for the same freedoms. The principle of freedom "belongs to all mankind" (D&C 98:5). Those who attempt to take away the freedom of others are "marshaled and disciplined for war" (D&C 87:4).

The remnants of the land, who "vex the Gentiles," (D&C 87:5) are those who survived the Nephite and the Lamanite battles to destruction (see Alma 45:14; Moroni 9:24). Many of the South and Central American countries of today, who are governed by European Gentile emigrants, have and are experiencing rebellions and revolutions of the native inhabitants of the land. These were not part of the Civil War.

The sword and bloodshed, the famine, plagues, and earthquakes (v. 6) were to come upon all the inhabitants of the earth, thus again, far more than prophecies about the Civil War. These atrocities have already commenced, in fact are well underway. The Lord suffers or allows these to come because of His indignation over their wickedness. They will not cease before the prophecy of Jeremiah comes to pass: "For I [am] with thee, saith the LORD, to save thee: though I make a full end of all nations whither I have scattered thee, yet will I not make a full end of thee: but I will correct thee in measure, and will not leave thee altogether unpunished" (Jeremiah 30:11). The house of Israel, or members of the Church will not have a full end, however they will be corrected and be punished for their wickedness (D&C 87:6). The righteous will not entirely escape, but their cry to the Lord over the blood of the Saints shall cease (v. 7). According to the prophet quoted by Nephi, probably Isaiah, they need not fear for they will be saved.

> 15 For behold, saith the prophet, the time cometh speedily that Satan shall have no more power over the hearts of the children of men; for the day soon cometh that all the proud and they who do wickedly shall be as stubble; and the day cometh that they must be burned.
>
> 16 For the time soon cometh that the fulness of the wrath of God shall be poured out upon all the children of men; for he will not suffer that the wicked shall destroy the righteous.
>
> 17 Wherefore, he will preserve the righteous by his power, even if it so be that the fulness of his wrath must come, and the righteous be

preserved, even unto the destruction of their enemies by fire. Wherefore, the righteous need not fear; for thus saith the prophet, they shall be saved, even if it so be as by fire. [1 Nephi 22:15–17]

In the meantime, they must stand in holy places, and be not moved (D&C 87:8). The holy places are of course the temples, but are wherever the Saints are gathered as instructed by the Presidency of the Church. The Prophet Joseph declared: "Look to the Presidency and receive instructions. Every man who is afraid, covetous, will be taken in a snare. The time is soon coming, when no man will have any peace but in Zion and her stakes" (*TPJS,* 161). More is said about the time preceding the Second Coming in the next revelation.

DOCTRINE AND COVENANTS 88:87–116

Historical Setting: "Two days after the preceding prophecy, on the 27th of December [1832], I received [Doctrine and Covenants 88]" (*HC,* 1:302). Since the topic of the verses in section 88 is about war, we will include this part of the revelation with the revelation on the wars that were to come.

SECTION 88 • OUTLINE

➤ 88:87–91   In not many days, the earth shall tremble as a drunken man, the sun refuse her light, the moon bathed in blood, and the stars fall as a fig off a tree.

       a.   After your testimony, comes wrath and indignation on the people (v. 88).

       b.   Earthquakes shall cause men to fall and not be able to stand (v. 89).

       c.   The voice of thunderings, lightnings, tempests, and the waves of the sea beyond their bounds shall come (v. 90).

       d.   All things shall be in commotion, and men's hearts fail them for fear (v. 91).

➤ 88:92–95   Angels shall fly through the heaven saying, Prepare for the Bridegroom, the judgment of God is come, go meet Him.

a. A great sign shall appear in heaven, and all people shall see it together (v. 93).

b. Another angel shall announce the great abominable church, the tares of the earth, are bound ready to be burned (v. 94).

c. There shall be silence for half an hour, and then the Lord's face will be unveiled (v. 95).

➤ 88:96–98   The Saints who are alive are caught up to meet Him.

a. The graves are opened, and those who slept are caught up to meet Him (v. 97).

b. They are Christ's, the first fruits (v. 98).

➤ 88:99–102   The second angel sounds and those who are Christ's are received in prison to receive the gospel and be judged.

a. The third angel sounds and the spirits who are under condemnation are judged, and live not again until the thousand years are ended (vv. 100–101).

b. The fourth angel sounds, those come who remain filthy unto the end (v. 102).

➤ 88:103–107   The fifth angel sounds, who committed the everlasting gospel, and says: Fear God and give him glory, for the hour of His judgment is come (v. 103–104).

a. The sixth angel sounds, saying: She is fallen who made all nations drink the wine of her fornication (v. 105).

b. The seventh angel sounds saying: It is finished, The Lamb of God has trodden the wine-press alone (v. 106).

c. The angels are crowned with glory, and the Saints filled with glory, receive their inheritance, and made equal with Christ (v. 107).

➤ 88:108–110   The first angel sounds to the living, and reveals the secret acts of men and the mighty works of God in the first thousand years.

a. The second angel through the sixth sounds, and reveals the secret acts of men, and the mighty works of God of each of the thousand years (v. 110).

b. The seventh angel sounds, and swears that time is no longer (v. 110).

    c.   Satan shall be bound and not loosed for a thousand years (v. 110).

➤ 88:111–116 Satan shall be loosed for a little season to gather his armies.

    a.   Michael, the seventh angel, shall gather his armies, the host of heaven (v. 112).

    b.   They come to battle, and the devil and his armies are cast into their own place and have power over the Saints no more (vv. 112–113).

    c.   Michael shall fight and overcome him who seeks the Lamb's throne (v. 114).

    d.   This is the glory of God, and the sanctified shall see death no more (v. 116).

TEXT AND COMMENTARY

D&C 88:87–91 • After Your Testimony Comes Wrath

87 For not many days hence and the earth shall tremble and reel to and fro as a drunken man; and the sun shall hide his face, and shall refuse to give light; and the moon shall be bathed in blood; and the stars shall become exceedingly angry, and shall cast themselves down as a fig that falleth from off a fig-tree.

88 And after your testimony cometh wrath and indignation upon the people.

89 For after your testimony cometh the testimony of earthquakes, that shall cause groanings in the midst of her, and men shall fall upon the ground and shall not be able to stand.

90 And also cometh the testimony of the voice of thunderings, and the voice of lightnings, and the voice of tempests, and the voice of the waves of the sea heaving themselves beyond their bounds.

91 And all things shall be in commotion; and surely, men's hearts shall fail them; for fear shall come upon all people.

"The day of the Lord" (D&C 87:8) is enlarged upon in this part of the revelation given two days later. The earth shall tremble and roll as a drunken man was prophesied by the prophet Isaiah: "The earth shall reel to and fro like a drunkard, and shall be removed like a cottage; and the transgression thereof shall be heavy upon it; and it shall fall, and not rise again" (Isaiah 24:20). The latter part of his prophecy will be fulfilled at His coming, or the beginning of the Millennium, and will be discussed later. Oliver Cowdery paraphrased this prophecy of Isaiah in noting which of the "many other passages of scriptures" the angel Moroni told Joseph Smith were about to be fulfilled (JS—H 1:41).[28] The Lord, speaking of the coming of the Son of Man, in an earlier revelation, gave us the same warning: "Wherefore, be not deceived, but continue in steadfastness, looking forth for the heavens to be shaken, and the earth to tremble and to reel to and fro as a drunken man, and for the valleys to be exalted, and for the mountains to be made low, and for the rough places to become smooth—and all this when the angel shall sound his trumpet" (D&C 49:23). In November of 1833, the Prophet Joseph said: ". . . when I consider that soon the heavens are to be shaken, and the earth tremble and reel to and fro; and that the heavens are to be unfolded as a scroll when it is rolled up; and that every mountain and Island are to be rolled away, I cry out in my heart, What manner of persons ought we to be in all holy conversation and godliness!" (*TPJS,* 29). Five months later, the Prophet again commented on these events:

> . . . The time is near when the sun shall be darkened and the moon turned to blood, and the stars fall from heaven, and the earth reel to and fro. Then, if this is the case, and if we are not sanctified and gathered to the places God has appointed, with all former professions and our great love of the Bible, we must fall; we cannot stand; we cannot be saved; for God will gather out his Saints from the Gentiles, and then comes desolation and destruction, and none can escape except the pure in heart who are gathered. [*TPJS,* 71]

The account in this revelation (D&C 88:87) gives a more specific account of how the heavens will shake. We will leave the interpretation of the more specifics on the sun, moon, and stars to Nephi's declaration concerning Isaiah's prophecies: ". . . nevertheless, in the days that the prophecies of Isaiah shall be fulfilled men shall know of a surety, at the times when they shall come to pass" (2 Nephi 25:7).

"And after your testimony" (D&C 88:88) seems to be the time spoken of by the Savior to the Nephites:

> 10 And thus commandeth the Father that I should say unto you: At

---

[28] *Messenger and Advocate* [Early Newspaper of the Church] April 1835, 111–12.

that day when the Gentiles shall sin against my gospel, and shall reject the fulness of my gospel, and shall be lifted up in the pride of their hearts above all nations, and above all the people of the whole earth, and shall be filled with all manner of lyings, and of deceits, and of mischiefs, and all manner of hypocrisy, and murders, and priestcrafts, and whoredoms, and of secret abominations; and if they shall do all those things, and shall reject the fulness of my gospel, behold, saith the Father, I will bring the fulness of my gospel from among them.

11 And then will I remember my covenant which I have made unto my people, O house of Israel, and I will bring my gospel unto them.

12 And I will show unto thee, O house of Israel, that the Gentiles shall not have power over you; but I will remember my covenant unto you, O house of Israel, and ye shall come unto the knowledge of the fulness of my gospel.

13 But if the Gentiles will repent and return unto me, saith the Father, behold they shall be numbered among my people, O house of Israel. [3 Ne 16:10–13]

The Saints will gather to their designated places mentioned above by the Prophet Joseph (see also 2 Nephi 24:1–2; compare Isaiah 14:1–2). The great division of the wicked and the righteous spoken of by Nephi will have taken place (see 2 Nephi 30:9), but another testimony from the Lord will be given before He comes.

Earthquakes, thunderings, lightnings, tempests, and the waves of the sea heaving beyond their bounds, will come after the testimony of the Lord's servants (D&C 88:89–90; compare 43:25). There will be great commotion and men's hearts shall fail them because of fear (v. 91). How much overlapping there will be within these two periods of "after your testimony" is not stated, but there will probably be some.

D&C 88:92–95 • Seven Angels Fly through Heaven

92 And angels shall fly through the midst of heaven, crying with a loud voice, sounding the trump of God, saying: Prepare ye, prepare ye, O inhabitants of the earth; for the judgment of our God is come. Behold, and lo, the Bridegroom cometh; go ye out to meet him.

93 And immediately there shall appear a great sign in heaven, and all people shall see it together.

94 And another angel shall sound his trump, saying: That great

church, the mother of abominations, that made all nations drink of the wine of the wrath of her fornication, that persecuteth the saints of God, that shed their blood—she who sitteth upon many waters, and upon the islands of the sea—behold, she is the tares of the earth; she is bound in bundles; her bands are made strong, no man can loose them; therefore, she is ready to be burned. And he shall sound his trump both long and loud, and all nations shall hear it.

95 And there shall be silence in heaven for the space of half an hour; and immediately after shall the curtain of heaven be unfolded, as a scroll is unfolded after it is rolled up, and the face of the Lord shall be unveiled;

Seven angels sounding their trumpets are recorded in the book of Revelation, chapters eight through ten. While these are probably the same angels, their messages given here are different than the ones recorded there. The interpretation of the Revelation angels were given to us, at least in part, by the Prophet Joseph Smith in Doctrine and Covenants 77, and correlated in chapter 2 of this work. While the messages are related, we will only comment on the message of the seven angels in this revelation (D&C 88:92–98).

The angels, plural, are apparently giving a message in unity: Prepare for the judgment of God, the Bridegroom of the parable of the ten virgins (D&C 88:92). This parable was mentioned and discussed in D&C 45, and discussed in volume 1, chapter 22, of this work. The Bridegroom is Christ, and the bride is the Church adorning herself for the wedding at His Second Coming. The inhabitants of the earth are invited to go out and meet Him (see Revelation 19:7–9).

The great sign in heaven does not appear to be the sign of the Second Coming, since the angels messages that follow are telling us what will happen before He comes. The Prophet Joseph said:

Judah must return, Jerusalem must be rebuilt, and the temple, and water come out from under the temple, and the Dead Sea healed. It will take some time to rebuild the walls of the city and the temple, &c.; and all this must be done before the Son of Man makes his appearance. There will be wars and rumors of wars, signs in the heavens above and on the earth beneath, the sun turned into darkness and the moon turned to blood, earthquakes in divers places, the seas heaving beyond their bounds; then will appear one grand sign of the Son of Man in heaven. But what will the world do? They will say it is a planet, a comet, etc. But the Son of Man will come as the sign of the Son of Man, which will be as the light of the morning cometh out of the east [April 7, 1843]. [*HC*, 5:337]

His comment seems to speak of two different signs. We do not know what the first sign will be, but it will be spectacular if all people see it together (D&C 88:93).

The first of the seven angels will make two announcements. The first is the binding of the great church, the mother of abominations, the tares of the parable of the wheat and tares bound and ready to be burned. She is not burned as yet, but ready to be. Her fall will come later as the wording suggests (see Revelation 14:8). Just as all people shall see the first sign, all nations shall hear the loud and long trumpet (D&C 88:94). The trumpet will be followed by "silence in heaven" for half an hour (v. 95). This silence is caused by the corruption "and the powers of darkness" that prevail on earth as the angels await the command to gather and burn the tares (see D&C 38:11–12). If this is the same silence spoken of in Revelation 8:1, which it may or may not be, it is after the opening of the 7th seal, or the beginning of the last thousand years of the earth's temporal existence (see Revelation 8:1). Using the Lord's time of a thousand years being one day (see Abraham 3:4; 2 Peter 3:8), half an hour out of a twenty-four hour day is slightly more than twenty years of earth's time. The curtain of heaven being "unfolded as a scroll" is using the terminology of Revelation 6:14 when "every mountain and island were moved out of their places." This brings us to the time of the Second Coming when the face of the Lord is unveiled (D&C 88:95).

D&C 88:96–98 • The Celestial Saints

96 And the saints that are upon the earth, who are alive, shall be quickened and be caught up to meet him.

97 And they who have slept in their graves shall come forth, for their graves shall be opened; and they also shall be caught up to meet him in the midst of the pillar of heaven—

98 They are Christ's, the first fruits, they who shall descend with him first, and they who are on the earth and in their graves, who are first caught up to meet him; and all this by the voice of the sounding of the trump of the angel of God.

The second announcement of the first angel blowing his trump is regarding the celestial Saints. Those who are alive will be caught up to meet the Savior as He returns (v. 96). They will be quickened which apparently means a temporary transfiguration, allowing them to transcend the laws of mortality. During the Millennium, which will then be ushered in, men "shall live to be an hundred years old [average?]" (JST, Isaiah 65:20). Therefore, the transfiguration does not seem to be a permanent change, but they will return to earth to live out their mortal years.

Those Saints who have died, and qualified for a celestial resurrection, will also be caught up to meet Christ at this time (v. 97). They will of course have a permanent body. They are Christ's the "first fruits" of the resurrection. They, and those who were caught up while yet alive, will descend with him (v. 98). Others will be resurrected, or changed "in the twinkling of an eye" as they close out their mortal existence (D&C 101:31).

D&C 88:99–102 • The Terrestrial, the Telestial, and Sons of Perdition

> 99 And after this another angel shall sound, which is the second trump; and then cometh the redemption of those who are Christ's at his coming; who have received their part in that prison which is prepared for them, that they might receive the gospel, and be judged according to men in the flesh.
>
> 100 And again, another trump shall sound, which is the third trump; and then come the spirits of men who are to be judged, and are found under condemnation;
>
> 101 And these are the rest of the dead; and they live not again until the thousand years are ended, neither again, until the end of the earth.
>
> 102 And another trump shall sound, which is the fourth trump, saying: There are found among those who are to remain until that great and last day, even the end, who shall remain filthy still.

At the second angel's trump, those who had qualified for a terrestrial resurrection will come forth. They had received a testimony of Christ either on earth or in the prison of the spirit world, but had not accepted the gospel in either place (see D&C 76:71–79 and comments). They have part in the first resurrection, but will follow the celestial resurrection (see D&C 45:54). How long into the Millennium before this resurrection will begin is not stated. Their glory is compared to the celestial Saints as the sun is comparable to the moon (see 1 Corinthians 15:40–42; D&C 76:96–97).

The third trump of an angel will then sound, and the telestial spirits will come forth and be condemned to the spirit prison for another thousand years (D&C 88:100–101). They rejected both the testimony of Christ and His gospel. They will be resurrected at the end of the thousand years, (see D&C 76:82–85).

The fourth angel's trump will call those who are the sons of perdition who will remain in their filthy state "until that great and last day" (D&C 88:102). Their final state has not and will not be revealed to man (see D&C 76:45–46).

D&C 88:103–107 • Fifth, Sixth, and Seventh Angels

103 And another trump shall sound, which is the fifth trump, which is the fifth angel who committeth the everlasting gospel—flying through the midst of heaven, unto all nations, kindreds, tongues, and people;

104 And this shall be the sound of his trump, saying to all people, both in heaven and in earth, and that are under the earth—for every ear shall hear it, and every knee shall bow, and every tongue shall confess, while they hear the sound of the trump, saying: Fear God, and give glory to him who sitteth upon the throne, forever and ever; for the hour of his judgment is come.

105 And again, another angel shall sound his trump, which is the sixth angel, saying: She is fallen who made all nations drink of the wine of the wrath of her fornication; she is fallen, is fallen!

106 And again, another angel shall sound his trump, which is the seventh angel, saying: It is finished; it is finished! The Lamb of God hath overcome and trodden the wine-press alone, even the wine-press of the fierceness of the wrath of Almighty God.

107 And then shall the angels be crowned with the glory of his might, and the saints shall be filled with his glory, and receive their inheritance and be made equal with him.

The fifth angel is undoubtedly Moroni, who has charge of the Book of Mormon going forth to all nations, kindreds, tongues, and people (v. 103; compare Revelation 14:6–7). He has appeared to some, "and shall appear unto many that dwell on the earth" (D&C 133:36). His trump

will declare his mission is completed and every knee will bow and everyone will confess, or acknowledge, that he has done his work, and that the judgment of God has come (D&C 88:104; compare Revelation 14:7). The sixth angel will then announce the fall of Babylon, the symbolic term of wickedness, and the mother of harlots, and abominations of the earth (D&C 88:105; compare Revelation 14:8; 17:5).

The seventh and last angel will announce that Christ has finished His work. He has trodden the winepress alone, or stomped out the telestial wickedness from the earth by the fierceness of an Almighty God (D&C 88:106; compare 76:107; Revelation 14:20). The symbolism of the winepress will be discussed in D&C 133:46–53. The angels being crowned with glory endorses the doctrine taught by the Prophet Joseph that: "there are no angels who minister to this earth but those who do belong or have belonged to it. The angels do not reside on a planet like this earth; But they reside in the presence of God, on a globe like a sea of glass and fire, where all things for their glory are manifest, past, present, and future, and are continually before the Lord" (D&C 130:5–7). Moroni was obviously the fifth angel. Adam is identified as the seventh angel (D&C 88:112). Others are and have been identified periodically. They will apparently be a part of the Saints being filled with glory, receiving an inheritance, and "made equal with God" (D&C 88:107).

D&C 88:108–110 • The Secret Acts of Men

108 And then shall the first angel again sound his trump in the ears of all living, and reveal the secret acts of men, and the mighty works of God in the first thousand years.

109 And then shall the second angel sound his trump, and reveal the secret acts of men, and the thoughts and intents of their hearts, and the mighty works of God in the second thousand years—

110 And so on, until the seventh angel shall sound his trump; and he shall stand forth upon the land and upon the sea, and swear in the name of him who sitteth upon the throne, that there shall be time no longer; and Satan shall be bound, that old serpent, who is called the devil, and shall not be loosed for the space of a thousand years.

As stated in 2 Nephi 27:11–12, the unsealed portion of the plates that were bound with the plates from which the Book of Mormon was translated contained a revelation from the beginning of the worlds to the end thereof, and are to be read from the house tops by the power of God. Whether this is the same incident as this revelation speaks or not is not known, but it obviously contains the same secret acts of men, and the mighty works of God that will be revealed. The sealed plates will verify the foreknowledge of God, since they were shown to the Brother of Jared, and written before they happened (see Ether 3:21–4:7). The seven angels will disclose all things that were thought to be secret. This reading will end the time of the temporal earth, and it will function on a different revolution during the Millennium (see Abraham 3:4–9).

The loosing of Satan (D&C 88:110) will come because of the wickedness of the people, probably in a gradual way as it happened among the Nephites who were all converted after the visit of Christ to the American continent. They gradually degenerated to almost total wickedness (see 4 Nephi 1:20–46). Just as the righteousness of the people binds Satan (see 1 Nephi 22:26), the opposite will loose him. Man will still have his agency during the Millennium.

D&C 88:111–116 • Loosed for a Season

111 And then he shall be loosed for a little season, that he may gather together his armies.

112 And Michael, the seventh angel, even the archangel, shall gather together his armies, even the hosts of heaven.

113 And the devil shall gather together his armies; even the hosts of hell, and shall come up to battle against Michael and his armies.

114 And then cometh the battle of the great God; and the devil and his armies shall be cast away into their own place, that they shall not have power over the saints any more at all.

115 For Michael shall fight their battles, and shall overcome him who seeketh the throne of him who sitteth upon the throne, even the Lamb.

116 This is the glory of God, and the sanctified; and they shall not any more see death.

The final battle between the devil and Michael [Adam] will be fought after the Millennium (vv. 111–115). This will be the end of the earth as a terrestrial planet. Its telestial status ended at the beginning of the Millennium, or the end of the world. We will learn about its becoming a celestial earth in the following chapter. The work and glory of God is

to sanctify the earth that it may gain immortality and eternal life as well as its eternal inhabitants (v. 116; compare Moses 1:39).

General Authority Quotes

—*Elder Marion G. Romney* • D&C 87:1–2, 6

That the Lord's purpose in revealing these unhappy impending calamities was not to condemn but to save mankind is evidenced by the fact that with the warning he identified the cause and revealed the means by which the calamities may be turned aside. [CR, April 1965, 104]

—*Bishop Joseph L. Wirthlin* • D&C 87:1–4

In many cases I am quite sure we all think that this has to do particularly with the slaves in the Southern States, but I believe . . . it was intended that this referred to slaves all over the world, . . . where the rights and the privilege to worship God and to come to a knowledge that Jesus Christ is his Son is denied them. [CR, October 1958, 32]

—*President Joseph Fielding Smith* • D&C 87:5

The history of the American continent also gives evidence that the Lamanites have risen up in their anger and vexed the Gentiles. This warfare may not be over. It has been the fault of people in the United States to think that this prophetic saying has reference to the Indians in the United States, but we must remember that there are millions of the "remnant" in Mexico, Central and South America. It was during our Civil War that the Indians in Mexico rose up and gained their freedom from the tyranny which Napoleon endeavored to inflict upon them contrary to the prediction of Jacob in the Book of Mormon, that there should no kings among the Gentiles on this land. The independence of Mexico and other nations to the south has been accomplished by the uprising of the "remnant" upon the land. However, let us not think that this prophecy has been completely fulfilled. [*Church History and Modern Revelation* (1946), 1:363]

—*President Harold B. Lee* • D&C 87:8

When an earthquake strikes, every person might be taken as he is then living—if at a movie, or a tavern, or in a drunken stupor, or whatever. But the true servants of God, those who are doing their duty, will be protected and preserved if they will do as the Lord has counseled: "stand ye in holy places, and be not moved," when these days should come (D&C 87:8). [*The Teachings of Harold B. Lee*, 411]

I bear you my witness in all humility that if your children and my children, our grandchildren, and our great-grandchildren remain faithful to this church, it will because you and I remained steadfast in the testimony that these men [the First Presidency and the Twelve] are prophets of the living God and that we must follow their counsel if we would be saved in the days of peril. Therefore "stand ye in holy places, and be not moved" (D&C 87:8), that we might abide the day of the coming of the Son of Man and be caught up in the clouds of heaven to meet our Redeemer when He comes on earth to reign, and reign with him a thousand years with our children and the redeemed of our Father's house. [*The Teachings of Harold B. Lee,* 521]

—*President Joseph Fielding Smith* • D&C 88:99–101

. . .There will come to pass another resurrection. This may be considered as a part of the first, although it comes later. In this resurrection will come forth those of the terrestrial order, who were not worthy to be caught up to meet him, but who are worthy to come forth to enjoy the millennial reign. . . .

This other class, which will also have right to the first resurrection. are those who are not members of the Church of the Firstborn, but who have led honorable lives, although they refused to accept the fullness of the gospel.

Also in this class will be numbered those who died without law and hence are not under condemnation for a violation of the commandments of the Lord. . . .

All liars, and sorcerers, and adulterers and all who love and make a lie, shall not receive a resurrection at this time, but for a thousand years shall be thrust down to hell where they shall suffer the wrath of God until they pay the price of their sinning, if it is possible, by the things which they shall suffer. . . .

This suffering will be a means of cleansing or purifying, and through it the wicked will be brought to a condition whereby they may, through the redemption of Jesus Christ, obtain immortality. Their spirits and bodies shall be again united, and they shall dwell in the telestial kingdom. But this resurrection will not come until the end of the world. [*Doctrines of Salvation,* 2:296–298]

Chapter Eight

The Olive Leaf

D&C 88:1–86, 117–141

DOCTRINE AND COVENANTS 88

*H*istorical Setting: "Two days after the preceding prophecy [D&C 87], on the 27ᵗʰ of December, I received [Doctrine and Covenants 88]" (*HC,* 1:302).

On January 14, 1833, the Prophet wrote to W. W. Phelps:

> I send unto you the "Olive Leaf" which we have plucked from the tree of Paradise, the Lord's message of peace to us; for though our brethren in Zion indulge in feelings towards us, which are not according to the requirements of the new covenant, yet, we have the satisfaction of knowing that the Lord approves of us, and has accepted us, and established His name in Kirtland for the salvation of the nations; for the Lord will have a place whence His word will go forth, in these last days, in purity. . . . [*HC,* 1:316]

> A conference of High Priests assembled in the translating room in Kirtland, Ohio on the 27ᵗʰ day of Dec, (1832), I received the following. Present: Joseph Smith, Sidney Rigdon, Orson Hyde, Joseph Smith Jun., Hyrum Smith, Samuel H. Smith, N. K. Whitney, F. G. Williams, Ezra Thayer & John Murdock commenced by prayer, then Bro. Joseph arose and said, to receive revelation and the blessings of heaven it was necessary to have our minds on god and exercise faith and become of one heart and of one mind. Therefore he recommended all present to pray separately and vocally to the Lord for to receive his will unto us concerning the upbuilding of Zion, & for the benefit of the saints and for the duty and employment of the Elders— Accordingly we all bowed down

before the Lord, after which arose and spoke in his turn his feelings, and determination to keep the commandments of God, and thus proceeded to receive a revelation concerning [not legible] above stated 9 o'clock P.M. the revelation not being finished the conference adjourned till tomorrow 9 o'clock A.M. — 27th [sic 28th] met according adjournment and commenced by Prayer thus proceeded to receive the residue of the above revelation and it being finished and there being no further business before the conference closed the meeting by prayer in harmony with the brethren and gratitude to our heavenly Father for the great manifestation of his holy Spirit during the setting of the conference.[29]

The section heading notes that portions of this revelation were received on December 27 and 28, 1832, and January 3, 1833. Verses 117–126 were published in the *Evening and Morning Star* (February 1833) and verses 117–137 (March 1833); an early Church newspaper. It appears that these verses may have been the ones [including vv. 138–141] received on January 3, 1833. Verses 138–141 may not have been included in the newspaper because of the instructions of the sacred ordinance of the washing of the feet.

DOCTRINE AND COVENANTS 88:1–86

SECTION 88 • OUTLINE

➤ 88:1–5   The prayers of those assembled have come up to the Lord, and are recorded in the book of the sanctified of the celestial world.

    a.   Another comforter is sent, the Holy Spirit of Promise, the same as promised in the testimony of John (v. 3).

    b.   It is the promise of eternal life, the glory of the celestial kingdom (v. 4).

    c.   The glory of the Church of the Firstborn, even God, through Jesus Christ (v. 5).

➤ 88:6–13   Christ ascended up on high, and below all things, and comprehended all things, to be in and through all things, the light of truth, and the Light of Christ.

---

[29] Kirtland Council Minute Book, 3, 4. This book is located in the Historical Department of the Church. A typewritten copy is in possession of the author. See also, Lyndon W. Cook, *The Revelations of the Prophet Joseph Smith* [1981], 181.

    a.   He is in the sun, the light of the sun and the power by which it was made (v. 7).

    b.   He is in the moon, the light of it and the power by which it was made (v. 8).

    c.   He is the light of the stars and the power by which they were made (v. 9).

    d.   The earth and the power thereof upon which you stand (v. 19).

    e.   Your light is through Him and quickens your understanding (v. 11).

    f.   The light proceeds from God to fill the immensity of space (v. 12).

    g.   The light is in all things and governs all things, even the power of God (v. 13).

88:14–20   Christ's redemption brought the resurrection of the dead.

    a.   The spirit and the body are the soul of man (v. 15).

    b.   The resurrection of the dead is the redemption of the soul (v. 16).

    c.   Christ decreed that the poor and the meek shall inherit the earth (v. 17).

    d.   The earth must be sanctified from all unrighteousness to be prepared for the celestial glory (v. 18).

    e.   After it fills the measure of its creation, it shall be crowned with the presence of the Father (v. 19).

    f.   Bodies of the celestial kingdom shall possess the earth forever and ever (v. 20).

88:21–24   Those not sanctified by Christ's law will have a terrestrial kingdom (v. 21–22).

    a.   Who cannot abide terrestrial law cannot abide a terrestrial kingdom (v. 23).

    b.   Who cannot abide a telestial law must abide a kingdom of no glory (v. 24).

88:25–33   The earth abides a celestial law and shall die and be quickened, and it shall be sanctified and inherited by the righteous.

    a.   Notwithstanding the righteous die, they shall rise as a spiritual body (v. 27).

    b.   A spirit shall receive its same body quickened by celestial glory (v. 28).

    c.   Those quickened by a portion of celestial glory shall receive a fulness (v. 29).

    d.   Those quickened by a portion of terrestrial glory shall receive a fulness (v. 30).

    e.   Those quickened by a portion of telestial glory shall receive a fulness (v. 31).

    f.   The remaining will return to their own place, they were not willing to enjoy what they might have received (v. 32).

    g.   What does it profit a man if a gift is bestowed and he receive not the gift (v. 33).

➤ 88:34–41   That which is governed by law is preserved, perfected, and sanctified by it.

    a.   That which becomes a law unto itself cannot be sanctified by law, mercy, justice, or judgment (v. 35).

    b.   All kingdoms have a law, there are many kingdoms, and a greater or lesser kingdom wherever there is space (vv. 36–37).

    c.   Every kingdom has a law, certain bounds, and conditions (v. 38).

    d.   All beings who abide not these conditions are not justified (v. 39).

    e.   Intelligence cleaves to intelligence, as also wisdom, truth, virtue, light, mercy, justice, and judgment (v. 40).

    f.   God comprehends all things, and all things are before Him, above, in, round about all things, and are by and of Him, even God forever and ever (v. 41).

➤ 88:42–50   God has given a law to all things to move in their times and seasons.

    a.   The courses of heaven and earth are fixed which comprehend the earth and all planets (v. 42).

    b.   They give light to each other in their times and seasons—all are one year with God, but not with man (v. 44).

    c.   The earth rolls, the sun gives light by day, the moon and stars by night (v. 45).

d. Any who have seen this has seen God moving in majesty and power (v. 47).

e. He came into his own and was not comprehended (v. 48).

f. The light shines in darkness, and the darkness does not comprehend, but they shall comprehend even God, being quickened by Him (v. 49).

g. Then shall ye know ye have seen me, and I am the true light in you (v. 50).

➤ 88:51–61 I will liken these kingdoms unto a man sending his servants to a field to dig.

a. He sent the first and said he would visit him in the first hour with joy (v. 52).

b. He sent the second and said he would visit him in the second hour (v. 53).

c. He sent the third through the twelfth with the same promise (vv. 54–55).

d. He visited the first to the twelfth in their hour, and was made glad (vv. 56–58).

e. He began from the first to the last, and from the last unto the first (v. 59).

f. Every man in his own hour that he might be glorified in him (v. 60).

g. The parable is like all these kingdoms according to the decree of God (v. 61).

➤ 88:62–66 Ponder these things in your heart with a commandment to call upon me while I am near. Draw near to me and I will draw near to you.

a. Seek and find; ask and receive; knock and it shall be opened (v. 63).

b. What you ask shall be given if expedient for you (v. 64).

c. Asking for what is not expedient shall turn to your condemnation (v. 65).

d. You hear a voice crying in the wilderness and you cannot see him, my voice is spirit and truth and abides forever (v. 66).

➤ 88:67–73 If your eye be single to my glory, your whole body shall be filled with light, which comprehends all things.

a. Sanctify yourselves and you shall see Him in His own time and own way (v. 68).

b. Cast away your idle thoughts and excess laughter far from you (v. 69).

c. Call a solemn assembly of the first laborers in this last kingdom (v. 70).

d. Let those who have been warned ponder it for a little season (v. 71).

e. I will care for your flocks, and raise up elders to send to you (v. 72).

f. I will hasten my work in its time (v. 73).

➤ 88:74–75   The Lord commands them to assemble, organize, prepare, and be sanctified.

a. Purify your hearts, cleanse your hands and feet, so I may make you clean (v. 74).

b. That he may testify to your Father, and your God, that you are clean from the blood of this wicked generation (v. 75).

➤ 88:76   The Lord commands them to continue in fasting and prayer from this time forth.

➤ 88:77–82   The Lord commands them to teach one another the doctrine of the kingdom.

a. Teach diligently and His grace shall attend you, to instruct more perfectly in all things pertaining to the kingdom (v. 78).

b. Teach things in heaven, on earth, under the earth, which are, must come to pass, at home, abroad, wars, judgments, and a knowledge of countries (v. 79).

c. That ye may be prepared when you are sent to your mission (v. 80).

d. You are sent to testify and warn the people, and every man warn his neighbor.

e. They are left without excuse, and their sins are on their own heads (v. 82).

➤ 88:83–86   He that seeks me early shall find me and not be forsaken.

   a.   Be perfected in your ministry among the Gentiles for the
        last time, to bind up the law and seal the testimony, and
        prepare the Saints for judgment (v. 84).

   b.   That their souls escape the desolation of abominations of
        the wicked (v. 85).

   c.   Abide ye in the liberty where you are made free, entangle
        not in sin (v. 86).

Introduction

The Lord had earlier admonished the Saints in Zion: "But learn that
he who doeth the works of righteousness shall receive his reward, even
peace in this world, and eternal life in the world to come" (D&C 59:23).
Doctrine and Covenants 88 gives us four teachings of the gospel of Jesus
Christ that is "the Lord's message of peace to us." The four principles will
be analyzed in this chapter. They are: (1) Another Comforter. (2) The
light of truth. (3) The resurrection of the dead. (4) Become perfected and
sanctified. These four principles will bring peace in this world, and eternal
life in the world to come.

TEXT AND COMMENTARY

D&C 88:1–5 • Another Comforter

1 Verily, thus saith the Lord unto you who have assembled yourselves
together to receive his will concerning you:

2 Behold, this is pleasing unto your Lord, and the angels rejoice over
you; the alms of your prayers have come up into the ears of the Lord of
Sabaoth, and are recorded in the book of the names of the sanctified,
even them of the celestial world.

3 Wherefore, I now send upon you another Comforter, even upon
you my friends, that it may abide in your hearts, even the Holy Spirit
of promise; which other Comforter is the same that I promised unto my
disciples, as is recorded in the testimony of John.

4 This Comforter is the promise which I give unto you of eternal
life, even the glory of the celestial kingdom;

5 Which glory is that of the church of the Firstborn, even of God,
the holiest of all, through Jesus Christ his Son—

Addressing the ten high priests who are assembled, the Lord expresses His pleasure with them, and that the angels rejoice over them. Their prayers have come into the ears of the Lord of Sabaoth,[30] "and are recorded in the book of the names of the sanctified" (v. 2). As it reads, the prayers were recorded and not the ten men's names. Why the prayers were recorded there is not stated, but because of the prayers, probably the ones they had given to request the revelation, the Lord says He will send upon them another Comforter. The promise recorded in the Testimony of John is later identified by the Prophet Joseph Smith after making the following comments:

> The other Comforter spoken of is a subject of great interest, and perhaps understood by few of this generation. After a person has faith in Christ, repents of his sins, and is baptized for the remission of sins and receives the Holy Ghost, (by laying on of hands), which is the first comforter, then let him continue to humble himself before God, hungering and thirsting after righteousness, and living by every word of God, and the Lord will soon say unto him, Son, thou shalt soon be exalted. When the Lord has thoroughly proved him, and finds that the man is determined to serve Him at all hazards, then the man will find his calling and election made sure, then it will be his privilege to receive the other Comforter, which the Lord has promised the Saints, as is recorded in the testimony of St. John, in the 14th chapter, from the 12th to the 27th verses.

> Note the 16, 17, 18, 21, 23rd verses:

> "16. And I will pray the Father, and he shall give you another Comforter, that he may abide with you forever;

> "17. Even the Spirit of truth; whom the world cannot receive, because it seeth him not, neither knoweth him: but ye know him; for he dwelleth with you, and shall be in you.

> "18. I will not leave you comfortless: I will come to you.

> "21. He that hath my commandments, and keepeth them, he it is that loveth me: and he that loveth me shall be loved of my Father, and I will love him, and will manifest myself to him.

> "23. If a man love me, he will keep my words: and my Father will

---

[30] The "Lord of Sabaoth" is the "Lord of Hosts," a title given to Jehovah in the Old Testament [1 Samuel 17:45; James 5:4]; see the Bible Dictionary, 764.

love him, and we will come unto him, and make our abode with him."
[*TPJS*, 150]

Both comforters are spoken of in these verses in John. The Prophet also identifies the first Comforter as the Holy Ghost on the previous page (*TPJS*, 149). John 14:16–17, 26 speaks of the first Comforter, while verses 21 and 23 speak of the other Comforter.[31] The Prophet continues his comments after quoting the above verses:

> Now what is the other Comforter? It is no more nor less than the Lord Jesus Christ Himself; and this is the sum and substance of the whole matter; that when any man obtains this last Comforter, he will have the personage of Jesus Christ to attend to him, or appear unto him from time to time, and even He will manifest the Father unto him, and they will take up their abode with him, and the visions of the heavens will be opened unto him, and the Lord will teach him face to face, and he may have a perfect knowledge of the mysteries of the Kingdom of God; and this is the state and place the ancients Saints arrived at when they had such glorious visions—Isaiah, Ezekiel, John upon the Isle of Patmos, St. Paul in the three heavens, and all the saints who had communion with the general assembly and Church of the Firstborn. [*TPJS*, 150–151]

The concluding verse of the testimony of John, cited by the Prophet Joseph says: "Peace I leave with you, my peace I give unto you: not as the world giveth, give I unto you. Let not your heart be troubled, neither let it be afraid" (John 14:27). This blessing is a beautiful tie-in with the concept of peace promised in D&C 88. Those who attain the glory of the celestial kingdom become members of "the church of the Firstborn," the heavenly Church (see D&C 88:5 and 76:54). This blessing is possible through Jesus Christ.

Some of the ten assembled high priests left the Church at various times following the reception of this revelation. Therefore, the question of their having their "calling and election made sure" may be raised. First, it may be asked if they all actually received this Comforter—or were they promised it for the future—and some may not have been given that blessing? If they were, which seems it was, we should remember what an earlier revelation said: "And we know also, that sanctification through the grace of our Lord and Savior Jesus Christ is just and true, to all those

---

[31] See *Doctrines of Salvation*, 1:55.

who love and serve God with all their mights, minds, and strength. But there is a possibility that man may fall from grace and depart from the living God; therefore let the church take heed and pray always, lest they fall into temptation; yea, and even let those who are sanctified take heed also" (D&C 20:31–34). The eternal status of those who fell away from the Church is in the hands of the Lord; we must not pass judgment. However, if they did fall from grace, the olive leaf of peace certainly was taken from them.

D&C 88:6–13 • The Light of Truth

6 He that ascended up on high, as also he descended below all things, in that he comprehended all things, that he might be in all and through all things, the light of truth;

7 Which truth shineth. This is the light of Christ. As also he is in the sun, and the light of the sun, and the power thereof by which it was made.

8 As also he is in the moon, and is the light of the moon, and the power thereof by which it was made;

9 As also the light of the stars, and the power thereof by which they were made;

10 And the earth also, and the power thereof, even the earth upon which you stand.

11 And the light which shineth, which giveth you light, is through him who enlighteneth your eyes, which is the same light that quickeneth your understandings;

12 Which light proceedeth forth from the presence of God to fill the immensity of space—

13 The light which is in all things, which giveth life to all things, which is the law by which all things are governed, even the power of God who sitteth upon his throne, who is in the bosom of eternity, who is in the midst of all things.

The light truth is the Light of Christ. He attained the light of truth by ascending up on high after He had descended below all things. He was able, though His premortal and mortal life, to comprehend all things "that he might be in all and through all things (v. 6). In the testimony of John, we learn that He became "the way, the truth, and the life" (John

14:6). As taught by Joseph Smith, He held the keys of the universe (see *TPJS,* 157; last sentence). His truth shines throughout the universe—the sun, the moon, the stars, and the earth (vv. 7–10). His light proceeds "from the presence of God to fill the immensity of space" (v. 12). Thus He is an eminent God, having three primary functions. The first is creative power. Through His power He created the sun, the moon, the stars, and the earth. "The word create came from the word *barau* [Hebrew] which does not mean to create out of nothing; it means to organize; the same as a man would organize materials and build a ship" (*TPJS,* 350). The elements obey the voice of God (see Helaman 12:7–17). Therefore, Christ spoke and the elements obeyed, and they came together to form the various planets (see Genesis 1:3, 6, 9, and more).

The second function of the Light of Christ is the quickening of your understanding. The light here refers to intelligence or intellect (v. 11). All people are born with "the true Light, which lighteth every man that cometh into the world" (John 1:9; see also D&C 84:46). The primary purpose of the light of truth is so that each person "may know good from evil." It invites everyone "to do good, and to persuade to believe in Christ" (Moroni 7:16). Those who hearken "to the voice of the Spirit cometh unto God, even the Father" (D&C 84:47).

Those who come unto the Father are taught by the Holy Ghost. They are brought to the covenant of baptism (see 3 Nephi 12:3; 21:6; 27:20), and given the gift of the Holy Ghost. Those who will receive that gift are taught further. However, "A man may receive the Holy Ghost, and it may descend upon him and not tarry with him" D&C 130:23). This is the first Comforter. The Prophet Joseph taught: "This first Comforter or Holy Ghost has no other effect than pure intelligence. It is more powerful in expanding the mind, enlightening the understanding, and storing the intellect with present knowledge . . . (*TPJS,* 149). The testimony of John says: "But the Comforter, [which is] the Holy Ghost, whom the Father will send in my name, he shall teach you all things, and bring all things to your remembrance, whatsoever I have said unto you" (John 14:26). Jesus taught the Nephites that the Holy Ghost comes through Christ, sustaining the Doctrine and Covenants revelation that the Holy Ghost is a part of the light of truth. "And after that ye were blessed then fulfilleth the Father the covenant which he made with Abraham, saying: In thy seed shall all the kindreds of the earth be blessed—unto the *pouring out of the Holy Ghost through me* upon the Gentiles" (3 Nephi 20:27; italics added). Thus the Holy Ghost comes through the Light of Christ, making a second witness of truth to those who will receive it.

The third function of the Light of Christ is to govern the earth. It gives "light to all things, which is the law by which all things are governed, even the power of God" (D&C 88:13). As taught in the New Testament, "in him we live, and move and have our being" (Acts 17:28). The concept of life bring sustained by Jesus Christ is enlarged upon in the Book of Mormon:[32] "if ye should serve him who has created you from the beginning, and is preserving you from day to day, by lending you breath, that ye may live and move and do according to your own will, and even supporting you from one moment to another—I say, if ye should serve him with all your whole souls yet ye would be unprofitable servants (Mosiah 2:21). As the governing power of the earth, He not only created it, but He gives light to its inhabitants, and enables them to live on it. Wherefore, He is "the light and life of the world" (3 Nephi 9:18).

D&C 88:14–20 • The Resurrection of the Dead

14 Now, verily I say unto you, that through the redemption which is made for you is brought to pass the resurrection from the dead.

15 And the spirit and the body are the soul of man.

16 And the resurrection from the dead is the redemption of the soul.

17 And the redemption of the soul is through him that quickeneth all things, in whose bosom it is decreed that the poor and the meek of the earth shall inherit it.

18 Therefore, it must needs be sanctified from all unrighteousness, that it may be prepared for the celestial glory;

19 For after it hath filled the measure of its creation, it shall be crowned with glory, even with the presence of God the Father;

20 That bodies who are of the celestial kingdom may possess it forever and ever; for, for this intent was it made and created, and for this intent are they sanctified.

The "Olive Leaf" revelation sheds much light on the third principle

---

[32] That Christ is the creator from the beginning is confirmed in Mormon 9:11–12. He is the Administrator of the plan of salvation (see Abraham 3:24–27).

that it testifies will bring peace to the soul—the redemption of the dead through Jesus Christ (v. 14). In his mortal probation upon the earth, man is composed of a spirit and a body (see D&C 93:33). In this revelation, the soul is defined as "the spirit and the body" (D&C 88:15). The soul is separated upon death, and reunited at "the resurrection from the dead;" therefore, it "is the redemption of the soul" (v. 16). The Redeemer has decreed that "the poor and the meek of the earth shall inherit it" (v. 17). The decree was given in the Sermon on the Mount in Galilee (see Matthew 5:5), and to the Nephites (see 3 Nephi 12:5). The poor and the meek will become celestial beings, and their home will be the celestial earth. The earth was created for this purpose (see 1 Nephi 17:36; compare Alma 12:24).

D&C 88:21–24 • Other Kingdoms

21 And they who are not sanctified through the law which I have given unto you, even the law of Christ, must inherit another kingdom, even that of a terrestrial kingdom, or that of a telestial kingdom.

22 For he who is not able to abide the law of a celestial kingdom cannot abide a celestial glory.

23 And he who cannot abide the law of a terrestrial kingdom cannot abide a terrestrial glory.

24 And he who cannot abide the law of a telestial kingdom cannot abide a telestial glory; therefore he is not meet for a kingdom of glory. Therefore he must abide a kingdom which is not a kingdom of glory.

Many of the earth's inhabitants will not qualify for celestial life upon the sanctified earth. Their lack of qualification would prevent them from living there; they could not abide the glory that will exist upon that planet (vv. 21–22). Furthermore, they would not be happy there even if they could abide the glory. Their environment would make them internally miserable and unhappy. As Moroni declares:

4 Behold, I say unto you that ye would be more miserable to dwell with a holy and just God, under a consciousness of your filthiness before him, than ye would to dwell with the damned souls in hell.

5 For behold, when ye shall be brought to see your nakedness before God, and also the glory of God, and the holiness of Jesus Christ, it will kindle a flame of unquenchable fire upon you. [Mormon 9:4–5]

The same misery would exist between the terrestrial and the telestial kingdom (v. 23). The sons of perdition are those who will have no glory (v. 24).

D&C 88:25–33

25 And again, verily I say unto you, the earth abideth the law of a celestial kingdom, for it filleth the measure of its creation, and transgresseth not the law—

26 Wherefore, it shall be sanctified; yea, notwithstanding it shall die, it shall be quickened again, and shall abide the power by which it is quickened, and the righteous shall inherit it.

27 For notwithstanding they die, they also shall rise again, a spiritual body.

28 They who are of a celestial spirit shall receive the same body which was a natural body; even ye shall receive your bodies, and your glory shall be that glory by which your bodies are quickened.

29 Ye who are quickened by a portion of the celestial glory shall then receive of the same, even a fulness.

30 And they who are quickened by a portion of the terrestrial glory shall then receive of the same, even a fulness.

31 And also they who are quickened by a portion of the telestial glory shall then receive of the same, even a fulness.

32 And they who remain shall also be quickened; nevertheless, they shall return again to their own place, to enjoy that which they are willing to receive, because they were not willing to enjoy that which they might have received.

33 For what doth it profit a man if a gift is bestowed upon him, and he receive not the gift? Behold, he rejoices not in that which is given unto him, neither rejoices in him who is the giver of the gift.

The glory of the God will be upon the celestial earth because the Father will dwell there, as stated above (D&C 88:19). In addition, the Lord tells us why it will become a celestial planet. It will have filled its purpose of creation, and did not transgress the law (v. 25). May we note further that our planet obeyed the voice of the Lord, as discussed above. Our planet was baptized with the waters of the flood, and will be baptized by fire at the beginning of the Millennium. "The earth will be renewed and receive its paradisiacal glory" (A of F 1:10), and be sanctified during the Millennium. Our earth "shall die" but "it shall be quickened again," or resurrected, as a celestial earth. The righteous, or the celestial beings, shall then inherit the earth (v. 26). It shall be a new earth, even a celestial earth.

The spiritual body (v. 27) is not the spirit body. As Amulek explained: ". . . concerning the death of the mortal body, and also concerning the resurrection of the mortal body. I say unto you that this mortal body is raised to an immortal body, that is from death, even from the first death unto life, that they can die no more; their spirits uniting with their bodies, never to be divided; thus the whole becoming spiritual and immortal, that they can no more see corruption" (Alma 11:45).

A resurrected body is a spiritual body. On May 17, 1843, the Prophet Joseph explained further: "There is no such thing as immaterial matter. All spirit is matter, but it is more fine or pure, and can only be discerned by purer eyes; we cannot see it; but when our bodies are purified we shall see that it is all matter" (D&C 131:7–8). Earlier he had taught (April 1, 1842):

> . . . we shall find a very material difference between the body and the spirit; the body is supposed to be organized matter, and the spirit, by many, is thought to be immaterial, without substance. With this latter statement we should beg leave to differ, and state the spirit is a subject; that it is material, but that it is more pure, elastic and refined matter than the body; that it existed before the body, can exist in the body; and will exist separate from the body, when the body is smoldering in the dust; and will in the resurrection be again united with it. [*TPJS,* 207]

On April 7, 1842, six days later: "To a remark of elder Orson Pratt's, that a man's body changes every seven years, President Joseph replied there is no fundamental principle belonging to a human system that ever goes into another in this world or in the world to come; I care not what the theories of men are. We have the testimony that God will raise us up, and he has the power to do it. If any one supposes that any part of our bodies, that is, the fundamental parts thereof, ever goes into another body, he is mistaken" (*HC,* 5:339). Therefore, all who receive a glory will be resurrected with their natural bodies becoming spiritual bodies of that glory that quickened your body (v. 28).

Each individual will be resurrected by "a portion" of that glory for which he or she has prepared their bodies to receive, and then in time receive a fulness of the same glory (vv. 29–31). How long that process will take is not stated. It may vary with individuals, depending on their own initiative and efforts.

Those who remain, the sons of perdition, will also be quickened or resurrected (v. 31). Some have erroneously claimed that these spirits will not be resurrected, and base their argument upon D&C 76:38: "the only ones who shall not be redeemed." However, not being redeemed has reference to their not receiving a glory as had the other classes of men. The scriptures clearly teach that **all** will be resurrected (bolding added; see John 5:29; Acts 24:15; 1 Corinthians 15:21–22; Alma 11:40–42).

The place to which the sons of perdition will return is not revealed. The revelation says only that they "return again to their own place, to enjoy that which they were willing to receive" (D&C 88:32). The word "enjoy" is misleading. Will they be happy? No! They will be with the devil who sought "evil before God . . . and had become miserable forever, [and] he sought also the misery of all mankind" (2 Nephi 2:17–18). They did not profit from the gift bestowed upon them (D&C 88:33). They have sinned against the Holy Ghost, and fought against God. They rejoiced not in the gift they had received nor in Christ (v. 33). Only those who are cast into this place will know of its condition (see D&C 76:43–48). All except the sons of perdition will receive a degree of glory.

D&C 88:34–41 • Become Perfected and Sanctified

34 And again, verily I say unto you, that which is governed by law is also preserved by law and perfected and sanctified by the same.

35 That which breaketh a law, and abideth not by law, but seeketh to become a law unto itself, and willeth to abide in sin, and altogether abideth in sin, cannot be sanctified by law, neither by mercy, justice, nor judgment. Therefore, they must remain filthy still.

36 All kingdoms have a law given;

37 And there are many kingdoms; for there is no space in the which there is no kingdom; and there is no kingdom in which there is no space, either a greater or a lesser kingdom.

38 And unto every kingdom is given a law; and unto every law there are certain bounds also and conditions.

39 All beings who abide not in those conditions are not justified.

40 For intelligence cleaveth unto intelligence; wisdom receiveth wisdom; truth embraceth truth; virtue loveth virtue; light cleaveth unto light; mercy hath compassion on mercy and claimeth her own; justice continueth its course and claimeth its own; judgment goeth before the face of him who sitteth upon the throne and governeth and executeth all things.

41 He comprehendeth all things, and all things are before him, and all things are round about him; and he is above all things, and in all things, and is through all things, and is round about all things; and all things are by him, and of him, even God, forever and ever.

The fourth principle for eternal peace outlined in the "Olive Leaf" is to become perfected and sanctified (v. 34). However, only one person who lived on this mortal earth was able to keep all the laws—the Lord Jesus Christ (see Hebrews 4:15). As Lehi taught Jacob: "By the law no flesh is justified. Those who seek to become a law unto itself are the sons of perdition of whom we have just spoken. They must remain filthy. The others who attain a degree of glory must do so by mercy, or justice, or judgment (v. 35). As all kingdoms have a law that must be met to abide therein (v. 36), the following interpretation is suggested:

The celestial kingdom may be attained by taking full advantage of the Atonement of Jesus Christ. Again citing Lehi's teaching to his son Jacob:

7 Behold, he offereth himself a sacrifice for sin, to answer the ends of the law, unto all those who have a broken heart and a contrite spirit; and unto none else can the ends of the law be answered.

8 Wherefore, how great the importance to make these things known unto the inhabitants of the earth, that they may know that there is no flesh that can dwell in the presence of God, save it be through the merits, and mercy, and grace of the Holy Messiah, who layeth down his life according to the flesh, and taketh it again by the power of the Spirit, that he may bring to pass the resurrection of the dead, being the first that should rise. [2 Nephi 2:7–8]

The celestial glory will be attained through the ever loving mercy of Christ who "suffered these things for all, that they might not suffer if they would repent" (D&C 19:16).

Mercy cannot rob justice. "Mercy claimeth the penitent," and "justice exerciseth all his demands," as men are "judged according to their works" on earth (Alma 42:22–25). The bounds and conditions of the terrestrial kingdom were to be honorable men and have a testimony of Jesus. However, if they rejected the gospel of Jesus Christ and the ordinances thereof, they "receive of his glory, but not of the fullness thereof" (D&C 76:75–76).

The bounds and conditions of the telestial kingdom are the judgment of a thousand years of suffering in the spirit world. They rejected both the testimony of Jesus and the gospel of Jesus Christ (see D&C 76: 82, 101). Although they acknowledge that He is the Christ (see D&C 88:110), their works were of darkness (see D&C 76:103). Their glory still "surpasses all understanding" (D&C 76:89). "Every man shall receive according to his own works, his own dominion, in the mansions which are prepared" (D&C 76:111).

God governs by law, and there are many kingdoms throughout space, and every space has a lesser or greater kingdom (D&C 88:37–38). Those who do not abide in the conditions of a higher kingdom are not justified to be there (v. 39). They did not add to their first estate (see Abraham 3:26). Those who did not cleave unto intelligence, receive wisdom, embrace truth, or love virtue must continue in the course of justice or judgment (D&C 88:40). These laws are eternal and are administered by God, who comprehends all things, governs all things, and is God forever and ever (v. 41).

D&C 88:42–50 • Times and Seasons

42 And again, verily I say unto you, he hath given a law unto all things, by which they move in their times and their seasons;

43 And their courses are fixed, even the courses of the heavens and the earth, which comprehend the earth and all the planets.

44 And they give light to each other in their times and in their seasons, in their minutes, in their hours, in their days, in their weeks, in their months, in their years—all these are one year with God, but not with man.

45 The earth rolls upon her wings, and the sun giveth his light by day, and the moon giveth her light by night, and the stars also give their light, as they roll upon their wings in their glory, in the midst of the power of God.

46 Unto what shall I liken these kingdoms, that ye may understand?

47 Behold, all these are kingdoms, and any man who hath seen any or the least of these hath seen God moving in his majesty and power.

48 I say unto you, he hath seen him; nevertheless, he who came unto his own was not comprehended.

49 The light shineth in darkness, and the darkness comprehendeth it not; nevertheless, the day shall come when you shall comprehend even God, being quickened in him and by him.

50 Then shall ye know that ye have seen me, that I am, and that I am the true light that is in you, and that you are in me; otherwise ye could not abound.

The eternal kingdoms are also governed by law, and are used to complement each other, and bring about the purposes and glory of God (vv. 88:42–45; compare Abraham 3 and Facsimile 3). To help mortal people understand, the Lord gives some comparisons. The first comparison is to what man may have seen. As the universe or the atom is viewed, the largest and the smallest observable models, one will recognize the pattern of "God moving in his might and power" (v. 47). Of particular interest to the author is the fifteen fixed planets or stars that are governed by one of the planets (Facsimile 2, figure 5). Does this not remind us of the First Presidency and the Quorum of the Twelve Apostles, or Abraham, Isaac, and Jacob, and the twelve tribes of Israel? Although most mortals do not comprehend God, even His own people [the Jews] to whom He came, the day will come when men will know that His power and majesty have been governing the universe (D&C 88:48–50). The second comparison is to a man visiting the various kingdoms (vv. 51–61).

D&C 88:51–61 • Parable of the Kingdoms

51 Behold, I will liken these kingdoms unto a man having a field, and he sent forth his servants into the field to dig in the field.

52 And he said unto the first: Go ye and labor in the field, and in the first hour I will come unto you, and ye shall behold the joy of my countenance.

53 And he said unto the second: Go ye also into the field, and in the second hour I will visit you with the joy of my countenance.

54 And also unto the third, saying: I will visit you;

55 And unto the fourth, and so on unto the twelfth.

56 And the lord of the field went unto the first in the first hour, and tarried with him all that hour, and he was made glad with the light of the countenance of his lord.

57 And then he withdrew from the first that he might visit the second also, and the third, and the fourth, and so on unto the twelfth.

58 And thus they all received the light of the countenance of their lord, every man in his hour, and in his time, and in his season—

59 Beginning at the first, and so on unto the last, and from the last unto the first, and from the first unto the last;

60 Every man in his own order, until his hour was finished, even according as his lord had commanded him, that his lord might be glorified in him, and he in his lord, that they all might be glorified.

61 Therefore, unto this parable I will liken all these kingdoms, and the inhabitants thereof—every kingdom in its hour, and in its time, and in its season, even according to the decree which God hath made.

As discussed in section 76 (chapter 3 of this work), this has reference to Christ visiting the other worlds, which were covered by His Atonement that was made upon planet earth.

In summary, the "Olive Leaf" revelation gave the early elders of the Church, and the Saints, four ways of obtaining eternal peace while in their mortal probation: (1) Another Comforter, even the personal appearance of Jesus Christ. (2) The light of truth, or the Light of Christ. (3) The resurrection of the dead. (4) The perfection and sanctification of man.

The Lord then gave four commandments to keep them from falling from grace, or the promise "of eternal life, even the glory of the celestial kingdom" (D&C 88:4). The four commandments were: (1) Call upon me while I am near. (2) Organize yourselves and assemble together. (3) Continue in fasting and prayer. (4) Teach one another the doctrine of the kingdom. Each of these commandments will be discussed separately.

D&C 88:62–66 • Call on Me while I Am Near

62 And again, verily I say unto you, my friends, I leave these sayings with you to ponder in your hearts, with this commandment which I give unto you, that ye shall call upon me while I am near—

63 Draw near unto me and I will draw near unto you; seek me diligently and ye shall find me; ask, and ye shall receive; knock, and it shall be opened unto you.

64 Whatsoever ye ask the Father in my name it shall be given unto you, that is expedient for you;

65 And if ye ask anything that is not expedient for you, it shall turn unto your condemnation.

66 Behold, that which you hear is as the voice of one crying in the wilderness—in the wilderness, because you cannot see him—my voice, because my voice is Spirit; my Spirit is truth; truth abideth and hath no end; and if it be in you it shall abound.

Addressing the ten high priests as His friends (v. 62), undoubtedly because they had done "whatsoever I command you" (John 15:13), the Savior commanded them to ponder His message of peace to them with the same commandment He had given to the prophet Isaiah (see Isaiah 55:6), "to call upon me while I am near. Isaiah had also received the other Comforter (see *TPJS,* 151; quoted above). The Lord was certainly near to them at that time, and was inviting them to continue to seek revelation. If they sought Him they would find Him verifies what Joseph Smith said: "When a man obtains this last Comforter, he will have the personage of Jesus Christ to attend him, or appear unto him from time to time" (*TPJS,* 151). It seems, from this statement that Christ may attend to someone without appearing to him. To seek is to study or contemplate in the mind. To ask is to pray. To knock is to do or live as required (D&C 88:63; see also Matthew 7:7; 3 Nephi 14:7; 2 Nephi 32:4, 7). With these efforts, whatsoever they asked would be given them (D&C 88:64; compare 3 Nephi 18:20; John 15:16). The warning to not ask for what was not expedient or it would turn to your condemnation (D&C 88:65) was similar to what was written in the New Testament: "Ye ask, and receive not, because ye ask amiss, that ye may consume [it] upon your lusts" (James 4:3).

The Lord continues by expounding upon another prophecy of Isaiah (40:3) that is usually associated with the mission of John the Baptist. Its inclusion here shows it was His voice that was directing John, and it was also applicable to others. The wilderness for John was in Judea, but to others it is a wilderness in that they "cannot see him." His voice was the spirit of truth and would abound, or be abundant to them, not just occasional. It was the still small voice of revelation (v. 66; see also D&C 85:6, 1 Kings 19:12). Thus another principle for obtaining peace, the spirit of truth, was expanded upon.

D&C 88:67–73 • An Eye Single to the Glory of God

67 And if your eye be single to my glory, your whole bodies shall be filled with light, and there shall be no darkness in you; and that body which is filled with light comprehendeth all things.

68 Therefore, sanctify yourselves that your minds become single to God, and the days will come that you shall see him; for he will unveil his face unto you, and it shall be in his own time, and in his own way, and according to his own will.

69 Remember the great and last promise which I have made unto you; cast away your idle thoughts and your excess of laughter far from you.

70 Tarry ye, tarry ye in this place, and call a solemn assembly, even of those who are the first laborers in this last kingdom.

71 And let those whom they have warned in their traveling call on the Lord, and ponder the warning in their hearts which they have received, for a little season.

72 Behold, and lo, I will take care of your flocks, and will raise up elders and send unto them.

73 Behold, I will hasten my work in its time.

The Lord expounds upon another New Testament teaching: "The light of the body is the eye: if therefore thine eye be single, thy whole body shall be full of light. But if thine eye be evil, thy whole body shall be full of darkness. If therefore the light that is in thee be darkness, how great [is] that darkness!" (Matthew 6:22–23). The revelation adds that the "body filled with light comprehendeth all things" (v. 67). As indicated in the next verse, this is the sanctification process. It will be fulfilled in stages or progressively as our "minds *become* single to God" (v. 68; italics added). Helaman described the process in the Book of Mormon: "Nevertheless they did fast and pray oft, and did wax stronger and stronger in their humility, and firmer and firmer in the faith of Christ, unto the filling their souls with joy and consolation, yea, even to the purifying and the sanctification of their hearts, which sanctification cometh because of their yielding their hearts unto God" (Helaman 3:35). The ultimate filling of the body will come in the resurrected state, but in this life, it may result in seeing Jesus Christ personally as Joseph Smith explained above. That blessing "shall be in his own time, and in his own way, and according to his own will" (v. 68).

The ten high priests, unto whom this revelation was addressed, were probably in the beginning stages of having their calling and election made sure. They had proven their determination to serve Him (see *TPJS*, 150), but the unveiling of His face was yet future, if they continued faithful. To see Him, they must overcome a few things. They must cast away their idle thoughts and excess laughter (D&C 88:69). They were to tarry in Kirtland, and call a solemn assembly (v. 70). This assembly was probably to discuss and listen to further instructions from the Prophet Joseph, and ponder over the great blessing they had been promised. Their remaining there would allow those whom they had recently taught to ponder over the restored gospel that these brethren had preached to them (v. 71). They were temporarily not to worry about those they were teaching, the Lord would watch over them and would raise up other elders and send to them (v. 72). Apparently, the Lord wanted His priesthood leaders to mature in their thinking and living as a preparation for their future work. The Lord would hasten His work when it was expedient to do so (v. 73).

D&C 88:74–76 • Assemble and Organize Yourselves

74 And I give unto you, who are the first laborers in this last kingdom, a commandment that you assemble yourselves together, and organize yourselves, and prepare yourselves, and sanctify yourselves; yea, purify your hearts, and cleanse your hands and your feet before me, that I may make you clean;

75 That I may testify unto your Father, and your God, and my God, that you are clean from the blood of this wicked generation; that I may

fulfil this promise, this great and last promise, which I have made unto you, when I will.

76 Also, I give unto you a commandment that ye shall continue in prayer and fasting from this time forth.

The mention of a solemn assembly (v. 70 above), and again to assemble and cleanse their hands and feet (v. 74) imply a temple to us now, but did not to them at that time, except perhaps Joseph Smith. The Lord's reason "that I may fulfill this promise, this great and last promise" (v. 75) shows once more that these ten brethren were only in the beginning stage of their receiving the "other Comforter." The second commandment, of the four commandments given to the ten men, is enlarged upon later in the revelation. This part of the revelation was given at a future date, as mentioned in the section heading. That the Lord was speaking of the temple is evident in those verses.

The third commandment to prevent the high priests from falling from grace was to continue in fasting and prayer (v. 76). These brethren had obviously been fasting and praying for the revelation, or for other things. The Lord makes no further comments.

D&C 88:77–82

77 And I give unto you a commandment that you shall teach one another the doctrine of the kingdom.

78 Teach ye diligently and my grace shall attend you, that you may be instructed more perfectly in theory, in principle, in doctrine, in the law of the gospel, in all things that pertain unto the kingdom of God, that are expedient for you to understand;

79 Of things both in heaven and in the earth, and under the earth; things which have been, things which are, things which must shortly come to pass; things which are at home, things which are abroad; the wars and the perplexities of the nations, and the judgments which are on the land; and a knowledge also of countries and of kingdoms—

80 That ye may be prepared in all things when I shall send you again to magnify the calling whereunto I have called you, and the mission with which I have commissioned you.

81 Behold, I sent you out to testify and warn the people, and it becometh every man who hath been warned to warn his neighbor.

82 Therefore, they are left without excuse, and their sins are upon their own heads.

The last of the four commandments, to prevent falling from grace, was to teach one another the doctrine of the kingdom (v. 77). The Lord gave the answers to three basic questions usually associated with teaching: how, what, and why. First, how: teach diligently (v. 78). To be diligent is to work hard, zealous, thorough, and careful. It is to put one's heart and soul into his preparation and presentation.

The second question, what to teach: teach "all things that pertain unto the kingdom of God, that are expedient for you to understand (v. 78). Note that the Lord approves of teaching theory. However, the principles, doctrines, and the law of the gospel that have been made known should not be theorized. It is not necessary to speculate on mysteries that "are not yet fully made known unto me" (Alma 37:11). On the other hand, the mysteries of God—things that are only revealed to those who seek to know them—should be studied out and taught to those who are ready to receive them (see 1 Nephi 10:12–19; Alma 26:21–22). Furthermore, the milk must be given before the meat, the basic principles first and then deeper doctrine as the learner matures (see 1 Peter 2:2; 1 Corinthians 3:2; Hebrews 5:12–14).

What does God consider pertinent to the kingdom? The disciplines mentioned (D&C 88:79) are extensive and all-inclusive. We need not enumerate them. However, why we should study the various disciplines does put some qualifications on them. Their study is primarily to prepare us to be better missionaries (v. 80). It is not only pertinent to be better missionaries, but required to magnify our calling, or their sins are upon our heads (vv. 81–82; see Jacob 1:19).

D&C 88:83–86 • The Last Time to the Gentiles

83 He that seeketh me early shall find me, and shall not be forsaken.

84 Therefore, tarry ye, and labor diligently, that you may be perfected in your ministry to go forth among the Gentiles for the last time, as many as the mouth of the Lord shall name, to bind up the law and seal up the testimony, and to prepare the saints for the hour of judgment which is to come;

85 That their souls may escape the wrath of God, the desolation of

abomination which awaits the wicked, both in this world and in the world to come. Verily, I say unto you, let those who are not the first elders continue in the vineyard until the mouth of the Lord shall call them, for their time is not yet come; their garments are not clean from the blood of this generation.

86 Abide ye in the liberty wherewith ye are made free; entangle not yourselves in sin, but let your hands be clean, until the Lord comes.

The Lord admonishes the high priests to seek Him early, meaning as soon as they could (v. 83). Earlier in the revelation, He told them to seek Him diligently (v. 63). Both were needed for them and are for us. Once more the Lord turns them to Isaiah, but with different emphasis: "Bind up the testimony, seal the law among my disciples" (Isaiah 8:16). In Isaiah's day, the law of Moses was the law to be followed, and the testimonies of the prophets were to remind them of future restorations. In the day of the Restoration, the law of the celestial kingdom was to be followed, and testimony of the Restoration was to be proclaimed. This is a possible explanation for the wording differences. Whatever the reason for differences was, the purpose was to help the Gentiles escape the "desolation and abomination which awaits the wicked" (v. 85). The high priests were to abide in their liberty of freedom from sin, and remain that way until the Lord comes (v. 86). The same advice is applicable to all members of The Church of Jesus Christ of Latter-day Saints.

Note: vv. 87–116 were included and discussed in the previous chapter.

DOCTRINE AND COVENANTS 88:117–141

SECTION 88 • OUTLINE

➢ 88:117–120 Call your solemn assembly as I have commanded you.

    a.   Teach wisdom out of the best books, learn by study and faith (v. 118).

    b.   Establish a house of prayer, of fasting, of faith, of learning, of glory of order; a house of God (v. 119).

    c.   Your incomings and outgoings be in the name of the Lord, and your salutations with uplifted hands unto the Most High (v. 120).

➢ 88:121–126 Cease from light speeches, all laughter, lustful desires, pride, light-mindedness, and all wicked doings.

a. Appoint a teacher, let one speak at a time and all listen and be edified (v. 122).

b. Love one another, cease covetousness, and impart one to another (v. 123).

c. Cease to be idle, unclean, sleeping longer than necessary, retire and arise early, that your bodies and minds be invigorated (v. 124).

d. Clothe you with a bond of charity, a mantle of perfectness and peace (v. 125).

e. Pray that you be not faint, until I come and receive you unto myself (v. 126).

➤ 88:127–131 The order of the School of the Prophets, from high priest down to deacon.

a. The president, or teacher, stand in place in the house prepared for him (v. 128).

b. He is first in the house of God, where all can hear his words carefully and distinctly, not with loud voice (v. 129).

c. An ensample, and should offer himself in prayer on his knees in remembrance of the everlasting covenant (vv. 130–131).

➤ 88:132–137 When any come in, arise with uplifted hands and salute his brethren.

a. I salute you in the name of the Lord, in token of the everlasting covenant, and receive you in fellowship to be your friend and brother (v. 133).

b. He that is unworthy shall not have place among you (v. 134).

c. The brethren that are faithful shall salute the president in the same way (v. 135).

d. An ensample for saluting one another in the house of God, or school (v. 136).

e. Do this by prayer and thanksgiving as the Spirit directs in all doings in the house or school, that it may be a sanctuary, a tabernacle of the Spirit (v. 137).

➤ 88:138–141 You shall not receive any save he is clean from the blood of this generation.

    a.   He shall be received by the ordinance of the washing of the feet (v. 139).

    b.   The ordinance is to be administered by the president or presiding elder (v. 140).

    c.   It is commenced by prayer, after partaking of bread and wine, he is to gird himself according to the pattern in John chapter thirteen (v. 141).

TEXT AND COMMENTARY

D&C 88:117–120

117 Therefore, verily I say unto you, my friends, call your solemn assembly, as I have commanded you.

118 And as all have not faith, seek ye diligently and teach one another words of wisdom; yea, seek ye out of the best books words of wisdom; seek learning, even by study and also by faith.

119 Organize yourselves; prepare every needful thing; and establish a house, even a house of prayer, a house of fasting, a house of faith, a house of learning, a house of glory, a house of order, a house of God;

120 That your incomings may be in the name of the Lord; that your outgoings may be in the name of the Lord; that all your salutations may be in the name of the Lord, with uplifted hands unto the Most High.

This revelation was given later, and the assembled brethren had had time to think about the revelation they had received before. One of the purposes of temples is to hold solemn assemblies (v. 117), as well as other purposes listed in this portion of the revelation. These four verses were later quoted in the dedicatory prayer of the Kirtland Temple (D&C 109:6–9; a confirmation that they are referring to the temple).

The best books, from which words of wisdom should be sought, would include the standard works, the Joseph Smith Translation, and the printed words of the latter-day Apostles and prophets (see D&C 124:89; 28:5; 52:9). These sources would give us learning by study. To learn by faith is to receive personal revelation. Revelation often comes as we study (see 1 Nephi 1:12–13; D&C 76:11–19; 138:1–11).

D&C 88:121–126

121 Therefore, cease from all your light speeches, from all laughter, from all your lustful desires, from all your pride and light-mindedness, and from all your wicked doings.

121 Therefore, cease from all your light speeches, from all laughter, from all your lustful desires, from all your pride and light-mindedness, and from all your wicked doings.

122 Appoint among yourselves a teacher, and let not all be spokesmen at once; but let one speak at a time and let all listen unto his sayings, that when all have spoken that all may be edified of all, and that every man may have an equal privilege.

123 See that ye love one another; cease to be covetous; learn to impart one to another as the gospel requires.

124 Cease to be idle; cease to be unclean; cease to find fault one with another; cease to sleep longer than is needful; retire to thy bed early, that ye may not be weary; arise early, that your bodies and your minds may be invigorated.

125 And above all things, clothe yourselves with the bond of charity, as with a mantle, which is the bond of perfectness and peace.

126 Pray always, that ye may not faint, until I come. Behold, and lo, I will come quickly, and receive you unto myself. Amen.

This is the third time the Lord has warned against laughter: "much laughter is sin" (D&C 59:15); "excess of laughter" (D&C 88:69); and "from all laughter" (D&C 88:121). These warnings should be taken in their context. The first warning was in a revelation about the Sabbath day. The second warning was in regards to becoming sanctified, and the third warning was regarding the temple. As Ecclesiastes 3:4 says: there is "a time to weep, and a time to laugh." Furthermore, there is a difference in loud, scornful, or vulgar laughter, and humorous or joyful laughter. A sense of humor is to sense when laughter or humor is appropriate and when it is not.

The teacher should be in control (D&C 88:122). While discussion is good, "every man may have an equal privilege" of expression—the teacher must insure that correct conclusions are drawn. If the conclusion is in accordance with the Spirit, those in tune will be edified together.

The bond of "charity is the pure love of Christ" (Moroni 7:47), as the bond of perfection and peace supports (88:125). Charity *preventeth* a multitude of sins (JST, 1 Peter 4:8, italics show the change). The other above verses are self-explanatory, or will be commented on elsewhere.

D&C 88:127–137 • The School of the Prophets

127 And again, the order of the house prepared for the presidency of the school of the prophets, established for their instruction in all things that are expedient for them, even for all the officers of the church, or in other words, those who are called to the ministry in the church, beginning at the high priests, even down to the deacons—

128 And this shall be the order of the house of the presidency of the school: He that is appointed to be president, or teacher, shall be found standing in his place, in the house which shall be prepared for him.

129 Therefore, he shall be first in the house of God, in a place that the congregation in the house may hear his words carefully and distinctly, not with loud speech.

130 And when he cometh into the house of God, for he should be first in the house—behold, this is beautiful, that he may be an example—

131 Let him offer himself in prayer upon his knees before God, in token or remembrance of the everlasting covenant.

132 And when any shall come in after him, let the teacher arise, and, with uplifted hands to heaven, yea, even directly, salute his brother or brethren with these words:

133 Art thou a brother or brethren? I salute you in the name of the Lord Jesus Christ, in token or remembrance of the everlasting covenant, in which covenant I receive you to fellowship, in a determination that is fixed, immovable, and unchangeable, to be your friend and brother through the grace of God in the bonds of love, to walk in all the commandments of God blameless, in thanksgiving, forever and ever. Amen.

134 And he that is found unworthy of this salutation shall not have place among you; for ye shall not suffer that mine house shall be polluted by him.

135 And he that cometh in and is faithful before me, and is a brother, or if they be brethren, they shall salute the president or teacher with uplifted hands to heaven, with this same prayer and covenant, or by saying Amen, in token of the same.

136 Behold, verily, I say unto you, this is an ensample unto you for a salutation to one another in the house of God, in the school of the prophets.

137 And ye are called to do this by prayer and thanksgiving, as the Spirit shall give utterance in all your doings in the house of the Lord, in the school of the prophets, that it may become a sanctuary, a tabernacle of the Holy Spirit to your edification.

This portion of the revelation was probably given on January 3, 1833 (see section heading). The instructions are for the meeting "in the house of God, in the school of the prophets" (v. 136). While there were schools known as the "School of the Prophets," and "School of the Elders," held in Kirtland before the temple was built,[33] the eventual school described in the revelation was for the meeting in the temple of the President of the Church with those who are invited. Since the meeting is a closed meeting in the temple, and only the General Authorities, or general officers of the Church, are invited, it is not applicable to comment, nor is there any further knowledge available to report.

D&C 88:138–141 • Ordinance of the Washing of Feet

138 And ye shall not receive any among you into this school save he is clean from the blood of this generation;

139 And he shall be received by the ordinance of the washing of feet, for unto this end was the ordinance of the washing of feet instituted.

140 And again, the ordinance of washing feet is to be administered by the president, or presiding elder of the church.

141 It is to be commenced with prayer; and after partaking of bread and wine, he is to gird himself according to the pattern given in the thirteenth chapter of John's testimony concerning me. Amen.

On November 12, 1835, before the temple was built, the Prophet Joseph Smith made these comments on the ordinance of the washing of feet:

The item to which I wish the more particularly to call your attention to-night, is the ordinance of washing of feet. This we have not done as yet, but it is necessary now, as much as it was in the days of the Savior;

---

[33] For more information on the schools in Kirtland see Lyndon W. Cook *The Revelations of the Prophet Joseph Smith* [1981], 185–190.

and we must have a place prepared, that we may attend to this ordinance aside from the world.

We have not desired so much from the hand of the Lord through the faith and obedience, as we ought to have done, yet we have enjoyed great blessings, and we are not so sensible of this as we should be. When or where has God suffered one of the witnesses or first elders to fall? Never, and nowhere. Amidst all the calamities and judgments that have befallen the inhabitants of the earth, His mighty arm has sustained us, men and devils have raged and spent their malice in vain. We must have all things prepared, and call our solemn assembly as the Lord has commanded us, that we may be able to accomplish His great work, and it must be done in God's own way. The house of the Lord must be prepared, and the solemn assembly called and organized in it, according to the order of the house of God; and in it we must attend to the ordinance of washing of feet. It was never intended for any but official members. It is calculated to unite our hearts, that we may be one in feeling and sentiment, and that our faith may be strong, so that Satan cannot overthrow us, nor have any power over us here. [*TPJS*, 90–91]

The pattern given in the thirteenth chapter of John, as now recorded, gives us no detail, but does show the reason it was done:

10 Jesus saith to him, He that is washed needeth not save to wash [his] feet, but is clean every whit: and ye are clean, but not all.

11 For he knew who should betray him; therefore said he, Ye are not all clean.

12 So after he had washed their feet, and had taken his garments, and was set down again, he said unto them, Know ye what I have done to you?

13 Ye call me Master and Lord: and ye say well; for [so] I am.

14 If I then, [your] Lord and Master, have washed your feet; ye also ought to wash one another's feet.

15 For I have given you an example, that ye should do as I have done to you.

16 Verily, verily, I say unto you, The servant is not greater than his lord; neither he that is sent greater than he that sent him.

17 If ye know these things, happy are ye if ye do them. [John 13:10–17]

If the Savior was willing to wash the Apostles feet, we should be willing to serve in whatever capacity we are called to serve. He that serves where and when he is called, and serves willingly and well shall find the peace promised in the "Olive Leaf" revelation.

General Authority Quotes

—President Joseph Fielding Smith • 88:2–4

Joseph Smith speaks of two Comforters: the first is the Holy Ghost, the second is the Son of God himself. He uses the 14th chapter of John as the basis of his discourse. Verses 16, 17, and 26 definitely refer to the Holy Ghost. They speak of the Spirit of Truth which "dwelleth in you, and shall be in you." Verses 18, 21, and 23 clearly refer to the Lord himself and his coming to man.

The Holy Spirit of Promise is not the Second Comforter. The Holy Spirit of Promise is the Holy Ghost who places the stamp of approval upon every ordinance that is done righteously; and when covenants are broken, he removes the seal.

There is no forgiveness for denying the First Comforter. But if a man received honor enough to have the presence of the Son, he would also have the knowledge of the First Comforter and should he turn away, his sin would be unpardonable. A man could not deny the Second Comforter any more than he could the first.

If a man gets knowledge enough to have the companionship of the Son of God, the chances are his call and election would be made sure. [*Doctrines of Salvation*, 1:55]

—Elder Bruce R. McConkie • D&C 88:3–5

. . . They [10 high priests] had then earned the right by faith and devotion to have the seal of divine acceptance placed on the conditional promises they had theretofore made. They now had the sure promise . . . of eternal life (D&C 88:4), which eternal life is the name of the kind of life which God our Heavenly and Eternal Father lives, and they were prepared to receive the Second Comforter. [*Doctrinal New Testament Commentary* (1965), 3:339]

—President Howard W. Hunter • D&C 88:12

We believe there is spiritual influence that emanates from the presence of God to fill the immensity of space (see D&C 88:12). All men share an inheritance of divine light. God operates among his children in all nations, and those who seek God are entitled to further light and knowledge, regardless of their race, nationality, or cultural traditions. [*The Teachings of Howard W. Hunter,* ed. Clyde J, Williams (1997), 101]

—*The Prophet Joseph Smith* • D&C 88:20–24

There are mansions for those who obey a celestial law, and there are other mansions for those who come short of the law every man in his own order. [*TPJS,* 366]

—*Elder Harold B. Lee* • D&C 88:20–24

. . . In the first place, we are our own judges of the place we shall have in the eternal world. Here and now in mortality, each one of us is having the opportunity of choosing the kind of laws we elect to obey. We are now living and obeying celestial laws that will make us candidates for celestial glory, or we are living terrestrial laws that will make us candidates for either terrestrial glory, or telestial law. The place we shall occupy in the eternal worlds will be determined by the obedience we yield to the laws of these various kingdoms during the time we have here in mortality upon this earth. [*The Teachings of Harold B. Lee,* 264]

—*President Brigham Young* • D&C 88:77–80

There are a great many branches of education: some go to college to learn languages, some to study law, some to study physics, and some to study astronomy, and various branches of science. We want every branch of science taught in this place that is taught in the world. But our favorite study is that branch which particularly belongs to the elders of Israel—namely, theology. Every Elder should become a profound theologian—should understand this branch better than all the world. [*Discourses of Brigham Young,* 258]

—*Elder Harold B. Lee* • D&C 88:117–141

There is a caution that I want to make about these ordinances in the temple. There is a difference between the revelations the Lord has given to us—that we might call "open" revelations that might be discussed in the world, and private or "safeguarded" revelations. The teachings which are contained in the four standard Church works which are taught as a part of the temple endowment anyone is free to talk about—section 76, section 88, section 110, other things that pertain to priesthood—all of that which is open revelations may be taught. But there are certain things that are solely reserved for teaching inside the temple walls, not to be discussed outside. [*The Teachings of Harold B. Lee,* 575–76]

Chapter Nine

The Weakest of All Saints

D&C 89

DOCTRINE AND COVENANTS 89

Historical Setting: All that is in the *History of the Church* is: "February 27 [1833].—I [Joseph] received the following revelation [D&C 89]."

Brigham Young: I think I am as well acquainted with the circumstances which led to the giving of the Word of Wisdom as any man in the Church, although I was not present at the time to witness them. The first school of the prophets was held in a small room situated over the Prophet Joseph's kitchen, in a house which belonged to Bishop Whitney, . . . Over this kitchen was situated the room in which the Prophet received revelations and in which he instructed his brethren. . . . When they assembled together in this room after breakfast, the first thing they did was to light their pipes, and, while smoking, talk about the great things of the kingdom, and spit all over the room, and as soon as the pipe was out of their mouths a large chew of tobacco would then be taken. Often when the Prophet entered the room to give the school instructions he would find himself in a cloud of tobacco smoke. This and the complaints of his wife at having to clean so filthy a floor, made the Prophet think upon the matter, and he inquired of the Lord relating to the conduct of the Elders in using tobacco, and the revelation known as the Word of Wisdom was the result of his inquiry. [*Journal of Discourses,* 12:158]

SECTION 89 • OUTLINE

➤ 89:1–3 A word of wisdom to the council of high priests in Kirtland, and Saints in Zion.

   a. Not by commandment but by revelation showing the order and will of God in the temporal salvation of the Saints in the last days (v. 2).

   b. A principal with a promise adapted to the weakest of Saints (v. 3).

➤ 89:4–9 A warning, in consequence of evils and designs which do and will exist in the hearts of conspiring men in the last days.

   a. Wine and strong drinks are not good, except in offering sacraments (v. 5).

   b. A sacrament should be pure wine of the grape, and of your own make (v. 6).

   c. Strong drinks are not for the body, but for washing of the body (v. 7).

   d. Tobacco is not good for man, but an herb for bruises and sick cattle (v. 8).

   e. Hot drinks are not for the body or belly (v. 9).

➤ 89:19–17 All wholesome herbs God made for the constitution, nature, and use of man.

   a. Each herb and fruit in their season, used in prudence and thanksgiving (v. 11).

   b. Flesh of beasts and fowls are made to use sparingly with thanksgiving (v. 12).

   c. It pleases God that they not be used, only in winter, cold, and famine (v. 13).

   d. All grain is made for the use of man and beasts for the staff of life (v. 14).

   e. Wild animals are for man's use in times of famine and excess hunger (v. 15).

   f. All grain, fruits of the vine, above and in the ground, is for man's use (v. 16).

   g. Wheat for man, corn for the ox, oats for the horse, rye for the fowls and swine, and all beasts of the field, barley for

useful animals, and mild drinks, as also other grains (v. 17).

89:18–21   All Saints who keep these commandments shall receive health in their naval and marrow in their bones.

     a.   Shall find wisdom and great treasures of knowledge, hidden treasures (v. 19).

     b.   They shall run and not be weary, and walk and not be faint (v. 20).

     c.   The destroying angel shall pass them by, and not slay them (v. 21).

Introduction

Each dispensation had its own word of wisdom. It was designed to meet the conditions or challenges of that time. Adam was a vegetarian: "And I, God, said unto man: Behold, I have given you every herb bearing seed, which is upon the face of all the earth, and every tree in the which shall be the fruit of a tree yielding seed; to you it shall be for meat" (Moses 2:29; see also v. 30 for other living creatures). Noah was given meat to eat but not blood: "Every moving thing that liveth shall be meat for you; even as the green herb have I given you all things. But flesh with the life thereof, [which is] the blood thereof, shall ye not eat" (Gen 9:3–4).

Moses was given detailed instructions—many due to their being in the wilderness for forty years where sanitation and disease control were major considerations (see Leviticus 11 for an example, but not all inclusive of their commandments). While Christ was under the law of Moses, he kept it, but apparently gave a more appropriate word of wisdom after His higher law was established. The eating of meat offered to idols was a big issue (see 1 Corinthians 8:7–13), and the controversy of His use of wine goes on (see John 2:1–11). Certainly, they were given guidelines, but we need not justify or own habits, or question others' style of living based on the little information we have of the period of the Church in the New Testament times. We need to concentrate on what He has revealed unto our day.

TEXT AND COMMENTARY

D&C 89:1–3 • By Revelation not Commandment

1 A Word of Wisdom, for the benefit of the council of high priests, assembled in Kirtland, and the church, and also the saints in Zion—

2 To be sent greeting; not by commandment or constraint, but by revelation and the word of wisdom, showing forth the order and will of God in the temporal salvation of all saints in the last days—

3 Given for a principle with promise, adapted to the capacity of the weak and the weakest of all saints, who are or can be called saints.

The Word of Wisdom given "by revelation" (v. 2) tells us that it came from God. "Not by commandment" is a pattern of the Lord that is learned from the children of Israel at Mount Sinai. The Lord offered them His higher law, but they rejected it and were given the law of Moses (see JST, Exodus 34:1–2; D&C 84:23–26). That the Word of Wisdom was to be taken seriously was confirmed by an assembly of the high council in February 1834, a year after the revelation was received. The council was assembled to consider "whether disobedience to the word of wisdom was a transgression sufficient to deprive an official member from holding office in the Church, after having it sufficiently taught him." After six elders had spoken on the subject, the President gave the decision: "No official member in this Church is worthy to hold an office, after having the Word of Wisdom properly taught him, and he, the official member, neglecting to comply with or obey it; which decision the Council confirmed by vote" (*HC*, 2:34–35).

According to President Joseph F. Smith: "the reason undoubtedly why the Word of Wisdom was given—as not by 'commandment or constraint' was that at that time, at least, if it had been given as a commandment it would have brought every man, addicted to the use of these noxious things, under condemnation; so the Lord was merciful and gave them a chance to overcome, before He brought them under the law. Later on, it was announced from this stand, by President Brigham Young that the Word of Wisdom was a revelation and a command of the Lord" (CR, October 1913).[34]

The temporal salvation (v. 2) is different than a temporal law, since all of God's laws are spiritual (see D&C 29:34). It must mean saved from temporal death or destruction.

D&C 89:4–9 • Conspiring Men in the Last Days

4 Behold, verily, thus saith the Lord unto you: In consequence of evils and designs which do and will exist in the hearts of conspiring men in the last days, I have warned you, and forewarn you, by giving unto you this word of wisdom by revelation—

5 That inasmuch as any man drinketh wine or strong drink among you, behold it is not good, neither meet in the sight of your Father, only in assembling yourselves together to offer up your sacraments before him.

6 And, behold, this should be wine, yea, pure wine of the grape of the vine, of your own make.

7 And, again, strong drinks are not for the belly, but for the washing of your bodies.

8 And again, tobacco is not for the body, neither for the belly, and is not good for man, but is an herb for bruises and all sick cattle, to be used with judgment and skill.

9 And again, hot drinks are not for the body or belly.

Conspiring men would include, but not be limited to advertisers, sales persons, and others who attempt to secure the "mighty dollar" through various means. In our day, it would also include drug growers and dealers who seek to get people addicted to their products, either as a means of getting them subject to them, or an assurance of a continuation of a demand for their products. "In the last days" indicated that things would continue to get worse, which they have. Undoubtedly, the Lord foresaw the curses of drug usage, and controlled substances illegally running rampant. Of course, Satan is behind all of them as a way of winning souls. He "seeks the misery of all mankind" (2 Nephi 2:18).

---

[34] The date of Brigham Young's proposal to make the Word of Wisdom a commandment was September 9, 1851, according to the *Millennial Star* of February 1, 1852; 35; taken from CES Institute Manual, 207. In 1859, he did command the Elders of Israel to cease getting drunk (*Discourses of Brigham Young*, 183).

The first negative warning from the Lord is the danger of wine and strong drink (v. 5). Alcoholism is one of the major plagues of the last days. It effects every phase of our lives both directly and indirectly. Physically, it causes loss of coordination, and creates an addiction to bodily needs that are harmful to many aspects of our strength and conditioning. Intellectually, it hampers our reasoning power, and dulls our mental reactions to harmful situations. Socially, it causes us to react in an unnatural way, and strains our relationship with others. Spiritually, it dulls our sensitivity to the Spirit, and leaves us vulnerable to sin and corruption. These effects are so generously supported by statistics that they need no further comment. Furthermore, it leads to addiction, and often is a forerunner to the use of drugs. The use of drugs leads to theft, and other crimes.

Alcohol does have positive uses. It is a symbol of the sacrament, the blood of Christ absorbed our sins as the garments absorbed the juice of the grapes by Him who treads the winepress (see D&C 133:48). The grapes are pressed when they are ripe, not when they have fermented and soured or spoiled. The blood of Christ absorbs our sins when we are fully repented, not after we die. "For behold, if ye have procrastinated the day of your repentance even until death, behold, ye have become subjected to the spirit of the devil, and he doth seal you his; therefore, the Spirit of the Lord hath withdrawn from you, and hath no place in you, and the devil hath all power over you; and this is the final state of the wicked (Alma 34:35). Thus we partake of the pure wine of the grape, of our own make (v. 6), when we have met the steps of repentance.

Strong drinks are for the washing of the body (v. 7). Alcohol preparations sterilize the skin surface, disinfecting the areas treated. By washing the body with alcohol, it will also lower the temperature, and bring comfort to the person. Obviously, there are other medical uses of which we were not aware in Joseph Smith's day.

The dangers of tobacco also fall into the category of being so well documented that it need not to be discussed, but its positive uses may not be as well known (v. 8). This writer has been told of its effect as a poultice for bruises, and has seen its use as an herb for sick cattle. Perhaps it would be used more if there was not a stigma attached to its being in one's possession, or its ability to be purchased in other types of packaging.

Hot drinks were interpreted by Hyrum Smith: ". . . There are many who wonder what [hot drinks] can mean; whether it refers to tea, or coffee, or not. I say it does refer to tea and coffee."[35] The controversial issue of caffeine drinks fall into the category of "it is not meet that I should command in all things; for he that is compelled in all things, the same is a slothful and not a wise servant" (D&C 58:26).

D&C 89:10–17 • The Constitution, Nature, and Use of Man

10 And again, verily I say unto you, all wholesome herbs God hath ordained for the constitution, nature, and use of man—

11 Every herb in the season thereof, and every fruit in the season thereof; all these to be used with prudence and thanksgiving.

12 Yea, flesh also of beasts and of the fowls of the air, I, the Lord, have ordained for the use of man with thanksgiving; nevertheless they are to be used sparingly;

13 And it is pleasing unto me that they should not be used, only in times of winter, or of cold, or famine.

14 All grain is ordained for the use of man and of beasts, to be the staff of life, not only for man but for the beasts of the field, and the fowls of heaven, and all wild animals that run or creep on the earth;

15 And these hath God made for the use of man only in times of famine and excess of hunger.

16 All grain is good for the food of man; as also the fruit of the vine; that which yieldeth fruit, whether in the ground or above the ground—

17 Nevertheless, wheat for man, and corn for the ox, and oats for the horse, and rye for the fowls and for swine, and for all beasts of the field, and barley for all useful animals, and for mild drinks, as also other grain.

The positive side of the word of wisdom is often neglected, or taken to extremes. Regardless of these positions, it is a health code that if followed, all will be benefited. The season thereof (v. 11) was stated before the art of refrigeration was developed. While the use of herbs and fruit is still followed, their use has been extended by refrigeration, canning, and other means of preservation. The generation of Joseph Smith used what was available to them at the time.

---

[35] *Times and Seasons*, vol.3. no.15, 800, City of Nauvoo. Illinois, June 1, 1842.

This revelation is the third one that endorses the use of meats for man (see D&C 59:16; 49:18–21). To use meat sparingly has not been defined specifically, but it is generally agreed that it should be eaten more in winter and cold than in the summer and warmer places. The argument of where the comma is placed in verse thirteen is not significant, according to my English expert friends. "Wild animals" seems to still be the subject of "the use of man only in times of famine and excess of hunger" (D&C 89:15). This also supports the concept of using other meats more in the cold and winter times.

Grain as the staff of life (v. 14), and all grain is good for the food of man (v. 15), seems to be widely accepted by dieticians. Likewise has the various relationships given between grains, and man and animals become accepted (v. 17). What is noteworthy to the author is the time frame when the revelation was given, and the scientific verifications that have come about since that time.

D&C 88:124 • Minds and Bodies Invigorated

124 Cease to be idle; cease to be unclean; cease to find fault one with another; cease to sleep longer than is needful; retire to thy bed early, that ye may not be weary; arise early, that your bodies and your minds may be invigorated.

Another element of wisdom was the Lord's instructions on sleep, given in the previous revelation. Too much or too little sleep was advised against. Sleep helps both the body and the mind. In our day of sleep apathy and sleep clinics, we should try the Lord's formula. It will undoubtedly confirm the old adage: "Early to bed and early to rise makes a man healthy, wealthy, and wise."

D&C 89:18–21 • The Blessings of the Word of Wisdom

18 And all saints who remember to keep and do these sayings, walking in obedience to the commandments, shall receive health in their navel and marrow to their bones;

19 And shall find wisdom and great treasures of knowledge, even hidden treasures;

20 And shall run and not be weary, and shall walk and not faint.

21 And I, the Lord, give unto them a promise, that the destroying

angel shall pass by them, as the children of Israel, and not slay them. Amen.

All that is known about the life of the Savior between the ages of twelve and thirty is: "And Jesus increased in wisdom and stature, and in favour with God and man" (Luke 12:52). However, we note that he grew in all four areas of life: in wisdom, intellectually; in stature, physically; in favour with God, spiritually; and in favor with man, socially. The promised blessings of the Word of Wisdom also extend to all four areas of our lives. Health in the naval, and marrow in the bones (v. 18) is today a measurement of our physical health. Wisdom and great treasures of knowledge (v. 19) is a blessing to the intellect of man. "Hidden treasures" suggests the acquisition of knowledge through revelation. While to run and not be weary (v. 20) appears to be another physical blessing—may we suggest that it is speaking of a social blessing. However, those who are actively involved in the Church, are usually involved in the community, their children's school activities, their business and professional obligations, and other social events. They are on the run in a different sense. The Lord is promising that they will be blessed with the ability to keep up their responsibilities as a citizen of the community, a family person, and be successful in their occupation. Last of all, the promise of the destroying angel passing over them, as with the Israelites when leaving Egypt (v. 21; see Exodus 12:21–23), is a spiritual blessing that has eternal consequences. It is indeed wisdom and spiritual to follow what the Lord has given us in his "Word of Wisdom."

General Authority Quotes

—President Joseph Fielding Smith • D&C 89:2

> The temporal salvation of the children of men is a most important thing, but sadly neglected by many religious teachers. The truth is that the spiritual salvation is dependent upon the temporal far more most men realize. The line of demarcation between the temporal, or physical, and the spiritual cannot be definitely seen. The Lord has said that he has not given a temporal commandment at any time. To men some of these commandments may be temporal, but they are spiritual to the Lord because they have a bearing on the spiritual or eternal welfare of mankind. [*Church History and Modern Revelation* (1948), 1:383]

—*President David O. McKay* • D&C 89:4

"Evils and designs which do and will exist in the hearts of conspiring men. . . ." The purport of that impressed me in the twenties and thirties of this century. I ask you to recall the methods employed by certain tobacco interests to induce woman to smoke cigarettes.

You remember how insidiously they launched their plan: First, by saying that it would reduce weight. They had a slogan: "Take a cigarette instead of a sweet."

Later, some of us who like the theatre noticed that they would have a young lady light the gentleman's cigarette. Following this a woman's hand would be shown on billboards lighting or taking a cigarette. A year or two passed, and soon they were brazen enough to show the lady on the screen or on the billboard smoking the cigarette.

I find here a clipping which I set aside in the early thirties, which corroborates this idea. This in 1931:

"It is a well known fact that the cigarette manufacturers are after the young women and girls, now. They say there are twenty-five million of them in the United States, and if they can popularize smoking among them, they will be able to increase their sales from three billions, six million dollars annually to six billion dollars. This is their claim and their aim."

Now it is common to see beautiful women depicted on billboards and in the popular journals advertising certain brands of cigarettes. [CR, September–October 1949] [*Gospel Ideals* (1953), 363]

—*The First Presidency* • D&C 89:5–7 • October 3, 1843

The world is smitten, nigh unto death, with great and grievous tribulations, following the commission of cardinal sins.

Over the earth, and it seems particularly in America, the demon drink is in control. Drunken with strong drink, men have lost their reason; their counsel has been destroyed; their judgment and vision are fled; they reel forward to destruction.

Drink brings cruelty into the home; it walks arm in arm with poverty; its companions are disease and plague; it puts chastity to flight; and it knows neither honesty nor fair dealing; it is a total stranger to truth; it drowns conscience; it is the bodyguard of evil; it curses all who touch it.

Drink has brought more woe and misery, broken more hearts,

wrecked more homes, committed more crimes, filled more coffins, than all the wars the world has suffered. . . .

But so great is the curse of drink that we should not be held guiltless did we not call all offending Saints to forsake it and banish it from their lives forever.

God has spoken against drink in our day, and has given to this, the Lord's own Church, a specific revelation concerning it, as a "word of wisdom by revelation—". . . [quotes D&C 89:5–7]

This declares the divine wisdom. It is God's law of health, and is binding on each and every one of us. We cannot escape its operation, for it is based upon eternal truth. Men may agree or disagree about this word of the Lord; if they agree it adds nothing; if they disagree, it means nothing. Beyond His word we cannot reach, and it is enough for every Latter-day Saint, willing and trying to follow divine guidance. . . . ["Messages of the First Presidency," as quoted in *The Latter-day Prophets and the Doctrine and Covenants,* comp. Roy W. Doxey (pamphlet, 1963), 3:233]

—President Heber J. Grant • D&C 89:7–9

I would like it known that if we as a people never used a particle of tea or coffee or of tobacco or of liquor, we would become one of the most wealthy people in the world. Why? Because we would have increased vigor of body, increased vigor of mind; we would grow spiritually; we would have a more direct line of communication with God, our Heavenly Father. [*Gospel Standards,* comp. Dr. G. Homer Durham (1969), 50]

Nearly always those who lose their virtue, first partake of those things that excite passions within them or lower their resistance and becloud their minds. Partaking of tobacco and liquor is calculated to make them a prey to those things which, if indulged in, are worse than death itself. There is no true Latter-day Saint who would not rather bury a son or daughter than to have her lose her virtue—realizing that virtue is of more value than anything else in the wide world. [*Gospel Standards,* 55]

—President Gordon B. Hinckley • D&C 89:7–9

We receive numerous letters inquiring whether this item or that item is proscribed in the Word of Wisdom. If we will avoid those things which are definitely and specifically defined, and beyond this observe the spirit of this great revelation, it will not involve a burden. It will, rather, bring a blessing. Do not forget: it is the Lord who has made the promise. [*Teachings of Gordon B. Hinckley*, 701]

—*Elder Howard W. Hunter* • D&C 89:9

We complicate the simplicity of the Word of Wisdom. The Lord said don't drink tea, coffee, or use tobacco or liquor and that admonition is simple. But we confuse it by asking if cola drinks are against the Word of Wisdom. The 89th section of the Doctrine and Covenants doesn't say anything about cola drinks, but we ask questions that go beyond the simplicity of the lesson that has been taught. We know that caffeine is taken out of coffee and used as an ingredient of cola drinks. It seems to me that if we really want to live the spirit of the law we probably wouldn't partake of that which had been taken from what we were told not to drink. [*The Teachings of Howard W. Hunter*, 105]

—*Elder Ezra Taft Benson* • D&C 89:17

In this great revelation known as the Word of Wisdom, he [revealed] not only what is good and what is not good for man, but he outlined a plan for the feeding of livestock which, through more than a hundred years, has gradually been sustained through scientific investigation of man. [*The Teachings of Ezra Taft Benson,* 287; quoted from *So Shall Ye Reap,* published in 1960 at the close of his service as the United States Secretary of Agriculture under President Dwight D. Eisenhower]

Chapter Ten

The First Presidency

D&C 81; 90

DOCTRINE AND COVENANTS 81 & 90

Historical Setting: Section 81 was one of four revelations received on or around March 1832. As noted in the section heading, Jesse Gause was the one to whom this revelation was originally given to serve as a counselor to Joseph Smith, but the call was subsequently transferred to Frederick G. Williams, since he was given the same calling. When Brother Gause was called, the office was called the Presidency of the High Priesthood.[36] All that is given in the *History of the Church* about section 90 is: "March 8 [1832] I received the following." The sections are combined here because of the subject of the First Presidency. The counselors were ordained on March 18, 1833 (section headings 81 and 90). The title of First Presidency was first used in D&C 102:26.

SECTIONS 81 & 90 • OUTLINE

➤ 81:1–7   Frederick G. Williams is called to be a high priest in the Church, and a counselor unto Joseph Smith.

    a.   Joseph has been given the keys which belong to the Presidency of the High Priesthood (v. 2).

    b.   Joseph and Frederick will be blessed as Frederick is faithful

---

[36] For more information on Jesse Gause and Frederick G. Williams, see Lyndon W. Cook, *The Revelations of the Prophet Joseph Smith* [1981], 105; or Hoyt W. Brewster Jr., *Doctrine and Covenants Encyclopedia* [1988], 203–204, 639.

      in counsel, vocal prayer and in his heart, in public and private, and proclaiming the gospel (v. 3).

  c. Frederick will thus do the greatest good for his fellow beings, and promote the glory of the Lord (v. 4).

  d. Stand in the office appointed; succor the weak, lift up the hands that fall down, and strengthen the feeble knees (v. 5).

  e. If faithful to the end, he will have a crown of immortality and eternal life (v. 6).

  f. These are the words of Alpha and Omega, even Jesus Christ (v. 7).

90:1–5   Joseph's sins are forgiven according to his prayers and the prayers of his brethren.

  a. He that holds the keys of the kingdom for the last time is blessed (v. 2).

  b. The keys shall never be taken while in the world or the world to come (v. 3).

  c. Through him the oracles shall be given to the Church (v. 4).

  d. Those who hold the oracles beware lest they stumble when storms come (v. 5

90:6–11   Sidney Rigdon and Frederick G. William's sins are forgiven, and are accounted equal in holding the keys for the last time.

  a. By their administration, the School of the Prophets was to be organized (v. 7).

  b. Thereby they may be perfected in the ministry for the salvation of Zion, and the nations of Israel and the Gentiles (v. 8).

  c. The Word was to go to the Gentiles first, and then to the Jews (v. 9).

  d. The heathen nations, the house of Joseph, would have the Lord revealed (v. 10).

  e. In that day, every nation shall hear the gospel in their own language (v. 11).

90:12–18   A commandment is given to continue in the ministry and presidency.

    a.   Finish the translation of the prophets, preside over the Church and school (v. 13).

    b.   Revelations to unfold the mysteries of the kingdom shall be given (v. 14).

    c.   Set in order the churches, learn, and become acquainted with languages (v. 15).

    d.   Preside in council, and set in order all the affairs of the Church (v. 16).

    e.   Be not ashamed nor confounded, be admonished in highness and pride (v. 17).

    f.   Set your homes in order, and be not slothful and unclean (v. 18).

➤ 90:19–21   Provide for Frederick, Sidney, and Joseph Smith Sen.

➤ 90:22–24   Let the bishop search for an agent that is a man of God, has riches, and will keep the storehouse from disrepute before the eyes of the people.

➤ 90:25–27   Let Joseph Smith Sen. family be small pertaining to those who are not family.

➤ 90:28–31   Give my handmaid money to go to the land of Zion.

➤ 90:32–37   Write a commandment to your brethren in Zion that you are called to preside also over Zion in mine own due time.

    a.   The brethren in Zion begin to repent, and the angels rejoice over them (v. 34).

    b.   The Lord is not pleased with some in Zion (v. 35).

    c.   The Lord will contend with Zion, and chasten her until she is clean (v. 36).

    d.   Zion shall not be moved out of her place (v. 37).

Introduction

You don't know me; you never knew my heart. No man knows my history. I cannot tell it: I shall never undertake it. I don't blame any one for not believing my history. If I had not experienced what I had, I could not have believed it myself. I never did harm any man since I was born in the world. My voice is always for peace.

I cannot lie down until my work is finished. I never think any evil, nor do anything to the harm of my fellow-man. When I am called by the trump of the archangel and weighed in the balance, you will all know me then. I add no more. God bless you all. Amen. [*TPJS,* 361–62]

Who was Joseph Smith? We learn more of this noble and great man in these revelations.

TEXT AND COMMENTARY

D&C 81:1–7 • Presidency of the High Priesthood

1 Verily, verily, I say unto you my servant Frederick G. Williams: Listen to the voice of him who speaketh, to the word of the Lord your God, and hearken to the calling wherewith you are called, even to be a high priest in my church, and a counselor unto my servant Joseph Smith, Jun.;

2 Unto whom I have given the keys of the kingdom, which belong always unto the Presidency of the High Priesthood:

3 Therefore, verily I acknowledge him and will bless him, and also thee, inasmuch as thou art faithful in counsel, in the office which I have appointed unto you, in prayer always, vocally and in thy heart, in public and in private, also in thy ministry in proclaiming the gospel in the land of the living, and among thy brethren.

4 And in doing these things thou wilt do the greatest good unto thy fellow beings, and wilt promote the glory of him who is your Lord.

5 Wherefore, be faithful; stand in the office which I have appointed unto you; succor the weak, lift up the hands which hang down, and strengthen the feeble knees.

6 And if thou art faithful unto the end thou shalt have a crown of immortality, and eternal life in the mansions which I have prepared in the house of my Father.

7 Behold, and lo, these are the words of Alpha and Omega, even Jesus Christ. Amen.

Joseph Smith was "ordained President of the High Priesthood" on January 25, 1832 (see section heading D&C 75). The President of the High Priesthood, and his two counselors, form a quorum, and jointly hold the keys of the kingdom (v. 2). More specific duties are given in section 90 that follows. The personal instructions and promised blessings to the counselor regarding prayer and proclaiming the gospel (vv. 3–4, 6) are self-explanatory. His instructions to "lift up the hands that hang down, and strengthen the feeble knees" (v. 5) is a quote from Isaiah 35:3. While the context of Isaiah's words is not plainly recognized, they are probably referring to the men who lead the Church in their older years. Although Joseph Smith was a young man, his successors have served well into their advanced years. President Spencer W. Kimball cited the Presidents of the Church as dying between the ages of 76 and 96 years of age, and then commented: "We may expect the Church President will always be an older man; young men have action, vigor, initiative; older men, stability strength and wisdom through experience and long communion with God" (CR, April 1970, 118–19). Thus the counselors are expected to lift and strengthen the older President. Therefore, these three men are those to whom the Prophet Joseph said we must "Look to the Presidency and receive instruction" (*TPJS*, 161). The quorum is dissolved upon the death of the President until the new President and his counselors are chosen (see *TPJS*, 106).

D&C 90:1–5 • The Keys Never Taken from Joseph

1 THUS saith the Lord, verily, verily I say unto you my son, thy sins are forgiven thee, according to thy petition, for thy prayers and the prayers of thy brethren have come up into my ears.

2 Therefore, thou art blessed from henceforth that bear the keys of the kingdom given unto you; which kingdom is coming forth for the last time.

3 Verily I say unto you, the keys of this kingdom shall never be taken from you, while thou art in the world, neither in the world to come;

4 Nevertheless, through you shall the oracles be given to another, yea, even unto the church.

5 And all they who receive the oracles of God, let them beware how they hold them lest they are accounted as a light thing, and are brought under condemnation thereby, and stumble and fall when the storms descend, and the winds blow, and the rains descend, and beat upon their house.

With the First Presidency about to be organized, the Lord confirms the giving of the keys, and that they are given for the last time (v. 2). The last dispensation is the "dispensation of the fullness of times" when "all things in Christ" will be gathered in one (Ephesians 1:10; see also D&C 112:30–31). The Lord also promises the Prophet Joseph that the keys shall never be taken from him in this "world or in the world to come" (v. 3). This was also another confirmation to the Church that Joseph was the Lord's mouthpiece (see D&C 21:5; 28:2). Just over two years earlier, the elders of the Church had been told that no one else but Joseph would be appointed to receive revelation for the Church, "for if it be taken from him he shall not have power except to appoint another in his stead" (D&C 43:4). Apparently, the Church was now prepared sufficiently, or soon would be, for the oracles, or the infallible authority, to be given to the Church (v. 4). The Prophet Joseph was the head of this last dispensation and would still be involved beyond the veil in its administration.

Prior to the death of the Savior, in New Testament Times, Jesus gave the keys to Peter, James, and John (see Matthew 17:1–5; *TPJS,* 158). These three Apostles would become the First Presidency of the New Testament Dispensation (see D&C 27:12–13). According to President Wilford Woodruff, the Prophet Joseph conferred all his keys upon the Quorum of the Twelve prior to his death:

> The last speech that Joseph Smith ever made to the quorum of the Apostles was in a building in Nauvoo, and it was such a speech as I never heard from mortal man before or since. He was clothed upon by the Spirit and power of God. His face was clear as amber. The room was filled as with consuming fire. He stood three hours upon his feet. Said he: "You Apostles of the Lamb of God have been chosen to carry out the purposes of the Lord on the earth. Now, I have received, as the Prophet, seer and revelator, standing at the head of this dispensation, every key, every ordinance, every principle and every Priesthood that belongs to the last dispensation and fulness of times. And I have sealed all these things upon your heads. Now, you Apostles, if you do not rise up and bear off this kingdom, as I have given it to you, you will be damned. [CR, April 1898, 89]

Every ordained member of the Quorum of the Twelve is given those keys, and the Quorum holds them collectively under the direction of the First Presidency. At the death of the Prophet, they have the oracles to appoint a new President and First Presidency. Thus, they hold off the storm, wind, and rains that Satan sends against the Church (v. 5). They

are the foundation upon which the Church is built with Jesus Christ as
the chief corner stone (see 3 Nephi 12–14; Matthew 5–7; Ephesians 1:20).

D&C 90:6–11 • Duties of the First Presidency

6 And again, verily I say unto thy brethren, Sidney Rigdon and
Frederick G. Williams, their sins are forgiven them also, and they are
accounted as equal with thee in holding the keys of this last kingdom;

7 As also through your administration the keys of the school of the
prophets, which I have commanded to be organized;

8 That thereby they may be perfected in their ministry for the
salvation of Zion, and of the nations of Israel, and of the Gentiles, as
many as will believe;

9 That through your administration they may receive the word, and
through their administration the word may go forth unto the ends of
the earth, unto the Gentiles first, and then, behold, and lo, they shall
turn unto the Jews.

10 And then cometh the day when the arm of the Lord shall be
revealed in power in convincing the nations, the heathen nations, the
house of Joseph, of the gospel of their salvation.

11 For it shall come to pass in that day, that every man shall hear
the fulness of the gospel in his own tongue, and in his own language,
through those who are ordained unto this power, by the administration
of the Comforter, shed forth upon them for the revelation of Jesus Christ.

The keys of the priesthood are the power to direct the priesthood
functions of the Church and kingdom (see President Joseph F. Smith in
"General Authority Quotes"). The two counselors in the First Presidency
are accounted equal with the Prophet in holding these keys (v. 6). One
of their primary duties is to administer the School of the Prophets (v. 7).
Since there was no Quorum of the Twelve at this time, the Prophet
organized and administered a school of invited priesthood holders. Today,
the First Presidency is responsible for the weekly meetings with all of the
General Authorities, through which other general offices of the Church
are administered. The purpose of these meetings is to help those called
to be perfected in their ministry, for the salvation of Zion, and for the
proclaiming of the gospel to all nations (v. 8). The Lord outlines the order
for proclaiming the gospel to the nations: The Gentiles, or the Christian
nations, those who believe in Christ (see 3 Nephi 16:6–7), are to be taken

the gospel first; and then to the Jews (v. 9). The Jews, as used here, is a generic term for all Israelites (see v. 8, "the nations of Israel," and D&C 19:27). In Joseph's day, the Jews were the only tribe of the twelve tribes of Israel that was recognized as being of Israel.

There is a sequence, stated in the Book of Mormon, for the nations of Israel to be given the gospel: "Graft in the branches; begin at the last that they may be first, and that the first may be last, and dig about the trees, both old and young, the first and the last; and the last and the first, that all may be nourished once again for the last time" (Jacob 5:63). The people of Lehi, the tribes of Ephraim and Manasseh, were the last ones taken away, and will be the first ones given the opportunity to return. The first ones taken away were the lost tribes, and will be the last ones to return. The third major group of Israel, the literal tribe of Judah, will be the second or middle group to be given the opportunity to return (see also Jacob 5:20–25).

The final group of nations to be given the opportunity to receive the gospel is the heathens. Since this is often used in a derogatory manner, they will be defined here as the non-Christian nations, or those who do not believe in Christ. Those who accept the gospel from this group will be adopted into the tribe of Joseph (v. 10). Apparently, Joseph will be given two portions of land in the last days for this reason (see Ezekiel 47:13). The Lord states that every man will hear the gospel in his own tongue in that day (v. 11). This was an incredible promise at that time, but with today's language techniques it is happening and will undoubtedly continue.

D&C 90:12–18 • Other Duties of the First Presidency

12 And now, verily I say unto you, I give unto you a commandment that you continue in the ministry and presidency.

13 And when you have finished the translation of the prophets, you shall from thenceforth preside over the affairs of the church and the school;

14 And from time to time, as shall be manifested by the Comforter, receive revelations to unfold the mysteries of the kingdom;

15 And set in order the churches, and study and learn, and become acquainted with all good books, and with languages, tongues, and people.

16 And this shall be your business and mission in all your lives, to preside in council, and set in order all the affairs of this church and kingdom.

17 Be not ashamed, neither confounded; but be admonished in all your high-mindedness and pride, for it bringeth a snare upon your souls.

18 Set in order your houses; keep slothfulness and uncleanness far from you.

Certain responsibilities that had been given to Joseph were to be continued, but with the assistance of his newly called counselors. Joseph was to continue his translation of the Bible. He was to finish the part of the Bible that he was now working on, the Prophets. This translation was important because they foretold the gospel being taken to the Gentiles and then to the House of Israel (see 3 Nephi 20:10–19; 23:1–6). It was a priority over the current affairs of the Church, and the School of the Prophets (v. 13). They could not teach them until they had been taught themselves. As they continued to learn, further "revelations would be given to unfold the mysteries of the kingdom" (v. 14).

They were to further prepare themselves by studying and becoming "acquainted with all good books, and with languages, tongues, and people" (v. 15). "Good books" are different than the "best books" referred to in D&C 88:118. The "best books" were defined above as the scriptures, and other words of the Apostles and prophets. Good books are implied by the Lord to be the books regarding "languages, tongues, and people." If the gospel is to be taught in every man's "own tongue, and in his own language, through those who are ordained unto this power" (D&C 90:11), the First Presidency must be the forerunner in preparing the gospel to be taught. They were not instructed to learn those languages, but to "become acquainted," or to become aware of their existence, location, and other characteristics of the people.

The three members of the First Presidency were lifetime appointments to administer the business and mission of the Church. While the counselors were to assist the President as they were directed by him, they were to be equal as they sat as a quorum, "to preside in Council, and set in order all the affairs of this church and kingdom" (v. 16). They were to discuss, consult, and advise one another as directed by the Comforter (v. 11). This heavy responsibility could not be carried out if they were shy [ashamed], not confident [confounded], not willing to be admonished by each other, or arrogant [high-minded] or prideful, which would be a snare to them individually as well as collectively as a Council (v. 17). They must also be an example to the Church through their own families [houses], habits [slothfulness], and personal living [uncleanness] (v. 18).

D&C 90:19–27 • Individual Instructions

19 Now, verily I say unto you, let there be a place provided, as soon as it is possible, for the family of thy counselor and scribe, even Frederick G. Williams.

20 And let mine aged servant, Joseph Smith, Sen., continue with his family upon the place where he now lives; and let it not be sold until the mouth of the Lord shall name.

21 And let my counselor, even Sidney Rigdon, remain where he now resides until the mouth of the Lord shall name.

22 And let the bishop search diligently to obtain an agent, and let him be a man who has got riches in store—a man of God, and of strong faith—

23 That thereby he may be enabled to discharge every debt; that the storehouse of the Lord may not be brought into disrepute before the eyes of the people.

24 Search diligently, pray always, and be believing, and all things shall work together for your good, if ye walk uprightly and remember the covenant wherewith ye have covenanted one with another.

25 Let your families be small, especially mine aged servant Joseph Smith's, Sen., as pertaining to those who do not belong to your families;

26 That those things that are provided for you, to bring to pass my work, be not taken from you and given to those that are not worthy—

27 And thereby you be hindered in accomplishing those things which I have commanded you.

The Church was currently attempting to further establish the law of consecration in Kirtland, as it had done in Zion. The personal needs of the counselors in the First Presidency were to be taken care of by the Church (vv. 19; 21). The agent appointed in the land of Zion was Sidney Gilbert (see D&C 57), but the Lord had directed them to appoint one in Kirtland to assist Bishop Newel K. Whitney (see D&C 72:8–10 and comments in chapter 3 of this volume) in Kirtland (D&C 84:113). The agent had not been appointed, and the Lord reminds them of the qualities needed and his duties. The Lord expects His Church to be above disrepute (vv. 22–24).

Joseph Smith Sen. was in his sixties, which was apparently slowing him down (vv. 20, 25). The size of his family, referring to those coming to Kirtland and living with church families, was to be kept small. The same was true for other officers of the Church who were being supported by the law of consecration, yet hindered from their duties by having guests living in their homes, especially those who were unworthy (vv. 26–27). The law of consecration was not a dole system.

D&C 90:28–31 • Vienna Jacques

28 And again, verily I say unto you, it is my will that my handmaid Vienna Jacques should receive money to bear her expenses, and go up unto the land of Zion;

29 And the residue of the money may be consecrated unto me, and she be rewarded in mine own due time.

30 Verily I say unto you, that it is meet in mine eyes that she should go up unto the land of Zion, and receive an inheritance from the hand of the bishop;

31 That she may settle down in peace inasmuch as she is faithful, and not be idle in her days from thenceforth.

Vienna Jacques was a convert to the Church who had come to Kirtland. She had apparently consecrated all that she had to the Church, and was to be assisted by the bishop and the storehouse in moving to Zion. She was faithful to the end.[37]

D&C 90:32–37 • Zion in the Lord's Own Due Time

32 And behold, verily I say unto you, that ye shall write this commandment, and say unto your brethren in Zion, in love greeting, that I have called you also to preside over Zion in mine own due time.

33 Therefore, let them cease wearying me concerning this matter.

---

[37] See Hoyt W. Brewster Jr., *Doctrine and Covenants Encyclopedia* [1988], 274–75.

34 Behold, I say unto you that your brethren in Zion begin to repent, and the angels rejoice over them.

35 Nevertheless, I am not well pleased with many things; and I am not well pleased with my servant William E. McLellin, neither with my servant Sidney Gilbert; and the bishop also, and others have many things to repent of.

36 But verily I say unto you, that I, the Lord, will contend with Zion, and plead with her strong ones, and chasten her until she overcomes and is clean before me.

37 For she shall not be removed out of her place. I, the Lord, have spoken it. Amen.

Again honoring the Prophet Joseph Smith as his mouthpiece, the Lord instructs that this revelation be sent to Zion (v. 32). The Lord will establish Zion in His own due time, but that time will also depend upon His people. The Lord will do His part through contending [correcting] with them, pleading [giving revelation] to her strong ones [leader's], and chastening them because of His love for them; but Zion must fully repent and become clean. Zion will not be removed out of her place (vv. 36–37).

General Authority Quotes
—President Joseph F. Smith • D&C 81:2

The Priesthood in general is the authority given to man to act for God. Every man ordained to any degree of the Priesthood, has this authority delegated to him.

But it is necessary that every act performed under this authority shall be done at the proper time and place, in the proper way, and after the proper order. The power of directing these labors constitutes the keys of the Priesthood. In their fulness, the keys are held by only one person at a time, the prophet and president of the Church. He may delegate any portion of this power to another, in which case that person holds the keys of that particular labor. [*Gospel Doctrine* (1959), 136]

—President Joseph Fielding Smith • D&C 81:2

Now, brethren, I think there is one thing which we should have exceedingly clear in our minds. Neither the President of the Church, nor the First Presidency, nor the united voice of the First Presidency and the twelve will ever lead the Saints astray or send forth counsel to the

world that is contrary to the mind and will of the Lord.

An individual may fall by the wayside, or have views, or give counsel which falls short of what the Lord intends. But the voice of the First Presidency and the united voice of those others who hold with them the keys of the kingdom shall always guide the Saints and the world in those paths where the Lord wants them to be. . . .

I testify that if we shall look to the First Presidency and follow their counsel and direction, no power on earth can stay or change our course as a church, and as individuals we shall gain peace in this life and be inheritors of eternal glory in the world to come. [Priesthood Session, CR, April 1972, 99]

—*President Harold B. Lee* • D&C 81:5

. . . As Moses sat upon a hill and raised the rod of his authority, or the keys of his priesthood, Israel prevailed over their enemies; but as the day wore on, his hands became heavy and began to droop at his side. And so they held up his hands so they would not be weakened and the rod would be lowered. He would be sustained so that the enemies of the church would not prevail over the saints of the Most High God (see Exodus 17:8–12).

I think that is the role that President Tanner and I should fulfill. The hands of President Smith may grow weary. They may tend to droop at times because of his heavy responsibilities; but as we uphold his hands, and as we lead under his direction, by his side, the gates of hell will not prevail against you and against Israel. Your safety and ours depends upon whether or not we follow the ones whom the Lord has placed to preside over his church. He knows whom he wants to preside over this church, and he will make no mistake. The Lord doesn't do things by accident. He has never done things accidentally. And I think the scientists and all the philosophers in the world have never discovered anything that God didn't already know. His revelations are more powerful, more meaningful, and have more substance than all the secular learning in the world.

Let's keep our eye on the President of the Church, and uphold his hands as President Tanner and I will continue to do. [CR, October 1970, 153]

—*President Brigham Young* • D&C 90:3

Is Joseph glorified? No, he is preaching to the spirits in prison. He will get his resurrection the first of any one in this Kingdom, for he is the first that God made choice of to bring forth the work of the last days.

His office is not taken from him, he has only gone to labor in another department of the operations of the Almighty. He is still an Apostle, still a Prophet, and is doing the work of an apostle and Prophet; he has gone one step beyond us and gained a victory that you and I have not gained, still he has not gone into the celestial kingdom, or, if he has, it has been by a direct command of the Almighty, and that, too, to return again as soon as the purpose has been accomplished. [*Discourses of Brigham Young,* 468]

—President Harold B. Lee • D&C 90:9–11

These missionary labors will be expanded in the Lord's own way, barriers will be broken down, and the honest in heart in every nation will hear the gospel in their own language, looking forward to the fulfillment of the prophecy that eventually "the word may go forth unto the ends of the earth, . . . in convincing the nations, the heathen nations, . . . that every man shall hear the fulness of the gospel in his own tongue, and in his own language" (D&C 90:9–11). [*The Teachings of Harold B. Lee,* 599]

—Elder Victor L. Brown • D&C 90:11

We feel this work [correlation program] is a literal fulfillment of prophecy. We are deeply grateful for the great privilege of being a small part in making it possible for many thousands to hear the fullness of the gospel in their own language. [CR, April 1967, 37]

Chapter Eleven

Know How and What
You Worship

D&C 93

DOCTRINE AND COVENANTS 93

Historical Setting: All the Prophet Joseph's history tells us is "that I [Joseph] received the [Doctrine and Covenants 93]" (*HC,* 1:343; May 6, 1833). He was probably working on the translation of the Bible. Two months earlier, he was "engaged in the translation of the Old Testament" and had asked about translating the Apocrypha (March 9, 1833; D&C 91; section heading). Although section 76 was given when the Prophet was translating the Testimony of John, in February of 1832, he was apparently working on it again because the opening verses contain several quotations from John. A study of Joseph's translation work concluded that: "The Prophet went over parts of the Bible more than once and made additional corrections each time."[38]

SECTION 93 • OUTLINE

➤ 93:1–19   The formula for understanding how to worship and what you worship.

a.   Forsake sins and come unto [Christ], call on my name,

---

[38] See Robert J. Matthews, *A Plainer Translation, Joseph Smith's Translation of the Bible, A History and Commentary* [1975], 214–215; see the entire chapter 10, 210–218.

> obey my voice, and keep my commandments, and you shall know that I am (v. 1).

    b.   He is the true light of every man, and one with the Father (vv. 2–5).

    c.   John the Baptist bore record of him (vv. 6–16).

    d.   If faithful, you shall receive the record of John (v. 18).

➤ 93:20–32   Christ is the Firstborn, and those begotten through Him are partakers of His glory, and of the Church of the Firstborn.

    a.   Ye were in the beginning with the Father, and of the Spirit of Truth (vv. 23–25).

    b.   John bore record that Christ received a fulness of all truth (vv. 26–28).

    c.   Intelligence was not created, and truth and all intelligence is independent to act for itself, which is the agency of man (vv. 29–32).

➤ 93:33–39   Man is spirit, the elements eternal, and when inseparably connected receive a fulness of joy.

    a.   Man is the tabernacle of God, and if defiled will be destroyed (v. 35).

    b.   The glory of God is intelligence, or light and truth, and forsakes evil (vv. 36–37).

    c.   The spirit of man was innocent in the beginning, and the wicked one takes away light and truth (vv. 38–39).

➤ 93:40–53   I command you to bring up your children in light and truth.

    a.   Frederick G. Williams is under condemnation (vv. 41–43).

    b.   Sidney Rigdon has not kept the commandments with his children (v. 44).

    c.   Joseph Smith must be rebuked (vv. 45–49).

    d.   Newel K. Whitney needs be chastened (v. 50).

    e.   My friends are given commandments to hasten the translation and obtain knowledge (vv. 51–53).

Introduction

Throughout the history of the world there have been many forms of worship introduced and followed, and many objects of worship. Isaiah describes the conditions of the world just prior to the Second Coming of Christ. He is describing our day, and it is an accurate description. "Their land is also full of idols; they worship the work of their own hands, that which their own fingers have made" (Isaiah 2:8). He is not describing the worshiping of literal idols as in Old Testament times, but is symbolically speaking of material things and human reasoning that is worshiped in our time (see D&C 124:84).

Male and female were created in the image and likeness of the only living and true God, and the only being whom they should worship (see D&C 20:18–19). There is no better way to come to worship God than to follow the instructions of his Only Begotten Son, through whom we worship Him. That instruction is given in section 93.

TEXT AND COMMENTARY

D&C 93:1–5 • Whom and What You Worship

1 Verily, thus saith the Lord: It shall come to pass that every soul who forsaketh his sins and cometh unto me, and calleth on my name, and obeyeth my voice, and keepeth my commandments, shall see my face and know that I am;

2 And that I am the true light that lighteth every man that cometh into the world;

3 And that I am in the Father, and the Father in me, and the Father and I are one—

4 The Father because he gave me of his fulness, and the Son because I was in the world and made flesh my tabernacle, and dwelt among the sons of men.

5 I was in the world and received of my Father, and the works of him were plainly manifest.

A promise to see the face of God was given slightly over four months previously. The Lord had promised ten high priests that he "would unveil his face unto [them], and it shall be in his own time, and in his own way, and according to his own will" (D&C 88:68; December 27, 1832). Perhaps they had been praying for that to happen, or the Lord was now giving them further encouragement to continue to seek after Him. For whatever reason, the revelation begins with a formula to see His face. There are five prerequisites in the above formula for seeing God: (1) The forsaking of sin is repentance. (2) To come unto Christ is to be baptized (3 Nephi 21:6; 27:20). (3) Calling on the Lord's name is a manner of prayer. (4) To obey His voice is to receive and accept revelation. (5) Keep the commandments, those recorded in the scriptures. The following of these five principles and ordinances are part of worshiping Christ.

The first purpose for the Lord giving this revelation was to show His Saints how to worship. The second purpose was to know what we worship (v. 19), or to learn about Christ and God the Father. Through learning about Christ, we can come to know Him face to face, and through His name come unto the Father and receive of His fulness, or obtain eternal life (D&C 93:1–4). Jesus taught this concept in the great Intercessory Prayer as he prepared himself to make the Atonement in Gethsemane: "And this is life eternal, that they might know thee the only true God, and Jesus Christ, whom thou hast sent" (John 17:3). After the formula was given to see the face of Christ, the revelation teaches us about Christ and His relationship to the Father.

We worship, in the words of the philosophers, an omnipotent (all powerful); omniscient (all knowing), omnipresent (in all presence) God. We also worship His Only Begotten Son who has also attained these eternal attributes. We learn of their divine natures in this revelation from the Son.

Jesus Christ bears testimony of what was recorded in the Gospel of John (1:9). He was "the true light that lighteth every man that cometh into the world" (D&C 93:2). The function of that light was earlier revealed to the Saints (D&C 84:45–46; and 88:6–13), and therefore will not be repeated here. The revelation continues by bearing record of Christ's oneness with the Father (D&C 93:3). The Gospel of John, or the Testimony of John as it is called in the JST, had also repeatedly borne record of Christ's oneness with the Father (see John 10:30; 14:10; 17:11, 20–22). The attribute of oneness is important to understand what or whom we worship. To worship one is to worship the other.[39] We must become one with Them in our worship. Earlier the Lord told the Church

[39] See Jerreld L. Newquist, *Gospel Truth, Discourses and Writings of President George Q. Cannon* [1974], 1:205.

through Joseph Smith, "Be one, and if ye are not one ye are not mine" (D&C 38:27).

Jesus testified to Philip that He [Jesus] "was in the Father and the Father [was] in him" (John 14:10). Abinadi, the Book of Mormon prophet, explained that Christ was the Father and the Son (Mosiah 15:1–4). Section 93 qualifies how He was considered to be both. "The Father because he gave me of his fulness, and the Son because I was in the world and made flesh my tabernacle, and dwelt among the sons of men" (D&C 93:4). Jesus' receiving the fulness of the Father was called the "divine investiture of authority" by the First Presidency and the Twelve,[40] in an explanation of how Christ is the Father. Other terms that may be applicable are "power of attorney," or the "administrator God." As taught in the Testimony of John, the Father "hath given him authority to execute judgment also, because he is the Son of man" (John 5:27; see also 5:22). Jesus being in the world in a tabernacle of flesh is also quoting John (1:14), and is explaining how He is the Son.

While Jesus was in His mortal ministry He was directed by the Father, "and the works of him were plainly manifest" (D&C 93:5). Once more the Testimony of John is being paraphrased, or quoted as it was originally written. In John 5:36, we read that the works that Jesus did were the ones His Father had given Him to finish, and bore witness of Him. Therefore, in the first five verses of section 93 Jesus had personally testified of who He was, and of His relationship to the Father and to the inhabitants of the earth. He was the true light of every man who came into the world. He was in complete oneness or unity with the Father. By divine investiture of authority from His Father, He was the Administrator God of this world. The works that He had done during His mortal ministry were done to carry out His Father's will.

D&C 93:6–10 • The Fulness of John's Record

> 6 And John saw and bore record of the fulness of my glory, and the fulness of John's record is hereafter to be revealed.

---

[40] James R. Clark, *Messages of the First Presidency*, "The Father and the Son, A Doctrinal Exposition by the First Presidency and the Twelve, June 30, 1916" [1971], 5:26–34.

7 And he bore record, saying: I saw his glory, that he was in the beginning, before the world was;

8 Therefore, in the beginning the Word was, for he was the Word, even the messenger of salvation—

9 The light and the Redeemer of the world; the Spirit of truth, who came into the world, because the world was made by him, and in him was the life of men and the light of men.

10 The worlds were made by him; men were made by him; all things were made by him, and through him, and of him.

Although most of what He said in these verses was also taught in the Gospel of John, He was not quoting it directly, at least as it is recorded today. Beginning with verse seven, and through verse 17, He quotes directly from John's record. John bore record of some additional attributes of Jesus as well as bearing record of some of the same things Jesus had said to help us know what or whom we worship. It was a second witness to the position Christ held in eternity and in the world.

Jesus begins quoting from the record of John to show us the position He had held in the premortal life: "I saw his glory, that he [Christ] was in the beginning, before the world was; . . . he was the Word, even the messenger of salvation" (vv. 7–8). The KJV of the Bible identifies the Word as God (John 1:1). The "messenger of salvation" was further qualified in the JST as "the gospel preached through the Son" in the beginning or in the premortal life (JST, John 1:1). He was not only a God in the premortal life, but was involved in the teaching of the gospel plan of salvation to those who were to come to the earth (see D&C 93:23 below).

His testimony of Christ being the Light of the World (D&C 93:9–10) is similar but more extensive than Christ's testimony of Himself as the true light (D&C 93:2). It is closer to the testimony given of the Light of Christ in the "Olive Leaf" as a creative, teaching, and governing light (see D&C 88:6–13). John's record identifies Christ as the Redeemer and the Spirit of Truth, as the Creator of this world and other worlds, and the Life (Governor) of the World, in addition to His being the light or source of truth that fills the universe as spoken of in section 88:12. The worlds and all things were created by Him (the administrator); through Him (others assisted under His directions), and of Him (according to

His knowledge and power) as revealed in D&C 76:24. The Gospel of John (KJV) records much of the same information, but is not as complete (see John 1:4, 10). It has lost (see D&C 93:12–14) a plain and precious part (see 1 Nephi 13:24–29).

93:11–14 • From Grace to Grace—a Fulness

> 11 And I, John, bear record that I beheld his glory, as the glory of the Only Begotten of the Father, full of grace and truth, even the Spirit of truth, which came and dwelt in the flesh, and dwelt among us.

> And the word was made flesh, and dwelt among us, (and we beheld his glory, the glory as of the only begotten of the Father), full of grace and truth. [John 1:14]

> 12 And I, John, saw that he received not of the fulness at the first, but received grace for grace;

> 13 And he received not of the fulness at first, but continued from grace to grace, until he received a fulness.

> 14 And thus he was called the Son of God because he received not of the fulness at first.

To receive "grace for grace" (v. 12) is to receive more from the Father as Christ shared His previous blessings with others. Thus He grew or "continued from grace to grace" (v. 13), or from one level of grace to a higher level of grace, until He had received the fulness of glory that was in the Father (v. 14). As described in section 88, He became perfected by keeping all of the law (D&C 88:34–35). During this process He was the Son of God because He was dwelling among the mortal inhabitants, and following the plan which they would be given an opportunity to follow. He was setting the example for them as He had later done among the Nephites (see 3 Nephi 27:21–22, 27).

D&C 93:15–17 • The Sign of the Dove

> 15 And I, John, bear record, and lo, the heavens were opened, and the Holy Ghost descended upon him in the form of a dove, and sat upon him, and there came a voice out of heaven saying: This is my beloved Son.

> 16 And I, John, bear record that he received a fulness of the glory of the Father;

17 And he received all power, both in heaven and on earth, and the glory of the Father was with him, for he dwelt in him.

The Savior received the Holy Ghost when He was baptized with water (v. 15). Joseph Smith taught: "the form of a dove" should be understood as "the sign of the dove," a witness of the Holy Ghost's presence, which the devil cannot duplicate (*TPJS,* 275–276). Thus Christ, the Eternal Being whom we worship, and through whom we worship the Father, had all power. He had grown from grace to grace until He had a fulness of knowledge, and the glory of the Father dwelt with Him giving Him the full presence of the glory of an Eternal God (vv. 16–17).

D&C 93:18 • The Fulness of John's Record

18 And it shall come to pass, that if you are faithful you shall receive the fulness of the record of John.

When Jesus began to quote from the record of John, he promised that "the fulness of John's record is hereafter to be revealed" (D&C 93:6). As He concluded His quote, He promised that the faithful would "receive the fulness of the record of John." To what record was Jesus referring? A careful reading of D&C 93:7–17 reveals that Jesus was referring to John the Baptist and not John the Revelator, the accepted author of the New Testament Gospel of John. Apparently, John the Baptist kept a record and it was used by John the Revelator to begin his own record.[41] Furthermore, John the Revelator had seen many of the same things of which the Baptist had written. Although John 1:35–40 implies that John the Baptist did not meet John the Revelator until the day after Jesus was baptized, the Revelator may have been present on the glorious occasion the previous day. This is implied in the Gospel of John. The Record of John (the Baptist) stated, "And I, John, bear record that I beheld his glory" (D&C 93:11). The Gospel of John testifies, "and we beheld his glory, the glory as of the only begotten of the Father" (John 1:14). The pronoun "we" tells us more than one person was present. If John the Revelator used the record of John the Baptist to write his testimony, the "we" suggests that

---

[41] The conclusion that the record of John referred to in D&C 93 is also the opinion of Sidney B. Sperry and Elder Bruce R. McConkie. See *Doctrine and Covenants Compendium* [1960], 472–73; and *The Mortal Messiah* [1981], 1:426–27.

both men were there and both were given a glorious manifestation. Section 93 promises to restore the Baptist's record. The JST restores some of the plain and precious parts lost from the Revelator's records as well as others. When these two records are fully restored, the faithful will learn more about these New Testament events. Section 93 concludes with an admonition to "hasten to translate my [Christ's] scriptures" (v. 53). Further knowledge was restored through the JST, but we don't have the record of John (the Baptist).

D&C 93:19–28 • The Fulness of the Father

19 I give unto you these sayings that you may understand and know how to worship, and know what you worship, that you may come unto the Father in my name, and in due time receive of his fulness.

20 For if you keep my commandments you shall receive of his fulness, and be glorified in me as I am in the Father; therefore, I say unto you, you shall receive grace for grace.

22 And all those who are begotten through me are partakers of the glory of the same, and are the church of the Firstborn.

23 Ye were also in the beginning with the Father; that which is Spirit, even the Spirit of truth;

24 And truth is knowledge of things as they are, and as they were, and as they are to come;

25 And whatsoever is more or less than this is the spirit of that wicked one who was a liar from the beginning.

26 The Spirit of truth is of God. I am the Spirit of truth, and John bore record of me, saying: He received a fulness of truth, yea, even of all truth;

27 And no man receiveth a fulness unless he keepeth his commandments.

28 He that keepeth his commandments receiveth truth and light, until he is glorified in truth and knoweth all things.

Jesus restored enough knowledge that we might better understand how to worship and what to worship in order that we "may come unto the Father in my [Christ's] name, and in due time receive of his [the Father's] fulness" (v. 19). He also revealed the process for us to come to that station while in mortality. The fulness of the Father does not come in a brief period of time as it did to the Savior. The Prophet Joseph Smith observed:

> We consider that God has created man with a mind capable of instruction, and a faculty which may be enlarged in proportion to the heed and diligence given to the light communicated from heaven to the intellect; and that the nearer man approaches perfection, the clearer are his views, and the greater his enjoyments, till he has overcome the evils of his life and lost every desire for sin; and like the ancients, arrives at that point of faith where he is wrapped in the power and glory of his Maker and is caught up to dwell with Him. But we consider that this is a station to which no man ever arrived in a moment, he must have been instructed in the government and laws of that kingdom by proper degrees, until his mind is capable in some measure of comprehending the propriety, justice, equality, and consistency of the same. [*TPJS,* 51]

In section 93 the Lord listed several but not all of the things that must be done to attain the fulness of the Father. Three of these requirements are discussed here.

The first requirement listed for mankind to attain a fulness of the Father is to keep the commandments which have been revealed (v. 20). We thus follow the same pattern that Christ followed in receiving grace for grace. As we keep the laws of God we are blessed. The Prophet Joseph gave this instruction: "There is a law, irrevocably decreed in heaven before the foundations of this world, upon which blessings are predicted—and when we obtain any blessing from God, it is by obedience to that law upon which it is predicated" (D&C 130:20–21). Obedience is the first law of heaven and of earth. The Lord is "bound when ye do what I say; but when ye do not what I say ye have no promise" (D&C 82:10). As we share those blessings with our associates, thus giving grace for grace, we are further blessed and rise to a higher level of grace. Therefore, we can grow from grace to grace until we receive a fulness, as did Christ.

The second requirement, given by Christ in this revelation, to attain a fulness of the Father was to become His sons and daughters through being born again (D&C 93:21–22). Those who are baptized with fire and the Holy Ghost are spiritually begotten sons and daughters of Christ (see Mosiah 5:7; Alma 36:24; Ether 3:14). As taught by Joseph Smith, "Being born again, comes by the Spirit of God through ordinances" (*TPJS,* 162). As the Firstborn spirit child of the Father, the heavenly Church is called "the church of the Firstborn" (D&C 93:22). Thus it

is named after Him just as the earthly Church is named after Him. His spiritually adopted children, who receive of the glory of the Father, become members of the heavenly Church, and are "given all things" (D&C 76:54–55).

The third requirement revealed by Christ for receiving the fulness of the Father was to receive a fulness of truth (D&C 93:23). As spirit offspring of our Father in Heaven (Hebrews 12:9), we lived with Christ and our Father in a premortal life. There we were taught truth or knowledge (Alma 13:3; Abraham 3:26). Pilate asked Jesus, "What is truth?" (John 18:38). The question had undoubtedly been asked many times before and has been asked many times since. Although the answer is given above, have we really comprehended the depth of the definition; to receive the fulness of the truth? From the context of this revelation, a "knowledge of things as they are" is a knowledge of things as they exist here in mortality. A knowledge of things as "they were" is a knowledge of our having a premortal life and what has been revealed regarding that life. A knowledge of things "as they are to come," is a knowledge of the postmortal life (D&C 93:24).

Similar definitions of truth are given in other scriptures. Jacob, brother of Nephi, spoke "concerning things which are, and which are to come." He then quoted Isaiah to tell of the future, things which are to come, and likened Isaiah's words to their situation in order that they may learn (2 Nephi 6:4–5). That Jacob was aware of the broader definition of truth given in section 93, is confirmed in his later writings:

"Behold, my brethren, he that prophesieth, let him prophesy to the understanding of men; for the Spirit speaketh the truth and lieth not. Wherefore, it speaketh of things as they really are, and of things as they really will be; wherefore, these things are manifested unto us plainly, for the salvation of our souls. But behold, we are not witnesses alone in these things; for God also spake them unto prophets of old" (Jacob 4:13).

A knowledge of things as they really are must include the past and the present. A knowledge of things as they really will be must include all things of the future. Although truth can be defined as knowledge of things past, present, and future, it would not be complete without including the premortal and the postmortal life. God chastised Job for his lack of knowledge and understanding in his arguments with his friends. A careful reading of the questions God asks of Job shows reference to the premortal life (Job 38:1–7; and following), the mortal life (Job 39:1–6; and following), and the knowledge of the last days that will usher in the millennial reign and bring many to the postmortal era (Job 40:6–10; and following). All truth must include a complete knowledge of all of these three stages of our life.

Satan's objective is to take away knowledge of these three stages of man's existence, or to embellish or theorize beyond what is known, and thus desecrate the truth. He too existed in the premortal life where he began his campaign against truth. He was thus a liar from the beginning (D&C 93:25). On the other hand, Christ is the champion of truth. "The Spirit of truth is of God. I am the Spirit of truth, . . . He received a fulness of truth, yea, even of all truth" (D&C 93:26). Jesus was taught in His mortal childhood by His Father as Isaiah had prophesied: "For he [Christ] shall grow up before [the Father] as a tender plant" (Isaiah 53:2). He confounded the learned doctors and astonished all who heard Him in the area of the temple, and further confirmed the source of His knowledge to his worried mother by asking, "wist ye not that I must be about my Father's business" (Luke 2:46–50). As he received the fulness of truth (from grace to grace), He had even all truth, and was prepared to begin His three-year mortal ministry. Of this accomplishment, John bore record above.

Having defined truth, Jesus emphasized that no man can receive a fulness of truth unless he keeps the commandments (D&C 93:27–28). The Prophet Joseph Smith emphasized that we must keep "*all* the commandments of God. But we cannot keep all the commandments without first knowing them, and we cannot expect to know all, or more than we now know unless we comply with or keep those we have already received" (*TPJS*, 255–56; emphasis added.) As the commandments are kept, and more knowledge is received, we will come to understand the three stages of life.

D&C 93:29–32 • The Agency and Condemnation of Man

29 Man was also in the beginning with God. Intelligence, or the light of truth, was not created or made, neither indeed can be.

30 All truth is independent in that sphere in which God has placed

it, to act for itself, as all intelligence also; otherwise there is no existence.

31 Behold, here is the agency of man, and here is the condemnation of man; because that which was from the beginning is plainly manifest unto them, and they receive not the light.

32 And every man whose spirit receiveth not the light is under condemnation.

The Lord continued to reveal truths about all three stages of life. In the premortal life (the first stage), the spirit or intelligence was organized[42] from an eternal matter called intelligence or the light of truth (v. 29). In the second stage, the spirit was given independence, and a place to act for itself (v. 30). The right to have freedom was an eternal principle for the premortal life as well as for earth life. This freedom is also called agency, but can also be "the condemnation of man" because truth is plainly manifest, "And every man whose spirit receiveth not the light is under condemnation" (vv. 31–32). With agency comes responsibility. Those spirits who accept light will grow toward the fulness of the Father, while those who reject it will be condemned eternally because they have not absorbed the light necessary for progression. The purpose of mortal life is for man to be tested and progress towards eternal glory (Abraham 3:25–26).

D&C 93:33–39 • The Fulness of Joy—the Celestial Home

33 For man is spirit. The elements are eternal, and spirit and element, inseparably connected, receive a fulness of joy;

34 And when separated, man cannot receive a fulness of joy.

35 The elements are the tabernacle of God; yea, man is the tabernacle of God, even temples; and whatsoever temple is defiled, God shall destroy that temple.

36 The glory of God is intelligence, or, in other words, light and truth.

37 Light and truth forsake that evil one.

38 Every spirit of man was innocent in the beginning; and God

---

[42] The Prophet Joseph taught: "The word create came from the [Hebrew] word *baurau* which does not mean to create out of nothing; it means to organize" (*TPJS*, 350).

having redeemed man from the fall, men became again, in their infant state, innocent before God.

39 And that wicked one cometh and taketh away light and truth, through disobedience, from the children of men, and because of the tradition of their fathers.

The fulness of joy comes in the third and final stage of man—the resurrected state—when "spirit and element [are] inseparably connected" (vv. 33–34). The spirit and the body constitute the soul of man (D&C 88:15). With the resurrection, the spirit and the body become one body, spiritual and immortal, or inseparably connected. No longer can the body and spirit be divided or separated. They are one eternal spiritual body (see Alma 11:45; D&C 88:27). The celestial nature of the body is brought about by receiving revelation and knowledge to the understanding of the mysteries and peaceable things of God (see D&C 42:61). Those who do not receive revelation and intelligence (the light of truth) will still receive a resurrection, but not of the same glory (see D&C 88:21–24). Only in the celestial kingdom of God—not in this world—is the fulness of joy experienced (2 Nephi 9:18; D&C 101:36).

The teaching of Paul that the body of man is the temple of God, and the spirit of God dwells in it (1 Corinthians 3:16) is confirmed: "man is the tabernacle of God, even temples; and whatsoever temple is defiled, God shall destroy that temple" (D&C 93:35). Paul also warned of the temple body being destroyed (see 1 Corinthians 3:17). However, as Lehi proclaimed, the purpose of mortal life was for man to attain joy (see 2 Nephi 2:25). The Prophet Joseph taught: "We came to this earth that we might have a body and present it pure before God in the Celestial kingdom. The great principle of happiness consists in having a body" (*TPJS,* 181). These teachings are consistent with the Lord's statement: "The glory of God is intelligence, or, in other words, light and truth" (D&C 93:36).

Some have speculated or interpreted the above verse as a declaration of the makeup of the intelligence from which the spirit children of our Father in Heaven were organized. That may well be, but we must remember that more or less than what truth has been revealed may be from the spirit of the wicked one (D&C 93:25). President Joseph Fielding Smith gave this caution: "The Latter-day Saints believe that man is a spirit clothed with a tabernacle of flesh and bone, the intelligent part of which was never created or made, but existed eternally. . . .

"Some of our writers have endeavored to explain what an intelligence is, but to do so is futile, for we have never been given any insight into this matter beyond what the Lord has fragmentarily revealed. We know, however, that there is something called intelligence which always existed. It is the real eternal part of man, which was not created or made. This intelligence combined with the spirit constitutes a spiritual identity or individual.[43]

Thus, the spirit of man is a combination of the intelligence and the spirit which is an entity begotten of God. In November of 1909, the First Presidency sent out a message to the Church on the "Origin of Man." The following excerpt from that message tells us all that really has ever been revealed about intelligence: "The doctrine of the pre-existence, —revealed so plainly, particularly in latter days, pours a wonderful flood of light upon the otherwise mysterious problem of man's origin. It shows that man, as a spirit, was begotten and born of heavenly parents, and reared to maturity in the eternal mansions of the Father, prior to coming upon the earth in a temporal body to undergo an experience in mortality. It teaches that all men existed in the spirit before any man existed in the flesh, and that all who have inhabited the earth since Adam have taken bodies and become souls in like manner."[44]

As mortality is experienced, it is important to know that "Light and truth forsake that evil one" (D&C 93:37). The evil one attempted to take away light and truth from God's children in the premortal life and continues to do so in earth life. Arguments have flared throughout the history of the world concerning the nature of mankind at birth. Are children born good or born evil? From this revelation we learn that they are not born good or evil, but are born innocent in both stages of life, the premortal and mortal beginning (v. 38). Spirits progressed at varying degrees in the premortal life, but their progress was not made known as they came into mortality. However, it was made known that they had been placed upon the earth based upon their premortal experience (see Deuteronomy 32:7–8; Acts 17:26; Alma 13:1–5; Abraham 3:22–23;

---

[43] Joseph Fielding Smith, *The Progress of Man* [1973], 10–11.

[44] James R. Clark *Messages of the First Presidency* [1970], 4:205.

TPJS, 365.) Nevertheless, they entered this life with a clean slate and were innocent in the eyes of God.

As children begin to experience mortality they become good or evil (see Moses 6:48–49, 55–56). Since it is natural to follow the ways of the world where they live, they fall by nature. Thus, fallen man is a natural man. The natural man is an enemy to God because he does not follow the Spirit and seek the fulness of the Father (see Mosiah 3:16, 19; 16:3–4). While Satan seeks to destroy the children, he is not the only cause of the loss of truth—light and truth are taken away because of the traditions of their fathers (see D&C 93:39).

D&C 93:40–50 • Bring up Your Children in Truth

40 But I have commanded you to bring up your children in light and truth.

41 But verily I say unto you, my servant Frederick G. Williams, you have continued under this condemnation;

42 You have not taught your children light and truth, according to the commandments; and that wicked one hath power, as yet, over you, and this is the cause of your affliction.

43 And now a commandment I give unto you—if you will be delivered you shall set in order your own house, for there are many things that are not right in your house.

44 Verily, I say unto my servant Sidney Rigdon, that in some things he hath not kept the commandments concerning his children; therefore, first set in order thy house.

45 Verily, I say unto my servant Joseph Smith, Jun., or in other words, I will call you friends, for you are my friends, and ye shall have an inheritance with me—

46 I called you servants for the world's sake, and ye are their servants for my sake—

47 And now, verily I say unto Joseph Smith, Jun.—You have not kept the commandments, and must needs stand rebuked before the Lord;

48 Your family must needs repent and forsake some things, and give more earnest heed unto your sayings, or be removed out of their place.

49 What I say unto one I say unto all; pray always lest that wicked one have power in you, and remove you out of your place.

50 My servant Newel K. Whitney also, a bishop of my church, hath need to be chastened, and set in order his family, and see that they are more diligent and concerned at home, and pray always, or they shall be removed out of their place.

A fourth requirement for obtaining the fulness of the Father, is to bring up your children in light and truth (v. 40). As the parents receive knowledge, they are to teach it, and then they will receive more knowledge. Thus, they will grow from grace to grace (D&C 93:20). Those who do not teach their children the truth will be hampered by the false traditions of their culture. The Lord likens these traditions to golden calves that we worship (see D&C 124:84), and He will also visit "the iniquity of the fathers upon the children unto the third and fourth generation of them that hate me" (Exodus 24:5). These visits, or punishments, come about naturally, as it takes three or four generations to correct them without the help of the gospel teachings.

The Lord chastised the leaders of the Church in 1833—the First Presidency and the bishop—because they were not teaching their children. These chastisements are self-explanatory, and will not be commented upon, except to note the high priority that the Lord places upon the raising of our children correctly. We must weigh the modern theories of child rearing very carefully against the teachings of the modern prophets and Apostles. However, it is observed that the Church leaders were still His friends and His servants (see D&C 93:41–51).

D&C 93:51–53 • Hasten to Translate and Obtain Knowledge

51 Now, I say unto you, my friends, let my servant Sidney Rigdon go on his journey, and make haste, and also proclaim the acceptable year of the Lord, and the gospel of salvation, as I shall give him utterance; and by your prayer of faith with one consent I will uphold him.

52 And let my servants Joseph Smith, Jun., and Frederick G. Williams make haste also, and it shall be given them even according to the prayer of faith; and inasmuch as you keep my sayings you shall not be confounded in this world, nor in the world to come.

53 And, verily I say unto you, that it is my will that you should hasten to translate my scriptures, and to obtain a knowledge of history, and of countries, and of kingdoms, of laws of God and man, and all this for the salvation of Zion. Amen.

The friends and servants of the Lord were given two other requirements that were necessary for them to receive the fulness of the Father.
The proclaiming of "the acceptable year of the Lord, and the gospel of
salvation," (v. 51) would bring about the fulfillment of Isaiah's prophecy
of the latter-days, and included many aspects of the gospel, and warning
of the day of vengeance (see Isaiah 61:1–2). Until the full gospel was
preached and practiced, and the day of vengeance came to destroy the
wicked, the year would not be acceptable to the Lord. The [Joseph Smith]
translation of the scriptures was also a high priority of the Lord. They
were told to "hasten to translate" and to fulfill other duties of the First
Presidency (D&C 93:53; compare D&C 90:13–15). As they had their
individual duties to fulfill, so does every member of His church if they
are to receive the fulness of the Father.

The Saints of the Church in May of 1833 had been given another
great revelation. The Lord had taught them truth from the premortal state,
concerning mortality, and about the life to come. They were given the
opportunity to receive revelation and knowledge of the mysteries and
peaceable things of God's kingdom. They could work further toward
receiving of His fulness.

General Authority Quotes

—President Lorenzo Snow • D&C 93:12–14

> When Jesus lay in the manger, a helpless infant, He knew not that
> he was the Son of God, and that formerly He created the earth. When
> the edict of Herod was issued, He knew nothing of it; He had not power
> to save Himself; and His father and mother had to take Him and fly into
> Egypt to preserve Him from the effects of that edict. Well He grew up
> to manhood, and during His progress it was revealed unto Him who
> He was, and for what purpose he was in the world. The glory and power
> He possessed before He came into the world was made known unto
> Him. . . .[CR, April 1901, 3]

—Elder Neal A. Maxwell • D&C 93:23–24

> For those who believe we are all going to be around forever, it is both
> natural and wise to concern ourselves with such questions and also with
> such principles which are also going to be around forever. The definition
> of truth given in 1833 [quotes D&C 93:24] is related to another

scripture [quotes Jacob 4:13 and included in our text]. Note the presence of the powerful adverb *really*. The gospel of Jesus Christ and The Church of Jesus Christ of Latter-day Saints deal plainly with realities—"things as they *really* are" and "things as they *really* will be." ["Eternalism vs. Secularism," *Ensign,* October 1974, 71]

—*The Prophet Joseph Smith* • D&C 93:24; 29–30

Happiness is the object and design of our existence; and will be the end thereof, if we pursue the path that leads to it; and this path is virtue, uprightness, faithfulness, holiness, and keeping all the commandments of God. But we cannot keep all the commandments without first knowing them, and we cannot know all, or more than we now know unless we comply with or keep those we have already received. That which is wrong under one circumstance, may be, and often is, right under another.

God said, "thou shalt not kill;" at another time He said, "Thou shalt utterly destroy." This is the principle on which the government of heaven is conducted—by revelation adapted to the circumstances in which the children of the kingdom are placed. Whatever God requires is right, no matter what it is, although we may not see the reason thereof till long after the events transpire. "If we seek first the kingdom of God, all good things will be added. [*TPJS,* 255–56]

The spirit of man is not a created being; it existed from eternity, and will exist into eternity. Anything created cannot be eternal; and earth, water, etc., had their existence in an elementary state, from eternity. [*TPJS,* 158]

—*President Spencer W. Kimball* • D&C 93:24, 29–30

There are absolute truths and relative truths. . . . Many scientific findings have changed from year to year. . . . There are many ideas advanced to the world that have been changed to meet the needs of the truth as it has been discovered. There are relative truths, and there are absolute truths which are the same yesterday, today, and forever—never changing. These absolute truths are not altered by the opinions of men. . . .

We learn about these absolute truths by being taught by the Spirit. These truths are "independent" in their spiritual sphere and are to be discovered spiritually, though they may be confirmed by experience and intellect (see D&C 93:30). . . .

If men are really humble, they will realize that they discover, but do not create, truth. . . . ["Absolute Truth," in *BYU 1977 Devotional Speeches Of The Year,* 137–138; also, *Ensign*, September 1978, 3–5]

Chapter Twelve

Zion Shall Be Great and Terrible

D&C 94–97

DOCTRINE AND COVENANTS 94

*H*istorical Setting: "May 6 [1833]—I [Joseph] received [Doctrine and Covenants 94]," is all that is written in the *History of the Church* (1:346). Section 93 was received earlier the same day. There is some evidence that section 97, which is dated August 2ⁿᵈ was received the same day.⁴⁵ Regardless, the message is still the same.

Introduction

The Prophet Joseph said: "The main object [of gathering the Jews] was to build unto the Lord a house whereby He could reveal unto His people the ordinances of His house and the glories of His kingdom, and teach the people the way of salvation; for there are certain ordinances and principles that, when they are taught and practiced must be done in a place or house built for that purpose" (*TPJS,* 308). We have seen several references to the temple in the previous revelations we have studied. On December 27–28, five months previous to this revelation, the Lord had commanded the Saints to build Him a house. The following revelations are the continuing saga of the temple being built.

TEXT AND COMMENTARY

---

⁴⁵ See Lyndon W. Cook, *The Revelations of the Prophet Joseph Smith* [1981], 195–97.

D&C 94:1–9 • A House for the Presidency

1 AND again, verily I say unto you, my friends, a commandment I give unto you, that ye shall commence a work of laying out and preparing a beginning and foundation of the city of the stake of Zion, here in the land of Kirtland, beginning at my house.

2 And behold, it must be done according to the pattern which I have given unto you.

3 And let the first lot on the south be consecrated unto me for the building of a house for the presidency, for the work of the presidency, in obtaining revelations; and for the work of the ministry of the presidency, in all things pertaining to the church and kingdom.

4 Verily I say unto you, that it shall be built fifty-five by sixty-five feet in the width thereof and in the length thereof, in the inner court.

5 And there shall be a lower court and a higher court, according to the pattern which shall be given unto you hereafter.

6 And it shall be dedicated unto the Lord from the foundation thereof, according to the order of the priesthood, according to the pattern which shall be given unto you hereafter.

7 And it shall be wholly dedicated unto the Lord for the work of the presidency.

8 And ye shall not suffer any unclean thing to come in unto it; and my glory shall be there, and my presence shall be there.

9 But if there shall come into it any unclean thing, my glory shall not be there; and my presence shall not come into it.

The foundation of the city of the stake of Zion was to begin with the Lord's house, according to the pattern given (vv. 1–2). Kirtland had been designated as a stake a year earlier, April 26, 1832, and the revelation had quoted Isaiah 54:2 and 52:1 as justification for the stake (D&C 82:13–14). A house for the presidency was also to be built, to receive revelations and for the work of the ministry (vv. 3–5). The house was to be dedicated to the Lord, and be kept clean so that the glory of the Lord would be there (vv. 6–9). This would be called a stake center today.

D&C 94:10–12 • A House for Printing

10 And again, verily I say unto you, the second lot on the south shall

be dedicated unto me for the building of a house unto me, for the work of the printing of the translation of my scriptures, and all things whatsoever I shall command you.

11 And it shall be fifty-five by sixty-five feet in the width thereof and the length thereof, in the inner court; and there shall be a lower and a higher court.

12 And this house shall be wholly dedicated unto the Lord from the foundation thereof, for the work of the printing, in all things whatsoever I shall command you, to be holy, undefiled, according to the pattern in all things as it shall be given unto you.

The importance of the Joseph Smith Translation to the Lord, and other materials to be printed, i.e., the Doctrine and Covenants, is again shown by His commandment to build a house for printing (v. 10). The Church has always been involved in printing in order to keep their members informed. Since the publications were scripturally oriented, they were to dedicate the building (v. 12).

D&C 94:13–17 • The Building Committee

13 And on the third lot shall my servant Hyrum Smith receive his inheritance.

14 And on the first and second lots on the north shall my servants Reynolds Cahoon and Jared Carter receive their inheritances—

15 That they may do the work which I have appointed unto them, to be a committee to build mine houses, according to the commandment, which I, the Lord God, have given unto you.

16 These two houses are not to be built until I give unto you a commandment concerning them.

17 And now I give unto you no more at this time. Amen.

Note that the building committee was to build houses (plural; v. 15). The pattern was set, and the building committee of the Church still exists. The hundreds of buildings each year illustrate the need of a building committee. A building is dedicated on an average of one a day (CR, October 2007).

DOCTRINE AND COVENANTS 95

*H*istorical Setting: "June 1—Great preparations were making to commence a house of the Lord; and notwithstanding the Church was poor, yet our unity, harmony, and charity abounded to strengthen us to do the commandments of God. The building of the house of the Lord in Kirtland was a matter that continued to increase in the hearts of the brethren, and the building committee issued the following circular to the different branches of the Church" (*HC*, 1:349).

"The same day [June 1ˢᵗ] I [Joseph] received [Doctrine and Covenants 95]" (*HC*, 1:350).

SECTION 95 • OUTLINE

➤ 95:1–7   The Lord chastens whom he loves that they be forgiven of their sins, and the Saints need to be rebuked.

   a. Ye have sinned in not building my house (v. 3).

   b. My Apostles must be prepared to prune the vineyard for the last time (v. 4).

   c. Many of you have been called, but few are chosen (v. 5).

   d. They sin grievously by walking in darkness at noonday (v. 6).

   e. For this cause I commanded you that your prayers would come to the Lord of Sabaoth, the creator of the first day (v. 7).

➤ 95:8–12 I commanded you to build a house in which I design to endow you with power from on high.

   a. I command you to tarry even as my Apostles in Jerusalem (v. 9).

   b. Contentions arose in the School of the Prophets, a grievous sin (v. 10).

   c. If you keep my commandments, you shall have power to build it (v. 11).

   d. If you don't keep them, you shall dwell in darkness (v. 12).

➤ 95:13–17 The wisdom of the Lord is to not build it after the manner of the world, but after the manner shown to the three appointed to this power.

a.   The lower part is for sacraments, prayers, and praying (v. 16).

b.   The higher part is for the School of the Apostles (v. 17).

TEXT AND COMMENTARY

D&C 95:1–7 • Whom I Love I Also Chasten

1 Verily, thus saith the Lord unto you whom I love, and whom I love I also chasten that their sins may be forgiven, for with the chastisement I prepare a way for their deliverance in all things out of temptation, and I have loved you—

2 Wherefore, ye must needs be chastened and stand rebuked before my face;

3 For ye have sinned against me a very grievous sin, in that ye have not considered the great commandment in all things, that I have given unto you concerning the building of mine house;

4 For the preparation wherewith I design to prepare mine apostles to prune my vineyard for the last time, that I may bring to pass my strange act, that I may pour out my Spirit upon all flesh—

5 But behold, verily I say unto you, that there are many who have been ordained among you, whom I have called but few of them are chosen.

6 They who are not chosen have sinned a very grievous sin, in that they are walking in darkness at noon-day.

7 And for this cause I gave unto you a commandment that you should call your solemn assembly, that your fastings and your mourning might come up into the ears of the Lord of Sabaoth, which is by interpretation, the creator of the first day, the beginning and the end.

The Lord's not having revealed a more specific purpose for the temple before was perhaps one of the reasons why many of the leadership of the Church were slow in beginning to construct the temple. The delay in starting to build the temple caused them to be severely chastised by the Lord, as stated above, five months after the original commandment had been given to build it. He chastened them because He loved them, and "that their sins may be forgiven, for with the chastisement I prepare a way for their deliverance in all things out of temptation" (vv. 1–2). Paul gave a similar reason for why the Lord chastens His people to the Hebrews, and it is also taught in the Old Testament (see Hebrews 12:5–8; Proverbs 13:24; 24:13–14).

As a part of the chastisement, the Lord specifies three specific purposes of the temple. The first purpose was to prepare His Apostles to prune His vineyard for the last time (v. 4) Though Joseph Smith and Oliver Cowdery had been called as Apostles (see D&C 20:2–3), the Quorum of the Twelve Apostles was not called and ordained until February 14, 1835 (see *HC,* 2:186–87; D&C 18:37–38). It seems apparent that the Apostles' pruning of the vineyard would refer to the First Presidency and the Quorum of the Twelve. Pruning the vineyard refers us to the allegory of the tame and wild olive trees originally given by the Old Testament prophet, Zenos. Although the writings of Zenos were a part of the plain and precious parts lost from the Bible (see 1 Nephi 13:24–29), his allegory is restored to us through the Book of Mormon prophet Jacob, brother of Nephi (Jacob chapter 5). In the allegory, the final act of pruning was to graft back the branches of Israel into the mother trunk, thus enabling the natural tree to again produce natural fruit unto the Lord (see Jacob 5:67–73).

As foretold by the Old Testament prophet Amos, the Lord promised that He would "not utterly destroy the house of Israel," but He "would sift [scatter] the house of Israel among all nations, like as corn is sifted in a sieve, yet shall not the least grain fall upon the earth" (Amos 9:8–9). In President Spencer W. Kimball's message in the December 1975 *Ensign* magazine, he quoted this prophecy and added at the end "and be lost." The grafting back of Israel began with the gathering of those who had been scattered back into the fold of the restored Church. The prophet Isaiah's admonition to "put on thy strength O Zion" (Isaiah 52:1) "had reference to those whom God should call in the last days, who should hold the power of priesthood to bring again Zion, and the redemption of Israel; and to put on her strength is to put on the authority of the priesthood, which she, Zion, has a right to by lineage, also to return to that power which she had lost" (D&C 113:7–8).

The strange act of pouring out His Spirit (v. 4) is a quote from Isaiah 28:21, which refers to His giving revelation to His servants. The receiving of revelation was certainly not a common practice to the world, and therefore strange to them. Of course, the whole Restoration of the gospel, and pouring the Spirit out on all flesh, was considered strange to the Christian world who believed that revelation ceased with the New Testament, even though it had been prophesied by the prophet Joel (see Joel 2:28–32). While the world may feel that Joel's prophecy was fulfilled in the day of Pentecost (see Acts 2:17), it was a dual prophecy, applying to both time periods—a common feature of the prophets—or else Peter was saying that what happened on that day was like unto what Joel said. We know that it was intended for Joseph Smith's day because the Angel Moroni quoted it to him saying, "this was not yet fulfilled, but was soon to be" (JS—H 1:41).

Many are called, but few are chosen (v. 5) is also a New Testament phrase (see Matthew 20:16; 22:14), and used several times in the Doctrine and Covenants. Their walking in darkness was because they were not receiving the light of revelation, and "at noon-day" was saying it was in a time period when revelation was most accessible to them—it was available to all flesh as stated above, and foretold by Joel. Through the building of the temple, it would be even more available as their prayers were answered by the Lord of Sabaoth (v. 7), or the Lord of Hosts (see the Bible Dictionary, 764).

D&C 95:8–12 • Endow the Chosen with Power

8 Yea, verily I say unto you, I gave unto you a commandment that you should build a house, in the which house I design to endow those whom I have chosen with power from on high;

9 For this is the promise of the Father unto you; therefore I command you to tarry, even as mine apostles at Jerusalem.

10 Nevertheless, my servants sinned a very grievous sin; and contentions arose in the school of the prophets; which was very grievous unto me, saith your Lord; therefore I sent them forth to be chastened.

11 Verily I say unto you, it is my will that you should build a house. If you keep my commandments you shall have power to build it.

12 If you keep not my commandments, the love of the Father shall not continue with you, therefore you shall walk in darkness.

The promise to be endowed with power was one of the purposes for coming to Kirtland from New York (see D&C 38:32). As the New Testament Apostles had been instructed to tarry in Jerusalem until "ye be endowed with power from on high" (Luke 24:49), the Saints were to tarry in Kirtland until they achieved the blessings of the temple (v. 9). Many were desirous to move to Missouri. The contentions in the School of the Prophets were caused by the "devil, who is the father of contention, and he stirreth up the hearts of men to contend with anger, one with another" (3 Nephi 11:29). The Kirtland leaders were heavily in debt, yet trying to raise the money for the temple. The Lord gives them a conditional promise—keep the commandments and they would have [be given] the power to build it, if not they shall remain in darkness, receiving no revelation (vv. 11–12).

D&C 95:13–17 • Not after the Manner of the World

13 Now here is wisdom, and the mind of the Lord—let the house be built, not after the manner of the world, for I give not unto you that ye shall live after the manner of the world;

14 Therefore, let it be built after the manner which I shall show unto three of you, whom ye shall appoint and ordain unto this power.

15 And the size thereof shall be fifty and five feet in width, and let it be sixty-five feet in length, in the inner court thereof.

16 And let the lower part of the inner court be dedicated unto me for your sacrament offering, and for your preaching, and your fasting, and your praying, and the offering up of your most holy desires unto me, saith your Lord.

17 And let the higher part of the inner court be dedicated unto me for the school of mine apostles, saith Son Ahman; or, in other words, Alphus; or, in other words, Omegus; even Jesus Christ your Lord. Amen.

Had the contention (v. 10) been over the way to build the temple? These verses seem to indicate this. The Lord gives His building committee a vote of confidence. These verses are self-explanatory. The purposes of the lower and higher parts of the temple are seen in the beautiful temple that is still standing.

According to Elder Orson Pratt, a revelation that was not included in the Doctrine and Covenants was given in a question and answer period. The first question was, "What is the name of God in the pure language?"

the answer was "Ahman" who is the Son of God.[46] This revelation (v. 17) supports the unpublished revelation. The three members of the Godhead were also defined in another question and answer period: "The Father has a body of flesh and bones as tangible as man's; the Son also; but the Holy Ghost has not a body of flesh and bones, but is a personage of Spirit. Were it not so, the Holy Ghost could not dwell in us. A man may receive the Holy Ghost, and it may descend upon him and not tarry with him" (D&C 130:22–23). The word Elohim—usually the name we use for the Father—is a plural masculine name, which was apparently translated as "the Gods" in the book of Abraham (see Abraham 4 and 5). The first article of faith declares our belief in three separate beings as the Godhead.

DOCTRINE AND COVENANTS 96

Historical Setting: "June 4 [1833]—A similar conference assembled . . . and took into consideration how the French farm should be disposed of. The conference could not agree who should take charge of it, but all agreed to inquire of the Lord; accordingly we received [Doctrine and Covenants 96]" (*HC,* 1:352).

D&C 96:1–9 • A Descendant of Joseph

1 Behold, I say unto you, here is wisdom, whereby ye may know how to act concerning this matter, for it is expedient in me that this stake that I have set for the strength of Zion should be made strong.

2 Therefore, let my servant Newel K. Whitney take charge of the place which is named among you, upon which I design to build mine holy house.

3 And again, let it be divided into lots, according to wisdom, for the benefit of those who seek inheritances, as it shall be determined in council among you.

4 Therefore, take heed that ye see to this matter, and that portion that is necessary to benefit mine order, for the purpose of bringing forth my word to the children of men.

5 For behold, verily I say unto you, this is the most expedient in me, that my word should go forth unto the children of men, for the purpose

---

[46] *Journal of Discourses,* 2:342.

of subduing the hearts of the children of men for your good. Even so. Amen.

6 And again, verily I say unto you, it is wisdom and expedient in me, that my servant John Johnson whose offering I have accepted, and whose prayers I have heard, unto whom I give a promise of eternal life inasmuch as he keepeth my commandments from henceforth—

7 For he is a descendant of Joseph and a partaker of the blessings of the promise made unto his fathers—

8 Verily I say unto you, it is expedient in me that he should become a member of the order, that he may assist in bringing forth my word unto the children of men.

9 Therefore ye shall ordain him unto this blessing, and he shall seek diligently to take away incumbrances that are upon the house named among you, that he may dwell therein. Even so. Amen.

The purpose of the pruning of the vineyard was enlarged upon. Newel K. Whitney was called to take charge of the French farm being divided into lots (vv. 1–5). This farm included the place where the Kirtland Temple was to be built. John Johnson was called "to assist in bringing forth my word unto the children of men" (v. 8). The Lord identified him as "a descendant of Joseph and a partaker of the blessings of the promise made unto his fathers" (D&C 96:7). The fathers of Joseph [who was sold into Egypt] were Abraham, Isaac, and Jacob. Jacob is the father of the twelve tribes of Israel.[47]

DOCTRINE AND COVENANTS 97

H istorical Setting: On the same day (July 23rd), while the brethren in Missouri were preparing to leave the county, through the violence of the mob, the corner stones of the Lord's house were laid in Kirtland, after the order of the holy priesthood.

---

[47] There are twenty-six different revelations in the Doctrine and Covenants that declare those being gathered were literal descendants of Israel. See Monte S. Nyman, "The Second Gathering of the Literal Seed" chapter 14, in *Doctrines for Exaltation, 1989 Sperry Symposium* [1989].

"August 2 [1833], I received [Doctrine and Covenants 97]." (*HC,* 1:400)

SECTION 97 • OUTLINE

➤ 97:1–9   The voice of my Spirit will show you my will concerning your brethren in Zion.

 a. I will show mercy to the meek and others to justify the day of judgment (v. 2).

 b. I am pleased with the school in Zion and with Parley P. Pratt (v. 3).

 c. He shall continue to preside over the school until I give commandment (v. 4).

 d. I will bless him in expounding the scriptures, mysteries and edification (v. 5).

 e. I will be merciful to the residue of the school, some must be chastened (v. 6).

 f. Every tree that bears not good fruit shall be hewn down and burned (v. 7).

 g. Those whose hearts are honest, broken, and will sacrifice are accepted (v. 8).

 h. The Lord will cause the accepted to bring forth a tree that bears fruit (v. 9).

➤ 97:10–17 The Lord desires to build a house in Zion like the pattern that has been given.

 a. It should be built by tithing and sacrifice, for the salvation of Zion (vv. 11–12).

 b. It is a place of thanksgiving for all Saints, instruction for those called to the ministry; they may be perfected in theory, principle, and doctrine (vv. 13–14).

 c. If it is not defiled, my glory shall rest upon it, and I will come unto it, and the pure in heart shall see God, but I will not come into unholy temples (vv. 15–17).

➤ 97:18–24 If Zion do these things, she shall become very great and very terrible.

 a. The nations shall honor her and say, Zion is the city of God, and cannot fail nor be moved, and by His power is her salvation and high tower (vv. 19–20).

b. Let Zion rejoice for she is the pure in heart, and the wicked shall mourn (v. 21).

c. Vengeance shall come upon the ungodly, and who shall escape (v. 22)?

d. His scourge shall be night and day, and not stayed until He comes (vv. 23–24).

➤ 97:25–28   Zion shall escape if she does as commanded, but if not I will visit her according to her works.

a. Nevertheless, the Lord has accepted her offerings, and if she sin no more, none of these things shall come upon her (v. 27).

b. I will bless her with a multiplicity of blessings for generations forever (v. 28).

TEXT AND COMMENTARY

D&C 97:1–9 • Zion Must Become a Fruitful Tree

1 VERILY I say unto you my friends, I speak unto you with my voice, even the voice of my Spirit, that I may show unto you my will concerning your brethren in the land of Zion, many of whom are truly humble and are seeking diligently to learn wisdom and to find truth.

2 Verily, verily I say unto you, blessed are such, for they shall obtain; for I, the Lord, show mercy unto all the meek, and upon all whomsoever I will, that I may be justified when I shall bring them unto judgment.

3 Behold, I say unto you, concerning the school in Zion, I, the Lord, am well pleased that there should be a school in Zion, and also with my servant Parley P. Pratt, for he abideth in me.

4 And inasmuch as he continueth to abide in me he shall continue to preside over the school in the land of Zion until I shall give unto him other commandments.

5 And I will bless him with a multiplicity of blessings, in expounding all scriptures and mysteries to the edification of the school, and of the church in Zion.

6 And to the residue of the school, I, the Lord, am willing to show mercy; nevertheless, there are those that must needs be chastened, and their works shall be made known.

7 The ax is laid at the root of the trees; and every tree that bringeth not forth good fruit shall be hewn down and cast into the fire. I, the Lord, have spoken it.

8 Verily I say unto you, all among them who know their hearts are honest, and are broken, and their spirits contrite, and are willing to observe their covenants by sacrifice—yea, every sacrifice which I, the Lord, shall command—they are accepted of me.

9 For I, the Lord, will cause them to bring forth as a very fruitful tree which is planted in a goodly land, by a pure stream, that yieldeth much precious fruit.

Two months later, the Lord gave another revelation on the purpose and blessings of the building of the temple. The Lord praised many of the brethren in Zion for their being "truly humble and are seeking diligently to learn wisdom and to find truth," promising blessings and "mercy unto all the meek, and upon all whomsoever I will, that I may be justified when I shall bring them unto judgment" (D&C 97:2–3). He was pleased with Parley P. Pratt, in particular, for his work in the school in Zion (vv. 4–5). He again chastised some of "the residue of the school," using the imagery of the tree that "bringeth not forth good fruit" being cut down and burned (Matthew 3:10). To those with whom He was pleased, He paraphrased Psalm 1:3 as He promised they would be "as a very fruitful tree which is planted in a goodly land, by a pure stream, that yieldeth much precious fruit" (D&C 97:7–9). This imagery confirms the interpretation given above of D&C 95:4 that the pruning of the vineyard had reference to the allegory of the house of Israel given by the prophet Zenos.

D&C 97:10–17 • The Pure in Heart Shall See God

10 Verily I say unto you, that it is my will that a house should be built unto me in the land of Zion, like unto the pattern which I have given you.

11 Yea, let it be built speedily, by the tithing of my people.

12 Behold, this is the tithing and the sacrifice which I, the Lord, require at their hands, that there may be a house built unto me for the salvation of Zion—

13 For a place of thanksgiving for all saints, and for a place of

instruction for all those who are called to the work of the ministry in all their several callings and offices;

14 That they may be perfected in the understanding of their ministry, in theory, in principle, and in doctrine, in all things pertaining to the kingdom of God on the earth, the keys of which kingdom have been conferred upon you.

15 And inasmuch as my people build a house unto me in the name of the Lord, and do not suffer any unclean thing to come into it, that it be not defiled, my glory shall rest upon it;

16 Yea, and my presence shall be there, for I will come into it, and all the pure in heart that shall come into it shall see God.

17 But if it be defiled I will not come into it, and my glory shall not be there; for I will not come into unholy temples.

The subject of the temple was again approached by the Lord. He reminded them "that it was my will that a house should be built unto me in the land of Zion, like unto the pattern which I have given you" (v. 10). Enlarging upon the principle of sacrifice, mentioned above in being a fruitful tree (vv. 8–9), he gives the source of financing for the building of the temple: "Let it be built speedily by the tithing of my people . . . the sacrifice which I, the Lord, require at their hands" (vv. 11–12). While this formula for building temples was and is still used, to the early Saints it was a tithing of their labor and time as well as what monetary sacrifice they could make. The women also sacrificed by making clothes for the workers, and also materials for the beautifying and enhancing the appearance of the temple.

With every sacrifice made unto the Lord there is a blessing that follows. In this case, it was an eternal blessing, "the salvation of Zion" (v. 12). Again the Lord gave some more specific blessings. A place of thanksgiving for all Saints (v. 13) is a part of the original commandment to build a temple, to establish a house of prayer. A place of instruction for all those who are called to the work of the ministry, in all things pertaining to the kingdom of God (v. 13) is also a part of the original commandment to build a temple, to establish a house of learning. A place where "they may be perfected in the understanding of their ministry, in theory, in principle, and in doctrine, in all things pertaining to the kingdom of God" (v. 14) is part of the original commandment to establish a house of order (D&C 88:119). The temple being a house of glory, as defined in the original commandment (D&C 88:119), was conditional upon the Saints not suffering [allowing] "any unclean thing to come into it, that it may not be defiled, [and] my glory shall rest upon it" (D&C 97:15). The individual salvation of the Saints was also promised by the Lord: "I will come into it, and all the pure in heart that shall come into it shall see God" (D&C 97:16; see also D&C 93:1). Salvation will therein be assured.

Without the Melchizedek Priesthood "no man can see the face of God, even the Father, and live" (D&C 84:19–22). Therefore, this promise was also conditional, "if it be defiled I will not come into it, and my glory shall not be there; for I will not come into unholy temples" (see D&C 97:17).

D&C 97:18–24 • Zion Is the Pure in Heart

18 And, now, behold, if Zion do these things she shall prosper, and spread herself and become very glorious, very great, and very terrible.

19 And the nations of the earth shall honor her, and shall say: Surely Zion is the city of our God, and surely Zion cannot fall, neither be moved out of her place, for God is there, and the hand of the Lord is there;

20 And he hath sworn by the power of his might to be her salvation and her high tower.

21 Therefore, verily, thus saith the Lord, let Zion rejoice, for this is Zion—THE PURE IN HEART; therefore, let Zion rejoice, while all the wicked shall mourn.

22 For behold, and lo, vengeance cometh speedily upon the ungodly as the whirlwind; and who shall escape it?

23 The Lord's scourge shall pass over by night and by day, and the report thereof shall vex all people; yea, it shall not be stayed until the Lord come;

24 For the indignation of the Lord is kindled against their abominations and all their wicked works.

These verses were a collective promise given to the Saints of Zion. The feminine pronoun is used for "mercy" because it is an attribute of women in general. It is possibly used to designate Zion (v. 18) for the following reasons. Zion is to be prepared for the Second Coming of

Christ. The Church is the bride and Christ is the Bridegroom in the marriage of the Lamb (Revelation 19:7–8; see also JST, Revelation 12:7). Apparently, Zion, as the center of the Church, is as women adorned for the Bridegroom. She was to become both great and terrible (v. 18). She would be great in the eyes of her people and the nations of the earth (vv. 19–20), but terrible to those who opposed her. The prophet Isaiah foretold of the nations of the world acknowledging Zion as the city of our God.

> 1 ARISE, shine [Zion, see Latter-day Saint Bible footnote]; for thy light is come, and the glory of the Lord is risen upon thee.
>
> 2 For, behold, the darkness shall cover the earth, and gross darkness the people: but the Lord shall arise upon thee, and his glory shall be seen upon thee.
>
> 3 And the Gentiles shall come to thy light, and kings to the brightness of thy rising. [Isaiah 60:1–3, see the entire chapter]

Therefore, Zion shall be built by the faithful Saints: "For this is Zion—THE PURE IN HEART; therefore, let Zion rejoice [for her greatness], while all the wicked shall mourn [for she is terrible]" (D&C 97:21).

The definition of Zion being "THE PURE IN HEART" should not be misunderstood. While whoever becomes pure in heart would have individual eternal salvation, the context of the blessing or promise is to those who are gathered to the city of our God, the New Jerusalem in Independence, Missouri (see D&C 84:4–5; 3 Nephi 21:22–23; Moses 7:62). The same blessing will also come upon other stakes of Zion, especially upon those where temples are built—the glory of the Lord will rest upon "every dwelling of mount Zion, and upon her assemblies, a cloud and smoke by day, and the shining of a flaming fire by night" (Isaiah 4:5–6; 2 Nephi 14:5–6). The righteous and the wicked will thus be separated, and the Saints will be protected (see D&C 115:5–6).

However, vengeance "shall not be stayed until the Lord come; for the indignation of the Lord is kindled against their abominations and all their wicked works" (D&C 97:22–24). The Lord's scourge will be similar to that which came upon Jerusalem in ancient days, but will come again. The Prophet Joseph Smith said: "The servants of God will not have gone over the nations of the Gentiles, with a warning voice, until the destroying angel will commence to waste the inhabitants of the earth, and as the prophet hath said, 'It shall be a vexation to hear the report' (*TPJS*, 87; quoting Isaiah 28:19).

D&C 97:25–28 • Zion Shall Escape If?

25 Nevertheless, Zion shall escape if she observe to do all things whatsoever I have commanded her.

26 But if she observe not to do whatsoever I have commanded her, I will visit her according to all her works, with sore affliction, with pestilence, with plague, with sword, with vengeance, with devouring fire.

27 Nevertheless, let it be read this once to her ears, that I, the Lord, have accepted of her offering; and if she sin no more none of these things shall come upon her;

28 And I will bless her with blessings, and multiply a multiplicity of blessings upon her, and upon her generations forever and ever, saith the Lord your God. Amen.

While Zion shall collectively escape (v. 25), as also shown from other scriptures, those who do not observe the Lord's commandments will be visited "according to all her works, with sore affliction, with pestilence, with plague, with sword, with vengeance, with devouring fire" (v. 26). The Lord then gives what is apparently a final warning to those who were collectively gathered, but who were not keeping the commandment to build the temple, "I the Lord have accepted of her offering; and if she sin no more none of these things shall come upon her" (v. 27). Those who were faithful would be blessed with "a multiplicity of blessings upon her, and upon her generations forever and ever" (v. 28). Therefore, "surely Zion cannot fall, neither be moved out of her place, for God is there, and the hand of the Lord is there" (v. 19). Zion must first be built, and the stakes surrounding her, that are well under way. The question we must answer is, are we doing our part to become pure in heart, and willing to fill the callings and offices we are given?

General Authority Quotes
—President Harold B. Lee • D&C 97:15; 94:8–9; 97:15, 21

Obedient to that instruction [97:15], these holy temples are carefully safeguarded, not because of the necessity of secrecy but because of the sacredness of the work performed therein, by forbidding those who by the Lord's standards may be considered "unclean" in that they do not keep his commandments. [*The Teachings of Harold B. Lee*, 579–80]

[After quoting D&C 94:8–9] Temple recommends should mean something. A nonmember sister wrote to me saying that she had a very dear friend who would soon be married in the temple. She asked if it wouldn't be possible to witness this wedding. I'm sure you know my response to her. . . .

Another young girl came to me upset that her intended husband could not receive a temple recommend from his bishop. She raved on, "Why can't my future husband receive a recommend?" I answered, "Dear sister, don't you see what a protection this is? Perhaps the bishop and stake president are aware of circumstances that you know nothing of, or that he can't tell you. This young man must measure up to these standards before he can enter the Lord's house."

Sometimes bishops and stake presidents lower their standards. How serious it is to let someone come into the temple unworthily! It would be more of a condemnation than a blessing. [*The Teachings of Harold B. Lee*, 580]

Now what do we mean when we use the word Zion? In some biblical references, and in modern scripture, Zion is referred to as a place—a city. In other places it is referred to as a continent; but in another sense, the Lord has spoken of Zion in these words: (quotes 97:21). In other words, he is saying again what the Master said: "The kingdom of God is within you." Here within the righteous heart of every member of the Church might be the seed-corn of the growth of the Church. The pure in heart is the beginning of the growth of Zion. [*The Teachings of Harold B. Lee*, 409]

—Elder Parley P. Pratt • D&C 97

In the latter part of summer and in the Autumn, I devoted almost my entire time in ministering among the churches; holding meetings; visiting the sick; comforting the afflicted, and giving counsel. A school of the Elders was also organized, over which I was called to preside. This class, to the number of about sixty, met for instruction once a week. The place of meeting was in the open air, under some tall trees, in a retired place in the wilderness, where we prayed, preached and prophesied, and exercised ourselves in the gifts of the Holy Spirit. Here great blessings were poured out, and many great and marvelous things were manifested and taught. The Lord gave me great wisdom and enabled me to teach

and edify the Elders, and comfort and encourage them in their preparations for the great work which lay before us. I was also edified and
strengthened. To attend the school I had to travel on foot, and sometimes
with bare feet at that, about six miles. This I did once a week, besides
visiting and preaching in five or six branches a week. (Elder Pratt then
quotes the entire 97th section.)

This revelation was not complied with by the leaders and Church
in Missouri as a whole; notwithstanding many were humble and faithful.
Therefore, the threatened judgment was poured out to the uttermost,
as the history of the following five years will show. (He then recounts
many of those events). [*Autobiography of Parley P. Pratt*, ed. his son Parley
P. Pratt (1970), 93–96]

—President Howard W. Hunter • D&C 97:15–18

The Lord desires that his people be a temple–motivated people. It
would be the deepest desire of my heart to have every member of the
Church be temple worthy. I would hope that every adult member would
be worthy of—and carry—a current temple recommend, even if
proximity to a temple does not allow immediate or frequent use of it.

Let us be a temple-attending and a temple loving people. Let us
hasten to the temple as frequently as time and means and personal
circumstances allow. Let us go not only for our kindred dead, but let
us go also for the personal blessing of temple worship, for the sanctity
and safety which is provided within those hallowed walls and consecrated
walls. The temple is a place of beauty, it is a place of revelation, it is a
place of peace. It is the house of the Lord. It should be holy unto us. [*The
Teachings of Howard W. Hunter*, 239]

—President Joseph Fielding Smith • D&C 97:25–26

This way of escape, insuring the protection of the Lord, is a very
simple one [do as commanded]. Unfortunately, many of the people of
Zion have refused to take advantage of this promise. [*Doctrines of
Salvation*, 3:32]

Chapter Thirteen

Concerning the Laws of the Land

D&C 98; 99; 134

DOCTRINE AND COVENANTS 98

*H*istorical Setting: "August 6th [1833],—I [Joseph] received [Doctrine and Covenants 98]" (*HC*, 1:403). As stated in the section heading, "This revelation came in consequence of the persecution upon the Saints in Missouri." On July 20, 1833, a mob came into Independence, Missouri and demanded that the members of the Church prepare to leave Jackson County. In response to the Saints' request for time to consider the demand, the mob granted them fifteen minutes. Destruction, beatings, and tarring and feathering of some of the leaders followed. Seventeen days later, Joseph received the above referenced revelation. As also stated in the section heading, due to the nine hundred miles separating Kirtland and Independence, "the seriousness of the situation (in Missouri) could have been known to [Joseph Smith] in Kirtland at this date only by revelation." The first part of the revelation (vv. 1–18) gave counsel to the friends of the Lord (Church members) in Missouri. The remainder of the revelation (vv. 19–49) addresses the Church at Kirtland.

SECTION 98 • OUTLINE

➤ 98:1–3   The Lord comforts His friends in Zion.

      a.   Their prayers have been heard, and shall be granted (v. 2).

      b.   Their afflictions shall work together for their good (v. 3).

➤ 98:4–18   The constitutional law of the land belongs to all mankind and is justifiable.

    a. Befriend the constitution, more or less than this is of evil (vv. 6–7).

    b. The law makes you free; when the wicked rule, the people mourn (vv. 8–9).

    c. Honest, good, and wise men should be sought and upheld, or evil comes (v. 10).

    d. You shall live by every word from God, line upon line to prove you (vv. 11–12).

    e. Those who lay down their lives in His cause shall have eternal life (vv. 13–15).

    f. Renounce war, proclaim peace, turn the hearts of the children to their fathers and the fathers to the children (v. 16).

    g. Turn the hearts of the Jews to the prophets, and the prophets to the Jews (v. 17).

    h. In my Father's house are many mansions prepared for you (v. 18).

➤ 98:19–22   The Lord is not pleased with many of the Church in Kirtland.

    a. He will chasten them if they do not repent (vv. 20–21).

    b. Keep my commandments, the gates of hell will not prevail against them (v. 22).

➤ 98:23–32   The law of retaliation concerning your families.

    a. Bear your afflictions three times and you will be rewarded (vv. 23–25).

    b. Three testimonies shall stand as a testimony against your enemies (vv. 26–31).

    c. The Lord gave this law to Nephi, and the biblical prophets and Apostles (v. 32).

➤ 98:33–38   The law of war given to the ancients: Do not go to war until I command.

    a. First lift the standard of peace unto them three times (vv. 34–35).

    b.   Bring the three testimonies, and the Lord, will fight their battles (vv. 36–37).

    c.   This is an ensample unto all people, and is justified before the Lord (v. 38).

➤ 98:39–48   The law of forgiveness: If your enemy repents, forgive him seventy times seven.

    a.   If he repents not three times, still forgive him (v. 41).

    b.   Do not forgive the fourth time, but bring the testimonies before the Lord and he will not be forgiven until he reward thee four-fold (vv. 44–45).

    c.   If he does not, the Lord will avenge thee an hundred-fold, and his children that hate me unto the third and fourth generation (vv. 45–46).

    d.   If children, or the children's children, turn to the Lord, forgive them (vv. 47–48).

Introduction

"We believe in being subject to kings, presidents, rulers, and magistrates, in obeying, honoring, and sustaining the law" (A of F 1:12). How does D&C 98 apply to this article of faith? In light of the persecution of the Saints in Missouri, was it still to be followed? The Lord answers this question and other related questions in this revelation.

TEXT AND COMMENTARY

D&C 98:1–3 • Afflictions Shall Work for Your Good

1 VERILY I say unto you my friends, fear not, let your hearts be comforted; yea, rejoice evermore, and in everything give thanks;

2 Waiting patiently on the Lord, for your prayers have entered into the ears of the Lord of Sabaoth, and are recorded with this seal and testament—the Lord hath sworn and decreed that they shall be granted.

3 Therefore, he giveth this promise unto you, with an immutable covenant that they shall be fulfilled; and all things wherewith you have been afflicted shall work together for your good, and to my name's glory, saith the Lord.

The Lord consoles his Missouri friends by telling them not to fear and to wait patiently on the Lord, for He has heard their prayers and promises a fulfillment of their requests (vv. 1–3). He concludes his words of comfort by reminding them that their recent afflictions "shall work together for your good, and to my names glory, saith the Lord." The same principle had been taught by the Apostle Paul to the Roman Saints (see Romans 8:15). Joseph and Sidney were also comforted similarly by the Lord about two months later (see D&C 100:15; October 12, 1833).

Some may question why the Lord allows His Saints to suffer or why He doesn't react quicker against the wicked. While there are several similar situations in the scriptures, the letter of General Moroni to the governor, Pahoran, gives us a clear and succinct answer:

> Do ye suppose that, because so many of your brethren have been killed it is because of their wickedness? I say unto you, if ye have supposed this ye have supposed in vain; for I say unto you, there are many who have fallen by the sword; and behold it is to your condemnation;
>
> For the Lord suffereth the righteous to be slain that his justice and judgment may come upon the wicked; therefore ye need not suppose that the righteous are lost because they are slain; but behold, they do enter into the rest of the Lord their God. [Alma 60:12–13]

Although none of the Saints in Missouri had been slain, justice and judgment will follow and those persecuted will be blessed for their faith and patience.

D&C 98:4–18 • The Laws of the Land

> 4 And now, verily I say unto you concerning the laws of the land, it is my will that my people should observe to do all things whatsoever I command them.
>
> 5 And that law of the land which is constitutional, supporting that principle of freedom in maintaining rights and privileges, belongs to all mankind, and is justifiable before me.
>
> 6 Therefore, I, the Lord, justify you, and your brethren of my church, in befriending that law which is the constitutional law of the land;
>
> 7 And as pertaining to law of man, whatsoever is more or less than this, cometh of evil.

8 I, the Lord God, make you free, therefore ye are free indeed; and the law also maketh you free.

9 Nevertheless, when the wicked rule the people mourn.

10 Wherefore, honest men and wise men should be sought for diligently, and good men and wise men ye should observe to uphold; otherwise whatsoever is less than these cometh of evil.

11 And I give unto you a commandment, that ye shall forsake all evil and cleave unto all good, that ye shall live by every word which proceedeth forth out of the mouth of God.

12 For he will give unto the faithful line upon line, precept upon precept; and I will try you and prove you herewith.

13 And whoso layeth down his life in my cause, for my name's sake, shall find it again, even life eternal.

14 Therefore, be not afraid of your enemies, for I have decreed in my heart, saith the Lord, that I will prove you in all things, whether you will abide in my covenant, even unto death, that you may be found worthy.

15 For if ye will not abide in my covenant ye are not worthy of me.

16 Therefore, renounce war and proclaim peace, and seek diligently to turn the hearts of the children to their fathers, and the hearts of the fathers to the children;

17 And again, the hearts of the Jews unto the prophets, and the prophets unto the Jews; lest I come and smite the whole earth with a curse, and all flesh be consumed before me.

18 Let not your hearts be troubled; for in my Father's house are many mansions, and I have prepared a place for you; and where my Father and I am, there ye shall be also.

The Lord desires His people to observe the laws of the land, especially this land of the United States of America (see D&C 58:19–22). The United States Constitution supports freedom and maintains rights and privileges for all. The Lord says it "belongs to all mankind, and is justifiable before [Him]" (vv. 4–5).

President George Albert Smith, as he dedicated the Idaho Falls Temple, prayed that all nations under heaven would adopt that constitutional system of government, that the prophecy of Isaiah and Micah might be fulfilled; that "out of Zion would go forth the law" (Isaiah 2:3; Micah

4:2).[48] The Savior taught the Nephites that the Gentiles "should be established in this land, and be set up as a free people by the power of the Father, that [the Book of Mormon] might come forth . . . that the covenant of the Father may be fulfilled which he hath covenanted with his people, O house of Israel" (3 Nephi 21:4). The Prophet Joseph Smith equated the law out of Zion with the purposes of God being accomplished where "the Lord shall be king over the whole earth" (*TPJS*, 252). He called the Constitution "a glorious standard; it is founded in the wisdom of God. It is a heavenly banner" (*TPJS*, 147). He called himself "the greatest advocate of the Constitution of the United States there is on the earth" and he praised its purposes (*TPJS*, 326–27; 278–79). The Lord endorsed it for the Missouri Saints: "in befriending that law which is the constitutional law of the land" (D&C 98:6). To befriend the Constitution is to support it and sustain it. While it is the law of the land, it is also, in essence, a law of God. Four months after this revelation was given, December 16, 1833, the Lord gave another revelation to those who had been driven out of Jackson County, Missouri. In this revelation, he referred to the "Constitution of the people, which I have suffered to be established" (D&C 101:77. More concerning this revelation is discussed in the following chapter.

The Constitution has had several amendments added to it. There has been and continues to be Supreme Court interpretations rendered concerning its meaning. These amendments and interpretations may or may not be the Lord's will. The Lord probably had these in mind when He said: "whatsoever is more or less than this cometh of evil" (D&C 98:7). It should be noted that the Lord warns of it being interpreted or amended too strictly or too loosely. The Lord desires freedom for all people and the constitutional "law also maketh you free" (v. 8).

The Lord next quotes a well-known proverb, "Nevertheless, when the wicked rule the people mourn" (D&C 98:9; Proverbs 29:2). The wicked take away freedom, which causes people to mourn. To prevent the wicked from ruling, the Lord tells us several things that we must do: "Honest men and wise men should be sought for diligently, and good men and wise men ye should observe to uphold; otherwise whatsoever

---

[48] See *Improvement Era*, October 1945, 564; or *Ensign*, November 1971, 15; as quoted in Monte S. Nyman, *Great are the Words of Isaiah* [1980], 30.

is less than these cometh of evil" (D&C 98:10). There are three characteristics that must be sought after to serve in government and sustain the principles of the Constitution. Note that the characteristics of honest and good must be combined with the attribute of being wise. A man may be honest, but not intellectually capable of understanding the political ramifications of government. A man may be a good man, yet not blessed with the intelligence necessary to govern. When dishonest men attain office their lack of integrity leads to deceit and corruption, and the people mourn. When evil men attain office their objectives are influenced by Satan who seeks the misery of all mankind (2 Nephi 2:18), and they are in a position to affect many, thus also causing people to mourn. The Lord wants us to elect men to office with the qualities above. In conclusion, the Lord says, "whatsoever is less than these cometh of evil" (D&C 98:10). A person cannot be too honest or too good, but there is no degree of dishonesty, evil, or stupidity allowable to the Lord. He does not "look upon sin with the least degree of allowance" (D&C 1:31).

Turning from the solution for governing of the nation, the Lord gives the formula for individuals to live under the rule of the wicked—He commanded them to "forsake all evil and cleave unto all good," and "live by every word" of God. He gives "the faithful line upon line, precept upon precept;" to try and prove them (vv. 11–12). Every word of the Lord includes continuous revelation (A of F 1:9). It may come through the Lord's anointed servants or to the individual. People are accountable before the Lord for their response to the revelations given to them.

For those who suffer because of the wickedness of others, because they are doing the will of the Lord, even to the loss of their life, the Lord gives a promise that He also gave to the people in Palestine as recorded in the New Testament. "And whoso layeth down his life in my cause, for my name's sake, shall find it again, even life eternal" (D&C 98:13; see also Luke 9:24). In addition to the Lord allowing the Saints to be persecuted that His justice and judgment may come upon the wicked (Alma 60:13; quoted above), the Saints are tried to see if they will keep the covenants which they have entered into with the Lord (D&C 98:14–15). The trials we encounter in this life, although not necessarily given to us by the Lord, are part of the plan in our coming to this earth (see Abraham 3:23–26).

It is easier to keep the Lord's covenants when there is less opposition.

Although the Lord at times commands His people to go to war as will be discussed later, the initial commandment is to renounce war and proclaim peace (D&C 98:16). The best preventative against war is to proclaim peace, which is done by teaching the gospel (see Words of Mormon 1:16–18; Ether 7:23–27).

The latter part of D&C 98:16 is apparently paraphrasing Malachi 4:6: "turn the hearts of the children to their fathers, and the hearts of the fathers to the children." This is a good example of dual prophecy. As used generally in the Church, Malachi was referring to "the Spirit of Elijah" moving upon people to do their genealogy and temple work for their ancestors, which is the primary interpretation. However, the message must be interpreted in the context of the revelation, which is the persecution against the members of the Church in Missouri. The basis of the Lord's message to the persecuted is the United State Constitution. The "fathers" to whom the inhabitants of the land are to turn their hearts (v. 16) are the Founding Fathers, who through inspiration, drafted the Constitution. To turn "the hearts of the [Founding] fathers to the children" suggests that they have some influence beyond the veil. Their appearance in the St. George Temple as reported by President Wilford Woodruff, President of the Quorum of the Twelve Apostles and of the St. George Temple, shows they are now a part of the kingdom in heaven:

> Those men who laid the foundation of this American Government and signed the Declaration of Independence were the best spirits the God of Heaven could find on the face of the earth. They were choice spirits, not wicked men. General Washington and all the men that labored for the purpose were inspired of the Lord. . . . I have a right to say it. Every one of those men that signed the Declaration of Independence with General Washington called upon me, as an Apostle of the Lord Jesus Christ, in the Temple at St. George two consecutive nights, and demanded at my hands that I should go forth and attend to the ordinances of the house of God for them.[49]

Wilford Woodruff recorded in his journal on August 21, 1877 that he ordained George Washington a high priest the following day and

---

[49] CR, April 1898, 89–90.

Benjamin Franklin the next day.[50] Certainly, these men and the others are interested and still working for the interest of the United States.

The order of preaching the gospel, recorded five months earlier, was "unto the Gentiles first, and then, behold, and lo, they shall turn unto the Jews" (D&C 90:9). Having given a formula for preserving peace in the Gentile nation of the United States, the Lord gives the formula for teaching the gospel to the Jews: "And again, the hearts of the Jews unto the prophets, and the prophets unto the Jews; lest I come and smite the whole earth with a curse, and all flesh be consumed before me" (D&C 98:17). The "prophets" refers to the second division of Jewish scriptures, or the Old Testament Prophets. These Prophets testify of Jesus Christ, and of the fulfilling of the covenants to the house of Israel (see 1 Nephi 19:23; Mosiah 13:33–35; 3 Nephi 23:1–6). The prophets also foretell of the coming forth of the Book of Mormon (see Isaiah 29; Ezekiel 37). To turn the hearts of the Jews to the Prophets is to acquaint them with these scriptures, and others foretelling the Restoration. To turn the Prophets to the Jews, is to interpret and apply the scripture as being fulfilled through the Jews. The gospel must go to all nations. Those who do not accept the gospel will be cursed or consumed at the Second Coming. However, the Lord reminds His people once more that there is more than one heaven and hell, there are "many mansions" (v. 18). To those who were persecuted and endured those trials, there is a place prepared for them with the Father and Christ. The eternal rewards are much more important than the mortal ones.

D&C 98:19–22 • The Church in Kirtland

19 Behold, I, the Lord, am not well pleased with many who are in the church at Kirtland;

20 For they do not forsake their sins, and their wicked ways, the pride of their hearts, and their covetousness, and all their detestable things, and observe the words of wisdom and eternal life which I have given unto them.

21 Verily I say unto you, that I, the Lord, will chasten them and will do whatsoever I list, if they do not repent and observe all things whatsoever I have said unto them.

---

[50] Mimeographed copy in the files of the writer, 368–369.

22 And again I say unto you, if ye observe to do whatsoever I command you, I, the Lord, will turn away all wrath and indignation from you, and the gates of hell shall not prevail against you.

Having answered the Prophet's concerns about the people in Missouri, the Lord speaks about those in Kirtland. He is not well pleased with them and calls them to repentance. If the Saints respond to His chastisement He will turn all wrath and indignation from them (D&C 98:19–22). Three laws are revealed which are to govern the people of the Lord:

D&C 98:23–32 • The Law of Retaliation

23 Now, I speak unto you concerning your families—if men will smite you, or your families, once, and ye bear it patiently and revile not against them, neither seek revenge, ye shall be rewarded;

24 But if ye bear it not patiently, it shall be accounted unto you as being meted out as a just measure unto you.

25 And again, if your enemy shall smite you the second time, and you revile not against your enemy, and bear it patiently, your reward shall be an hundredfold.

26 And again, if he shall smite you the third time, and ye bear it patiently, your reward shall be doubled unto you four-fold;

27 And these three testimonies shall stand against your enemy if he repent not, and shall not be blotted out.

28 And now, verily I say unto you, if that enemy shall escape my vengeance, that he be not brought into judgment before me, then ye shall see to it that ye warn him in my name, that he come no more upon you, neither upon your family, even your children's children unto the third and fourth generation.

29 And then, if he shall come upon you or your children, or your children's children unto the third and fourth generation, I have delivered thine enemy into thine hands;

30 And then if thou wilt spare him, thou shalt be rewarded for thy righteousness; and also thy children and thy children's children unto the third and fourth generation.

31 Nevertheless, thine enemy is in thine hands; and if thou rewardest him according to his works thou art justified; if he has sought thy life, and thy life is endangered by him, thine enemy is in thine hands and thou art justified.

32 Behold, this is the law I gave unto my servant Nephi, and thy fathers, Joseph, and Jacob, and Isaac, and Abraham, and all mine ancient prophets and apostles.

The first law was concerning families or individuals being smitten. A man is justified if he retaliates when smitten, but loses the blessings of the Lord. He has taken matters into his own hands rather than turning the matter over to the Lord. The same is true for a second and a third smiting by the same person. However, the blessings of the Lord are multiplied at innumerable proportions, the second being a hundredfold, and the third doubled four-fold more (D&C 98:25–26). The mathematical calculation of these blessings seems to be saying that the Lord's blessings are beyond human calculation.

A further action of the Lord concerns the offender. If he does not repent after the third smiting the Lord will send His vengeance upon the enemy. The Lord's vengeance may be severe enough to end further aggression of the offender. To be "brought into judgment before [Christ]" strongly implies death and appearance before the judgment bar. If the Lord spares the offender, the offended has the responsibility to warn the enemy in the name of Christ to come no more against him or his family "unto the third and fourth generation" (D&C 98:27–28). If the enemy comes upon anyone of this family, the following three generations (the fourth), the Lord will deliver their enemy into the hands of those offended (v. 29). Once more, blessings are promised if mercy is extended (v. 30), but the offended is justified in retaliating. The Lord adds another stipulation, "if [the offender] has sought thy life, and thy life is endangered by him, thine enemy is in thine hands and thou art justified" (v. 31). The Lord concludes the law of retaliation with a declaration that He gave this law "unto my servant Nephi, and thy fathers, Joseph, and Jacob, and Isaac, and Abraham, and all mine ancient prophets and apostles" (v. 32). While the many people named shows the eternal nature of the law, the Lord's beginning with Nephi is extremely important.

One of the frequent criticisms of the Book of Mormon is the account of Nephi slaying Laban (1 Nephi 4:1–18). The critics cannot understand how a servant of the Lord would kill another person, but more troubling is the fact that the Spirit had commanded Nephi to commit the act. The usual answer given by faithful members of the Church is, "Behold the

Lord slayeth the wicked to bring forth his righteous purposes. It is better that one man should perish than that a nation should dwindle and perish in unbelief" (1 Nephi 4:13). While this is certainly a true principle and applicable to the situation, the real answer to the critics is given to us in the law of retaliation analyzed above.

Nephi knew that prior to the Spirit commanding him to slay Laban, that Laban was guilty of these offenses against him. "And the Spirit said unto me again: Behold the Lord hath delivered him into thy hands. Yea, and I also knew that he had sought to take away mine own life; yea, and he would not hearken unto the commandments of the Lord; and he also had taken away our property" (1 Nephi 4:11).

A review of 1 Nephi 3 sustains what Nephi said he knew. All three of the offenses by Laban were also against the Lord, or against what the Lord had commanded Nephi to do. Laban had sought to take Nephi's life (1 Nephi 3:13, 25). Secondly, he would not hearken to the Lord's commandments to give them the records (1 Nephi 3:12–13, 24–25). Thirdly, Laban had taken away their property (1 Nephi 3:26). Thus, the Lord had brought vengeance upon Laban through Nephi, and Laban was about to be brought before the judgment bar of Christ (D&C 98:28; see Alma 40:11). The law of retaliation was given to Nephi. When the scriptures are restored, it will be clearly shown that this law was also revealed to Joseph, Jacob, Isaac, and Abraham, and all the ancient prophets and Apostles (D&C 98:32). There are other accounts of prophets taking the lives of others as directed by the Lord (see Numbers 25:5; 31:17; 1 Kings 18:40).

D&C 98:33–38 • The Law of War

33 And again, this is the law that I gave unto mine ancients, that they should not go out unto battle against any nation, kindred, tongue, or people, save I, the Lord, commanded them.

34 And if any nation, tongue, or people should proclaim war against them, they should first lift a standard of peace unto that people, nation, or tongue;

35 And if that people did not accept the offering of peace, neither the second nor the third time, they should bring these testimonies before the Lord;

36 Then I, the Lord, would give unto them a commandment, and justify them in going out to battle against that nation, tongue, or people.

37 And I, the Lord, would fight their battles, and their children's battles, and their children's children's, until they had avenged themselves on all their enemies, to the third and fourth generation.

38 Behold, this is an ensample unto all people, saith the Lord your God, for justification before me.

The law of war was also given unto the Lord's ancients (v. 33). This statement is sustained in the Book of Mormon (see Alma 43:45–47). As outlined in this revelation, there are three important parts of the law of war that are also recorded in the Bible and sustained in the Book of Mormon.

The Lord told the ancients to "not go out to battle against any nation, kindred, tongue, or people, save I, the Lord, commanded" (D&C 98:33). Joshua was commanded of the Lord to go against all the land of Canaan (Joshua 1:2–5). An example of a specific commandment for Joshua to go against a nation is that of Ai (Joshua 8). In the Book of Mormon, Mormon recorded that God would make it known where to go to defend themselves against their enemies (Alma 48:16). Other specific examples are given in the war chapters, Alma chapters 43–62 (see also Alma 60:33).

Secondly, the Lord said, "And if any nation, tongue, or people should proclaim war against them, they should first lift a standard of peace unto that people, nation, or tongue" (D&C 98:34). As in the law of war, this statement of peace was to be lifted up three times before they would be commanded of the Lord to go to battle (vv. 35–36). In Deuteronomy we read, "when thou comest nigh unto a city to fight against it, then proclaim peace unto it" (Deuteronomy 20:10; see also vv. 11–12). General Moroni lifted the standard of liberty three times to the Lamanites (Alma 43–44; see other examples in the war chapters, e.g., 54:6).

Thirdly, the Lord said he "would fight their battles . . . to the third and fourth generation" (D&C 98:37). The Lord told King Hezekiah, through Isaiah, that he would defend Jerusalem "for mine own sake, and for my servant David's sake" (Isaiah 37:35). Although the Book of Mormon makes no direct statement that the Lord would fight their battles, it does attribute their victories to Him (see Alma 44:3; 46:20; 48:15; 56:46–47; 58:10–12, 37). The law of war was certainly known among the ancients and is "an example unto all people" (D&C 98:38).

D&C 98:39–48 • The Law of Forgiveness

39 And again, verily I say unto you, if after thine enemy has come upon thee the first time, he repent and come unto thee praying thy forgiveness, thou shalt forgive him, and shalt hold it no more as a testimony against thine enemy—

40 And so on unto the second and third time; and as oft as thine enemy repenteth of the trespass wherewith he has trespassed against thee, thou shalt forgive him, until seventy times seven.

41 And if he trespass against thee and repent not the first time, nevertheless thou shalt forgive him.

42 And if he trespass against thee the second time, and repent not, nevertheless thou shalt forgive him.

43 And if he trespass against thee the third time, and repent not, thou shalt also forgive him.

44 But if he trespass against thee the fourth time thou shalt not forgive him, but shalt bring these testimonies before the Lord; and they shall not be blotted out until he repent and reward thee four-fold in all things wherewith he has trespassed against thee.

45 And if he do this, thou shalt forgive him with all thine heart; and if he do not this, I, the Lord, will avenge thee of thine enemy an hundred-fold;

46 And upon his children, and upon his children's children of all them that hate me, unto the third and fourth generation.

47 But if the children shall repent, or the children's children, and turn to the Lord their God, with all their hearts and with all their might, mind, and strength, and restore four-fold for all their trespasses wherewith they have trespassed, or wherewith their fathers have trespassed, or their father's fathers, then thine indignation shall be turned away;

48 And vengeance shall no more come upon them, saith the Lord thy God, and their trespasses shall never be brought any more as a testimony before the Lord against them. Amen.

Following the same formula as the law of retaliation and the law of war, the law of forgiveness requires us to forgive someone who has sinned against us and asks our forgiveness, not only three times, but for as many times as he asks, "until seventy times seven" (vv. 39–40; see also Matthew

18:21–22). However, even if our offenders trespass against us and are not repentant, we must forgive them the first three times. President Joseph F. Smith cautioned us that although we may forgive our enemies and pray for them to repent, we are not obligated to associate with them and allow them to continue to sin against us.[51] After those three times the Lord says: "the fourth time thou shalt not forgive him, but shalt bring these testimonies before the Lord; and they shall not be blotted out until he repent and reward thee four-fold," and then "thou shalt forgive him with all thine heart; and if he do this, I, the Lord, will avenge thee of thine enemy an hundred-fold (D&C 98:44–45). The Lord had spoken earlier on the principle of forgiveness (D&C 64:8–13).[52]

The "children and the children's children" gives us a broader view of the word "families." The law of forgiveness extends to generations not just immediate families. As the Lord declared in the second of the Ten Commandments, "the iniquity of the fathers" extends to "the third and fourth generations of them that hate me" (Exodus 20:5). As explained under D&C 93:39, this is natural to follow the traditions of the fathers, or their culture, if they do not repent (see chapter 11). The same is true in D&C 98:46. Note that if the next, or the third generation, repents and meets the conditions required, they shall be forgiven (v. 47)—the testimony of the transgression shall never be brought before the Lord (v. 48).

What we have learned about the United States Constitution, the taking of the gospel to the Gentiles and the Jews in order to proclaim peace, and the laws of retaliation, war, and forgiveness certainly qualify section 98 as a great revelation. The revelation is diversified and an in-depth treatise of the laws of God to govern us collectively and individually. We would do well to study it seriously and repeatedly.

DOCTRINE AND COVENANTS 99

This revelation is placed, by the writer, in the same category as D&C

---

[51] Joseph F. Smith, *Gospel Doctrine*, 337–38.

[52] This principle was discussed in chapter twenty-eight of vol. 1, *More Precious Than Gold*, and should be reviewed in light of this revelation.

79 and 80 mentioned in chapter 1 of this work. It calls John Murdock on a mission to the eastern countries. Although important at the time it was given, it has no doctrinal or historical significance to include here.

DOCTRINE AND COVENANTS 134

Historical Setting: "A general assembly of the Church of Latter-day Saints was held at Kirtland on the 17th of August, 1835, to take into consideration the labors of a committee appointed by a general assembly of the Church on the 24th of September, 1834, for the purpose of arranging the items of the doctrine of Jesus Christ for the government of the Church" (*HC,* 2:243)

"President Oliver Cowdery then read the following article [D&C 134] on "Governments and Laws in General," which was accepted and adopted and ordered to be printed in [the Doctrine and Covenants], by a unanimous vote" (*HC,* 2:247)

"That our belief with regard to earthly governments and laws in general may not be misinterpreted nor misunderstood, we have thought proper to present, at the close of this volume, our opinions concerning the same [first paragraph of the article—it was included as the section heading in the first edition of the Doctrine and Covenants and in subsequent editions]" (D&C 134; section heading).

Introduction

Although not a revelation, it has been accepted as an official position of the Church since 1835. It is included with D&C 98 because both give the position of the Church on the laws of the land.

TEXT AND COMMENTARY

D&C 134:1–3 • The Place of Governments

1 WE believe that governments were instituted of God for the benefit of man; and that he holds men accountable for their acts in relation to them, both in making laws and administering them, for the good and safety of society.

2 We believe that no government can exist in peace, except such laws are framed and held inviolate as will secure to each individual the free exercise of conscience, the right and control of property, and the protection of life.

3 We believe that all governments necessarily require civil officers and magistrates to enforce the laws of the same; and that such as will administer the law in equity and justice should be sought for and upheld by the voice of the people if a republic, or the will of the sovereign.

Governments being instituted by God (v. 1) is verified by the Book of Mormon: "He raiseth up a righteous nation, and destroyeth the nations of the wicked" (1 Nephi 17:37). He inspires men to govern by his law (see Mosiah 29:25). Men have their agency, and so do governments. If wrong choices are made by men of the nations, he does not destroy them until they are ripened in iniquity (see 1 Nephi 17:35; Genesis 15:16). Therefore, there may be much iniquity before they are destroyed. He does hold their destiny (see D&C 117:6).

The "free exercise of conscience, the right and control of property, and the protection of life" (v. 2) is called "due process" in the language of the courts. Governments can exist in peace through this process, and by doing "the works of righteousness" (D&C 59:23).

If the officers and magistrates are honest, good, and wise men (D&C 98:10), they will enforce the laws in equity and justice (v. 3), and will usually be upheld by the majority of the people if the laws are given by the Lord (see Mosiah 29:26).

D&C 134:4–6 • Religion and Man

4 We believe that religion is instituted of God; and that men are amenable to him, and to him only, for the exercise of it, unless their religious opinions prompt them to infringe upon the rights and liberties of others; but we do not believe that human law has a right to interfere in prescribing rules of worship to bind the consciences of men, nor dictate forms for public or private devotion; that the civil magistrate should restrain crime, but never control conscience; should punish guilt, but never suppress the freedom of the soul.

5 We believe that all men are bound to sustain and uphold the respective governments in which they reside, while protected in their inherent and inalienable rights by the laws of such governments; and

that sedition and rebellion are unbecoming every citizen thus protected, and should be punished accordingly; and that all governments have a right to enact such laws as in their own judgments are best calculated to secure the public interest; at the same time, however, holding sacred the freedom of conscience.

6 We believe that every man should be honored in his station, rulers and magistrates as such, being placed for the protection of the innocent and the punishment of the guilty; and that to the laws all men show respect and deference, as without them peace and harmony would be supplanted by anarchy and terror; human laws being instituted for the express purpose of regulating our interests as individuals and nations, between man and man; and divine laws given of heaven, prescribing rules on spiritual concerns, for faith and worship, both to be answered by man to his Maker.

These verses are an expression of the eleventh article of faith, and advocate a separation of church and state, or government and religion. Religion is between man and his God, and man is accountable to Him, and cannot infringe upon "the rights and liberties of others (v. 4). All men will be at the judgment bar of Christ to answer for their works done in the body, whether they were good or evil (see 2 Corinthians 5:10; Mormon 3:20).

Loyalty to whatever government one is living under is vital, and sedition and rebellion are not sanctioned (D&C 134:5). It should be remembered that the Saints were under persecution at the time this section was written, and the government was not protecting "their inherent and inalienable rights" (v. 5). Correction of such wickedness that "seek to destroy the church of God, and to destroy the foundation of liberty" (Alma 46:10) should be sought for peaceably, which the Saints had done to some extent. However, at times God will command man to fight "in memory of our God, our religion, and freedom, and our peace, our wives, and our children" (Alma 46:12). That process was given above in the law of war (D&C 98:33–39), and supported in the Book of Mormon (see Alma 43:45–46). The laws of man should, and the laws of God do protect the innocent and punish the guilty (see D&C 134:6), if not in this life in the next.

D&C 134:7–9 • Free Exercise of Belief

7 We believe that rulers, states, and governments have a right, and are bound to enact laws for the protection of all citizens in the free exercise of their religious belief; but we do not believe that they have a right in justice to deprive citizens of this privilege, or proscribe them in their opinions, so long as a regard and reverence are shown to the laws and such religious opinions do not justify sedition nor conspiracy.

8 We believe that the commission of crime should be punished according to the nature of the offense; that murder, treason, robbery, theft, and the breach of the general peace, in all respects, should be punished according to their criminality and their tendency to evil among men, by the laws of that government in which the offense is committed; and for the public peace and tranquility all men should step forward and use their ability in bringing offenders against good laws to punishment.

9 We do not believe it just to mingle religious influence with civil government, whereby one religious society is fostered and another proscribed in its spiritual privileges, and the individual rights of its members, as citizens, denied.

The eleventh article of faith is again evident in the declaration that as long as the citizen does not break the civil law, they should have the privilege to worship "according to the dictates of their own conscience," as long as they don't deprive other citizens of that privilege (v. 7). The Lord instructed His Saints, in the "law of the church," to let the law of the land judge and punish most of the crimes referred to in verse eight (see D&C 42:79–86). Again, the article (D&C 134) separates the church and the state, but adds the principle of equality for all religious societies (v. 9).

D&C 134:10–12 • Religious Societies Rights

10 We believe that all religious societies have a right to deal with their members for disorderly conduct, according to the rules and regulations of such societies; provided that such dealings be for fellowship and good standing; but we do not believe that any religious society has authority to try men on the right of property or life, to take from them this world's goods, or to put them in jeopardy of either life or limb, or to inflict any physical punishment upon them. They can only excommunicate them from their society, and withdraw from them their fellowship.

11 We believe that men should appeal to the civil law for redress of all wrongs and grievances, where personal abuse is inflicted or the right of property or character infringed, where such laws exist as will protect the same; but we believe that all men are justified in defending themselves, their friends, and property, and the government, from the unlawful assaults and encroachments of all persons in times of exigency, where immediate appeal cannot be made to the laws, and relief afforded.

12 We believe it just to preach the gospel to the nations of the earth, and warn the righteous to save themselves from the corruption of the world; but we do not believe it right to interfere with bond-servants, neither preach the gospel to, nor baptize them contrary to the will and wish of their masters, nor to meddle with or influence them in the least to cause them to be dissatisfied with their situations in this life, thereby jeopardizing the lives of men; such interference we believe to be unlawful and unjust, and dangerous to the peace of every government allowing human beings to be held in servitude.

The right to excommunicate, but not to inflict other punishments, was also outlined in "the law of the church," and in the Book of Mormon. Those who do not comply with the moral and ethical standards of the Church shall be "cast out," or their names blotted out (D&C 42:20–21, 26; Moroni 6:7). The appeal for redress (v. 11) was made later by the Prophet Joseph, but to no avail. We will leave further discussion of that to a study of Church history. The people's rights to defend themselves was mentioned above under verses four through six and the law of war among the Nephites. The preaching of the gospel to the nations of the earth is a commandment of God (v. 12; Mark 16:15–16; D&C 90:9), and would or should not violate the laws of nations. Joseph Smith, in his *Views of the Powers and policy of the Government of the United States,* said about bond-servants (v. 12):

Petition; also, ye goodly inhabitants of the slave States, your legislators to abolish slavery by the year 1850, or now, and save the abolitionists from reproach and ruin, infamy and shame.

Pray congress to pay every man a reasonable price for his slaves out of the surplus revenue arising from the sale of public lands, and from the reduction of pay from the members of congress.

Break off the shackles of the poor black man, and hire him to labor like other human beings, "for an hour of virtuous liberty on earth is worth a whole eternity of bondage. . . .[*HC,* 6:205)]

Although not a revelation, the above points are a brief endeavor to show that the views expressed in this section of the Doctrine and Covenants are based on ancient and modern scripture, and the views of the Prophet Joseph Smith.

General Authority Quotes

—*The Prophet Joseph Smith* • D&C 98:5–6

I am the greatest advocate of the Constitution of the United states there is on earth. In my feelings I am ready to die for the protection of the weak and oppressed rights. The only fault I find with the Constitution is, it is not broad enough to cover the whole ground.

Although it provides that all men shall enjoy religious freedom, yet it does not provide the manner by which that freedom can be preserved, nor for the punishment of Government officers who refuse to protect the people in their religious rights, or punish those mobs, states, or communities who interfere with the rights of the people on account of their religion. Its sentiments are good, but it provides no means of enforcing them. It has but this one fault. [*TPJS,* 326–27]

—*President David O. McKay* • D&C 98:5–6; 134:1–2

The two most important documents affecting the destiny of America are the Declaration of Independence and the Constitution of the United States. Both of these inspired, immortal papers relate primarily to the freedom of individual. Founded upon that principle of free enterprise fostered by these documents, the United States of America, in less than two centuries, has achieved a greatness that far exceeds any other country in the world. [CR, October 1966, 5]

Preach that the plan of salvation involves the belief that governments were instituted of God for the benefit of man. Man was not born for the benefit of the state. [quotes 134:2]. [CR, October 1966, 7]

—*President Spencer W. Kimball* • D&C 98:5–6

The Mormon people who are citizens of [the United States of] America today are intensely loyal to its Constitution and desire in every way to promote the god-given freedoms it was designed to protect. They have had experience with the tragedy that results when those freedoms are not protected, but this only feeds their determination to do all within their power to protect these freedoms, both for themselves and others. . . .

We do not endorse any candidates, but we hope you will vote for good men and women of character, integrity, and ability. You are to be the judge, further, we hope our Church buildings and our church organizations will not be used to advance the candidacy or policies of any of the candidates. . . .

Please avoid, even by implication, involving the Church in political issues. It is so easy, if we are not careful, to project our personal preference as the position of the Church on an issue. [*The Teachings of Spencer W. Kimball*, 405–06]

—*President Ezra Taft Benson* • D&C 98:6

Only in this foreordained land, under its God-inspired Constitution and the resulting environment of freedom, was it possible to have established the restored Church.[53] It is our responsibility to see that this freedom is perpetuated so that the Church may more easily flourish in the future [quotes D&C 98:6]. . . .

How then can we best befriend the Constitution in this critical hour and secure the blessings of liberty and ensure the protection and guidance of our Father in Heaven?

First and foremost, we must be righteous. John Adams said, "Our Constitution was made only for a moral and religious people. It is wholly inadequate to the government of any other." If the Constitution is to have continuance, this American nation, and especially the Latter-day Saints, must be virtuous. [Quotes 2 Nephi 1:7; Ether 2:9, 12]. . . .

Second, we must learn the principles of the Constitution in the tradition of the Founding Fathers. Have we read the Federalist Papers? Are we reading the Constitution and pondering it? Are we aware of its principles? Are we abiding by these principles and teaching them to others? Could we defend the Constitution? Can we recognize when a law is constitutionally unsound? Do we know what the Prophets have said about the Constitution and the threats to it?

As Jefferson said, "If a nation expects to be ignorant and free . . . it expects what never was and never will be."

Third, we must become involved in civic affairs to see that we are properly represented. [quotes D&C 134:1 and 98:10]. . . .

Fourth, we must make our influence felt by our vote, our letters, our teaching, and our advice. We must become accurately informed and then let others know how we feel. The Prophet Joseph Smith said: "It is our

[53] See 3 Nephi 21:4.

duty to concentrate all our influence to make popular that which is sound and good, and unpopular that which is unsound. Tis right, politically, for a man who has influence to use it. . . . From henceforth I will maintain all the influence I can get" (*History of the Church*, 5:286).

I have faith that the Constitution will be saved, as prophesied by Joseph Smith. It will be saved by the righteous citizens of this nation, who love and cherish freedom. It will be saved by the enlightened members of this Church—among others—men and women who understand and abide the principles of the Constitution. . . .

We are fast approaching that moment prophesied by Joseph Smith when he said: "Even this nation will be on the very verge of crumbling to pieces and tumbling to the ground, and when the Constitution is upon the brink of ruin, this people will be the staff upon which the nation will lean, and they shall bear the constitution away from the very verge of destruction" (Church Historian's Office, Salt Lake City, July 19, 1840). [*The Teachings of Ezra Taft Benson*, 621–622, 624]

. . . We read that we should seek out men who are wise, good, and honest. When I first read these criteria years ago, they seemed quite general to me; they don't now. Too often leaders can lead men astray because they lack one or more of these qualities. A leader can be bright but dishonest, and a leader can be honest and conceptually inadequate. A man may be a good man and yet lack the wisdom to cope with complex circumstances that can come upon him. This triad of virtues, for me, is a significant guide to selecting future leaders in any representative government. ["The Lonely Sentinels of Democracy," *New Era*, July 1972, 47]

—President Harold B. Lee • D&C 98:16; 134:3

In our generation the true Christian's position on war is clearly set forth by a declaration in which the Lord says, "Therefore renounce war and proclaim peace." [D&C 98:16]

What is the position of the Church with respect to war? A declaration of the First Presidency given during World War II is still applicable in our time. The statement said: "The Church is and must be against war. The Church itself cannot wage war, unless and until the Lord shall issue new commands. It cannot regard war as a righteous means of settling international disputes; these should and could be settled—the nations agreeing— peaceful negotiations and adjustment (In CR, April 1942, 252). [*The Teachings of Harold B. Lee*, 358]

I can't think of more trouble I could get into than by answering as I would feel, but I said, "I'll tell you how to vote. You read the 134ᵗʰ section of the Doctrine and Covenants, where the Lord has said to an inspired prophet [Oliver Cowdery], (quotes 134:30)." I said "now that's your first guide. Then you turn to Mosiah, the twenty-ninth chapter, and read what King Mosiah advised concerning the voice of the majority of the people. The reason why we get into the hands of autocrats in politics is because many of us criticize and stay home and don't go to our district meetings. And we don't allow ourselves to become candidates, or representatives to vote for those who will represent in the nation, or the county, or the state. Well," I said, "you study those two and then pray about it. You'll know who to vote for." [*The Teachings of Harold B. Lee*, 367]

Chapter Fourteen

The Lord's Jewels

D&C 100–101

DOCTRINE AND COVENANTS 100

Historical Setting: "October 5, [1833]—I [Joseph] started on a journey to the east and to Canada, in company with Elders Rigdon and Freeman Nickerson" (*HC,* 1:416).

On the 12th [October, 1833] arrived at Father Nickerson's at Perrysburg, New York, where I received [Doctrine and Covenants 100]" (*HC,* 1:419–20).

SECTION 100 • OUTLINE

➤ 100:1–2   Sidney and Joseph's families are well and in my hands.

     a.   I will do with them as seems good, I have all power (v. 1).

     b.   Follow me and listen to my counsel.

➤ 100:3–8   There are much people in the region, I have sent you for the salvation of souls.

     a.   In the very moment, speak the thoughts I shall give you (vv. 5–6).

     b.   Declare it in my name, and the Holy Ghost shall bear record (vv. 7–8).

➤ 100:9–12   Sidney shall be a spokesman for Joseph.

     a.   Joseph shall have power to be mighty in testimony (v. 10).

>   b.   Sidney shall expound the scriptures, and Joseph be a revelator (vv. 11–12).

➤ 100:13–17   Zion shall be redeemed, although she is chastened for a little season.

      a.   Orson and John shall work for the sanctification of the Church (vv. 14–15).

      b.   I will raise up a pure people, who shall be saved (vv. 16–17).

Introduction

A jewel is a precious stone that has withstood the natural physical forces of intense heat and pressure that have hardened it through the ages of the world. When these stones are mined, cut out, and polished, they glisten and are radiant, reflecting the various rays of light that shine upon them. In contrast, other stones will crack or crumble having become weakened and rough and do not reflect light. The world is full of ordinary looking rough stones, and many of those rough stones would become beautiful if they were cut and polished. Is there a similar process taking place among the inhabitants of the world? Does the Lord periodically gather His precious jewels from the world through His mining process? In the book of Malachi we read:

> Then they that feared the Lord spake often one to another: and the Lord hearkened, and heard *it*, and a book of remembrance was written before him for them that feared the Lord, and that thought upon his name.
>
> And they shall be mine, saith the Lord of hosts, in that day when I make up my jewels; and I will spare them, as a man spareth his own son that serveth him.
>
> Then shall ye return, and discern between the righteous and the wicked, between him that serveth God and him that serveth him not. [Malachi 3:16–18; 3 Nephi 24:16–18]

The following chapter of Malachi shows that those who "feared the Lord, and that thought upon his name" and "serveth God" had reference to those who will be spared at the cleansing at the Second Coming. Prior to the Second Coming, the Lord's people will become refined and polished under the pressure and persecutions of the world. As they endure these experiences, they reflect the light of the Lord, and stand as examples of what mankind can become as they endure the trials of their lifetime. The two sections of the Doctrine and Covenants being considered in this chapter exemplify this symbolic process.

TEXT AND COMMENTARY

D&C 100:1–2 • Pressure of the World

1 Verily, thus saith the Lord unto you, my friends Sidney and Joseph, your families are well; they are in mine hands, and I will do with them as seemeth me good; for in me there is all power.

2 Therefore, follow me, and listen to the counsel which I shall give unto you.

The people in Missouri had been through trials and tribulations, and the Lord was using them as His jewels, to reflect His light. The concern for the families of Sidney and Joseph was first alleviated (v. 1), and they were in the Lord's hands. As the maker of jewels, He knew when to relieve the pressure, and when to cut and polish. He was also working with Joseph and Sidney, and He invited them to listen to His counsel (v. 2).

D&C 100:3–8 • It Shall Be Given What to Say

3 Behold, and lo, I have much people in this place, in the regions round about; and an effectual door shall be opened in the regions round about in this eastern land.

4 Therefore, I, the Lord, have suffered you to come unto this place; for thus it was expedient in me for the salvation of souls.

5 Therefore, verily I say unto you, lift up your voices unto this people; speak the thoughts that I shall put into your hearts, and you shall not be confounded before men;

6 For it shall be given you in the very hour, yea, in the very moment, what ye shall say.

7 But a commandment I give unto you, that ye shall declare whatsoever thing ye declare in my name, in solemnity of heart, in the spirit of meekness, in all things.

8 And I give unto you this promise, that inasmuch as ye do this the Holy Ghost shall be shed forth in bearing record unto all things whatsoever ye shall say.

The Lord had many people for them to gather from the area of their mission, and bring about the "salvation of souls" (v. 3–4). The missionaries were to reflect the Lord's light. The Lord's instructions told them how to accomplish their mission—"speak the thoughts that I shall put in your hearts" (v. 5). The Savior had given the same instructions to his Apostles whom He had chosen to reflect His light in Jerusalem (Matthew 10:19–20).

An account of Elder Jedediah M. Grant, as he preached the gospel in the southern states, shows how the Lord gives His servants the words they shall speak—and when spoken are not confounded before men:

> In the early part of President Grant's ministry in that country, he gained quite a reputation as a ready speaker, frequently responding to invitations to preach from such subjects or texts as might be selected at the time of commencing his sermon, by those inviting him.
>
> In time it became a matter of wonder with many as to how and when he prepared his wonderful sermons. In reply to their queries he informed them that he *never* prepared his sermons as other ministers did. He said, "Of course, I read and store my mind with a knowledge of gospel truths, but I never study up a sermon."
>
> Well, they did not believe he told the truth, for, as they thought, it was impossible for a man to preach such sermons without careful preparation. So, in order to prove it, a number of persons decided to put him to the test, and asked him if he would preach at a certain time and place, and from a text selected by them. They proposed to give him the text on his arrival at the place of meeting, thus giving him no time to prepare.
>
> To gratify them, he consented.
>
> The place selected was Jeffersonville, the seat of Tazewell County, at that time the home of the late John B. Floyd (who subsequently became secretary of war), and many other prominent men.
>
> The room chosen was in the court house. At the hour appointed the house was packed to its utmost capacity.
>
> Mr. Floyd and a number of lawyers and ministers were present, and occupied front seats.
>
> Elder Grant came in, walked to the stand and opened the meeting as usual. At the close of the second hymn, a clerk, appointed for the occasion, stepped forward and handed a paper (the text) to Elder Grant.

Brother Grant unfolded the paper and found it to be blank. Without any mark of surprise, he held the paper up before the audience, and said:

"My friends, I am here to-day according to agreement, to preach from such a text as these gentlemen might select for me. I have it here in my hand. I don't wish you to become offended at me, for I am under promise to preach from the text selected; and if any one is to blame, you must blame those who selected it. I knew nothing of what text they would choose, but of all the texts this is my favorite one.

"You see the paper is blank" (at the same time holding it up to view).

"You sectarians down there believe that out of nothing God created all things, and now you wish me to create a sermon from nothing, for this paper is blank.

"Now, you sectarians believe in a God that has neither body, parts nor passions. Such a God I conceive to be a perfect blank, just as you find my text is.

"You believe in a church without prophets, apostles, evangelists, etc. Such a church would be a perfect blank, as compared with the church of Christ, and this agrees with my text.

"You have located your heaven beyond the bounds of time and space. It exists no where, and consequently your heaven is blank, like unto my text."

Thus he went on until he had torn to pieces all the tenets of faith professed by his hearers; and then he proclaimed the principles of the gospel in great power.

He wound up by asking, "Have I stuck to the text, and does that satisfy you?"

As soon as he sat down Mr. Floyd jumped up and said: "Mr. Grant, if you are not a lawyer you ought to be one." Then, turning to the people, he added: "Gentlemen, you have listened to a wonderful discourse, and with amazement."[54]

As the Lord's servants, His jewels, have these experiences, they are commanded to speak in the name of the Lord. The Prophet Nephi taught the same doctrine, "For when a man speaketh by the power of the Holy Ghost the power of the Holy Ghost carrieth it unto the hearts of the children of men" (2 Nephi 33:1). The Holy Ghost is the Lord's messenger, His witness, or Testator (see *TPJS*, 323, 190).

---

[54] T. B. Lewis, *A String of Pearls, Anecdotes of Elder Grant* [1880], 36–37.

D&C 100:9–12 • Sidney a Spokesman unto Joseph

9 And it is expedient in me that you, my servant Sidney, should be a spokesman unto this people; yea, verily, I will ordain you unto this calling, even to be a spokesman unto my servant Joseph.

10 And I will give unto him power to be mighty in testimony.

11 And I will give unto thee power to be mighty in expounding all scriptures, that thou mayest be a spokesman unto him, and he shall be a revelator unto thee, that thou mayest know the certainty of all things pertaining to the things of my kingdom on the earth.

12 Therefore, continue your journey and let your hearts rejoice; for behold, and lo, I am with you even unto the end.

Just as different jewels have different uses, the Lord calls His people to serve in various callings, but still coordinates their duties. Sidney Rigdon is called as a spokesman for Joseph, the Prophet. The calling had originally been Oliver Cowdery's (see D&C 28:3 and 2 Nephi 3:18–19), but with the growth of the Church and the expansion of other duties, Oliver was no longer to serve as Joseph's spokesman. Sidney had earlier been called to write for Joseph, to preach the gospel, and call on the prophecies of the holy prophets to prove the things Joseph had been inspired to prophesy (D&C 35:20–23). These duties, given three years earlier, were now expanded, but were still dependent upon Joseph. The Prophet was the one mighty in testimony and the revelator to Sidney. Although Sidney could expound *all* scripture (italics added), it was through Joseph that he was to come to know of the certainty of the things of the kingdom.

D&C 100:13–17 • Zion Shall Be Redeemed

13 And now I give unto you a word concerning Zion. Zion shall be redeemed, although she is chastened for a little season.

14 Thy brethren, my servants Orson Hyde and John Gould, are in my hands; and inasmuch as they keep my commandments they shall be saved.

15 Therefore, let your hearts be comforted; for all things shall work together for good to them that walk uprightly, and to the sanctification of the church.

16 For I will raise up unto myself a pure people, that will serve me in righteousness;

17 And all that call upon the name of the Lord, and keep his commandments, shall be saved. Even so. Amen.

Although the founding of the center place of Zion (D&C 57:3) had been temporarily delayed, the Lord emphatically declared that "Zion shall be redeemed, although she is chastened for a little season" (D&C 100:13). The Lord's servants, who were laboring in Zion, would be saved if they kept the commandments (v. 14). He would turn their afflictions to His good, and make the whole Church a jewel, a sanctified stone that reflected the Lord's light (v. 15; D&C 101:3). There would yet be a pure people to serve Him and keep His commandments (D&C 100:16–17).

DOCTRINE AND COVENANTS 101

*H*istorical Setting:

December 12.[1833]—An express arrived . . . from Van Buren county, with information that those families, which had fled from Jackson County, and located there, were about to be driven from that county, after building their houses and carting their winter's store of provisions, grain, etc,. forty or fifty miles. Several families are already fleeing from thence. . . .The destruction of crops, household furniture, and clothing is very great, and much of their stock is lost. The main body of the church is now in Clay county, where the people are as kind and accommodating as could reasonably be expected. The continued threats of death to individuals of the Church, if they make their appearance in Jackson county, prevent the most of them, even at this day, from returning to that county, to secure personal property, which they were obliged to leave in their flight. [*HC,* 1:456–57]

"*December* 16—I [Joseph Smith] received [Doctrine and Covenants 101]." [*HC,* 1:458]

SECTION 101 • OUTLINE

➤ 101:1–10   I have suffered afflictions because of transgression, but they will be mine when I make up my jewels.

       a.   They must be chastened as Abraham was commanded to offer his son (vv. 4–5).

       b.   They polluted their inheritance, and were slow to hearken unto God (vv. 6–7).

       c.   In peace they esteemed lightly my counsel, but in trouble feel after me (v. 8).

       d.   I will not utterly cast them off, nor let the sword fall (vv. 9–10).

➤ **101:11–16**   Mine indignation shall soon be poured out upon all nations.

       a.   In that day all Israel shall be saved, those scattered shall be gathered (vv. 12–13).

       b.   They who mourned be comforted, and gave their lives be crowned (vv. 14–15).

       c.   Be comforted concerning Zion, for all flesh is in my hands (v. 16).

➤ **101:17–21**   Zion shall not be moved out of her place, the pure in heart shall return.

       a.   All these things shall fulfill the words of the prophets (v. 19).

       b.   There is no other place appointed, neither shall be for the gathering (v. 20).

       c.   When there is no more room, stakes shall be appointed (v. 21).

➤ **101:22–38**   All that worship according to the everlasting gospel will gather to holy places.

       a.   To prepare for the revelation when all flesh shall see me together (v. 24).

       b.   All corruptible thing consumed, the elements melt, all becomes new (vv. 24–25).

       c.   The enmity of man and beasts will cease before my face (v. 26).

       d.   Whatever man shall ask, it shall be given, and Satan shall have no power to tempt man (vv. 27–28).

       e.   There shall be no sorrow because there shall be no death (vv. 29–31).

       f.   All things shall be revealed (vv. 32–36).

    g.   Care not for the body, but for the life of the soul and eternal life (vv. 37–38).

➤ 101:39–42   When men are called and covenant to the everlasting gospel they are the salt of the earth, and the savor of men.

    a.   If the salt lose its savor, it is good only to be trodden of men (v. 40).

    b.   He that exalts himself shall be abased, he that abases himself exalted (vv. 41–42).

➤ 101:43–62   The parable of the redemption of Zion: The noble man and the choice land.

    a.   What the nobleman [the Lord] commanded His servants (v. 44–45).

    b.   What the servants did (vv. 46–51).

    c.   What the Lord said (vv. 52–62).

➤ 101:63–75   The parable of the gathering of my Saints: the wheat and the tares.

    a.   The wheat secured in the garners to possess eternal life (v. 65).

    b.   The tares bound in bundles to be burned (v. 66).

    c.   Continue to gather and purchase lands (vv. 67–74).

    d.   There is now sufficient to redeem Zion, would they hearken to the Lord (v. 75).

➤ 101:76–80   Continue to importune for redress and redemption to the rulers in authority.

    a.   According to the Constitution which I suffered to be established (vv. 77–79).

    b.   For this purpose I established the Constitution by the hands of wise men (v. 80).

➤ 101:81–95   Parable of the woman and the unjust judge.

    a.   Pray always and not faint (vv. 82–91).

    b.   Why to pray and persist (vv. 92–95).

➤ 101:96–101 It is contrary to my commandment to sell the storehouse in Jackson county.

    a.   It is my will to lay claim on what is appointed, even if not dwelling there (v. 99).

    b.   If they bring forth fruits and works, they shall dwell there (v. 100).

    c.   They shall build, plant vineyards, and eat the fruit (v. 101).

TEXT AND COMMENTARY

D&C 101:1–10 • Tested as Abraham

1 VERILY I say unto you, concerning your brethren who have been afflicted, and persecuted, and cast out from the land of their inheritance—

2 I, the Lord, have suffered the affliction to come upon them, wherewith they have been afflicted, in consequence of their transgressions;

3 Yet I will own them, and they shall be mine in that day when I shall come to make up my jewels.

4 Therefore, they must needs be chastened and tried, even as Abraham, who was commanded to offer up his only son.

5 For all those who will not endure chastening, but deny me, cannot be sanctified.

6 Behold, I say unto you, there were jarrings, and contentions, and envyings, and strifes, and lustful and covetous desires among them; therefore by these things they polluted their inheritances.

7 They were slow to hearken unto the voice of the Lord their God; therefore, the Lord their God is slow to hearken unto their prayers, to answer them in the day of their trouble.

8 In the day of their peace they esteemed lightly my counsel; but, in the day of their trouble, of necessity they feel after me.

9 Verily I say unto you, notwithstanding their sins, my bowels are filled with compassion towards them. I will not utterly cast them off; and in the day of wrath I will remember mercy.

10 I have sworn, and the decree hath gone forth by a former commandment which I have given unto you, that I would let fall the sword of mine indignation in behalf of my people; and even as I have said, it shall come to pass.

The Lord allowed the persecution to come because of their transgressions (v. 2), but assures them they are still candidates for exaltation (v. 3). "When ye do not what I say, ye have no promise" (D&C 82:10). Concerning Abraham's trial of offering up his son Isaac (v. 4), the Prophet Joseph taught: "The sacrifice required of Abraham in the offering up of Isaac, shows that if a man would attain to the keys of the kingdom of an endless life, he must sacrifice all things. When God offers a blessing or knowledge to a man, and he refuses to receive it, he will be damned" (*TPJS,* 322). Abraham's test was also in similitude of the Atonement of Jesus Christ (see Jacob 4:5). The mention of it here could have been a reminder of this Book of Mormon teaching. Many of the Saints in Missouri would pass their tests and become sanctified (D&C 101:5). Others would not endure their chastening, and unless they repented would not get the full benefit of the Atonement. The chastening of the Lord came because their personal reactions to each other, and wrongful desires, had "polluted their inheritances" (v. 6). Personal revelation must be followed, or the Lord will cease to respond (v. 7). The answers to prayer are also based on worthiness: "The effectual fervent prayer of a righteous man availeth much" (James 5:16). Prayers are for guidance and prevention as well as for trouble solving (D&C 101:8). Those who were guilty of the above were still assured of some blessings. They had not endured enough to be celestial jewels, but had apparently met the terrestrial requirements. They would not be utterly cast off (v. 9). These people, because of the sufferings they had experienced, would escape the destruction of the telestial people if the Lord came at that time (v. 10).

D&C 101:11–16 • Be Still and Know that I Am God

11 Mine indignation is soon to be poured out without measure upon all nations; and this will I do when the cup of their iniquity is full.

12 And in that day all who are found upon the watch-tower, or in other words, all mine Israel, shall be saved.

13 And they that have been scattered shall be gathered.

14 And all they who have mourned shall be comforted.

15 And all they who have given their lives for my name shall be crowned.

16 Therefore, let your hearts be comforted concerning Zion; for all

flesh is in mine hands; be still and know that I am God.

"In that day" (v. 12) refers to the time when the Lord's indignation would "be poured out without measure upon all nations" (v. 11), or his Second Coming. Those who are found upon the watch tower (v. 12) would be those Saints who have been watching for the signs of His coming as foretold in the parable of the fig tree (see JS—Matthew 1:38–39; Luke 21:25–32). The saving of all Israel (v. 12) is in fulfillment of a prophecy of Isaiah (45:17). Those of the house of Israel who had been scattered, and not yet gathered, would be gathered (v. 13), showing that all would not be gathered before the Millennium would come. Those who mourned because of their persecutions, or had even given their lives would receive full reward for the sacrifices they had endured (vv. 14–15). Justice and mercy are not fully realized until the day the Lord comes. The same is true of the collective blessings promised to come upon the Saints. The Lord assured His Saints of the eventual blessings to come upon Zion (v. 16). "Be still [patient], and know that I [am] God" is a quote from Psalm 46:10.

D&C 101:17–21 • The Prophets Might Be Fulfilled

17 Zion shall not be moved out of her place, notwithstanding her children are scattered.

18 They that remain, and are pure in heart, shall return, and come to their inheritances, they and their children, with songs of everlasting joy, to build up the waste places of Zion—

19 And all these things that the prophets might be fulfilled.

20 And, behold, there is none other place appointed than that which I have appointed; neither shall there be any other place appointed than that which I have appointed, for the work of the gathering of my saints—

21 Until the day cometh when there is found no more room for them; and then I have other places which I will appoint unto them, and they shall be called stakes, for the curtains or the strength of Zion.

The Lord had previously revealed, through the record of Enoch, that all flesh was in His hands, or that He was in control of the destiny of the inhabitants of the earth (Moses 6:32; see also a later confirmation, D&C 117:6). The place for Zion to be built had also been revealed previously, and the Lord affirms that it will still be built there. Those who endure the persecutions will receive their inheritance, and then will another prophecy of Isaiah be fulfilled, the pure in heart will return to Zion "with song or everlasting love" (see Isaiah 51:11; 2 Nephi 8:11). Thus, the Lord's words, whether spoken by Him or His servants the prophets will be brought to pass (D&C 101:19; see D&C 1:38).

The wording of Doctrine and Covenants 101:20–21 might be interpreted that there will be no stakes established until after the gathering to Zion had completely filled up the area. However, "when there is found no more room for them" seems, from other revelations, to refer to a time when all have been driven out of Missouri. Kirtland had been designated as a place to establish a stake of Zion (D&C 82:13; 94:1). Other stakes would be established until they were established all around the center place of Zion.[55] These are "the curtains or the strength of Zion" (v. 21) The stakes of Zion will be established all around the city of Zion, the New Jerusalem, to raise the tent of Israel. The city of Zion will be the center pole (see D&C 57:3) from which the cords will be extended to the stakes. The strength of these stakes will support the curtains that engulf the city. As Zion grows in the Millennium, the cords will be lengthened and the stakes strengthened (see Isaiah 54:1–2; 3 Nephi 22:1–2). Those of the house of Israel who endure the pressure of the world, will be solidified and purified, and will firmly establish Zion and her stakes.

D&C 101:22–31 • The Intense Light of the Lord

22 Behold, it is my will, that all they who call on my name, and worship me according to mine everlasting gospel, should gather together, and stand in holy places;

23 And prepare for the revelation which is to come, when the veil of the covering of my temple, in my tabernacle, which hideth the earth, shall be taken off, and all flesh shall see me together.

24 And every corruptible thing, both of man, or of the beasts of the field, or of the fowls of the heavens, or of the fish of the sea, that dwells upon all the face of the earth, shall be consumed;

25 And also that of element shall melt with fervent heat; and all things shall become new, that my knowledge and glory may dwell upon all the earth.

---

[55] This concept of Zion being surrounded by stakes will be discussed in section 103.

26 And in that day the enmity of man, and the enmity of beasts, yea, the enmity of all flesh, shall cease from before my face.

27 And in that day whatsoever any man shall ask, it shall be given unto him.

28 And in that day Satan shall not have power to tempt any man.

29 And there shall be no sorrow because there is no death.

30 In that day an infant shall not die until he is old; and his life shall be as the age of a tree;

31 And when he dies he shall not sleep, that is to say in the earth, but shall be changed in the twinkling of an eye, and shall be caught up, and his rest shall be glorious.

It was the Lord's will that His people be gathered to holy places (Zion and her stakes) in preparation for the Second Coming of Christ (v. 22). Just as natural jewels have been subjected to the intense heat of the internal earth, the pouring out of the glory of the Lord at the beginning of the Millennium will be endured by those who have prepared themselves for that event. As the Lord appears, all of the inhabitants of the earth will see Christ (v. 23). This is the final appearance to the whole world. He will have previously appeared in His temples and to the Jews.[56] As He appears, those who are not able to endure the glory will be eliminated. The animal kingdom and all flesh that are not of the celestial or terrestrial creations will also be taken away (v. 24). Even the corruptible parts of the earth shall be removed, and the earth refined into a planet able to endure the additional knowledge and glory of the Lord Jesus Christ.

The beasts that have filled the measure of their creation will live in a spirit of peace. "The enmity of man, and the enmity of beasts" shall cease (v. 26). The increase of the Spirit of the Lord will change their carnal nature to peaceful lovable creatures. The change in their nature will fulfill a prophecy of Isaiah (see 11:6–8; 65:25). Another prophecy of Isaiah will also be fulfilled: "Whatsoever any man shall ask, it shall be given unto him" (D&C 101:27). Isaiah says "that before they call, I will answer, and while they are yet speaking, I will hear" (Isaiah 65:24). The promise now given to the Apostles of receiving whatsoever they ask (John 15:16; 3 Nephi 27:28) shall be extended to all the righteous. Satan shall be

---

[56] See Malachi 3:1 (3 Nephi 24:1) and D&C 45:47–53; Zachariah 14:4.

bound, and "not have power to tempt any man" (D&C 101:28; compare Isaiah 14:7, 15–19; D&C 43:30–31).

The final prophecy of Isaiah mentioned in this section of the revelation will then come to pass. "There shall be no sorrow because there is no death" (vv. 29–31). JST, Isaiah 65:20 is a better parallel of the revelation than the KJV. "In those days there shall be no more thence an infant of days, nor an old man that hath not filled his days; for the child shall not die, but live to be an hundred years old; but the sinner, living to be an hundred years old, shall be accursed." Those who are able to endure all of these changes, brought about by the glory of the Lord being poured out, will be a lot closer to becoming the Lord's jewels permanently. However, there is one more major step. An earlier revelation further qualified how death would cease during the Millennium. "Wherefore, children shall grow up until they become old; old men shall die; but they shall not sleep in the dust, but they shall be changed in the twinkling of an eye" (D&C 63:51). Thus they will pass from mortality into a resurrected state instantaneously.

D&C 101:32–38 • The Polished Stones—All Things Revealed

32 Yea, verily I say unto you, in that day when the Lord shall come, he shall reveal all things—

33 Things which have passed, and hidden things which no man knew, things of the earth, by which it was made, and the purpose and the end thereof—

34 Things most precious, things that are above, and things that are beneath, things that are in the earth, and upon the earth, and in heaven.

35 And all they who suffer persecution for my name, and endure in faith, though they are called to lay down their lives for my sake yet shall they partake of all this glory.

36 Wherefore, fear not even unto death; for in this world your joy is not full, but in me your joy is full.

37 Therefore, care not for the body, neither the life of the body; but care for the soul, and for the life of the soul.

38 And seek the face of the Lord always, that in patience ye may possess your souls, and ye shall have eternal life.

The final process in making a jewel out of a rock is to polish it. In the symbolism of the Lord, the Lord's polishing of His jewels is also in the last stages of life or of the world. After quoting verses 32–34, President Harold B. Lee made this observation regarding the creation: "If you and I are there when the Lord reveals all this, then I will answer your questions—how the earth was made, how man came to be placed upon this earth. Until that time all we have is the support and security that we have in the scriptures, and we must accept the rest by faith."[57] If the Lord is going to reveal all things when He comes again, it is obvious that we do not know all things now. The same is true of many other topics. The Millennium will be a time of great revelation "for the earth shall be full of the knowledge of the Lord" (Isaiah 11:9). The things reserved for future generations, such as the sealed portion of the plates from which the Book of Mormon was translated (see D&C 5:9); the plates of brass obtained from Laban by Nephi (see 1 Nephi 5:18–19); the fuller record of Jesus' visit among the Nephites (see 3 Nephi 26:9–11); and many other ancient records (see D&C 8:1; 9:2). Knowledge is a polishing power of the Lord to make the children of men His jewels.

A second polishing effort for the Lord's jewels is the fulness of the Lord's glory. The receiving of His glory is a process where we grow from grace to grace (see D&C 93:20). The fulness is not achieved in this world, but comes through Christ. If our lives are cut short (vv. 35–36), we can still reach the plateau of the fulness of His glory. Therefore, "care for the soul, and for the life of the soul. And seek the face of the Lord always, that in patience ye may possess your souls, and ye shall have eternal life" (D&C 101:35–38). The things of the soul are the most important. The Prophet Nephi was well aware of the things important to the soul, and wrote of them eloquently in 2 Nephi 4:15–35. We should read his stirring soliloquy periodically. Those things that delight the soul such as "the scriptures" and "other things of the Lord," as termed by Nephi, will polish us and make us "partakers of the divine nature" as expressed by Peter (2 Peter 2:4; see the whole chapter).

---

[57] *Ensign*, December 1972.

D&C 101:39–42 • The Salt, the Savor of Men

39 When men are called unto mine everlasting gospel, and covenant with an everlasting covenant, they are accounted as the salt of the earth and the savor of men;

40 They are called to be the savor of men; therefore, if that salt of the earth lose its savor, behold, it is thenceforth good for nothing only to be cast out and trodden under the feet of men.

41 Behold, here is wisdom concerning the children of Zion, even many, but not all; they were found transgressors, therefore they must needs be chastened—

42 He that exalteth himself shall be abased, and he that abaseth himself shall be exalted.

A third source for polishing our souls that we may become the Lord's jewels is to receive and magnify the priesthood as we learned in D&C 84. The Savior used this symbolism of salt in the Sermon on the Mount (Matthew 5:13). To savor is to season, or if on the receiving side, to taste and enjoy. The priesthood is to season the earth with the gospel teachings and ordinances (to be saviors of men; D&C 103:9–10). As we magnify our callings we become polished in the service of the Lord. If we do not magnify our callings and use improper seasoning, or misuse the priesthood, we lose the savor that we once had and are good for nothing in the Lord's work.

As a final method of polishing, we must accept the chastisement of the Lord. The Lord chastises those whom He loves (see D&C 95:1; Hebrews 12:6). "Many, but not all" of the children of Israel, then and now, "were found transgressors, therefore they must be chastened—he that exalteth himself shall be abased, and he that abaseth himself shall be exalted" (D&C 101:41–42; see Luke 14:11). Those who acknowledge the Lord as the source of their knowledge and power in His service will become polished, and become the Lord's jewels in eternity.

D&C 101:43–45 • A Parable Concerning Zion

> 43 And now, I will show unto you a parable, that you may know my will concerning the redemption of Zion.
>
> 44 A certain nobleman had a spot of land, very choice; and he said unto his servants: Go ye unto my vineyard, even upon this very choice piece of land, and plant twelve olive-trees;
>
> 45 And set watchmen round about them, and build a tower, that one may overlook the land round about, to be a watchman upon the tower, that mine olive-trees may not be broken down when the enemy shall come to spoil and take upon themselves the fruit of my vineyard.

Having chastised and comforted the individuals who had been solely persecuted and tried, the Lord turns to the subject of the redemption of Zion, the center place of the Lord from whence they had been driven. He spoke in parables that he "who hath ears to hear" may hear (Matthew 13:9).

The first parable is lengthy (D&C 101:44–62) and will be broken into three parts. It is similar to the parable of the wicked husbandman in the New Testament (Matthew 21:33–41), but yet quite different. The following imagery of the parable will help you understand as you read. The first part should need no further comment.

NOBLEMAN AND THE CHOICE LAND • D&C 101:43–62

WHAT THE NOBLEMAN [LORD] COMMANDED HIS SERVANTS

Go to a choice piece of land	=	Independence, Mo. (D&C 57:3)
Plant 12 olive trees	=	Men prepared to be Apostles
Set watchmen	=	Appoint priesthood leaders
Build a tower	=	Temple
Be a watchman upon the tower	=	Protect the olive trees

D&C 101:46–51 • What the Servants Did,

> 46 Now, the servants of the nobleman went and did as their lord commanded them, and planted the olive-trees, and built a hedge round about, and set watchmen, and began to build a tower.
>
> 47 And while they were yet laying the foundation thereof, they began to say among themselves: And what need hath my lord of this tower?

48 And consulted for a long time, saying among themselves: What need hath my lord of this tower, seeing this is a time of peace?

49 Might not this money be given to the exchangers? For there is no need of these things.

50 And while they were at variance one with another they became very slothful, and they hearkened not unto the commandments of their lord.

51 And the enemy came by night, and broke down the hedge; and the servants of the nobleman arose and were affrighted, and fled; and the enemy destroyed their works, and broke down the olive-trees.

Planted the olive trees	=	Potential Apostles [tested]
Built a hedge	=	Purchased the land
Set watchmen	=	At variance with one another
Laid the tower foundation	=	Temple cornerstone
Frightened and fled	=	Enemy broke down the hedge

The testing of men to be called as apostles will be shown in chapter 16. The interpretation of the hedge is taken from the commandment to obtain the land by purchase, not by blood (see D&C 63:29–31). The servants questioning what the Lord had commanded fit the watchmen being at variance (D&C 101:47–50). The enemy that caused the Saints to leave being the mob that drove them out seems evident (v. 50).

D&C 101:52–54 • What the Lord Said

52 Now, behold, the nobleman, the lord of the vineyard, called upon his servants, and said unto them, Why! what is the cause of this great evil?

53 Ought ye not to have done even as I commanded you, and—after ye had planted the vineyard, and built the hedge round about, and set watchmen upon the walls thereof—built the tower also, and set a watchman upon the tower, and watched for my vineyard, and not have fallen asleep, lest the enemy should come upon you?

54 And behold, the watchman upon the tower would have seen the enemy while he was yet afar off; and then ye could have made ready and kept the enemy from breaking down the hedge thereof, and saved my vineyard from the hands of the destroyer.

Not fallen asleep	=	Ignored the commandments
Watchmen seen the enemy	=	Leaders recognized the problems
Saved the vineyard	=	Not driven out

The Lord said they should have kept the commandments (v. 53). The leaders would have been receptive to the Lord's warning revelation of the enemy (v. 54). The mob would not have been able to drive them out (v. 54).

D&C 101:55–62 • What the Lord Said to Do

55 And the lord of the vineyard said unto one of his servants: Go and gather together the residue of my servants, and take all the strength of mine house, which are my warriors, my young men, and they that are of middle age also among all my servants, who are the strength of mine house, save those only whom I have appointed to tarry;

56 And go ye straightway unto the land of my vineyard, and redeem my vineyard; for it is mine; I have bought it with money.

57 Therefore, get ye straightway unto my land; break down the walls of mine enemies; throw down their tower, and scatter their watchmen.

58 And inasmuch as they gather together against you, avenge me of mine enemies, that by and by I may come with the residue of mine house and possess the land.

59 And the servant said unto his lord: When shall these things be?

60 And he said unto his servant: When I will; go ye straightway, and do all things whatsoever I have commanded you;

61 And this shall be my seal and blessing upon you—a faithful and wise steward in the midst of mine house, a ruler in my kingdom.

62 And his servant went straightway, and did all things whatsoever his lord commanded him; and after many days all things were fulfilled.

Gather my warriors	=	Priesthood holders in Zion's camp
Redeem my vineyard	=	Repossess the land of Zion
When will it be?	=	When the Lord wills
A faithful and wise steward	=	Joseph Smith

The interpretation of the last part of the parable was given later. Joseph Smith, Jun. was the servant of the Lord (v. 61), the young men and warriors (v. 55) were the priesthood holders known as Zion's Camp (D&C 103:21–28).

The mission of Zion's camp was to redeem Zion, or repossess the land (vv. 56–58). Further discussion of these men will be given in D&C 103 where the Lord gives the interpretation.

D&C 101:63–66 • A Parable of Gathering—the Wheat and the Tares

63 Again, verily I say unto you, I will show unto you wisdom in me concerning all the churches, inasmuch as they are willing to be guided in a right and proper way for their salvation—

64 That the work of the gathering together of my saints may continue, that I may build them up unto my name upon holy places; for the time of harvest is come, and my word must needs be fulfilled.

65 Therefore, I must gather together my people, according to the parable of the wheat and the tares, that the wheat may be secured in the garners to possess eternal life, and be crowned with celestial glory, when I shall come in the kingdom of my Father to reward every man according as his work shall be;

66 While the tares shall be bound in bundles, and their bands made strong, that they may be burned with unquenchable fire.

The second parable was given concerning the salvation of the various branches of the Church that had not gathered to Zion (v. 63). The work of the gathering was to continue and build up "holy places; for the time of harvest is come, and my word must needs be fulfilled" (v. 64). The gathering was to be done according to the parable of the wheat and the tares (v. 65; Matthew 13:24–30, 36–43). The wheat was to be gathered and crowned with celestial glory, and the tares were to be burned (vv. 65–66).[58]

D&C 101:67–75 • A Commandment to All Churches

67 Therefore, a commandment I give unto all the churches, that they shall continue to gather together unto the places which I have appointed.

---

[58] The 86th section of the Doctrine and Covenants also enlarged upon our knowledge of the parable of the wheat and tares.

68 Nevertheless, as I have said unto you in a former commandment, let not your gathering be in haste, nor by flight; but let all things be prepared before you.

69 And in order that all things be prepared before you, observe the commandment which I have given concerning these things—

70 Which saith, or teacheth, to purchase all the lands with money, which can be purchased for money, in the region round about the land which I have appointed to be the land of Zion, for the beginning of the gathering of my saints;

71 All the land which can be purchased in Jackson county, and the counties round about, and leave the residue in mine hand.

72 Now, verily I say unto you, let all the churches gather together all their moneys; let these things be done in their time, but not in haste; and observe to have all things prepared before you.

73 And let honorable men be appointed, even wise men, and send them to purchase these lands.

74 And the churches in the eastern countries, when they are built up, if they will hearken unto this counsel they may buy lands and gather together upon them; and in this way they may establish Zion.

75 There is even now already in store sufficient, yea, even an abundance, to redeem Zion, and establish her waste places, no more to be thrown down, were the churches, who call themselves after my name, willing to hearken to my voice.

The "holy places" or "the places which I have appointed" (v. 67) were the stakes of Zion where the Saints were to gather rather than the center place of Zion (see D&C 94:1; 109:59; 105:23–24). The gathering was not to "be in haste, nor by flight; but let all things be prepared before you" (D&C 101:68). The Lord was quoting Isaiah (52:12), who was contrasting the hasty exodus of Israel out of Egypt with the latter-day gathering. They were to take time to gather "in order that all things be prepared before you" (D&C 101:69). They had previously been commanded to purchase land (see D&C 63:27), and that commandment was still in effect for both Jackson County, Missouri, and the regions round about. Honorable and wise men were to be appointed to make the purchases (see D&C 101:70–73). The eastern branches of the Church (in the United States) were also to participate in the purchasing of lands. There were sufficient people and funds to fulfill this commandment if the voice of the Lord was hearkened unto (vv. 74–75).

D&C 101:76–80 • A Parable of Scattered Israel

76 And again I say unto you, those who have been scattered by their enemies, it is my will that they should continue to importune for redress, and redemption, by the hands of those who are placed as rulers and are in authority over you—

77 According to the laws and constitution of the people, which I have suffered to be established, and should be maintained for the rights and protection of all flesh, according to just and holy principles;

78 That every man may act in doctrine and principle pertaining to futurity, according to the moral agency which I have given unto him, that every man may be accountable for his own sins in the day of judgment.

79 Therefore, it is not right that any man should be in bondage one to another.

80 And for this purpose have I established the Constitution of this land, by the hands of wise men whom I have raised up unto this very purpose, and redeemed the land by the shedding of blood.

The Saints had earlier been commanded to befriend the "constitutional law of the land" (D&C 98:5–6). The Saints were to "importune for redress," or seek compensation, according to this law (vv. 76–77). The Lord acknowledges that He was behind the establishment of that inspired document (v. 77), and that it was based upon "moral agency" for every man to be accountable for his sins (v. 78). Its purpose was to prevent any man to "be in bondage to another" (v. 79). It had come from the hands of "wise men whom [He] had raised up unto this very purpose, and redeemed the land by the shedding of blood" (v. 80). The shedding of blood referred to the American War of Independence. However, the law had not been honored in the driving of the Saints from Missouri. He wanted it to be tested again.

D&C 101:81–88 • Parable of the Woman and the Unjust Judge

81 Now, unto what shall I liken the children of Zion? I will liken them unto the parable of the woman and the unjust judge, for men ought always to pray and not to faint, which saith—

82 There was in a city a judge which feared not God, neither regarded man.

83 And there was a widow in that city, and she came unto him, saying: Avenge me of mine adversary.

84 And he would not for a while, but afterward he said within himself: Though I fear not God, nor regard man, yet because this widow troubleth me I will avenge her, lest by her continual coming she weary me.

85 Thus will I liken the children of Zion.

86 Let them importune at the feet of the judge;

87 And if he heed them not, let them importune at the feet of the governor;

88 And if the governor heed them not, let them importune at the feet of the president;

The Lord reiterates another parable he had given in the New Testament, the Woman and the Unjust Judge (Luke 18:1–8). The two parables have only minor differences. Its purpose at this time was to show what could and should be done concerning Zion. Again we will only outline an interpretation:

PRAY ALWAYS AND FAINT NOT (PERSISTENCE) • 101:81–91

The judge	=	The mob (local leaders)
The widow	=	The children of Zion
Governor	=	Missouri Governor Boggs
Be a watchman upon the tower	=	Protect the olive trees
President	=	U.S. President Van Buren

The mob had taken matters into their own hands, ignoring the justice of the U.S. Constitution. The children are likened to the woman (vv. 81 and 85). Boggs was the governor of Missouri (v. 87), Van Buren was the President of the United States.

D&C 101:89–95 • Why Pray and Persist?

89 And if the president heed them not, then will the Lord arise and come forth out of his hiding place, and in his fury vex the nation;

90 And in his hot displeasure, and in his fierce anger, in his time, will cut off those wicked, unfaithful, and unjust stewards, and appoint

them their portion among hypocrites, and unbelievers;

91 Even in outer darkness, where there is weeping, and wailing, and gnashing of teeth.

92 Pray ye, therefore, that their ears may be opened unto your cries, that I may be merciful unto them, that these things may not come upon them.

93 What I have said unto you must needs be, that all men may be left without excuse;

94 That wise men and rulers may hear and know that which they have never considered;

95 That I may proceed to bring to pass my act, my strange act, and perform my work, my strange work, that men may discern between the righteous and the wicked, saith your God.

The nation may have been vexed by the Civil War because of the slave question, or man being in bondage (vv. 89–92; see v. 79, above; D&C 130:12–13). Because of their moral agency (v. 78, above), the Lord wants all men left without excuse (v. 94), or leave them without any reasonable justification for their actions, and will provide ways to make them accountable. Through the importuning to the governor and president these supposedly "wise men and rulers may hear and know that which they have never considered" (v. 94). The Lord is again quoting Isaiah (52:15). The Restoration of the gospel is to leave all men without excuse, and so the Lord wants to "proceed to bring to pass my strange act" (v. 95). The Restoration, which is strange to the ways of the world, was also prophesied by Isaiah (28:21), and will enable men to "discern between the righteous and the wicked" (v. 95), because of the restored truths that are now available to them and the Light of Christ that all men have.

D&C 101:96–101 • Do Not Sell Lands in Jackson County

96 And again, I say unto you, it is contrary to my commandment and my will that my servant Sidney Gilbert should sell my storehouse, which I have appointed unto my people, into the hands of mine enemies.

97 Let not that which I have appointed be polluted by mine enemies, by the consent of those who call themselves after my name;

98 For this is a very sore and grievous sin against me, and against my

people, in consequence of those things which I have decreed and which are soon to befall the nations.

99 Therefore, it is my will that my people should claim, and hold claim upon that which I have appointed unto them, though they should not be permitted to dwell thereon.

100 Nevertheless, I do not say they shall not dwell thereon; for inasmuch as they bring forth fruit and works meet for my kingdom they shall dwell thereon.

101 They shall build, and another shall not inherit it; they shall plant vineyards, and they shall eat the fruit thereof. Even so. Amen.

The revelation closes with the Lord's instruction to not sell the storehouse in Jackson County, the seriousness of the sins against Him and His people, and His decrees which would soon "befall the nations" (vv. 96–98). Although the Saints had been driven out, His final declaration was: "it is my will that my people should claim, and hold claim upon that which I have appointed unto them, though they shall not be permitted to dwell thereon" v. 99). The Lord again assures them that they could dwell there if "they shall bring forth fruit and works meet for [His] kingdom" (v. 100). The saints in Missouri did not meet that requirement, but the time will come when the Lord's people will dwell in the land of Zion. When Zion will be redeemed is the subject of the following chapter. When it is redeemed, another prophecy of Isaiah will be fulfilled: "They shall plant vineyards, and they shall eat the fruit thereof" (v. 101; see Isaiah 65:21).

General Authority Quotes
—President John Taylor • D&C 101:4

. . . It is necessary that we pass through certain ordeals, and that we be tried. But why is it that we should be tried? There is just the same necessity for it now that there was in former times. I heard the Prophet Joseph say, in speaking of the Twelve on one occasion: "You will have all kinds of trials to pass through. And it is quite as necessary for you to be tried as it was for Abraham and other men of God, and (said he) god will feel after you, and he will take hold of you and wrench your very heart strings, and if you cannot stand it you will not be fit for an inheritance in the Celestial Kingdom of God." Some people have wondered why so many of the Twelve fell away. God tries people according to the position they occupy. Joseph Smith never had many months of peace after he received the truth, and finally he was murdered in Carthage jail. [*Journal of Discourses*, 24:196–97]

—President George Q. Cannon • D&C 101:4

. . . Here comes the command of god to [Abraham] who has been taught so scrupulously about the sinfulness of murder and human sacrifice, to do these very things. Now, why did the Lord ask such things of Abraham? Because, knowing what his future would be and that he would be the father of an innumerable posterity, he was determined to test him. God did not do this for his own sake; for he knew by his foreknowledge what Abraham would do [Abraham 1:22–23]; but the purpose was to impress upon Abraham a lesson, and to enable him to attain unto knowledge that he could not obtain in any other way. That is why God tries all of us. It is not for his own knowledge for he knows all things before hand. He knows all your lives and everything you will do. But he tries us for our own good, that we may know ourselves, for it is most important that a man should know himself. He required Abraham to submit to this trial because he intended to give him glory, exaltation and honor; He intended to make him a king and a priest, to share with Himself the glory, power and dominion He exercised. [CR, April 1899, 66–67]

—Elder Boyd K. Packer • D&C 101:4

Abraham did not have to kill Isaac, you know. He only had to be willing to. Once that was known, that he would sacrifice his only begotten, he was known to be godlike and the blessings poured out upon him. [*That All May Be Edified* (1982), 286]

—President Wilford Woodruff • D&C 101:77–80

I will say here before closing, that two weeks before I left St. George, the spirits of the dead gathered around me wanting to know why we did not redeem them. Said they: "You have had the use of the Endowment House for a number of years and yet nothing has been done for us. We laid the foundation of the government you now enjoy, and we never apostatized from it, but we remained true to it and were faithful to God." These were the signers of the Declaration of Independence, and they waited on me for two days and two nights. . . .I suppose, that heretofore our minds were reaching after our more immediate friends and relatives. I straightway went into the baptismal font and called upon Brother McCallister to baptize me for the signers of the Declaration of Independence, and fifty other eminent men, making one hundred in all, including John Wesley, Columbus, and others. I then baptized him for every President of the United States except three; and when their cause is just, somebody will do the work for them. [General Conference, September 16, 1877; *Journal of Discourses,* 19:229]

I am going to bear my testimony to this assembly, if I never do it again in this life, that those men who laid the foundation of this American Government and signed the Declaration of Independence were the best spirits the God of Heaven could find on the face of the earth. They were choice spirits, not wicked men. General Washington and all the men that labored for the purpose were inspired of the Lord.

Another thing I am going to say here, because I have a right to say it. Every one of those men that signed the Declaration of Independence with General Washington called upon me, as an Apostle of the Lord Jesus Christ, in the Temple at Saint George two consecutive nights, and demanded at my hands that I should go forth and attend to the ordinances of the house of God for them. Men are here, I believe that know of this. . . . Brother McCallister baptized me for all these men, and I then told these brethren that it was their duty to go into the temple and labor until they got endowments for all of them. They did it. Would those spirits have called upon me, as an Elder in Israel, to perform that work if they had not been noble spirits of God? They would not.

I bear testimony because it is true. The spirit of God bore record to myself and the brethren while we were laboring in that way. [CR, April 10, 1898, 89–90]

—*President Harold B. Lee* • D&C 98:77–80

I have often wondered what that expression meant, that out of Zion should go forth the law [Micah 4:2; Isaiah 2:3]. Years ago I went with the Brethren to the Idaho Falls temple, and I heard in that inspired prayer of the First Presidency a definition of the meaning of that term. . . .Note what they said: "We thank thee that thou hast revealed to us that those who gave us our constitutional form of government were men wise in thy sight and that thou didst raise them up for the very purpose of putting forth that sacred document [as revealed in D&C 101]. . . .We pray that kings and rulers and the peoples of all nations under heaven may be persuaded of the blessings enjoyed by the people of this land by reason of their freedom under thy guidance and be constrained to adopt similar governmental systems, thus to fulfill the ancient prophecy of Isaiah [and Micah] that out of Zion shall go forth the law and the word of the Lord from Jerusalem." [*THBL,* 377]

Chapter Fifteen

The Constitution of the High Council

D&C 102; 107:76, 81–84

DOCTRINE AND COVENANTS 102

Historical Setting:

On the 18th of January I reviewed and corrected the minutes of the organization of the High Council, and on the 19th of February, the Council assembled according to adjournment, from the 17th, (Oliver Cowdery and Orson Hyde, clerks,) when the revised minutes were presented and read to the Council. I urged the necessity of prayer, that the Spirit might be given, that the things of the Spirit might be judged thereby, because the carnal mind cannot discern the things of God. The minutes were read three times, and unanimously adopted and received for a form and constitution of the High Council of the Church of Christ hereafter; with this provision, thas [sic that] if the President should discover anything lacking in the same, he should be privileged to supply it. [Verses 30–32, having to do with the Council of the Twelve Apostles, were added by the Prophet Joseph Smith in 1835 when he prepared this section for publication in the Doctrine and Covenants. See section heading.] [*HC*, 2:31]

SECTION 102 • OUTLINE

➤ 102:1–5   The organization of the twelve member council.

➤ 102:6–8   The twelve high councilors cannot act without seven of their members or appointed successors.

    a.   The seven may appoint other worthy and capable high priests to act for those absent (v. 7).

    b.   Death or removal from office vacancies are filled by nomination of the president, or presidents, and sanctioned by a general council of high priests (v. 8).

> 102:9–11   The President of the Church presides over the Council of the Church assisted by the two other presidents [counselors].

    a.   In the absence of one or both assistants, the President may preside without assistants (v. 11).

    b.   In the absence of the President, both or either president may preside (v. 11).

> 102:12–18   The twelve councilors are to draw lots as to who speaks first.

    a.   The councilors shall determine whether it is a difficult case or not, and if not only two shall speak (v. 13).

    b.   If a difficult case, four shall speak, if more difficult, six shall speak, but never more than six (v. 14).

    c.   One-half of the councilors (those drawing even numbers) shall speak in behalf of the accused to prevent insult or injustice (vv. 15, 17).

    d.   Those appointed to speak are to present the evidence in its true light according to equity and justice (v. 16).

    e.   The accuser and the accused have the right to speak for themselves (v. 18).

> 102:19–23   After the evidences are heard, the president shall give a decision and call upon the twelve to sanction it by vote.

    a.   If a councilor manifests an error, the case shall have a rehearing (v. 20).

    b.   After a careful rehearing, the decision can be altered accordingly (v. 21).

    c.   If no additional light is given, the decision shall stand (v. 22).

    d.   In a case of difficulty respecting doctrine or principle, the president can call on the Lord for revelation (v. 23).

> 102:24–29   High priests abroad can organize a council after the same manner to settle difficulties when parties request it.

a. That council has power to appoint one of their own number to preside (v. 25).

b. A copy of the proceedings and their decision shall be sent immediately to the council of the First Presidency (v. 26).

c. If either party is dissatisfied, they may appeal to the First Presidency (v. 27).

d. The First Presidency Council should only be called upon difficult cases (v. 28).

e. The traveling high priests have power to say if a rehearing is necessary (v. 29).

➤ 102:30–33   There is a difference between high priests traveling abroad, and the High Quorum of the Twelve Apostles, in their decisions.

a. From the former there can be an appeal, but not from the latter (v. 31).

b. The latter can only be called in question by the General Authorities in case of transgression (v. 32).

c. The president or presidents of the First Presidency have power to determine whether a case may have a rehearing (v. 33).

➤ 102:34   The twelve councilors cast their ballot.

Introduction

Some sins are so serious that repentance can only be brought about by proper Church discipline administered by the priesthood. Priesthood discipline is administered by revelation according to the pattern given in section 102.

Note: Because of the sensitivity of church discipline, commentary will be limited.

TEXT AND COMMENTARY

D&C 102:1–5 • Organization of the High Council

1 THIS day a general council of twenty-four high priests assembled at the house of Joseph Smith, Jun., by revelation, and proceeded to organize the high council of the church of Christ, which was to consist

of twelve high priests, and one or three presidents as the case might require.

2 The high council was appointed by revelation for the purpose of settling important difficulties which might arise in the church, which could not be settled by the church or the bishop's council to the satisfaction of the parties.

3 Joseph Smith, Jun., Sidney Rigdon and Frederick G. Williams were acknowledged presidents by the voice of the council; and Joseph Smith, Sen., John Smith, Joseph Coe, John Johnson, Martin Harris, John S. Carter, Jared Carter, Oliver Cowdery, Samuel H. Smith, Orson Hyde, Sylvester Smith, and Luke Johnson, high priests, were chosen to be a standing council for the church, by the unanimous voice of the council.

4 The above-named councilors were then asked whether they accepted their appointments, and whether they would act in that office according to the law of heaven, to which they all answered that they accepted their appointments, and would fill their offices according to the grace of God bestowed upon them.

5 The number composing the council, who voted in the name and for the church in appointing the above-named councilors were forty-three, as follows: nine high priests, seventeen elders, four priests, and thirteen members.

Individual members of the Church should solve their differences between themselves. Jesus gave these instructions:

15 Moreover if thy brother shall trespass against thee, go and tell him his fault between thee and him alone: if he shall hear thee, thou hast gained thy brother.

16 But if he will not hear [thee, then] take with thee one or two more, that in the mouth of two or three witnesses every word may be established.

17 And if he shall neglect to hear them, tell [it] unto the church: but if he neglect to hear the church, let him be unto thee as an heathen man and a publican. [Matthew 18:15–17; see also D&C 42:88–92]

The solving of differences by the Church is referred to as Church discipline. The purpose of Church discipline, among the Nephites, was described by Moroni: "And they were strict to observe that there should be no iniquity among them; and whoso was found to commit iniquity, and three witnesses of the church did condemn them before the elders, and if they repented not, and confessed not, their names were blotted out, and they were not numbered among the people of Christ. But as oft as they repented and sought forgiveness, with real intent, they were forgiven" (Moroni 6:7–8).

The Prophet Joseph Smith gave instructions on "the process of laboring with members: We are to deal with them precisely as the Scriptures direct. If thy brother trespass against thee, take him between him and thee alone; if he make thee satisfaction, thou hast saved thy brother; and if not, proceed to take another with thee, etc., and when there is no Bishop, they are to be tried by the voice of the Church; and if an Elder, or a High Priest be present, he is to take the lead in managing the business; but if not, such as have the highest authority should preside" (*TPJS,* 21).

The bishop is the judge in Israel, and responsible for solving differences between the people of his ward. However, the sins committed by Melchizedek Priesthood holders are the responsibility of the stake president, who is also a judge in Israel. He is assisted by the high council as organized by the Prophet Joseph Smith. The Nephites, described above, were also disciplined on the Melchizedek Priesthood level as indicated by their being condemned "before the elders" (Moroni 6:7), rather than "the bishops council" (D&C 102:2). The extent, or the limitations, of the discipline was outlined in another section of the Doctrine and Covenants:

> 10 We believe that all religious societies have a right to deal with their members for disorderly conduct, according to the rules and regulations of such societies; provided that such dealings be for fellowship and good standing; but we do not believe that any religious society has authority to try men on the right of property or life, to take from them this world's goods, or to put them in jeopardy of either life or limb, or to inflict any physical punishment upon them. They can only excommunicate them from their society, and withdraw from them their fellowship. [D&C 134:10]

As instructed in the revelation known as the "Law of the Church," those who break the laws of the land are to be "dealt with according to the laws of the land (D&C 42:79–82).

D&C 102:6–8 • Councilors Nominated by the President

6 Voted: that the high council cannot have power to act without seven of the above-named councilors, or their regularly appointed successors are present.

7 These seven shall have power to appoint other high priests, whom they may consider worthy and capable to act in the place of absent councilors.

8 Voted: that whenever any vacancy shall occur by the death, removal from office for transgression, or removal from the bounds of this church government, of any one of the above-named councilors, it shall be filled by the nomination of the president or presidents, and sanctioned by the voice of a general council of high priests, convened for that purpose, to act in the name of the church.

The selection of members of the high council is one form of doing the [Church] business by the "voice of the people" (see Mosiah 29:26). The twelve men are selected by the president by revelation (D&C 102:2), but approved by the general council of high priests (v. 8), and sustained by all the people in a general conference of the Church. The majority of these twelve select men must be present, and they will select other "worthy and capable" high priests to fill in for the absentees or to replace needed vacancies (v. 7). This procedure is to assure that honest, wise, and good men (see D&C 98:10) will "act in the office according to the law of heaven" (D&C 102:4), and in the name of the Church (v. 8).

D&C 102:9–11

9 The president of the church, who is also the president of the council, is appointed by revelation, and acknowledged in his administration by the voice of the church.

10 And it is according to the dignity of his office that he should preside over the council of the church; and it is his privilege to be assisted by two other presidents, appointed after the same manner that he himself was appointed.

11 And in case of the absence of one or both of those who are appointed to assist him, he has power to preside over the council without an assistant; and in case he himself is absent, the other presidents have power to preside in his stead, both or either of them.

Once more the hand of the Lord must be recognized in the high council. The president, or presidents have been called by revelation, and are to run the council under the same principle of revelation.

D&C 102:12–18

12 Whenever a high council of the church of Christ is regularly organized, according to the foregoing pattern, it shall be the duty of the twelve councilors to cast lots by numbers, and thereby ascertain who of the twelve shall speak first, commencing with number one and so in succession to number twelve.

13 Whenever this council convenes to act upon any case, the twelve councilors shall consider whether it is a difficult one or not; if it is not, two only of the councilors shall speak upon it, according to the form above written.

14 But if it is thought to be difficult, four shall be appointed; and if more difficult, six; but in no case shall more than six be appointed to speak.

15 The accused, in all cases, has a right to one-half of the council, to prevent insult or injustice.

16 And the councilors appointed to speak before the council are to present the case, after the evidence is examined, in its true light before the council; and every man is to speak according to equity and justice.

17 Those councilors who draw even numbers, that is, 2, 4, 6, 8, 10, and 12, are the individuals who are to stand up in behalf of the accused, and prevent insult and injustice.

18 In all cases the accuser and the accused shall have a privilege of speaking for themselves before the council, after the evidences are heard and the councilors who are appointed to speak on the case have finished their remarks.

The selection of men by casting lots to see who speaks, and who is to represent the accused or the accuser, is to prevent insult and injustice to the accused, and equity and justice within the Church (vv. 15–16). Without particular preparation for one side or the other, they must become familiar with the case and also know the doctrines and principles of the Church and the Lord. This again requires good, honest, and wise men. For more difficult cases, the numbers are increased for both sides of the issue, which is to assure that the true light will come before the council and the presidents (v. 16). Further-more, both the accused and the accuser are allowed to present their own case. The procedure is designed to get all of the truth before the council, and not to see who can have more influence on the decision, or in the worlds view to win or lose the issue.

D&C 102:19–23 • The Decision Made by the President

19 After the evidences are heard, the councilors, accuser and accused have spoken, the president shall give a decision according to the understanding which he shall have of the case, and call upon the twelve councilors to sanction the same by their vote.

20 But should the remaining councilors, who have not spoken, or any one of them, after hearing the evidences and pleadings impartially, discover an error in the decision of the president, they can manifest it, and the case shall have a re-hearing.

21 And if, after a careful re-hearing, any additional light is shown upon the case, the decision shall be altered accordingly.

22 But in case no additional light is given, the first decision shall stand, the majority of the council having power to determine the same.

23 In case of difficulty respecting doctrine or principle, if there is not a sufficiency written to make the case clear to the minds of the council, the president may inquire and obtain the mind of the Lord by revelation.

The president who presides is the one who makes the decision, and that decision is to be based upon revelation from the Lord. The twelve high councilors must then sanction the decision. (v. 19). There is another assurance factor built in. If any one of the council feels there has been an error, or an oversight, they may call for a re-hearing on the issue (v. 20). If more truth is brought forth, the decision can be altered or adjusted accordingly (v. 21). If the decision remains the same, the entire council must support the decision. If there still remains questions in the minds of the councilors due to lack of understanding of doctrine or principles of the gospel, the president may ask for further revelation on the matter (v. 23). However, the presidents and the council are expected to know the doctrine and principles of the gospel. In a letter written by the Prophet regarding the receiving of revelation, nearly a year earlier, he declared: ". . . We never inquire at the hand of God for special revelation only in case of their [*sic*] being no previous revelation to suit the case; and that in a council of high priests.

"It is a great thing to inquire at the hands of God, or to come into His presence; and we feel fearful to approach Him on subjects that are of little or no consequence, to satisfy the queries of individuals, especially about things the knowledge of which men ought to obtain in all sincerity, before God, for themselves, in humility by the prayer of faith; and more especially a teacher or a High Priest in the Church. I speak these things not by way of reproach, but by way of instruction" (*TPJS*, 22).

D&C 102:24–29 • Traveling High Priests Abroad

24 The high priests, when abroad, have power to call and organize a council after the manner of the foregoing, to settle difficulties, when the parties or either of them shall request it.

25 And the said council of high priests shall have power to appoint one of their own number to preside over such council for the time being.

26 It shall be the duty of said council to transmit, immediately, a copy of their proceedings, with a full statement of the testimony accompanying their decision, to the high council of the seat of the First Presidency of the Church.

27 Should the parties or either of them be dissatisfied with the decision of said council, they may appeal to the high council of the seat of the First Presidency of the Church, and have a re-hearing, which case shall there be conducted, according to the former pattern written, as though no such decision had been made.

28 This council of high priests abroad is only to be called on the most difficult cases of church matters; and no common or ordinary case is to be sufficient to call such council.

29 The traveling or located high priests abroad have power to say whether it is necessary to call such a council or not.

The high priests traveling abroad were given power to organize a council to settle differences where stakes were not organized. The word *abroad* may be misleading. This would have been anywhere the high priest was traveling as a missionary, except Zion, in Missouri; and Kirtland. In today's world, a good example might be a mission president presiding over an area where no stakes were organized, and he has the power to organize a council in that area. Another example might be in the military where a chaplain, or a member, might be an ordained high priest and have the power to set up a council. All such councils are immediately reviewed by the First Presidency.

D&C 102:30–32

> 30 There is a distinction between the high council or traveling high priests abroad, and the traveling high council composed of the twelve apostles, in their decisions.
>
> 31 From the decision of the former there can be an appeal; but from the decision of the latter there cannot.
>
> 32 The latter can only be called in question by the general authorities of the church in case of transgression.

As stated above, these verses were added after the Quorum of the Twelve was organized in February of 1835, and before the Doctrine and Covenants was published. Obviously, this quorum has more authority than a stake high council, and thus their decisions cannot be appealed unless in a case of transgression of one of its members where the General Authorities call it in question (v. 32). The Quorum of Twelve Apostles is equal in authority and power to the First Presidency (see D&C 107:24).

D&C 102:34 • The First Casting of Lots

> 34 The twelve councilors then proceeded to cast lots or ballot, to ascertain who should speak first, and the following was the result, namely: 1, Oliver Cowdery; 2, Joseph Coe; 3, Samuel H. Smith; 4, Luke Johnson; 5, John S. Carter; 6, Sylvester Smith; 7, John Johnson; 8, Orson Hyde; 9, Jared Carter; 10, Joseph Smith, Sen.; 11, John Smith; 12, Martin Harris.
>
> After prayer the conference adjourned.
>
>

OLIVER COWDERY,
ORSON HYDE,
Clerks

In a later revelation, the Lord gave these instructions:

D&C 107:76, 81–84 • None Exempted from Justice

76 But a literal descendant of Aaron has a legal right to the presidency of this [Aaronic] priesthood, to the keys of this ministry, to act in the office of bishop independently, without counselors, except in a case where a President of the High Priesthood, after the order of Melchizedek, is tried, to sit as a judge in Israel. . . .

81 There is not any person belonging to the church who is exempt from this council of the church.

82 And inasmuch as a President of the High Priesthood shall transgress, he shall be had in remembrance before the common council of the church, who shall be assisted by twelve counselors of the High Priesthood;

83 And their decision upon his head shall be an end of controversy concerning him.

84 Thus, none shall be exempted from the justice and the laws of God, that all things may be done in order and in solemnity before him, according to truth and righteousness.

For further commentary on these verses, see D&C 42:16–21 in volume 1 of this work. They are quoted here to show that the Lord has provided a system where even His prophet is subject to the discipline of the Church. In fact, the Prophet Joseph Smith was investigated under the direction of Bishop Newel K. Whitney for accusations "made by Elder Sylvester Smith, one of the high councilors of this Church" and determined that Brother Sylvester was the one in error, which he later acknowledged (see *HC*, 2:142–144).

General Authority Quotes

Note: These selected quotes are important for an understanding of Church discipline.

—President Spencer W. Kimball

I should like to address a few words to our executive officers, particularly the bishops and stake presidents, who are "common judges" in Israel.

I will read for you the words of prophets and the president of the Church in an earlier century. President John Taylor is quoted as saying:

"Furthermore, I have heard of some Bishops who have been seeking to cover up the iniquities of men: I tell them, in the name of God, they will have to bear them themselves, and meet that judgment; and I tell you that any man who tampers with iniquity, he will have to bear that iniquity, and if any of you want to partake of the sins of men, or uphold them, you will have to bear them. Do you hear it, you Bishops and you Presidents? God will require it at your hands. You are not placed in positions to tamper with principles of righteousness nor to cover up the infamies and corruptions of men." (CR, April 1880, 78.)

I read further from George Q. Cannon, who was also in the First Presidency:

"The Spirit of God would undoubtedly be so grieved that it would forsake not only those who are guilty of these acts, but it would withdraw itself from those who would suffer them to be done in our midst unchecked and unrebuked; and from the President of the Church down, through the entire ranks of the Priesthood, there would be a loss of the Spirit of God, a withdrawal of His gifts and blessings and His power, because of their not taking measures to check and to expose their iniquity." (*Journal of Discourses*, 26:139)

Now, brethren, we could quote many others of the Brethren in this same vein.

We are concerned that too many times the interviewing leader in his personal sympathies for the transgressor, and his love perhaps for the family of the transgressor, is inclined to waive the discipline which that transgressor demands.

Too often a transgressor is forgiven and all penalties waived when that person should have been disfellowshipped or excommunicated. Too often a sinner is disfellowshipped when he or she should have been excommunicated. [CR, April 1975, 115–116]

—Statement by The Council of the First Presidency and The Quorum of the Twelve Apostles of the Church of Jesus Christ of Latter-day Saints

In light of extensive publicity given to six recent Church disciplinary councils in Utah, we believe it helpful to reaffirm the position of the First Presidency and the Quorum of the Twelve Apostles.

We deeply regret the loss of Church membership on the part of anyone. The attendant consequences felt over time by the individuals and their families are very real.

In their leadership responsibilities, local Church leaders may seek clarification and other guidance from General Authorities of the Church.

General Authorities have an obligation to teach principles and policies and to provide information that may be helpful in counseling members for whom local leaders are responsible. In matters of Church discipline, the General Authorities do not direct the decisions of local disciplinary councils. Furthermore, the right to appeal is open to anyone who feels he or she has been unfairly treated by a disciplinary council.

It is difficult to explain Church disciplinary action to representatives of the media. Considerations of confidentiality restrain public comment by Church leaders in such private matters. We have the responsibility to preserve the doctrinal purity of the Church. We are united in this objective. The Prophet Joseph taught an eternal principle when he explained: "That man who rises up to condemn others, finding fault with the Church, saying that they are out of the way, while he himself is righteous, then know assuredly, that that man is in the high road to apostasy." (Joseph Smith, *Teachings of the Prophet Joseph Smith*, sel. Joseph Fielding Smith [1976], 156). In instructing His Twelve Disciples in the New World about those who would not repent, the Savior said, But if he repent not he shall not be numbered among my people, that he shall not destroy my people . . ." (3 Nephi 18:31, see also Mosiah 26:36, and Alma 5:39). The Prophet also remarked that "from apostates the faithful have received the severest persecutions." This continues to be the case today [Quotes D&C 134:10, quoted previously in this chapter] . . . . [*Teachings of the Prophet Joseph Smith*, 67]

Faithful members of the Church can distinguish between mere differences of opinion and those activities formally defined as apostasy. Apostasy refers to Church members who "(1) repeatedly act in clear, open and deliberate public opposition to the Church or its leaders; or (2) persist in teaching as Church doctrine information that is not Church doctrine after being corrected by their bishops or higher authority, or (3) continue to follow the teachings of apostate cults (such as those who advocate plural marriage) after being corrected by their bishops or higher authority." [*General Handbook of Instructions*, 10–3.]

The general and local officers of the Church will continue to do their duty, and faithful Church members will understand.

As leaders of The Church of Jesus Christ of Latter-day Saints, we reach out in love to all and constantly pray that the Lord, whose Church this is, will bless those who love and seek divine truth. [*The Council of the First Presidency and the Quorum of the Twelve Apostles*, Published in the *Deseret News*, October 17, 1993]

—President N. Eldon Tanner

With all the evil present in the world today, it is important that those that are responsible conduct proper interviews.

Let us always remember that our main purpose, assignment, and responsibility is to save souls.

It is important that those we interview realize that they are *spirit children of God* and that *we love them*, and *let them know that we love them* and are interested in their welfare and in helping them succeed in life.

It is a great responsibility for a bishop or a stake president to conduct a worthiness interview. There is equal responsibility, however, upon the member who is interviewed. Careful, searching interviews need to be conducted always individually and privately. . . . [CR, October 1978, 59]

—Elder James A. Cullimore

[after quoting Alma 42:24–25 on mercy and justice] How plain, then, is the logic as to the necessity of taking appropriate action in case of serious transgression. The need is to cleanse the Church and to help bring about full repentance to the individual.

President [Harold B.] Lee said as he spoke to the Brethren in 1972: "Now, this doesn't mean when we have to take action that we turn our backs on him who has sinned . . . we don't do [that]—we should try not to do it. But we have to be like fathers—sometimes we have to discipline . . . , we have to spank them, then we have to love them. It is the doctrine of the Lord, and we should do that in kindness. It seems to me, that there comes a time in the lives of those who have sinned so seriously that, short of disciplinary action, I think some men can't repent until they are turned over to the buffetings of Satan by the loss of the Spirit of the Lord." [Priesthood Board Meeting, March 1, 1972, 12]

—Elder Robert L. Simpson

. . . May I take a few minutes at this session of our conference to discuss what I believe is perhaps the most misunderstood meeting of all the meetings that convene in the Church. . . .[After describing an excommunication by a high council, he continues].

This young man had just taken his first giant step back. As an excommunicated member of the Church and with his heart determined to make things right, he was far better off than just a few days before with his membership record intact but carrying deceit in his heart that seemed to shout the word hypocrite with every move he made toward doing something in the Church. . . .

Priesthood courts of the Church are not courts of retribution. They are courts of love. Oh that members of the Church could understand this one fact. . . .

Few, if any, men have the strength to walk that hill alone, and please be assured, it is uphill all the way. There needs to be help—someone who really loves you, someone who has been divinely commissioned to assist you confidentially, quietly, assuredly—and may I re-emphasize the word *confidentially*, for here again, Satan has spread the false rumor that confidences are rarely kept. . . .

Even excommunication from this Church is not the end of the world; and if this process is necessary in carrying out true justice, I bear you my personal and solemn witness that even this extreme penalty of excommunication can be the first giant step back, provided there follows a sincere submission to the Spirit and faith in the authenticity of God's plan. [CR, April, 1972, 31–33; this talk was later approved by the First Presidency and the Council of the Twelve and sent to local leaders of the Church with some added comments, including the statements of President John Taylor and President George Q. Cannon quoted by President Spencer W. Kimball above.]

Chapter Sixteen

When Will Zion Be Redeemed?[59]

D&C 103; 105

DOCTRINE AND COVENANTS 103

Historical Setting: "February 24 [1834]—I received [Doctrine and Covenants 103]" (*HC,* 2:36; no more is written in the Prophet's history).

"This revelation was received after the arrival in Kirtland, Ohio, of Parley P. Pratt and Lyman Wight, who had come from Missouri to counsel with the Prophet as to the restoration of the saints to their land in Jackson County" (section heading).

SECTION 103 • OUTLINE

➤ 103:1–10   A revelation and commandment for the salvation and redemption of Zion.

     a.   The Lord will pour wrath on His enemies when their iniquities are full (vv. 2–3).

     b.   Those who call themselves by my name will be chastened a little season (v. 4).

     c.   If they hearken to my counsel, they shall prevail against the enemy (vv. 5–7).

     d.   If they don't keep them, the kingdoms of the world shall prevail (v. 8).

---

[59] This chapter was originally given as a paper at the 25th Annual Sidney B. Sperry Symposium, 1996. It has been revised.

    e.   They were to be a light to the world, and saviors of men (v. 9).

    f.   If the salt has lost its savor, they shall be trodden by men (vv. 9–10).

➤ 103:11–14   I have decreed that your brethren return and build up the waste places.

    a.   After much tribulation comes the blessing (v. 12).

    b.   After tribulation, you shall return to Zion, never to be thrown down (vv. 13–14).

➤ 103:15–20   The redemption of Zion must come by power.

    a.   I will raise a man like Moses to lead you out of bondage (vv. 16–18).

    b.   Angels and my presence shall go before you (vv. 19–20).

➤ 103:21–29   Joseph Smith is the man in the parable to gather warriors to go to the Zion.

    a.   All the churches send wise men with money to purchase lands (v. 23).

    b.   If enemies come against you, I will curse them (vv. 24–26).

    c.   No man be afraid to lay down his life, for he shall find it again (vv. 27–28).

    d.   Sidney shall lift his voice to the eastern churches about the redemption (v. 29).

➤ 103:30–40   Requirements for Zion's camp journey to Zion.

    a.   Go by companies of ten, twenty, fifty, and a hundred: total five hundred (v. 30).

    b.   If not five hundred, three hundred, but no less than one hundred (vv. 31–34).

    c.   Pray for Joseph to go with you; other assignments (vv. 37–40).

Introduction

When will Zion be redeemed? From the very beginning of the history of the Church, when the concept of the building of a Zion society was introduced, there has been much speculation, much misinformation, and many ideas put forth about when and how Zion will be redeemed. The Lord invites the members of the Church to search the scriptures and avoid the confusion of speculation. As we seek an answer to our question, we must first determine the meaning of the term *Zion*.

President David O. McKay said, "Zion means, literally, a 'sunny place,' or 'sunny mountain.' It first designated an eminence in Palestine on which Jerusalem is built. In the Doctrine and Covenants, Zion has three designations: first, the land of America; second, a specific place of gathering; and third, the pure in heart."[60] Each one of these Doctrine and Covenants definitions given by President McKay will be briefly analyzed, but the redemption of Zion, the "specific place of gathering," or city of the New Jerusalem, will be emphasized.

ZION AS THE LAND OF AMERICA

"You know there has been great discussion in relation to Zion—where it is, and where the gathering of the dispensation is, and which I am now going to tell you. The Prophets have spoken and written about it; but I will make a proclamation that will cover a broader ground. *The whole of America is Zion itself from north to south, and is described by the Prophets, who declare that it is the Zion where the mountain of the Lord should be, and that it should be in the center of the land.* When Elders shall take up and examine the old prophecies in the Bible, they will see it." (*TPJS*, 362).

The whole of North and South America is Zion. General Moroni also understood the definition of Zion. In Alma we read, "And it came to pass that when he had poured out his soul to God, he [General Moroni] named all the land which was south of the land Desolation, yea, and in fine, all the land, both on the north and on the south—a chosen land, and the land of liberty" (Alma 46:17). When we accept this definition of Zion, we can understand the prophecies spoken by the ancient prophets in a new light.

---

[60] David O. McKay, "Zion Shall Flourish," *Instructor*, February 1959, 33.

A SPECIFIC PLACE OF GATHERING

The Lord revealed to the Latter-day Saints that the specific place of gathering was Independence, Jackson County, Missouri, the center place of Zion (D&C 57:3). The center place introduces another scripture related to the gathering of the Saints. The prophet Isaiah spoke of enlarging the tent of Israel—of lengthening its cords and strengthening its stakes (see Isaiah 54:2). At the time of Moses, the tabernacle was a tent, which was picked up and carried. It was, in effect, a portable temple. After that time, the concept of Israel being gathered into a tent was familiar among the prophets.

No other group in the Christian world uses the term *stake*, but we speak of the thousands of stakes of Zion. This term has direct reference to the tent of Israel. To set up a tent, particularly a large tent, you must have at least one large center pole held up by the cords or ropes secured to stakes driven into the ground. The center pole, or the center place, cannot be set up until there are stakes established all the way around it. Similarly, Zion must have stakes all the way around the New Jerusalem (Independence, Missouri) before the tent of Israel will be established.

We now have many places of gathering, stakes established all around Jackson County, and are coming to the time of establishing a center place. Every state in the United States has one or more stakes, and there are stakes in Canada, Mexico, and Central American countries. Stakes are also established throughout other parts of the world, but the Lord defined Independence, Missouri, as the center of the land "and the place for the city of Zion" (D&C 57:1–2). Therefore, it seems that the tent concept refers to the Americas and specifically to North America, the initial place appointed for the gathering. After the New Jerusalem is established, and the Church is enlarged, it will be necessary to "lengthen [the] cords and strengthen [the] stakes" (Isaiah 54:2).

THE PURE IN HEART

The Doctrine and Covenants describes the people who inherit the land of Zion as the pure in heart (D&C 97:21). Becoming pure in heart is a process. The formula for becoming pure in heart was given in D&C

88:67–68, and discussed in chapter 8 (see also D&C 97:8–17; chapter 12). When the formula is followed, the beatitude: "Blessed are all the pure in heart, for they shall see God" (3 Nephi 12:8; Matthew 5:8) will be fulfilled.

To establish a center place of Zion, the Lord must have a Zion people. Therefore, the place to begin to establish Zion is in the individual. The whole idea of the gospel is to make ourselves pure in heart. When enough people seeking to become pure in heart gather together in a designated place, a stake of Zion is established. When a center place is established, surrounded by stakes of Zion, the stakes will be strengthened and the cords will be lengthened to include North and South America and even the whole world as part of the Zion of our God.[61] The Prophet Joseph said, "We ought to have the building up of Zion as our greatest object" (*TPJS,* 160). Every dispensation in the history of the world has been given the same commandment to "seek to bring forth and establish the cause of Zion" (D&C 6:6). It will be accomplished in this dispensation, although the early members of the Church were given the opportunity and failed.

TEXT AND COMMENTARY

D&C 103:1–10 • Salvation and Redemption of Zion

1 VERILY I say unto you, my friends, behold, I will give unto you a revelation and commandment, that you may know how to act in the discharge of your duties concerning the salvation and redemption of your brethren, who have been scattered on the land of Zion;

2 Being driven and smitten by the hands of mine enemies, on whom I will pour out my wrath without measure in mine own time.

3 For I have suffered them thus far, that they might fill up the measure of their iniquities, that their cup might be full;

4 And that those who call themselves after my name might be chastened for a little season with a sore and grievous chastisement,

---

[61] Brigham Young taught that "Zion will extend, eventually, all over the earth;" in *Journal of Discourses* [1954–86], 9:138. Because this is a millennial condition and will happen following the establishment of the city of the New Jerusalem, it is only mentioned here.

because they did not hearken altogether unto the precepts and commandments which I gave unto them.

5 But verily I say unto you, that I have decreed a decree which my
people shall realize, inasmuch as they hearken from this very hour unto
the counsel which I, the Lord their God, shall give unto them.

6 Behold they shall, for I have decreed it, begin to prevail against mine
enemies from this very hour.

7 And by hearkening to observe all the words which I, the Lord their
God, shall speak unto them, they shall never cease to prevail until the
kingdoms of the world are subdued under my feet, and the earth is given
unto the saints, to possess it forever and ever.

8 But inasmuch as they keep not my, and hearken not to observe all
my words, the kingdoms of the world shall prevail against them.

9 For they were set to be a light unto the world, and to be the saviors
of men;

10 And inasmuch as they are not the saviors of men, they are as salt
that has lost its savor, and is thenceforth good for nothing but to be cast
out and trodden under foot of men.

About two months after the Saints had been driven out of Jackson
County, February 1834, the Lord gave the early members of the Church
the opportunity to go back and redeem their brethren who were driven
from Zion (vv. 1–2). He decreed then that if they would hearken unto
His counsel, they should "begin to prevail against mine enemies from this
very hour" (vv. 5–6). It was promised to be a permanent Zion establishment (v. 7). The Lord reminded them of being a light to the world and
the "saviors of men" (v. 9). In the revelation two months before, he had
called them to be the "savor of men" (D&C 101:39–40). Salt is used as
a seasoning, and is an essential need of the body. The gospel brings
seasoning, or understanding to the purpose of life. The priesthood
ordinances are necessary for salvation in the kingdom of God. Salt that
is polluted, or mixed with other ingredients, is no more useful for either
seasoning or for the body. In ancient Israel, they used polluted salt for
housetops and walkways, thus it was trodden under foot. (D&C 103:10;
101:40). If Church members do not act as savors, spread the gospel, or
as saviors, administer the priesthood ordinances where appropriate, they
could be trodden down at the Second Coming, or before.

D&C 103:11–14 • After Tribulation Comes Blessings

11 But verily I say unto you, I have decreed that your brethren which have been scattered shall return to the lands of their inheritances, and shall build up the waste places of Zion.

12 For after much tribulation, as I have said unto you in a former commandment, cometh the blessing.

13 Behold, this is the blessing which I have promised after your tribulations, and the tribulations of your brethren—your redemption, and the redemption of your brethren, even their restoration to the land of Zion, to be established, no more to be thrown down.

14 Nevertheless, if they pollute their inheritances they shall be thrown down; for I will not spare them if they pollute their inheritances.

The building of the waste places of Zion (v. 11) was a prophecy of the last days made by the Old Testament prophet Amos (Amos 9:11–15). The former commandment concerning Zion and tribulation (v. 12) was D&C 58:4. It was really a warning of tribulation to come, but probably wasn't recognized as such. The Lord was offering the blessing now (v. 13), after the great tribulation they had been through. Again he warns them against polluting their inheritance (v. 14).

D&C 103:15–20 • A Man Like unto Moses

15 Behold, I say unto you, the redemption of Zion must needs come by power;

16 Therefore, I will raise up unto my people a man, who shall lead them like as Moses led the children of Israel.

17 For ye are the children of Israel, and of the seed of Abraham, and ye must needs be led out of bondage by power, and with a stretched-out arm.

18 And as your fathers were led at the first, even so shall the redemption of Zion be.

19 Therefore, let not your hearts faint, for I say not unto you as I said unto your fathers: Mine angel shall go up before you, but not my presence.

20 But I say unto you: Mine angels shall go up before you, and also my presence, and in time ye shall possess the goodly land.

The man like unto Moses is the President of the Church, the President of the High Priesthood (D&C 107:91–92). That man is the mouthpiece of the Lord, as was Moses. Other men may receive personal revelation, but the one to whom the Lord speaks directly to guide His Church is its president (Numbers 12). Elder John A. Widtsoe has verified scripturally that the man like unto Moses is the President of the Church:

> Yet, the meaning as set forth in the scriptures is very simple. In modern revelation, the President of the Church is frequently compared to Moses. Soon after the organization of the Church, the Lord said, "no one shall be appointed to receive commandments and revelations in this church excepting my servant Joseph Smith, Jun., for he receiveth them even as Moses" (D&C 28:2). In one of the greatest revelations upon Priesthood, this is more specifically expressed: "The duty of the President of the office of the High Priesthood is to preside over the whole church, and to be like unto Moses." [D&C 107:91]
>
> The discussion of this question among the Saints, led to the following statement in the *Times and Seasons* (6:922) by John Taylor, then the editor: "The President [of the Church] stands in the Church as Moses did to the children of Israel, according to the revelations the man like unto Moses in the Church is the President of the Church."[62]

The Lord will raise up the man who will lead the children of Israel back to build up the city of the New Jerusalem (D&C 103:16). That man is the President of the Church. He may be the present president of the Church or any one of his successors.

The Lord promises to lead the modern nation of gathered Israel out of bondage even as he had their fathers (v. 17). To whom were they in bondage? To the Gentile nations who were persecuting them. He had promised ancient Israel (Moses; Exodus 33:1–4) that his "angel shall go up before you, but not my presence." To modern Israel He promised that "his angels shall go up before you, and also my presence (D&C 103:19–20). Ancient Israel functioned under the Aaronic Priesthood, therefore, they could only endure the presence of angels. Modern Israel had been given the Melchizedek Priesthood, and thus could, if worthy,

---

[62] John A. Widtsoe, *Evidences and Reconciliations*, arr. G. Homer Durham [1960], 248.

have the presence of angels and the presence of the Lord (see D&C 67:10–14; 84:19–26).

D&C 103:21–29 • Gather Warriors for Zion

21 Verily, verily I say unto you, that my servant Joseph Smith, Jun., is the man to whom I likened the servant to whom the Lord of the vineyard spake in the parable which I have given unto you.

22 Therefore let my servant Joseph Smith, Jun., say unto the strength of my house, my young men and the middle aged—Gather yourselves together unto the land of Zion, upon the land which I have bought with money that has been consecrated unto me.

23 And let all the churches send up wise men with their moneys, and purchase lands even as I have commanded them.

24 And inasmuch as mine enemies come against you to drive you from my goodly land, which I have consecrated to be the land of Zion, even from your own lands after these testimonies, which ye have brought before me against them, ye shall curse them;

25 And whomsoever ye curse, I will curse, and ye shall avenge me of mine enemies.

26 And my presence shall be with you even in avenging me of mine enemies, unto the third and fourth generation of them that hate me.

27 Let no man be afraid to lay down his life for my sake; for whoso layeth down his life for my sake shall find it again.

28 And whoso is not willing to lay down his life for my sake is not my disciple.

29 It is my will that my servant Sidney Rigdon shall lift up his voice in the congregations in the eastern countries, in preparing the churches to keep the commandments which I have given unto them concerning the restoration and redemption of Zion.

The imagery of the parable of the nobleman and the choice land (see D&C 101:43–62) previously identified Joseph Smith as the leader of the men who were to go to seek the redemption of Zion. It is a good example of the Lord commanding His Saints to go to war (see D&C 98:36). The purchasing of more lands (v. 23) confirms the seriousness of the Lord in His quest for returning to Zion. Collectively, He would curse the enemy, and avenge them for the previous persecutions (vv. 24–26). Individually, those who gave their lives in this courageous battle would gain eternal life (vv. 27–28). Sidney Rigdon was to inform the churches in the east of this program (v. 29). While in His foreknowledge, He knew they would fail, it would not be His fault when they did so.

D&C 103:30–40 • Zion's Camp

30 It is my will that my servant Parley P. Pratt and my servant Lyman Wight should not return to the land of their brethren, until they have obtained companies to go up unto the land of Zion, by tens, or by twenties, or by fifties, or by an hundred, until they have obtained to the number of five hundred of the strength of my house.

31 Behold this is my will; ask and ye shall receive; but men do not always do my will.

32 Therefore, if you cannot obtain five hundred, seek diligently that peradventure you may obtain three hundred.

33 And if ye cannot obtain three hundred, seek diligently that peradventure ye may obtain one hundred.

34 But verily I say unto you, a commandment I give unto you, that ye shall not go up unto the land of Zion until you have obtained a hundred of the strength of my house, to go up with you unto the land of Zion.

35 Therefore, as I said unto you, ask and ye shall receive; pray earnestly that peradventure my servant Joseph Smith, Jun., may go with you, and preside in the midst of my people, and organize my kingdom upon the consecrated land, and establish the children of Zion upon the laws and commandments which have been and which shall be given unto you.

36 All victory and glory is brought to pass unto you through your diligence, faithfulness, and prayers of faith.

37 Let my servant Parley P. Pratt journey with my servant Joseph Smith, Jun.

38 Let my servant Lyman Wight journey with my servant Sidney Rigdon.

39 Let my servant Hyrum Smith journey with my servant Frederick G. Williams.

40 Let my servant Orson Hyde journey with my servant Orson Pratt, whithersoever my servant Joseph Smith, Jun., shall counsel them, in obtaining the fulfilment of these commandments which I have given unto you, and leave the residue in my hands. Even so. Amen.

Zion's Camp, as it became known, was no easy task. They were to march about one thousand miles under difficult circumstances. They were inexperienced and untrained warriors, but went on their faith in the Lord. He promised if they would ask they would receive (vv. 31, 35). He promised them victory if they were diligent and faithful (v. 36). The Lord asked for five hundred men and would go with less, but not fewer than one hundred (vv. 30, 32–34). There were two hundred and nine men, plus a few women, who undertook this difficult task. We will leave more details to a study of Church history.

DOCTRINE AND COVENANTS 105

*H*istorical Setting: "June 19 [1834]. . . Many of my little band sheltered in an old meeting house through this night, and in the morning the water in Big Fishing river was about forty feet deep, where, the previous evening, it was no more than to our ankles, and our enemies swore that the water rose thirty feet in thirty minutes in Little Fishing river. They reported the one of their men was killed by lightning, and that another had his hand torn off by his horse drawing his hand between the logs of a corn crib while he was holding him on the inside. They declared that if that was the way God fought for the Mormons, they might as well go about their business [God will fight their battles—D&C 98:37]" (*HC*, 2:105).

"I received [Doctrine and Covenants 105]—*Revelation given on Fishing River, Missouri, June 22, 1834*" (*HC*, 2:108; see the section heading of D&C 105 for a summation of *HC*, 2:94–105)

SECTION 105 • OUTLINE

➤ 105:1–8   Were it not for the transgression of my people collectively, Zion might have been redeemed now.

     a. They are not obedient, and do not impart their substance to the poor (v. 3).

     b. They are not united according to the law of the celestial kingdom (vv. 4–5).

     c. They must be chastened until they learn obedience (v. 6).

    d.   The first elders are not under condemnation (v. 7).

    e.   The churches abroad say: God will deliver them or we keep our money (v. 8).

➤ 105:9–13   Because of transgressions, they must wait a little season for Zion's redemption.

    a.   They must be prepared, taught, know more perfectly, have experience (v. 10).

    b.   Mine elders must be endowed with power from on high (vv. 11–12).

➤ 105:14–19   The Lord will fight their battles for Zion.

    a.   Satan will lay waste the enemies, and they will not pollute the heritages (v. 15).

    b.   The warriors did not hearken to my voice to throw down the towers (vv. 16–17).

    c.   A blessing of the endowment is prepared for the faithful (vv. 18–19).

➤ 105:20–26   A commandment to stay in the regions as Joseph appoints them.

    a.   Reveal not the things I have revealed unto them (v. 23).

    b.   Talk not of judgments, nor boast, gather consistent to people's feelings (v. 24).

    c.   I will give favor in the people's eyes, that the army of Israel is great (vv. 25–26).

➤ 105:27–30   I will soften the people's hearts, that the strength of my house be gathered.

    a.   Send wise men to purchase lands to be possessed by consecration (vv. 28–29).

    b.   The armies of Israel may possess the lands previously purchased (v. 30).

➤ 105:31–32   First, let the army become very great and be sanctified before me.

    a.   The kingdoms of this world may acknowledge the kingdom of Zion (v. 32).

    b.   They will become subject unto her laws (v. 32).

➤ 105:33–37   The day of calling is past, the day of choosing the worthy will
come.

    a.   The first elders are to be endowed in the Lord's house in
Kirtland (v. 33).

    b.   The commandments and laws of Zion shall be executed
and fulfilled (v. 34).

    c.   It will be manifest to my servant those chosen, they will
be sanctified (v. 36).

    d.   They shall have power after many days to bring about
Zion (v. 37).

➤ 105:38–41   The Church must sue for peace to those who smote you, and
to all people.

    a.   Lift up an ensign, and a proclamation of peace to the ends
of the earth (v. 39).

    b.   Make proposals to those who smote, as given by the Spirit
(vv. 40–41).

TEXT AND COMMENTARY

D&C 105:1–8 • Zion Built by the Law of the Celestial Kingdom

1 VERILY I say unto you who have assembled yourselves together that
you may learn my will concerning the redemption of mine afflicted
people—

2 Behold, I say unto you, were it not for the transgressions of my
people, speaking concerning the church and not individuals, they might
have been redeemed even now.

3 But behold, they have not learned to be obedient to the things
which I required at their hands, but are full of all manner of evil, and
do not impart of their substance, as becometh saints, to the poor and
afflicted among them;

4 And are not united according to the union required by the law of
the celestial kingdom;

5 And Zion cannot be built up unless it is by the principles of the
law of the celestial kingdom; otherwise I cannot receive her unto myself.

6 And my people must needs be chastened until they learn obedience,
if it must needs be, by the things which they suffer.

7 I speak not concerning those who are appointed to lead my people, who are the first elders of my church, for they are not all under this condemnation;

8 But I speak concerning my churches abroad—there are many who will say: Where is their God? Behold, he will deliver them in time of trouble, otherwise we will not go up unto Zion, and will keep our moneys.

Zion's Camp was organized to redeem Zion. Four months later, June 1834, after they had failed in their attempt, the Lord gave them additional counsel. In this revelation, He repeats that they had not been obedient, they had been full of all manner of evil, they would not impart of their substance to the poor, (v. 3) and they had not been united according to the law of the celestial kingdom, as was required (v. 4). He further stated that the only way that Zion will ever be built up is upon the principles of the law of the celestial kingdom (v. 5). The coming chastisement was because of the disobedience and attitude of many of the Church members, not the leaders (vv. 6–8). The Lord deals with the Church collectively, not individually, when the issues concern the whole Church.

D&C 105:9–13 • Prerequisites for Redeeming Zion

9 Therefore, in consequence of the transgressions of my people, it is expedient in me that mine elders should wait for a little season for the redemption of Zion—

10 That they themselves may be prepared, and that my people may be taught more perfectly, and have experience, and know more perfectly concerning their duty, and the things which I require at their hands.

11 And this cannot be brought to pass until mine elders are endowed with power from on high.

12 For behold, I have prepared a great endowment and blessing to be poured out upon them, inasmuch as they are faithful and continue in humility before me.

13 Therefore it is expedient in me that mine elders should wait for a little season, for the redemption of Zion.

The Lord's elders must wait for a little season before Zion will be redeemed (v. 9). He did not define the length of a "little season," but outlined *eight more* things that must be accomplished before that redemption will come to pass. The Lord had revealed the *first* thing to be accomplished, in a revelation previously received. He promised those who would gather to return to Missouri (Zion's Camp) that "the redemption of Zion must needs come by power; therefore, I will raise up unto my people a man, who shall lead them like as Moses led the children of Israel. For ye are the children of Israel, and of the seed of Abraham, and ye must needs be led out of bondage by power, and with a stretched-out arm" (D&C 103:15–17). Joseph was the man in Zion's Camp, but a future president will be raised up after the little season.

The *second* prerequisite was the people must receive and be taught through their temple endowment. The Lord instituted the endowment to prepare "my people," teach them "more perfectly, . . . and know more perfectly concerning their duty, and the things which I require at their hands." This experience would not "be brought to pass until mine elders are endowed with power from on high" (D&C 105:10–11). The Lord had commanded them to go the Ohio so that they "shall be endowed with power from on high" (D&C 38:32). Zion will never be established except by a people who receive and live up to their temple endowment, which is to help them become pure in heart and perfected in their ministry (D&C 97:12–16). This revelation was given in 1834, and the Kirtland Temple was completed two years later, in 1836. The dedication of the temple on April 3, 1836 was a great historical incident spoken of by the prophets. The collective outpouring of the Spirit accompanied this dedication (see *HC,* 2:427–28 and chapter 19 of this work). Yet that endowment of spiritual power does not fulfill the prophecy; each member must be personally endowed as well.

The people must also be taught the fulness of the gospel of Jesus Christ more perfectly through the temple of the Lord. The temple is the Lord's university. It is a degree-granting university, fully accredited in every aspect, in which we prepare ourselves for the celestial degree. Therefore, when the Lord stated that the Saints must be taught more perfectly, he was referring to the building of the temple and the receiving of personal endowments which the Lord had prepared (v. 12). In the temple endowment, we are instructed how to live; then we covenant to live as we have been instructed. To bring our ancestors out of the spirit world, we must vicariously perform their temple ordinances. That is a vital and integral doctrine of the gospel. We are also beneficiaries because we have a constant reminder of those covenants, better enabling us to know how to live and what the Lord requires at our hands. With this knowledge, we may become a pure people, a Zion people, and be ready to establish the center place of Zion in the tent of Israel. If the relatively few Saints in 1833, who had not received their temple endowments, could have redeemed Zion had they hearkened to the Lord (see D&C 105:2), certainly we now have enough temples built, and people endowed, for Zion to be redeemed if the rest of the Lord's prerequisites are met.

D&C 105:14–19 • The Lord Will Fight Your Battles

14 For behold, I do not require at their hands to fight the battles of Zion; for, as I said in a former commandment, even so will I fulfil—I will fight your battles.

15 Behold, the destroyer I have sent forth to destroy and lay waste mine enemies; and not many years hence they shall not be left to pollute mine heritage, and to blaspheme my name upon the lands which I have consecrated for the gathering together of my saints.

16 Behold, I have commanded my servant Joseph Smith, Jun., to say unto the strength of my house, even my warriors, my young men, and middle-aged, to gather together for the redemption of my people, and throw down the towers of mine enemies, and scatter their watchmen;

17 But the strength of mine house have not hearkened unto my words.

18 But inasmuch as there are those who have hearkened unto my words, I have prepared a blessing and an endowment for them, if they continue faithful.

19 I have heard their prayers, and will accept their offering; and it is expedient in me that they should be brought thus far for a trial of their faith.

The *third* prerequisite of the redemption of Zion is that when the people are prepared, the Lord will fight the Saints' battles for them (v. 14). The former commandment [D&C 98:37] was part of the law of war, as stated previously. The Lord had fulfilled His promise by raising up Joseph Smith and his warriors, but collectively they had not lived up to their commitment (vv. 16–17). He again showed His mercy with the promise of the endowment (v. 18). The Lord had told Zion's Camp four months earlier that from that very day He would give them power to prevail over

their enemies (see D&C 103:6). The same promise is applicable to us. From this very day, if we become the Zion people that we have the potential of being, the Lord will fight our battles. But if we again let "jarrings and contentions, and envyings, and strifes, and lustful and covetous desires" (D&C 101:6), and the designs of the world enter our lives, the Lord will not redeem Zion.

The destroyer sent to destroy the Lord's enemies (D&C 105:15) may have dual applications, or be more than one time or event. We occasionally hear that Heber C. Kimball prophesied that there would not be a yellow dog left to wag its tail in resistance to the Saints' return to Jackson County.[63] This prophecy has been tied to another prophecy—that Zion will be swept clean. These are actually two separate prophecies and should not be linked together. The sweeping clean of Missouri may have already been fulfilled. During the Civil War, opposing factions called the Bushwhackers and Jayhawkers battled in Missouri. Through these and other battles, Zion, or Missouri, was swept clean, leaving only chimneys in place of farms and houses.[64] The yellow dog prophecy may be referring to another kind of resistance. The return of specified Saints to Missouri will come about in a natural way; they will have no resistance from the inhabitants. Today, many members live happily in Missouri without resistance. The Lord said He would fight our battles; He will take care of whatever resistance is raised if we trust Him.

Although Zion's Camp failed collectively to qualify for the Lord to fight their battles, individually the Lord had brought them "thus far for a trial of their faith" (D&C 105:19). They were tested for their worthiness to hold offices of the soon to be organized apostles and seventies. We will discuss this further in chapter 18.

D&C 105:20–26 • The Army of Israel Becomes Great

20 And now, verily I say unto you, a commandment I give unto you,

---

[63] *Deseret News,* May 23, 1931, as cited in Roy W. Doxey, *Zion in the Last Days* [1965], 55.

[64] The destruction of Missouri fulfilled a prophecy of Joseph Smith to General Doniphan. See B. H. Roberts, *A Comprehensive History of The Church of Jesus Christ of Latter-day Saints* [1930], vol. 1, chapter 39.

that as many as have come up hither, that can stay in the region round about, let them stay;

21 And those that cannot stay, who have families in the east, let them tarry for a little season, inasmuch as my servant Joseph shall appoint unto them;

22 For I will counsel him concerning this matter, and all things whatsoever he shall appoint unto them shall be fulfilled.

23 And let all my people who dwell in the regions round about be very faithful, and prayerful, and humble before me, and reveal not the things which I have revealed unto them, until it is wisdom in me that they should be revealed.

24 Talk not of judgments, neither boast of faith nor of mighty works, but carefully gather together, as much in one region as can be, consistently with the feelings of the people;

25 And behold, I will give unto you favor and grace in their eyes, that you may rest in peace and safety, while you are saying unto the people: Execute judgment and justice for us according to law, and redress us of our wrongs.

26 Now, behold, I say unto you, my friends, in this way you may find favor in the eyes of the people, until the army of Israel becomes very great.

The *fourth* prerequisite for redeeming Zion is the establishment of stakes around the center place, New Jerusalem. The Lord commanded to "stay in the region round about," and "those that cannot stay" to "tarry for a little season," as directed by Joseph (vv. 20–21). The people dwelling in the regions round about seems to refer to the establishment of stakes around the New Jerusalem for the center place, or center pole, of the tent of Israel to be put in place. Earlier, when the members of the Church were under great persecution, the Lord had declared that Zion would "not be moved out of her place, notwithstanding her children are scattered" (D&C 101:17). The pure in heart would return "that the prophets might be fulfilled" (D&C 101:19). Then He would appoint other places of gathering, which would "be called stakes, for the curtains or the strength of Zion" (D&C 101:21; note again the association with the tabernacle of Moses).

To understand the Lord's instructions not to disclose or boast of the revelation concerning Zion (D&C 105:23–24), we must know the background of what had taken place there. In 1831, the Saints arrived in Independence in the midst of a rough group of settlers. There, they boasted of building up Zion and implied that they were going to drive out all of the inhabitants. This attitude undoubtedly contributed to their being driven out. The Lord chastised the Saints for their behavior and admonished them to go about their future building up of stakes quietly, without conceit, living the gospel and preparing for the Second Coming.

The *fifth* prerequisite for the redemption is the Lord's promise to help the people "find favor [and grace] in [the people's] eyes, until the army of Israel becomes very great" (D&C 105:26). Estimates of the number of people driven out of Missouri range from approximately three thousand to twelve thousand. The total membership of the Church at the time is not known, but lower estimates seem more correct. Still, when we compare the larger number (twelve thousand) to our present Church membership (about thirteen million), we can see that the army of Israel has become very great. We do not know how many soldiers the Lord requires in His army of Israel, but it is obvious that His ranks have grown tremendously. As Church membership continues to grow, we need not fear that the Lord will have sufficient men and women to bring to pass His great work of redeeming Zion. He has already demonstrated He could have done it with the small number in Zion's camp (see historical setting; D&C 105).

D&C 105:27–30

27 And I will soften the hearts of the people, as I did the heart of Pharaoh, from time to time, until my servant Joseph Smith, Jun., and mine elders, whom I have appointed, shall have time to gather up the strength of my house,

28 And to have sent wise men, to fulfil that which I have commanded concerning the purchasing of all the lands in Jackson county that can be purchased, and in the adjoining counties round about.

29 For it is my will that these lands should be purchased; and after they are purchased that my saints should possess them according to the laws of consecration which I have given.

30 And after these lands are purchased, I will hold the armies of Israel guiltless in taking possession of their own lands, which they have previously purchased with their moneys, and of throwing down the

towers of mine enemies that may be upon them, and scattering their watchmen, and avenging me of mine enemies unto the third and fourth generation of them that hate me.

The *sixth* prerequisite of the redemption of Zion concerns the purchase, not conquest, of the land of New Jerusalem. The Church has very quietly purchased land in Missouri. Much speculation has been made about how much land has been bought, but though the amount of land in Missouri that is owned by the Church is not generally known, we can be assured that the work is progressing (vv. 27–28).

A few years ago, 1978, the governor of Missouri issued a decree abolishing the extermination order issued by former Governor Lilburn W. Boggs, which had stated that no Mormon was welcome in Missouri. This is a noteworthy example of the heart being softened (v. 27). Other events have taken place, and will yet take place, to that same effect. Again, how much more is required will be known when the Lord reveals it.

Earlier, the Lord revealed that the only way Zion will be built up is by purchase or by blood, and the Lord forbade the shedding of blood (see D&C 63:27–31). Therefore, the Lord instructed the Saints in other areas to send money to the land of Zion to make purchases. The faithful would receive an inheritance in Zion (see D&C 63:37–41, 47–48). Just as David was forbidden to build the temple because he was a man of war (1 Chronicles 28:2–3), it seems that we, as a people, will also be forbidden to enter Zion if we attempt to obtain the land by force. The land in Missouri will be purchased, not conquered (D&C 105:28–29). What lands the Church had purchased and will again have possession of will be known when it happens (see 2 Nephi 25:7).

D&C 105:31–32 • Banners to the World

31 But first let my army become very great, and let it be sanctified before me, that it may become fair as the sun, and clear as the moon, and that her banners may be terrible unto all nations;

32 That the kingdoms of this world may be constrained to acknowledge that the kingdom of Zion is in very deed the kingdom of our God and his Christ; therefore, let us become subject unto her laws.

The *seventh* prerequisite is that the Church and the kingdom of God will become banners to the world. The Lord's "army [will] become very great" and become pure and holy, or sanctified before the Lord, (v. 31).[65] The banner of Zion, the ensign—the Book of Mormon and the Church—must be waved for the world to see. Eventually, the New Jerusalem will become the banner acknowledged by the Gentiles, or the world (see Isaiah 60:3). When that happens, the army of Israel will have become great, and also become sanctified. In our day, for instance, political leaders and dignitaries of the United States, and of foreign countries, who come to Utah visit the Prophet and the First Presidency. Though some visits may be mere political moves, nonetheless, they are a recognition of the kingdom of Zion (v. 32). The character of the people of the Church, both individually and collectively, will lead other nations to recognize the hand of God upon Zion (D&C 45:64–71). Although this prophecy is not yet fulfilled, the recognition of the Church and kingdom by the people and nations of the world is coming to pass.

D&C 105:33–37 • A Day of Choosing

33 Verily I say unto you, it is expedient in me that the first elders of my church should receive their endowment from on high in my house, which I have commanded to be built unto my name in the land of Kirtland.

34 And let those commandments which I have given concerning Zion and her law be executed and fulfilled, after her redemption.

35 There has been a day of calling, but the time has come for a day of choosing; and let those be chosen that are worthy.

36 And it shall be manifest unto my servant, by the voice of the Spirit, those that are chosen; and they shall be sanctified;

37 And inasmuch as they follow the counsel which they receive, they shall have power after many days to accomplish all things pertaining to Zion.

The *eighth* prerequisite will be the reinstitution of the law of consecration in Zion, the New Jerusalem. The commandment "concerning Zion

---

[65] This is an allusion to the Song of Solomon. Most people are aware that Joseph Smith said the Song of Solomon was not inspired; they may wonder why the Lord used it here. Perhaps the author of the Song of Solomon was quoting from something else or perhaps some things in it are inspired.

and her law" is that law (v. 34). The Lord commanded the early Saints called to move to Missouri to covenant to live the law of consecration (see D&C 72). The day of calling (v. 35) was when the Gentiles were invited to help build Zion in 1831 (see D&C 58). The day of choosing is the day when the Lord will ask the Church to build the New Jerusalem.

Some have believed that all the members of the Church would leave their homes and go to Missouri; however, that concept is clearly not taught in the scriptures. We cannot establish the center place without having stakes. Those who will go to Jackson County will be called in an orderly manner. They will be called through the voice of the Spirit manifest to the Lord's servant. The call will come on an individual basis as people are needed to establish the center place of Zion. But there will be multitudes that will not be called. Bear in mind that those who are not called are not necessarily unworthy or less worthy than those who are called. The stakes must be maintained, and leadership will be needed in those stakes. The call to Jackson County is simply a different steward-ship that a person will be given for establishing the Zion society there. Those people will be united in living the principles of the law of the celestial kingdom, including the law of consecration (D&C 105:29).

D&C 105:38–41 • An Ensign of Peace

38 And again I say unto you, sue for peace, not only to the people that have smitten you, but also to all people;

39 And lift up an ensign of peace, and make a proclamation of peace unto the ends of the earth;

40 And make proposals for peace unto those who have smitten you, according to the voice of the Spirit which is in you, and all things shall work together for your good.

41 Therefore, be faithful; and behold, and lo, I am with you even unto the end. Even so. Amen.

The *ninth* prerequisite requires us to do missionary work in the meantime. To "sue for peace" is to "lift up an ensign of peace, and make a proclamation of peace unto the ends of the earth" (vv. 38–39). Those who preach the gospel are the publishers of peace (see Mosiah 15:13–18). The Latter-day Saints are to preach the gospel to the world. Today we have about 60,000 missionaries in many countries of the world. Still other countries are being prepared by the Lord. Missionary work will continue into the Millennium, and the Lord will proclaim when enough people have heard the gospel message for Zion to be established.

Of the nine prerequisites outlined by the Lord for the redemption of Zion, all have been met partially or fully, and many Saints are prepared to be chosen, if the Lord reveals it through His servant, the Prophet. To prepare for the redemption of Zion on an individual basis, we must make ourselves a Zion people, live the principles of the gospel, fulfill our temple covenant, and preach the gospel to all the world. In summary:

1. A man will be raised up like unto Moses to lead the people out of bondage.

2. The people have been prepared and taught more perfectly, and have experience, and know more perfectly concerning their duty through the temple endowment.

3. The Lord will fight the battle for Zion.

4. Many in the regions round about are faithful and prayerful and humble before the Lord, and reveal not the things which the Lord has revealed to them.

5. The army of Israel has become very great.

6. The Lord has softened the hearts of the people, and wise men have purchased lands.

7. Many of the army of Israel have become sanctified, and the kingdoms of this world are recognizing that the kingdom of Zion is in the kingdom of God and His Christ.

8. Many are worthy, and when manifest to the Lord's servant, will return and live the celestial law of Zion (law of consecration).

9. The members of the Church are proclaiming peace to many people by lifting up an ensign of peace, and making a proclamation of peace unto the ends of the earth.

"May the kingdom of God go forth, that the kingdom of heaven may come" (D&C 65:6).

General Authority Quotes

—President Spencer W. Kimball • D&C 105:5

Zion can be built up only among those who are pure in heart, not a people torn by covetousness or greed, but a pure and selfless people. Not a people who are pure in appearance, rather a people who are pure in heart. Zion is to be in the world and not of the world, not dulled by a sense of carnal security, nor paralyzed by materialism. No, Zion is not things of the lower, but of the higher order, things that exalt the mind and sanctify the heart. [*The Teachings of Spencer W. Kimball*, 363]

—The Prophet Joseph Smith • D&C 105:6–8 (December 5, 1833)

Now there are two things of which I am ignorant; and the Lord will not show them unto me, perhaps for a wise purpose in Himself—I mean in some respects—and they are these: Why God has suffered so great a calamity to come upon Zion, and what the great moving cause of this great affliction is; and again, by what means He will return her back to her inheritance, with songs of everlasting joy upon her head. These two things, brethren, are in part kept back that they are not plainly shown unto me; but there are some things that are plainly manifest which have incurred the displeasure of the Almighty. [*TPJS*, 34; these two things are at least partially answered in this revelation]

—Elder Bruce R. McConkie • D&C 105:9, 29

And so we wait, wondering the while how long the "little season" is destined to last. As to its length, we cannot say. This much only do we know: the "little season" is the appointed period of preparation for the Latter-day Saints. In it we must [obtain] the same spiritual stature enjoyed by those who built the original Zion. Then and only then will we build our latter-day City of Holiness.

Those who gather in the perfect Zion must be qualified to live the law of consecration, and obedience to that law is the very way in which the New Jerusalem will be built. As it is well known, the early saints attempted to live the law of consecration through a United Order, but they failed. And up to this point we are living only the lesser law of tithing, though some of the principles of consecration are found in the Church Welfare Program. [*A New Witness for the Articles of Faith* (1985), 616, 618]

—President Joseph Fielding Smith • D&C 105:28

We accept the fact that the center place where the City New Jerusalem is to be built is in Jackson County, Missouri. It was never the intention to substitute Utah or any other place for Jackson County. But we do hold that Zion, when reference is made to the land, is as broad as America, both North and South—all of it is Zion. [*Doctrines of Salvation,* 3:72]

—President Ezra Taft Benson • D&C 105:31

My dear brethren and sisters, we must prepare to redeem Zion. It is essentially the sin of pride that kept us from establishing Zion in the days of the Prophet Joseph Smith. It was the same sin of pride that brought consecration to an end among the Nephites (see 4 Nephi 1:24–25.

Pride is the great stumbling block to Zion. I repeat: Pride is the great stumbling block to Zion.

We must cleanse the inner vessel by conquering pride (see Alma 6:2–4; Matthew 23:25–26.). . . . [quotes Mosiah 3:19]. [CR, April 1989, 7]

Chapter Seventeen

The Law of Tithing

D&C 104; 119–120

DOCTRINE AND COVENANTS 104

Historical Setting: "April 23, [1834]—Assembled in Council with Elders Sidney Rigdon, Frederick G. Williams, Newel K. Whitney, John Johnson, Oliver Cowdery; and united in asking the Lord to give Elder Zebedee Coltrin influence over Brother Myers, to obtain the money which he has gone to borrow for us, or cause him to come to this place and bring it himself. I also received [Doctrine and Covenants 104]" (*HC*, 2:54).

SECTION 104 • OUTLINE

➤ 104:1–13   Counsel and commandment for properties as a united order of the Church.

    a.   A multitude of blessing were promised (v. 2).

    b.   Some were nigh to cursing, and some were cursed (vv. 3–4).

    c.   The covenant breakers will be cursed, the Lord will not be mocked (vv. 5–6).

    d.   The innocent will not be condemned with the unjust, nor the guilty escape (v. 7).

    e.   The transgressors are cut off and delivered to the buffetings of Satan (vv. 8–10).

    f.   Organize, appoint stewardships, and every man will be accountable (vv. 11–13).

➤ 104:14–18   The earth was organized to provide for the Lord's Saints, in His way.

    a.   His way is to exalt the poor and the rich be made low (v. 16).

    b.   The earth is full, has enough to spare, and all men are their own agents (v. 17).

    c.   Those who attain abundance shall impart his portion to the poor and needy, or be in torment with the wicked in hell (v. 18).

➤ 104:19–46   Concerning the properties of the order.

    a.   Sidney Rigdon and Martin Harris' stewardships (vv. 20–26).

    b.   Frederick G. Williams and Oliver Cowdery's stewardships (vv. 27–33).

    c.   John Johnson and Newel K. Whitney's stewardships (vv. 34–42).

    d.   Joseph Smith Jun. and Joseph Smith Sen. stewardships (vv. 43–46).

➤ 104:47–53   The United Order of the Stake of Zion, the City of Kirtland; and the United Order of the City of Zion shall be organized in their own names, and their own business.

    a.   This is for the salvation of both because of being driven out of Zion (v. 51).

    b.   The covenants are broken, you are dissolved as brethren (vv. 52–53).

➤ 104:54–59   A commandment concerning the United Order of Kirtland.

    a.   All these properties are the Lord's, and ye are stewards (vv. 55–56).

    b.   You are stewards over mine own house (temple) (v. 57).

    c.   I have commanded you to print my scriptures and revelations (vv. 58–59).

➤ 104:60–66   Prepare a treasury and consecrate it to the name of Christ.

    a.   Appoint and ordain one to keep the treasury (v. 61).

    b.   There shall be a seal on it for all sacred things, and it belongs to you all (v. 62).

    c.   It is appointed for the printing of these sacred things (v. 63).

    d.   It shall not be used nor taken out nor the seal broken unless commanded (v. 64).

    e.   It shall be called the sacred treasury of the Lord, and be kept holy and consecrated unto the Lord (v. 66).

➤ 104:67–77   Another treasury shall be prepared and a treasurer appointed and it be sealed.

    a.   All money from stewardships, properties shall be kept in it (vv. 68–69).

    b.   Let no man say it is his own, or any part of it (v. 70).

    c.   No part shall be used or taken except by common consent of the order (v. 71).

    d.   Any one in need of help shall ask and it shall be given (vv. 72–73).

    e.   A transgressor, unfaithful, or unwise, shall be subject to the order (vv. 74–76).

    f.   If the treasurer is found unfaithful or unwise he shall be removed (v. 77).

➤ 104:78–86   Concerning debts, it is the Lord's will that ye pay them.

    a.   If you are diligent and humble, the Lord will soften the hearts of your debtors, and send means for your deliverance (vv. 80–82).

    b.   Write speedily to New York as dictated by the Spirit, and the Lord will soften the hearts of your debtors, and deliver you from bondage (vv. 81–83).

    c.   If you obtain a chance to loan money this once, the Lord will deliver you from bondage and not let His house be broken up (vv. 84–86).

Introduction

The section heading: "The United Order at Kirtland was to be temporarily dissolved and reorganized." The reorganization was needed because the Saints in Jackson County, Missouri had been driven out of their homes and land. This revelation gives instructions concerning the law of consecration which those Saints had been trying to live.

TEXT AND COMMENTARY

D&C 104:1–13 • The Covenant Broken

1 VERILY I say unto you, my friends, I give unto you counsel, and a commandment, concerning all the properties which belong to the order which I commanded to be organized and established, to be a united order, and an everlasting order for the benefit of my church, and for the salvation of men until I come—

2 With promise immutable and unchangeable, that inasmuch as those whom I commanded were faithful they should be blessed with a multiplicity of blessings;

3 But inasmuch as they were not faithful they were nigh unto cursing.

4 Therefore, inasmuch as some of my servants have not kept the commandment, but have broken the covenant through covetousness, and with feigned words, I have cursed them with a very sore and grievous curse.

5 For I, the Lord, have decreed in my heart, that inasmuch as any man belonging to the order shall be found a transgressor, or, in other words, shall break the covenant with which ye are bound, he shall be cursed in his life, and shall be trodden down by whom I will;

6 For I, the Lord, am not to be mocked in these things—

7 And all this that the innocent among you may not be condemned with the unjust; and that the guilty among you may not escape; because I, the Lord, have promised unto you a crown of glory at my right hand.

8 Therefore, inasmuch as you are found transgressors, you cannot escape my wrath in your lives.

9 Inasmuch as ye are cut off for transgression, ye cannot escape the buffetings of Satan until the day of redemption.

10 And I now give unto you power from this very hour, that if any man among you, of the order, is found a transgressor and repenteth not of the evil, that ye shall deliver him over unto the buffetings of Satan; and he shall not have power to bring evil upon you.

11 It is wisdom in me; therefore, a commandment I give unto you, that ye shall organize yourselves and appoint every man his stewardship;

12 That every man may give an account unto me of the stewardship which is appointed unto him.

13 For it is expedient that I, the Lord, should make every man accountable, as a steward over earthly blessings, which I have made and prepared for my creatures.

Those who had broken the covenants of the law of consecration were some who had been driven from Missouri. They had forfeited the promised blessings (v. 2), and were now undergoing the curse of the Lord (v. 4). While many of the Saints were innocent of these charges, they were the victims of those who were guilty. It seems the Lord was allowing these persecutions at this time as a protection against future further persecutions. He also reminds the innocent of their promised future crown of glory at His right hand (v. 7). The guilty would not escape the buffetings of Satan except they repent (vv. 9–10). The buffetings of Satan are the mental anguish that comes after the Spirit of the Lord has withdrawn and being subjected to the torments of hell (see Alma 15:3, 5). That these blessings, curses, and torments are on an individual basis is shown from another reminder, every man is accountable for his newly appointed stewardship under the law of consecration and all earthly blessings (vv. 11–13).

D&C 104:14–18

14 I, the Lord, stretched out the heavens, and built the earth, my very handiwork; and all things therein are mine.

15 And it is my purpose to provide for my saints, for all things are mine.

16 But it must needs be done in mine own way; and behold this is the way that I, the Lord, have decreed to provide for my saints, that the poor shall be exalted, in that the rich are made low.

17 For the earth is full, and there is enough and to spare; yea, I prepared all things, and have given unto the children of men to be agents unto themselves.

18 Therefore, if any man shall take of the abundance which I have made, and impart not his portion, according to the law of my gospel, unto the poor and the needy, he shall, with the wicked, lift up his eyes in hell, being in torment.

The Lord's purpose for creating the earth was to provide for his Saints (v. 15). This purpose is further verified in the Book of Mormon. "Behold, the Lord hath created the earth that it should be inhabited; and he hath created his children that they should possess it" (1 Nephi 17:36). The best way to provide for His Saints was through the law of consecration which exalts the poor and brings down the rich (D&C 104:16). Man was commanded to multiply and replenish, or fill the earth, and subdue it (see Genesis 1:28). By subduing the earth, or bringing it to produce for them, there was more than enough to care for all of its inhabitants (see D&C 104:17). However, they were granted their agency and must choose how to manage the earth. Should they raise children and learn how to gain more production from the earth, or practice birth control and find ways to limit the earth's production? It seems that many advocate the latter instead of the original commandment. Should we Latter-day Saints live the law of consecration individually, even though it is not commanded to live it collectively at this time, by importing our portion to the poor and needy through fast offering, food storage, and other welfare programs of the Church, or endorse the dole systems of socialism advocated by the world? We must seek the crown of glory in this life, or we will lift up our eyes in torment later (v. 18).

D&C 104:19–23 • Sidney Rigdon's Properties

19 And now, verily I say unto you, concerning the properties of the order—

20 Let my servant Sidney Rigdon have appointed unto him the place where he now resides, and the lot of the tannery for his stewardship, for his support while he is laboring in my vineyard, even as I will, when I shall command him.

21 And let all things be done according to the counsel of the order, and united consent or voice of the order, which dwell in the land of Kirtland.

22 And this stewardship and blessing, I, the Lord, confer upon my servant Sidney Rigdon for a blessing upon him, and his seed after him;

23 And I will multiply blessings upon him, inasmuch as he will be humble before me.

Although Sidney is a counselor to the Prophet, he is still blessed to have a stewardship for his temporal duties (vv. 20–21). He is also expected to follow the counsel of the order with the conditional promise of blessings (vv. 21–23).

D&C 104:24–26 • Martin Harris' Stewardship

24 And again, let my servant Martin Harris have appointed unto him, for his stewardship, the lot of land which my servant John Johnson obtained in exchange for his former inheritance, for him and his seed after him;

25 And inasmuch as he is faithful, I will multiply blessings upon him and his seed after him.

26 And let my servant Martin Harris devote his moneys for the proclaiming of my words, according as my servant Joseph Smith, Jun., shall direct.

Martin is likewise given a stewardship, but is expected to contribute his money as the Prophet directs.

D&C 104:27–33 • Frederick and Oliver

27 And again, let my servant Frederick G. Williams have the place upon which he now dwells.

28 And let my servant Oliver Cowdery have the lot which is set off joining the house, which is to be for the printing office, which is lot number one, and also the lot upon which his father resides.

29 And let my servants Frederick G. Williams and Oliver Cowdery have the printing office and all things that pertain unto it.

30 And this shall be their stewardship which shall be appointed unto them.

31 And inasmuch as they are faithful, behold I will bless, and multiply blessings upon them.

32 And this is the beginning of the stewardship which I have appointed them, for them and their seed after them.

33 And, inasmuch as they are faithful, I will multiply blessings upon them and their seed after them, even a multiplicity of blessings.

Frederick was a counselor to Joseph, and Oliver was the assistant president. Their stewardship of the printing office was presently of top priority (see D&C 104:58–59).

D&C 104:34–38 • John Johnson's Stewardship

34 And again, let my servant John Johnson have the house in which he lives, and the inheritance, all save the ground which has been reserved for the building of my houses, which pertains to that inheritance, and those lots which have been named for my servant Oliver Cowdery.

35 And inasmuch as he is faithful, I will multiply blessings upon him.

36 And it is my will that he should sell the lots that are laid off for the building up of the city of my saints, inasmuch as it shall be made known to him by the voice of the Spirit, and according to the counsel of the order, and by the voice of the order.

37 And this is the beginning of the stewardship which I have appointed unto him, for a blessing unto him and his seed after him.

38 And inasmuch as he is faithful, I will multiply a multiplicity of blessings upon him.

John had been instrumental in the Kirtland area, and supportive of the Prophet. He was to be an important part of the new order.

D&C 104:39–42 • Newel K. Whitney's Stewardship

39 And again, let my servant Newel K. Whitney have appointed unto him the houses and lot where he now resides, and the lot and building on which the mercantile establishment stands, and also the lot which is on the corner south of the mercantile establishment, and also the lot on which the ashery is situated.

40 And all this I have appointed unto my servant Newel K. Whitney for his stewardship, for a blessing upon him and his seed after him, for the benefit of the mercantile establishment of my order which I have established for my stake in the land of Kirtland.

41 Yea, verily, this is the stewardship which I have appointed unto my servant N. K. Whitney, even this whole mercantile establishment, him and his agent, and his seed after him.

42 And inasmuch as he is faithful in keeping my commandments, which I have given unto him, I will multiply blessings upon him and his seed after him, even a multiplicity of blessings.

As the bishop of the Kirtland Order, Newel, and the appointed agent, were the key figures in the business end, as these words imply.

D&C 104:43–46 • Joseph Jun. & Joseph Sen.

43 And again, let my servant Joseph Smith, Jun., have appointed unto him the lot which is laid off for the building of my house, which is forty rods long and twelve wide, and also the inheritance upon which his father now resides;

44 And this is the beginning of the stewardship which I have appointed unto him, for a blessing upon him, and upon his father.

45 For behold, I have reserved an inheritance for his father, for his support; therefore he shall be reckoned in the house of my servant Joseph Smith, Jun.

46 And I will multiply blessings upon the house of my servant Joseph Smith, Jun., inasmuch as he is faithful, even a multiplicity of blessings.

As mentioned above, Joseph Sen. was beginning to show his age, and his son Joseph was to be a support for him. Note that many of the above stewardship blessings include promises to their families and seed.

D&C 104:47–53 • Separate United Orders

47 And now, a commandment I give unto you concerning Zion, that you shall no longer be bound as a united order to your brethren of Zion, only on this wise—

48 After you are organized, you shall be called the United Order of the Stake of Zion, the City of Kirtland. And your brethren, after they are organized, shall be called the United Order of the City of Zion.

49 And they shall be organized in their own names, and in their own name; and they shall do their business in their own name, and in their own names;

50 And you shall do your business in your own name, and in your own names.

51 And this I have commanded to be done for your salvation, and also for their salvation, in consequence of their being driven out and that which is to come.

52 The covenants being broken through transgression, by covetousness and feigned words—

53 Therefore, you are dissolved as a united order with your brethren, that you are not bound only up to this hour unto them, only on this wise, as I said, by loan as shall be agreed by this order in council, as your

circumstances will admit and the voice of the council direct.

There were still members of the Church in Missouri, and whatever ties to the order that could be maintained should be, but they were to be separate units. This individuality was a part of the law of consecration as new stakes were organized under the law (see D&C 51:10–11; the churches in these verses refer to other units, not denominations).

D&C 104:54–59

54 And again, a commandment I give unto you concerning your stewardship which I have appointed unto you.

55 Behold, all these properties are mine, or else your faith is vain, and ye are found hypocrites, and the covenants which ye have made unto me are broken;

56 And if the properties are mine, then ye are stewards; otherwise ye are no stewards.

57 But, verily I say unto you, I have appointed unto you to be stewards over mine house, even stewards indeed.

58 And for this purpose I have commanded you to organize yourselves, even to print my words, the fulness of my scriptures, the revelations which I have given unto you, and which I shall, hereafter, from time to time give unto you—

59 For the purpose of building up my church and kingdom on the earth, and to prepare my people for the time when I shall dwell with them, which is nigh at hand.

These verses remind us of the 24th Psalm: "The earth is the LORD's, and the fulness thereof; the world, and they that dwell therein" (v. 1). As His stewards, or managers of the earth, we are to do as He directs (D&C 104:56–57). Jesus set the example for us when He went into Gethsemane to make the Atonement: "And he went a little further, and fell on his face, and prayed, saying, O my Father, if it be possible, let this cup pass from me: nevertheless not as I will, but as thou wilt" (Matthew 26:39). His scriptures give us directions, as His stewards. They are to be printed for our benefit. "The fullness of my scripture" apparently refers to the Joseph Smith Translation of the Bible, which Joseph was continually working upon. The revelations, given and to be given, were obviously referring to the first edition of the Doctrine and Covenants which was printed in 1835 (D&C 104:58). The whole purpose of these scriptures was to help us as stewards to build up His "church and kingdom" before His soon coming millennial reign (v. 59).

D&C 104:60–66 • The Sacred Treasury

60 And ye shall prepare for yourselves a place for a treasury, and consecrate it unto my name.

61 And ye shall appoint one among you to keep the treasury, and he shall be ordained unto this blessing.

62 And there shall be a seal upon the treasury, and all the sacred things shall be delivered into the treasury; and no man among you shall call it his own, or any part of it, for it shall belong to you all with one accord.

63 And I give it unto you from this very hour; and now see to it, that ye go to and make use of the stewardship which I have appointed unto you, exclusive of the sacred things, for the purpose of printing these sacred things as I have said.

64 And the avails of the sacred things shall be had in the treasury, and a seal shall be upon it; and it shall not be used or taken out of the treasury by any one, neither shall the seal be loosed which shall be placed upon it, only by the voice of the order, or by commandment.

65 And thus shall ye preserve the avails of the sacred things in the treasury, for sacred and holy purposes.

66 And this shall be called the sacred treasury of the Lord; and a seal shall be kept upon it that it may be holy and consecrated unto the Lord.

The "sacred treasury" shall be established for the printing of those scriptures (v. 63), and all the materials that pertained to their being printed were to be kept therein. The seal upon it was a lock being placed upon it (v. 64). These things were "for sacred and holy purposes," and were to be sealed because they were to be "holy and consecrated to the Lord" (vv. 65–66).[66] These scriptures belonged to the order, or to the

---

[66] The following lines which follow verse 59 in the "Kirtland Revelation Book" [p. 111] are not part of the present text of section 104 of the Doctrine and Covenants. "Therefore a commandment I give unto you that you shall take the books of Mormon and also the copyright which shall be secured of the Articles and Covenants [Doctrine and Covenants] in which covenants all my commandments which it is my will should

(continued...)

whole Church (v. 62). Thus, they are our scriptures, this dispensation's scriptures.

D&C 104:67–77 • Another Treasury Prepared

67 And again, there shall be another treasury prepared, and a treasurer appointed to keep the treasury, and a seal shall be placed upon it;

68 And all moneys that you receive in your stewardships, by improving upon the properties which I have appointed unto you, in houses, or in lands, or in cattle, or in all things save it be the holy and sacred writings, which I have reserved unto myself for holy and sacred purposes, shall be cast into the treasury as fast as you receive moneys, by hundreds, or by fifties, or by twenties, or by tens, or by fives.

69 Or in other words, if any man among you obtain five dollars let him cast them into the treasury; or if he obtain ten, or twenty, or fifty, or an hundred, let him do likewise;

70 And let not any among you say that it is his own; for it shall not be called his, nor any part of it.

71 And there shall not any part of it be used, or taken out of the treasury, only by the voice and common consent of the order.

72 And this shall be the voice and common consent of the order—that any man among you say to the treasurer: I have need of this to help me in my stewardship—

73 If it be five dollars, or if it be ten dollars, or twenty, or fifty, or a hundred, the treasurer shall give unto him the sum which he requires to help him in his stewardship—

74 Until he be found a transgressor, and it is manifest before the council of the order plainly that he is an unfaithful and an unwise steward.

75 But so long as he is in full fellowship, and is faithful and wise in his stewardship, this shall be his token unto the treasurer that the treasurer shall not withhold.

---

[66] (...continued)
be printed, shall be printed, as it shall be made known unto you; and also the copyright of the new translation of the scripture; and this I say that others may not take the blessings away from you which I have conferred upon you." Lyndon W. Cook, *The Revelations of the Prophet Joseph Smith* [1981], 212; an example of holy things consecrated to the Lord.

76 But in case of transgression, the treasurer shall be subject unto the council and voice of the order.

77 And in case the treasurer is found an unfaithful and an unwise steward, he shall be subject to the council and voice of the order, and shall be removed out of his place, and another shall be appointed in his stead.

The second treasury was the same as the bishops' storehouse. Why it was not called the storehouse may have been because the Lord did not want it confused with the storehouse of the Zion United Order. They were both for the same purposes, and having been commented upon before, will not be repeated here.

D&C 104:78–86 • Pay All Your Debts

78 And again, verily I say unto you, concerning your debts—behold it is my will that you shall pay all your debts.

79 And it is my will that you shall humble yourselves before me, and obtain this blessing by your diligence and humility and the prayer of faith.

80 And inasmuch as you are diligent and humble, and exercise the prayer of faith, behold, I will soften the hearts of those to whom you are in debt, until I shall send means unto you for your deliverance.

81 Therefore write speedily to New York and write according to that which shall be dictated by my Spirit; and I will soften the hearts of those to whom you are in debt, that it shall be taken away out of their minds to bring affliction upon you.

82 And inasmuch as ye are humble and faithful and call upon my name, behold, I will give you the victory.

83 I give unto you a promise, that you shall be delivered this once out of your bondage.

84 Inasmuch as you obtain a chance to loan money by hundreds, or thousands, even until you shall loan enough to deliver yourself from bondage, it is your privilege.

85 And pledge the properties which I have put into your hands, this once, by giving your names by common consent or otherwise, as it shall seem good unto you.

86 I give unto you this privilege, this once; and behold, if you proceed to do the things which I have laid before you, according to my command-

ments, all these things are mine, and ye are my stewards, and the master will not suffer his house to be broken up. Even so. Amen.

Previously, the Lord had said: "Behold, it is said in my laws, or forbidden, to get in debt to thine enemies" (D&C 64:27). There is no direct quote of this wording in the present day Bible. Although the quote has apparently been lost, the Lord wants His Saints free from debt (D&C 104:78). Earlier He had instructed them to get an agent: "That thereby he may be enabled to discharge every debt; that the storehouse of the Lord may not be brought into disrepute before the eyes of the people" (D&C 90:23). The formula for getting the Lord's help in removing debt is diligence, humility, and the prayer of faith (vv. 79–80). The specifics of the debts in New York (v. 81) are not known to this writer, but Brigham Young made great efforts to find and settle any unknown ones.[67] That the Lord had advised them previously against debt is implied by His offer to deliver them "this once out of your bondage" (v. 83), and to pledge their properties as security to loan [borrow] money as a "privilege this once" (vv. 85–86).

DOCTRINE AND COVENANTS 119 & 120

*H*istorical Setting: "The three revelations which I received January 12, 1838, the day I left Kirtland, were read in the public congregation at Far West, and the same day I inquired of the Lord, 'O Lord! Show unto thy servant; how much thou requirest of the properties of thy people for a tithing,' and received [Doctrine and Covenants 119–120]; which was also read in public" (*HC*, 3:44).

"The three revelations here referred to do not appear in the Doctrine and Covenants nor in any other publication. Diligent search also has been made for them through the several packages of Church documents in the Historians Office, but they have not been found" (*HC*, 3:44; footnote).

Section 119 heading: The law of tithing, as understood today, had not been given to the Church previous to this revelation. The term "tithing"

---

[67] See *Journal of Discourses,* 18:242; reporting in 1874, but referring to the time Joseph was in Kirtland.

in the prayer just quoted and in previous revelations (64:23; 85:3; 97:11) had meant not just one tenth, but all free-will offerings, or contributions to the Church funds. The Lord had previously given to the Church the law of consecration and stewardship of property, which members (chiefly the leading elders) entered into by covenant that was to be everlasting. Because of failure on the part of many to abide by this covenant, the Lord withdrew it for a time, and gave instead the law of tithing to the whole Church. The Prophet asked the Lord how much of their property he required for sacred purposes. The answer was this revelation.

TEXT AND COMMENTARY

D&C 119:1–7 • All Surplus Property

1 Verily, thus saith the Lord, I require all their surplus property to be put into the hands of the bishop of my church in Zion,

2 For the building of mine house, and for the laying of the foundation of Zion and for the priesthood, and for the debts of the Presidency of my Church.

3 And this shall be the beginning of the tithing of my people.

4 And after that, those who have thus been tithed shall pay one-tenth of all their interest annually; and this shall be a standing law unto them forever, for my holy priesthood, saith the Lord.

5 Verily I say unto you, it shall come to pass that all those who gather unto the land of Zion shall be tithed of their surplus properties, and shall observe this law, or they shall not be found worthy to abide among you.

6 And I say unto you, if my people observe not this law, to keep it holy, and by this law sanctify the land of Zion unto me, that my statutes and my judgments may be kept thereon, that it may be most holy, behold, verily I say unto you, it shall not be a land of Zion unto you.

7 And this shall be an ensample unto all the stakes of Zion. Even so. Amen.

The surplus properties to be put into the hands of the bishop (v. 1) were those which had been consecrated to the Lord, and deeded to the steward to manage and earn his livelihood. Under the law of tithing, the steward could earn a good living without the use of some of his property. These properties could then be sold, traded, disposed of in some other way, or kept for the building of the temple, laying the foundation of Zion, other priesthood uses, and to reduce the debts of the Presidency of the Church (v. 2). The beginning of the tithing of His people was not the first time of tithing, it was the present law of financing the Church, and was to be observed by all members of the Church after they had settled their united properties into individual ownerships. It may be compared to the law of Moses which "was added" to the children of Israel "because of transgression" (Galatians 3:19). The Prophet Joseph commented on this verse, asking, "What we ask, was it added to, if it was not added to the gospel? It must be plain that it was added to the gospel, since we learn that they had the gospel preached to them" (*TPJS,* 60; having previously quoted Hebrews 4:2). While tithing in one sense had been a part of the law of consecration, as verified in the verses quoted in the section 119 heading, it was now defined as "one-tenth of all their interest annually" (v. 4). The Prophet and Oliver had already covenanted, March 29, 1834, to "give a tenth to be bestowed upon the poor in His Church, or as He shall command" (*TPJS,* 70).

Those who had not covenanted to live the law of consecration, but came to Zion, or Missouri, were to "be tithed of their surplus properties," and observe the law [tithing] if they were to be "worthy to abide among" the members in Zion (v. 5; note the use of the word tithe with their surplus properties). If the law of tithing was not observed there, it would not become a land of Zion for them (v. 6). Zion was to be "an ensample [example] unto all the stakes of Zion" (v. 7). Tithing has always been, and will always be, a law of the Lord's people (see Genesis 14:20; 28:22; Malachi 3:8–19; Alma 13:15; 3 Nephi 24:8–10).

D&C 120 • A Council and Mine Own Voice

> Verily, thus saith the Lord, the time is now come, that it shall be disposed of by a council, composed of the First Presidency of my Church, and of the bishop and his council, and by my high council; and by mine own voice unto them, saith the Lord. Even so. Amen.

The council is composed of the best men in the Church and in the world, yet this governing body is still guided by the voice of the Lord, or by revelation. The Church was in the best hands financially that it could be, but they still had their agency.

General Authority Quotes

—Elder Harold B. Lee • (after quoting D&C 104:14–18)

... Not the government's way, not some crackpot philosopher's way, but it is to be done in the Lord's way. ...

There are your fast offerings, there is your tithing. Now what does He mean by this phrase? His way is, "that the poor shall be exalted, in that the rich are made low.

Exalt, in the language of the dictionary, and the definition that the Lord is trying to convey, means: "To lift up with pride and joy to success."

That is how we lift the poor up ... and how are we to do it? By the rich being made low.

Now do not mistake that word rich. That does not always mean a man with a lot of money. That man may be poor in money, but he may be rich in skill. He may be rich in judgment. He may be rich in good example. He may be rich in splendid optimism, and in a lot of other qualities that are necessary. And when individual priesthood quorum members unite themselves together, we usually find all those rare qualities necessary to lift up the needy and the distressed with pride and joy to success in the accomplishment. There could not be a more perfect working of the Lord's plan than that. [*The Teachings of Harold B. Lee* (1996), 310–11]

—President Ezra Taft Benson • D&C 104:17

A major trend is to rationalize the commandment to procreate, saying that the earth cannot support this great number of unrestricted births, or that it is not financially possible to support a great number of children today. The Lord said ... [quotes 104:17].

A major reason why there is famine in some parts of the world is because evil men have used the vehicle of government to abridge the freedom that men need to produce abundantly. True to form, many of the people who desire to frustrate God's purposes of giving mortal tabernacles to His spirit children through world wide birth control are the same people who support the kinds of government that perpetuate famine. They advocate an evil to cure the results of the wickedness they support. [*The Teachings of Ezra Taft Benson*, 540]

—*President J. Reuben Clark* • D&C 104:78–86

Interest never sleeps nor sickens nor dies; it never goes to the hospital; it works on Sundays and holidays; it never takes a vacation; it never visits nor travels; it takes no pleasure; it is never laid off work nor discharged from employment; it never works on reduced hours; it never has short crops or droughts; it never pays taxes; it buys no food; it wears no clothes; it is unhoused and without home and so has no repairs, no replacements, no shingling, plumbing, painting, or whitewashing; it has neither wife, children, father, mother, nor kinfolk to watch over and care for; it has no expense of living; it has neither weddings nor births nor deaths; it has no love, no sympathy; it is as hard and soulless as a granite cliff. Once in debt, interest is your companion every minute of the day and night; you cannot shun it or slip away from it; you cannot dismiss it; it yields neither to entreaties, demands, or orders; and whenever you get in its way or cross its course or fail to meet its demands, it crushes you.

So much for the interest we pay. Whoever borrows should understand what interest is; it is with you every minute of the day and night. [*J. Reuben Clark, Selected Papers*, ed. David H. Yarn (1984), 193]

—*President Lorenzo Snow* • D&C 119:3–4

The time has now come for every Latter-day Saint, who calculates to be prepared for the future and to hold his feet strong upon a strong foundation, to do the will of the Lord and pay his tithing in full. That is the word of the Lord to you, and it will be the word of the Lord to every settlement throughout the land of Zion. After I leave you and you get to thinking about this, you will see yourselves that the time has come when every man should stand up and pay his tithing in full. The Lord has blessed us and has had mercy upon us in the past; but there are times coming when the lord requires us to stand up and do that which he has commanded and not leave it any longer. What I say to you in this stake of Zion I will say to every stake of Zion that has been organized. There is no man or woman that now hears what I am saying who will feel satisfied if he or she fails to pay a full tithing. [*The Teachings of Lorenzo Snow*, comp. Clyde J. Williams (1984), 155]

—*President Harold B. Lee* • D&C 119:3–4

Notice tithing is "one-tenth of all their interest," and that has always been interpreted to mean income, a tenth of income is a tithe. We are now living that, and in addition we have the welfare program. . . .

We heard President [J. Reuben Clark] say something that I have

thought about as the brethren have talked today. He said, in effect, "If you think about it clearly, when you think about our storehouses where we are putting in all our surpluses we can, when we are paying a full tithing, when we are giving assistance in the health services, when we are giving assistance in the programs by which we reach out to those who are far afield, teaching them how to take care of themselves, we will not be far from living the united order. [*The Teachings of Harold B. Lee*, 207]

Chapter Eighteen

Even a Great Revelation

D&C 106–108

DOCTRINE AND COVENANTS 106

Similar to Doctrine and Covenants 79 and 80, part of chapter 1 of this work, section 106 calling Warren Cowdery as presiding high priest in the land of freedom is not considered doctrinally valuable to our study; only two verses are included below without comment.

> 4 And again, verily I say unto you, the coming of the Lord draweth nigh, and it overtaketh the world as a thief in the night—
>
> 5 Therefore, gird up your loins, that you may be the children of light, and that day shall not overtake you as a thief. [D&C 106:5–6]

DOCTRINE AND COVENANTS 107

Historical Setting: The winter of 1834–35 was an exciting time in the Church. Many new priesthood offices were revealed, and previously revealed offices were solidified. The Lectures on Faith were delivered at the School of the Elders, Oliver Cowdery was ordained Assistant President (*HC,* 2:175–76), and on February 14, 1835, the Quorum of the Twelve Apostles was chosen by the Three Witnesses to the Book of Mormon under the direction of the Prophet (see D&C 18:37). They were selected from among those faithful who had traveled to Missouri in Zion's Camp. Six weeks later, March 28, 1835, the Twelve met in council and asked for "even a great revelation."

This afternoon the Twelve met in council, and had a time of general confession. On reviewing our past course we are satisfied, and feel to confess also, that we have not realized the importance of our calling to that degree that we ought; we have been light-minded and vain, and in many things have done wrong. For all these things we have asked forgiveness of our Heavenly Father; and wherein we have grieved or wounded the feelings of the Presidency, we ask their forgiveness. The time when we are about to separate is near; and when we shall meet again, God only knows; we therefore feel to ask of him whom we have acknowledged to be our Prophet and Seer, that he inquire of God for us, and obtain a revelation, (if consistent) that we may look upon it when we are separated that our hearts may be comforted. Our worthiness has not inspired us to make this request, but our unworthiness. We have unitedly asked God our Heavenly Father to grant us through His Seer, a revelation of His mind and will concerning our duty the coming season, even a great revelation, that will enlarge our hearts, comfort us in adversity, and brighten our hopes amidst the powers of darkness. ORSON HYDE, WM. E. MCLELLIN, Clerks.

To President Joseph Smith, Jun., Kirtland, Ohio.

In compliance with the above request, I inquired of the Lord, and received for answer [Doctrine and Covenants 107]. [*HC*, 2:209–210]

The Prophet inquired of the Lord and the revelation was given in the presence of the Twelve. As noted in the section heading, parts of the revelation were received at sundry times. The first 52 verses and verse 58 were given at this time. According to the Kirtland Council Minute Book, verses 59 through 100 were given in November 1831 and added by the Prophet with various other additions within the body of these verses.[68] Some of the various additions will be identified as they are discussed.

SECTION 107 • OUTLINE

➤ 107:1–12   There are two priesthoods in the Church, the Melchizedek and the Aaronic.

       a.   The first called Melchizedek because he was such a great high priest (vv. 2–4).

---

[68] See Lyndon W. Cook, *The Great Revelations of the Prophet Joseph Smith* [1981], 215–16, 326–29.

b. All offices are appendages to this priesthood, but has two divisions (vv. 5–6).

c. The elder, and the right of presidency to administer in the spiritual (vv. 7–8).

d. The High Priesthood Presidency can officiate in all offices in the Church (v. 9).

e. High priests officiate in all offices by direction of the presidency (vv. 10–12).

➤ 107:13–20   The Aaronic Priesthood is an appendage to the Melchizedek and administers in outward ordinances.

a. The bishopric is the presidency and holds the keys of authority (v. 15).

b. Aaron's literal descendant has a right, but a high priest can officiate (vv. 16–17).

c. Melchizedek holds the keys of the spiritual blessings of the Church (vv. 18–19).

d. Aaronic holds the keys of ministering of angels and outward ordinances (v. 20).

➤ 107:21–26   Presidents or presiding officers are ordained in these two priesthoods.

a. Three Presiding High Priests are the Presidency of the Church (v. 22).

b. Twelve Apostles are a quorum equal in authority and power (vv. 23–24).

c. The Seventy are a quorum equal in authority to the Twelve (vv. 25–26).

➤ 107:27–32   Every decision of these quorums must be a unanimous decision.

a. A majority may act when circumstances render it impossible (vv. 28–29).

b. Decisions must be made in righteousness, holiness, and charity (vv. 30–32).

➤ 107:33–38   The Twelve are a Traveling Presiding High Council under direction of the Presidency.

a. The Seventy act under the direction of the Twelve (v. 34).

b.   The Twelve hold the keys of preaching the gospel to Gentiles and Jews (v. 35).

c.   The stake high council of Zion, the high council of Zion, are equal in their decisions to the presidency or traveling high council (vv. 36–37).

d.   The traveling high council call on the Seventy if they need assistance (v. 38).

e.   The Twelve ordain evangelical ministers in all large branches (v. 39).

> 107:39–57   The evangelical order of the priesthood belongs to the literal descendants of the chosen seed.

a.   Adam installed it to his posterity (vv. 41–52).

b.   Three years prior to Adam's death he bestowed his last blessing (v. 53).

c.   The Lord blessed Adam, Michael, the prince, the archangel (vv. 54–55).

d.   Adam predicted what would befall his posterity to the last generation (v. 56).

e.   It was written in the book of Enoch, to be revealed in due time (v. 57).

> 107:58–67   The Twelve are to ordain and set in order all other officers of the Church.

a.   Presiding elders, priests, teachers, and deacons (vv. 60–63).

b.   One must be appointed as President of the High Priesthood (vv. 64–66).

c.   Ordinances and blessings are administered by laying on of hands (v. 67).

> 107:68–76   The office of bishop is to administer all temporal things.

a.   He is from the High Priesthood unless a literal descendant of Aaron (vv. 69–71).

b.   A judge in Israel, does the Church business, assisted by counselors (vv. 72, 74).

c.   A literal descendant of Aaron can act without counselors except when a President of the High Priesthood is tried (v. 76).

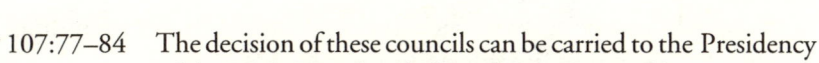

➤ 107:77–84   The decision of these councils can be carried to the Presidency of the High Priesthood if satisfaction is not felt.

      a.   No member of the Church is exempt from the councils of the Church (v. 81).

      b.   If the President of the High Priesthood is found in transgression, the common council is assisted by the twelve counselors (v. 82).

➤ 107:85–90   The duties of the presiding officers of the deacons, teachers, and priests, of whom the president is the bishop.

      a.   The presiding officer over ninety-six elders (v. 89).

      b.   The elders differ, they do not travel (v. 90).

➤ 107:91–100 The President of the High Priesthood presides over the Church like Moses.

      a.   A seer, a revelator, a translator, a prophet, having all the gifts of God (v. 92).

      b.   The Seventy have seven presidents, the seventh presiding over the other six, and choose other seventies until seven times seventy (vv. 93–97).

      c.   Officers, not of the Twelve or Seventy, may hold responsible offices (v. 98).

      d.   Let every man learn his duty, and act in the office appointed (vv. 99–100).

Introduction

What is a great revelation? Any revelation from the Lord is great for those to whom it is given, but as stated in the introduction of this book, all revelations are not of the same value to the collective members of the Church.[69] We learn some characteristics of a great revelation from Nephi, son of Lehi. He instructed his younger brother Jacob to engraven "preaching which was sacred, or *revelation which was great*, or prophesying" upon the plates from which the Book of Mormon was translated (Jacob 1:4; italics added). If all revelations were equal, he would have just said to include all revelation. Therefore we will define great revelation as that which answers many questions, or gives much instruction that

---

[69] Ezra Taft Benson, CR, April 1986, 100.

helps people to better serve the Lord and keep His commandments. Section 107 certainly fits this definition.

Text and Commentary

D&C 107:1–6 • Two Priesthoods in the Church

1 There are, in the church, two priesthoods, namely, the Melchizedek and Aaronic, including the Levitical Priesthood.

2 Why the first is called the Melchizedek Priesthood is because Melchizedek was such a great high priest.

3 Before his day it was called *the Holy Priesthood, after the Order of the Son of God.*

4 But out of respect or reverence to the name of the Supreme Being, to avoid the too frequent repetition of his name, they, the church, in ancient days, called that priesthood after Melchizedek, or the Melchizedek Priesthood.

5 All other authorities or offices in the church are appendages to this priesthood.

6 But there are two divisions or grand heads—one is the Melchizedek Priesthood, and the other is the Aaronic or Levitical Priesthood. [italics added]

Little is learned about Melchizedek, the great high priest (v. 2), from the Bible (see Hebrews 7:1–21 for the most comprehensive statement about him). The name of the priesthood being the order of the Son of God before the day of Melchizedek, and the greatness of him (vv. 3–4) is confirmed in the Book of Mormon (see Alma 13:7–19). The JST, Genesis 14:25–40 is a third source of modern revelation to learn of him. The Prophet also added some significant things in JST, Hebrews 7:3, 19–21, 25–26. Many questions are answered and instructions given to help us serve the Lord in all of the above sources, but the first six verses of the revelation certainly qualify as being great.

D&C 107:7–12 • The Melchizedek Priesthood

7 The office of an elder comes under the priesthood of Melchizedek.

8 The Melchizedek Priesthood holds the right of presidency, and has power and authority over all the offices in the church in all ages of the

world, to administer in spiritual things.

9 The Presidency of the High Priesthood, after the order of Melchizedek, have a right to officiate in all the offices in the church.

10 High priests after the order of the Melchizedek Priesthood have a right to officiate in their own standing, under the direction of the presidency, in administering spiritual things, and also in the office of an elder, priest (of the Levitical order), teacher, deacon, and member.

11 An elder has a right to officiate in his stead when the high priest is not present.

12 The high priest and elder are to administer in spiritual things, agreeable to the covenants and commandments of the church; and they have a right to officiate in all these offices of the church when there are no higher authorities present.

The Melchizedek Priesthood was restored to the earth before the Church was organized in 1830. The exact date of the restoration of the keys of the Melchizedek Priesthood is not known. We do know from D&C 18:9 that Oliver Cowdery and David Whitmer had received their apostolic calling, an office of the Melchizedek Priesthood, by June 1829. "The office of an elder comes under the priesthood of Melchizedek" (v. 7); and "an apostle is an elder" (D&C 20:38). In other words, many officers in the Church, holding the Melchizedek Priesthood may be titled "elder."

The new revelation gives four functions of the Melchizedek Priesthood: (1) The right of presidency. (2) Power and authority over all the officers in the Church in all ages of the world. (3) It is to administer in spiritual things of the Church. (4) A right to officiate in all the offices in the Church (D&C 107:8–9). Joseph Smith was sustained and ordained President of the High Priesthood three years earlier, on January 25, 1832 (see D&C 75 heading). His counselors Sidney Rigdon and Frederick G. Williams were ordained about one year later, March 18, 1833 (D&C 90 heading; 90:6).

The presidency of the High Priesthood "have the right to officiate in all the offices in the church" (D&C 107:9). Other high priests of the Melchizedek Priesthood may administer under the direction of the presidency in "spiritual things, and also in the office of an elder, priest (of the Levitical order), teacher, deacon, and member" (v.10). An elder may officiate in spiritual things "when the high priest" or "no higher authorities" are present, but the administration must be "agreeable to the covenants and commandments of the Church" (vv. 11–12).

D&C 107:13–20 • The Aaronic Priesthood

13 The second priesthood is called the Priesthood of Aaron, because it was conferred upon Aaron and his seed, throughout all their generations.

14 Why it is called the lesser priesthood is because it is an appendage to the greater, or the Melchizedek Priesthood, and has power in administering outward ordinances.

15 The bishopric is the presidency of this priesthood, and holds the keys or authority of the same.

16 No man has a legal right to this office, to hold the keys of this priesthood, except he be a literal descendant of Aaron.

17 But as a high priest of the Melchizedek Priesthood has authority to officiate in all the lesser offices, he may officiate in the office of bishop when no literal descendant of Aaron can be found, provided he is called and set apart and ordained unto this power by the hands of the Presidency of the Melchizedek Priesthood.

18 The power and authority of the higher, or Melchizedek Priesthood, is to hold the keys of all the spiritual blessings of the church—

19 To have the privilege of receiving the mysteries of the kingdom of heaven, to have the heavens opened unto them, to commune with the general assembly and church of the Firstborn, and to enjoy the communion and presence of God the Father, and Jesus the mediator of the new covenant.

20 The power and authority of the lesser, or Aaronic Priesthood, is to hold the keys of the ministering of angels, and to administer in outward ordinances, the letter of the gospel, the baptism of repentance for the remission of sins, agreeable to the covenants and commandments.

John the Baptist appeared to Joseph Smith and Oliver Cowdery on May 15, 1829 and restored the Aaronic Priesthood. He informed them that the Aaronic Priesthood held "the keys of the ministering of angels, and of the gospel of repentance, and of baptism by immersion for the remission of sins" (D&C 13). The great revelation to the Twelve revealed that the priesthood of Aaron was conferred upon Aaron and his seed throughout all their generations and was called the lesser priesthood because it is an appendage to the Melchizedek Priesthood, "and has power in administering outward ordinances" (D&C 107:13–14). Furthermore, the bishopric was "the presidency of this priesthood and holds the keys or authority of the same." A literal descendent of Aaron "has a legal right to this office" (vv. 15–16). In another revelation given in November, 1831, the Lord had qualified that the "legal right to the bishopric" and "the presidency over this priesthood, and the keys or authority of the same belonged to the firstborn among the sons of Aaron." He must also "be designated by [the First] Presidency and found worthy, and anointed, and ordained under [their] hands." The Lord revealed that the legal heir must prove his lineage or "ascertain it by revelation from the Lord under the hands of the above-named presidency" (D&C 68:15–21).[70]

The revelation in section 68 gives evidence that the lineage of the firstborn of Aaron was not known to the Church or to the world at that time, nor has it been revealed publicly since that time. Therefore, the stipulation is still in force that "a high priest of the Melchizedek Priesthood . . . may officiate in the office of bishop when no literal descendant of Aaron can be found, provided he is called and set apart and ordained under this power by the hands of the Presidency of the Melchizedek Priesthood" (D&C 107:17; see also vv. 68–71; and D&C 68:19).

In the great revelation to the Twelve, the Lord repeated the keys of the Aaronic Priesthood as stated by John the Baptist (D&C 13), and to those revealed in D&C 84:26–27. The Lord referred to "the keys of the ministering of angels, and to administer in outward ordinances, the letter of the gospel, the baptism of repentance for the remission of sins, agreeable to the covenant and commandments" (D&C 107:20). He also stated that the office of bishop was to administer "all temporal things" (v. 68). Thus the keys of the Aaronic Priesthood, the lesser priesthood, the power to have angels minister, the power to preach the gospel of repentance, and to administer in all temporal things has been restored in this dispensation. All of these powers, however, were in preparation for the greater priesthood that was to follow.

---

[70] The revelation partially quoted above (D&C 68:15–21) may have been revealed at the same time as D&C 107:59–100, and the Prophet Joseph only recorded part of it in 1831. He would then have later added the rest of the revelation to section 107. This supposition is drawn from the fact that both section 68:15–21 and D&C 107:59–100 were given in November, 1831 and on the same subject.

D&C 107:21–26 • Presiding Councils

21 Of necessity there are presidents, or presiding officers growing out of, or appointed of or from among those who are ordained to the several offices in these two priesthoods.

22 Of the Melchizedek Priesthood, three Presiding High Priests, chosen by the body, appointed and ordained to that office, and upheld by the confidence, faith, and prayer of the church, form a quorum of the Presidency of the Church.

23 The twelve traveling councilors are called to be the Twelve Apostles, or special witnesses of the name of Christ in all the world—thus differing from other officers in the church in the duties of their calling.

24 And they form a quorum, equal in authority and power to the three presidents previously mentioned.

25 The Seventy are also called to preach the gospel, and to be especial witnesses unto the Gentiles and in all the world—thus differing from other officers in the church in the duties of their calling.

26 And they form a quorum, equal in authority to that of the Twelve special witnesses or Apostles just named.

The Lord outlined three councils within the Melchizedek Priesthood whose members are now known as "General Authorities," because they are appointed to govern the whole Church. He also speaks of a local council. There is a hierarchy formed by the three higher general councils. "Three Presiding High Priests. . . form a quorum of the Presidency of the Church" (v. 22).

THE FIRST PRESIDENCY

The First Presidency is to "receive the oracles for the whole church" (D&C 124:126). The oracles constitute the infallible authority, or the final voice in the earthly kingdom of God. These three men jointly hold the "keys of the kingdom, which belong always unto the Presidency of the High Priesthood" (D&C 81:2). Those who treat the oracles lightly are under condemnation and will fall if they do not repent (D&C 90:5). Peter, James, and John formed this quorum in the meridian of time (D&C 13 preface), and they have passed their keys to this dispensation (D&C 27:12–13). They received these keys from Jesus Himself (D&C

7:7). Today, three Presiding High Priests govern The Church of Jesus Christ of Latter-day Saints.

THE QUORUM OF THE TWELVE

Oliver Cowdery and David Whitmer, when called as Apostles, were told that there were others who were "called to declare my gospel, both unto Gentile and unto Jew; yea, even Twelve" (D&C 18:26–27). Cowdery and Whitmer were then, June 1829, called to search out the Twelve (v. 37). As stated earlier, these Twelve were called and organized as a quorum on February 14, 1835, and then sought for this great revelation (*HC,* 2:210). This revelation refers to the twelve traveling counselors being "called to be the Twelve Apostles, or special witnesses of the name of Christ in all the world—thus differing from other officers in the Church in the duties of their calling" (D&C 107:23). President J. Reuben Clark, a past member of the First Presidency, reminded us that:

> . . . it should be in mind that some of the General Authorities have had assigned to them a special calling; they possess a special gift; they are sustained as prophets, seers, and revelators, which gives them a special spiritual endowment in connection with their teaching of the people. They have the right, the power, and authority to declare the mind and will of God to his people, subject to the over-all power and authority of the Presidency of the Church. Others of the General Authorities are not given this special spiritual endowment and authority covering their teaching; they have a resulting limitation, and the resulting limitation upon their power and authority in teaching applies to every other officer and member of the Church, for none of them is spiritually endowed as a prophet, seer and a revelator. Furthermore, as just indicated, the President of the Church has a further and special spiritual endowment in this respect, for he is the Prophet, Seer, and Revelator for the whole Church.[71]

To qualify for this special spiritual endowment, Cowdery and Whitmer had been told, the Twelve who they were to choose, must "desire to take upon them my name [Christ] with full purpose of heart" (D&C 18:27–28). Though the Twelve had not yet been called, the Lord spoke to them and testified that:

---

[71] David H. Yarn Jr., *J. Reuben Clark, Selected Papers* [1984], 100–101.

34 These words are not of men nor of man, but of me; wherefore, you shall testify they are of me and not of men;

35 For it is my voice which speaketh them unto you; for they are given by the Spirit unto you, and by my power you can read them one to another; and save it were by my power you could not have them;

36 Wherefore, you can testify that you have heard my voice, and know my words. [D&C 18:34–36]

"These words" (v. 34) imply that the endowment given to the Twelve consists of a special revelation to them. After the Twelve were chosen, Oliver Cowdery instructed them: "Never cease striving until you have seen God face to face. Strengthen your faith; cast off your doubts, your sins, and all your unbelief; and nothing can prevent you from coming to God. Your ordination is not full and complete till God has laid His hand upon you" (*HC*, 2:196). Such experiences are certainly sacred, and not for public expression, but each man, in his own way, becomes a "special [witness] of the name of Christ in all the world" (D&C 107:23).

These twelve men "form a quorum, equal in authority and power to the three presidents [First Presidency] previously mentioned" (v. 24). As explained by the Prophet Joseph, "Where I am not, there is no first presidency over the Twelve" (*TPJS*, 106). Therefore, this council's authority is not exercised until the First Presidency is dissolved upon the death of the President.[72] The Twelve as a council then have authority to organize again the First Presidency. This doctrine was followed precisely upon the death of Joseph Smith, and upon the death of every succeeding President of the Church.

THE SEVENTY

The third body of general church level administration is the Seventy. This quorum consists of seventy men who are to be presided over by seven presidents chosen from among the seventy men, and one of the seven presidents is to preside over the other six presidents (D&C 107:93–94). This quorum is equal in authority to that of the Quorum of the Twelve Apostles (D&C 107:26). The members of this quorum "are to act in the name of the Lord under the direction of the Twelve," and the Twelve

---

[72] Wilford Woodruff, CR, 1898, 89.

are to call upon them when they need assistance in "building up the church and regulating all the affairs of the same," and in filling their "several calls for preaching and administering the gospel" (D&C 107:34, 38). Thus it seems obvious that their quorum being "equal in authority" (v. 26) would be only upon the possibility of the First Presidency and the Quorum of the Twelve being inoperative due to multiple deaths or calamities that dissolved the two higher quorums. In such instances the keys of the kingdom would still be operative.

D&C 107:27–32 • The Decisions of These Quorums

> 27 And every decision made by either of these quorums must be by the unanimous voice of the same; that is, every member in each quorum must be agreed to its decisions, in order to make their decisions of the same power or validity one with the other—

> 28 A majority may form a quorum when circumstances render it impossible to be otherwise—

> 29 Unless this is the case, their decisions are not entitled to the same blessings which the decisions of a quorum of three presidents were anciently, who were ordained after the order of Melchizedek, and were righteous and holy men.

> 30 The decisions of these quorums, or either of them, are to be made in all righteousness, in holiness, and lowliness of heart, meekness and long suffering, and in faith, and virtue, and knowledge, temperance, patience, godliness, brotherly kindness and charity;

> 31 Because the promise is, if these things abound in them they shall not be unfruitful in the knowledge of the Lord.

> 32 And in case that any decision of these quorums is made in unrighteousness, it may be brought before a general assembly of the several quorums, which constitute the spiritual authorities of the church; otherwise there can be no appeal from their decision.

The First Presidency, as stated earlier, is the final authority of the earthly kingdom. The Quorum of the Twelve and the First Quorum of Seventy have equal authority provided certain criteria are met. All of their decisions "must be by unanimous voice" or every member must be agreed to the quorum decision (v. 27). "A majority may form a quorum when circumstances render it impossible to be otherwise" (v. 28). Circumstances rendering it impossible to have the quorum at full capacity would be due to death or unavailability of some of its members. The First Presidency of righteous and holy men, as in ancient days, will sustain their decisions, and they will be blessed (v. 29).

The decisions of either the Twelve or Seventy "are to be made in all righteousness, in holiness, and lowliness of heart, meekness and long suffering, and in faith, and virtue, and knowledge, temperance, patience, godliness, brotherly kindness and charity" (v. 30). With such attributes, they are promised their decisions "shall not be unfruitful in the knowledge of the Lord (v. 31), or those decisions shall be made by revelation. In this case, the decisions will not be "made in unrighteousness," the spiritual authorities of the Church will sustain them, and "there can be no appeal from their decision" (v. 32).

D&C 107:33–38 • More Duties of the Twelve and Seventy

33 The Twelve are a Traveling Presiding High Council, to officiate in the name of the Lord, under the direction of the Presidency of the Church, agreeable to the institution of heaven; to build up the church, and regulate all the affairs of the same in all nations, first unto the Gentiles and secondly unto the Jews.

34 The Seventy are to act in the name of the Lord, under the direction of the Twelve or the traveling high council, in building up the church and regulating all the affairs of the same in all nations, first unto the Gentiles and then to the Jews;

35 The Twelve being sent out, holding the keys, to open the door by the proclamation of the gospel of Jesus Christ, and first unto the Gentiles and then unto the Jews.

36 The standing high councils, at the stakes of Zion, form a quorum equal in authority in the affairs of the church, in all their decisions, to the quorum of the presidency, or to the traveling high council.

37 The high council in Zion form a quorum equal in authority in the affairs of the church, in all their decisions, to the councils of the Twelve at the stakes of Zion.

38 It is the duty of the traveling high council to call upon the Seventy, when they need assistance, to fill the several calls for preaching and administering the gospel, instead of any others.

The Prophet Joseph Smith gave the unique qualification of this "Traveling Presiding High Council" (v. 33): "They are the Twelve

Apostles, who are called to the office of the Traveling High Council, who are to preside over the churches of the Saints, among the Gentiles, where there is no presidency established; and they are to travel and preach among the Gentiles, until the Lord shall command them to go to the Jews. They are to hold the keys of this ministry, to unlock the door of the Kingdom of heaven unto all nations, and to preach the Gospel to every creature. This is the power, authority, and virtue of their apostleship" (*TPJS,* 74).

The building up and regulating the affairs of the Church by the Twelve (v. 33) were to be done "according to the power of the Holy Ghost which is in you, and according to the callings and gifts of God unto men" (D&C 18:32). The latter part of this admonition implies that it is the Twelve's calling to determine and ordain those who have been foreordained by the Lord to the various callings. The Seventy's assist as noted before. The sequence of the Gentiles and then the Jews (vv. 33–34) is the same as in the New Testament (Luke 13:28–30), the Book of Mormon, 3 Nephi 16:10–11, and previous Doctrine and Covenants references (19:27; 90:9).

The Twelve hold "the keys, to open the door by the proclamation of the gospel of Jesus Christ, and first unto the Gentiles and then unto the Jews" (D&C 107:35). The Lord revealed to Thomas B. Marsh, who was serving in that office, that the keys for this work were held by the President of the Quorum of the Twelve. This responsibility was under the direction of the First Presidency. It is the duty of the President of the Twelve to open the door of Christ's kingdom to the various nations of the world as sent by the First Presidency (D&C 112:16–20). Brigham Young was later called to be the President of the Quorum of the Twelve, and the Lord affirmed to him and the Twelve that they have the responsibility of holding "the keys to open up the authority of my kingdom upon the four corners of the earth, and after that to send [the Lord's] word to every creature" (D&C 124:127–28).

The stake that was formed at Kirtland (see D&C 94:1) was also governed by a high council (see D&C 102:1–2). Other high councils in other stakes of Zion (see D&C 107:36), as they would be organized, were to govern as revealed by the Lord. The high council of Zion (v. 37) was apparently a local council in addition to the Twelve Apostles. Their decisions were valid on the local level just as the decisions of the above three quorums were to the general population of the Church.

The Prophet Joseph made the following distinction between the Quorum of the Twelve Apostles and the standing high council or stake high councils:

> President Joseph Smith stated that the Twelve will have no right to go into Zion, or any of the stakes, and there undertake to regulate the affairs thereof, where there is a standing high council; but it is their duty to go abroad and regulate all matters relative to the different branches of the Church. When the Twelve are together, or a quorum of them, in any church, they will have authority to act independently, and make decisions, and those decisions will be valid. But where there is not a quorum, they will have to do business by the voice of the Church. No standing High Council has authority to go into the churches abroad, and regulate the matters thereof, for this belongs to the Twelve. No standing High Council will ever be established only in Zion, or one of her stakes. When the Twelve pass a decision, it is in the name of the Church, therefore it is valid. [*TPJS,* 74]

D&C 107:39–52 • Evangelic Ministers—Patriarchs

39 It is the duty of the Twelve, in all large branches of the church, to ordain evangelical ministers, as they shall be designated unto them by revelation—

40 The order of this priesthood was confirmed to be handed down from father to son, and rightly belongs to the literal descendants of the chosen seed, to whom the promises were made.

41 This order was instituted in the days of Adam, and came down by lineage in the following manner:

42 From Adam to Seth, who was ordained by Adam at the age of sixty-nine years, and was blessed by him three years previous to his (Adam's) death, and received the promise of God by his father, that his posterity should be the chosen of the Lord, and that they should be preserved unto the end of the earth;

43 Because he (Seth) was a perfect man, and his likeness was the express likeness of his father, insomuch that he seemed to be like unto his father in all things, and could be distinguished from him only by his age.

44 Enos was ordained at the age of one hundred and thirty-four years and four months, by the hand of Adam.

45 God called upon Cainan in the wilderness in the fortieth year of his age; and he met Adam in journeying to the place Shedolamak. He was eighty-seven years old when he received his ordination.

46 Mahalaleel was four hundred and ninety-six years and seven days old when he was ordained by the hand of Adam, who also blessed him.

47 Jared was two hundred years old when he was ordained under the hand of Adam, who also blessed him.

48 Enoch was twenty-five years old when he was ordained under the hand of Adam; and he was sixty-five and Adam blessed him.

49 And he saw the Lord, and he walked with him, and was before his face continually; and he walked with God three hundred and sixty-five years, making him four hundred and thirty years old when he was translated.

50 Methuselah was one hundred years old when he was ordained under the hand of Adam.

51 Lamech was thirty-two years old when he was ordained under the hand of Seth.

52 Noah was ten years old when he was ordained under the hand of Methuselah.

Another major function of the Twelve was to ordain evangelical ministers [patriarchs] in all large branches of the Church as "designated unto them by revelation" (v. 39). The Prophet Joseph declared that "An Evangelist is a patriarch, even the oldest man of the blood of Joseph or the seed of Abraham" (*TPJS*, 151). As the name suggests, the ordination was "to be handed down from father to son." The chosen seed designates the covenant posterity of Abraham. This part of the Melchizedek Priesthood was "an order instituted in the days of Adam" and carried out in subsequent generations (v. 41). The order of the priesthood traced in these verses is patriarchal. In August 1843, the Prophet Joseph said: There are three grand orders of priesthood. The first was Melchizedek. "The second Priesthood is Patriarchal authority (the third was Levitical or Aaronic). Go to and finish the temple, and God will fill it with power, and you will then receive more knowledge concerning this priesthood" (*TPJS*, 323). Upon the completion of the temple, the [patriarchal] order of the priesthood was revealed "by the hand of Elijah the Prophet" as prophesied by Malachi in the Old Testament (Malachi 4:5–6; D&C 2:1;

D&C 110:13–15).[73] The power to seal families and to bind one generation to the next was thus restored. The lineage traced in the revelation
to the twelve (vv. 41–52) is the patriarchal line, while the authority of
the Melchizedek Priesthood is traced in D&C 84:6–16. The patriarchal
line has varying ages of when this priesthood was received. The variance
was probably due to their being ordained at the same time, three years
previous to Adam's death, except for Lamech and Noah who were later
ordained (D&C 107:51–52). The order was to come through Seth, who
"was a perfect man" and in the "express likeness of his father [Adam]"
(vv. 42–43). We have little other information about Seth. The tradition
of Enoch being translated is also verified in the tracing of the lineage
(v. 49).

D&C 107:53–57 • Adam Bestows His Last Blessing

53 Three years previous to the death of Adam, he called Seth, Enos,
Cainan, Mahalaleel, Jared, Enoch, and Methuselah, who were all high
priests, with the residue of his posterity who were righteous, into the
valley of Adam-ondi-Ahman, and there bestowed upon them his last
blessing.

54 And the Lord appeared unto them, and they rose up and blessed
Adam, and called him Michael, the prince, the archangel.

55 And the Lord administered comfort unto Adam, and said unto
him: I have set thee to be at the head; a multitude of nations shall come
of thee, and thou art a prince over them forever.

56 And Adam stood up in the midst of the congregation; and,
notwithstanding he was bowed down with age, being full of the Holy
Ghost, predicted whatsoever should befall his posterity unto the latest
generation.

57 These things were all written in the book of Enoch, and are to
be testified of in due time.

---

[73] The wording of D&C 2:1, as quoted, is that of Moroni quoting Malachi 4:5
when he appeared to Joseph Smith on the morning of September 22, 1823 at
Manchester, New York. The wording was apparently changed to give Joseph and
eventually the members of the Church a plainer translation. This conclusion is drawn
from the Prophet's statement in a letter to the Saints on September 6, 1842 when he
quoted Malachi 4:5–6 as recorded in the King James Bible, but explained that he could
have given a plainer translation (D&C 128:17–18).

Verses 53–55 were revealed to the Prophet Joseph on December 18, 1833, while blessing his father when he conferred upon him "the office and Priesthood of Patriarch of the Church." "The J. Reuben Clark Selected Papers, were open to his view," and he blessed his father to "be numbered among those who hold the right of Patriarchal Priesthood, even the keys of that ministry." He saw, and the words fell from his lips (*TPJS*, 38–39), that it was written of Adam in the book of Enoch (D&C 107:57) that he had blessed the seven high priests in the valley of Adam-ondi-Ahman (v. 53). The Lord appeared unto the people who were gathered there, "and they rose up and blessed Adam, and called him Michael, the prince, the archangel" (v. 54). The names that the people called Adam are used throughout the scriptures. They are probably names he was already known by. He is called Michael, and the prince of all, as one who will attend the last great sacrament meeting with other leaders of dispensations (see D&C 27:11). Michael is called "mine archangel" as the one who "shall sound his trump" and "all the dead" will awake (D&C 29:26). The Lord had set him "to be at the head" (v. 55) and the one to bring forth the dead since he is the father of "the whole human family" (Mormon 3:20; see also 2 Nephi 9:21). Thus the Patriarchal Priesthood was conferred upon Joseph Smith, Sen. and the Seer, Joseph, Jun., was shown in vision Adam blessing his posterity (D&C 107:56). Joseph apparently inserted these verses (53–57) in the revelation to the Twelve.

Joseph Jun. then said:

> So shall it be with my father: he shall be called a prince over his posterity, holding the keys of the patriarchal Priesthood over the kingdom of God on earth even the Church of the Latter-day Saints, and he shall sit in the general assembly of Patriarchs, even in council with the Ancient of Days when he shall sit and all the Patriarchs with him and shall enjoy his right and authority under the direction of the Ancient of Days.
>
> And blessed also, is my mother, for she is a mother in Israel, and shall be a partaker with my father in all his patriarchal blessings.
>
> And blessed, also, are my brothers and my sisters, for they shall yet find redemption in the house of the Lord, and their off springs shall be a blessing, a joy and a comfort unto them. [*TPJS*, 39]

The things written in the book of Enoch will "be testified of in due time" (D&C 107:57). The Prophet had had many other things from the book of Enoch given to him by revelation as he translated the Bible (see Moses 6:21–8:2). He was apparently inspired to include verse 56 to complete the account of Adam, and then identified his source (v. 57). The verses given in this revelation shed extensive light on the lineage and office of the Patriarchal Priesthood. We look forward to the many other things that the book of Enoch will shed light upon.

D&C 107:58–67 • President of the High Priesthood

58 It is the duty of the Twelve, also, to ordain and set in order all the other officers of the church, agreeable to the revelation which says:

59 To the church of Christ in the land of Zion, in addition to the church laws respecting church business—

60 Verily, I say unto you, saith the Lord of Hosts, there must needs be presiding elders to preside over those who are of the office of an elder;

61 And also priests to preside over those who are of the office of a priest;

62 And also teachers to preside over those who are of the office of a teacher, in like manner, and also the deacons—

63 Wherefore, from deacon to teacher, and from teacher to priest, and from priest to elder, severally as they are appointed, according to the covenants and commandments of the church.

64 Then comes the High Priesthood, which is the greatest of all.

65 Wherefore, it must needs be that one be appointed of the High Priesthood to preside over the priesthood, and he shall be called President of the High Priesthood of the Church;

66 Or, in other words, the Presiding High Priest over the High Priesthood of the Church.

67 From the same comes the administering of ordinances and blessings upon the church, by the laying on of the hands.

All other officers of the Church were to be ordained and set in order by the Twelve agreeable to the revelation (v. 58). "The revelation" probably has reference to the verses that follow (vv. 59–63) that were revealed to Joseph in November of 1831 as stated above. Wherefore, he included them in the revelation to the Twelve.

The one appointed to preside over the High Priesthood, "the greatest

of all" (v. 64), and "called the President of the High Priesthood of the Church; or, in other words, the Presiding High Priest over the High Priesthood of the Church" (vv. 64–66) is the same office as the President of the Church.[74] The Presiding High Priest administers the "ordinances and blessings upon the church, by the laying on of hands' (v. 67). Thus, the right of presidency was restored in these latter days.

D&C 107:68–76 • The Presiding Officers of the Aaronic Priesthood

68 Wherefore, the office of a bishop is not equal unto it; for the office of a bishop is in administering all temporal things;

69 Nevertheless a bishop must be chosen from the High Priesthood, unless he is a literal descendant of Aaron;

70 For unless he is a literal descendant of Aaron he cannot hold the keys of that priesthood.

71 Nevertheless, a high priest, that is, after the order of Melchizedek, may be set apart unto the ministering of temporal things, having a knowledge of them by the Spirit of truth;

72 And also to be a judge in Israel, to do the business of the church, to sit in judgment upon transgressors upon testimony as it shall be laid before him according to the laws, by the assistance of his counselors, whom he has chosen or will choose among the elders of the church.

73 This is the duty of a bishop who is not a literal descendant of Aaron, but has been ordained to the High Priesthood after the order of Melchizedek.

74 Thus shall he be a judge, even a common judge among the inhabitants of Zion, or in a stake of Zion, or in any branch of the church where he shall be set apart unto this ministry, until the borders of Zion are enlarged and it becomes necessary to have other bishops or judges in Zion or elsewhere.

75 And inasmuch as there are other bishops appointed they shall act in the same office.

76 But a literal descendant of Aaron has a legal right to the presidency

---

[74] President Joseph Fielding Smith states: ". . . The keys of this authority are held by the President of the Church, who is the president of the High Priesthood, 'and there is never but one on the earth at a time on whom this power and the keys of this priesthood are conferred'" (D&C 132:7). [*Doctrines of Salvation,* 3:135]

of this priesthood, to the keys of this ministry, to act in the office of bishop independently, without counselors, except in a case where a President of the High Priesthood, after the order of Melchizedek, is tried, to sit as a judge in Israel.

Two of the offices belonging unto the high priesthood "are elders and bishop" (D&C 84:29). It is generally assumed that the office of bishop is the highest office of the Aaronic Priesthood. This conclusion is drawn from D&C 68:16–18; and 107:69–70). A careful reading of the three revelations (sections 68, 84, 107) offer some other considerations for the office of presidency over the Aaronic Priesthood.

While the revelations say the office of a bishop belongs to the firstborn literal sons of Aaron (v. 69), they do not say that the "literal descendant" will not hold the office of a high priest in the Melchizedek Priesthood. The office of a bishop belongs to the family of Aaron. What office of the priesthood did Aaron and his successors hold? The high priest (Aaron and his successors) went into the holy of holies alone once a year, on the Day Of Atonement (Hebrews 9:7, 25; Exodus 36:10). The high priest was the only one allowed in the holy of holies. The ark of the covenant was the only furniture in the holy of holies. The mercy seat was placed above the ark. The mercy seat was the place God would come and commune with the high priest. "And there I will meet with thee, and I will commune with them from above the mercy seat, from between the two cherubims which are upon the ark of the testimony, of all things which I will give thee in commandment unto the children of Israel" (Exodus 25:22). The Melchizedek Priesthood was required for the manifestation of the power of Godliness, or to see the face of God and live (D&C 84:20–22). Therefore the office of the bishop who holds the keys of the Aaronic Priesthood, or the high priest under the law of Moses, seems to have been a holder of the Melchizedek Priesthood.

The Prophet Joseph taught: "The Bishop is a High Priest, and necessarily so, because he is to preside over the particular branch of Church affairs, that is denominated the lesser priesthood, and because we have no direct lineal descendant of Aaron, to whom it would of right belong" (*TPJS*, 112). Whether a direct descendant or not, he is still to preside over the lesser priesthood. He is, however, to minister in temporal things, be a judge in Israel, do the business of the church, sit in judgment upon transgressors, "by the assistance of his counselors, whom he has chosen or will choose among the elders of the church" (D&C 107:71–72). The literal first-born son of Aaron could "act without counselors, except in a case where a President of the High Priesthood, after the order of Melchizedek, is tried, to sit as a judge in Israel" (v. 76). His calling is a high and holy calling whether a descendant of Aaron or a high priest ordained after the order of Melchizedek.

D&C 107:77–84

77 And the decision of either of these councils, agreeable to the commandment which says:

78 Again, verily, I say unto you, the most important business of the church, and the most difficult cases of the church, inasmuch as there is not satisfaction upon the decision of the bishop or judges, it shall be handed over and carried up unto the council of the church, before the Presidency of the High Priesthood.

79 And the Presidency of the council of the High Priesthood shall have power to call other high priests, even twelve, to assist as counselors; and thus the Presidency of the High Priesthood and its counselors shall have power to decide upon testimony according to the laws of the church.

80 And after this decision it shall be had in remembrance no more before the Lord; for this is the highest council of the church of God, and a final decision upon controversies in spiritual matters.

81 There is not any person belonging to the church who is exempt from this council of the church.

82 And inasmuch as a President of the High Priesthood shall transgress, he shall be had in remembrance before the common council of the church, who shall be assisted by twelve counselors of the High Priesthood;

83 And their decision upon his head shall be an end of controversy concerning him.

84 Thus, none shall be exempted from the justice and the laws of God, that all things may be done in order and in solemnity before him, according to truth and righteousness.

The judiciary system of the Lord allows for appeals to, or reviews by, the higher councils of the Church. They were discussed above (see D&C 107:30–33). However, once it has reached the highest council [The First

Presidency] it is the "final decision," and "an end to controversy" (vv. 80, 83). We learn from this revelation that no person belonging to the Church is exempt from a trial for his worthiness (vv. 81, 84).

D&C 107:85–90

85 And again, verily I say unto you, the duty of a president over the office of a deacon is to preside over twelve deacons, to sit in council with them, and to teach them their duty, edifying one another, as it is given according to the covenants.

86 And also the duty of the president over the office of the teachers is to preside over twenty-four of the teachers, and to sit in council with them, teaching them the duties of their office, as given in the covenants.

87 Also the duty of the president over the Priesthood of Aaron is to preside over forty-eight priests, and sit in council with them, to teach them the duties of their office, as is given in the covenants—

88 This president is to be a bishop; for this is one of the duties of this priesthood.

89 Again, the duty of the president over the office of elders is to preside over ninety-six elders, and to sit in council with them, and to teach them according to the covenants.

90 This presidency is a distinct one from that of the seventy, and is designed for those who do not travel into all the world.

The size of the Aaronic Priesthood quorums, and the elders quorum are given, but no reasons are stated for their size. It is interesting that the size doubles as they advance in age, at least under our present age of ordaining. It is suggested that this ratio is to give more individual attention to the younger boys, but as they increase in age they are expected to assume more responsibility and also accountability. It should be remembered that the Aaronic Priesthood is a training period to receive the Melchizedek Priesthood (see D&C 84:106–108).

D&C 107:91–92 • The Man Like unto Moses

91 And again, the duty of the President of the office of the High Priesthood is to preside over the whole church, and to be like unto Moses—

92 Behold, here is wisdom; yea, to be a seer, a revelator, a translator,

and a prophet, having all the gifts of God which he bestows upon the head of the church.

In November 1831, the Lord revealed that the duty of the President of the High Priesthood "is to preside over the whole church, and to be like unto Moses—" (D&C 107:91). Moses was the Lord's spokesman, the man to whom he spoke "mouth to mouth, even apparently [directly], and not in dark speeches; and the similitude of the Lord [would Moses] behold" (Numbers 12:8). Such is the Lord's prophet today. He is to "be a seer, a revelator, a translator, and a prophet, having all the gifts of God which he bestows upon the whole church" (D&C 107:92). He is the first elder and the presiding elder over all the Church of Christ (D&C 20:2; 124:125). He is the only one who holds all the keys and powers of the High Priesthood over all the offices of the Church (D&C 124:123; 132:7).

The words that are spoken as the Prophet receives them from the Lord are to be received in patience and faith "as if from [the Lord's] own mouth (D&C 21:4–5). "No one shall be appointed to receive commandments and revelations [for] this church" except the Prophet (D&C 28:2), and the Church is not to receive the teachings of any others who come before them as revelations or commandments for the entire Church (see D&C 43:3, 5). He is the spiritual administrator of the things of God for the Church.

D&C 107:93–97 • The Vision of the Seventy

93 And it is according to the vision showing the order of the Seventy, that they should have seven presidents to preside over them, chosen out of the number of the seventy;

94 And the seventh president of these presidents is to preside over the six;

95 And these seven presidents are to choose other seventy besides the first seventy to whom they belong, and are to preside over them;

96 And also other seventy, until seven times seventy, if the labor in the vineyard of necessity requires it.

97 And these seventy are to be traveling ministers, unto the Gentiles first and also unto the Jews.

The members of the Seventy are "called to preach the gospel, and to be especial witnesses unto the Gentiles and in all the world—thus differing from other officers in the church in the duties of their calling" (D&C 107:25). They "are to be traveling ministers, unto the Gentiles first and also unto the Jews" (v. 97; D&C 124:139). As the kingdom grows and "the labor in the vineyard" requires more traveling ministers, the seven presidents, who preside over the first quorum (v. 93), are to call other seventy, even seven times seventy (D&C 107:95–96). The members of these quorums are called to travel continually and have no responsibility to preside (D&C 124:140).

The flexibility of this quorum, or eventual quorums, to meet the needs of a growing church, has been demonstrated throughout the history of the Church, and particularly in the past several years. On October 3, 1975, other Seventies were called as General Authorities in addition to the First Council of the Seventy, constituting the First Quorum of Seventy. The Second Quorum of the Seventy was organized on April 1, 1989, with members called as General Authorities for a period of five years.[75] New members are periodically called to fill the needs of the Church.

D&C 107:98–100 • Other Officers of the Church

> 98 Whereas other officers of the church, who belong not unto the Twelve, neither to the Seventy, are not under the responsibility to travel among all nations, but are to travel as their circumstances shall allow, notwithstanding they may hold as high and responsible offices in the church.
>
> 99 Wherefore, now let every man learn his duty, and to act in the office in which he is appointed, in all diligence.
>
> 100 He that is slothful shall not be counted worthy to stand, and he that learns not his duty and shows himself not approved shall not be counted worthy to stand. Even so. Amen.

The Lord left the door of the Church organization open as He concluded the great revelation to the Twelve. Such officers as Assistants

---

[75] In the April 1997 General Conference of the Church, the Third, Fourth, and Fifth Quorums of the Seventy were organized. The quorums comprised Area Authorities of geographical parts of the earth.

to the Twelve, additional counselors to the First Presidency, or Regional Representatives of the Twelve, would fall under this category of other officers (v. 98).[76] The Lord concluded the great revelation on priesthood to the Twelve with an admonition and a warning. Not only is it important for every man to learn his duty, he must also understand how the presiding officers are to govern, and how one is to be governed (v. 99). Without this knowledge one cannot fully understand his duty or always diligently act in his office. Those who are slothful shall not be counted worthy and those who are diligent will reap eternal life (v. 100).

The revelation given above is a great example of revelation given line upon line, precept upon precept, as the Church grows (see Isaiah 28:13; 2 Nephi 28:30–31; D&C 98:12). The Church organization is as perfect for the time and the place as possible for the circumstances, but the officers who are called may not be perfect, and thus make human errors. As the Prophet Joseph declared: "I never told you I was perfect, but there is no error in the revelations which I have taught" (*TPJS*, 368).

The Twelve had requested "even a great revelation" (*HC*, 2:209–10). Certainly the Lord honored their request and revealed the answer to many questions regarding the governing of the Church. He also gave much instruction to help those who govern, and those being governed, to attain immortality and eternal life in the celestial kingdom of God.

DOCTRINE AND COVENANTS 108

This revelation giving Lyman Sherman comfort concerning his spiritual standing is not considered of doctrinal value to our study and will not be considered here.

General Authority Quotes
—*Elder Harold B. Lee* • D&C 107

There are two great revelations which must be read and understood and almost committed to memory if you would understand the priesthood. I refer first to one of the greatest of all the revelations we have ever had, the 107th section of the Doctrine and Covenants, and then to the eighty-fourth section. There are other scriptures which deal with the

---

[76] Harold B. Lee, *Stand Ye in Holy Places* [1974], 300.

priesthood, but those are the two great revelations on the subject. [*The Teachings of Harold B. Lee,* 481]

—President Spencer W. Kimball • D&C 107:5

The power of this priesthood is not with the General Authorities, with the apostles, with the stake presidents, with the bishops alone. It is for every man who is given the Melchizedek Priesthood and made an elder. He is entitled, if he lives for it, to have these blessings.

How privileged we are to hold this precious priesthood, which is greater than that held by kings and emperors. How wonderful it is for every boy to have this privilege with his brothers and father. [*The Teachings of Spencer W. Kimball,* 495]

There is no limit to the power of the priesthood which you hold. The limit comes in you, if you do not live in harmony with the Spirit of the Lord and you limit yourselves in the power you exert. [*The Teachings of Spencer W. Kimball,* (1982), 498]

—President Joseph F. Smith • D&C 107:8

There is no office growing out of this priesthood that is or can be greater than the priesthood itself. It is from the priesthood that the office derives its authority and power. No office gives authority to the priesthood. But all offices in the Church derive their power, their virtue, their authority, from the priesthood. . . . Which is the greater—the high priest or the seventy? I tell you that neither of them is the greater, and neither of them is the lesser. Their callings lie in different directions, but they are from the same priesthood. [*Gospel Doctrine,* (1959), 148]

—The Prophet Joseph Smith • D&C 107:10

The duty of the High Priest is to administer in spiritual and holy things, and to commune with God; but not to exercise monarchial government, or to appoint meetings for the Elders without their consent. And again, it is the High Priest's duty to be better qualified to teach principles and doctrines, than the Elders; for the office of Elder is an appendage to the High Priesthood, and it concentrates and centers in one. [*TPJS,* 21]

If the first Seventy are all employed, and there is a call for more laborers, it will be the duty of the seven presidents of the first Seventy to call and ordain other Seventy and send them forth to labor in the vineyard, until, if needs be, they set apart seven times seventy, and even

until there are one hundred and forty-four thousand thus set apart for the ministry.

The Seventy are not to attend the conferences of the Twelve, unless they are called upon or requested so to do by the Twelve. The Twelve and the Seventy have particularly to depend upon their ministry for their support, and that of their families; and they have the right, by virtue of their offices, to call upon the churches to assist them. [*TPJS*, 75]

—*President Howard W. Hunter* • D&C 107:21

A man who holds the priesthood accepts his wife as a partner in the leadership of the home and family with full knowledge of and full participation in all decisions relating thereto. Of necessity there must be in the Church and in the home a presiding officer (see D&C 107:21). By divine appointment, the responsibility to preside in the home rests upon the priesthood holder (see Moses 4:22). The Lord intended that the wife be a helpmeet for man (*meet* means equal)—that is, a companion equal and necessary in full partnership. Presiding in righteousness necessitates a shared responsibility between husband and wife; together you act with knowledge and participation in all family matters. For a man to operate independent of or without regard to the feelings and counsel of his wife in governing the family is to exercise unrighteous dominion. [*The Teachings of Howard W. Hunter*, 152–53]

—*President Harold B. Lee* • D&C 107:22

All members of the First Presidency and the Twelve are regularly sustained as "prophets, seers, and revelators," as you have done today. This means that any of the Apostles, so chosen and ordained, could preside over the Church if he were "chosen by the body [which has been interpreted to mean the entire Quorum of the Twelve], appointed and ordained to that office, and upheld by the confidence, faith, and prayer of the church," to quote from a revelation on this subject, on one condition, and that he was the senior member, or the president, of that body (see D&C 107:22).

Occasionally the question is asked as to whether or not one other than the senior member of the Twelve could become President. Some thought on the matter would suggest that any other than the senior member could become President of the Church only if the Lord reveals to that President of the Twelve that someone other than himself could be selected. [*The Teachings of Harold B. Lee*, 535]

—President Ezra Taft Benson • D&C 107:35 (after quoting it);107:53–55

Proselyting the gospel in the nations of the world only occurs when a member of the First Presidency or the Twelve dedicates the land for that purpose. The Church works within the laws of each nation to ensure that Church practices do not conflict with the law or the customs of that nation. We do not proselyte where the laws of that country prohibit the practice. [*The Teachings of Ezra Taft Benson*, 185]

Many great events have transpired in this land of destiny. This is the land where Adam dwelt; this was the place where the Garden of Eden was; it was here that Adam met with a body of high priests at Adam-ondi-Ahman shortly before his death and gave them his final blessing, and the place to which he will return to meet with the leaders of his people (D&C 107:52–57). This was the place of three former civilizations: that of Adam, that of the Jaredites, and that of the Nephites. This is also the place where our Heavenly Father and His Son, Jesus Christ, appeared to Joseph Smith, inaugurating the last dispensation. [*The Teachings of Ezra Taft Benson*, 587–88]

—President Harold B. Lee • D&C 107:99–199

Now, this last sentence indicates that where you find leaders that do not respond, then there must be changes, but not until we have done everything in our power to teach them in their duties as to how they may be carried out more effectively. [*The Teachings of Harold B. Lee*, 513]

Chapter Nineteen

The Keys of this Dispensation

D&C 109–110

DOCTRINE AND COVENANTS 109 & 110

*H*istorical Setting: "The following prayer was given by Revelation to Joseph, the Seer, and was Repeated in the Kirtland Temple at the time of its Dedication, March 27, 1836" (*HC*, 2:420).

SECTIONS 109 & 110 • OUTLINE

➤ 109:1–33   A request to accept the house they were commanded to build.

   a. The purpose of the temple as revealed in D&C 88:117–120 (vv. 6–21).

   b. A request to arm the servants to go forth in power (vv. 22–23).

   c. A request for protection from their enemies (vv. 24–33).

➤ 109:34–46 Jehovah is asked for a repeat of the day of Pentecost.

   a. Put the testimony of the covenant upon the servants (v. 38).

   b. Let the people receive the testimony, and gather to Zion (vv. 30–41).

   c. Deliver thy people from the calamity of the wicked (vv. 42–46).

➤ 109:47–67 Remember the inhabitants driven from Jackson County.

   a. Have mercy upon the wicked mob (vv. 50–53).

    b.   Have mercy upon the nations of the earth (vv. 54–57).

    c.   The sons of Jacob to gather the righteous to build the holy city (v. 58).

    d.   Appoint other stakes to gather and cut short thy work in righteousness (v. 59).

    e.   Those identified with the Gentiles and scattered upon the mountains (vv. 60–61).

    f.   May the children of Judah return to the land of Abraham (vv. 62–64).

    g.   Cause the remnants of Jacob to be converted to the gospel (vv. 65–66).

    h.   May all scattered remnants driven to the ends of the earth be redeemed (v. 67).

➤ 109:68–71   Remember Joseph Smith Jun., and his covenant with Jehovah.

    a.   Have mercy that his wife and children may be exalted (v. 69).

    b.   Have mercy upon all their immediate connections (v. 70).

    c.   All the presidents of thy church and their families for generations (v. 71).

➤ 109:72–76   Remember all the Church, with their families and all, that the kingdom set up without hands may fill the whole earth.

    a.   May the Church come out of the wilderness and shine forth (v. 73).

    b.   Be adorned as a bride when the heavens are unveiled (v. 74).

    c.   Be caught up to meet Christ, and be clothed with robes and crowns (vv. 75–76).

➤ 109:77–80   Hear our petitions and answer us from heaven. Accept the dedication of this house, the work of our hands, built unto Thee.

    a.   Help us by the Spirit to mingle our voices in praise to God and Christ (v. 79).

    b.   Let Thine anointed ones be clothed with salvation (v. 80).

➤ 110:1–10   The Lord appears and accepts the house.

    a.   Your sins are forgiven, let your hearts rejoice (vv. 5–6).

> b. Hearts of tens of thousands will be blessed with this endowment (v. 9).
>
> c. The fame of this house will spread to foreign lands (v. 10).

➤ 110:11–15   Moses appears with the keys of the gathering.

> a. Elias appears with the keys of the gospel of Abraham (v. 13).
>
> b. Elijah appears with the keys of turning the hearts of the fathers to the children, and the children to the fathers (vv. 13–15).

➤ 110:16   The keys of this dispensation are committed before the day of the Lord.

Introduction

The building of the Kirtland Temple was a milestone in the Restoration of the gospel of Jesus Christ. In December of 1830, the Lord had commanded the Church to "assemble together at the Ohio" (D&C 37:3) to receive His law (D&C 42) "and there you shall be endowed with power from on high" (D&C 38:32; January 2, 1831). Three days later the Lord promised that: "inasmuch as my people shall assemble themselves at the Ohio, I have kept in store a blessing such as is not known among the children of men, and it shall be poured forth upon their heads. And from thence men shall go forth into all nations" (D&C 39:15). Two years later, December 27, 1832, the Lord commanded the Saints to build "a house of God" (D&C 88:119). About five months later, June 1, 1833, the Lord chastened His people for "a very grievous sin, in that ye have not considered the great commandment in all things, that I have given unto you concerning the building of mine house" (D&C 95:3). Shortly thereafter, construction began and was completed less than three years later, March of 1836. Six years later, while work was underway on the Nauvoo Temple, the Prophet Joseph declared "that the church is not fully organized, in its proper order, and cannot be, until the Temple is completed where places will be provided for the administration of the ordinances of the priesthood" (*TPJS*, 224). An analysis of the prayer, that was given by revelation (see section heading), and the appearance of the Lord and angelic beings confirm the Prophet's statement. The prayer and its fulfillment are considered together.

TEXT AND COMMENTARY

D&C 109:1–21 • Accept the Work of Our Hands

1 THANKS be to thy name, O Lord God of Israel, who keepest covenant and showest mercy unto thy servants who walk uprightly before thee, with all their hearts—

2 Thou who hast commanded thy servants to build a house to thy name in this place [Kirtland].

3 And now thou beholdest, O Lord, that thy servants have done according to thy commandment.

4 And now we ask thee, Holy Father, in the name of Jesus Christ, the Son of thy bosom, in whose name alone salvation can be administered to the children of men, we ask thee, O Lord, to accept of this house, the workmanship of the hands of us, thy servants, which thou didst command us to build.

5 For thou knowest that we have done this work through great tribulation; and out of our poverty we have given of our substance to build a house to thy name, that the Son of Man might have a place to manifest himself to his people.

6 And as thou hast said in a revelation, given to us, calling us thy friends, saying—Call your solemn assembly, as I have commanded you;

7 And as all have not faith, seek ye diligently and teach one another words of wisdom; yea, seek ye out of the best books words of wisdom, seek learning even by study and also by faith;

8 Organize yourselves; prepare every needful thing, and establish a house, even a house of prayer, a house of fasting, a house of faith, a house of learning, a house of glory, a house of order, a house of God;

9 That your incomings may be in the name of the Lord, that your outgoings may be in the name of the Lord, that all your salutations may be in the name of the Lord, with uplifted hands unto the Most High—

10 And now, Holy Father, we ask thee to assist us, thy people, with thy grace, in calling our solemn assembly, that it may be done to thine honor and to thy divine acceptance;

11 And in a manner that we may be found worthy, in thy sight, to secure a fulfilment of the promises which thou hast made unto us, thy people, in the revelations given unto us;

12 That thy glory may rest down upon thy people, and upon this

thy house, which we now dedicate to thee, that it may be sanctified and consecrated to be holy, and that thy holy presence may be continually in this house;

13 And that all people who shall enter upon the threshold of the Lord's house may feel thy power, and feel constrained to acknowledge that thou hast sanctified it, and that it is thy house, a place of thy holiness.

14 And do thou grant, Holy Father, that all those who shall worship in this house may be taught words of wisdom out of the best books, and that they may seek learning even by study, and also by faith, as thou hast said;

15 And that they may grow up in thee, and receive a fulness of the Holy Ghost, and be organized according to thy laws, and be prepared to obtain every needful thing;

16 And that this house may be a house of prayer, a house of fasting, a house of faith, a house of glory and of God, even thy house;

17 That all the incomings of thy people, into this house, may be in the name of the Lord;

18 That all their outgoings from this house may be in the name of the Lord;

19 And that all their salutations may be in the name of the Lord, with holy hands, uplifted to the Most High;

20 And that no unclean thing shall be permitted to come into thy house to pollute it;

21 And when thy people transgress, any of them, they may speedily repent and return unto thee, and find favor in thy sight, and be restored to the blessings which thou hast ordained to be poured out upon those who shall reverence thee in thy house.

The dedicatory prayer begins by asking the Lord to accept the house that had been built "that the Son of Man might have a place to manifest himself to his people" (vv. 1–5). It then quotes the revelation that commanded them to build the house (vv. 6–9; D&C 88:117–120). The Father is then asked to assist His people in obtaining the blessings promised in the revelation just quoted (D&C 109:10–21).

D&C 109:22–33 • An Endowment of Power

22 And we ask thee, Holy Father, that thy servants may go forth from this house armed with thy power, and that thy name may be upon them, and thy glory be round about them, and thine angels have charge over them;

23 And from this place they may bear exceedingly great and glorious tidings, in truth, unto the ends of the earth, that they may know that this is thy work, and that thou hast put forth thy hand, to fulfil that which thou hast spoken by the mouths of the prophets, concerning the last days.

24 We ask thee, Holy Father, to establish the people that shall worship, and honorably hold a name and standing in this thy house, to all generations and for eternity;

25 That no weapon formed against them shall prosper; that he who diggeth a pit for them shall fall into the same himself;

26 That no combination of wickedness shall have power to rise up and prevail over thy people upon whom thy name shall be put in this house;

27 And if any people shall rise against this people, that thine anger be kindled against them;

28 And if they shall smite this people thou wilt smite them; thou wilt fight for thy people as thou didst in the day of battle, that they may be delivered from the hands of all their enemies.

29 We ask thee, Holy Father, to confound, and astonish, and to bring to shame and confusion, all those who have spread lying reports abroad, over the world, against thy servant or servants, if they will not repent, when the everlasting gospel shall be proclaimed in their ears;

30 And that all their works may be brought to naught, and be swept away by the hail, and by the judgments which thou wilt send upon them in thine anger, that there may be an end to lyings and slanders against thy people.

31 For thou knowest, O Lord, that thy servants have been innocent before thee in bearing record of thy name, for which they have suffered these things.

32 Therefore we plead before thee for a full and complete deliverance from under this yoke;

33 Break it off, O Lord; break it off from the necks of thy servants,

by thy power, that we may rise up in the midst of this generation and
do thy work.

The prayer next asked for an endowment of power upon the Lord's
servants as they went forth unto the ends of the earth (vv. 22–23). To
be "endowed with power from on high" was one of the purposes for their
going to the Ohio (D&C 38:32). It was also a requirement for the
redemption of Zion (D&C 105:10–11). This request was followed by
another one for protection from their enemies as foretold by Isaiah (54:17;
see also 1 Nephi 14:3, 22:14). The Lord is also requested to fight their
battles (D&C 109:24–28). The Holy Father is asked "to confound and
astonish," and to bring "to shame and confusion, all those who spread
lying reports" against the Lord's people, and to break the yoke off the
necks of His servants (vv. 29–33). Therefore, the first part of the prayer
requests the blessings promised concerning the temple and the purposes
for which it was built.

D&C 110:1–10 • The Lord Accepts the House

1 THE veil was taken from our minds, and the eyes of our understanding were opened.

2 We saw the Lord standing upon the breastwork of the pulpit, before
us; and under his feet was a paved work of pure gold, in color like amber.

3 His eyes were as a flame of fire; the hair of his head was white like
the pure snow; his countenance shone above the brightness of the sun;
and his voice was as the sound of the rushing of great waters, even the
voice of Jehovah, saying:

4 I am the first and the last; I am he who liveth, I am he who was
slain; I am your advocate with the Father.

5 Behold, your sins are forgiven you; you are clean before me;
therefore, lift up your heads and rejoice.

6 Let the hearts of your brethren rejoice, and let the hearts of all my
people rejoice, who have, with their might, built this house to my name.

7 For behold, I have accepted this house, and my name shall be here;
and I will manifest myself to my people in mercy in this house.

8 Yea, I will appear unto my servants, and speak unto them with mine
own voice, if my people will keep my commandments, and do not pollute
this holy house.

9 Yea the hearts of thousands and tens of thousands shall greatly rejoice in consequence of the blessings which shall be poured out, and the endowment with which my servants have been endowed in this house.

10 And the fame of this house shall spread to foreign lands; and this is the beginning of the blessing which shall be poured out upon the heads of my people. Even so. Amen.

The prayer was answered on April 3, 1836, when the Lord appeared to Joseph Smith and Oliver Cowdery in the temple (vv. 1–2). The description of Jehovah (v. 3) is symbolic. It is very similar to Ezekiel's when the Lord appeared to him (Ezekiel 1:26–28). The glory of the Lord cannot be explained adequately in human words. As their advocate with the Father, their grievous sins of not building the house were now forgiven (vv. 4–6). The house was accepted and the Son of Man had a place to manifest Himself to His people (v. 7). His promise to appear unto His servants (v. 8) was fulfilled.[77] The hearts of tens of thousands have rejoiced over the endowment (v. 9). The fame of the Kirtland Temple has spread to foreign lands, and, as the Lord said; "this is the beginning of the blessing" (v. 10). His appearance was as Malachi had prophesied, it was not scheduled or expected, but He "suddenly [came] to his temple" (Malachi 3:1).

D&C 109:34–46 • The Day of Pentecost

34 O Jehovah, have mercy upon this people, and as all men sin forgive the transgressions of thy people, and let them be blotted out forever.

35 Let the anointing of thy ministers be sealed upon them with power from on high.

36 Let it be fulfilled upon them, as upon those on the day of Pentecost; let the gift of tongues be poured out upon thy people, even cloven tongues as of fire, and the interpretation thereof.

37 And let thy house be filled, as with a rushing mighty wind, with thy glory.

38 Put upon thy servants the testimony of the covenant, that when they go out and proclaim thy word they may seal up the law, and prepare

---

[77] See Karl Ricks Anderson, *Joseph Smith's Kirtland* (1989), 111.

the hearts of thy saints for all those judgments thou art about to send, in thy wrath, upon the inhabitants of the earth, because of their transgressions, that thy people may not faint in the day of trouble.

39 And whatsoever city thy servants shall enter, and the people of that city receive their testimony, let thy peace and thy salvation be upon that city; that they may gather out of that city the righteous, that they may come forth to Zion, or to her stakes, the places of thine appointment, with songs of everlasting joy;

40 And until this be accomplished, let not thy judgments fall upon that city.

41 And whatsoever city thy servants shall enter, and the people of that city receive not the testimony of thy servants, and thy servants warn them to save themselves from this untoward generation, let it be upon that city according to that which thou hast spoken by the mouths of thy prophets.

42 But deliver thou, O Jehovah, we beseech thee, thy servants from their hands, and cleanse them from their blood.

43 O Lord, we delight not in the destruction of our fellow men; their souls are precious before thee;

44 But thy word must be fulfilled. Help thy servants to say, with thy grace assisting them: Thy will be done, O Lord, and not ours.

45 We know that thou hast spoken by the mouth of thy prophets terrible things concerning the wicked, in the last days—that thou wilt pour out thy judgments, without measure;

46 Therefore, O Lord, deliver thy people from the calamity of the wicked; enable thy servants to seal up the law, and bind up the testimony, that they may be prepared against the day of burning.

Returning to the next segment of the dedicatory prayer, the Prophet appealed to Jehovah (v. 34). In the previous mentioning of Deity, he had addressed the Holy Father (D&C 109:4, 10, 22, 24, 29), and in the formal salutation had done so in the name of Jesus Christ (D&C 109:4), although he had given thanks to the Lord God of Israel in the opening verse. Was Joseph now directly communicating with Jehovah? When Jesus appeared to the Nephites they prayed unto Him "calling him their Lord and their God" (3 Nephi 19:18). As Jesus departed from the Nephites, He prayed to the Father, and explained that "they pray unto me because

I am with them" (vv. 22). It appears that Joseph was communicating directly to Jehovah at this time.

The Prophet appeals in the prayer for the gift of tongues to "be poured out upon thy people, even cloven tongues as of fire, and the interpretation thereof. And let [Jehovah's] house be filled, as with a rushing mighty wind, with [Jehovah's] glory" as on the day of Pentecost in Jerusalem (D&C 109:34–37; see Acts 2:1–4). The Lord had promised earlier that His glory would rest upon the temple if "it be not defiled" and that "my presence shall be there, for I will come into it, and all the pure in heart that shall come into it shall see God" (D&C 97:15–16). The purpose of the Pentecostal experience was to prepare for the day of burning [Second Coming] (D&C 109:38–46). This part of the prayer was also fulfilled.

At the dedication of the Temple on March 27, 1836, during the opening prayer, President Frederick G. Williams testified that an angel entered the window and sat between Father Smith and himself. David Whitmer saw angels and after the Hosanna Shout, "President Brigham Young gave a short address in tongues, and David W. Patten interpreted, and gave a short exhortation in tongues himself. The Prophet Joseph then recorded:

> Do not quench the Spirit, for the first one that opens his mouth shall receive the Spirit of Prophecy.
>
> Brother George A. Smith arose and began to prophesy, when a noise was heard like the sound of a rushing mighty wind, which filled the Temple, and all the congregation simultaneously arose, being moved upon by an invisible power; many began to speak in tongues and prophesy; others saw glorious visions; and I beheld the Temple was filled with angels, which fact I declared to the congregation. The people of the neighborhood came running together (hearing an unusual sound within, and seeing a bright light like a pillar of fire resting upon the Temple), and were astonished at what was taking place, This continued until the meeting closed at eleven p.m. [HC, 2:427–28]

The latter-day Pentecost had occurred. "The anointing of [Jehovah's] ministers" was "sealed upon them with power from on high" (D&C 109:35). The Lord's house had been filled "with [His] glory" (v. 37).

D&C 109:47–59 • Pleas for Mercy

47 We ask thee, Holy Father, to remember those who have been driven by the inhabitants of Jackson county, Missouri, from the lands of their inheritance, and break off, O Lord, this yoke of affliction that has been put upon them.

48 Thou knowest, O Lord, that they have been greatly oppressed and afflicted by wicked men; and our hearts flow out with sorrow because of their grievous burdens.

49 O Lord, how long wilt thou suffer this people to bear this affliction, and the cries of their innocent ones to ascend up in thine ears, and their blood come up in testimony before thee, and not make a display of thy testimony in their behalf?

50 Have mercy, O Lord, upon the wicked mob, who have driven thy people, that they may cease to spoil, that they may repent of their sins if repentance is to be found;

51 But if they will not, make bare thine arm, O Lord, and redeem that which thou didst appoint a Zion unto thy people.

52 And if it cannot be otherwise, that the cause of thy people may not fail before thee may thine anger be kindled, and thine indignation fall upon them, that they may be wasted away, both root and branch, from under heaven;

53 But inasmuch as they will repent, thou art gracious and merciful, and wilt turn away thy wrath when thou lookest upon the face of thine Anointed.

54 Have mercy, O Lord, upon all the nations of the earth; have mercy upon the rulers of our land; may those principles, which were so honorably and nobly defended, namely, the Constitution of our land, by our fathers, be established forever.

55 Remember the kings, the princes, the nobles, and the great ones of the earth, and all people, and the churches, all the poor, the needy, and afflicted ones of the earth;

56 That their hearts may be softened when thy servants shall go out from thy house, O Jehovah, to bear testimony of thy name; that their prejudices may give way before the truth, and thy people may obtain favor in the sight of all;

57 That all the ends of the earth may know that we, thy servants, have heard thy voice, and that thou hast sent us;

58 That from among all these, thy servants, the sons of Jacob, may gather out the righteous to build a holy city to thy name, as thou hast commanded them.

59 We ask thee to appoint unto Zion other stakes besides this one which thou hast appointed, that the gathering of thy people may roll on in great power and majesty, that thy work may be cut short in righteousness.

The dedicatory prayer continues with a plea for those driven from Jackson County, Missouri, and for the mobs who had driven them to repent or suffer the indignation of justice (D&C 109:47–53). The Prophet prayed for his enemies, those "whom despitefully use you and persecute you" as the Savior had taught (Matthew 5:44; 3 Nephi 12:44). He then pled for mercy upon all nations of the earth, and for the principles of the United States Constitution to be extended to all (D&C 109:54–55). This was the law to come forth out of Zion (Isaiah 2:3), and belonged to all mankind (D&C 98:5). He prayed that the truth may spread—or the gospel of Jesus Christ—and gather the people to build up stakes of Zion and a holy city unto the Lord (D&C 109:54–59). The holy city was the New Jerusalem (see Moses 7:62, 3 Nephi 21:23). The establishing of Zion and her stakes would cut short the work of the destruction of the wicked at the Second Coming of Christ (see D&C 84:96–97).

D&C 109:60–67 • The Various Tribes of Israel Gathered

60 Now these words, O Lord, we have spoken before thee, concerning the revelations and commandments which thou hast given unto us, who are identified with the Gentiles.

61 But thou knowest that thou hast a great love for the children of Jacob, who have been scattered upon the mountains for a long time, in a cloudy and dark day.

62 We therefore ask thee to have mercy upon the children of Jacob, that Jerusalem, from this hour, may begin to be redeemed;

63 And the yoke of bondage may begin to be broken off from the house of David;

64 And the children of Judah may begin to return to the lands which thou didst give to Abraham, their father.

65 And cause that the remnants of Jacob, who have been cursed and

smitten because of their transgression, be converted from their wild and savage condition to the fulness of the everlasting gospel;

66 That they may lay down their weapons of bloodshed, and cease their rebellions.

67 And may all the scattered remnants of Israel, who have been driven to the ends of the earth, come to a knowledge of the truth, believe in the Messiah, and be redeemed from oppression, and rejoice before thee.

Although the modern day Saints, who had already been gathered, were of the house of Israel, they were "identified with the Gentiles" (v. 60). They were basically of the house of Israel who had been scattered "among all nations" (Amos 9:8–9; D&C 86:8–10; 103:17). Since they had lost their identity as Israelites, they were now considered to be Gentiles among whom they had lived for hundreds of years. The prayer speaks of them as "the children of Jacob, who have been scattered upon the mountains for a long time, in a cloudy and dark day" (D&C 109:61). The mountains refer to the everlasting hills of the Americas (see Genesis 49:22–26). While some had been gathered, many more were yet to be. Thus they were nationally, or culturally Gentiles. Similarly, Nephi was of the tribe of Manasseh (Alma 10:3), but was nationally or culturally a Jew since he had lived among the Jews all his life (see 2 Nephi 30:4; 33:8).

The prayer asked for mercy upon the children of Judah that they may *begin* to "return to the lands" given to Abraham their father, that the yoke of bondage may *begin* to be broken and Jerusalem *begin* to be redeemed (D&C 109:62–64). Judah was to begin to gather from the hour of the temple dedication (v. 62). The prayer also requested the conversion of the Lamanites "from their wild and savage condition," and all the scattered remnants of Israel, who have been scattered to the end of the earth (including the lost ten tribes but not limited to them), "come to a knowledge of the truth believe in the Messiah, and be redeemed" (vv. 65–67). The prayer was answered.

D&C 110:11 • Moses and the Keys of Gathering Israel

11 After this vision closed, the heavens were again opened unto us; and Moses appeared before us, and committed unto us the keys of the gathering of Israel from the four parts of the earth, and the leading of the ten tribes from the land of the north.

Following the Savior's appearance to Joseph and Oliver, Moses appeared to them. The keys of the gathering of Israel were now restored and the work commenced.

The gathering of those among the Gentiles, scattered upon the mountains, continued. The Prophet Joseph, in the April conference of 1840, sent Elder Orson Hyde, of the Quorum of the Twelve Apostles, to dedicate the land of Jerusalem for the return of Judah to Jerusalem. Elder Hyde had been told by the Prophet Joseph many years before that "in due time thou shalt go to Jerusalem, the land of thy fathers, and be a watchman unto the house of Israel; and by thy hands shall the Most High do a great work, which shall prepare the way and greatly facilitate the gathering together of that people." In March of 1840, Elder Hyde had a glorious vision of his mission to Jerusalem (*HC*, 4:375–76). The prayer of the temple dedication said the redemption of Jerusalem was to begin "from this hour" and Elder Hyde left Nauvoo April 15, 1840, and traveled east. Elder John E. Page was called to accompany him, but did not go. Elder Hyde traveled through Europe visiting many of the Jewish communities. After arriving in Jerusalem on October 21, 1841, he dedicated the land three days later, October 24, 1841, for the return of Judah. From this time the Jews have "begun" to physically gather, and as Nephi prophesied, "the Jews which are scattered also shall begin to believe in Christ; and they shall begin to gather in upon the face of the land; and as many as shall believe in Christ shall also become a delightsome people" (2 Nephi 30:7).

The attitude of the Jewish people towards Christ has changed gradually since the dedication. They do not accept Him as the Messiah but many do look upon Him as a great teacher, or even a prophet. As they have begun to believe, they have begun to gather. The time will come when the gospel will be preached to them (Isaiah 18; 26:1–2; 3 Nephi 20:29–42). The Lamanites have begun to accept the gospel, but many more will yet come into the fold (2 Nephi 30:4–6), and the others of Israel (the lost tribes) will be the last ones gathered (Jacob 5:63; D&C 133:26–34). The keys to gather Israel or to preach the gospel to all the nations of the earth—one of the three primary missions of the Church—was given to the Prophet and Oliver by Moses in the Kirtland Temple on April 3, 1836.

D&C 109:68–71 • Joseph and All the Presidents

68 O Lord, remember thy servant, Joseph Smith, Jun., and all his afflictions and persecutions—how he has covenanted with Jehovah, and vowed to thee, O Mighty God of Jacob—and the commandments which thou hast given unto him, and that he hath sincerely striven to do thy will.

69 Have mercy, O Lord, upon his wife and children, that they may be exalted in thy presence, and preserved by thy fostering hand.

70 Have mercy upon all their immediate connections, that their prejudices may be broken up and swept away as with a flood; that they may be converted and redeemed with Israel, and know that thou art God.

71 Remember, O Lord, the presidents, even all the presidents of thy church, that thy right hand may exalt them, with all their families, and their immediate connections, that their names may be perpetuated and had in everlasting remembrance from generation to generation.

The dedicatory prayer then turned to the Prophet Joseph Smith and the covenant he had made with Jehovah, his wife and children, and "all their immediate connections" (D&C 109:68–70). Jehovah later covenanted with the Prophet that "the kindreds of the earth [would] be blessed" even as He had covenanted with Abraham (D&C 124:58; 103:17; 132:30–32). The "immediate connections" seems to refer to the extended family of the Smiths, and especially those who were not amenable to the mission of Joseph, but also to those who came into the covenant through the waters of baptism. Their conversion and redemption with Israel was requested. The prayer was again answered.

D&C 110:12 • Elias and the Gospel of Abraham

12 After this, Elias appeared, and committed the dispensation of the gospel of Abraham, saying that in us and our seed all generations after us should be blessed.

There have been varying opinions about who Elias is. While there are many Eliases, including Jesus (JST, John 1:20–30; D&C 77:14), the Elias spoken of here was identified by President Joseph Fielding Smith as Noah:

Elias came and restored the gospel of Abraham. Who was Elias? Well,

Elias was Noah, who came and restored his keys . . . .Noah, who is Gabriel, . . . stands next in authority to Adam in the priesthood; he was called of God to this office, and was the father of all living in his day, and to him was given the dominion. These men held keys first on earth, and then in heaven (*DHC* 3:385–86). It was Gabriel who appeared to Zacharias and promised him a son, and who appeared to Mary and announced the coming of the Son of God as recorded by Luke. It was also Gabriel as an Elias who is mentioned in the Doctrine and Covenants, section 27, verse 7. It was Gabriel or Noah, who stands next to Michael or Adam in the priesthood. [CR, April 1960, 72]

As the personage preserved by God through the flood, he seems to be the one commissioned to restore all things after the flood.

The keys committed by Elias, or Noah, were for "the dispensation of the gospel of Abraham." The gospel of Abraham is administered through the ministry and priesthood of the literal seed of the body of Abraham (see Abraham 2:9–11). Therefore, as a literal descendant of Abraham, Joseph Smith and his associates, "all generations after [them] should be blessed" (D&C 110:12). Through the temple ordinances for the living, the second mission of the Church—the perfection of the Saints—will be furthered.

13 For a place of thanksgiving for all saints, and for a place of instruction for all those who are called to the work of the ministry in all their several callings and offices;

14 That they may be perfected in the understanding of their ministry, in theory, in principle, and in doctrine, in all things pertaining to the kingdom of God on the earth, the keys of which kingdom have been conferred upon you. [D&C 97:13–14]

The temple ordinances are the culminating blessing of the gospel, but the obeying of all other principles and ordinances will be necessary to become perfect even as Christ (3 Nephi 12:48; Matthew 5:48).

The Lord was asked to remember all the Presidents of the Church and their families and immediate connections with all their families from generation to generation (D&C 109:71). Again we return to the dedicatory prayer.

D&C 109:72–76 • The Church Shine Forth

72 Remember all thy church, O Lord, with all their families, and all their immediate connections, with all their sick and afflicted ones, with all the poor and meek of the earth; that the kingdom, which thou hast set up without hands, may become a great mountain and fill the whole earth;

73 That thy church may come forth out of the wilderness of darkness, and shine forth fair as the moon, clear as the sun, and terrible as an army with banners;

74 And be adorned as a bride for that day when thou shalt unveil the heavens, and cause the mountains to flow down at thy presence, and the valleys to be exalted, the rough places made smooth; that thy glory may fill the earth;

75 That when the trump shall sound for the dead, we shall be caught up in the cloud to meet thee, that we may ever be with the Lord;

76 That our garments may be pure, that we may be clothed upon with robes of righteousness, with palms in our hands, and crowns of glory upon our heads, and reap eternal joy for all our sufferings.

The Lord was asked to remember the Church and kingdom that had been set up without hands that it "may become a great mountain and fill the whole earth" (see Daniel 2:44–45), and "come forth out of the wilderness" (D&C 1:30; Revelation 12:7) and become the kingdom of Zion (D&C 105:31–32) that it was destined to become (D&C 109:72–76). These requests were honored by the next appearance in the temple.

D&C 110:13–15 • Elijah and the Keys of the Patriarchal Priesthood

13 After this vision had closed, another great and glorious vision burst upon us; for Elijah the prophet, who was taken to heaven without tasting death, stood before us, and said:

14 Behold the time has fully come, which was spoken of by the mouth of Malachi—testifying that he [Elijah] should be sent, before the great and dreadful day of the Lord come—

15 To turn the hearts of the fathers to the children, and the children to the fathers, lest the whole earth be smitten with a curse—

The Prophet Elijah was the last of the ancient prophets to appear in the Kirtland Temple. The Lord, as promised, sent Elijah the prophet to restore the patriarchal authority (D&C 110:13–15). His mission was twofold: first, to plant in the hearts of the people the promises that had been made to people of earlier dispensations who had their "eye fixed on the restoration of the priesthood, the glories to be revealed in the last days" as did Malachi the prophet (D&C 128:17).

As revealed to President Joseph F. Smith, this planting was "foreshadowing the great work to be done in the temples of the Lord in the dispensation of the fulness of time, for the redemption of the dead, and the sealing of the children to their parents" (D&C 138:48). This great work was the second part of Elijah's mission, to provide "a welding link of some kind or other between the fathers and the children" (D&C 128:18).

D&C 109:77–80 • Hear Our Plea, Answer Us from Heaven

77 O Lord God Almighty, hear us in these our petitions, and answer us from heaven, thy holy habitation, where thou sittest enthroned, with glory, honor, power, majesty, might, dominion, truth, justice, judgment, mercy, and an infinity of fulness, from everlasting to everlasting.

78 O hear, O hear, O hear us, O Lord! And answer these petitions, and accept the dedication of this house unto thee, the work of our hands, which we have built unto thy name;

79 And also this church, to put upon it thy name. And help us by the power of thy Spirit, that we may mingle our voices with those bright, shining seraphs around thy throne, with acclamations of praise, singing Hosanna to God and the Lamb!

80 And let these, thine anointed ones, be clothed with salvation, and thy saints shout aloud for joy. Amen, and Amen.

The keys for the third mission of the Church—the redemption of the dead—were restored. The Lord had heard their petitions from the heavens and accepted the dedication of the house of the Lord, the first one in this dispensation. The Lord and three of "those bright, shining seraphs around the throne" had brought the keys necessary for the salvation of the Saints (D&C 109:77–80).

D&C 110:16 • The Keys of This Dispensation

16 Therefore the keys of this dispensation are committed into your hands; and by this ye may know that the great and dreadful day of the Lord is near, even at the doors" (D&C 110:16).

The temple was now built and the Church was fully organized. The keys of the last dispensation would enable the Church to fulfill its three fold mission, which was confirmed by the First Presidency and the Twelve in 1981: "To proclaim the gospel of the Lord Jesus Christ to every nation, kindred, tongue, and people; To perfect the Saints by preparing them to receive the ordinances of the gospel and by instructions and discipline to gain exaltation; To redeem the dead performing vicarious ordinances of the gospel for those who had lived on earth.[78] The organization of the Church was now complete—a place was provided "for the administration of the ordinances of the priesthood" (*TPJS,* 224; see also *HC,* 2:432).

General Authority Quotes

—*The Prophet Joseph Smith* • D&C 109:36 (March 30, 1836—after the first day of dedication, but before the appearances of the Savior and the three ancient prophets)

I then observed to the quorums, that I had now completed the organization of the Church, and we had passed through the necessary ceremonies, that I had given them all the instructions they needed, and that they were now at liberty, . . . to go forth and build up the kingdom of God, and that it was expedient for me and the Presidency to retire, having spent the night previously in waiting upon the Lord in His temple, and having to attend another dedication on the morrow. . . .

I left the meeting in charge of the Twelve, and retired about nine o'clock in the evening. The brethren continued exhorting, prophesying, and speaking in tongues until five o'clock in the morning. The Savior made his appearance to some, while angels ministered to others, and it was a Pentecost and an endowment indeed, long to be remembered, for the sound shall go forth from this place into all the world, and the occurrences of this day shall be handed down upon the pages of sacred history, to all generations; as the day of Pentecost, so shall this day be numbered and celebrated as a year of Jubilee, and a time of rejoicing to the Saints of the Most High God. [*HC,* 2:432–33]

---

[78] CR, April 1981, 3.

—*President Gordon B. Hinckley* • D&C 109:72–73; 110:8–10

We are witnessing the answer to that remarkable pleading. Increasingly the Church is being recognized at home and abroad for what it truly is. There are still those, not a few, who criticize and rebel, who apostatize and lift their voices against this work. We have always had them. They speak their piece as they walk across the stage of life, and then they are soon forgotten. I suppose we will always have them as long as we are trying to do the work of the Lord. The honest in heart will detect that which is true and that which is false. We go forward, marching as an army with banners emblazoned with the everlasting truth. We are a cause that is militant for truth and goodness. We are a body of Christian soldiers "marching as to war, with the cross of Jesus going on before" (*Hymns*, 246). [*Teachings of Gordon B. Hinckley*, 295–96]

But it was also a marvelous and miraculous season, a time of Pentecostal outpouring.

Sixty-two of the revelations found in the Doctrine and Covenants were received in that Ohio and environment. During that time the Kirtland Temple was constructed, with all of the miraculous incidents that occurred incident to its dedication. Moses, Elias, and Elijah came, bestowing eternal priesthood keys. The Son of God appeared to his servants, who bore testimony of him. The work was strengthened and integrated in a remarkable manner.

Of that season Orson Pratt wrote: "God was there, his angels were there, the Holy Ghost was in the midst of the people, the visions of the Almighty were opened to the minds of the servants of the living God; the veil was taken from the minds of many; they saw the heavens opened, they beheld the angels of God; they heard the voice of the Lord; and they were filled from the crown of their heads to the soles of their feet with the power and inspiration of the Holy Ghost. [*Teachings of Gordon B. Hinckley*, 102–03]

—*President Howard W. Hunter* • D&C 110:16

All of our efforts in proclaiming the gospel, perfecting the Saints, and redeeming the dead lead to the holy temple. This is because the temple ordinances are absolutely crucial; we cannot return to God's presence without them. [*The Teachings of Howard W. Hunter*, 237–38]

Chapter Twenty

Truth Will Prevail

D&C 112; 114; 118

DOCTRINE AND COVENANTS 112

*H*istorical Setting:

. . . The [seven] brethren went to Preston [England], about thirty miles from Liverpool, and as they alighted from the coach a large flag was unfurled nearly over their heads, with this inscription, in letters of gold, "Truth will prevail," it being election day for members of Parliament. King William the Fourth had recently died and Queen Victoria was about to organize her cabinet. . . . The Elders had an interview that evening with the Rev. James Fielding, brother of Joseph Fielding, who had a chapel in that place, where all the brethren went to hear him preach on Sunday, 23rd. After his sermon in the morning Mr. Fielding gave notice to his congregation that there were present some ministers from America, and they would occupy his pulpit in the afternoon. This unexpected offer was unsolicited but joyfully received, and in the afternoon President Kimball gave a brief relation of the Church from the commencement, followed by Elder Hyde, who bore testimony of the same; thus was the key turned and the door of salvation opened to the inhabitants of England. . . .

The same day that the Gospel was first preached in England I received [Doctrine and Covenants 112].

Revelation given at Kirtland, Ohio, July 23rd, 1837. The word of the Lord unto Thomas B. Marsh, concerning the Twelve Apostles of the Lamb. [*HC*, 2:498–499]

SECTION 112 • OUTLINE

➤112:1–9 The Lord has heard Elder Marsh's prayers and his alms for his brethren who have been called to bear testimony of Christ's name.

    a. The Lord is not well pleased with a few things in his heart and with him (v. 2).

    b. He has abased himself and shall be exalted, his sins are forgiven (v. 3).

    c. He shall bear record to the Gentiles, the Jews, and to the ends of the earth (v. 4).

    d. Let thy warning voice keep the earth's inhabitants from slumber (v. 5).

    e. Let thy habitation be known in Zion, the Lord has a great work for him (v. 6).

    f. Gird thy loins and shoe thy feet to go among the mountains and nations (v. 7).

    g. By thy word many high ones shall be brought low and low ones exalted (v. 8).

    h. Thy voice shall be a rebuke to the transgressor (v. 9).

➤ 112:10–13 Be humble and the Lord will lead you and answer your prayers.

    a. Be not partial of thy brethren in love, and to all men (v. 11).

    b. Pray for the Twelve, admonish them sharply for my sake, and their sins (v. 12).

    c. After temptations and tribulations, they will be converted and healed (v. 13).

➤ 112:14–15 The Lord speaks to all of the Twelve.

    a. Gird up your loins, take up your cross, follow me, and feed my sheep (v. 13).

    b. Rebel not against Joseph who has the keys until Christ comes (v. 14).

➤ 112:16–22 Thomas holds the keys of the kingdom of the Twelve among the nations.

    a. To unlock the doors where Joseph, Sidney, and Hyrum cannot go (vv. 17–18).

   b. Where they send you go in my name, an effectual door shall be opened (v. 19).

   c. Those who receive my word receive the First Presidency, my counselors (v. 20).

   d. The Twelve you authorize, have power to open the door where sent (vv. 21–22).

➤ 112:23–29   Darkness covers the earth and the minds of the people, and all flesh is corrupt.

   a. Vengeance comes soon upon the earth, a day of burning and desolation (v. 24).

   b. From my house it shall begin and go forth (v. 25).

   c. First among you who profess my name and blaspheme me (v. 26).

   d. Trouble not about my Church in this place (v. 27).

   e. Purify your heart and preach my gospel to whoever has not received it (v. 28).

   f. He that believes and is baptized shall be saved, and if not, condemned (v. 29).

➤ 112:30–34   The Twelve and the First Presidency, with Joseph, is given the power of the priesthood for the dispensation of the fulness of times.

   a. This power is in connection with all other dispensations (v. 31).

   b. The keys have come down from the fathers unto you (v. 32).

   c. Clean your hearts and garments, or this generation's blood be required of you (v. 33).

   d. I come quickly and will recompense every man (v. 34).

Introduction

Apostles were first called and ordained before the Church was organized. Oliver Cowdery and David Whitmer were called, and commissioned to search out the Twelve (see D&C 18:9, 37). As special witnesses of Christ's name themselves (see D&C 107:23), they were apparently qualified to recognize those who were potential candidates for this high and noble calling. On the day the Church was organized, April 6, 1830,

Joseph Smith and Oliver Cowdery were designated as Apostles, and the first and second elders of the Church respectively (see D&C 20:2–3). They had been ordained previously (see D&C 27:12). Thus the Church was "built upon the foundation of apostles and prophets, Jesus Christ being the chief corner stone" as explained by the Apostle Paul (Ephesians 2:20). However, the Quorum of the Twelve Apostles was not organized until February 14; 1835. Thomas B. Marsh was called as the president of this quorum, and D&C 112 was addressed to him. It is also addressed to whoever is called to that same position. It also addresses the members of that quorum, and is an important doctrinal section for Church members.

TEXT AND COMMENTARY

D&C 112:1–9 • Bear Record of My Name unto the Ends of the Earth

1 VERILY thus saith the Lord unto you my servant Thomas: I have heard thy prayers; and thine alms have come up as a memorial before me, in behalf of those, thy brethren, who were chosen to bear testimony of my name and to send it abroad among all nations, kindreds, tongues, and people, and ordained through the instrumentality of my servants,

2 Verily I say unto you, there have been some few things in thine heart and with thee with which I, the Lord, was not well pleased.

3 Nevertheless, inasmuch as thou hast abased thyself thou shalt be exalted; therefore, all thy sins are forgiven thee.

4 Let thy heart be of good cheer before my face; and thou shalt bear record of my name, not only unto the Gentiles, but also unto the Jews; and thou shalt send forth my word unto the ends of the earth.

5 Contend thou, therefore, morning by morning; and day after day let thy warning voice go forth; and when the night cometh let not the inhabitants of the earth slumber, because of thy speech.

6 Let thy habitation be known in Zion, and remove not thy house; for I, the Lord, have a great work for thee to do, in publishing my name among the children of men.

7 Therefore, gird up thy loins for the work. Let thy feet be shod also, for thou art chosen, and thy path lieth among the mountains, and among many nations.

8 And by thy word many high ones shall be brought low, and by thy word many low ones shall be exalted.

9 Thy voice shall be a rebuke unto the transgressor; and at thy rebuke let the tongue of the slanderer cease its perverseness.

The Quorum had been functioning for over two years when this revelation was given. Thomas had done and desired things with which the Lord was not well pleased (v. 2). However he had abased himself, or lowered his estimation of his own abilities, and learned to depend upon the Lord for guidance. Therefore, the Lord had forgiven him (v. 3). Furthermore, he expanded his ministry to include the Jews as a people, and to the ends of the earth as the territory (v. 4). We know President Marsh never traveled to the Palestine area, nor is there any record of his bearing record to Jewish people in the United States. His foreordained mission to the Jews may have been fulfilled by Elder Orson Hyde, who was sent to Palestine in 1840, a relative short time after President Marsh was excommunicated from the Church in 1839.

His warning voice to keep the inhabitants from sleeping (v. 5) was probably related to what the Lord declared later in this revelation about the impending vengeance to come (see v. 24). His great work was also among Church members, or Zion (v. 6), as well as "high ones," and transgressors brought to repentance (vv. 8–9). How much greater would have been his joy had he remained faithful (see D&C 18:16). This great work extending to the mountains (D&C 112:7) is an early recognition by the Lord that the Saints would be driven west to the mountains. As President of the Twelve, he would have been sent among many nations to open the doors for preaching the gospel (see 112:17). It is unfortunate that Thomas B. Marsh did not live up to his calling. A study of his life shows the suffering that he went through as a result of his apostasy. Hell is a knowledge of the man one might have been. May we all learn from his experience, and take the necessary precautions. Succeeding Presidents of the Twelve have done, and will do, what he failed to do, and were and will be greatly blessed.

D&C 112:10–13 • The Lord Shall Lead Thee by the Hand

10 Be thou humble; and the Lord thy God shall lead thee by the hand, and give thee answer to thy prayers.

11 I know thy heart, and have heard thy prayers concerning thy brethren. Be not partial towards them in love above many others, but let thy love be for them as for thyself; and let thy love abound unto all men, and unto all who love my name.

12 And pray for thy brethren of the Twelve. Admonish them sharply for my name's sake, and let them be admonished for all their sins, and be ye faithful before me unto my name.

13 And after their temptations, and much tribulation, behold, I, the Lord, will feel after them, and if they harden not their hearts, and stiffen not their necks against me, they shall be converted, and I will heal them.

As the leader of the Lord's quorum of special witnesses, much is expected of him. The Lord would lead him, but only on the condition of humility (v. 10). All of us are commanded to "love thy neighbors as thyself" (Matthew 22:39), but we often think of our neighbor as those to whom we are closest. As the parable of the good Samaritan shows, all our associates are our neighbors (Luke 10:30–37). As the President of the Quorum of Twelve, he was to be totally impartial and love all men, especially all who love the name of Christ (see D&C 112:11). Admonishing the Twelve sharply means to be precise in his constructive criticism, not in anger. As Apostles, the people will expect them to be perfect, but all of us are human, and mistakes will be made. President Marsh was expected to correct and encourage them (v. 12). As members of the Church, we have a tendency to think our leaders are above temptations and tribulations, but Satan probably works on them harder than he does us. Elder Harold B. Lee, while a member of the Quorum of the Twelve noted:

> I have been in a position since I was called to the Council of the Twelve to observe some things among my brethren, and I want to say to you: Every man who is my junior in the Council of the Twelve I have seen submitted, as though by Providence, to these same tests of loyalty, and I have wondered some times whether they were going to pass the tests. The reasons they are here today is because they did, and our Father has honored them.

> It is my conviction that every man who will be called to a high place in the Church will have to pass tests not devised by human hands, by which our Father numbers them as a united group of leaders willing to follow the prophets of the living God and be loyal and true as witnesses

and exemplars of the truths they teach.[79]

Following their tests, the mantle of conversion to be a special witness falls upon them and the Lord heals them (v. 13).

D&C 112:14–15 • I Say Unto All the Twelve

14 Now, I say unto you, and what I say unto you, I say unto all the Twelve: Arise and gird up your loins, take up your cross, follow me, and feed my sheep.

15 Exalt not yourselves; rebel not against my servant Joseph; for verily I say unto you, I am with him, and my hand shall be over him; and the keys which I have given unto him, and also to youward, shall not be taken from him till I come.

To "gird up your loins" is a New Testament term meaning to prepare for battle. The Twelve must battle Satan and his evil ways that come against the Saints. To "take up your cross" is for a man "to deny himself all ungodliness, and every worldly lust, and keep my commandments" (JST, Matthew 16:26). To "follow me" is to go where the Lord directs, and to "feed my sheep" is to teach the principles and doctrines of the kingdom to the members of the Church (D&C 112:14). Such is the role of every member of the Quorum of the Twelve.

The Twelve must and do give their total support and confidence to the President of the Church. In Joseph's case, he is the head of the dispensation, as will be shown later. The Twelve hold the keys with him, and will not relinquish them until the Lord comes, although there will be deaths and additions within the Quorum (v. 15).

D&C 112:16–22 • Open the Door of My Kingdom

16 Verily I say unto you, my servant Thomas, thou art the man whom I have chosen to hold the keys of my kingdom, as pertaining to the Twelve, abroad among all nations—

17 That thou mayest be my servant to unlock the door of the kingdom in all places where my servant Joseph, and my servant Sidney, and my servant Hyrum, cannot come;

---

[79] *The Teachings of Harold B. Lee*, 526–27.

18 For on them have I laid the burden of all the churches for a little season.

19 Wherefore, whithersoever they shall send you, go ye, and I will be with you; and in whatsoever place ye shall proclaim my name an effectual door shall be opened unto you, that they may receive my word.

20 Whosoever receiveth my word receiveth me, and whosoever receiveth me, receiveth those, the First Presidency, whom I have sent, whom I have made counselors for my name's sake unto you.

21 And again, I say unto you, that whosoever ye shall send in my name, by the voice of your brethren, the Twelve, duly recommended and authorized by you, shall have power to open the door of my kingdom unto any nation whithersoever ye shall send them—

22 Inasmuch as they shall humble themselves before me, and abide in my word, and hearken to the voice of my Spirit.

Jesus said to the Jerusalem Twelve: "Go ye into all the world, and preach the gospel to every creature" (Mark 16:15). The same mission is given the Twelve in this last dispensation (D&C 112:16). They are to represent the First Presidency wherever they are unable to go (v. 17). Hyrum was now serving as an assistant counselor in place of Frederick G. Williams, who had been excommunicated. The First Presidency's first priority at this time was the Church in Kirtland, where much work was needed (v. 18). Those who received the word of the Lord received the Lord. The same connection was given to the Jerusalem Twelve (see Matthew 10:40). In this latter day, those who received the Twelve also received the First Presidency. The First Presidency are counselors to the Twelve (D&C 112:20). They give direction and counsel to them as they send them out. Thus they are "duly recommended and authorized by the First Presidency" (v. 21). They are also to be directed by the Spirit (v. 22).

D&C 112:23-29 • Darkness Covers the Earth

23 Verily, verily, I say unto you, darkness covereth the earth, and gross darkness the minds of the people, and all flesh has become corrupt before my face.

24 Behold, vengeance cometh speedily upon the inhabitants of the earth, a day of wrath, a day of burning, a day of desolation, of weeping, of mourning, and of lamentation; and as a whirlwind it shall come upon all the face of the earth, saith the Lord.

25 And upon my house shall it begin, and from my house shall it go forth, saith the Lord;

26 First among those among you, saith the Lord, who have professed to know my name and have not known me, and have blasphemed against me in the midst of my house, saith the Lord.

27 Therefore, see to it that ye trouble not yourselves concerning the affairs of my church in this place, saith the Lord.

28 But purify your hearts before me; and then go ye into all the world, and preach my gospel unto every creature who has not received it;

29 And he that believeth and is baptized shall be saved, and he that believeth not, and is not baptized, shall be damned.

The Lord again affirms that there is a complete apostasy in the world, except for His newly established Church (v. 23). Because of the completeness of the apostasy, the Lord is going to cleanse the earth of its corruption. He cleansed the earth in Noah's day by water (see Genesis 7), but in this day He will do it by fire. The burning by fire will be a sad day for the earth's inhabitants—weeping, mourning, and lamentation (v. 24), but before He cleanses the earth, He must cleanse His own house, or the Church (v. 25). Those who have taken Christ's name upon themselves, through baptism, but have really not known Him, or have blasphemed will be taken away (v. 26).

This place (v. 27) refers to Kirtland where an apostasy was currently occurring within the Church members. The First Presidency was working on this problem and the Twelve were not to be concerned (v. 28). They were to go into the world, and preach the gospel, and save those who would be baptized (v. 29; compare Mark 16:16).

D&C 112:30–34 • The Keys of the Dispensation of the Fulness of Times

30 For unto you, the Twelve, and those, the First Presidency, who are appointed with you to be your counselors and your leaders, is the power of this priesthood given, for the last days and for the last time, in the which is the dispensation of the fulness of times.

31 Which power you hold, in connection with all those who have received a dispensation at any time from the beginning of the creation;

32 For verily I say unto you, the keys of the dispensation, which ye have received, have come down from the fathers, and last of all, being sent down from heaven unto you.

33 Verily I say unto you, behold how great is your calling. Cleanse your hearts and your garments, lest the blood of this generation be required at your hands.

34 Be faithful until I come, for I come quickly; and my reward is with me to recompense every man according as his work shall be. I am Alpha and Omega. Amen.

The power of the priesthood was committed to the leaders of the Church for the dispensation of the fulness of times (v. 30). The keys committed to the Quorum of the Twelve in 1843 was to have the continuity of the oracles as long as they were in the world, but at death would be given to others, or unto the Church (see D&C 90:2–4 and comments). The oracles means the source of their authority (D&C 112:30). This authority was connected with all previous dispensations of the gospel (v. 31). It had come down from the fathers (v. 32) by angelic bestowal as exemplified by Moses, Elias, and Elijah in the Kirtland Temple (see D&C 110). The cleansing of the heart and the garments (v. 33) was to be done by taking the responsibility to teach everyone possible the gospel (see Jacob 1:19; 2 Nephi 9:44). Those who were offered the gospel still had their agency to accept or reject, but would all stand before the Judgment Bar of Christ to be judged by the things done in the body (see 2 Corinthians 5:10; Mormon 3:18–20) This judgment is the recompense spoken of in D&C 112:34.

DOCTRINE AND COVENANTS 114

*H*istorical Setting: "April 17 [1838]—I received [Doctrine and Covenants 114]: *Revelation Given at Far West*" (*HC,* 3:23).

TEXT AND COMMENTARY

D&C 114:1–2 • Others Planted in Their Stead

1 VERILY thus saith the Lord: It is wisdom in my servant David W. Patten, that he settle up all his business as soon as he possibly can, and

make a disposition of his merchandise, that he may perform a mission unto me next spring, in company with others, even twelve including himself, to testify of my name and bear glad tidings unto all the world.

2 For verily thus saith the Lord, that inasmuch as there are those among you who deny my name, others shall be planted in their stead and receive their bishopric. Amen.

David Patten's mission was to England the next spring (v. 1), which was also the subject of Doctrine and Covenants 118 below. The more important item of this revelation is "others shall be planted in their stead and receive their bishopric" (v. 2). The Lord is apparently quoting Psalm 109:8 in this revelation, which was also quoted in Acts 1:20 when a replacement for Judas Iscariot was chosen. Nevertheless, most of the Christian world believe that their church is still based on the original Twelve Apostles of Jerusalem, and Judas' replacement was the only exception. However, the New Testament records the appointment of several Apostles after Matthias was chosen to replace Judas. James, the brother of the Lord (Galatians 1:20); Paul (Romans 1:1; 1 Corinthians 1:1); and Barnabas (1 Corinthians 9:5–6) are examples. David Patten was killed in the battle of Crooked River in October of 1838, and another was appointed in his office (see D&C 118; below). The Book of Mormon adds a second witness to the replacement of disciples, or apostles, as they pass on: ". . . even an hundred years had passed away, and the disciples of Jesus, whom he had chosen, had all gone to the paradise of God, save it were the three who should tarry; and there were other disciples ordained in their stead; and also many of that generation had passed away" (4 Nephi 1:14).

DOCTRINE AND COVENANTS 118

*H*istorical Setting: This revelation was given the same day as section 114 just discussed. The *History of the Church*, 3:46, records only what is in the section heading: "*Revelation given through Joseph Smith the Prophet, at Far West, Missouri, July 8, 1838, in response to the supplication [in answer to the question in HC]: "Show us thy will, O Lord, concerning thy Twelve."*

Text and Commentary

D&C 118:1–6 • Replacements for the Twelve

1 Verily, thus saith the Lord: Let a conference be held immediately; let the Twelve be organized; and let men be appointed to supply the place of those who are fallen.

2 Let my servant Thomas remain for a season in the land of Zion, to publish my word.

3 Let the residue continue to preach from that hour, and if they will do this in all lowliness of heart, in meekness and humility, and long-suffering, I, the Lord, give unto them a promise that I will provide for their families; and an effectual door shall be opened for them, from henceforth.

4 And next spring let them depart to go over the great waters, and there promulgate my gospel, the fulness thereof, and bear record of my name.

5 Let them take leave of my saints in the city of Far West, on the twenty-sixth day of April next, on the building-spot of my house, saith the Lord.

6 Let my servant John E. Taylor, and also my servant John E. Page, and also my servant Wilford Woodruff, and also my servant Willard Richards, be appointed to fill the places of those who have fallen, and be officially notified of their appointment.

In the spring of 1939, the Twelve did leave from the temple lot in Far West (v. 5) even though the Saints had been driven out, and threats had been made that any Apostle who returned would be killed.[80] Four brethren (v. 6) were called to replace William E. McLellin, Luke S. Johnson, John F. Boynton, and Lyman E. Johnson. Others were called to replace David Patten and others as vacancies occurred. Apostles of the Lord Jesus Christ were again on the earth after an absence of about seventeen hundred years.

---

[80] See Daniel H. Ludlow, *A Companion to Your Study of the Doctrine and Covenants* [1978], 1:592–93.

General Authority Quotes

—Elder Bruce R. McConkie • D&C 112:14–21

[Apostles] is the supreme office in the church in all dispensations because those so ordained hold both the fulness of the priesthood and all the keys of the kingdom of God on the earth. The President of the Church serves in that high and exalted position because he is the senior apostle of God on earth and thus can direct the manner in which all other apostles and priesthood holders use their priesthood. An apostle is an ordained office in the Melchizedek Priesthood, and those so ordained (with an occasional exception that does not rank the person so involved along with those whom Paul writes and of whom the other revelations speak) are set apart as members of the Quorum of the Twelve and are given the keys and power to preside over the church and kingdom and regulate all of the affairs of God on earth. . . . [quotes D&C 107:23, 33]. [*A New Witness for the Articles of Faith* (1985), 348–49]

—President Joseph Fielding Smith • D&C 112:14–34

In the year 1835, when the Twelve Apostles were chosen and their duties defined, the Lord declared that they were equal with the Presidency as a quorum. That is, *in case of the dissolution or destruction of the First Presidency of the Church, the Twelve should succeed to the Presidency,* and thus would act until such time and place as the Lord revealed that the First Presidency should be again organized. *And whenever the First Presidency should be disorganized, it would devolve upon the quorum of the Apostles to set in order and direct the affairs of the Church.* . . .

When the First Presidency is disorganized, the Twelve Apostles become the presiding quorum of the church until the presidency is again organized, and during that time they are virtually the presidency of the church—the presiding quorum. [*Doctrines of Salvation,* 1:254–55] .

—The Prophet Joseph Smith • D&C 112:23

Consider for a moment, brethren, the fulfillment of the words of the prophet; for we behold that darkness covers the earth, and gross darkness the minds of the inhabitants thereof—that crimes of every description are increasing among men—vices of great enormity are practiced—the rising generation growing up in the fullness of pride and arrogance—the aged losing every age of conviction, and seemingly banishing every thought of a day of retribution—intemperance, immorality, extravagance, pride, blindness of heart, idolatry, the loss of natural affection; the love of the world, and indifference toward the things of eternity increasing among those who profess a belief in the religion of heaven, and infidelity spreading itself in consequence of the same—men giving themselves up to commit acts of the foulest kind, and deeds of the blackest dye, blaspheming, defrauding, blasting the reputation of neighbors, stealing, robbing, murdering; advocating error and opposing the truth, forsaking the covenants of heaven, and denying the faith of Jesus—and in the midst of all this, the day of the Lord fast approaching when none except those who have won the wedding garment will be permitted to eat and drink in the presence of the Bridegroom, the Prince of Peace. [*TPJS*, 47; January, 1834]

Chapter Twenty-One

The Destinies of All Nations

D&C 111; 115–117

DOCTRINE AND COVENANTS 111

*H*istorical Setting:

In July, of 1836, in the midst of the greatest financial distress at Kirtland, the Prophet, with his brother Hyrum, Sidney Rigdon and Oliver Cowdery made a journey to Salem Massachusetts, where they hired a house during the month of August and spent their time in teaching the people from house to house and preaching publicly, as opportunity presented. Visiting occasionally sections of the surrounding country which are rich in the history of the Pilgrim Fathers of New England, in Indian warfare, religious superstitions, bigotry, persecution and learned ignorance. . . . The *Times and Seasons*, states that the journey to Salem arose from these circumstances. There came to Kirtland a brother by the name of Burgess who stated that he had knowledge of a large sum of money secreted in the cellar of a certain house in Salem Massachusetts, which belonged to a widow (then deceased), and thought he was the only person who had knowledge of it, or of the location of the house. The brethren accepting the representations of Burgess as true made the journey to secure, if possible, the treasure. Burgess. . . claimed that time had wrought such changes in the town that he could not for certainty point out the house "and soon left". . . . While in Salem the prophet received [Doctrine and Covenants 111]. [B. H. Roberts, *A Comprehensive History of The Church of Jesus Christ of Latter-day Saints* (1930), 1:411]

SECTION 111 • OUTLINE

➤ 111:1–5 The Lord is not displeased with your journey notwithstanding your follies.

     a.   I have much treasure in this city, and many people to gather out in due time, for the benefit of Zion (v. 2).

     b.   Make acquaintance with the men of this city as you shall be led (v. 3).

     c.   In due time, I will give this city into your hands, and they shall not discover your secret parts; and its wealth in gold and silver shall be yours (v. 4).

     d.   Concern not about your debts, I will give you power to pay them (v. 5).

➤ 111:6–11 Concern not about Zion, I will deal mercifully with her.

     a.   Tarry here and the regions round about (v. 7).

     b.   The place to tarry will be signaled by peace and the power of my Spirit (v. 8).

     c.   Inquire about the more ancient inhabitants and founders of this city (v. 9).

     d.   There are more treasures than one in this city (v. 10).

     e.   Be wise as serpents and without sin, and all things shall be for your good (v. 11).

Introduction

The events spoken of in the four revelations discussed in this chapter are mainly still in the future. While we may not know what the future holds, we do know who holds the future. "Do I [the Lord] not hold the destinies of all the armies of the nations of the earth?" (D&C 117:6). Herein He gives us insights to the future.

TEXT AND COMMENTARY

D&C 111:1–5 • An Honest Mistake

1 I, the Lord your God, am not displeased with your coming this journey, notwithstanding your follies.

2 I have much treasure in this city for you, for the benefit of Zion,

and many people in this city, whom I will gather out in due time for the benefit of Zion, through your instrumentality.

3 Therefore, it is expedient that you should form acquaintance with men in this city, as you shall be led, and as it shall be given you.

4 And it shall come to pass in due time that I will give this city into your hands, that you shall have power over it, insomuch that they shall not discover your secret parts; and its wealth pertaining to gold and silver shall be yours.

5 Concern not yourselves about your debts, for I will give you power to pay them.

A folly (v. 1) is an honest mistake. Obviously, Joseph and his companions were only concerned with the debts that had incurred in Kirtland, and not in their own wealth. The treasures, and the people in the city to be gathered, both for the benefit of Zion, has probably not as yet happened (v. 2). Although there is some evidence that the prophecy was fulfilled by the successful mission in the early 1840s of young Elder Erastus Snow, later to be an Apostle, when the Salem branch grew to ninety members of the Church.[81] The promised "benefit of Zion" suggests it will happen after the city of Zion, or the New Jerusalem, is built in these latter days. Perhaps there will be a dual fulfillment, which is so prevalent in Old Testament prophecy. Joseph's admonition to get acquainted with the "men in this city" as he is led (v. 3) is a good example of his later teaching that "all these things shall give thee experience, and shall be for thy good" (D&C 122:7). The people not discovering their secret parts (v. 4) may be a hint of the establishing of temple ordinances that were yet to be revealed. Perhaps someday a temple will be built there. The infamous "witchcraft of Salem" may be Satan's counterpart to the firm establishing of the kingdom there. Regardless, the Lord was aware of their debts, and consoles them in their disappointment by promising them power to pay them (v. 5).

D&C 111:6–11 • More Treasures than One

6 Concern not yourselves about Zion, for I will deal mercifully with her.

7 Tarry in this place, and in the regions round about;

---

[81] See Kenneth W. Godfrey, *Hearken O Ye People* [1984], 191–204.

8 And the place where it is my will that you should tarry, for the main, shall be signalized unto you by the peace and power of my Spirit, that shall flow unto you.

9 This place you may obtain by hire. And inquire diligently concerning the more ancient inhabitants and founders of this city;

10 For there are more treasures than one for you in this city.

11 Therefore, be ye as wise as serpents and yet without sin; and I will order all things for your good, as fast as ye are able to receive them. Amen.

Zion was another problem that Joseph was worried about, and again the Lord consoled him (v. 6). The significance of the place to tarry that would be signaled to Joseph (vv. 7–8) is not known, but again may become significant as the promises to the area are unfolded. The ancient inhabitants of the city and the founders of the city (v. 9) have usually been interpreted to be some of the Founding Fathers of our great nation. Again, which ones of these fathers it refers to have not been specifically identified, but again may be someday. These people are usually tied to our doing their genealogical work. While these are certainly valid interpretations, there may be another key here that has been generally overlooked. Could the ancient inhabitants be a separate people, and not the founders of the city? Could they be the Nephites of old that inhabited this area? While the Book of Mormon is not a history book, there is certainly enough evidence to keep this possibility open. Someday we will get more of their records that will certainly shed more light on their geographical borders. There is more than one treasure in this city (v. 10).

The Prophet Joseph changed the biblical imagery of "wise as serpents" to be "wise servants" (JST, Matthew 10:16), but the Lord may have used the present imagery because the JST was not available to the Church as yet. Regardless, the Lord cautions Joseph to be wise and without sin (v. 11). This advise is good at any time and in any place. Joseph learned a lot from his folly.

DOCTRINE AND COVENANTS 115

*H*istorical Setting: "April 26 [1838]—I received [Doctrine and Covenants 115]: *Revelation Given at Far West making known the will of God concerning the building up of that place, and of the Lord's house*" (*HC,* 3:23).

SECTION 115 • OUTLINE

➤ 115:1–7   The Lord to Joseph and all the presiding officers of the Church and people.

    a.   My Church shall be called in the last days, The Church of Jesus Christ of Latter-day Saints (v. 4).

    b.   Let thy light shine forth, and be a standard for the nations (v. 5).

    c.   The gathering upon the land of Zion and her stakes shall be a defense and a refuge from the storm poured out upon the whole earth (v. 6).

    d.   Let Far West be a holy, consecrated land, and be called holy, for it is holy (v. 7).

➤ 115:8–16   I command you to build a house unto me for gathering of my Saints to worship.

    a.   Let July 4, [1839] be the beginning, and labor diligently (vv. 9–10).

    b.   In one year, recommence laying the foundation, labor until finished (vv. 11–12).

    c.   Let Joseph, Sidney, and Hyrum not get into debt anymore to build it (v. 13).

    d.   If the house is built as I will show you, I will accept it (vv. 14, 16).

    e.   If it is not that pattern, I will not accept it (v. 15).

➤ 115:17–19   Again, the city of Far West should be built speedily by the Saints gathering.

    a.   Other stakes shall be appointed in the regions as manifested to Joseph (v. 18).

    b.   I will sanctify him, for I have given him the keys of the kingdom (v. 19).

TEXT AND COMMENTARY

D&C 115:1–7 • The Name of the Church

1 VERILY thus saith the Lord unto you, my servant Joseph Smith, Jun., and also my servant Sidney Rigdon, and also my servant Hyrum Smith, and your counselors who are and shall be appointed hereafter;

2 And also unto you, my servant Edward Partridge, and his counselors;

3 And also unto my faithful servants who are of the high council of my church in Zion, for thus it shall be called, and unto all the elders and people of my Church of Jesus Christ of Latter-day Saints, scattered abroad in all the world;

4 For thus shall my church be called in the last days, even The Church of Jesus Christ of Latter-day Saints.

5 Verily I say unto you all: Arise and shine forth, that thy light may be a standard for the nations;

6 And that the gathering together upon the land of Zion, and upon her stakes, may be for a defense, and for a refuge from the storm, and from wrath when it shall be poured out without mixture upon the whole earth.

7 Let the city, Far West, be a holy and consecrated land unto me; and it shall be called most holy, for the ground upon which thou standest is holy.

The exact name of the restored Church was not given until eight years after it was officially organized. Why? Probably because Joseph had not asked, and no one had asked him. A similar situation had happened among the Nephites after Jesus had ministered unto them. In one of His many appearances to them after His three-day ministry (see 3 Nephi 26:13), they had asked what "we shall call this church, for there are disputations among the people." He replied:

5 Have they not read the scriptures, which say ye must take upon you the name of Christ, which is my name? For by this name shall ye be called at the last day;

6 And whoso taketh upon him my name, and endureth to the end, the same shall be saved at the last day.

7 Therefore, whatsoever ye shall do, ye shall do it in my name;

therefore ye shall call the church in my name; and ye shall call upon the Father in my name that he will bless the church for my sake.

8 And how be it my church save it be called in my name? For if a church be called in Moses' name then it be Moses' church; or if it be called in the name of a man then it be the church of a man; but if it be called in my name then it is my church, if it so be that they are built upon my gospel [3 Nephi 27:3–8]

The name "Latter-day Saints" (vv. 3–4) differentiates between the Church from former-day Saints of other dispensations.

Verses 5 and 6 are actually the fulfillment of the prophet Isaiah's prophecies. In Isaiah we read: (note the tie of verse 2 with D&C 112:23.)

2 For, behold, the darkness shall cover the earth, and gross darkness the people: but the LORD shall arise upon thee, and his glory shall be seen upon thee.

3 And the Gentiles shall come to thy light, and kings to the brightness of thy rising.

4 Lift up thine eyes round about, and see: all they gather themselves together, they come to thee: thy sons shall come from far, and thy daughters shall be nursed at [thy] side.

5 Then thou shalt see, and flow together, and thine heart shall fear, and be enlarged; because the abundance of the sea shall be converted unto thee, the forces of the Gentiles shall come unto thee. [Isaiah 60:2–5]

The storm (D&C 115:6) will be the one that cleanses the earth (D&C 112:24), and the Saints will gather out from the world. The Prophet Joseph Smith declared: "The time is soon coming, when no man will have any peace but in Zion and her stakes" (*TPJS*, 161). The Saints will gather for a defense and refuge from that storm. Far West will be a stake of Zion at that time (v. 7), and the temple will be built there (see the next verses below). It is probably holy ground because of what had happened there to other peoples in previous dispensations.

D&C 115:8–16 • A Temple in Far West

8 Therefore, I command you to build a house unto me, for the gathering together of my saints, that they may worship me.

9 And let there be a beginning of this work, and a foundation, and

a preparatory work, this following summer;

10 And let the beginning be made on the fourth day of July next; and from that time forth let my people labor diligently to build a house unto my name;

11 And in one year from this day let them re-commence laying the foundation of my house.

12 Thus let them from that time forth labor diligently until it shall be finished, from the corner stone thereof unto the top thereof, until there shall not anything remain that is not finished.

13 Verily I say unto you, let not my servant Joseph, neither my servant Sidney, neither my servant Hyrum, get in debt any more for the building of a house unto my name;

14 But let a house be built unto my name according to the pattern which I will show unto them.

15 And if my people build it not according to the pattern which I shall show unto their presidency, I will not accept it at their hands.

16 But if my people do build it according to the pattern which I shall show unto their presidency, even my servant Joseph and his counselors, then I will accept it at the hands of my people.

As one who has stood on that holy and consecrated land (v. 7) where the temple shall be built (v. 8), the Spirit, on each occasion, has confirmed the sanctity of the site. The author looks forward to the time when the building of that edifice shall re-commence according to the pattern that will be shown to the Presidency (v. 14). Those who prevented its previously being built will answer to their God, and when the time is right that command will be reissued.

D&C 115:17–19 • The City of Far West Shall Be Built

17 And again, verily I say unto you, it is my will that the city of Far West should be built up speedily by the gathering of my saints;

18 And also that other places should be appointed for stakes in the regions round about, as they shall be manifested unto my servant Joseph, from time to time.

19 For behold, I will be with him, and I will sanctify him before the people; for unto him have I given the keys of this kingdom and ministry. Even so. Amen.

The driving of the Saints from Missouri did not cancel the gathering of the Saints to Far West, it only postponed the time. The establishing of stakes in the regions round about (v. 18) has quietly, and slowly continued in these latter days. Joseph was sanctified before his people, and his successors were given the keys of the kingdom (v. 19). The word of the Lord will be fulfilled.

DOCTRINE AND COVENANTS 116

H istorical Setting:

> . . . We pursued our course up the [Grand] river, mostly through timber, for about eighteen miles, when we arrived at Colonel Lyman Wight's home. He lives at the foot of Tower Hill (a name I gave the place in consequence of the remains of an old Nephite altar or tower that stood there), where we camped for the Sabbath.
>
> In the afternoon I went up the river about half a mile to Wight's ferry, accompanied by President Rigdon, and my clerk, George W. Robinson, for the purpose of selecting and laying claim to a city plat. . . which the brethren called "Spring Hill," but by the mouth of the Lord it was named Adam-ondi-Ahman, because said he [Doctrine and Covenants 116]. [*HC,* 3:35]
>
> This is not the first time that the name or phrase "Adam-ondi-Ahman" is used in the revelations of the Lord. Some six years before this, viz., in the year 1832 it is used incidentally in one of the revelations. . . "and be made rulers over many kingdoms, saith the Lord God, the Holy One of Zion, who hath established the foundations of *Adam-ondi-Ahman* [D&C 78:15]. [*HC,* 3:35; footnote]

TEXT AND COMMENTARY

D&C 116

1 SPRING HILL is named by the Lord Adam-ondi-Ahman, because, said he, it is the place where Adam shall come to visit his people, or the Ancient of Days shall sit, as spoken of by Daniel the prophet.

According to Elder Orson Pratt, *Adam-ondi Ahman* "means the place where Adam dwelt. 'Ahman' signifies God. The whole term means Valley of God where Adam dwelt. It is in the original language spoken by Adam, as revealed to the Prophet Joseph."[82] While most people believe Adam dwelt on the eastern hemisphere, the Doctrine and Covenants places the Garden of Eden in Missouri (note references below).

> 53 Three years previous to the death of Adam, he called Seth, Enos, Cainan, Mahalaleel, Jared, Enoch, and Methuselah, who were all high priests, with the residue of his posterity who were righteous, into the valley of Adam-ondi-Ahman, and there bestowed upon them his last blessing.
>
> 54 And the Lord appeared unto them, and they rose up and blessed Adam, and called him Michael, the prince, the archangel.
>
> 55 And the Lord administered comfort unto Adam, and said unto him: I have set thee to be at the head; a multitude of nations shall come of thee, and thou art a prince over them forever.
>
> 56 And Adam stood up in the midst of the congregation; and, notwithstanding he was bowed down with age, being full of the Holy Ghost, predicted whatsoever should befall his posterity unto the latest generation.
>
> 57 These things were all written in the book of Enoch, and are to be testified of in due time (D&C 107:53–57).

When the book of Enoch is fully restored—we have part of it in Moses 6:25–7:69—we will have more confirmation on the geographical location of Adam-ondi-Ahman. We will also learn more about the Book of Mormon geography, and the Nephite altar identified by Joseph Smith, when more Book of Mormon records are given to us (see 3 Nephi 26:9). Adam's visit to his people in the last days will take place prior to the Second Coming. Christ will come and partake of the sacrament again on earth with Adam and other past prophets and Apostles (see D&C 27:1–14), as Daniel the prophet testified, calling Adam the Ancient of Days:

> 9 I beheld till the thrones were cast down, and the Ancient of days did sit, whose garment [was] white as snow, and the hair of his head like the pure wool: his throne [was like] the fiery flame, [and] his wheels [as] burning fire.
>
> 10 A fiery stream issued and came forth from before him: thousand

---

[82] *Journal of Discourses*, 18:343.

thousands ministered unto him, and ten thousand times ten thousand stood before him: the judgment was set, and the books were opened. [Daniel 7:9–10]

The Prophet Joseph commented on these verses:

> Daniel in his seventh chapter speaks of the Ancient of days; he means the oldest man, our Father Adam, Michael, he will call his children together and hold a council with them to prepare them for the coming of the Son of Man. He (Adam) is the father of all the human family and presides over the spirits of all men, and all that have had the keys must stand before him in this grand council. . . . The Son of Man stands before him, and there is given him glory and dominion. Adam delivers up his stewardship to Christ, that which was delivered to him as holding the keys of the universe, but retains his standing as head of the human family. [*TPJS,* 157]

According to Elder Bruce R. McConkie, "the thousand thousands" [one million] (Daniel 7:10) are those who held priesthood authority in all dispensations, and the ten thousand times ten thousand are [one hundred million] before whom the books were opened (v. 11) are the faithful servants of all dispensations (see under McConkie, "General Authority Quotes," end of chapter).

Daniel's prophecy continues:

> 13 I saw in the night visions, and, behold, one like the Son of man came with the clouds of heaven, and came to the Ancient of days, and they brought him near before him.
>
> 14 And there was given him dominion, and glory, and a kingdom, that all people, nations, and languages, should serve him: his dominion is an everlasting dominion, which shall not pass away, and his kingdom that which shall not be destroyed." [Daniel 7:13–14]

The Prophet Joseph explained: "He (Adam) is the head, and was told to multiply. The keys were first given to him, and by him to others. He will have to give an account of his stewardship, and they to him" (*TPJS,* 158). Elder LeGrand Richards observed: "Now it is obvious that a kingdom cannot be delivered unto the Son of Man when he comes to take his rightful place to rule over all nations unless a kingdom is prepared for him. The kingdom, according to Daniel, is to be given to the saints of the Most High, that they might possess it forever and ever."[83] All this is to happen at Adam-ondi-Ahman.

Again we turn to Daniel: "I beheld, and the same horn made war with the saints, and prevailed against them; until the Ancient of days came, and judgment was given to the saints of the most High; and the time came that the saints possessed the kingdom" (Daniel 7:21–22). The war is undoubtedly the condition of corruption described in D&C 112:23, and is the beast spoken of in Revelation 13:7 who was "to make war with the saints." The Prophet Joseph was probably referring to this Revelation chapter when he said: "The last revelation says, Ye shall not have time to have gone over the earth, until these things come. It will come as did the cholera, war, fires, and earthquakes; one pestilence after another, until the ancient of days comes, then judgment will be given to the Saints" (*TPJS*, 160–61). Much is associated with the coming of the Ancient of Days.

Doctrine and Covenants 117

Historical Setting: This revelation was the third of the four revelations received on July 8, 1838, with no further comments in the *History of the Church*.

Section 117 • Outline

➤ 117:1–11   William Marks and Newel K. Whitney are to settle their business in Kirtland and journey to Zion.

       a.   Do not tarry or it shall not be well with thee (vv. 2–3).

       b.   Repent of all your sins and covetous desires, what is property to me (v. 4).

       c.   Let Kirtland property be turned out to debt, or kept in your hands (v. 5).

       d.   I hold the destinies of all nations of the earth (v. 6).

       e.   I will make the solitary places bring forth in abundance (v. 7).

---

[83] *A Marvelous Work and A Wonder* [1976], 133–34.

    f.   Do not covet that which is a drop and neglect the more weighty matters (v. 8).

    g.   Let William be fruitful, a ruler, and preside in Far West, and be blessed (v. 10).

    h.   Let Newel be ashamed of the Nicolaitane band and his littleness of soul, and be a bishop not in name but in deed.

➤ 117:12–16   Oliver Granger's name shall be had in sacred remembrance from generation to generation, forever and ever.

    a.   Let him contend for the First Presidency's redemption of my Church (v. 13).

    b.   When he falls, arise, and his sacrifice more sacred than his increase (v. 13).

    c.   Come to Zion and he shall be a merchant for the benefit of my people (v. 14).

    d.   No man despise, but let a blessing of my people be on him forever (v. 15).

    e.   Let all my servants in Kirtland remember the Lord and mine house, and overthrow the moneychangers in mine own due time (v. 16).

TEXT AND COMMENTARY

D&C 117:1–11 • I Hold the Destinies of All Nations

1 VERILY thus saith the Lord unto my servant William Marks, and also unto my servant Newel K. Whitney, let them settle up their business speedily and journey from the land of Kirtland, before I, the Lord, send again the snows upon the earth.

2 Let them awake, and arise, and come forth, and not tarry, for I, the Lord, command it.

3 Therefore, if they tarry it shall not be well with them.

4 Let them repent of all their sins, and of all their covetous desires, before me, saith the Lord; for what is property unto me? saith the Lord.

5 Let the properties of Kirtland be turned out for debts, saith the Lord. Let them go, saith the Lord, and whatsoever remaineth, let it remain in your hands, saith the Lord.

6 For have I not the fowls of heaven, and also the fish of the sea, and the beasts of the mountains? Have I not made the earth? Do I not hold

the destinies of all the armies of the nations of the earth?

7 Therefore, will I not make solitary places to bud and to blossom, and to bring forth in abundance? saith the Lord.

8 Is there not room enough on the mountains of Adam-ondi-Ahman, and on the plains of Olaha Shinehah, or the land where Adam dwelt, that you should covet that which is but the drop, and neglect the more weighty matters?

9 Therefore, come up hither unto the land of my people, even Zion.

10 Let my servant William Marks be faithful over a few things, and he shall be a ruler over many. Let him preside in the midst of my people in the city of Far West, and let him be blessed with the blessings of my people.

11 Let my servant Newel K. Whitney be ashamed of the Nicolaitane band and of all their secret abominations, and of all his littleness of soul before me, saith the Lord, and come up to the land of Adam-ondi-Ahman, and be a bishop unto my people, saith the Lord, not in name but in deed, saith the Lord.

The Lord had given up on Kirtland. They were apparently ripened in iniquity, and he was leading "the righteous into precious lands" of Zion (v. 9), and had "cursed the land of Kirtland with a very sore and grievous curse" (1 Nephi 17:38; D&C 104:4). Those exiting were also to repent, and the properties they owned, or managed, were to be turned out for debt, or just left (D&C 117:4–5). The Lord was still in control, in fact, the fowls, the fish, the beasts, and all the armies of the nations of the earth are in His hands (v. 6). He blesses the solitary places to produce, as well as curses the lands of the wicked (v. 7). He again identifies Adam-ondi-Ahman as the land of Adam (v. 8). In the book of Abraham we learn: "This is Shinehah, which is the sun. . . . Olea, which is the moon" (Abraham 3:13). These two words are probably from the language of Adam, and "Olaha" is possibly another spelling for Olea. Therefore, the Lord in this revelation, is referring to the plains under the sun and the moon (D&C 117:8). Jesus gave a similar admonition about the weightier matters of the law (v. 8) to the scribes and Pharisees: ". . . hypocrites! for ye pay tithe of mint and anise and cummin, and have omitted the weightier [matters] of the law, judgment, mercy, and faith: these ought ye to have done, and not to leave the other undone" (Matthew 23:23).

William Marks was called to preside in Far West (v. 10), and was to become the stake president, but the Saints were driven out and he never was ordained to that position. He did serve in that position in Nauvoo.[84] The Nicolaitane band (v. 11) was a form of a secret combination at the time of John the Revelator (see Revelation 2:6, 15). Apparently, Bishop Whitney had entertained some of those practices in Kirtland that were not in keeping with his role as a bishop (v. 11). The remark of "overthrow the moneychangers" (v. 16 below) is a further indication of this supposition. He must not have been too involved, or fully repented, for he was called to the same office in Far West. As with brother Marks, he did not serve in Far West, but did serve in Illinois, and Utah.[85]

D&C 117:12–16 • Sacred Remembrance of Oliver Granger

12 And again, I say unto you, I remember my servant Oliver Granger; behold, verily I say unto him that his name shall be had in sacred remembrance from generation to generation, forever and ever, saith the Lord.

13 Therefore, let him contend earnestly for the redemption of the First Presidency of my Church, saith the Lord; and when he falls he shall rise again, for his sacrifice shall be more sacred unto me than his increase, saith the Lord.

14 Therefore, let him come up hither speedily, unto the land of Zion; and in the due time he shall be made a merchant unto my name, saith the Lord, for the benefit of my people.

15 Therefore let no man despise my servant Oliver Granger, but let the blessings of my people be on him forever and ever.

16 And again, verily I say unto you, let all my servants in the land of Kirtland remember the Lord their God, and mine house also, to keep and preserve it holy, and to overthrow the moneychangers in mine own due time, saith the Lord. Even so. Amen.

Oliver Granger was unto the Lord and the Prophet Joseph as Sam was to his brother Nephi, always a true friend and supporter, but usually behind the scenes (see 2 Nephi 4:11). He was defined by the First

---

[84] See Lyndon W. Cook, *The Revelations of the Prophet Joseph Smith*, 230–31.

[85] See Hoyt W. Brewster Jr. *Doctrine and Covenants Encyclopedia* [1988], 633–34.

Presidency as "a man of the most strict integrity and moral virtue; and in fine, a man of God."[86]

General Authority Quotes

—President Harold B. Lee • D&C 115:4–6

> When [he Lord] revealed the name by which the Church was to be called, He used some interesting expressions. (quotes D&C 115:4) The word the is significant: not just Church of Jesus Christ of Latter-day Saints, because to say "The Church" distinguishes this as the only true church on the face of the earth [see D&C 1:30]. He didn't say Mormon Church; He didn't say Latter-day Saint Church, but the clear, firm, unequivocal statement, "even The Church of Jesus Christ of Latter-day Saints." [*The Teachings of Harold B. Lee*, 383]

> This inspired gathering of former years [to build the kingdom] was necessary for those earlier years. In the wisdom of the Lord it was desired that converts from throughout the world gather to unitedly build the kingdom. In recent years it has been the inspired policy of the Church to urge converts to stay in their own lands, to build up Zion within their own numbers, "that thy light may be a standard for the nations" (D&C 115:5) to all who surround them. And so even before they had temples and the full programs of the Church, they have throughout the years created Zion in their own hearts and homes as the Lord promised, for after all Zion is where the pure in heart are to be found. They have suffered much with war, persecutions, hunger, and deprivations, but the Lord has been mindful of their sufferings. . . . [*The Teachings of Harold B. Lee*, 384–85]

> What is the defense program as far as the Lord is concerned? It is the gathering together of the Saints into stakes of Zion. I need not remind you what a stake organization is and of its subdivisions. A stake is composed of priesthood quorums, the Relief Society organization, and the auxiliary organizations—a group of workers prepared for whatever might be necessary to advance the interests of the Church temporally or spiritually. [*The Teachings of Harold B. Lee*, 566]

---

[86] Cook, op. cit., 230.

—*President Joseph Fielding Smith* • D&C 116

In accord with the revelations given to the Prophet Joseph Smith, we teach that *the Garden of Eden was on the American continent located where the city Zion, or the New Jerusalem will be built.* When Adam and Eve were driven out of the garden, they eventually dwelt at a place called *Adam-ondi-Ahman*, situated in what is now Davies County, Missouri. Three years before the death of Adam he called the righteous of his posterity at this place, and blessed them, and it is at this place where Adam, or Michael, will sit as we read in the 7th chapter of Daniel. [*Doctrines of Salvation,* 3:74]

—*Elder Bruce R. McConkie* • D&C 116

We now come to the least known and least understood thing connected with the Second Coming. It might well be termed the best-kept secret set forth in the revealed word. It is something about which the world knows nothing; it is a doctrine that has scarcely dawned on most Latter-day Saints themselves; and yet it is set forth in holy writ and in the teachings of the Prophet Joseph Smith with substantially the same clarity as any of the doctrines of the kingdom. . . .

Before the Lord Jesus descends openly and publicly in the clouds of glory, attended by all the hosts of heaven. . . before all flesh shall see him together; before any of his appearances, which taken together comprise the Second Coming of the Son of God—before all these, there is to be a secret appearance to selected members of the Church. He will come in private to his prophet and to the apostles then living. Those who have held keys and powers and authorities in all ages from Adam to the present will also be present. And further, all the faithful members of the Church then living, and all the faithful saints of all ages past will be present. It will be the greatest congregation of faithful saints ever assembled on planet earth. It will be a sacrament meeting. It will be a day of judgment for the faithful of all ages. And it will take place. . . at a place called Adam-ondi-Ahman. . . . [*The Millennial Messiah* (1982), 578–79]

Who are the "thousand thousands" who "ministered unto him"? Are not these the millions who held keys and powers and authorities in all dispensations? Are they not the ones who are called to report their stewardships and to give an accounting of how and in what manner they have exercised the keys of the kingdom in their days? Will not every steward be called upon to tell what he has done with the talents with which he was endowed? Truly, it shall be so; and those who minister unto the Ancient of Days are indeed the ministers of Christ reporting their labors to their immediate superiors, even back to Adam, who held the keys of salvation over all the earth for all ages.

And who are the "ten thousand times ten thousand" who stand before him? Are not these the one hundred million and more who have been faithful and true in the days of their mortal probation? Are they not the same "ten thousand times ten thousand" who are "kings and priests," and who will live and reign with Christ a thousand years? Are they not the ones who will sing in that great day the song of the redeemed, saying, "Worthy is the Lamb that was slain to receive power, and riches, and wisdom, and strength, and honour, and glory, and blessing."

. . . And we need not suppose that all these things [transpired at Adam-ondi-Ahman] at one single meeting or at one single hour in time. It is proper to hold numerous meetings at a general conference, some for the instruction of leaders, others for the edification of the Saints. . . . [*The Millennial Messiah*, 584–85]

Chapter Twenty-Two

Prayer and Prophecies

D&C 121–123

DOCTRINE AND COVENANTS 121–123

*H*istorical Setting: "Prayer and prophecies [excerpts from a letter] written by Joseph Smith the Prophet, while he was a prisoner in the jail at Liberty, Missouri, dated March 20, 1839 [begun on the 20th and completed on the 25th]. The Prophet with several companions had been months [since late November 1838] in prison. Their petitions and appeals directed to the executive officers and judiciary had failed to bring them relief" (D&C 121; section heading).

SECTIONS 121–123 • OUTLINE

Note: To understand these sections, they should be studied with the letter. As Joseph wrote to the Saints, he was moved upon by the Spirit and wrote the things that came to him by revelation.

➤ 121:1–6   How long will the hand of the Lord be stayed; remember thy suffering Saints.

      a.   Let thy anger be kindled against our enemies (vv. 4–5).

      b.   Remember thy suffering Saints, and thy servants will rejoice (v. 6).

➤ 121:7–25   Thine afflictions shall be but a small moment, and if endured well God shall exalt thee, and you shall triumph over all your enemies.

     a. Thy friends stand by thee; thou art not yet as Job (vv. 9–11).

     b. God will change the times and seasons that they not understand (vv. 12–15).

     c. Cursed are those who lift their heel against his anointed (vv. 16–18).

     d. Wo to those who offend my little ones, better they were drowned (vv. 19–25).

➤ 121:26–32   God shall give you knowledge by his Holy Spirit, nothing shall be withheld.

     a. Which our forefathers have awaited anxiously to be revealed (vv. 26–31).

     b. According to what was ordained in the Council of the Eternal God (v. 32).

➤ 121:33   The Almighty will pour down knowledge upon the Latter-day Saints.

➤ 121:34–46   Many Are called, but few are chosen.

     a. The rights of the priesthood are controlled by righteousness (vv. 36–38).

     b. Those who exercise unrighteousness dominion are not chosen (vv. 39–40).

     c. The way to obtain the power and influence of the priesthood (vv. 41–45).

     d. The blessings that accompany the proper use of the priesthood (vv. 45–46).

➤ 122:1–9   The ends of the earth shall inquire after thy name, and thy people shall never be turned against thee.

     a. The pure in heart shall seek counsel and authority under thy hand (v. 2).

     b. Traitors shall cast you into trouble, but God shall stand by thee (vv. 3–4).

     c. All these things shall give thee experience, and be for thy good (vv. 5–7).

     d. The Son of Man has descended below them all (v. 8).

     e. Thy days are numbered and shall not be less (v. 9).

➤ 123:1–10   Gather the facts, sufferings, and abuses against the Saints as a testimony against the offenders.

     a.   Publish them to all the world, and present them to heads of government to leave them without excuse (v. 6).

     b.   It is a duty we owe to God, angels, our wives and children, widows and fatherless (vv. 7–10).

➤ 123:11–17   It is an imperative duty to the rising generation, and the pure in heart.

     a.   Many are kept from the truth because they know not where to find it (v. 12).

     b.   We should bring to light things of darkness revealed from heaven (vv. 13–16).

     c.   Cheerfully do all things in our power to see the salvation of God (v. 17).

Introduction

According to President Joseph Fielding Smith, the letter from which the excerpts were taken to formulate Doctrine and Covenants 121, 122, and 123 "is one of the greatest letters that was ever penned by the hand of man. It is a prayer and a prophecy and an answer by revelation from the Lord"[87] An examination of the three sections drawn from the letter will verify President Smith's statement. We will include a synopsis of the contents of the letter that preceded the prayers and the prophecies that came from the Prophet's pen.

TEXT AND COMMENTARY

Letter: "... I think it cannot be found among the wild and ferocious beasts of the forest—that a man should be mangled for sport! Women be robbed of all that they have—their last morsel for subsistence, and then be violated to gratify the hellish desires of the mob, and finally left to perish with their helpless offspring clinging around their necks. ...

They practice these things upon the Saints, who have done them no wrong, who are innocent and virtuous; who loved the Lord their God, and were willing to forsake all things for Christ's sake. These things are

---

[87] *Church History and Modern Revelation* [1947], 2:176.

awful to relate, but they are verily true. It must be that offences come, but woe unto them by whom they come [Matthew 18:7]" (*HC,* 3:290–91; or *TPJS*, 131).

D&C 121:1–6 • The Prophet's Plea

1 O God, where art thou? And where is the pavilion that covereth thy hiding place?

2 How long shall thy hand be stayed, and thine eye, yea thy pure eye, behold from the eternal heavens the wrongs of thy people and of thy servants, and thine ear be penetrated with their cries?

3 Yea, O Lord, how long shall they suffer these wrongs and unlawful oppressions, before thine heart shall be softened toward them, and thy bowels be moved with compassion toward them?

4 O Lord God Almighty, maker of heaven, earth, and seas, and of all things that in them are, and who controllest and subjectest the devil, and the dark and benighted dominion of Sheol—stretch forth thy hand; let thine eye pierce; let thy pavilion be taken up; let thy hiding place no longer be covered; let thine ear be inclined; let thine heart be softened, and thy bowels moved with compassion toward us.

5 Let thine anger be kindled against our enemies; and, in the fury of thine heart, with thy sword avenge us of our wrongs.

6 Remember thy suffering saints, O our God; and thy servants will rejoice in thy name forever.

Joseph is not the first Prophet to make such a plea to the Lord. The Old Testament prophet Habakkuk cried: "O LORD, how long shall I cry, and thou wilt not hear! even cry out unto thee of violence, and thou wilt not save!" (Habakkuk 1:2; see the whole chapter). Jeremiah asks a similar question: "RIGHTEOUS art thou, O LORD, when I plead with thee: yet let me talk with thee of thy judgments: wherefore doth the way of the wicked prosper? wherefore are all they happy that deal very treacherously?" (Jeremiah 12:1; see the whole chapter). The Lord answered those prophets, and when Joseph was prepared, He answered him.

Letter: "We received some letters last evening—one from Emma, one from Don C. Smith, and one from Bishop Partridge—all breathing a kind and consoling spirit. . . but those who have not been enclosed in the walls of prison without cause or provocation, can have but little idea how sweet

the voice of a friend is; one token of friendship from any source whatever awakens and calls into action every sympathetic feeling; . . . until finally all enmity, malice and hatred, and past differences, misunderstandings and mismanagements are slain victorious at the feet of hope; and when the heart is sufficiently contrite, then the voice of inspiration steals along and whispers" (*HC*, 3:293; or *TPJS*, 134).

D&C 121:7–15 • Thy Friends Do Still Stand by Thee

7 My son, peace be unto thy soul; thine adversity and thine afflictions shall be but a small moment;

8 And then, if thou endure it well, God shall exalt thee on high; thou shalt triumph over all thy foes.

9 Thy friends do stand by thee, and they shall hail thee again with warm hearts and friendly hands.

10 Thou art not yet as Job; thy friends do not contend against thee, neither charge thee with transgression, as they did Job.

11 And they who do charge thee with transgression, their hope shall be blasted, and their prospects shall melt away as the hoar frost melteth before the burning rays of the rising sun;

12 And also that God hath set his hand and seal to change the times and seasons, and to blind their minds, that they may not understand his marvelous workings; that he may prove them also and take them in their own craftiness;

13 Also because their hearts are corrupted, and the things which they are willing to bring upon others, and love to have others suffer, may come upon themselves to the very uttermost;

14 That they may be disappointed also, and their hopes may be cut off;

15 And not many years hence, that they and their posterity shall be swept from under heaven, saith God, that not one of them is left to stand by the wall.

A small moment of adversity and afflictions (v. 7) is speaking of the Lord's time; one day is equal to a thousand years of man (see 2 Peter 3:8). While it seems a long time to people living on the earth, it is very brief in the Lord's time. The Lord's reference to Job (vv. 10–11) was to comfort Joseph as he reflected upon the many friends who remembered him at this time of suffering. The book of Job is about a righteous man who had many afflictions. In a day when it was believed that afflictions were because of man's sins, Jobs friends came to him and urged him to confess his sins in order for his afflictions to come to an end (see Job chapters 2–26). Joseph learned the value of friends throughout his life. As Joseph prepared to ride to Carthage, where he would be martyred, he replied to those who accused him of deserting his people: "If my life is of no value to my friends, it is of none to myself" (*TPJS*, 377).

The Lord changing the times and seasons (vv. 12–13) should not be taken out of context. The Lord is saying their will come situations that will have negative effects upon the mob and others. They will not understand His ways, and will be caught in their own acts of wickedness. In the words of the angel that spoke to Nephi: "And that great pit, which hath been digged for them by that great and abominable church, which was founded by the devil and his children, that he might lead away the souls of men down to hell—yea, that great pit which hath been digged for the destruction of men shall be filled by those who digged it, unto their utter destruction" (1 Nephi 14:3, see also 22:14). Their wickedness will affect their posterity as well (v. 15). This will again be the natural effect of their wickedness, "visiting the iniquity of the fathers upon the children unto the third and fourth generation of them that hate me" (Exodus 20:5). Of course those of the posterity who repent will be given mercy (see Exodus 20:6).

D&C 121:16–25 • Shall Not Have the Priesthood

16 Cursed are all those that shall lift up the heel against mine anointed, saith the Lord, and cry they have sinned when they have not sinned before me, saith the Lord, but have done that which was meet in mine eyes, and which I commanded them.

17 But those who cry transgression do it because they are the servants of sin, and are the children of disobedience themselves.

18 And those who swear falsely against my servants, that they might bring them into bondage and death—

19 Wo unto them; because they have offended my little ones they shall be severed from the ordinances of mine house.

20 Their basket shall not be full, their houses and their barns shall perish, and they themselves shall be despised by those that flattered them.

21 They shall not have right to the priesthood, nor their posterity after them from generation to generation.

22 It had been better for them that a millstone had been hanged about their necks, and they drowned in the depth of the sea.

23 Wo unto all those that discomfort my people, and drive, and murder, and testify against them, saith the Lord of Hosts; a generation of vipers shall not escape the damnation of hell.

24 Behold, mine eyes see and know all their works, and I have in reserve a swift judgment in the season thereof, for them all;

25 For there is a time appointed for every man, according as his works shall be.

The little ones that were offended (v. 19) are the Lord's little children, the members of the Church. Verses 16–18 are describing the actions of the mobs. The Lord knew what they had done. Their baskets and barns not being full is the temporal or financial effects upon the mobs. The Lord will withhold the blessings of the elements (see Amos 4:6–10). They shall be despised by those that flattered them is a social stigma that will be a result of their actions (v. 20). The priesthood rights for them and their posterity being withdrawn (v. 21) is another example of the natural effects of their actions. Remember that one of the purposes of the Restoration was "that every man might speak in the name of the Lord [priesthood]" D&C 1:20).

A millstone hanged about their neck (v. 22) is quoting from the Savior's castigation of some in the New Testament (see Matthew 18:6). What he is saying is that they would have been farther ahead in eternity if they had suffered death before they performed such wickedness. Now, they will not escape "the damnation of hell" (v. 23). Again the Lord bears witness of His knowledge of the actions of the mobs, and returns to the season and their time appointed (vv. 24–25). The seasons are programmed by the Lord to enable man to grow his crops. In the imagery used by the Lord, He will not give the mob the normal opportunities to grow spiritually that they could have had. Their time to be on earth will also be altered in length or place, or both. Just as a farmer must prepare his ground to plant, the mob had let his ground become full of weeds and clods. They were not ready for the planting, and there would be no crop to harvest. Their works had affected their future; all of the persecutors of the Saints would have "a swift judgment" (v. 24).

Letter: ". . . God hath said that He would have a tried people, that He would purge them as gold, now we think that this time He has chosen His own crucible, wherein we have been tried. . . . We trust that a ram may be caught in the thicket speedily, to relieve the sons and daughters of Abraham from their great anxiety, . . .

We would say beware of pride also. . . . Flattery is also a deadly poison. . . . Let honesty, and sobriety, and candor, and solemnity, and virtue, and pureness, and meekness, and simplicity crown our heads in every place; and in fine become as little children, without malice, guile or hypocrisy (*HC,* 3:294–296; or *TPJS,* 135–138).

D&C 121:26–32 • Ordained in the Council of the Eternal God

26 God shall give unto you knowledge by his Holy Spirit, yea, by the unspeakable gift of the Holy Ghost, that has not been revealed since the world was until now;

27 Which our forefathers have awaited with anxious expectation to be revealed in the last times, which their minds were pointed to by the angels, as held in reserve for the fulness of their glory;

28 A time to come in the which nothing shall be withheld, whether there be one God or many gods, they shall be manifest.

29 All thrones and dominions, principalities and powers, shall be revealed and set forth upon all who have endured valiantly for the gospel of Jesus Christ.

30 And also, if there be bounds set to the heavens or to the seas, or to the dry land, or to the sun, moon, or stars—

31 All the times of their revolutions; all the appointed days, months, and years, and all the days of their days, months, and years, and all their glories, laws, and set times, shall be revealed in the days of the dispensation of the fulness of times—

32 According to that which was ordained in the midst of the Council of the Eternal God of all other gods before this world was, that should be reserved unto the finishing and the end thereof, when every man shall enter into his eternal presence and into his immortal rest.

The forefathers who have anxiously been waiting for revelation (v. 27) seem to be the Founding Fathers of the nation who established the U.S. Constitution. This conclusion is drawn from the ending of this letter written by Joseph Smith (see the conclusion of this letter at the end of this chapter), and other things known about them. They were promised great things, and apparently were then aware of the future events.

The various questions that would be answered (vv. 28–31) are still in the future, although there were limited answers given for some of the questions in the book of Abraham (chapter three), and by the Prophet Joseph Smith. We will not attempt to expound on any of them here. When these answers will be made fully known to the general Church populace was determined in the Council of the Eternal God. Some of the questions will be apparently answered on an individual basis, but every man shall know when he enters "into [God's] eternal presence and into his eternal rest" (v. 32), if he has not learned before.

Letter: "Letter: . . . ignorance, superstition and bigotry placing itself where it ought not, is oftentimes in the way of the prosperity this Church" (*HC,* 3:296; or *TPJS,* 138).

D&C 121:33 • The Almighty Will Pour Down Knowledge

33 How long can rolling waters remain impure? What power shall stay the heavens? As well might man stretch forth his puny arm to stop the Missouri river in its decreed course, or to turn it up stream, as to hinder the Almighty from pouring down knowledge from heaven upon the heads of the Latter-day Saints.

The stopping of the Missouri River by a man's arm is impossible, and so is any attempt to prevent revelation coming from God, if he wants to send it. He does want to send it because, as Joseph Smith said: "You know very well that the Lord has led this Church by revelation" (*TPJS,* 362).

Letter: ". . . If there are any among you who aspire after their own aggrandizement, and seek their own opulence, while their brethren are groaning in poverty, and are under sore trials and temptations, they cannot be benefited by the intercession of the Holy Spirit, which maketh intercession for us day and night with groanings that cannot be uttered [see Romans 8:26].

We ought at all times to be very careful that such high-mindedness shall never have place in our hearts; but condescend to men of low estate, and with all long-suffering beat the infirmities of the weak" (*HC,* 3:299; or *TPJS,* 141).

D&C 121:34–40 • The Priesthood Inseparably Connected with Heaven

34 Behold, there are many called, but few are chosen. And why are they not chosen?

35 Because their hearts are set so much upon the things of this world, and aspire to the honors of men, that they do not learn this one lesson—

36 That the rights of the priesthood are inseparably connected with the powers of heaven, and that the powers of heaven cannot be controlled nor handled only upon the principles of righteousness.

37 That they may be conferred upon us, it is true; but when we undertake to cover our sins, or to gratify our pride, our vain ambition, or to exercise control or dominion or compulsion upon the souls of the children of men, in any degree of unrighteousness, behold, the heavens withdraw themselves; the Spirit of the Lord is grieved; and when it is withdrawn, Amen to the priesthood or the authority of that man.

38 Behold, ere he is aware, he is left unto himself, to kick against the pricks, to persecute the saints, and to fight against God.

39 We have learned by sad experience that it is the nature and disposition of almost all men, as soon as they get a little authority, as they suppose, they will immediately begin to exercise unrighteous dominion.

40 Hence many are called, but few are chosen.

The phrase "many are called, but few are chosen" was used by Christ in the New Testament in referring to those who were invited to the wedding feast. The phrase was used in Doctrine and Covenants 95:5 to show why some who were ordained to the priesthood were not chosen to bring to pass the Lord's work. The revelation received, as Joseph wrote this letter, gives other reasons why their priesthood power is not obtained. Their hearts are set upon the things of the world, and the honors of men (D&C 121:35). They had not learned that the rights of the priesthood were inseparably connected with the powers of heaven and could only be controlled upon the principles of righteousness (v. 36). When a

priesthood holder sins, or seeks dominion over the souls of men, the heavens withdraw, the Spirit is grieved, and the priesthood authority is gone (v. 37). Being left alone, without the Spirit, he persecutes the Saints and fights against God (v. 38). The nature and disposition of almost all men is to exercise unrighteous dominion as they get a little authority (v. 39). Hence, many who receive the priesthood are not chosen to carry on the Lord's work (v. 40).

D&C 121:41–46 • The Constitution of the Priesthood

41 No power or influence can or ought to be maintained by virtue of the priesthood, only by persuasion, by long-suffering, by gentleness and meekness, and by love unfeigned;

42 By kindness, and pure knowledge, which shall greatly enlarge the soul without hypocrisy, and without guile—

43 Reproving betimes with sharpness, when moved upon by the Holy Ghost; and then showing forth afterwards an increase of love toward him whom thou hast reproved, lest he esteem thee to be his enemy;

44 That he may know that thy faithfulness is stronger than the cords of death.

45 Let thy bowels also be full of charity towards all men, and to the household of faith, and let virtue garnish thy thoughts unceasingly; then shall thy confidence wax strong in the presence of God; and the doctrine of the priesthood shall distil upon thy soul as the dews from heaven.

46 The Holy Ghost shall be thy constant companion, and thy scepter an unchanging scepter of righteousness and truth; and thy dominion shall be an everlasting dominion, and without compulsory means it shall flow unto thee forever and ever.

The five principles for using the priesthood given above (vv. 41–45) are defined by the author as; *first,* "quiet dignity." Dignity is to be distinctive, but to not make an out-ward show. Unfeigned means not pretended or insincere (v. 41). The Apostle Paul used almost these same words (vv. 41–42) as guidelines for the Corinthians to be "ministers of God" (2 Corinthians 6:4–6). Paul's source must have also been revelation from God.

The *second* principle for using the priesthood is "by revelation," the only source of unwritten pure knowledge. Hypocrisy is to say one thing and do another. The priesthood holder must be an example of the gospel in action. Guile is to be cunning or deceitful. The priesthood holder must be of impeccable character (v. 42).

The *third* principle for proper priesthood use is to "be sharp." This principle is sometimes interpreted as an excuse to become angry, or associated with anger. Laman and Lemuel accused Nephi of being angry, but Lehi said," his sharpness was the sharpness of the power of the word of God" (2 Nephi 1:26). Therefore, we interpret the sharpness of the priesthood to be exact, clear, or be certain of clarity in your speech and actions. Reproof means to rebuke, to chastise, to reprimand, with intent to correct. Reproof, if used with principle number one, will be used in kindness, and patience. The Lord chastens those He loves, and priesthood holders should do likewise. He must love them enough to correct them. Betimes means to do it early, or without delay. Showing an increase of love implies that love has already been shown (D&C 121:43–44).

The *fourth* principle for priesthood use is "charity," the pure love of Christ. This principle is defined in Moroni 7:45, and 1 Corinthians 13:4–7, and has similar characteristics as principle number one, but will be defined here as doing what the Savior would do in the same situation. He did chastise, reprove, and reprimand (see Matthew 23), as the incidents required. Priesthood holders should do the same in faith that the Spirit will witness the truth to those being corrected (D&C 121:45).

The *fifth* principle is "virtue." Definitions of virtue include moral excellence, and manly strength and courage. Jesus was not effeminate, or backward. To garnish is to add color or attractiveness. The thoughts of the priesthood holder must be pure, and directed toward the purposes of the kingdom. He must be doing the right thing for the right reason (see Moroni 7:5). The five principles used together will bring forth the power of the priesthood in our wards and stakes. As a constitution is the basic laws of a nation, the above verses are the constitution of the priesthood.

There are five blessings promised to those who follow the five principles just discussed. There is no correlation between the numbering of the principles and the blessings. The blessings come according to the need and the circumstances. The *first* blessing is "confidence." To call on the power of the Lord, one must have a trust and an assurance that the Lord will do what the priesthood holder declares. This assurance comes from the revelation, or pure knowledge, that he has been given by the Spirit.

The giving of the Spirit is the *second* promised blessing, the "doctrine of the priesthood." Doctrine is knowledge and it distils upon the soul (v. 45) line upon line, precept upon precept (see 2 Nephi 28:30; Isaiah 28:13). The priesthood holder must carefully and slowly pronounce the knowledge that is given to him; having the courage to say what he is given, but not saying more than is given. Therefore, there may be pauses as he proceeds.

The *third* blessing that comes from the proper use of the priesthood is "The Holy Ghost shall be thy constant companion" (D&C 121:46). While this blessing was given when confirmed a member of the Church, the Spirit "may descend upon him and not tarry with him" (D&C 130:23). When using the priesthood correctly, that companionship will be there. If not used correctly, the Spirit withdraws (D&C 121:37).

The scepter is the emblem of authority used by a political leader in some forms of government. As an emblem of the priesthood it is the *fourth* promised blessing; a mantle of "righteousness and truth" that rests upon the priesthood holder. While not recognizable to the naked eye, it is discerned by the Spirit to the other members of the Church as they associate with the priesthood holder in his dominion, or in his office and calling.

The *fifth* blessing promised for proper use of priesthood power is an eternal one. It is the "everlasting dominion" of the priesthood (v. 46). Just as the improper use of the priesthood is an "Amen to the priesthood of that man" (v. 38), the proper use of the priesthood extends not only into this life, but into the eternities. It becomes an everlasting power of God flowing in thy soul forever.

D&C 122:1–9 • Thy People Shall Never Be Turned Against Thee

1 THE ends of the earth shall inquire after thy name, and fools shall have thee in derision, and hell shall rage against thee;

2 While the pure in heart, and the wise, and the noble, and the

virtuous, shall seek counsel, and authority, and blessings constantly from under thy hand.

3 And thy people shall never be turned against thee by the testimony of traitors.

4 And although their influence shall cast thee into trouble, and into bars and walls, thou shalt be had in honor; and but for a small moment and thy voice shall be more terrible in the midst of thine enemies than the fierce lion, because of thy righteousness; and thy God shall stand by thee forever and ever.

5 If thou art called to pass through tribulation; if thou art in perils among false brethren; if thou art in perils among robbers; if thou art in perils by land or by sea;

6 If thou art accused with all manner of false accusations; if thine enemies fall upon thee; if they tear thee from the society of thy father and mother and brethren and sisters; and if with a drawn sword thine enemies tear thee from the bosom of thy wife, and of thine offspring, and thine elder son, although but six years of age, shall cling to thy garments, and shall say, My father, my father, why can't you stay with us? O, my father, what are the men going to do with you? and if then he shall be thrust from thee by the sword, and thou be dragged to prison, and thine enemies prowl around thee like wolves for the blood of the lamb;

7 And if thou shouldst be cast into the pit, or into the hands of murderers, and the sentence of death passed upon thee; if thou be cast into the deep; if the billowing surge conspire against thee; if fierce winds become thine enemy; if the heavens gather blackness, and all the elements combine to hedge up the way; and above all, if the very jaws of hell shall gape open the mouth wide after thee, know thou, my son, that all these things shall give thee experience, and shall be for thy good.

8 The Son of Man hath descended below them all. Art thou greater than he?

9 Therefore, hold on thy way, and the priesthood shall remain with thee; for their bounds are set, they cannot pass. Thy days are known, and thy years shall not be numbered less; therefore, fear not what man can do, for God shall be with you forever and ever.

The earth inquiring after thy name and fools have thee in derision, and the people of Joseph Smith seeking counsel and authority from him (vv. 1–2), is basically the same prophecy as the Angel Moroni gave on September 22, 1823: "that my name should be had for good and evil among all nations, kindreds, and tongues, or that it should be both good and evil spoken of among all people" (JS—H 1:33). Both prophecies have certainly come to pass. His voice more terrible than a fierce lion (v. 4) reminds us of his imprisonment in the Richmond, Missouri jail in November of 1838. Parley P. Pratt, who was imprisoned with him, wrote of this incident:

> In one of these tedious nights we had lain as if in sleep till the hour of midnight had passed, and our ears and hearts had been pained, while we had listened for hours to the obscene jests, the horrid oaths, the dreadful blasphemies and filthy language of our guards, . . . They even boasted of defiling by force wives, daughters and virgins, and of shooting or dashing out the brains of men, women, and children.
>
> . . . On a sudden [Joseph] arose to his feet, and spoke in a voice of thunder, or as the roaring lion, uttering as near as I can recollect, the following words:
>
> "SILENCE, ye fiends of the infernal pit. In the name of Jesus Christ I rebuke you, and command you to be still; I will not take another minute and hear such language. Cease such talk, or you or I die THIS INSTANT!"
>
> He ceased to speak. He stood erect in terrible majesty. Chained, and without weapon; calm, unruffled and dignified as an angel, he looked upon the quailing guards, whose weapons were lowered or dropped to the ground; whose knees smote together, and who, shrinking into a corner, or crouching at his feet, begged his pardon, and remained quiet till a change of guards.
>
> I have seen the ministers of justice, clothed in magisterial robes, and criminals arraigned before them, while life was suspended on a breath, in the courts of England; I have witnessed congress in solemn session to give laws to nations; I have tried to conceive of kings, of royal courts, of thrones and crowns; and of emperors assembled to decide the fate of kingdoms; but dignity and majesty have I seen but *once*, as it stood in chains, at midnight, in a dungeon in an obscure village of Missouri.[88]

The tribulations and perils given as possibilities in verses 5–8 were actual things that did happen to him in the following four years. The Lord revealing them as possible was probably to prepare him, but not to discourage him. His gaining of experience, and being benefited by these

---

[88] *Autobiography of Parley P. Pratt,* ed. his son Parley P. Pratt [1970], 210–11.

experiences, was the same principle given to the Romans by the Apostle Paul: "And we know that all things work together for good to them that love God, to them who are the called according to his purpose" (Romans 8:28). This principle had been stated in two previous revelations concerning other men, but with conditions of righteousness attached (see D&C 90:24; 100:15). The Lord knew that Joseph could handle them in righteousness. The question, comparing the Son of Man's tribulations with Joseph's (D&C 121:8), seems to be a way of strengthening Joseph to endure those events at the time they happened. Jehovah knows "the end from the beginning" (Abraham 2:8; Isaiah 46:10), and he assures Joseph that his life will be protected until his mission is completed (D&C 122:9). Joseph made several statements, after this assurance was given unto him, that he would not be taken until his mission was completed (see *TPJS,* 258, 274, 328). There were other assurances given to Joseph, but this one, under the circumstances he was in, was undoubtedly a major influence on his knowing his life was in the hands of the Lord.

Letter:

We have reason to believe that many things were introduced among the Saints before God had signified the times; and notwithstanding the principles and plans may have been good, yet aspiring men, or in other words, men who had not the substance of godliness about them, perhaps to handle edged tools. Children, you know, are fond of tools, while they are not yet able to use them.

Time and experience, however, are the only safe remedies against such evil. There are many teachers, but, perhaps, not many fathers. There are times coming when God will signify many things that are expedient for the well-being of the Saints; but the time has not yet come, but will come, as fast as there can be found place and reception for them. [*HC,* 3: 301–302; or *TPJS,* 144]

D&C 123:1–10 • An Imperative Duty to God and Angels

1 AND again, we would suggest for your consideration the propriety of all the saints gathering up a knowledge of all the facts, and sufferings and abuses put upon them by the people of this State;

2 And also of all the property and amount of damages which they have sustained, both of character and personal injuries, as well as real property;

3 And also the names of all persons that have had a hand in their

oppressions, as far as they can get hold of them and find them out.

4 And perhaps a committee can be appointed to find out these things, and to take statements and affidavits; and also to gather up the libelous publications that are afloat;

5 And all that are in the magazines, and in the encyclopedias, and all the libelous histories that are published, and are writing, and by whom, and present the whole concatenation of diabolical rascality and nefarious and murderous impositions that have been practised upon this people—

6 That we may not only publish to all the world, but present them to the heads of government in all their dark and hellish hue, as the last effort which is enjoined on us by our Heavenly Father, before we can fully and completely claim that promise which shall call him forth from his hiding place; and also that the whole nation may be left without excuse before he can send forth the power of his mighty arm.

7 It is an imperative duty that we owe to God, to angels, with whom we shall be brought to stand, and also to ourselves, to our wives and children, who have been made to bow down with grief, sorrow, and care, under the most damning hand of murder, tyranny, and oppression, supported and urged on and upheld by the influence of that spirit which hath so strongly riveted the creeds of the fathers, who have inherited lies, upon the hearts of the children, and filled the world with confusion, and has been growing stronger and stronger, and is now the very mainspring of all corruption, and the whole earth groans under the weight of its iniquity.

8 It is an iron yoke, it is a strong band; they are the very handcuffs, and chains, and shackles, and fetters of hell.

9 Therefore it is an imperative duty that we owe, not only to our own wives and children, but to the widows and fatherless, whose husbands and fathers have been murdered under its iron hand;

10 Which dark and blackening deeds are enough to make hell itself shudder, and to stand aghast and pale, and the hands of the very devil to tremble and palsy.

The suffering of the Saints has been published, and is available to the world (vv. 1–6), but is only generally known to most members of the Church and a few others. The heads of the government of the United States of America, at the time of Joseph Smith, were presented with the facts and were left without excuse (v. 6). The influence of the creeds, and lies that were inherited by the fathers of the various churches, is still prevalent among the people of the Christian world, and still handcuff them. The widows and orphans are still testimonies against those who are in hell (vv. 7–10).

D&C 123:11–17 • Still Many Are Kept from the Truth

11 And also it is an imperative duty that we owe to all the rising generation, and to all the pure in heart—

12 For there are many yet on the earth among all sects, parties, and denominations, who are blinded by the subtle craftiness of men, whereby they lie in wait to deceive, and who are only kept from the truth because they know not where to find it—

13 Therefore, that we should waste and wear out our lives in bringing to light all the hidden things of darkness, wherein we know them; and they are truly manifest from heaven—

14 These should then be attended to with great earnestness.

15 Let no man count them as small things; for there is much which lieth in futurity, pertaining to the saints, which depends upon these things.

16 You know, brethren, that a very large ship is benefited very much by a very small helm in the time of a storm, by being kept workways with the wind and the waves.

17 Therefore, dearly beloved brethren, let us cheerfully do all things that lie in our power; and then may we stand still, with the utmost assurance, to see the salvation of God, and for his arm to be revealed.

It is now about one hundred and seventy years since these atrocities were committed, and many generations (v. 11) have passed. Many among those generations have found where to obtain the truth (v. 12), but the work of the Lord must go on in "great earnestness" (vv. 13–14). There are still many who do not know where to find the truth. Many of the things that pertained to the Saints have come about (v. 15). The small helm [the Church] (v. 16) is now much bigger, and the ship [world population] has also grown. We must continue to "cheerfully do all things that lie in our power" to prepare "to see the salvation of God." His arm will be revealed at His Second Coming (v. 17). The ending of the letter written from the prison follows:

Letter: (conclusion)

". . . The Constitution of the United States is a glorious standard; it is founded in the wisdom of God. It is a heavenly banner; it is to all those who are privileged with the sweets of liberty, like the cooling shades and refreshing waters of a great rock in a thirsty and weary land. It is like a great tree under whose branches men from every cline can be shielded from the burning rays of the sun. . . .

We say that God is true; that the Constitution of the United States is true; that the Bible is true; that the Book of Mormon is true; that the Book of Covenants is true; that Christ is true; that the ministering angels sent forth from God are true, and that we know that we have an house not made with hands eternal in the heavens; whose builder and maker is God; a consolation which our oppressors cannot feel, when fortune, or fate, shall lay its iron hand on them as it has us. Now, we ask, what is man? Remember, brethren, that time and chance happen to all men. [*HC*, 3:304–305; or *TPJS*, 147–148]

General Authority Quotes

—*President Harold B. Lee* • D&C 121:34–44

. . . There are many who were foreordained before the world was to a greater state than they have prepared themselves for here. Even though they might have been among the noble and great, from among whom the Father declared He would make His chosen leaders, they may fail of that calling here in mortality. Then the Lord poses the question: "And why are they not chosen?" (D&C 121:34)

Two answers were given: First, "Because their hearts are set so much upon the things of this world." And second, they "aspire to the honors of men." (D&C 121:35) [*The Teachings of Harold B. Lee*, 185]

[After quoting D&C 121:35–38]

That, it seems to me, is about the progressive way that men begin to fall away. They first begin to "kick against the pricks." I have wondered what that means. These no doubt are the pricks of the gospel. I wonder, perhaps, if they are not those things referred to by President J. Reuben Clark Jr. as "restraints"—the restraints of the Word of Wisdom, the restraints imposed in keeping the Sabbath day holy, injunctions against card playing, the restraints imposed by following the welfare program, and so on. These are the restraints against which some people seem to rebel and are kicking constantly against—the "pricks" of the gospel.

I remember in this connection what somebody said in classifying humankind. He said there were only three kinds of people in the world—"Saints, Aint's, and Complaints," and perhaps the "Complaints" would represent those who seem to be kicking against the pricks. These are they who "persecute the Saints" and finally, "fight against God." [*The Teachings of Harold B. Lee*, 391–92]

. . . (see D&C 121:41–43). In all our priesthood callings we must never forget that the business of the Church and kingdom of God is to save souls, and that all over whom we preside are our Father's children, and He will aid us in our endeavors to save every one. [*The Teachings of Harold B. Lee*, 501]

The greater your authority, the greater care you must have lest you use that authority unrighteously. . . . [quotes D&C 121:43, 39–40] Force is an ultimate resource that maintains itself by being seldom employed. [*The Teachings of Harold B. Lee*, 510]

—President Gordon B. Hinckley • D&C 121:36–37

Brethren, let us be worthy of the priesthood which we hold. Let us live nearer to the Lord. Let us be good husbands and fathers.

Any man who is a tyrant in his own home is unworthy of the priesthood. He cannot be a fit instrument in the hands of the Lord when he does not show respect and kindness and love toward the companion of his choice.

Likewise, any man who is a bad example for his children, who cannot control his temper, or who is involved in dishonest or immoral practices will find the power of the priesthood nullified.

I remind you . . . [quotes D&C 121 36–37].

Brethren, let us be good men as those favored of the Lord with a bestowal of His divine power upon us. [CR, October 2001, 65–66]

—President Hugh B. Brown • D&C 121:45–46

I should like to say to you fathers tonight that our conduct in the home determines in large measure our worthiness to hold and exercise the priesthood, which is the power of God delegated to man. Almost any man can make a good showing when on parade before the public, but one's integrity is tested when "off duty." The real man is seen and known in the comparative solitude of the home. An office or title will not erase a fault nor guarantee a virtue. [CR, April 1962, 88]

—*President Spencer W. Kimball* • D&C 123:6

. . . We have had a delightful message from Christopher S. Bond, governor of the state of Missouri, who advised us that he has rescinded the 138-year-old executive order of Governor Lilburn W. Boggs calling for the extermination or expulsion of the Mormons from the state of Missouri. Governor Bond, present Missouri governor, writes:

"Expressing on behalf of all Missourians our deep regret for the injustice and undue suffering which was caused by this 1838 order, I hereby rescind Executive Order No. 44 dated October 27, 1838, issued by Governor Lilburn W. Boggs."

To Governor Bond and the people of Missouri, we extend our deep appreciation for this reversal and for the present friendly associations between the membership of The Church of Jesus Christ of Latter-day Saints and the people of Missouri as it is now in effect.

In Missouri now we have five stakes in fifty-one communities, with approximately 15,000 members of the Church, who, we are confident, are law-abiding citizens of the state of Missouri. Thank you, Governor Bond. [CR, October 1976, 4–5]

Chapter Twenty-Three

Proclamation to the World

D&C 124–126

*H*istorical Setting: "I received [Doctrine and Covenants 124]. . . . *Revelation Given to Joseph Smith at Nauvoo, January 19ᵗʰ 1841*" (*HC*, 4:274).

"Because of increasing persecutions and illegal procedures against them by public officers, the saints had been compelled to leave Missouri. The exterminating order issued by Lilburn W. Boggs, Governor of Missouri, dated October 27, 1838, had left them no alternative. See *HC* 3:175. In 1841, when this revelation was given, the city of Nauvoo, occupying the site of the former village of Commerce, Illinois, had been built up by the saints, and here the headquarters of the Church had been established" (section 124 heading).

SECTION 124 • OUTLINE

➤ 124:1–11 Joseph is commanded to make a proclamation to the leaders of the nations of the world, written by the power of the Holy Ghost.

    a. Give heed to the light and glory of Zion, for my day comes speedily (vv. 6–10).

    b. Come with your gold and silver and help my people (v. 11).

➤ 124:12–21 Stewardships given to various individuals.

a.   Robert B. Thompson to help Joseph write the proclamation (vv. 12–14).

b.   Hyrum Smith is loved because of the integrity of his heart (v. 15).

c.   John C. Bennett is to help Joseph in sending the proclamation (vv. 16–17).

d.   Lyman Wight is to continue preaching in Zion, that he be received (vv. 18–19).

e.   George Miller called to be bishop like unto Edward Partridge (vv. 20–21).

➤ 124:22–24   A [Nauvoo] house for boarding of strangers to be built.

a.   My servant Joseph shall show you (v. 22).

b.   It shall be built unto my name, and be holy for the Lord to dwell in (v. 24).

➤ 124:25–55   Build a house [temple] to my name for the Most High to dwell.

a.   Bring gold and silver that the fulness of the priesthood be restored (vv. 26–28).

b.   Build a baptismal font to do baptisms for the dead (vv. 29–36).

c.   The ordinances were hid from before the foundations of the world (vv. 37–41).

d.   Joseph shall be shown the place, blessings or cursings will follow (vv. 42–55).

➤ 124:56–71   Joseph to have place in the boarding house from generation to generation.

a.   Joseph to bless the kindreds of the earth as did Abraham (vv. 57–61).

b.   Stock to sell for not more than 15 thousand, nor less than 50 dollars (vv. 62–72).

➤ 124:72–90   Instructions to various individuals concerning their stewardships.

a.   Answer to those requesting who should buy stocks (vv. 72–81).

     b.   Instructions to William Law and Almon Babbitt (vv. 82–90).

➤ 124:91–102   New offices in the priesthood appointed.

     a.   William Law replaces Hyrum as counselor to Joseph Smith (vv. 91, 97–102).

     b.   Hyrum Smith replaces his father as patriarch and Oliver Cowdery (vv. 91–96).

➤ 124:103–110   Sidney Rigdon called to repentance as a counselor to Joseph.

     a.   Lift up his voice and be a spokesman, and assist Joseph (vv. 104–107).

     b.   Do the Lord's will and not remove his family to eastern lands (vv. 108–110).

➤ 124:111–118   The stewardships of Amos Davies and Robert D. Foster.

➤ 124:119–122   No man pay stock for the Nauvoo House unless he believes in the Book of Mormon and the revelations.

     a.   More or less than this cometh of evil, and will have curses not blessings (v. 120).

     b.   A just recompense shall be paid for labors on the Nauvoo House (vv. 121–22)

➤ 124:123–145   Officers belonging to my priesthood, to hold the keys thereof.

     a.   Hyrum Smith the sealing blessings of the Church (v. 124).

     b.   Joseph the presiding elder, his two counselors, the First Presidency, to receive the oracles of the whole Church (vv. 124–126).

     c.   Brigham Young and the Twelve, open the four corners of the earth (vv. 127–30).

     d.   The high council for the corner stone of Zion (vv. 131–32).

     e.   Don C. Smith president of high priests as standing presidents (vv. 133–36).

     f.   A quorum of elders to be standing ministers (v. 137).

g.   Seven seventies as traveling elders to travel continually (vv. 138–40).

h.   Three to preside over the bishopric (v. 141).

i.   Presidents of priests, teachers, and deacons, and the presidents of stakes (v. 142).

j.   These offices are for the work of the ministry; and the perfecting of the Saints, to be approved at general conference (vv. 144–45).

Introduction

There are no revelations recorded in the Doctrine and Covenants for the past twenty-two months, since March 1839. However, there were many received, but not placed in the Doctrine and Covenants. They probably could be described as did Jarom in the Book of Mormon: "I shall not write the things of my prophesying, nor of my revelations. For what could I write more than my fathers have written? For have not they revealed the plan of salvation? I say unto you, Yea; and this sufficeth me" (Jarom 1:2). Section 124 is the longest revelation in the Doctrine and Covenants, and is over ten pages long. The longest chapter in the Book of Mormon, Jacob 5, is only a little more than half that long. We will emphasis the more important points that are revealed.

TEXT AND COMMENTARY

D&C 124:1–11 • A Proclamation to the World

1 Verily, thus saith the Lord unto you, my servant Joseph Smith, I am well pleased with your offering and acknowledgments, which you have made; for unto this end have I raised you up, that I might show forth my wisdom through the weak things of the earth.

2 Your prayers are acceptable before me; and in answer to them I say unto you, that you are now called immediately to make a solemn proclamation of my gospel, and of this stake which I have planted to be a cornerstone of Zion, which shall be polished with the refinement which is after the similitude of a palace.

3 This proclamation shall be made to all the kings of the world, to the four corners thereof, to the honorable president-elect, and the high-minded governors of the nation in which you live, and to all the nations of the earth scattered abroad.

4 Let it be written in the spirit of meekness and by the power of the Holy Ghost, which shall be in you at the time of the writing of the same;

5 For it shall be given you by the Holy Ghost to know my will concerning those kings and authorities, even what shall befall them in a time to come.

6 For, behold, I am about to call upon them to give heed to the light and glory of Zion, for the set time has come to favor her.

7 Call ye, therefore, upon them with loud proclamation, and with your testimony, fearing them not, for they are as grass, and all their glory as the flower thereof which soon falleth, that they may be left also without excuse—

8 And that I may visit them in the day of visitation, when I shall unveil the face of my covering, to appoint the portion of the oppressor among hypocrites, where there is gnashing of teeth, if they reject my servants and my testimony which I have revealed unto them.

9 And again, I will visit and soften their hearts, many of them for your good, that ye may find grace in their eyes, that they may come to the light of truth, and the Gentiles to the exaltation or lifting up of Zion.

10 For the day of my visitation cometh speedily, in an hour when ye think not of; and where shall be the safety of my people, and refuge for those who shall be left of them?

11 Awake, O kings of the earth! Come ye, O, come ye, with your gold and your silver, to the help of my people, to the house of the daughters of Zion.

The proclamation that was commanded to be written was sent to the world April 6, 1845, about four years later. It was the first of five proclamations that has been sent since the Church was organized. Three of those five proclamations have been sent in the past thirty some years. At the October 1975 General Conference, President Ezra Taft Benson, President of the Quorum of the Twelve, reaffirmed the great truths of the first proclamation to all the nations of the world (see CR October 1975, 46–49). On April 6, 1980, President Spencer W. Kimball, sent a proclamation to the world from the First Presidency and the Quorum of the Twelve Apostles. This proclamation was sent from the reconstructed Peter Whitmer farmhouse on the sesquicentennial commemoration [150 years] of the organization of the Church at this site. This fourth proclamation is printed in the Conference Report of October 1980, 75–77. The fifth was from the First Presidency and the Quorum of the Twelve Apostles: "The Family: A Proclamation to the World" to all nations. This proclamation was not published in the October 1995 Conference Report, but has been widely disseminated thereafter.

The invitation to give heed to the light and glory of Zion (v. 6) was a prophecy, yet to be fulfilled, given by Isaiah: "ARISE, shine; for thy light is come, and the glory of the LORD is risen upon thee. For, behold, the darkness shall cover the earth, and gross darkness the people: but the LORD shall arise upon thee, and his glory shall be seen upon thee" (Isaiah 60:1–2). The gross darkness of the apostasy, prophesied by Isaiah, was paraphrased in the revelation to the Twelve promising them the keys to unlock the doors of the nations of the earth (see D&C 112:23). The comparison of the people of the nations with grass and flowers is also a paraphrase of Isaiah (40:6–7), and in the same context of the burning at the Second Coming (D&C 124:10). The Gentiles coming to the light of truth (D&C 124:7) is a paraphrase of Isaiah 60:5, and the invitation to come with their gold and silver (D&C 124:11) is a paraphrase of Isaiah 60:7. It seems obvious that the Lord is basing the proclamation to the world He commands them to write, on the prophecies of Isaiah.

D&C 124:12–21 • Stewardships and Love

12 And again, verily I say unto you, let my servant Robert B. Thompson help you to write this proclamation, for I am well pleased with him, and that he should be with you;

13 Let him, therefore, hearken to your counsel, and I will bless him with a multiplicity of blessings; let him be faithful and true in all things from henceforth, and he shall be great in mine eyes;

14 But let him remember that his stewardship will I require at his hands.

15 And again, verily I say unto you, blessed is my servant Hyrum Smith; for I, the Lord, love him because of the integrity of his heart, and because he loveth that which is right before me, saith the Lord.

16 Again, let my servant John C. Bennett help you in your labor in sending my word to the kings and people of the earth, and stand by you, even you my servant Joseph Smith, in the hour of affliction; and his reward shall not fail if he receive counsel.

17 And for his love he shall be great, for he shall be mine if he do

this, saith the Lord. I have seen the work which he hath done, which I accept if he continue, and will crown him with blessings and great glory.

18 And again, I say unto you that it is my will that my servant Lyman Wight should continue in preaching for Zion, in the spirit of meekness, confessing me before the world; and I will bear him up as on eagles' wings; and he shall beget glory and honor to himself and unto my name.

19 That when he shall finish his work I may receive him unto myself, even as I did my servant David Patten, who is with me at this time, and also my servant Edward Partridge, and also my aged servant Joseph Smith, Sen., who sitteth with Abraham at his right hand, and blessed and holy is he, for he is mine.

20 And again, verily I say unto you, my servant George Miller is without guile; he may be trusted because of the integrity of his heart; and for the love which he has to my testimony I, the Lord, love him.

21 I therefore say unto you, I seal upon his head the office of a bishopric, like unto my servant Edward Partridge, that he may receive the consecrations of mine house, that he may administer blessings upon the heads of the poor of my people, saith the Lord. Let no man despise my servant George, for he shall honor me.

The stewardship of Robert Thompson needs no comment. In our day, we hear a lot about unconditional love. We note in the above verses the conditions of His love for the people mentioned. He loved Hyrum because of the integrity of his heart, and Hyrum's love for the right before God (v. 15). John C. Bennett receiving God's love was conditional on "if he received counsel," and his continuing to do so (vv. 16–17). Lyman Wight was promised, "I will bear him up as on eagles wings" if he continued to preach for Zion (vv. 18–19). The eagle wings imagery is once more from Isaiah (40:31). David Patten, Edward Partridge, and Joseph Smith Sen. had passed away and were with the Lord (D&C 124:19). George Miller, who replaced Bishop Partridge, was loved because he was without guile; and "because of the integrity of his heart" (vv. 20–21).

God loves all His children, but gives His love, or His blessings, to them on the conditions of their keeping His commandments (D&C 82:10). He is an eternal God, and cannot give His love to those who do not keep the eternal law that is predicated for that blessing (see D&C 130:20–21). He loves "those who will have him to be their God" (1 Nephi

17:40). He hated the Lamanites "because their deeds have been evil continually" (Helaman 15:4). "If you keep not my commandments, the love of the Father shall not continue with you" (D&C 95:12). Christ and the Father have perfect love as described by the Apostle John: "God is love; and he that dwelleth in love dwelleth in God, and God in him. Herein is our love made perfect, that we may have boldness in the day of judgment: because as he is, so are we in this world. There is no fear in love; but perfect love casteth out fear: because fear hath torment. He that feareth is not made perfect in love. We love him, because he first loved us" (1 John 4:16–19). The Prophet Joseph said: "Until we have perfect love we are liable to fall" (*TPJS,* 9). He also said: "I love you all; but I hate some of your deeds" (*TPJS,* 361). Unconditional love implies that he will love us, and bless us, regardless of what we do. Perfect love may bring blessings and chastisements as needed to help the individual.[89] If we were saved in our sins, Moroni explained:

"Behold, I say unto you that ye would be more miserable to dwell with a holy and just God, under a consciousness of your filthiness before him, than ye would to dwell with the damned souls in hell.

"For behold, when ye shall be brought to see your nakedness before God, and also the glory of God, and the holiness of Jesus Christ, it will kindle a flame of unquenchable fire upon you" (Mormon 9:4–5).

D&C 124:22–24 • The Nauvoo House

22 Let my servant George, and my servant Lyman, and my servant John Snider, and others, build a house unto my name, such a one as my servant Joseph shall show unto them, upon the place which he shall show unto them also.

23 And it shall be for a house for boarding, a house that strangers may come from afar to lodge therein; therefore let it be a good house, worthy of all acceptation, that the weary traveler may find health and safety while he shall contemplate the word of the Lord; and the corner-stone I have appointed for Zion.

24 This house shall be a healthful habitation if it be built unto my name, and if the governor which shall be appointed unto it shall not

---

[89] See Elder Russell M. Nelson, "Divine Love," *Ensign,* February 2003, 20; and excerpts in "General Authority Quotes" at the end of this chapter.

suffer any pollution to come upon it. It shall be holy, or the Lord your God will not dwell therein.

The house the Lord commands to be built (v. 22) is later given the name of Nauvoo House (v. 60). Its purpose was for strangers to be made comfortable and contemplate the word of the Lord (vv. 23–24), or to become acquainted with the latter-day movement of the Restoration. The lodging place would be comparable with the Hotel Utah, adjacent to the temple in Salt Lake City, Utah, which was built for a similar purpose.

D&C 124:25–28 • The House for the Most High

25 And again, verily I say unto you, let all my saints come from afar.

26 And send ye swift messengers, yea, chosen messengers, and say unto them: Come ye, with all your gold, and your silver, and your precious stones, and with all your antiquities; and with all who have knowledge of antiquities, that will come, may come, and bring the box-tree, and the fir-tree, and the pine-tree, together with all the precious trees of the earth;

27 And with iron, with copper, and with brass, and with zinc, and with all your precious things of the earth; and build a house to my name, for the Most High to dwell therein.

28 For there is not a place found on earth that he may come to and restore again that which was lost unto you, or which he hath taken away, even the fulness of the priesthood.

The temple that had been built in Kirtland had been left by the Saints, and Nauvoo was now the main gathering place of the Lord's people (v. 25).Although the temple had been completed in Kirtland, part of, but not the fulness of, the priesthood ordinances had been administered there (v. 28). The Prophet Joseph later taught: "The main object [of the gathering] was to build unto the Lord a house whereby He could reveal unto His people the ordinances of His house and the glories of His Kingdom, and teach the people the way of salvation; for there are certain ordinances and principles that, when they are taught and practiced, must be done in a place built for that purpose" (*TPJS*, 307–08).

D&C 124:29–36 • Baptisms for the Dead

29 For a baptismal font there is not upon the earth, that they, my

saints, may be baptized for those who are dead—

30 For this ordinance belongeth to my house, and cannot be acceptable to me, only in the days of your poverty, wherein ye are not able to build a house unto me.

31 But I command you, all ye my saints, to build a house unto me; and I grant unto you a sufficient time to build a house unto me; and during this time your baptisms shall be acceptable unto me.

32 But behold, at the end of this appointment your baptisms for your dead shall not be acceptable unto me; and if you do not these things at the end of the appointment ye shall be rejected as a church, with your dead, saith the Lord your God.

33 For verily I say unto you, that after you have had sufficient time to build a house to me, wherein the ordinance of baptizing for the dead belongeth, and for which the same was instituted from before the foundation of the world, your baptisms for your dead cannot be acceptable unto me;

34 For therein are the keys of the holy priesthood ordained, that you may receive honor and glory.

35 And after this time, your baptisms for the dead, by those who are scattered abroad, are not acceptable unto me, saith the Lord.

36 For it is ordained that in Zion, and in her stakes, and in Jerusalem, those places which I have appointed for refuge, shall be the places for your baptisms for your dead.

The Prophet Joseph "first mentioned the doctrine [baptism for the dead] in public when preaching the funeral sermon of Brother Seymour Brunson [August 19, 1840]: and have since given general instructions in the Church on the subject" (*TPJS,* 179; October 19, 1840). This revelation, January 19, 1841, supports what Joseph had been teaching the past few months. Baptisms were performed in the Mississippi River for a time, but would not be acceptable after the time for the building of the Nauvoo Temple was expired (D&C 124:31). The Church met that dead line and baptisms for the dead were performed in the temple. The Church was not rejected (v. 32). The places for baptisms for the dead, other temples, have been established, but the Jerusalem temple is yet to be built (v. 36). Today well over one hundred temples are carrying on the work that was begun in 1840.

D&C 124:37–41 • Why Moses Built a Tabernacle

37 And again, verily I say unto you, how shall your washings be acceptable unto me, except ye perform them in a house which you have built to my name?

38 For, for this cause I commanded Moses that he should build a tabernacle, that they should bear it with them in the wilderness, and to build a house in the land of promise, that those ordinances might be revealed which had been hid from before the world was.

39 Therefore, verily I say unto you, that your anointings, and your washings, and your baptisms for the dead, and your solemn assemblies, and your memorials for your sacrifices by the sons of Levi, and for your oracles in your most holy places wherein you receive conversations, and your statutes and judgments, for the beginning of the revelations and foundation of Zion, and for the glory, honor, and endowment of all her municipals, are ordained by the ordinance of my holy house, which my people are always commanded to build unto my holy name.

40 And verily I say unto you, let this house be built unto my name, that I may reveal mine ordinances therein unto my people;

41 For I deign to reveal unto my church things which have been kept hid from before the foundation of the world, things that pertain to the dispensation of the fulness of times.

The ordinances which are hid from the world (v. 37) are other ordinances of the temple. They were hidden because they were sacred: "Give not that which is holy unto the dogs, neither cast ye your pearls before swine, lest they trample them under their feet, and turn again and rend you" (3 Nephi 14:6; Matthew 7:6). The general public would not understand these ordinances, would probably ridicule them.

The tabernacle built by Moses was a transportable temple (v. 38). The Prophet Joseph taught:

. . . There are certain ordinances and principles that, when they are taught and practiced, must be done in a place or house built for that purpose.

It was the design of the councils of heaven before the world was, that the principles and laws of the priesthood should be predicated upon the gathering of the people in every age of the world. Jesus did everything to gather the people, and they would not be gathered, and He therefore poured out curses upon them. Ordinances instituted in the heavens before the foundation of the world, in the priesthood, for the salvation of men, are not to be altered or changed. All must be saved on the same principles.

It is for the same purpose that God gathers together His people in the last days, to build unto the Lord a house to prepare them for the ordinances and endowments, washings and anointings, etc. One of the ordinances of the house of the Lord is baptism for the dead. God decreed before the foundation of the world that that ordinance should be administered in a font prepared for that purpose in the house of the Lord. [*HC*, 5:423]

The various items listed in verse 39 are done in the temple, and pertain unto this last dispensation (v. 41).

D&C 124:42–55 • When the Lord Requires No More?

42 And I will show unto my servant Joseph all things pertaining to this house, and the priesthood thereof, and the place whereon it shall be built.

43 And ye shall build it on the place where you have contemplated building it, for that is the spot which I have chosen for you to build it.

44 If ye labor with all your might, I will consecrate that spot that it shall be made holy.

45 And if my people will hearken unto my voice, and unto the voice of my servants whom I have appointed to lead my people, behold, verily I say unto you, they shall not be moved out of their place.

46 But if they will not hearken to my voice, nor unto the voice of these men whom I have appointed, they shall not be blest, because they pollute mine holy grounds, and mine holy ordinances, and charters, and my holy words which I give unto them.

47 And it shall come to pass that if you build a house unto my name, and do not do the things that I say, I will not perform the oath which I make unto you, neither fulfil the promises which ye expect at my hands, saith the Lord.

48 For instead of blessings, ye, by your own works, bring cursings, wrath, indignation, and judgments upon your own heads, by your follies, and by all your abominations, which you practise before me, saith the Lord.

49 Verily, verily, I say unto you, that when I give a commandment to any of the sons of men to do a work unto my name, and those sons

of men go with all their might and with all they have to perform that work, and cease not their diligence, and their enemies come upon them and hinder them from performing that work, behold, it behooveth me to require that work no more at the hands of those sons of men, but to accept of their offerings.

50 And the iniquity and transgression of my holy laws and commandments I will visit upon the heads of those who hindered my work, unto the third and fourth generation, so long as they repent not, and hate me, saith the Lord God.

51 Therefore, for this cause have I accepted the offerings of those whom I commanded to build up a city and a house unto my name, in Jackson county, Missouri, and were hindered by their enemies, saith the Lord your God.

52 And I will answer judgment, wrath, and indignation, wailing, and anguish, and gnashing of teeth upon their heads, unto the third and fourth generation, so long as they repent not, and hate me, saith the Lord your God.

53 And this I make an example unto you, for your consolation concerning all those who have been commanded to do a work and have been hindered by the hands of their enemies, and by oppression, saith the Lord your God.

54 For I am the Lord your God, and will save all those of your brethren who have been pure of heart, and have been slain in the land of Missouri, saith the Lord.

55 And again, verily I say unto you, I command you again to build a house to my name, even in this place, that you may prove yourselves unto me that ye are faithful in all things whatsoever I command you, that I may bless you, and crown you with honor, immortality, and eternal life.

The Lord showed Moses the pattern of the tabernacle that he was to build (see Exodus 25:8–9; 40), and he built it as shown (see Exodus 39:43). Joseph Smith was likewise shown where and how to build the temple in Nauvoo, as he was promised (D&C 124:42–43). The temple was consecrated and made holy (v. 44). In spite of its later destruction, it was rebuilt in our day, and has become holy again. The promised blessings and curses are self-explanatory (vv. 45–48).

The Lord had earlier explained that He commands and revokes commandments (D&C 56:3–4). In this revelation, He explains some of the conditions of His revoking commandments. When the enemy prevents that commandment from being fulfilled, after diligent efforts to do so, He requires that work no more, but those who prevent it will be punished unto the third and fourth generation (D&C 124:49–50). This is another example of natural consequences of wickedness, their children suffer. The temple commanded to be built in Jackson County, Missouri was now revoked (vv. 51–52). It too will be built at a later date, and will be a holy place (see D&C 84:4–5; 3 Nephi 21:23; Moses 7:62). A further declaration of comfort was given to the Saints; those who were pure in heart, but had been slain in Missouri, would be saved (D&C 124:54). The repeat of the commandment to build the temple in Nauvoo (v. 55) implies that the saving ordinances that they had not received, because of the enemy, would be done for them.

D&C 124:56–61 • The Covenant Made to Abraham Fulfilled

56 And now I say unto you, as pertaining to my boarding house which I have commanded you to build for the boarding of strangers, let it be built unto my name, and let my name be named upon it, and let my servant Joseph and his house have place therein, from generation to generation.

57 For this anointing have I put upon his head, that his blessing shall also be put upon the head of his posterity after him.

58 And as I said unto Abraham concerning the kindreds of the earth, even so I say unto my servant Joseph: In thee and in thy seed shall the kindred of the earth be blessed.

59 Therefore, let my servant Joseph and his seed after him have place in that house, from generation to generation, forever and ever, saith the Lord.

60 And let the name of that house be called Nauvoo House; and let it be a delightful habitation for man, and a resting-place for the weary traveler, that he may contemplate the glory of Zion, and the glory of this, the corner-stone thereof;

61 That he may receive also the counsel from those whom I have set to be as plants of renown, and as watchmen upon her walls.

A careful reading of the covenant made to Abraham reveals that it was never fully fulfilled (see Abraham 2:9–11). For example, the land promised to Abraham, "from the river of Egypt unto the great river, the river Euphrates" (Genesis 15:18) has never been fully occupied by his seed as a covenant people of the Lord. There are other parts of the covenants that are not yet fulfilled as well.[90] Joseph Smith is designated as the man who will begin the fulfillment of this covenant in these latter days (D&C 124:57–58). The building of the Nauvoo House was to be a part of the covenant fulfillment, Nauvoo being a corner stone of the glory of Zion (v. 60). Those who were watchmen on the walls, who would give counsel to the weary traveler (v. 61), are the Church leaders of that area whenever the Church is built up there. The commencement of that corner-stone of Zion being laid is again underway.

D&C 124:62–71 • Stock for the Nauvoo House

62 Behold, verily I say unto you, let my servant George Miller, and my servant Lyman Wight, and my servant John Snider, and my servant Peter Haws, organize themselves, and appoint one of them to be a president over their quorum for the purpose of building that house.

63 And they shall form a constitution, whereby they may receive stock for the building of that house.

64 And they shall not receive less than fifty dollars for a share of stock in that house, and they shall be permitted to receive fifteen thousand dollars from any one man for stock in that house.

65 But they shall not be permitted to receive over fifteen thousand dollars stock from any one man.

66 And they shall not be permitted to receive under fifty dollars for a share of stock from any one man in that house.

67 And they shall not be permitted to receive any man, as a stock-holder in this house, except the same shall pay his stock into their hands at the time he receives stock;

68 And in proportion to the amount of stock he pays into their hands he shall receive stock in that house; but if he pays nothing into their hands he shall not receive any stock in that house.

69 And if any pay stock into their hands it shall be stock in that house, for himself, and for his generation after him, from generation to generation, so long as he and his heirs shall hold that stock, and do not sell or convey the stock away out of their hands by their own free will

---

[90] See Monte S. Nyman, "The Covenant of Abraham," In *The Pearl of Great Price: Revelations from God,* eds. H. Donl Peterson and C. Tate. [1989],155.

and act, if you will do my will, saith the Lord your God.

70 And again, verily I say unto you, if my servant George Miller, and my servant Lyman Wight, and my servant John Snider, and my servant Peter Haws, receive any stock into their hands, in moneys, or in properties wherein they receive the real value of moneys, they shall not appropriate any portion of that stock to any other purpose, only in that house.

71 And if they do appropriate any portion of that stock anywhere else, only in that house, without the consent of the stockholder, and do not repay fourfold for the stock which they appropriate anywhere else, only in that house, they shall be accursed, and shall be moved out of their place, saith the Lord God; for I, the Lord, am God, and cannot be mocked in any of these things.

The limits on stock purchased may have been to control the operation of the Nauvoo House. Those who paid more may have attempted to dictate how it was to function, while the minimum amount was to prevent too many being involved in its management. To not sell the stock was probably to keep it under the control of the Church members. The revelation gives no reason for the limits.

D&C 124:72–83 • The Individuals Who May Buy Stock

72 Verily I say unto you, let my servant Joseph pay stock into their hands for the building of that house, as seemeth him good; but my servant Joseph cannot pay over fifteen thousand dollars stock in that house, nor under fifty dollars; neither can any other man, saith the Lord.

73 And there are others also who wish to know my will concerning them, for they have asked it at my hands.

74 Therefore, I say unto you concerning my servant Vinson Knight, if he will do my will let him put stock into that house for himself, and for his generation after him, from generation to generation.

75 And let him lift up his voice long and loud, in the midst of the people, to plead the cause of the poor and the needy; and let him not fail, neither let his heart faint; and I will accept of his offerings, for they shall not be unto me as the offerings of Cain, for he shall be mine, saith the Lord.

76 Let his family rejoice and turn away their hearts from affliction; for I have chosen him and anointed him, and he shall be honored in the midst of his house, for I will forgive all his sins, saith the Lord. Amen.

77 Verily I say unto you, let my servant Hyrum put stock into that house as seemeth him good, for himself and his generation after him, from generation to generation.

78 Let my servant Isaac Galland put stock into that house; for I, the Lord, love him for the work he hath done, and will forgive all his sins; therefore, let him be remembered for an interest in that house from generation to generation.

79 Let my servant Isaac Galland be appointed among you, and be ordained by my servant William Marks, and be blessed of him, to go with my servant Hyrum to accomplish the work that my servant Joseph shall point out to them, and they shall be greatly blessed.

80 Let my servant William Marks pay stock into that house, as seemeth him good, for himself and his generation, from generation to generation.

81 Let my servant Henry G. Sherwood pay stock into that house, as seemeth him good, for himself and his seed after him, from generation to generation.

82 Let my servant William Law pay stock into that house, for himself and his seed after him, from generation to generation.

83 If he will do my will let him not take his family unto the eastern lands, even unto Kirtland; nevertheless, I, the Lord, will build up Kirtland, but I, the Lord, have a scourge prepared for the inhabitants thereof.

Why the individuals in this revelation are especially mentioned about buying stock is because they had asked about it (v. 73). The Lord probably began with Joseph Smith to show that there were no exceptions to the limits of stock purchase (v. 72). Vinson Knight being told to plead the cause of the poor may have been connected with his call "to preside over the bishopric" which was given later in the revelation (v. 141). Cain's offering was rejected by the Lord (see Genesis 4:3–5; Hebrews 11:4; *TPJS,* 58–59, 169), and was used as an example to Brother Knight. Other callings are mentioned, but are not commented on here (v. 79). The scourge that was prepared for the inhabitants of Kirtland was lifted on October 14, 1979 by the President of the Quorum of the Twelve Apostles, Ezra Taft Benson, as ground was broken for a "meeting house in Kirtland, the first building of the Church since the temple was completed in 1836."[91]

D&C 124:84–90 • Worship the Golden Calf

84 And with my servant Almon Babbitt, there are many things with which I am not pleased; behold, he aspireth to establish his counsel instead of the counsel which I have ordained, even that of the Presidency of my Church; and he setteth up a golden calf for the worship of my people.

85 Let no man go from this place who has come here essaying to keep my commandments.

86 If they live here let them live unto me; and if they die let them die unto me; for they shall rest from all their labors here, and shall continue their works.

87 Therefore, let my servant William put his trust in me, and cease to fear concerning his family, because of the sickness of the land. If ye love me, keep my commandments; and the sickness of the land shall redound to your glory.

88 Let my servant William go and proclaim my everlasting gospel with a loud voice, and with great joy, as he shall be moved upon by my Spirit, unto the inhabitants of Warsaw, and also unto the inhabitants of Carthage, and also unto the inhabitants of Burlington, and also unto the inhabitants of Madison, and await patiently and diligently for further instructions at my general conference, saith the Lord.

89 If he will do my will let him from henceforth hearken to the counsel of my servant Joseph, and with his interest support the cause of the poor, and publish the new translation of my holy word unto the inhabitants of the earth.

90 And if he will do this I will bless him with a multiplicity of blessings, that he shall not be forsaken, nor his seed be found begging bread.

Nothing is said about Almon Babbitt buying stock, but it seems to be a refusal until he would receive counsel from "the Presidency of my Church" (v. 84). President Spencer W. Kimball later used his example as an admonition to the Church.

William Law is admonished to hearken to the counsel of Joseph

---

[91] See Karl Ricks Anderson, *Joseph Smith's Kirtland* (1989), 246–47.

Smith, but it is apparently in relation to his new calling as counselor to the Prophet Joseph, announced in verse 91. He was also to support the cause of publishing "the new translation of my holy word" (v. 89) or the Bible. Its publication was also a revoking of a previous commandment to not publish it until it was finished (D&C 42:57). He now commands them to finish it because it would not be finished before Joseph's martyrdom. The Lord undoubtedly knew this before, but the Church, and those who had been working on it, did not know it. The Lord wanted it worked on to get as much done as they could before publishing it. It was a vital part of the Restoration.

D&C 124:91–102 • New Appointments in the Priesthood

91 And again, verily I say unto you, let my servant William be appointed, ordained, and anointed, as counselor unto my servant Joseph, in the room of my servant Hyrum, that my servant Hyrum may take the office of Priesthood and Patriarch, which was appointed unto him by his father, by blessing and also by right;

92 That from henceforth he shall hold the keys of the patriarchal blessings upon the heads of all my people,

93 That whoever he blesses shall be blessed, and whoever he curses shall be cursed; that whatsoever he shall bind on earth shall be bound in heaven; and whatsoever he shall loose on earth shall be loosed in heaven.

94 And from this time forth I appoint unto him that he may be a prophet, and a seer, and a revelator unto my church, as well as my servant Joseph;

95 That he may act in concert also with my servant Joseph; and that he shall receive counsel from my servant Joseph, who shall show unto him the keys whereby he may ask and receive, and be crowned with the same blessing, and glory, and honor, and priesthood, and gifts of the priesthood, that once were put upon him that was my servant Oliver Cowdery;

96 That my servant Hyrum may bear record of the things which I shall show unto him, that his name may be had in honorable remembrance from generation to generation, forever and ever.

97 Let my servant William Law also receive the keys by which he may ask and receive blessings; let him be humble before me, and be without guile, and he shall receive of my Spirit, even the Comforter,

which shall manifest unto him the truth of all things, and shall give him, in the very hour, what he shall say.

98 And these signs shall follow him—he shall heal the sick, he shall cast out devils, and shall be delivered from those who would administer unto him deadly poison;

99 And he shall be led in paths where the poisonous serpent cannot lay hold upon his heel, and he shall mount up in the imagination of his thoughts as upon eagles' wings.

100 And what if I will that he should raise the dead, let him not withhold his voice.

101 Therefore, let my servant William cry aloud and spare not, with joy and rejoicing, and with hosannas to him that sitteth upon the throne forever and ever, saith the Lord your God.

102 Behold, I say unto you, I have a mission in store for my servant William, and my servant Hyrum, and for them alone; and let my servant Joseph tarry at home, for he is needed. The remainder I will show unto you hereafter. Even so. Amen.

William Law was called as a counselor to Joseph Smith, and replaced Hyrum Smith who had been serving since the excommunication of Frederick G. Williams. Hyrum was called to be the patriarch to the Church to replace his father who had passed away four months previously. Just prior to his death, Joseph Sen. blessed his son Hyrum:

"My son, Hyrum, I seal upon your head your patriarchal blessing, which I placed upon your head before, for that shall be verified. In addition to this I now give you my dying blessing. You shall have a season of peace, so that you shall have sufficient rest to accomplish the work which God has given you to do. You shall be as firm as the pillars of heaven unto the end of your days. I now seal upon your head the patriarchal power, and you shall bless the people. This is my dying blessing upon your head in the name of Jesus. Amen."[92] This revelation "by blessing" (v. 91) confirms the blessing of his father.

Hyrum is also called to replace Oliver Cowdery as Assistant President, or second elder of the Church (vv. 94–95). The office of Assistant President is not understood by many members of the Church. It was an office that was no longer needed after the martyrdom, but needed until

---

[92] *History of Joseph Smith, By His Mother, Lucy Mack Smith* [1958], 309.

that time as a second witness of the Restoration. More will be said of this office in chapter 28, under the discussion of D&C 136:36–39 (see also "General Authority Quotes," Joseph Fielding Smith). Note that he was to be "a prophet, and a seer, and a revelator unto my church, as well as my servant Joseph" (D&C 124:94), and "that he may bear record of the things which I shall show unto him" (v. 95). The things he was to be shown were apparently the things that Oliver had seen to qualify him as a second witness with Joseph (see D&C 6:36–37).

Further instructions were also given to William Law. As a member of the First Presidency, he was an Apostle and has the blessings that were given to them. The truth of all things, and the signs to follow even to the raising of the dead, were some of those blessings (D&C 124:97–100). The callings of William and Hyrum were special for them (v. 102).

D&C 124:103–110 • Sidney Repent

103 And again, verily I say unto you, if my servant Sidney will serve me and be counselor unto my servant Joseph, let him arise and come up and stand in the office of his calling, and humble himself before me.

104 And if he will offer unto me an acceptable offering, and acknowledgments, and remain with my people, behold, I, the Lord your God, will heal him that he shall be healed; and he shall lift up his voice again on the mountains, and be a spokesman before my face.

105 Let him come and locate his family in the neighborhood in which my servant Joseph resides.

106 And in all his journeyings let him lift up his voice as with the sound of a trump, and warn the inhabitants of the earth to flee the wrath to come.

107 Let him assist my servant Joseph, and also let my servant William Law assist my servant Joseph, in making a solemn proclamation unto the kings of the earth, even as I have before said unto you.

108 If my servant Sidney will do my will, let him not remove his family unto the eastern lands, but let him change their habitation, even as I have said.

109 Behold, it is not my will that he shall seek to find safety and refuge out of the city which I have appointed unto you, even the city of Nauvoo.

110 Verily I say unto you, even now, if he will hearken unto my

voice, it shall be well with him. Even so. Amen.

Sidney was given a conditional blessing. He was to do the thing that he had been called and ordained to do. He was to be a counselor to Joseph, a spokesman for Joseph, help with the proclamation to the world, and not move to the east (vv. 103–109). If he did these things, it would be well for him (v. 110). If he did not do them, it is implied that it would not be well for him. Unfortunately, he chose not to follow counsel, and it was not well for him. We will leave further comment to a study of Church history.

D&C 124:111–118 • Two More Stewardships

111 And again, verily I say unto you, let my servant Amos Davies pay stock into the hands of those whom I have appointed to build a house for boarding, even the Nauvoo House.

112 This let him do if he will have an interest; and let him hearken unto the counsel of my servant Joseph, and labor with his own hands that he may obtain the confidence of men.

113 And when he shall prove himself faithful in all things that shall be entrusted unto his care, yea, even a few things, he shall be made ruler over many;

114 Let him therefore abase himself that he may be exalted. Even so. Amen.

115 And again, verily I say unto you, if my servant Robert D. Foster will obey my voice, let him build a house for my servant Joseph, according to the contract which he has made with him, as the door shall be open to him from time to time.

116 And let him repent of all his folly, and clothe himself with charity; and cease to do evil, and lay aside all his hard speeches;

117 And pay stock also into the hands of the quorum of the Nauvoo House, for himself and for his generation after him, from generation to generation;

118 And hearken unto the counsel of my servants Joseph, and Hyrum, and William Law, and unto the authorities which I have called to lay the foundation of Zion; and it shall be well with him forever and ever. Even so. Amen.

Both Amos Davies and Robert D. Thompson are admonished to

accept counsel from Joseph, and Brother Foster was also to receive counsel from Hyrum and William Law (vv. 112, 118). Note that Sidney, a member of the First Presidency, was not included. Both men were invited to buy stock. The other admonitions are self-explanatory.

D&C 124:119–122 • Requirements for Stock Holders

119 And again, verily I say unto you, let no man pay stock to the quorum of the Nauvoo House unless he shall be a believer in the Book of Mormon, and the revelations I have given unto you, saith the Lord your God;

120 For that which is more or less than this cometh of evil, and shall be attended with cursings and not blessings, saith the Lord your God. Even so. Amen.

121 And again, verily I say unto you, let the quorum of the Nauvoo House have a just recompense of wages for all their labors which they do in building the Nauvoo House; and let their wages be as shall be agreed among themselves, as pertaining to the price thereof.

122 And let every man who pays stock bear his proportion of their wages, if it must needs be, for their support, saith the Lord; otherwise, their labors shall be accounted unto them for stock in that house. Even so. Amen.

Only those who believed in the Book of Mormon, and the revelations [the Doctrine and Covenants] was another safeguard to keep control of the Nauvoo House within the Church (v. 119). The curses are not specified, but would probably be related to the love of money (see 1 Timothy 6:10). The just recompense of wages for labor is a principle of consecration and stewardship that is from the Lord (D&C 42:72).

D&C 124:123–126 • The Keys of the Priesthood Held

123 Verily I say unto you, I now give unto you the officers belonging to my Priesthood, that ye may hold the keys thereof, even the Priesthood which is after the order of Melchizedek, which is after the order of mine Only Begotten Son.

124 First, I give unto you Hyrum Smith to be a patriarch unto you, to hold the sealing blessings of my church, even the Holy Spirit of promise, whereby ye are sealed up unto the day of redemption, that ye

may not fall notwithstanding the hour of temptation that may come upon you.

125 I give unto you my servant Joseph to be a presiding elder over all my church, to be a translator, a revelator, a seer, and prophet.

126 I give unto him for counselors my servant Sidney Rigdon and my servant William Law, that these may constitute a quorum and First Presidency, to receive the oracles for the whole church.

Keys are the directing power of the priesthood. The priesthood is the power of God given to man, but it must be used as directed. The power is delegated through Jesus Christ, whose power it is. As stated before, the priesthood was originally "called the Holy Priesthood, after the Order of the Son of God. But out of respect or reverence to the name of the Supreme Being, to avoid the too frequent repetition of his name, they, the church, in ancient days, called that priesthood after Melchizedek, or the Melchizedek Priesthood" (D&C 107:3–4).

Hyrum was given the keys to bless the Church (v. 124). His blessings did not seal the people unto eternal life, but gave them directions to follow to obtain that blessing unto the day of redemption. In the words of President Joseph Fielding Smith: "The Holy Spirit of Promise is not the Second Comforter. The Holy Spirit of Promise is the stamp of approval upon every ordinance that is done righteously; and when covenants are broken he removes the seal."[93] It was a blessing also to direct one from temptation.

As stated periodically throughout the Doctrine and Covenants, Joseph was the presiding elder of the Church, with all his other titles (v. 125; see also 90:2; 43:2–3; 28:1–2; 21:4–5). With his two counselors, the quorum of the First Presidency, he holds the oracles, the infallible authority, or the keys for the whole Church. It is the authority not the man that is infallible. The Church is organized to protect it from losing those keys, as discussed in Doctrine and Covenants 107).

D&C 124:127–130

127 I give unto you my servant Brigham Young to be a president over the Twelve traveling council;

---

[93] *Doctrines of Salvation*, 1:55.

128 Which Twelve hold the keys to open up the authority of my kingdom upon the four corners of the earth, and after that to send my word to every creature.

129 They are Heber C. Kimball, Parley P. Pratt, Orson Pratt, Orson Hyde, William Smith, John Taylor, John E. Page, Wilford Woodruff, Willard Richards, George A. Smith;

130 David Patten I have taken unto myself; behold, his priesthood no man taketh from him; but, verily I say unto you, another may be appointed unto the same calling.

Brigham Young, as the President of the Twelve traveling high council, or the Twelve Apostles (v. 127; see 107:23), held the keys to open the doors of the nations unto the four corners of the earth, to take unto them the kingdom of God, or the restored gospel (D&C 124:128; see 112:21). The Twelve Apostles named here are not the original Twelve, as many had apostatized, and David Patten had been killed. Others had been appointed in their stead (v. 130; see 118:6). About six months later, July 9, 1841, Brigham was given a revelation, at his house (*HC,* 4:382), through the Prophet Joseph.

D&C 126 • Brigham Young

1 DEAR and well-beloved brother, Brigham Young, verily thus saith the Lord unto you: My servant Brigham, it is no more required at your hand to leave your family as in times past, for your offering is acceptable to me.

2 I have seen your labor and toil in journeyings for my name.

3 I therefore command you to send my word abroad, and take especial care of your family from this time, henceforth and forever. Amen.

Brigham's commandment to remain with his family, at this time, seems to be a preparatory period for him to be ready to lead the church after the martyrdom of the Prophet. His labors as a member of the Twelve had proved his worthiness and qualities for the next step in his mortal probation.

D&C 124:131–132 • The High Council of Zion

131 And again, I say unto you, I give unto you a high council, for the corner-stone of Zion—

132 Namely, Samuel Bent, Henry G. Sherwood, George W. Harris, Charles C. Rich, Thomas Grover, Newel Knight, David Dort, Dunbar Wilson—Seymour Brunson I have taken unto myself; no man taketh his priesthood, but another may be appointed unto the same priesthood in his stead; and verily I say unto you, let my servant Aaron Johnson be ordained unto this calling in his stead—David Fullmer, Alpheus Cutler, William Huntington.

The high council of Zion was probably named as such, instead of the Nauvoo Stake of Zion, because of the designation of the stake as a cornerstone of Zion (D&C 124:2, 23). It apparently had the same function as a stake high council. A corner stake of a tent, depending on the shape of the tent, usually has more pressure placed against it. When the New Jerusalem is established as the center place of Zion (see D&C 57:3), the high council may have a different function—although certainly related—than a regular stake high council.

D&C 124:133–142 • Other Councils

133 And again, I give unto you Don C. Smith to be a president over a quorum of high priests;

134 Which ordinance is instituted for the purpose of qualifying those who shall be appointed standing presidents or servants over different stakes scattered abroad;

135 And they may travel also if they choose, but rather be ordained for standing presidents; this is the office of their calling, saith the Lord your God.

136 I give unto him Amasa Lyman and Noah Packard for counselors, that they may preside over the quorum of high priests of my church, saith the Lord.

137 And again, I say unto you, I give unto you John A. Hicks, Samuel Williams, and Jesse Baker, which priesthood is to preside over the quorum of elders, which quorum is instituted for standing ministers; nevertheless they may travel, yet they are ordained to be standing ministers to my church, saith the Lord.

138 And again, I give unto you Joseph Young, Josiah Butterfield, Daniel Miles, Henry Herriman, Zera Pulsipher, Levi Hancock, James Foster, to preside over the quorum of seventies;

139 Which quorum is instituted for traveling elders to bear record of my name in all the world, wherever the traveling high council, mine

apostles, shall send them to prepare a way before my face.

140 The difference between this quorum and the quorum of elders is that one is to travel continually, and the other is to preside over the churches from time to time; the one has the responsibility of presiding from time to time, and the other has no responsibility of presiding, saith the Lord your God.

141 And again, I say unto you, I give unto you Vinson Knight, Samuel H. Smith, and Shadrach Roundy, if he will receive it, to preside over the bishopric; a knowledge of said bishopric is given unto you in the book of Doctrine and Covenants.

142 And again, I say unto you, Samuel Rolfe and his counselors for priests, and the president of the teachers and his counselors, and also the president of the deacons and his counselors, and also the president of the stake and his counselors.

The high priests presidency is to qualify, or prepare, men to serve as standing presidents (v. 134). Standing presidents are stake presidents, or bishops who are not literal descendants of Aaron, who are called to serve as bishops of local wards. These officers do not travel to other areas. Men who are called as mission presidents are also high priests who are called to travel for the duration of their mission call (see v. 135). Today, the stake president is the high priest president, and is responsible for the training and selection of men to be bishops, and other leadership roles in the stake and wards.

The seventies are the traveling elders who are called to travel continually under the direction of the Twelve Apostles (vv. 139–140). Their function has changed as the Church has grown. Today there are two quorums who serve as General Authorities and travel throughout the world. Other quorums serve as Regional Authorities, and travel throughout their assigned region. As the Church grows, the number of these quorums will increase. The elders preside from time to time as called to do so.

Edward Partridge was called as the first bishop of the Church (D&C 41:9). Newel K. Whitney was later called as the bishop in Kirtland (D&C 72:8). The call of George Miller, in this revelation, was to replace Edward Partridge D&C 124:20). Therefore, Vinson Knight's call was to serve as a presiding bishop (v. 141).[94] Perhaps Edward Partridge fulfilled both roles during his appointed ministry, but the two offices are now separated. No comment is needed on verse 142.

D&C 124:143–145 • The Purpose of Keys

143 The above offices I have given unto you, and the keys thereof, for helps and for governments, for the work of the ministry and the perfecting of my saints.

144 And a commandment I give unto you, that you should fill all these offices and approve of those names which I have mentioned, or else disapprove of them at my general conference;

145 And that ye should prepare rooms for all these offices in my house when you build it unto my name, saith the Lord your God. Even so. Amen.

The offices and keys of the priesthood were given for helps [assistance] and government [administering], for the work of the ministry, and for the perfection of the Saints (v. 143). A similar statement was made by Paul to the Saints at Ephesus (4:11–13). The needed unity for the Church to become perfected comes through the priesthood.

DOCTRINE AND COVENANTS 125

*H*istorical Setting: "On March 30, 1841, the Prophet asked and received the answer" (*HC*, 4:311).

1 WHAT is the will of the Lord concerning the saints in the Territory of Iowa?

2 Verily, thus saith the Lord, I say unto you, if those who call themselves by my name and are essaying to be my saints, if they will do my will and keep my commandments concerning them, let them gather themselves together unto the places which I shall appoint unto them by my servant Joseph, and build up cities unto my name, that they may be prepared for that which is in store for a time to come.

3 Let them build up a city unto my name upon the land opposite

---

[94] According to President John Taylor, this call was as the first Presiding Bishop of the Church (see *Journal of Discourses,* 22:200).

the city of Nauvoo, and let the name of Zarahemla be named upon it.

4 And let all those who come from the east, and the west, and the north, and the south, that have desires to dwell therein, take up their inheritance in the same, as well as in the city of Nashville, or in the city of Nauvoo, and in all the stakes which I have appointed, saith the Lord.

[the answer needs no commentary]

General Authority Quotes

—*Elder Russell M. Nelson* • D&C 124:15

While divine love can be called perfect, infinite, enduring, and universal, it cannot correctly be characterized as *unconditional*. The word does not appear in the scriptures. On the other hand, many verses affirm that the higher levels of love the Father and the Son feel for each of us—and certain divine blessings stemming from that love—are *conditional*.

Several forms of conditional expression may be found in the scriptures:

- "*If*. . . [certain conditions exist], *then*. . . [certain consequences follow]." (The indicators if and then may be written or implied.)

- "*Inasmuch as*. . . [certain conditions exist], . . . [certain consequences follow]."

- "*Except*. . . *cannot*. . . "

- "*Prove*. . . , *if*. . . " For example, a verse pertaining to our creation reveals a prime purpose for our sojourn here in mortality: "We will *prove* them herewith, to see *if* they will do all things whatsoever the Lord their God shall command them. Life here is a period of mortal probation. Our thoughts and actions determine whether our mortal probation can merit heavenly approbation. [Many examples and footnotes follow, but are not included here]. . . .

Why is divine love conditional? Because God loves us and wants us to be happy. "Happiness is the object and design of our existence; and will be the end thereof if we pursue the path that leads to it; and this path is virtue, uprightness, faithfulness, holiness, and keeping all the commandments of God." [*TPJS*, 255–56; emphasis added]

Understanding that divine love and blessings are not truly "unconditional" can defend us against common fallacies such as these: "Since God's love is unconditional, He will love me regardless. . . "; or "Since 'God is love,' He will love me unconditionally, regardless. . . "

These arguments are used by anti-Christs to woo people with deception. . . .[quotes Alma 1:4; 41:10; 3 Nephi 12:20]

Does this mean that God does not love the sinner? Of course not. Divine love is infinite and universal. The Savior loves both saints and sinners. ["Divine Love," *Ensign*, February 2003, 20–25; see the entire article, if available]

—President Joseph Fielding Smith • D&C 124:28–32, 94–95

The Kirtland Temple holds a peculiar place in the annals of temple building. It is not like other temples. It was built primarily for the restoration of keys of authority. In the receiving of these keys the fullness of the gospel ordinances is revealed. The keys of salvation and exaltation for both the living and the dead were given within its sacred walls. An endowment, such as was necessary at the time, was also given. This was not as complete as the endowment later revealed.

In the Kirtland Temple there was no provision made for the salvation of the dead. It had no baptismal font, for it was only a preparatory temple. It had no provision for the endowment ordinances which were later revealed. It was a temple, however, and fully answered the purpose of its creation. [*Doctrines of Salvation,* 2:242]

Some of those who destroy the work of God, have declared that the Church was rejected with its dead, because the temple at Nauvoo was not finished; and, say they, the Lord, by revelation, declared that he would give the saints sufficient time to build a house (temple) unto him, and if they failed to build it in the sufficient time, they would be rejected with their dead. The fact is, the Nauvoo Temple was built, and many of the saints received their endowments in it and labored for their dead before they were finally driven from Nauvoo by their enemies.

But the meaning of this revelation is perverted; the Lord did not say he would reject the Church, with its dead, if they failed to build the temple, but that they would be rejected if they did not perform the ordinances for their dead in the temple when it was prepared for that purpose. [*Doctrines of Salvation,* 2:171]

The Prophet Joseph Smith was alone in his first vision. He was alone when the angel Moroni first came to him and revealed the Book of Mormon, but whenever keys were to be bestowed, when the Lord had light and information to reveal in which the power of the priesthood was to play a part, Joseph Smith and one other witness received the blessings.

It was Oliver Cowdery who was appointed to stand with Joseph

Smith to hold the keys of this dispensation [Recounts the bestowel of the Aaronic and the Melchizedek Priesthood, and the Kirtland Temple receiving of keys]. . . .

. . . In this manner Oliver Cowdery was appointed and ordained to stand with the Prophet Joseph Smith as an associate and witness, holding all the authority and keys of this glorious of all dispensations—the dispensation of the fulness of times. . . .

. . . By revelation through Joseph Smith, Hyrum was called and ordained to the priesthood and standing once held by Oliver Cowdery. Hyrum received a double portion, not only was he called to become the Patriarch of the Church, which was his birthright, but at the same time, the Lord said to him [quotes D&C 124:94–96]. . . .

In accord with this calling and commandment, the Prophet Joseph Smith conferred all the keys, authority and gifts of the priesthood which he, the Prophet, held, and which were formerly held by Oliver Cowdery. The Lord also revealed to Hyrum Smith all that was necessary to make him and to a full degree, a witness his brother Joseph, as a prophet, seer, revelator and president of the Church, and to stand at all time and all eternity at the head of this dispensation with his brother Joseph, a witness for Jesus Christ. [*Doctrines of Salvation,* 1:217–219]

—President Howard W. Hunter • D&C 124:45

To those who have not received their temple blessings, or who do not hold a current temple recommend, may I encourage you in humility and love to work towards the day that you can enter into the house of the Lord. He has promised those who are faithful to their covenants "And if my people will hearken unto my voice, and unto the voice of my servants whom I have appointed to lead my people, behold, verily I say unto you, they shall not be moved out of their place" (D&C 124:45).

—President Spencer W. Kimball • D&C 124:84

We fear that never in the history of the world has there ever been so many people bowing to the god of lust than there were bowing to golden calves and the images of wood and stone and metal. This idolatry, so closely associated with the destruction of mind and body, could inundate the world. [CR, April 1975, 7]

Chapter Twenty-Four

Baptisms for the Dead

D&C 127–130

DOCTRINE AND COVENANTS 127–130

Historical Setting: "September 1, 1842. . . . A letter from the Prophet to the Saints at Nauvoo—Directions on Baptism for the dead" (*HC*, 5:142; now Doctrine and Covenants 127).

SECTION 127 • OUTLINE

➢ 127:1–4   Joseph leaves for a short season because his enemies are in pursuit; his agents and clerks will take care of his business.

    a.   His perils may be because of his being foreordained for some good (v. 2).

    b.   He feels like Paul, to glory in tribulation; God will deliver him. (vv. 2–3).

    c.   Let the temple work continue; if they persecute you, so persecuted they the prophets, and there is a reward in heaven (v. 4).

➢ 127:5–8   A word in relation to the baptism for your dead.

    a.   A recorder should be an eye-witness of your baptisms (v. 6).

    b.   Whatsoever you bind on earth shall be bound in heaven (v. 7).

    c.   The Lord is about to restore many things pertaining to the priesthood (v. 8).

⮞ 127:9–12   All the records are to be put in the archives of the temple, and
              held in remembrance for generations.

    a.   I will write the words of the Lord from time to time
         (v. 10).

    b.   The prince of the world comes, but he has nothing in me
         (v. 11).

    c.   My prayer is that you all may be saved (v. 12).

Introduction

As Jesus met with His Apostles at the Last Supper, He said: "I have
yet many things to say unto you, but ye cannot bear them now" (John
16:12). When did He tell them these things? The answer is in the book
of Acts: "To whom also he shewed himself alive after his passion by many
infallible proofs, being seen of them forty days, and speaking of the things
pertaining to the kingdom of God" (Acts 1:3).

In 1895, a Coptic [Egyptian] manuscript was discovered that tells
of the teachings of Jesus Christ during His forty-day ministry in Jerusalem
following His resurrection. His message introduced work for the dead.
Two of the most learned modern church historians of the New Testament
Church era promptly declared the manuscript authentic, and not Gnostic
or of the Egyptian Church. One of these scholars produced a number
of other manuscript fragments matching the Coptic text word for word,
in a half dozen languages.[95] Therefore, Jesus did instruct His Apostles
further, and His subject was doing work for the dead. Joseph Smith here
instructs the Church members on the subject.

TEXT AND COMMENTARY

D&C 127:1–4 • Joseph Takes Leave

1 FORASMUCH as the Lord has revealed unto me that my enemies,
both in Missouri and this State, were again in the pursuit of me; and
inasmuch as they pursue me without a cause, and have not the least
shadow or coloring of justice or right on their side in the getting up of

---

[95] Hugh Nibley, a series of articles published in the *Improvement Era,* December
1948 through April 1949; later published in *The World And The Prophets* [1954],
149–156.

their prosecutions against me; and inasmuch as their pretensions are all founded in falsehood of the blackest dye, I have thought it expedient and wisdom in me to leave the place for a short season, for my own safety and the safety of this people. I would say to all those with whom I have business, that I have left my affairs with agents and clerks who will transact all business in a prompt and proper manner, and will see that all my debts are canceled in due time, by turning out property, or otherwise, as the case may require, or as the circumstances may admit of. When I learn that the storm is fully blown over, then I will return to you again.

2 And as for the perils which I am called to pass through, they seem but a small thing to me, as the envy and wrath of man have been my common lot all the days of my life; and for what cause it seems mysterious, unless I was ordained from before the foundation of the world for some good end, or bad, as you may choose to call it. Judge ye for yourselves. God knoweth all these things, whether it be good or bad. But nevertheless, deep water is what I am wont to swim in. It all has become a second nature to me; and I feel, like Paul, to glory in tribulation; for to this day has the God of my fathers delivered me out of them all, and will deliver me from henceforth; for behold, and lo, I shall triumph over all my enemies, for the Lord God hath spoken it.

3 Let all the saints rejoice, therefore, and be exceedingly glad; for Israel's God is their God, and he will mete out a just recompense of reward upon the heads of all their oppressors.

4 And again, verily thus saith the Lord: Let the work of my temple, and all the works which I have appointed unto you, be continued on and not cease; and let your diligence, and your perseverance, and patience, and your works be redoubled, and you shall in nowise lose your reward, saith the Lord of Hosts. And if they persecute you, so persecuted they the prophets and righteous men that were before you. For all this there is a reward in heaven.

Joseph was foreordained (v. 2), and it was foreknown that he would be known for evil and persecuted (see JS—H 1:33, D&C 122:6). The Lord spoke to him as he wrote (see D&C 128:2). He reminded him that previous prophets had been persecuted (see Matthew 5:12), but they would have a reward in heaven (v. 4).

D&C 127:5–8 • A Word on Baptism for Your Dead

5 And again, I give unto you a word in relation to the baptism for your dead.

6 Verily, thus saith the Lord unto you concerning your dead: When any of you are baptized for your dead, let there be a recorder, and let him be eye-witness of your baptisms; let him hear with his ears, that he may testify of a truth, saith the Lord;

7 That in all your recordings it may be recorded in heaven; whatsoever you bind on earth, may be bound in heaven; whatsoever you loose on earth, may be loosed in heaven;

8 For I am about to restore many things to the earth, pertaining to the priesthood, saith the Lord of Hosts.

A recorder is a second witness (v. 6), and meets the law of the Lord (see Matthew 18:16; Deuteronomy 19:15). The binding power on earth being bound in heaven (v. 7) was also a power given to the Apostle Peter (see Matthew 16:19). It means to hold securely. Bound in heaven is to be firmly fixed and eternally secured together. The promise to restore other things, pertaining to the priesthood (v. 8), was probably referring to other temple ordinances.

D&C 127:9–12 • The Archives of the Holy Temple

9 And again, let all the records be had in order, that they may be put in the archives of my holy temple, to be held in remembrance from generation to generation, saith the Lord of Hosts.

10 I will say to all the saints, that I desired, with exceedingly great desire, to have addressed them from the stand on the subject of baptism for the dead, on the following Sabbath. But inasmuch as it is out of my power to do so, I will write the word of the Lord from time to time, on that subject, and send it to you by mail, as well as many other things.

11 I now close my letter for the present, for the want of more time; for the enemy is on the alert, and as the Savior said, the prince of this world cometh, but he hath nothing in me.

12 Behold, my prayer to God is that you all may be saved. And I subscribe myself your servant in the Lord, prophet and seer of the Church of Jesus Christ of Latter-day Saints.

The records have been stored in the archives for many years (v. 9), and are available for future generations to know what work has been done. Joseph writing the word of the Lord from time to time (v. 10) was met partially five days later when the current Doctrine and Covenants 128 was written. The prince of this world (v. 11) is Satan. This verse is a quote from John 14:30. The Joseph Smith Translation makes the verse much clearer: "Hereafter I will not talk much with you; for the prince of *darkness, who* is of this world, cometh, *but* hath *no power over me, but he hath power over you*" (italics show changes).

DOCTRINE AND COVENANTS 128

Historical Setting: "Tuesday, September 6, 1842. Letter of the Prophet to the Church—Further directions on Baptism for the Dead" (*HC*, 5:148)

The Prophet Joseph Smith said: "If there is one word of the Lord that supports the doctrine of baptism for the dead, it is enough to establish it as a true doctrine" (*TPJS*, 201). The revelations studied in this chapter give several scriptural supports, as well as other instructions on the subject.

SECTION 128 • OUTLINE

➤ 128:1–5   Joseph resumes the subject of baptism for the dead since pursued by enemies.

     a.   Let a recorder be appointed in each ward of the city (v. 3).

     b.   Let a general recorder enter the record on the general Church book (v. 4).

     c.   It is the will of the Lord for the salvation of the dead without knowledge (v. 5).

➤ 128:6–9   Revelation 29:12 explained.

➤ 128:10–13   Matthew 16:18–19 explained.

➤ 128:13–15   1 Corinthians 15:46–48 explained.

➤ 128:16   1 Corinthians 15:29 quoted.

➤ 128:17–18   Malachi 4:5–6 explained.

➤ 128:19–21   Voices from heaven, Moroni, God, and other.

➤ 128:22–23   Brethren let us go forward and not backward in so great a
cause.
  a.   Let the dead speak praise to the King Immanuel (v. 22).
  b.   Let the mountains and valleys tell the wonders of your
       Eternal King (v. 23).
  c.   Let the morning stars sing together, and the sons of God
       shout for joy (v. 23).

➤ 128:24–25   The great day of the Lord is at hand, who can abide the day
of His coming.
  a.   Let us offer a righteous offering of a book of the records
       of our dead (v. 24).
  b.   Joseph will continue the subject another time (v. 25).

TEXT AND COMMENTARY

128:1–5 • Baptism for the Dead Resumed

1 AS I stated to you in my letter before I left my place, that I would
write to you from time to time and give you information in relation to
many subjects, I now resume the subject of the baptism for the dead,
as that subject seems to occupy my mind, and press itself upon my
feelings the strongest, since I have been pursued by my enemies.

2 I wrote a few words of revelation to you concerning a recorder. I
have had a few additional views in relation to this matter, which I now
certify. That is, it was declared in my former letter that there should be
a recorder, who should be eye-witness, and also to hear with his ears,
that he might make a record of a truth before the Lord.

3 Now, in relation to this matter it would be very difficult for one
recorder to be present at all times, and to do all the business. To obviate
this difficulty, there can be a recorder appointed in each ward of the city,
who is well qualified for taking accurate minutes; and let him be very
particular and precise in taking the whole proceedings, certifying in his
record that he saw with his eyes, and heard with his ears, giving the date,
and names, and so forth, and the history of the whole transaction;
naming also some three individuals that are present, if there be any

present, who can at any time when called upon certify to the same, that in the mouth of two or three witnesses every word may be established.

4 Then, let there be a general recorder, to whom these other records can be handed, being attended with certificates over their own signatures, certifying that the record they have made is true. Then the general church recorder can enter the record on the general church book, with the certificates and all the attending witnesses, with his own statement that he verily believes the above statement and records to be true, from his knowledge of the general character and appointment of those men by the church. And when this is done on the general church book, the record shall be just as holy, and shall answer the ordinance just the same as if he had seen with his eyes and heard with his ears, and made a record of the same on the general church book.

5 You may think this order of things to be very particular; but let me tell you that it is only to answer the will of God, by conforming to the ordinance and preparation that the Lord ordained and prepared before the foundation of the world, for the salvation of the dead who should die without a knowledge of the gospel.

The subject occupying his mind (v. 1) is evident from the previous letter written five days before (Doctrine and Covenants 127). It was mentioned publicly two years prior to these letters, August 10, 1840, as stated before, but was not recorded. On October 19, 1840, he mentioned that he had spoken of it then, and added some comments (see the "General Authority Quotes" for those and a few of his subsequent recorded comments). He had heard the voice of the Lord on January 21, 1836 regarding his brother Alvin and others who had died not having heard the gospel, being heirs of the celestial kingdom (D&C 137:7–8).

His explanation of each ward having a recorder, and there being a general church recorder (vv. 3–4) seem self-explanatory. The will of God, that was ordained and prepared before the foundation of the world (v. 5), exemplifies that He is a just and merciful God.

D&C 128:6–9 • Revelation 20:12, the First Scripture As Evidence

6 And further, I want you to remember that John the Revelator was contemplating this very subject in relation to the dead, when he declared, as you will find recorded in Revelation 20:12—And I saw the dead, small and great, stand before God; and the books were opened; and another

book was opened, which is the book of life; and the dead were judged out of those things which were written in the books, according to their works.

7 You will discover in this quotation that the books were opened; and another book was opened, which was the book of life; but the dead were judged out of those things which were written in the books, according to their works; consequently, the books spoken of must be the books which contained the record of their works, and refer to the records which are kept on the earth. And the book which was the book of life is the record which is kept in heaven; the principle agreeing precisely with the doctrine which is commanded you in the revelation contained in the letter which I wrote to you previous to my leaving my place—that in all your recordings it may be recorded in heaven.

8 Now, the nature of this ordinance consists in the power of the priesthood, by the revelation of Jesus Christ, wherein it is granted that whatsoever you bind on earth shall be bound in heaven, and whatsoever you loose on earth shall be loosed in heaven. Or, in other words, taking a different view of the translation, whatsoever you record on earth shall be recorded in heaven, and whatsoever you do not record on earth shall not be recorded in heaven; for out of the books shall your dead be judged, according to their own works, whether they themselves have attended to the ordinances in their own *propria persona,* or by the means of their own agents, according to the ordinance which God has prepared for their salvation from before the foundation of the world, according to the records which they have kept concerning their dead.

9 It may seem to some to be a very bold doctrine that we talk of—a power which records or binds on earth and binds in heaven. Nevertheless, in all ages of the world, whenever the Lord has given a dispensation of the priesthood to any man by actual revelation, or any set of men, this power has always been given. Hence, whatsoever those men did in authority, in the name of the Lord, and did it truly and faithfully, and kept a proper and faithful record of the same, it became a law on earth and in heaven, and could not be annulled, according to the decrees of the great Jehovah. This is a faithful saying. Who can hear it?

The books, plural, kept on earth, that will judge the dead (v. 7), are the genealogical records officially placed in the general church book (v. 4, above). The book of life is the record kept in heaven. The different view of the translation, given by Joseph, substitutes the word "record" for the scriptural "bind" (v. 8). There must be an official record kept on earth before a record is made in heaven. This system requires the proper use of the priesthood, as Joseph had written; two witnesses on earth, the ordinance performer, and a recorder, that the ordinance was performed, whether applying to the person or to those who had died (v. 8). Therefore, a priesthood holder cannot go do work for someone without conforming to the law of the Church, and the law of God. The priesthood is the power of God delegated to man, and if in conformity with the great Jehovah it is binding in heaven (v. 9).

D&C 128:10–13 • The Second Scriptural Evidence

10 And again, for the precedent, Matthew 16:18, 19: And I say also unto thee, That thou art Peter, and upon this rock I will build my church; and the gates of hell shall not prevail against it. And I will give unto thee the keys of the kingdom of heaven: and whatsoever thou shalt bind on earth shall be bound in heaven; and whatsoever thou shalt loose on earth shall be loosed in heaven.

11 Now the great and grand secret of the whole matter, and the *summum bonum* of the whole subject that is lying before us, consists in obtaining the powers of the Holy Priesthood. For him to whom these keys are given there is no difficulty in obtaining a knowledge of facts in relation to the salvation of the children of men, both as well for the dead as for the living.

12 Herein is glory and honor, and immortality and eternal life—The ordinance of baptism by water, to be immersed therein in order to answer to the likeness of the dead, that one principle might accord with the other; to be immersed in the water and come forth out of the water is in the likeness of the resurrection of the dead in coming forth out of their graves; hence, this ordinance was instituted to form a relationship with the ordinance of baptism for the dead, being in likeness of the dead.

13 Consequently, the baptismal font was instituted as a similitude of the grave, and was commanded to be in a place underneath where the living are wont to assemble, to show forth the living and the dead, and that all things may have their likeness, and that they may accord one with another—that which is earthly conforming to that which is heavenly, as Paul hath declared, 1 Corinthians 15:46, 47, and 48:

The ordinance of the baptism by water being in the likeness of the dead being resurrected (v. 12) was taught by the Apostle Paul to the Romans:

3 Know ye not, that so many of us as were baptized into Jesus Christ were baptized into his death?

4 Therefore we are buried with him by baptism into death: that like as Christ was raised up from the dead by the glory of the Father, even so we also should walk in newness of life.

5 For if we have been planted together in the likeness of his death, we shall be also [in the likeness] of [His] resurrection:

6 Knowing this, that our old man is crucified with [Him], that the body of sin might be destroyed, that henceforth we should not serve sin. [Romans 6:3–6]

The baptismal fonts in the temples are therefore always in the basements as a similitude of the grave, and explains what Paul was talking about to the Corinthians (v. 13).

D&C 128:14–15 • A Third Scriptural Evidence

14 Howbeit that was not first which is spiritual, but that which is natural; and afterward that which is spiritual. The first man is of the earth, earthy; the second man is the Lord from heaven. As is the earthy, such are they also that are earthy; and as is the heavenly, such are they also that are heavenly. And as are the records on the earth in relation to your dead, which are truly made out, so also are the records in heaven. This, therefore, is the sealing and binding power, and, in one sense of the word, the keys of the kingdom, which consist in the key of knowledge.

15 And now my dearly beloved brethren and sisters, let me assure you that these are principles in relation to the dead and the living that cannot be lightly passed over, as pertaining to our salvation. For their salvation is necessary and essential to our salvation, as Paul says concerning the fathers—that they without us cannot be made perfect—neither can we without our dead be made perfect.

Paul's words are sometimes hard to understand, as Peter acknowledged (see 2 Peter 3:15–16). Paul explains that the first man, Adam, was first an earthly man, or a temporal man, and became a heavenly man, or a spiritual man. The second man, the Lord, was a heavenly man. The earthly men are like Adam, and may become like the Lord. Joseph Smith then states that the records on earth follow the same pattern, if they are correctly made out, they become the spiritual record in heaven (v. 14).

Joseph emphasized the importance of the records of our dead. We must do the ordinances for them, to obtain our own salvation (v. 15). He paraphrases Hebrews 11:40 as the validity for this doctrine; we cannot be saved without our dead.[96] The family is the basic unit of the Church, and of eternity. As Joseph later in this letter explained, there must be a welding link of generations (v. 18), and that link is between prophets. The link between the dead is families, and the families are patriarchal, or from father to son. Both the resurrection and eternal life are dependent upon the family unit.[97]

D&C 128:16 • A Fourth Scriptural Evidence

> 16 And now, in relation to the baptism for the dead, I will give you another quotation of Paul, 1 Corinthians 15:29: Else what shall they do which are baptized for the dead, if the dead rise not at all? Why are they then baptized for the dead?

The Apostle Paul is giving evidence to the Corinthians of Christ having been resurrected. There are three things he cites. First, he recounts the many people who saw Him after He was resurrected, including Himself (1 Corinthians 15:4–8). The second evidence he cites was the practice of baptizing for the dead (D&C 124:16). The third thing he cites was a question. "Why would he have fought with wild beasts at Ephesus if he didn't know there was a resurrection?" (1 Corinthians 15:30–31). Paul's reference to the baptisms for the dead was a matter of fact, as if to say, "everybody knows about this practice among us." Of a later time, the Prophet Joseph comments: "Chrysostum says that the Marchionites practiced baptism for their dead. 'After a catechumen was dead, they had a living man under the bed of the deceased; then coming to the dead man, they asked him whether he would receive baptism, and he making no answer, the other answered for him, and said that he would be baptized in his stead; and so they practiced the living for the dead.' The church of course at that time was degenerate, and the particular form might be

---

[96] Although Joseph changed the wording of Hebrews 11:40 in his translation of the Bible (JST), his paraphrase here is a good example of applying the scriptures to ourselves (see 1 Nephi 19:23).

[97] See Monte S. Nyman, *The Record of Alma: Book of Mormon Commentary* [2004], 4:318–335.

incorrect, but the thing is sufficiently plain in the scriptures [quotes 1 Corinthians 15:29]. [*TPJS*, 222]

This practice, and similar apostate practices, described by Joseph, are probably the source for the recognition among Christian sects today that it was practiced, but it was by cults. The Lord, through Joseph Smith, has given us plenty of evidence that it was originally a true principle of the gospel in earlier times as well as now.

D&C 128:17–18 • A Fifth Scriptural Evidence

17 And again, in connection with this quotation I will give you a quotation from one of the prophets, who had his eye fixed on the restoration of the priesthood, the glories to be revealed in the last days, and in an especial manner this most glorious of all subjects belonging to the everlasting gospel, namely, the baptism for the dead; for Malachi says, last chapter, verses 5th and 6th: Behold, I will send you Elijah the prophet before the coming of the great and dreadful day of the Lord: And he shall turn the heart of the fathers to the children, and the heart of the children to their fathers, lest I come and smite the earth with a curse.

18 I might have rendered a plainer translation to this, but it is sufficiently plain to suit my purpose as it stands. It is sufficient to know, in this case, that the earth will be smitten with a curse unless there is a welding link of some kind or other between the fathers and the children, upon some subject or other—and behold what is that subject? It is the baptism for the dead. For we without them cannot be made perfect; neither can they without us be made perfect. Neither can they nor we be made perfect without those who have died in the gospel also; for it is necessary in the ushering in of the dispensation of the fulness of times, which dispensation is now beginning to usher in, that a whole and complete and perfect union, and welding together of dispensations, and keys, and powers, and glories should take place, and be revealed from the days of Adam even to the present time. And not only this, but those things which never have been revealed from the foundation of the world, but have been kept hid from the wise and prudent, shall be revealed unto babes and sucklings in this, the dispensation of the fulness of times.

Doctrine and Covenants 2 was probably the plainer translation to which the Prophet Joseph referred (v. 18). It is the words of Malachi as quoted by the Angel Moroni when he appeared to the Prophet in September, 1823. The link of baptism for the dead between the fathers and the children was mentioned above (v. 16). The whole and complete, and perfect union (v. 18) has been restored and been functioning in our temples and genealogical societies for over one hundred and seventy years. The wise and prudent of the world still do not understand these doctrines, but the babes and sucklings of this dispensation, the faithful members of the Church, have them within their grasp.

D&C 128:19–21 • Voices from Heaven

19 Now, what do we hear in the gospel which we have received? A voice of gladness! A voice of mercy from heaven; and a voice of truth out of the earth; glad tidings for the dead; a voice of gladness for the living and the dead; glad tidings of great joy. How beautiful upon the mountains are the feet of those that bring glad tidings of good things, and that say unto Zion: Behold, thy God reigneth! As the dews of Carmel, so shall the knowledge of God descend upon them!

20 And again, what do we hear? Glad tidings from Cumorah! Moroni, an angel from heaven, declaring the fulfilment of the prophets—the book to be revealed. A voice of the Lord in the wilderness of Fayette, Seneca county, declaring the three witnesses to bear record of the book! The voice of Michael on the banks of the Susquehanna, detecting the devil when he appeared as an angel of light! The voice of Peter, James, and John in the wilderness between Harmony, Susquehanna county, and Colesville, Broome county, on the Susquehanna river, declaring themselves as possessing the keys of the kingdom, and of the dispensation of the fulness of times!

21 And again, the voice of God in the chamber of old Father Whitmer, in Fayette, Seneca county, and at sundry times, and in divers places through all the travels and tribulations of this Church of Jesus Christ of Latter-day Saints! And the voice of Michael, the archangel; the voice of Gabriel, and of Raphael, and of divers angels, from Michael or Adam down to the present time, all declaring their dispensation, their rights, their keys, their honors, their majesty and glory, and the power of their priesthood; giving line upon line, precept upon precept; here a little, and there a little; giving us consolation by holding forth that which is to come, confirming our hope!

The gospel which the Church has received (v. 19) was in the pages of the Book of Mormon. It was revealed by an angel from heaven. Its truths were translated by the power of God from records long hidden in the earth. "Glad tidings" is the Hebrew translation of gospel. The gospel brings joy to the dead in the spirit world, and to the living as the gospel is preached on the earth. The feet of those upon the mountains [of Israel] are the prophets and the missionaries who have, do, and yet will preach the gospel of the founder of peace to the nations of the earth (see Mosiah 15:13–18; Isaiah 52:7). They recognize their God as His knowledge descends upon them.

The glad tidings from Cumorah, seems to be the teachings of Moroni as he schooled and prepared Joseph to receive and translate the book to be revealed (v. 20).

The testimony of the Three Witnesses which they received from the voice of God is printed in every copy of the Book of Mormon and bears record of the book. We do not have a record of the voice of Michael [Adam] detecting the devil, but we know it happened. Finally, the voice of Peter, James, and John at the Susquehanna river commemorates the restoration of the priesthood in this dispensation. Thus, we have the audible witnesses as well as the scriptural testimonies of this great latter day work.

God and every angel from all dispensations have likewise restored their keys, authority, and power line upon line as Isaiah said it would come (see 2 Nephi 28:30; Isaiah 28:10). We indeed are living in the dispensation of the fulness of times when "all things in Christ" in heaven and on earth are gathered in one (Ephesians 1:9–10).

D&C 128:22–23 • Go Forward and Not Backward

22 Brethren, shall we not go on in so great a cause? Go forward and not backward. Courage, brethren; and on, on to the victory! Let your hearts rejoice, and be exceedingly glad. Let the earth break forth into singing. Let the dead speak forth anthems of eternal praise to the King Immanuel, who hath ordained, before the world was, that which would enable us to redeem them out of their prison; for the prisoners shall go free.

23 Let the mountains shout for joy, and all ye valleys cry aloud; and all ye seas and dry lands tell the wonders of your Eternal King! And ye rivers, and brooks, and rills, flow down with gladness. Let the woods and all the trees of the field praise the Lord; and ye solid rocks weep for joy! And let the sun, moon, and the morning stars sing together, and let all the sons of God shout for joy! And let the eternal creations declare his

name forever and ever! And again I say, how glorious is the voice we hear from heaven, proclaiming in our ears, glory, and salvation, and honor, and immortality, and eternal life; kingdoms, principalities, and powers!

This eloquent tribute to the King Immanuel, the Son of God (see Isaiah 7:14), given to motivate Joseph's brethren, is one of the most moving acknowledgments in all of holy writ. The Psalmist gave a tribute to the Lord's creation of the earth: "The earth is the LORD's, and the fulness thereof; the world, and they that dwell therein. For he hath founded it upon the seas, and established it upon the floods" (Psalm 24:1–2). Job, whom the Prophet quotes (Job 38:7), gave the longest and certainly the best tribute of all, but his written words are what the Lord himself spoke to Job (Job 38–41). Who could have written it except a prophet, moved upon by the Holy Ghost? Joseph Smith was indeed a prophet.

D&C 128:24–25 • The Great Day of the Lord

24 Behold, the great day of the Lord is at hand; and who can abide the day of his coming, and who can stand when he appeareth? For he is like a refiner's fire, and like fuller's soap; and he shall sit as a refiner and purifier of silver, and he shall purify the sons of Levi, and purge them as gold and silver, that they may offer unto the Lord an offering in righteousness. Let us, therefore, as a church and a people, and as Latter-day Saints, offer unto the Lord an offering in righteousness; and let us present in his holy temple, when it is finished, a book containing the records of our dead, which shall be worthy of all acceptation.

25 Brethren, I have many things to say to you on the subject; but shall now close for the present, and continue the subject another time. I am, as ever, your humble servant and never deviating friend, JOSEPH SMITH.

Joseph ends the epistle with Malachi's questions that conclude the Old Testament (Malachi 3:1–3). He does so to teach the Lord's people of the sacrifice they must make in these latter days; a book containing the records of our dead (D&C 128:24). A sacrifice is giving something up for, or to, something else. In this case, it is to sacrifice time and talents to the acquiring of information about our ancestors, and recording it correctly that it may be presented in the temples for a proxy to receive the ordinances and endowment of the Lord for that ancestor. As Joseph hid from his enemies, his thoughts and prayers were still concentrating on the Lord's work.

DOCTRINE AND COVENANTS 129

*H*istorical Setting: "Revelation. *Three grand keys by which Good or Bad Angels or Spirits may be Known—Revealed to Joseph the Prophet, at Nauvoo, Illinois, February 9, 1843*" (*HC*, 5:267)

"A man came to me in Kirtland, and told me he had seen an angel, and described his dress. I told him he had seen no angel, and that there was no such dress in heaven. He grew mad, and went into the street and commanded fire to come down out of heaven and consume me. I laughed at him, and said, You are one of Baal's prophets; your God does not hear you; jump up and cut yourself: and he commanded fire from heaven to consume my house [see 1 Kings 18:17–46]" [*HC*, 5:267–68]

TEXT AND COMMENTARY

D&C 129:1–9 • Three Grand Keys to Detect Angels

1 THERE are two kinds of beings in heaven, namely: Angels, who are resurrected personages, having bodies of flesh and bones—

2 For instance, Jesus said: Handle me and see, for a spirit hath not flesh and bones, as ye see me have.

3 Secondly: the spirits of just men made perfect, they who are not resurrected, but inherit the same glory.

4 When a messenger comes saying he has a message from God, offer him your hand and request him to shake hands with you.

5 If he be an angel he will do so, and you will feel his hand.

6 If he be the spirit of a just man made perfect he will come in his glory; for that is the only way he can appear—

7 Ask him to shake hands with you, but he will not move, because it is contrary to the order of heaven for a just man to deceive; but he will still deliver his message.

8 If it be the devil as an angel of light, when you ask him to shake

hands he will offer you his hand, and you will not feel anything; you may therefore detect him.

9 These are three grand keys whereby you may know whether any administration is from God.

The handshake is the first key to discern an angel. The second key is the glory that attends the personage. Eight months after this revelation was given, October 9, 1843, the Prophet taught: "Spirits can only be revealed in flaming fire and glory. Angels have advanced further, their light and glory being tabernacled; and hence they appear in bodily shape. The spirits of just men are made ministering servants to those who are sealed unto eternal life, and it is through them that the sealing power comes down" (*TPJS*, 325). Joseph had taught some of these principles before (see *TPJS*, 162; 191). Paul admonished the Saints to: "Be not forgetful to entertain strangers: for thereby some have entertained angels unawares" (Hebrews 13:2). Therefore, it is possible for an angel to minister and not identify himself as an angel. The third key is to discern the devil. He may try to appear as an angel of light, but he cannot. When he appeared to Moses, Moses was able to discern the difference, and asked: "Who art thou? For behold, I am a son of God, in the similitude of his Only Begotten; and where is thy glory, that I should worship thee? For behold, I could not look upon God, except his glory should come upon me, and I were transfigured before him. But I can look upon thee in the natural man. Is it not so, surely?" (Moses 1:13–14). The Book of Mormon also shows there is a difference: "we become devils, angels to a devil, to be shut out from the presence of our God, and to remain with the father of lies, in misery, like unto himself; yea, to that being who beguiled our first parents, who transformeth himself **nigh** unto an angel of light," (2 Nephi 9:9, bold added). The handshake is for those who have not seen a just man made perfect.

Joseph Smith had the qualifications to speak about angels. As we learned in Doctrine and Covenants 128:21, every angel who held any keys in previous dispensations from Adam to his present time had appeared to him.

DOCTRINE AND COVENANTS 130

*H*istorical Setting: "Heard Elder Hyde preach. . . . Alluding to the coming of the Savior, he said, 'When He shall appear, we shall be like Him, &c. He will appear on a white horse as a warrior, and maybe we shall have some of the same spirit. Our god is a warrior. (John 14:23). It is our privilege to have the Father and Son dwelling in our hearts, &c.'

We dined with my sister Sophronia McCleary, when I told Elder Hyde that I was going to offer some corrections to his sermon this morning. He replied, "They shall be thankfully received."

"Important Items of Instruction given by Joseph the Prophet at Ramus, Illinois, April 2nd 1843" (*HC,* 5:323).

These items of instructions have largely been discussed in previous chapters, and those already discussed will be referred to where they were discussed.

TEXT AND COMMENTARY

D&C 130:1–3 • Appearing of the Father and the Son

1 WHEN the Savior shall appear we shall see him as he is. We shall see that he is a man like ourselves.

2 And that same sociality which exists among us here will exist among us there, only it will be coupled with eternal glory, which glory we do not now enjoy.

3 John 14:23—The appearing of the Father and the Son, in that verse, is a personal appearance; and the idea that the Father and the Son dwell in a man's heart is an old sectarian notion, and is false.

Mormon and the Apostle John add: "When he shall appear we shall be like him, for we shall see him as he is; that we may have this hope; that we may be purified even as he is pure. Amen (Moroni 7:48; 1 John 3:1–2). The sociality that will exist (vv. 1–2) speaks of His dwelling with us in the Millennium.

D&C 130:4–8

• Quoted in chapter 2, under D&C 77:1

D&C 130:9–11

• Quoted in chapter 2, under D&C 77:1

D&C 130:12–13

• Quoted in chapter 7, under D&C 87:1–3

D&C 130:14–17 • When Joseph Was 85 Years Old?

14 I was once praying very earnestly to know the time of the coming of the Son of Man, when I heard a voice repeat the following:

15 Joseph, my son, if thou livest until thou art eighty-five years old, thou shalt see the face of the Son of Man; therefore let this suffice, and trouble me no more on this matter.

16 I was left thus, without being able to decide whether this coming referred to the beginning of the Millennium or to some previous appearing, or whether I should die and thus see his face.

17 I believe the coming of the Son of Man will not be any sooner than that time.

Joseph would have been 85 years old on December 23, 1890, and the Second Coming did not come, nor has it yet, well over one hundred years after this date. What the Lord is apparently saying is that if the world would have accepted him, instead of murdering him, Joseph could have prepared the world for His coming by that date.

D&C 130:18–19

• Quoted in chapter 25, under D&C 131:7–8

D&C 130:29–21

• Quoted in chapter 4, under D&C 82:5–10

D&C 130:22–23

• Quoted in chapter 12, under D&C 95:17; and v. 22 is quoted in chapter 8, under D&C 88:11

General Authority Quotes

—*The Prophet Joseph Smith* • D&C 128:5; 129:1–8

. . . The Saints have the privilege of being baptized for those of their relatives who are dead, whom they believe would have embraced the gospel, if they had been privileged with hearing it, and who have received the gospel in the Spirit, through the instrumentality of those who have been commissioned to preach to them while in prison.

Without enlarging on the subject, you will undoubtedly see its consistency and reasonableness; and it presents the gospel of Christ in probably a more enlarged scale than some have imagined it. But as the performance of this right is more particularly confined to this place, it will not be necessary to enter into particulars; at the same time, I always feel glad to give all the information in my power, but my space will not allow me to do it. [*TPJS,* 179–80; October 19, 1840]

President Joseph Smith, by request of the Twelve Apostles, gave instructions on the doctrine of baptism for the dead, which was listened to with intense interest by the large assembly. He presented baptism for the dead as the only way that men can appear as saviors on Mount Zion. . . . [*TPJS,* 191]

This doctrine presents in a clear light the wisdom and mercy of God in preparing an ordinance for the salvation of the dead, being baptized by proxy, their names recorded in heaven and they judged according to deeds done in the body. This doctrine was the burden of the scriptures. Those Saints who neglect it in behalf of their deceased relatives, do it at the peril of their own salvation. The dispensation of the fullness of times will bring to light the things that have been revealed in all former dispensations; also other things that have not been before revealed. He shall send Elijah, the Prophet, &c., and restore all things. . . . [*TPJS,* 193; October 3, 1841]

. . . Our Savior says, that all manner of sin and blaspheme shall be forgiven men wherewith they shall blaspheme; but the blasphemy against the Holy Ghost shall not be forgiven, neither in this world nor in the world to come, evidently showing that there are sins which may be forgiven in the world to come, . . . [quotes 1 Peter 3:19–20]. Here then we have an account of our Savior preaching to the spirits in prison, . . . and what did He preach to them? . . . [quotes Luke 4:18 and Isaiah 42:7] It is very evident from this that He not only went to preach to them, but to deliver them, or bring them out of the prison house. . . . [quotes Isaiah 24:20–22] Thus we find that God will deal with all the human family equally, and that as the antediluvians had their day of visitation, so will those characters referred to by Isaiah, have their time of visitation and deliverance; after having been many days in prison. [*TPJS,* 219; April 15, 1842]

. . . It is not only necessary that you should be baptized for your dead, but you will have to go through all the ordinances for them, the same as you have gone through for them. . . . [*TPJS,* 366; May 2, 1844]

. . . An angel of God never has wings. Some will say that they have seen a spirit; that he offered him his hand, but they did not touch it. This is a lie. First it is contrary to the plan of God; a spirit cannot come but in glory; an angel has flesh and bones; we see not their glory. The devil may appear as an angel of light. Ask God to reveal it; if it be of the devil, he will flee from you; if of God, He will manifest Himself, or make it manifest. We may come to Jesus and ask Him; He will know all about it; if he comes to a little child, he will adapt himself to the language and capacity of a little child. [*TPJS,* 162]

—*President Gordon B. Hinckley* • D&C 128:24

There are today many genealogical and family history societies in the world. I think they have all come into existence subsequent to the visit of Elijah. . . .

When the Utah Genealogical Society was organized in 1894, the charter members contributed eleven volumes. That original root stock has grown to a library of 258,000 books. Each month another thousand volumes are added to this collection.

The collection also includes 1.8 million rolls of microfilm to which are added 5,000 rolls monthly. It has become the world's largest collection of family history data.

Only a handful of our people used the modest family resources of the Church around the turn of the century. How things have changed! During each of the last five years more than 750,000 researchers have used the main library here in Salt Lake City and the more than 2,200 family history centers scattered across the world. Approximately 40 percent of those using the Family History Library and 60 percent of the patrons using the local centers are not members of the Church. We offer a tremendous service to those not of our faith.

There is nothing else to compare with this treasury of family history. . . . I feel the Lord has designed that it should be so. This is His church which carries His name, and one of its purposes is to make available to the millions beyond the veil of death the full blessings that lead to eternal life. (Utah Genealogical Society Fireside, November 13, 1994.) [*Teachings of Gordon B. Hinckley,* 210–11]

Chapter Twenty-Five

The New and Everlasting Covenant of Marriage

D&C 131–132

DOCTRINE AND COVENANTS 131

Historical Setting: "Tuesday, [May] 16. . . . Remarks of the Prophet at Ramus—Lives that are Hid with God in Christ—Importance of the Eternity of the Marriage Covenant" (*HC,* 5:391).

"Wednesday, [May] 17. . . . Items of Doctrine by the Prophet" (*HC,* 5:392).

TEXT AND COMMENTARY

D&C 131:1–4 • Celestial Glory—Three Heavens

1 IN the celestial glory there are three heavens or degrees;

2 And in order to obtain the highest, a man must enter into this order of the priesthood [meaning the new and everlasting covenant of marriage];

3 And if he does not, he cannot obtain it.

4 He may enter into the other, but that is the end of his kingdom; he cannot have an increase.

About two months before section 132 was recorded—it was given long before (see section heading below)—the Prophet Joseph taught the above doctrine. He also taught that to have an increase is to have children after a husband and wife are resurrected. "Except a man and his wife enter into an everlasting covenant and be married for eternity, while in this probation, by the power and authority of the Holy Priesthood, they will cease when they die; that is, they will not have any children after the resurrection. But those who are married by the power and authority of the priesthood in this life, will continue to increase and have children in the celestial glory."[98]

Therefore, there is no marriage in the lower two kingdoms of the celestial glory, or in the terrestrial or telestial glory.

D&C 131:5–8 • You Cannot Be Saved in Ignorance

5 (May 17th, 1843.) The more sure word of prophecy means a man's knowing that he is sealed up unto eternal life, by revelation and the spirit of prophecy, through the power of the Holy Priesthood.

6 It is impossible for a man to be saved in ignorance.

7 There is no such thing as immaterial matter. All spirit is matter, but it is more fine or pure, and can only be discerned by purer eyes;

8 We cannot see it; but when our bodies are purified we shall see that it is all matter.

The more sure word of prophecy is another term for having your calling and election made sure, or receiving the Second Comforter. This subject was discussed in chapter 8 under Doctrine and Covenants 88:1–5. It comes by revelation and through the power of the priesthood (vv. 5–6). It is a sacred calling, and not discussed openly. Only those who have the experience know about it, but one cannot be saved without it.[99]

The Prophet Joseph stated a month earlier: "Salvation is nothing more nor less than to triumph over all our enemies and put them under our feet. And when we have power to put all enemies under our feet in this

---

[98] *TPJS*, 300–301. The verses in the Doctrine and Covenants (D&C 131:1–4) and Joseph's explanatory comments were given at the same time in Ramus, Illinois, May 16, 1843. The explanatory verses were not selected to be part of the Doctrine and Covenants.

[99] The best commentary on the subject is Bruce R. McConkie, *Doctrinal New Testament Commentary* [1973], 3:323–350.

world, and a knowledge to triumph over all evil spirits in the world to come, then are we saved, as in the case of Jesus, who was to reign until He had put all enemies under His feet, and the last enemy was death" (*TPJS*, 297).

The "more fine or pure" matter (vv. 7–8) was also commented on by the Prophet about a year earlier: ". . . The spirit is a substance; that it is material, but that it is more pure, elastic and refined matter than the body; that it existed before the body, can exist in the body; and will exist separate from the body, when the body will be mouldering in the dust; and will in the resurrection, be again united with it" (*TPJS*, 207). The Prophet's statement in the previous section seems to fit well with these statements: "Whatever principle of intelligence we attain unto in this life, it will rise with us in the resurrection.

And if a person gains more knowledge and intelligence in this life through his diligence and obedience than another, he will have so much the advantage in the world to come" (D&C 130:18–19). Not only will the spirit and the body be reunited, but all that the spirit has learned on earth will be retained in the soul—"The glory of God is intelligence, or, in other words, light and truth" (D&C 93:36)—"the spirit and the body are the soul of man" (D&C 88:15). Celestial souls will be on the path to become like God.

DOCTRINE AND COVENANTS 132

*H*istorical Setting: *"Revelation on the Eternity of the Marriage Covenant, including the Plurality of Wives. Given through Joseph the Seer, in Nauvoo, Hancock County, Illinois, July 12ᵗʰ, 1843"* (HC, 5:501).

Although the revelation was recorded in 1843, it is evident from the historical records that the doctrines and principles involved in this revelation had been known by the Prophet since 1831 (see section heading).

SECTION 132 • OUTLINE

➤ 132:1–6   The Lord reveals a new and everlasting covenant concerning many wives and concubines.

     a. No one can reject the covenant and enter into my glory (v. 4).

     b. It was initiated for the fulness of my glory (v. 6).

➤ 132:7–20 All covenants must be sealed by the Holy Spirit of Promise.

     a. Only one man has the power and keys to confer these covenants (vv. 7–11).

     b. Everything that is not done by the Lord does not remain after death (vv. 12–14).

     c. Those married for only this world are angels who minister to others (vv. 15–17).

     d. Those married for time and eternity without authority are void (v. 18).

     e. A marriage sealed by the Holy Spirit receives exaltation and glory (vv. 19–20).

➤ 132:21–27 If ye cannot abide my law ye cannot abide my glory.

     a. Strait is the gate and narrow the way to eternal life, and few find it (vv. 22–23).

     b. Eternal lives is to know God and Jesus Christ (v. 24).

     c. Broad is the gate and wide is the way that leads to death (v. 25).

     d. A marriage sealed by the Holy Spirit, and commits sin are delivered to the buffetings of Satan (v. 26).

     e. The blasphemy against the Holy Ghost after receiving the new and everlasting covenant are damned (v. 27).

➤ 132:28–33 The law of the Holy Priesthood was ordained before the world was.

     a. Abraham received all things by revelation and commandment and has entered unto his exaltation (v. 29).

     b. Joseph Smith is of Abraham's seed and is given this promise (vv. 30–31).

     c. The Father glorifies himself through this law (v. 32).

     d. If you receive not this law you cannot receive the promise of Abraham (v. 33).

➤ 132:34–40 God commanded Abraham to marry Hagar from whom came many people.

a. Abraham was commanded to offer Isaac and it was righteous (v. 36).

b. Abraham received concubines and they bore him children (v. 37).

c. Isaac and Jacob did as commanded and have entered their exaltation (v. 37).

d. David, Solomon, Moses, and many others did as commanded (v. 38).

e. David sinned in the case of Uriah and fell from exaltation (v. 39).

f. Joseph Smith was to restore all things according to the word of God (v. 40).

➤ 132:41–45   If a man receives a wife under the new and everlasting covenant and she commits adultery she shall be destroyed.

a. If a woman or man, not under covenant, is with another it's adultery (vv. 42–43).

b. If the woman has not committed adultery, Joseph has power to give her to another man who is faithful (vv. 44–45).

➤ 132:46–50   Whatever Joseph seals on earth shall be sealed in heaven.

a. The Lord will be with Joseph until the end of the earth, and he is exalted (v. 49).

b. The Lord has seen his sacrifice and has made way his escape (v. 50).

➤ 132:51–57   Emma Smith should not partake of what was commanded, it was to prove her.

a. She is to receive all who were given to Joseph and are virtuous (v. 52).

b. Joseph shall be made ruler over many things for he was faithful (v. 53).

c. Emma shall cleave unto Joseph or be destroyed (vv. 54–55).

d. Emma shall forgive Joseph for his trespasses and she shall be forgiven (v. 56).

e. Satan seeks to destroy Joseph, but the Lord is with him even as Abraham (v. 57).

➤ 132:58–65   Joseph was called by revelation, and has the keys of the priesthood.

     a.   If a man desires a virgin, and the first gives her consent, he is justified, even ten virgins (vv. 61–62).

     b.   If any of the ten virgins commits adultery, they shall be destroyed, for they were given to multiply and replenish the earth (v. 63).

     c.   If a man teaches his wife the law of the priesthood, she shall believe and administer to him, or become the transgressor (v. 64–65).

➤ 132:66   The Lord will reveal more unto you hereafter.

Introduction

Marriage is a sacred and crowning ordinance of the gospel of Jesus Christ. Whom to marry is one of, if not the most important decision that is made in this mortal probation. Furthermore, the decision is and should be made when one is young and inexperienced in life. Yet, as with other important decisions, the Lord has not left us without guidance in the matter. Through revelation the right decision can be made and direction given in the years that follow.

In another revelation, regarding the teachings of the Shakers (United Society of Believers in Christ's Second Appearing) regarding marriage, the Lord declared: "And again, verily I say unto you, that whoso forbiddeth to marry is not ordained of God, for marriage is ordained of God unto man. Wherefore, it is lawful that he should have one wife, and they twain shall be one flesh, and all this that the earth might answer the end of its creation; and that it might be filled with the measure of man, according to his creation before the world was made" (D&C 49:15–17).

A major purpose of marriage, but not the only one, is to have children and raise them up unto the Lord. Thus, the eternal perspective of the commandment to marry and have children was revealed to the Prophet Joseph early in his ministry.

As noted in the section heading, the doctrines and principles involved in the revelations under consideration in this chapter were known to the Prophet Joseph since 1831, but were not recorded until July 12, 1843 in Nauvoo. Apparently, Joseph was reluctant to make the revelation public because part of the revelation was about plural marriage, and Emma, Joseph's wife, was finding it difficult to accept. According to William Clayton, Joseph's private secretary:

> On the morning of the 12th of July, 1834; Joseph and Hyrum Smith came into the office in the upper story of the brick store, on the bank of the Mississippi River. They were talking on the subject of plural marriage. Hyrum said to Joseph, "If you will write the revelation on celestial marriage, I will take it and read it to Emma, and I believe I can convince her of its truth, and you will hereafter have peace." Joseph smiled and remarked, "You do not know Emma as well as I do." Hyrum repeated his opinion, and further remarked, "The doctrine is so plain, I can convince any reasonable man or woman of its truth, purity and heavenly origin," or words to that effect. Joseph then said, "Well, I will write the revelation and we will see." He then requested me to get paper and prepare to write. Hyrum very urgently requested Joseph to write the revelation by means of the Urim and Thummim, but Joseph in reply, said he did not need to, for he knew the revelation perfectly from beginning to end.
>
> Joseph and Hyrum then sat down and Joseph commenced to dictate the revelation on celestial marriage, and I wrote it, sentence by sentence, as he dictated. After the whole was written, Joseph asked me to read it through, slowly and carefully, which I did, and he pronounced it correct. He then remarked that there was much more that he could write on the same subject, but what was written was sufficient for the present.
>
> Hyrum then took the revelation to read to Emma. Joseph remained with me in the office until Hyrum returned. When he came back, Joseph asked him how he had succeeded, Hyrum replied that he had never received a more severe talking to in his life, that Emma was very bitter and full of resentment and anger.[100]

It is important to recognize that the first part of the revelation is teaching the new and everlasting covenant of [eternal] marriage (vv. 2–33), and that plural marriage is spoken of in some of the subsequent verses.

D&C 132:1–6 • Celestial Marriage

1 Verily, thus saith the Lord unto you my servant Joseph, that inasmuch as you have inquired of my hand to know and understand

---

[100] *HC,* 5: xxxii–xxxiii.

wherein I, the Lord, justified my servants Abraham, Isaac, and Jacob, as also Moses, David and Solomon, my servants, as touching the principle and doctrine of their having many wives and concubines—

2 Behold, and lo, I am the Lord thy God, and will answer thee as touching this matter.

3 Therefore, prepare thy heart to receive and obey the instructions which I am about to give unto you; for all those who have this law revealed unto them must obey the same.

4 For behold, I reveal unto you a new and an everlasting covenant; and if ye abide not that covenant, then are ye damned; for no one can reject this covenant and be permitted to enter into my glory.

5 For all who will have a blessing at my hands shall abide the law which was appointed for that blessing, and the conditions thereof, as were instituted from before the foundation of the world.

6 And as pertaining to the new and everlasting covenant, it was instituted for the fulness of my glory; and he that receiveth a fulness thereof must and shall abide the law, or he shall be damned, saith the Lord God.

The initial verse of the revelation implies that the revelation was probably given while Joseph Smith was working on the translation of the Old Testament. Another possibility is that it was revealed about the same time as the revelation partially quoted above (D&C 45; March 1831). The question of plural marriage being practiced in Old Testament time, asked by Joseph (D&C 132:1) may have been triggered by the Lord's statement, "it is lawful that he should have one wife" (D&C 49:16).

In answering Joseph (v. 2), the Lord first explained the principle of eternal marriage. He undoubtedly knew some background was needed before Joseph and his followers would be able to understand the answer to the Old Testament practice in question.

A similar background may be needed today for people to understand the revelation given to Joseph Smith. In today's Christian world, marriages are basically performed for "until death do you part." However, the concept of eternal marriage is not unique to Joseph Smith's followers. It was clearly taught by the New Testament Apostles. Peter declared that husband and wife were "heirs together of the grace of life" (1 Peter 3:7). Paul taught that "neither is the man without woman, neither the woman without the man, in the Lord" (1 Corinthians 11:11). It is not our purpose to expound on these teachings, but merely show that they were understood back then. The Apostles' teachings along with modern day revelations quoted above, will also give us insight into other teachings of Jesus as He ministered in Palestine that are often misunderstood. We will mention some of these later.

Some have interpreted the verses quoted in D&C 132:3–5 to say that all who learn of plural marriage must practice it, either on earth or if they attain the celestial kingdom. This interpretation is not the context of the revelation, or what has been taught by the Church through the years. The law of the Lord is revealing the eternal nature of the institution of marriage (vv. 4–6). Those who marry "until death do they part" have ended their marriage covenant at death, and their eternal progression is stopped or dammed. A dam is used to hold back water or stop the progress of the water. Therefore, they will not receive the blessings that were instituted before the foundation of the world. Therefore, those who are damned are those in the lower two kingdoms of the celestial glory or in the terrestrial or telestial glory.

D&C 132:7–11 • The Conditions of the Law

7 And verily I say unto you, that the conditions of this law are these: All covenants, contracts, bonds, obligations, oaths, vows, performances, connections, associations, or expectations, that are not made and entered into and sealed by the Holy Spirit of promise, of him who is anointed, both as well for time and for all eternity, and that too most holy, by revelation and commandment through the medium of mine anointed, whom I have appointed on the earth to hold this power (and I have appointed unto my servant Joseph to hold this power in the last days, and there is never but one on the earth at a time on whom this power and the keys of this priesthood are conferred), are of no efficacy, virtue, or force in and after the resurrection from the dead; for all contracts that are not made unto this end have an end when men are dead.

8 Behold, mine house is a house of order, saith the Lord God, and not a house of confusion.

9 Will I accept of an offering, saith the Lord, that is not made in my name?

10 Or will I receive at your hands that which I have not appointed?

11 And will I appoint unto you, saith the Lord, except it be by law,

even as I and my Father ordained unto you, before the world was?

The Lord's "house is a house of order . . . and not a house of confusion" (v. 8) Offerings and appointments must be made in the name of Christ as he and his Father ordained unto the inhabitants of the earth "before the world was" (vv. 9–11). The conditions of the law of marriage ordained there were: First, the marriage must be sealed by the Holy Spirit of Promise (v. 7); second, it must be performed by a man who holds the keys and power of the priesthood (v. 7). This power, held by the President of the High Priesthood (D&C 107:92), may be delegated to another priesthood holder. The sealing of the Holy Spirit of Promise is the Holy Ghost's stamp of approval on every ordinance and action of the gospel.[101] The power held by Joseph Smith has been given to each of his successors. Therefore, the authority to seal marriages for eternity is still upon the earth, "and all contracts that are not made unto this end [expire] when men are dead" (D&C 132:7).

D&C 132:12–14 • Things Not of God Are Destroyed

12 I am the Lord thy God; and I give unto you this commandment—that no man shall come unto the Father but by me or by my word, which is my law, saith the Lord.

13 And everything that is in the world, whether it be ordained of men, by thrones, or principalities, or powers, or things of name, whatsoever they may be, that are not by me or by my word, saith the Lord, shall be thrown down, and shall not remain after men are dead, neither in nor after the resurrection, saith the Lord your God.

14 For whatsoever things remain are by me; and whatsoever things are not by me shall be shaken and destroyed.

The "commandment—that no man shall come unto the Father but by [Christ] or by [His] word" (v. 12) is still in effect. All other things not of Christ "shall be shaken and destroyed" (v. 14).

D&C 132:15–17 • A Marriage Not of God

15 Therefore, if a man marry him a wife in the world, and he marry

---

[101] See Joseph Fielding Smith, *Doctrines of Salvation,* 1:55, in "General Authority Quotes," end of chapter.

her not by me nor by my word, and he covenant with her so long as he is in the world and she with him, their covenant and marriage are not of force when they are dead, and when they are out of the world; therefore, they are not bound by any law when they are out of the world.

16 Therefore, when they are out of the world they neither marry nor are given in marriage; but are appointed angels in heaven, which angels are ministering servants, to minister for those who are worthy of a far more, and an exceeding, and an eternal weight of glory.

17 For these angels did not abide my law; therefore, they cannot be enlarged, but remain separately and singly, without exaltation, in their saved condition, to all eternity; and from henceforth are not gods, but are angels of God forever and ever.

The first marriage, not of Christ or His word, ends with death (v. 15). These people "neither marry nor are given in marriage; but are appointed angels in heaven, which are ministering servants, to minister for those who are worthy of a far more, and an exceeding, and an eternal weight of glory" (v. 16). Because they did not abide the law, they "remain separately and singly, without exaltation" and "are not gods, but are angels of God forever and ever" (vv. 16–17). The wording of this example of an earthly marriage contains some phrases almost identical to Jesus' teachings in the New Testament.

"The Sadducees, which say there is no resurrection" (Matthew 22:23), came to Jesus and presented a hypothetical situation of the Levite marriage under the law of Moses. Under this law, if a man died, his brother was responsible to marry his wife and raise his children unto his brother (see Deuteronomy 25:5–10). The Sadducees' question was, if a woman was married to seven brothers, all of whom died, whose wife would she be in the resurrection? "Jesus answered and said unto them, Ye do err, not knowing the scriptures, nor the power of God. For in the resurrection they neither marry, nor are given in marriage, but are as the angels of God in heaven (Matthew 22:24–30). From His answer has come the Christian dogma that there are no marriages in the heavens, it is only "til death do we part." An analogy of the entire answer would show otherwise.

The Sadducees were attempting to trick Jesus into supporting their belief in there not being a resurrection. The following verses refute their attempt. He taught that Abraham, Isaac, and Jacob were still alive and awaiting the time of the resurrection: "But as touching the resurrection of the dead, have ye not read that which was spoken unto you by God, saying, I am the God of Abraham, and the God of Isaac, and the God of Jacob? God is not the God of the dead, but of the living" (Matthew 22:31–32).

The Luke account of the incident above is even more pronounced in supporting the concept taught in the revelation to Joseph: "And Jesus answering said unto them, The children of this world marry, and are given in marriage: But they which shall be accounted worthy [servants] to obtain that [celestial] world, and the resurrection from the dead, neither marry, nor are given in marriage: Neither can they die any more; for they are equal unto the angels; and are the children of God, being the children of the resurrection" (Luke 20:34–36). The people of this world have not come into the new and everlasting covenant of marriage, but marry according to the covenants of man. Those worthy of "that world" speaks of those who have lived a life worthy to be in the celestial kingdom and are the children of God. However, having not entered into the everlasting covenant of marriage, which the law of Moses did not include, they will be in the same category as those spoken of by the Lord in the revelation to Joseph. They are appointed angels to minister to those worthy of a more excellent glory (D&C 132:16). We will not consider at this time other opportunities—that might come to them while in the spirit—and vicarious work for the dead.

D&C 132:18 • A Second Example Not of God

> 18 And again, verily I say unto you, if a man marry a wife, and make a covenant with her for time and for all eternity, if that covenant is not by me or by my word, which is my law, and is not sealed by the Holy Spirit of promise, through him whom I have anointed and appointed unto this power, then it is not valid neither of force when they are out of the world, because they are not joined by me, saith the Lord, neither by my word; when they are out of the world it cannot be received there, because the angels and the gods are appointed there, by whom they cannot pass; they cannot, therefore, inherit my glory; for my house is a house of order, saith the Lord God.

The second example of a marriage not of God was when a man marries a wife "for time and for all eternity," but the covenant was not made by [Christ] or by [His] word." The covenant was "not valid neither of force when they are out of the world," and they cannot inherit the glory of the Lord God. Such a marriage would be someone using the words of the "time and all eternity," but not holding the priesthood authority to perform that marriage. Another example would be a marriage properly performed by a priesthood holder, but the marriage was not sealed by the Holy Spirit of Promise because one or both of the marriage partners did not live up to the conditions of the covenant. The sealing of a marriage does not come at the time of the marriage, although the Spirit may testify of the approval of the marriage, but is based upon faithfulness to those covenants.

D&C 132:19–20 • A Marriage that is of God

19 And again, verily I say unto you, if a man marry a wife by my word, which is my law, and by the new and everlasting covenant, and it is sealed unto them by the Holy Spirit of promise, by him who is anointed, unto whom I have appointed this power and the keys of this priesthood; and it shall be said unto them—Ye shall come forth in the first resurrection; and if it be after the first resurrection, in the next resurrection; and shall inherit thrones, kingdoms, principalities, and powers, dominions, all heights and depths—then shall it be written in the Lamb's Book of Life, that he shall commit no murder whereby to shed innocent blood, and if ye abide in my covenant, and commit no murder whereby to shed innocent blood, it shall be done unto them in all things whatsoever my servant hath put upon them, in time, and through all eternity; and shall be of full force when they are out of the world; and they shall pass by the angels, and the gods, which are set there, to their exaltation and glory in all things, as hath been sealed upon their heads, which glory shall be a fulness and a continuation of the seeds forever and ever.

20 Then shall they be gods, because they have no end; therefore shall they be from everlasting to everlasting, because they continue; then shall they be above all, because all things are subject unto them. Then shall they be gods, because they have all power, and the angels are subject unto them.

Those who marry "by [Christ's] word, which is [His] law, and by the new and everlasting covenant, and it is sealed unto them by the Holy Spirit of Promise, by him who is anointed" by him who has the "power and the keys of this priesthood . . . shall come forth in the first resurrection; and if it be after the first resurrection, in the next resurrection; and shall inherit thrones, kingdoms, principalities, and powers, dominions, all heights and depths." Their covenant "shall be of full force when they are out of the world" and shall have the exaltation and glory that was "sealed upon their heads . . . a fulness and a continuation of the seeds forever and ever." They shall "be gods, because they have all power, and the angels are subject unto them" (vv. 19–20). This is the eternal law of marriage that all should seek for and live to attain. But it isn't automatic.

D&C 132:21–27 • Few There Be that Find It

21 Verily, verily, I say unto you, except ye abide my law ye cannot attain to this glory.

22 For strait is the gate, and narrow the way that leadeth unto the exaltation and continuation of the lives, and few there be that find it, because ye receive me not in the world neither do ye know me.

23 But if ye receive me in the world, then shall ye know me, and shall receive your exaltation; that where I am ye shall be also.

24 This is eternal lives—to know the only wise and true God, and Jesus Christ, whom he hath sent. I am he. Receive ye, therefore, my law.

25 Broad is the gate, and wide the way that leadeth to the deaths; and many there are that go in thereat, because they receive me not, neither do they abide in my law.

26 Verily, verily, I say unto you, if a man marry a wife according to my word, and they are sealed by the Holy Spirit of promise, according to mine appointment, and he or she shall commit any sin or transgression of the new and everlasting covenant whatever, and all manner of blasphemies, and if they commit no murder wherein they shed innocent blood, yet they shall come forth in the first resurrection, and enter into their exaltation; but they shall be destroyed in the flesh, and shall be delivered unto the buffetings of Satan unto the day of redemption, saith the Lord God.

27 The blasphemy against the Holy Ghost, which shall not be forgiven in the world nor out of the world, is in that ye commit murder wherein ye shed innocent blood, and assent unto my death, after ye have received my new and everlasting covenant, saith the Lord God; and he that abideth not this law can in nowise enter into my glory, but shall be damned, saith the Lord.

Only those who abide the law of Christ, or the new and everlasting law of marriage, can attain His glory (v. 21). The strait gate is a restricted entry way that requires effort to get to and enter into. The narrow way again requires a careful and undeviating course to follow, and leads unto the exaltation and continuation of the lives, and few there be that find it. It does not allow us to take with us the things of the world, but the things made known to us by Christ as we get to know Him (v. 22). The continuation of lives refers to the husband and wife who receive their exaltation. They will be exalted together (v. 23) and thereby qualify for an increase or spiritual offspring. "This is eternal lives—to know the only wise and true God, and Jesus Christ, whom he hath sent. I am he. Receive ye, therefore, my law" (v. 24). Those who attain eternal lives also receive a seal upon their children as clarified by the Prophet Joseph:

> That which hath been hid from before the foundation of the world is revealed to babes and sucklings in the last days.
>
> The world is reserved unto burning in the last days. He shall send Elijah the prophet, and he shall reveal the covenants of the fathers in relation to the children, and the covenants of the children in relation to the fathers.
>
> Four destroying angels holding power over the four quarters of the earth until the servants of God are sealed in their foreheads, which signifies sealing the blessing upon their heads, meaning the everlasting covenant, thereby making their calling and election made sure. When a seal is put upon the father and mother, it secures their posterity, so that they cannot be lost, but will be saved by virtue of the covenant of their father and mother. [*TPJS,* 321]

It is reported that the Prophet Joseph taught the same principle on another occasion:

> The Prophet Joseph declared—and he never taught a more comforting doctrine—that the eternal sealings of faithful parents and the divine promise made to them for valiant service in the cause of truth, would save not only themselves, but likewise their posterity. Though some of the sheep may wander, the eye of the Shepherd is upon them, and sooner or later they will feel the tentacles of Divine Providence reaching out after them and drawing them back to the fold. Either in this life or the life to come, they will return. They will have to pay their debt to justice; they will suffer for their sins; they may tread a thorny path, but if it leads them at last, like the penitent Prodigal, to a loving and forgiving father's heart and home, the painful experience will not have been in vain. Pray for

your careless and disobedient children; hold on to them with your faith. Hope on, trust on, till you see the salvation of God.[102]

The prophet does not make any statement about the final outcome of the children. They will undoubtedly be judged upon their own works but may not be exalted, however, they will still be sealed to the faithful family. Those who do not receive Christ and the law of marriage suffer spiritual deaths as they enter into the broad gate and wide path rather than the strait and narrow one (D&C 132:24; compare 3 Nephi 14:13–14).

The revelation makes another qualification on the covenant of marriage. To be sealed by the Holy Spirit is to be sealed unto eternal life as a man and wife. It is not just having been married in the temple, which is a conditional promise. Once a person (or persons) has been sealed unto eternal life, they become accountable for their own sins and must suffer for them personally (Hebrews 10:26)—with the exception of murder or the shedding of innocent blood. The payment is made by suffering the buffetings of Satan (see D&C 78:12; 84:21). The Lord gives a further explanation of the shedding of innocent blood. There seem to be two sins of murder mentioned by the Lord concerning those who are sealed to eternal life; verse 26 is speaking of a physical murder, while verse 27 speaks of being a murderer by assenting to the death of Christ or crucifying Him afresh. Alma also speaks of the second type of murder: "Yea, and I had murdered many of his children, or rather led them away unto destruction" (Alma 36:14). As the following testimony of Alma shows, he received forgiveness after suffering or paying somewhat the demand of justice (see Alma 36:15–21).

D&C 132:28–33 • The Law of Christ's Holy Priesthood

28 I am the Lord thy God, and will give unto thee the law of my Holy Priesthood, as was ordained by me and my Father before the world was.

29 Abraham received all things, whatsoever he received, by revelation and commandment, by my word, saith the Lord, and hath entered into his exaltation and sitteth upon his throne.

---

[102] Orson F. Whitney, CR, April 1929, 110, as quoted by Elder Boyd K. Packer, CR, April 1992, 94.

30 Abraham received promises concerning his seed, and of the fruit of his loins—from whose loins ye are, namely, my servant Joseph—which were to continue so long as they were in the world; and as touching Abraham and his seed, out of the world they should continue; both in the world and out of the world should they continue as innumerable as the stars; or, if ye were to count the sand upon the seashore ye could not number them.

31 This promise is yours also, because ye are of Abraham, and the promise was made unto Abraham; and by this law is the continuation of the works of my Father, wherein he glorifieth himself.

32 Go ye, therefore, and do the works of Abraham; enter ye into my law and ye shall be saved.

33 But if ye enter not into my law ye cannot receive the promise of my Father, which he made unto Abraham.

The original question to the Lord submitted by the Prophet Joseph was about Abraham and others having many wives (v. 1). Having explained the everlasting covenant of marriage, the Lord gives background information on Abraham and the law of the priesthood that "was ordained by [Christ] and [His] Father before the world was" (v. 28). Abraham received all things by revelation and commandment, "and hath entered into his exaltation and sitteth upon his throne" (v. 29). Isaiah was told that Abraham was a friend of God (Isaiah 41:8). God's friends are those who keep His commandments (see John 15:14). Because of Abraham's faithfulness, the Lord extended His blessings to the seed (D&C 132:30). The promises made to Abraham concerning his seed was part of the covenant made to him (Abraham 2:11). The promises were made because of God's knowledge of Abraham and his seed (see Genesis 18:18–19).

Since Joseph Smith was from Abraham's loins, the promise of Abraham was extended through him (D&C 124:31). On January 19, 1841, Joseph had been told by the Lord that the promise to Abraham of all "the kindreds of the earth" being blessed would be fulfilled through him and his posterity (D&C 124:57–58; see Genesis 12:3). Through the law of the Holy Priesthood, "the continuation of the works of [the] Father, wherein he glorified himself" (D&C 132:31) was promised to Joseph. The Father's works were "to bring to pass the immortality and eternal life of man" (Moses 1:39). God progresses in glory as He brings others to glory. Joseph Smith explained about the work of Christ in bringing others to be heirs of God and joint heirs with Him:

> What is [a joint heir]? To inherit the same power, the same glory and the same exaltation, until you arrive at the station of a God, and ascend the throne of eternal power, the same as those who have gone before. What did Jesus do? Why, I do the things I saw my Father do when worlds come rolling into existence. My Father worked out his kingdom with fear and trembling, and when I get my kingdom, I shall present it to my Father, so that he may obtain kingdom upon kingdom, and it will exalt him in glory. He will then take a higher exaltation, and I will take his place, and thereby become exalted myself. So that Jesus treads in the tracks of his Father, and inherits what God did before; and God is thus glorified and exalted in the salvation and exaltation of all his children. [*TPJS*, 347–48]

Therefore, Joseph was commanded to "do the works of Abraham; enter into my law and ye shall be saved." Joseph would therefore fulfill Abraham's promise (D&C 132:32–33).

D&C 132:34–40 • Abraham Fulfills the Law

34 God commanded Abraham, and Sarah gave Hagar to Abraham to wife. And why did she do it? Because this was the law; and from Hagar sprang many people. This, therefore, was fulfilling, among other things, the promises.

35 Was Abraham, therefore, under condemnation? Verily I say unto you, Nay; for I, the Lord, commanded it.

36 Abraham was commanded to offer his son Isaac; nevertheless, it was written: Thou shalt not kill. Abraham, however, did not refuse, and it was accounted unto him for righteousness.

37 Abraham received concubines, and they bore him children; and it was accounted unto him for righteousness, because they were given unto him, and he abode in my law; as Isaac also and Jacob did none other things than that which they were commanded; and because they did none other things than that which they were commanded, they have entered into their exaltation, according to the promises, and sit upon thrones, and are not angels but are gods.

38 David also received many wives and concubines, and also Solomon and Moses my servants, as also many others of my servants, from the beginning of creation until this time; and in nothing did they sin save in those things which they received not of me.

39 David's wives and concubines were given unto him of me, by the hand of Nathan, my servant, and others of the prophets who had the keys of this power; and in none of these things did he sin against me save in the case of Uriah and his wife; and, therefore he hath fallen from his exaltation, and received his portion; and he shall not inherit them out of the world, for I gave them unto another, saith the Lord.

40 I am the Lord thy God, and I gave unto thee, my servant Joseph, an appointment, and restore all things. Ask what ye will, and it shall be given unto you according to my word.

The Lord, having given the necessary background for proper understanding, now answers the request of Joseph, "to know and understand . . . the principle and doctrine of having many wives and concubines" (v. 1). "God commanded Abraham, and Sarah gave Hagar to Abraham to wife. And why did she do it? Because this was the law; and from Hagar sprang many people. This, therefore, was fulfilling, among other things, the promises" (v. 34). The Lord commanded and Abraham received the revelation (v. 35; compare v. 29). Sarah gave her consent and obeyed. As revealed in the Book of Mormon, the reason the Lord commanded plural marriage is to "raise up seed unto [Him]" (Jacob 2:30). Otherwise, "there shall not any man among you have save it be one wife; and concubines he shall have none" (Jacob 2:27). The purpose of the Lord, to raise up seed, was fulfilled through Abraham and Hagar, and Joseph Smith was commanded to do likewise. While there are many theories advocated for the purposes and benefits of plural marriage, there is only one reason given in the scriptures, to raise up seed unto the Lord. The Prophet Joseph "gave instructions to try those persons who were preaching, teaching, or practicing the doctrine of plurality of wives; for there is never but one on earth at a time on whom the power and its keys are conferred; and I have constantly said no man shall have but one wife at a time, unless the Lord directs otherwise" (*TPJS,* 324).

A second example of Abraham's obedience was his willingness "to offer his son Isaac" (D&C 132:36). Again, the Lord had a purpose, to teach the people of the future Atonement of Jesus Christ. Isaac's sacrifice was "a similitude of God and his Only Begotten Son" (Jacob 4:5). The Lord apparently included it in this revelation to show Joseph the importance of following the revelation of God, even though it may seemingly be in conflict with other written commandments.

A third example of Abraham's righteousness was his receiving concubines (D&C 132:37). Since the word is plural, this seems to be a reference back to Hagar and to Keturah, a future wife Abraham took after Sarah's death. The book of Genesis uses the word concubine similarly in speaking of Isaac and Abraham's other children (Genesis 25:1–6). The Lord implies that Isaac and Jacob practiced plural marriage with His approval also. He states that they "did none other things than that which they were commanded;" and because of this, "they have entered into their exaltation, according to the promises, and sit upon thrones, and are not angels but are gods" (D&C 132:37).

Jacob had four wives, but much of the life of Jacob has been misrepresented in the present day Bible. We have no record of Isaac living in plural marriage, but apparently he did. There being no record is probably because the Old Testament has suffered the loss of many plain and precious parts (2 Nephi 13:24–29). As the Prophet Joseph declared: "I believe the Bible as it read when it came from the pen of the original writers. Ignorant translators, careless transcribers, or designing and corrupt priests have committed many errors" (*TPJS*, 327). When the plain and precious parts are restored, we will come to "know and understand" better the righteousness of Abraham, Isaac, and Jacob, in their practice of plural marriage, and why they are now exalted.

There were other periods of time when the Lord commanded marriage (vv. 38–39). Moses was married to Zipporah, daughter of Reuel [Jethro], the priest of Midian (Exodus 2:16–17); to an Ethiopian woman (see Numbers 12:1); and perhaps others. Solomon had many wives and concubines, but, as the revelation states, some were not received from the Lord (see 1 Kings 11:1–8). The Bible also supports the revelation concerning David falling from his exaltation and having his wives given to others (v. 39; see 2 Samuel 12:7–12; 1 Kings 15:5).

The Lord reminds Joseph that he is the Lord's servant and has been given an appointment. The Lord will restore all things (D&C 132:40). This dispensation is the dispensation of the fulness of times when all things must be restored (Ephesians 1:10). The law of plural marriage must therefore be restored. As Joseph asked the Lord's will, it was made known and the law was restored.

D&C 132:41–45 • Concerning Adultery

41 And as ye have asked concerning adultery, verily, verily, I say unto you, if a man receiveth a wife in the new and everlasting covenant, and if she be with another man, and I have not appointed unto her by the holy anointing, she hath committed adultery and shall be destroyed.

42 If she be not in the new and everlasting covenant, and she be with another man, she has committed adultery.

43 And if her husband be with another woman, and he was under a vow, he hath broken his vow and hath committed adultery.

44 And if she hath not committed adultery, but is innocent and hath not broken her vow, and she knoweth it, and I reveal it unto you, my servant Joseph, then shall you have power, by the power of my Holy Priesthood, to take her and give her unto him that hath not committed adultery but hath been faithful; for he shall be made ruler over many.

45 For I have conferred upon you the keys and power of the priesthood, wherein I restore all things, and make known unto you all things in due time.

Joseph had asked concerning adultery (v. 41). The Lord's answer makes a distinction between those who have received a wife or husband in the new and everlasting covenant and those who have not. Those given a wife in marriage by the power of the Holy Priesthood were not guilty of adulterous living unless it was with someone "not appointed unto her" (v. 41). The Lord had previously[103] revealed the consequences of adultery under the law unto the Church (D&C 42:24–26, 80–83). The temple endowment had not at that time been revealed, and thus D&C 42 was pertaining to those who had not entered into the new and everlasting covenant of marriage. Therefore, the penalty given in section 132 makes this distinction between those who had entered the eternal marriage covenant and those who had not. The penalty is much more severe for those under the covenant.[104]

Although the penalty for adultery under the law of Moses was death

---

[103] D&C 42, the law unto the Church was given February 9, 1831. It is assumed that being early in the year, and in much more detail concerning adultery than D&C 132, that it was given first or earlier in the year than D&C 132.

[104] Joseph Fielding Smith, *Doctrines of Salvation*, 2:93–94. See "General Authority Quotes," end of chapter.

(see Leviticus 20:10; Deuteronomy 22:22), "shall be destroyed" (D&C 132:41), the penalty for adultery under the new and everlasting covenant, may mean spiritual destruction. The word "shall" suggests the future. The Lord had later revealed (August 1831) that "he that looketh on a woman to lust after her . . . shall not have the Spirit, but shall deny the faith and shall fear" (D&C 63:16). In other words, they would deny the faith and fear their destruction at the judgment day. Those who committed adultery and had not entered into the new and everlasting covenant of marriage were to be dealt with as stated in the law unto the Church (D&C 42). The innocent, under the new and everlasting covenant of marriage, were to be given to another who was faithful, as had the wives of David (D&C 132:44). Joseph had therefore been given the keys and power of the priesthood through which all things were to be restored (v. 45).

D&C 132:46–50 • The Sealing Power

46 And verily, verily, I say unto you, that whatsoever you seal on earth shall be sealed in heaven; and whatsoever you bind on earth, in my name and by my word, saith the Lord, it shall be eternally bound in the heavens; and whosesoever sins you remit on earth shall be remitted eternally in the heavens; and whosesoever sins you retain on earth shall be retained in heaven.

47 And again, verily I say, whomsoever you bless I will bless, and whomsoever you curse I will curse, saith the Lord; for I, the Lord, am thy God.

48 And again, verily I say unto you, my servant Joseph, that whatsoever you give on earth, and to whomsoever you give any one on earth, by my word and according to my law, it shall be visited with blessings and not cursings, and with my power, saith the Lord, and shall be without condemnation on earth and in heaven.

49 For I am the Lord thy God, and will be with thee even unto the end of the world, and through all eternity; for verily I seal upon you your exaltation, and prepare a throne for you in the kingdom of my Father, with Abraham your father.

50 Behold, I have seen your sacrifices, and will forgive all your sins; I have seen your sacrifices in obedience to that which I have told you. Go, therefore, and I make a way for your escape, as I accepted the offering of Abraham of his son Isaac.

The Holy Priesthood had the power to seal on earth and in heaven

(v. 46). The Lord would bless those whom Joseph blessed, and curse those whom Joseph cursed (v. 47). Blessings would follow whatever Joseph did by the Lord's "word and according to [His] law" (v. 48). These promises were given to Joseph because he had been faithful as had Abraham (vv. 49–50).

Joseph had his exaltation sealed upon him. He had received the more sure word of prophecy, or had his calling and election made sure (see D&C 131:5–6 above). Although Joseph still suffered much after this knowledge was given him in 1831, the Lord did repeatedly "make a way for his escape" until his mission was complete (D&C 132:50). Joseph was also not ignorant of this promise to him. He repeatedly said he would be preserved until his mission in this life was fully accomplished (see *TPJS*, 258, 274, 328, 361).

D&C 132:51–57 • Emma's Commandment

51 Verily, I say unto you: A commandment I give unto mine handmaid, Emma Smith, your wife, whom I have given unto you, that she stay herself and partake not of that which I commanded you to offer unto her; for I did it, saith the Lord, to prove you all, as I did Abraham, and that I might require an offering at your hand, by covenant and sacrifice.

52 And let mine handmaid, Emma Smith, receive all those that have been given unto my servant Joseph, and who are virtuous and pure before me; and those who are not pure, and have said they were pure, shall be destroyed, saith the Lord God.

53 For I am the Lord thy God and ye shall obey my voice; and I give unto my servant Joseph that he shall be made ruler over many things; for he hath been faithful over a few things, and from henceforth I will strengthen him.

54 And I command mine handmaid, Emma Smith, to abide and cleave unto my servant Joseph, and to none else. But if she will not abide this commandment she shall be destroyed, saith the Lord; for I am the Lord thy God, and will destroy her if she abide not in my law.

55 But if she will not abide this commandment, then shall my servant Joseph do all things for her, even as he hath said; and I will bless him and multiply him and give unto him an hundredfold in this world, of fathers and mothers, brothers and sisters, houses and lands, wives and children, and crowns of eternal lives in the eternal worlds.

56 And again, verily I say, let mine handmaid forgive my servant Joseph his trespasses; and then shall she be forgiven her trespasses, wherein she has trespassed against me; and I, the Lord thy God, will bless her, and multiply her, and make her heart to rejoice.

57 And again, I say, let not my servant Joseph put his property out of his hands, lest an enemy come and destroy him; for Satan seeketh to destroy; for I am the Lord thy God, and he is my servant; and behold, and lo, I am with him, as I was with Abraham, thy father, even unto his exaltation and glory.

The revelation gives four commandments to Emma, Joseph's wife, and one to Joseph. The first commandment to Emma was actually a cancellation of a commandment that had been given to Joseph as a test for both of them. It is not known what that commandment was, but both of them had apparently passed the test (v. 51).

The second commandment was for Emma to receive all the plural wives "that have been given unto my servant Joseph, and who are virtuous and pure" before the Lord (v. 52). "Those that have been given" him seems to refer to a premortal assignment since the revelation was known as early as 1831. As Emma had been reluctant to accept the revelation, the Lord was apparently forewarning her. Through this law of marriage, Joseph was to "be made ruler over many things; for he had been faithful over a few things" (v. 53). The promise to Joseph was the same given by Jesus in the parable of the talents (Matthew 25:21, 14–30).

The third commandment was an extension of the second commandment. Emma was "to abide and cleave unto [Christ's] servant Joseph, and to none else" (D&C 132:54). In July of 1830, Emma had been told by revelation to "continue in the spirit of meekness, and beware of pride. Let thy soul delight in thy husband, and the glory which shall come upon him. Keep my commandments continually, and a crown of righteousness thou shalt receive. And except thou do this, where I am you cannot come" (D&C 25:14–15). The sharing of her husband with others was certainly a test of her meekness. If her pride caused her to reject the commandments she would be destroyed, but Joseph would still be given the blessings he had been promised (D&C 132:55). That the threatened destruction was of a spiritual nature is shown by the Lord's admonition to Joseph to still do all things for her as he had said. The hundredfold increase of eternal blessings is again a promise given by Jesus in His mortal ministry to those who left all and followed Him (see Mark 10:28–30). Joseph had certainly given all and had followed the Savior.

The fourth commandment to Emma was for her to forgive her husband of his trespasses, "and then shall she be forgiven her trespasses" against the Lord (D&C 132:56). Perhaps Emma was justifying or rationalizing that Joseph was not perfect, therefore, she need not keep the Lord's commandments. Whatever the reason, the Lord was teaching her to forgive others that she may be forgiven (see Matthew 6:14–15; D&C 64:9–10). The Lord concludes His commandments to Emma with a promise to "bless her, and multiply her, and make her heart to rejoice" (D&C 132:56). Certainly Emma was to be a benefactor if she would hearken to the Lord.

The Lord warned Joseph to not "put his property out of his hands" lest Satan be successful in seeking to destroy him. The Lord promised to be with Joseph as He had been "with Abraham, thy Father, even unto his exaltation and Glory" (v. 57). Joseph had asked about Abraham. The Lord therefore compared Joseph to Abraham especially since Joseph was to fulfill the covenant to Abraham.

D&C 132:58–65 • The Law of Sarah

58 Now, as touching the law of the priesthood, there are many things pertaining thereunto.

59 Verily, if a man be called of my Father, as was Aaron, by mine own voice, and by the voice of him that sent me, and I have endowed him with the keys of the power of this priesthood, if he do anything in my name, and according to my law and by my word, he will not commit sin, and I will justify him.

60 Let no one, therefore, set on my servant Joseph; for I will justify him; for he shall do the sacrifice which I require at his hands for his transgressions, saith the Lord your God.

61 And again, as pertaining to the law of the priesthood—if any man espouse a virgin, and desire to espouse another, and the first give her consent, and if he espouse the second, and they are virgins, and have vowed to no other man, then is he justified; he cannot commit adultery for they are given unto him; for he cannot commit adultery with that that belongeth unto him and to no one else.

62 And if he have ten virgins given unto him by this law, he cannot

commit adultery, for they belong to him, and they are given unto him; therefore is he justified.

63 But if one or either of the ten virgins, after she is espoused, shall be with another man, she has committed adultery, and shall be destroyed; for they are given unto him to multiply and replenish the earth, according to my commandment, and to fulfil the promise which was given by my Father before the foundation of the world, and for their exaltation in the eternal worlds, that they may bear the souls of men; for herein is the work of my Father continued, that he may be glorified.

64 And again, verily, verily, I say unto you, if any man have a wife, who holds the keys of this power, and he teaches unto her the law of my priesthood, as pertaining to these things, then shall she believe and administer unto him, or she shall be destroyed, saith the Lord your God; for I will destroy her; for I will magnify my name upon all those who receive and abide in my law.

65 Therefore, it shall be lawful in me, if she receive not this law, for him to receive all things whatsoever I, the Lord his God, will give unto him, because she did not believe and administer unto him according to my word; and she then becomes the transgressor; and he is exempt from the law of Sarah, who administered unto Abraham according to the law when I commanded Abraham to take Hagar to wife.

The Lord prefaced His further explanation of the original question concerning many wives and concubines with a statement about the law of the priesthood, and the call of Joseph Smith. Under the priesthood, any man who was called by God as was Aaron, and did "anything in [Christ's] name, and according to [Christ's] law and by [Christ's] word, he will not commit sin, and I will justify him" (D&C 132:58–59). Joseph had been called as was Aaron, by revelation (see *TPJS*, 272), and the Lord was with him (D&C 132:60). Therefore the law of the priesthood would direct Joseph in the initiation of the "law of Sarah" when it was appropriately introduced. If a man desired a second wife, "and the first give her consent," and they were virtuous and had "vowed to no other man," then he was justified, and was not committing adultery. He could not "commit adultery with that that belongeth unto him and to no one else" (v. 61).

The same law pertained if the man had ten virgins given unto him (v. 62). The first wife is to give her consent as did Sarah (v. 34), and as Emma was commanded (v. 52). The virgins shall not commit adultery, but are to multiply and replenish the earth to raise up seed unto the Lord as he had commanded (see Jacob 2:30). This commandment would bring them "exaltation in the eternal worlds" (D&C 132:63). Another point of the law was that the first wife, who had been taught the law, was to "believe and administer unto him, or she shall be destroyed" (v. 64). The Lord recognizes her agency, but warns that if she becomes the transgressor, the husband is exempt from the law of Sarah because of his wife (v. 65). The Lord will undoubtedly bless him in eternity as He has promised through other covenants, but he is to honor the covenant with her in this life (compare D&C 124:49–50).

D&C 132:66 • More Revealed Later

> 66 And now, as pertaining to this law, verily, verily, I say unto you, I will reveal more unto you, hereafter; therefore, let this suffice for the present. Behold, I am Alpha and Omega. Amen.

The Lord ended the revelation with a promise to reveal more hereafter (D&C 132:66). The promise was fulfilled, at least partially, through President Wilford Woodruff before the Manifesto, or Official Declaration—1, was given (see Doctrine and Covenants, p. 291–292). The Lord revealed His will to him, the President of the High Priesthood. He was shown "by vision and revelation" what would happen and what he was to do (see Excerpts from Three Addresses by President Wilford Woodruff Regarding the Manifesto, Doctrine and Covenants, p. 292–293). The practice of plural marriage was introduced by revelation. The Lord gave His will to His servant Wilford Woodruff. Its purpose was to raise up seed unto the Lord and it accomplished that end. It was restored as part of the restoration of all things in the dispensation of the fulness of times. It is just as serious, or perhaps more so, for the people of this Church to practice it today against the will of the Lord, as it was for those who had it revealed to them and rejected it at the time of Joseph Smith, Brigham Young, John Taylor, or Wilford Woodruff. One of the tests for us today is, do we believe in ongoing revelation?

General Authority Quotes

—The First Presidency and Quorum of the Twelve Apostles • D&C 131:1–4

> The family is ordained of God. Marriage between man and woman is essential to His eternal plan. Children are entitled to birth within the

bonds of matrimony, and to be reared by a father and mother who honor marital vows with complete fidelity. Happiness in family life is most likely to be achieved when founded upon the teachings of the Lord Jesus Christ. ["The Family: A Proclamation to the World," *Ensign,* November 1995, 102]

—*Elder Melvin J. Ballard* • D&C 131:1–4

Those who are denied endless increase cannot be what God is because that, in connection with other things, makes him God. The eternity of the marriage covenant ought to be understood by Latter-day Saints clearly to be the sealing of at least one woman to one man for time and for all eternity. Then do not get confused on that point and imagine that it necessarily means more than one woman. It may be, certainly, but it does mean at least that one man and one woman are sealed together by the power of the Holy Priesthood and by the sealing approval of the Holy Ghost for time and for all eternity, and then that they keep their covenants, before they will be candidates for the highest degree of the celestial glory, and unto them only of all these groups of our Father's children is the promise made of endless or eternal increase.

What do we mean by eternal increase? We mean that through the righteousness and faithfulness of men and women who keep the commandments of God they will come forth with celestial bodies, fitted and prepared to enter into their great, high and eternal glory in the celestial kingdom of God; and unto them, through their preparation, there will come children, who will be spirit children. I don't think that is very difficult to comprehend and understand. The nature of the offspring is determined by the nature of the substance that flows in the veins of the being. When blood flows in the veins of the being, the offspring will be what blood produces, which is tangible flesh and bone, but when that which flows in the veins is spirit matter, a substance which is more refined and pure and glorious than blood, the offspring of such beings will be spirit children. By that I mean they will be in the image of the parents. They will have a spirit body and have the spark of the eternal or divine that always did exist in them. [Bryant S. Hinckley, *Sermons and Missionary Services of Melvin J. Ballard* (1949), 239–40]

—*The Prophet Joseph Smith* • D&C 131:6

. . . A man is saved no faster than he gets knowledge, for if he does not get knowledge, he will be brought into captivity by some evil power in the other world, as evil spirits will have more knowledge, and consequently more power than many men on earth. Hence it needs revelation to assist us, and give us knowledge of the things of God. [*TPJS*, 217]

Add to your faith knowledge, etc. The principle of knowledge is the principle of salvation. This principle can be comprehended by the faithful and diligent; and every one that does not obtain knowledge sufficient to be saved will be condemned. The Principle of salvation is given through the knowledge of Jesus Christ. [*TPJS*, 297]

—*President Howard W. Hunter* • D&C 131:6

When the Prophet said, "A man is saved no faster than he gets knowledge," he had reference not to the temporal knowledge flowing from research, but to the eternal knowledge coming by revelation. Hence it needs revelation to assist us, he continued, "and gives us knowledge of the things of God." [*TPJS*, 217]

When he said, "It is impossible for a man to be saved in ignorance" (D&C 131:6), he meant there could be no ignorance of Jesus Christ and the saving principles of the gospel. [*The Teachings of Howard W. Hunter*, 181]

—*Elder Richard G. Scott* • D&C 132:5

If you are now ready to receive the ordinances of the temple, prepare carefully for that crowning event. Before entering the temple, you will be interviewed by your bishop and stake president for your temple recommend. Be honest and candid with them. That interview is not a test to get passed but an important step to confirm that you have the maturity and spirituality to receive the supernal ordinances and make and keep the edifying covenants offered in the house of the Lord. Personal worthiness is an essential requirement to enjoy the blessings of the temple. Anyone foolish enough to enter the temple unworthily will receive condemnation. [CR, April 1999, 31]

—*President Joseph Fielding Smith* • D&C 132:7, 41

The Holy Spirit of Promise is not the Second Comforter. The Holy Spirit of Promise is the Holy Ghost who places his stamp of approval upon every ordinance that is done righteously; and when covenants are broken he removes the seal. [*Doctrines of Salvation,* 1:55]

. . . In the Doctrine and Covenants, 42:24–26, the Lord has given us a key to this situation. If a person commits adultery and then repents with all his heart, he may be forgiven. If he repeats the offense, he is not to be forgiven, but is to be cast out. As I read it, the Lord has not provided that, under these circumstances, he can come back again.

Now this revelation was given before the endowment was made known. Since that time when a man is married in the temple, he takes a solemn covenant before God, angels, and witnesses that he will keep the law of chastity. Then if he violates that covenant it is not easy to receive forgiveness. I call your attention to this statement by the Prophet Joseph Smith: If a man commit adultery; he cannot receive the celestial kingdom of God. Even if he is saved in any kingdom, it cannot be the celestial kingdom.

Of course, a man may, according to the doctrine and covenants, 132:26, receive forgiveness, if he is willing to pay the penalty for such a crime: that is he "shall be destroyed in the flesh, and shall be delivered unto the buffetings of Satan unto the day of redemption," which is the time of the resurrection. . . . [*Doctrines of Salvation*, 2:93–94]

—President Harold B. Lee • D&C 132:6–7, 26

The Lord has given the inspired truth that "it is impossible to be saved in ignorance" (D&C 131:6). Does this mean that one must be a college graduate or a man of letters to be saved? Not at all. Man cannot be saved in ignorance of those saving principles of the gospel of Jesus Christ [even] if he were to have all the book learning in the world. [*The Teachings of Harold B. Lee*, 336]

There is [one course of] safety for you to follow. In the Doctrine and Covenants the Lord says (and I quote this with great humility because I stand in the position that the Lord is talking about): "I have appointed. . . but one on the earth at a time on whom this power and the keys of this priesthood are conferred" (D&C 132:7). There is only one man who holds all the keys of the priesthood at one time on the earth. He may delegate them to some but he may withhold them from others. [*The Teachings of Harold B. Lee*, 532–33]

Among us there are folks who are interpreting the twenty-sixth verse of the 132nd section of the Doctrine and Covenants to mean that if by some hook or crook we can get into the temple and be married, we are sure of an exaltation regardless of what we may do hereafter, short of committing the unpardonable sin. Have you ever heard that doctrine? The Lord means that we can be forgiven of all kinds of sin except the unpardonable sin, if we truly repent, and shall be forgiven. That is all he meant to tell us. But we will have to suffer the penalty for our sins. But some people construe it otherwise and so are saying [quotes 2 Nephi 28:9]. [*The Teachings of Harold B. Lee*, 111]

—*President Spencer W. Kimball* • D&C 132

It is the normal thing to marry. It was arranged by God in the beginning, long before this world's mountains were ever formed. Remember: "Neither is man without the woman, neither the woman without the man." (1 Corinthians 11:11). . . . Every person should want to be married. There are some who might not be able to. But every person should want to be married because that is what God in heaven planned for us. [*The Teachings of Spencer W. Kimball*, 291]

There are some men who fail to marry through their own choice. They deprive themselves. There may be many women who also deprive themselves of blessings. There are others who never marry because they had no opportunity. We know of course, that the Lord will make ample provision and that no one will ever be condemned for something he or she could not help.

Some might say, "well I'd be satisfied to just become an angel," but you would not. One never would be satisfied just to be a ministering angel to wait on other people when he could be the king himself. [*The Teachings of Spencer W. Kimball*, 292–93]

To the large group of young [unmarried] women in this category, we can only say, you are making a great contribution to the world as you serve your families and the Church and the world. You must remember that the Lord loves you and the Church loves you. We have no control over the heartbeats or the affections of men, but pray that you may find total fulfillment. And in the meantime, we promise you that insofar as your eternity is concerned, that no soul will be deprived of rich, eternal blessings for anything which that person could not help; that eternity is a long time, and that the Lord never fails in his promises and that every righteous woman will receive eventually all to which she is entitled which she has not forfeited through any fault of her own. [*The Teachings of Spencer W. Kimball*, 294]

Chapter Twenty-Six

The Appendix

D&C 133

Doctrine and Covenants 133

Historical Setting: "... A special conference was appointed for the first of November [1831; the publication of the revelations known as the Book of Commandments was to be considered]" (*HC,* 1:221–22).

"... At this time there were many things which the Elders desired to know relative to preaching the Gospel to the inhabitants of the earth, and concerning the gathering; and in order to walk by the true light, and be instructed from on high, on the 3rd of November, 1831, I inquired of the Lord and received the following important revelation [Doctrine and Covenants 133], which has since been added to the book of Doctrine and Covenants, and called the Appendix [due to mob persecutions, it was not added to the Book of Commandments]" (*HC,* 1:229).

Section 133 • Outline

➤ 133:1–3   The Lord will suddenly come to His temple, and will come upon the world with a curse to judgment.

     a.   He shall make bare His holy arm in the eyes of all nations (v. 3).

     b.   All the ends of the earth shall see the salvation of their God (v. 3).

➤ 133:4–11   The people of His Church are to gather upon the land of Zion and be sanctified.

    a.   Go out from Babylon and be clean as ye bear the Lord's vessels (vv. 5, 7).

    b.   Call solemn assemblies, and call upon the name of the Lord (v. 6).

    c.   Send the elders to the nations of the Gentiles, and then the Jews (v. 8).

    d.   Cry to the people to go to Zion, enlarge her borders, strengthen her stakes (v. 9).

    e.   Cry, arise and meet the Bridegroom, prepare for the day of the Lord (vv. 10–11).

➤ 133:12–15   Those among the Gentiles are to flee unto Zion, and those of Judah flee unto Jerusalem, the mountain of the Lord's house (vv. 12–13).

    a.   Go from the nations of Babylon, or the midst of spiritual wickedness (v. 14).

    b.   Let not your flight be in haste, but be prepared and do not look back (v. 15).

➤ 133:16–20   Listen to the elders, the Lord calls all men and commands them to repent.

    a.   He has sent His angel saying, prepare for the Lord's coming (v. 17).

    b.   The Lamb will stand upon Mount Zion with 144,000 (v. 18).

    c.   The Bridegroom will stand on mount Olivet, the mighty ocean, the islands of the sea, and the land of Zion (v. 20).

➤ 133:21–24   He will speak out of Zion, and from Jerusalem, and be heard by all people.

    a.   His voice will break down the mountains, and the valleys not be found (v. 22).

    b.   The great deep be driven to the north countries, and the islands becomes one land (v. 23).

    c.   Jerusalem and Zion will be in their own place like before they were divided (v. 24).

➤ 133:25–35   The Savior will stand in the midst of His people and reign over all flesh.

    a.   Those in the north countries will come to the Lord, their prophets hear His voice, smite the rocks and ice flows down at their presence (v. 26).

    b.   A highway comes up in the great deep, and enemies become their prey (vv. 27–28).

    c.   Pools of living water come in the barren deserts for the parched lands (v. 29).

    d.   They bring rich treasures to Ephraim, and the everlasting hills tremble (v. 39).

    e.   They fall down in Zion and are crowned with glory by the servants, Ephraim, and filled with everlasting joy (vv. 32–33).

    f.   This blessing is upon Israel, the richer blessing on the head of Ephraim (v. 34).

    g.   Judah, after their pain, will be sanctified to dwell with the Lord (v. 35).

➤ 133:36–56   The Lord has sent His angel with the everlasting gospel, who has appeared unto some and will appear unto many.

    a.   This gospel will be preached to every nation, kindred, tongue, and people (v. 37).

    b.   The servants of God shall say (quotes Revelation 14:7) (vv. 38–39).

    c.   They call on the Lord to fulfill the original text of Isaiah 64:1–4 (vv. 40–45).

    d.   It shall be said: (quotes Isaiah 63:1–9 with some variations) (vv. 46–53).

    e.   Enoch to John, and the Apostles, shall be in the Lamb's presence (vv. 54–55).

    f.   The graves will be opened, and they come and sing the song of the Lamb (v. 56).

➤ 133:57–74   The everlasting gospel was to make man partakers of glories revealed.

    a.   Make the weak to confound the wise, thrash the nations by His Spirit (vv. 58–61).

    b.   He that repents and sanctifies himself will be given eternal life (v. 62).

c. Those who hearken not shall be cut off as Moses said (v. 63).

d. The proud and wicked shall burn as Malachi wrote (v. 64).

e. The Lord's answer to the wicked: (Isaiah 50:2–3, 7) (vv. 65–71).

f. The servants sealed up the testimony and bound up the law, and the wicked were delivered unto outer darkness (vv. 72–74).

Introduction

A preface has a subject, a plan, and a purpose as discussed in the preface to the Doctrine and Covenants, section 1. This section, 133, the Appendix to the Doctrine and Covenants can also fit into this pattern, as will be shown in the following analysis.

TEXT AND COMMENTARY

D&C 133:1–3 • The Subject

1 Hearken, O ye people of my church, saith the Lord your God, and hear the word of the Lord concerning you—

2 The Lord who shall suddenly come to his temple; the Lord who shall come down upon the world with a curse to judgment; yea, upon all the nations that forget God, and upon all the ungodly among you.

3 For he shall make bare his holy arm in the eyes of all the nations, and all the ends of the earth shall see the salvation of their God.

The subject is the Second Coming of the Lord Jesus Christ. He was yet to come to His temple when this revelation was given (v. 2), but in the sequence of the published revelations, the appendix being placed at the end, he has now suddenly appeared, on April 3, 1836, in the Kirtland Temple (D&C 110:1–10). When He comes down upon the world, He will curse the nations that had forgotten God, and all the ungodly individuals among those who profess Him (v. 2). To "make bare his holy arm" is the imagery of a man flexing his muscles to show his physical strength. His appearance in glory to the world will show His power in descending without the help of instruments or machines made by man.

Those who cannot abide His glory that attends Him, or His power, will be destroyed, and those who can abide it "shall see the salvation of their God (v. 3).

D&C 133:4–11 • The Plan—Gather and Sanctify

4 Wherefore, prepare ye, prepare ye, O my people; sanctify yourselves; gather ye together, O ye people of my church, upon the land of Zion, all you that have not been commanded to tarry.

5 Go ye out from Babylon. Be ye clean that bear the vessels of the Lord.

6 Call your solemn assemblies, and speak often one to another. And let every man call upon the name of the Lord.

7 Yea, verily I say unto you again, the time has come when the voice of the Lord is unto you: Go ye out of Babylon; gather ye out from among the nations, from the four winds, from one end of heaven to the other.

8 Send forth the elders of my church unto the nations which are afar off; unto the islands of the sea; send forth unto foreign lands; call upon all nations, first upon the Gentiles, and then upon the Jews.

9 And behold, and lo, this shall be their cry, and the voice of the Lord unto all people: Go ye forth unto the land of Zion, that the borders of my people may be enlarged, and that her stakes may be strengthened, and that Zion may go forth unto the regions round about.

10 Yea, let the cry go forth among all people: Awake and arise and go forth to meet the Bridegroom; behold and lo, the Bridegroom cometh; go ye out to meet him. Prepare yourselves for the great day of the Lord.

11 Watch, therefore, for ye know neither the day nor the hour.

The Lord quotes extensively from the scriptures in the appendix, probably as a witness to the Church that the Restoration was a fulfillment of prophecy. The prophecy to go out from Babylon (v. 5), or the wickedness of the world (see v. 14 below), was a prophecy given by Isaiah (Isaiah 52:11). Those who bear the vessels of the Lord are the priesthood holders and leaders of the Church. The calling of solemn assemblies (v. 6) is one of the functions of the temple (see D&C 88:117). To let every man call on the name of the Lord (D&C 133:6) is one of the purposes of the Restoration, the offering of the priesthood to every worthy member male in the Church (see the preface; D&C 1:20). Through the priesthood holders, the voice of the Lord was to give the opportunity to gather out from all the nations of the earth (v. 7). The elders were to call upon all the nations, but upon the Gentiles before the Jews [and other Israel tribes] (v. 8). To enlarge the borders of Zion, and to strengthen her stakes (v. 9) is a quote from Isaiah 54:2. The coming of the Bridegroom (vv. 10–11) is the fulfilling of the Savior's parable of the ten virgins (see Matthew 25:1–13), for which coming the Saints were to prepare.

D&C 133:12–15 • Two Gathering Places

12 Let them, therefore, who are among the Gentiles flee unto Zion.

13 And let them who be of Judah flee unto Jerusalem, unto the mountains of the Lord's house.

14 Go ye out from among the nations, even from Babylon, from the midst of wickedness, which is spiritual Babylon.

15 But verily, thus saith the Lord, let not your flight be in haste, but let all things be prepared before you; and he that goeth, let him not look back lest sudden destruction shall come upon him.

The mountains [plural] of the Lord's house (v. 12–13) is the imagery used by the Lord to depict temples. A temple is yet to be built in Zion [Independence, Missouri] and in Jerusalem.[105] The word "flee" implies a sudden movement. It reminds us of a future time spoken of by the Prophet Joseph: "The time is soon coming, when no man will have any peace but in Zion and her stakes" (*TPJS,* 161). The imagery of Babylon as spiritual wickedness (D&C 133:13) is based on the extreme wickedness of ancient Babylon. To not flee in haste (v. 14) seems to contradict the sudden movement stated above. However, it is explaining that before the people will flee, all things must be prepared in those two places, Zion and Jerusalem. They will not necessarily flee at the same time either. The surrounding stakes must be established in Zion (see D&C 115:6, 18), and the cities of Zion and Jerusalem become holy (see Ether 13:8–11). The Lord now returns to the time of fleeing when He exhorts them to not look back (v. 15). This reminds us of the account of Lot and his wife (see Genesis 19:17–26). We must "look to the Presidency and receive instruction" (*TPJS*) to know when to build and when to flee.

---

[105] See Monte S. Nyman, *Great Are the Words of Isaiah,* 26–29, for a further explanation of the imagery and the building of these two temples.

D&C 133:16–20

16 Hearken and hear, O ye inhabitants of the earth. Listen, ye elders of my church together, and hear the voice of the Lord; for he calleth upon all men, and he commandeth all men everywhere to repent.

17 For behold, the Lord God hath sent forth the angel crying through the midst of heaven, saying: Prepare ye the way of the Lord, and make his paths straight, for the hour of his coming is nigh—

18 When the Lamb shall stand upon Mount Zion, and with him a hundred and forty-four thousand, having his Father's name written on their foreheads.

19 Wherefore, prepare ye for the coming of the Bridegroom; go ye, go ye out to meet him.

20 For behold, he shall stand upon the mount of Olivet, and upon the mighty ocean, even the great deep, and upon the islands of the sea, and upon the land of Zion.

The elders of Israel are called by the Lord to declare repentance to all men everywhere (v. 16). As further evidence of this declaration, the Lord confirms the visit of the angel [Moroni] to prepare the way of the Lord. The Lord's path cannot be made straight unless those who prepare it have repented and are walking a straight path (v. 17). This was John the Baptist's mission before His first coming (see Isaiah 40:3–5), and having brought His priesthood to the earth again (D&C 13), his mission which originally extended to the fulness of times is to be completed:

3 The voice of him that crieth in the wilderness, Prepare ye the way of the Lord, make straight in the desert a highway for our God.

4 Every valley shall be exalted, and every mountain and hill shall be made low; and the crooked shall be made straight, and the rough places plain;

5 And the glory of the Lord shall be revealed, and all flesh shall see it together; for the mouth of the Lord hath spoken it. [JST, Isaiah 40:3–5; see also JST, Luke 3:4–8]

Having delivered His keys to man in this dispensation, the elders were to do the earthly part of it. The time of His coming is again declared to be nigh (v. 17). This is in the Lord's time, but is even closer almost one hundred and eighty years later.

When He comes, He will stand upon Mount Zion with one hundred forty-four thousand of the Father's servants from this and other dispensations (see Revelation 7:4–8; D&C 77:11; and comments). The location of Mount Zion is not identified; it is certainly in America, perhaps the New Jerusalem temple area. Joseph Smith declared: "The selection of persons to form that number had already commenced" (*HC,* 6:196), implying that high priests from this dispensation will be included in that number. Those who go out to meet Him (v. 19) will be the living and not a part of that number, while those who come with Him will have left their mortal probation, and are a part of the total number. It does not say whether the high priests will be with Him on the other four places where He will stand (v. 20). While the mount of Olivet [Olives] in Jerusalem is a literal mountain, we know that it will split and form a great valley, and water shall come out from the temple (see Zechariah 14:4–11; Joel 3:18; D&C 45:48). We have no specific details of His standing on the ocean, the islands of the sea, and the land of Zion, but will know when it is fulfilled (see 2 Nephi 25:7).

D&C 133:21–24 • The Islands Become One Land

> 21 And he shall utter his voice out of Zion, and he shall speak from Jerusalem, and his voice shall be heard among all people;
>
> 22 And it shall be a voice as the voice of many waters, and as the voice of a great thunder, which shall break down the mountains, and the valleys shall not be found.
>
> 23 He shall command the great deep, and it shall be driven back into the north countries, and the islands shall become one land;
>
> 24 And the land of Jerusalem and the land of Zion shall be turned back into their own place, and the earth shall be like as it was in the days before it was divided.

The voice out of Zion and out of Jerusalem that will be heard by all people (v. 21) will possibly be the effects of the changing mountains and valleys. As cited above, the Mount of Olives will be divided, but the change in this verse seems to be a later change. We have no specifics on the changes, but they must be extensive and will be on both the eastern and the western continents (v. 22). The Prophet Joseph said: "The whole of America is Zion itself from north to south, and is described by the

Prophets" (*TPJS,* 362; see also Alma 46:17).

The great deep (v. 23) is apparently the Atlantic Ocean. The borders on its east side and its west side seem to fit together naturally if the ocean were removed. The prophet Isaiah made what appears to be the same prophecy:

> 1 FOR Zion's sake will I not hold my peace, and for Jerusalem's sake I will not rest, until the righteousness thereof go forth as brightness, and the salvation thereof as a lamp [that] burneth.
>
> 2 And the Gentiles shall see thy righteousness, and all kings thy glory: and thou shalt be called by a new name, which the mouth of the LORD shall name.
>
> 3 Thou shalt also be a crown of glory in the hand of the LORD, and a royal diadem in the hand of thy God.
>
> 4 Thou shalt no more be termed Forsaken; neither shall thy land any more be termed Desolate: but thou shalt be called Hephzibah, and thy land Beulah: for the LORD delighteth in thee, and thy land shall be married. [Isaiah 62:1–4]

The context of Isaiah—Zion and Jerusalem, the crown of glory, and the marriage of the lands—are the same context as the revelation we are now considering. The word *Hephzibah* means "desire or delight in her," and *Beulah* means "union or married" (see biblical footnotes in any versions). The earth obeys when the Lord speaks to it (D&C 133:23; and Helaman 12:8–19). The earth was divided (v. 24) in the days of Peleg (Genesis 10:25). While most Bible commentaries will explain that this division was a political or social one, the Doctrine and Covenants is a second witness that it was a literal physical division.

D&C 133:25–35 • Ephraim, Servants of the Lord

> 25 And the Lord, even the Savior, shall stand in the midst of his people, and shall reign over all flesh.
>
> 26 And they who are in the north countries shall come in remembrance before the Lord; and their prophets shall hear his voice, and shall no longer stay themselves; and they shall smite the rocks, and the ice shall flow down at their presence.
>
> 27 And an highway shall be cast up in the midst of the great deep.
>
> 28 Their enemies shall become a prey unto them,

29 And in the barren deserts there shall come forth pools of living water; and the parched ground shall no longer be a thirsty land.

30 And they shall bring forth their rich treasures unto the children of Ephraim, my servants.

31 And the boundaries of the everlasting hills shall tremble at their presence.

32 And there shall they fall down and be crowned with glory, even in Zion, by the hands of the servants of the Lord, even the children of Ephraim.

33 And they shall be filled with songs of everlasting joy.

34 Behold, this is the blessing of the everlasting God upon the tribes of Israel, and the richer blessing upon the head of Ephraim and his fellows.

35 And they also of the tribe of Judah, after their pain, shall be sanctified in holiness before the Lord, to dwell in his presence day and night, forever and ever.

The Savior reigning over all flesh (v. 25) strongly suggests the Millennium. Those who are in the north countries (v. 26) are apparently the lost tribes, also commonly called the ten tribes. Therefore, it seems that at least some of the ten tribes are still somewhere in a body of people together. It should also be remembered that during a conference of the Church in June 1831, according to John Whitmer's *History of the Church* (chapter 5): "The Spirit of the Lord fell upon Joseph in an unusual manner, and he prophesied that John the Revelator was then among the Ten Tribes of Israel who had been led away by Shalmaneser, king of Assyria, to prepare them for their return from their long dispersion. To again possess the land of their fathers" (*HC,* 1:176; footnote).

The Book of Mormon also supports their return being after the New Jerusalem is built and the Millennium is ushered in:

24 And then shall they assist my people that they may be gathered in, who are scattered upon all the face of the land, in unto the New Jerusalem.

25 And then shall the power of heaven come down among them; and I also will be in the midst.

26 And then shall the work of the Father commence at that day, even when this gospel shall be preached among the remnant of this people.

> Verily I say unto you, at that day shall the work of the Father commence among all the dispersed of my people, yea, even the tribes which have been lost, which the Father hath led away out of Jerusalem. [3 Nephi 21:24–26]

Again we turn to Isaiah for the same prophecy as given in the appendix: "And the ransomed of the LORD shall return, and come to Zion with songs and everlasting joy upon their heads: they shall obtain joy and gladness, and sorrow and sighing shall flee away" (Isaiah 35:10). Doctrine and Covenants 133:33 quotes the part about songs of everlasting joy. The Apocrypha—which the Lord told Joseph Smith had "many things contained therein that are true, and mostly translated correctly"—has as well "many things that are not true." To understand it, one must read it by the Spirit and obtain the benefit (see D&C 91). It tells of the ten tribes being taken into the north countries, a great distance, and dwelling there "until the last time" and then describes similar miracles on their return as are described in this appendix (D&C 133:26–29; see 2 Esdras 13:46–50). We will leave this as a possibility, and note what Nephi said about the prophecies of Isaiah, and apply it to the Apocrypha: "In the days that the prophecies of Isaiah [2 Esdras] shall be fulfilled men shall know of a surety, at the times when they shall come to pass" (2 Nephi 25:7). How the great highway in the midst of the great deep (v. 27) relates to the two continents becoming one we will put in the same category, but note that the ocean shall be driven into the north countries, from where those people [ten tribes?] will return.

The rich treasures, brought with those people from the north countries (v. 30), and their being crowned with glory in Zion (v. 32), has usually been interpreted to be their genealogical records, and the receiving of their temple endowments from the children of Ephraim. This interpretation is certainly valid, but should not be limited to that only. They are to also bring their scriptures with them:

> 12 For behold, I shall speak unto the Jews and they shall write it; and I shall also speak unto the Nephites and they shall write it; and I shall also speak unto the other tribes of the house of Israel, which I have led away, and they shall write it; and I shall also speak unto all nations of the earth and they shall write it.
>
> 13 And it shall come to pass that the Jews shall have the words of the Nephites, and the Nephites shall have the words of the Jews; and

the Nephites and the Jews shall have the words of the lost tribes of Israel; and the lost tribes of Israel shall have the words of the Nephites and the Jews. [2 Nephi 29:12–13]

"When the [three] nations shall run together the testimony of the [three] nations shall run together also" (2 Nephi 29:8). The boundaries of the everlasting hills trembling at their presence suggests a large number of them coming from the north.

Ephraim, the Lord's servant (D&C 133:30, 32) and birthright holder (1 Chronicles 5:1), is the prominent tribe of the Restoration. The appendix refers to them as the "richer blessing upon the head of Ephraim and his fellows" (D&C 133:34). They are the mother trunk into which the other branches are to be grafted (see Jacob 5:54–63). Their tribal patriarchal blessing, given to them by Moses, was: "His glory is like the firstling of his bullock, and his horns are like the horns of unicorns: with them he shall push the people together to the ends of the earth: and they are the ten thousands of Ephraim, and they are the thousands of Manasseh" (Deuteronomy 33:17). That this was to be fulfilled by the elders of the Church today was confirmed in August, 1831. "For, behold, [the elders] shall push the people together from the ends of the earth" (D&C 58:45).

The Lord also recognizes the tribe of Judah (v. 35), the third group of Israel, to include all of the basic tribes of Israel. Their pain probably refers to their persecution, their becoming "a hiss and a by-word, and be hated among all nations" where they were scattered (1 Nephi 19:14). They will also be gathered again, and become a sanctified people and dwell in His presence (v. 35).

D&C 133:36–39 • The Everlasting Gospel to All

36 And now, verily saith the Lord, that these things might be known among you, O inhabitants of the earth, I have sent forth mine angel flying through the midst of heaven, having the everlasting gospel, who hath appeared unto some and hath committed it unto man, who shall appear unto many that dwell on the earth.

37 And this gospel shall be preached unto every nation, and kindred, and tongue, and people.

38 And the servants of God shall go forth, saying with a loud voice:

Fear God and give glory to him, for the hour of his judgment is come;

39 And worship him that made heaven, and earth, and the sea, and the fountains of waters—

Again the Lord confirms the mission of the angel Moroni. This time He quotes Revelation 14:6–7, verifying that John the Revelator was speaking of Moroni in that passage of scripture. However, He adds a dimension that is not known or recognized even among most Church members. Moroni had "appeared unto some," more than just Joseph, and "shall yet appear unto many that dwell on the earth" (v. 36). Elder Pratt, not disclosing his sources, called him "the guardian of America:"

> It was by the agency of that same angel of God that appeared unto Joseph Smith, and revealed unto him the history [record] of the early inhabitants of this country, whose mounds, bones, and remains of towns, cities, and fortifications speak from the dust in the ears of the living with the voice of undeniable truth. This same angel presides over the destinies of America, and feels a lively interest in all our doings. He was in the camp of Washington; and, by an invisible hand, led on our fathers to conquest and victory; and all this to open and prepare the way for the Church and kingdom of God to be established on the western hemisphere, for the redemption of Israel and the salvation of the world.
>
> This same angel was with Columbus, and gave him deep impressions, by dreams and impressions, respecting this New World. Trammeled by poverty and by an unpopular cause, yet his persevering and unyielding heart would not allow an obstacle in his way too great for him to overcome; and the angel of God helped him—was with him on the stormy deep, calmed the troubled elements, and guided his frail vessel to the desired haven. Under the guardianship of this same angel, or prince of America, have the United States grown, increased, and flourished, like the sturdy oak by the rivers of water.[106]

Since the Book of Mormon was to go to every nation, kindred, tongue, and people; it was undoubtedly his stewardship to oversee it's being taken to places outside of America, and may have appeared invisibly, or visibly, to many others in those places of the earth. From this quote of Revelation 14:7 (vv. 38–39), it is apparent that this verse is the message for the servants of God to take to the world.

---

[106] H. Donl Peterson, *Ancient Prophet, Modern Messenger* [1983], 79–80.

D&C 133:40–45 • Isaiah 64:1–4 Fulfilled

40 Calling upon the name of the Lord day and night, saying: O that thou wouldst rend the heavens, that thou wouldst come down, that the mountains might flow down at thy presence.

41 And it shall be answered upon their heads; for the presence of the Lord shall be as the melting fire that burneth, and as the fire which causeth the waters to boil.

42 O Lord, thou shalt come down to make thy name known to thine adversaries, and all nations shall tremble at thy presence—

43 When thou doest terrible things, things they look not for;

44 Yea, when thou comest down, and the mountains flow down at thy presence, thou shalt meet him who rejoiceth and worketh righteousness, who remembereth thee in thy ways.

45 For since the beginning of the world have not men heard nor perceived by the ear, neither hath any eye seen, O God, besides thee, how great things thou hast prepared for him that waiteth for thee.

The message of the servants continues, and the Lord quotes Isaiah 64:1–4, showing that the Old Testament prophet had also foretold this great movement of the Restoration. We will not compare the two texts at this time, but merely note that the Doctrine and Covenants has the more complete text.[107] Whether it is the original text, or made more clear by the Lord is not certain, but the Doctrine and Covenants text should take precedence when studying either one. We just summarize here that the servants are pleading for the Lord to come down and cleanse the earth, a terrible thing for the wicked (v. 43), but a glorious event for the righteous (vv. 44–45).

D&C 133:46–53 • Isaiah 63:1–9 Fulfilled

46 And it shall be said: Who is this that cometh down from God in heaven with dyed garments; yea, from the regions which are not known, clothed in his glorious apparel, traveling in the greatness of his strength?

47 And he shall say: I am he who spake in righteousness, mighty to save.

---

[107] For a comparison of the texts, and some commentary, see Monte S. Nyman, *Great Are the Words of Isaiah* [1980], 241–243.

48 And the Lord shall be red in his apparel, and his garments like him that treadeth in the wine-vat.

49 And so great shall be the glory of his presence that the sun shall hide his face in shame, and the moon shall withhold its light, and the stars shall be hurled from their places.

50 And his voice shall be heard: I have trodden the wine-press alone, and have brought judgment upon all people; and none were with me;

51 And I have trampled them in my fury, and I did tread upon them in mine anger, and their blood have I sprinkled upon my garments, and stained all my raiment; for this was the day of vengeance which was in my heart.

52 And now the year of my redeemed is come; and they shall mention the loving kindness of their Lord, and all that he has bestowed upon them according to his goodness, and according to his loving kindness, forever and ever.

53 In all their afflictions he was afflicted. And the angel of his presence saved them; and in his love, and in his pity, he redeemed them, and bore them, and carried them all the days of old;

Verse 46 begins the quoting of the first half of the previous chapter of Isaiah (63:1–9). Once more there are some variations in the text. Both texts begin with a question, but the Doctrine and Covenants makes it a general comment of some who see the Lord descend at his Second Coming. The Isaiah text names the places from whence He comes, but the modern revelation says He comes from God in heaven the unknown regions (v. 46). Thus Isaiah is using imagery in his description. The Lord's response to the question is given in the Doctrine and Covenants, but not in Isaiah. He describes Himself by His past speech and His mission to save rather than giving His name (v. 47). The Isaiah text asks a question about His apparel, and the appendix merely describes it (v. 48).

The description of His garments being red often raises the question about the literalness of the color of His clothes. "Like him that treadeth the wine-vat" (v. 48; Isaiah 62:2) certainly suggests a figurative expression. The clothes of those who tread the grapes for the making of wine would absorb the color of the juice and identify what they were or had been doing. The symbolism, or the literalness, of His clothing color both refer to His having made the Atonement and absorbed the stain of their sins with His blood shed in Gethsemane. The following verse (D&C 133:49) is not in Isaiah, and may have been lost from His text or added to further clarify His coming. The verse seems to be a paraphrase of Isaiah 13:10 and 13, and Isaiah 24:23. The book of Revelation also gives a similar account (see Revelation 19:13, 15; 14:20). The greatness of the glory attending His presence shall exceed the light of the sun or the moon, and stars will be hurled from their traditional places. In this writer's mind, this further confirms that the clothing color is figurative; why would, or could, the color be noticeable in such brilliance at His coming? Regardless, does it matter? The Atonement that He had made is the intended message, and we should not be distracted from that priceless doctrine.

The Isaiah text is longer. The Doctrine and Covenants is more succinct. It first describes the day of His vengeance upon the wicked (vv. 50–51), followed by the loving kindness of the afflictions He suffered in His making the Atonement for all the inhabitants of the earth through-out all the days of their existence (vv. 52–53).[108]

D&C 133:54–56 • Those Who Came with the Savior

54 Yea, and Enoch also, and they who were with him; the prophets who were before him; and Noah also, and they who were before him; and Moses also, and they who were before him;

55 And from Moses to Elijah, and from Elijah to John, who were with Christ in his resurrection, and the holy apostles, with Abraham, Isaac, and Jacob, shall be in the presence of the Lamb.

56 And the graves of the saints shall be opened; and they shall come forth and stand on the right hand of the Lamb, when he shall stand upon Mount Zion, and upon the holy city, the New Jerusalem; and they shall sing the song of the Lamb, day and night forever and ever.

The names given here were the heads of their dispensations and were covered by the Atonement, along with the righteous who lived at that time. These were with Him at the resurrection that came after His death in the meridian of time (vv. 54–55). There could be others added from the Nephites (see 3 Nephi 23:9–13), and undoubtedly the lost tribes (see 3 Nephi 17:4). The holy Apostles were still living at the time of the beginning of the First Resurrection, but will be in His presence when He comes again. While some have been resurrected since that time—Moroni

---

[108] Ibid., 238–241.

was a resurrected being and lived after the First Resurrection (see *TPJS,* 119)—there will be many resurrected at the time of His coming to Mount Zion and the New Jerusalem (D&C 133:56).

D&C 133:57–62 • The Weak Confound the Wise

> 57 And for this cause, that men might be made partakers of the glories which were to be revealed, the Lord sent forth the fulness of his gospel, his everlasting covenant, reasoning in plainness and simplicity—
>
> 58 To prepare the weak for those things which are coming on the earth, and for the Lord's errand in the day when the weak shall confound the wise, and the little one become a strong nation, and two shall put their tens of thousands to flight.
>
> 59 And by the weak things of the earth the Lord shall thrash the nations by the power of his Spirit.
>
> 60 And for this cause these commandments were given; they were commanded to be kept from the world in the day that they were given, but now are to go forth unto all flesh—
>
> 61 And this according to the mind and will of the Lord, who ruleth over all flesh.
>
> 62 And unto him that repenteth and sanctifieth himself before the Lord shall be given eternal life.

The remainder of this revelation gives several purposes of the restoration of the fulness of the gospel, His everlasting covenant. The first purpose was for men to be partakers of the glories to be revealed (v. 57). These glories—the celestial, the terrestrial, and the telestial—were revealed about three and a half months later (February 1832; D&C 76).

The second purpose of the Restoration was to prepare the weak to confound the wise in the coming days (D&C 133:58). Paul gave the same principle to the Corinthians of his day (see 1 Corinthians 1:27). "The little one become a strong nation" was quoting from Isaiah 60:22. "The weak things of the earth shall thrash the nations by the power of his Spirit" (v. 59) was a phrase used by the Lord in an earlier revelation (D&C 35:13–14), and may have been paraphrasing from Isaiah 41:15, or even quoting from an earlier Isaiah text that had been lost. Quotes from Isaiah are very prevalent in the appendix.

A third purpose of the Restoration was for those who would repent and sanctify themselves to gain eternal life (vv. 60–62). What time period the commandments had been withheld from the world is not stated, but seems to be speaking of the apostasy following Christ's ministry on earth. While the reason for it being withheld is also not given, it was probably for their own good. It was the mind and will of the Lord (v. 61) whose work and glory is "to bring o pass the immortality and eternal life of man" (Moses 1:39). The Lord knew when was the best time for them to have a full opportunity for the gospel, then or in the spirit world.

D&C 133:63–64 • Fulfill Moses and Malachi

> 63 And upon them that hearken not to the voice of the Lord shall be fulfilled that which was written by the prophet Moses, that they should be cut off from among the people.
>
> 64 And also that which was written by the prophet Malachi: For, behold, the day cometh that shall burn as an oven, and all the proud, yea, and all that do wickedly, shall be stubble; and the day that cometh shall burn them up, saith the Lord of hosts, that it shall leave them neither root nor branch.

The quote of Moses (v. 63) is Deuteronomy 18:18–19, and was quoted by Peter as referring to Christ (see Acts 3:22–23). It was also quoted by Nephi as referring to Christ (see 1 Nephi 22:20–21), and by the angel Moroni to Joseph Smith and identified as Christ (JS—H 1:40). However, Jesus quoted it to the Nephites as referring to the Gentiles rejecting the Book of Mormon (see 3 Nephi 21:11). Since the words of the Book of Mormon were revealed through Christ, it was applicable to Moses' warning.

Malachi's quote is from his writings (Malachi 4:1), and was quoted by Jesus to the Nephites (3 Nephi 25:1), and by the angel Moroni to the young boy Joseph Smith, "though with a little variation" (JS—H 1:36–37). It speaks of the Second Coming and will be fulfilled when He appears in glory, and those who are not prepared to receive His glory will be burned. The roots refer to the ancestors, and the branches refer to the posterity of those burned. They will not have any eternal connections with their family.

D&C 133:65–71 • The Lord Answers the Wicked

65 Wherefore, this shall be the answer of the Lord unto them:

66 In that day when I came unto mine own, no man among you received me, and you were driven out.

67 When I called again there was none of you to answer; yet my arm was not shortened at all that I could not redeem, neither my power to deliver.

68 Behold, at my rebuke I dry up the sea. I make the rivers a wilderness; their fish stink, and die for thirst.

69 I clothe the heavens with blackness, and make sackcloth their covering.

70 And this shall ye have of my hand—ye shall lie down in sorrow.

71 Behold, and lo, there are none to deliver you; for ye obeyed not my voice when I called to you out of the heavens; ye believed not my servants, and when they were sent unto you ye received them not.

Jesus had been rejected by the Jews when He came to them as a mortal (v. 66). Isaiah 50:1 is apparently referring to His coming to them. At His Second Coming, the text of Isaiah 50:2–11 will then be fulfilled (D&C 133:67–70). The Book of Mormon text, 2 Nephi 7, of Jacob, son of Lehi, quoting Isaiah 50, shows that Isaiah is speaking to those of the house of Israel who rejected the Restoration, and that their rejection was not because He did not have the power, but it is His power that will place them where He is not, and they will reap sorrow (v. 67). Why the Lord quotes the King James Bible text rather than the better 2 Nephi text is not known, but it is possible that He wants to show the house of Israel, who rejected Him, that the Bible they professed belief in had the same message. They had rejected the Lord and His servants, and no one else had the power to deliver them from their misery (v. 71).

D&C 133:72–74 • The Servants' Testimony Sealed

72 Wherefore, they sealed up the testimony and bound up the law, and ye were delivered over unto darkness.

73 These shall go away into outer darkness, where there is weeping, and wailing, and gnashing of teeth.

74 Behold the Lord your God hath spoken it. Amen.

The subject of these verses is the servants of God (see vv. 71 and 38). These servants had been given the power to seal up the unbelieving and the rebellious unto the day when the wrath of God would be poured out upon the wicked. The appendix, placed at the end of the Doctrine and Covenants, is describing the day when that power had been exercised (vv. 72–73). The darkness may refer to the spirit world during the Millennium where the telestial beings would be for a thousand years awaiting the resurrection, or it may be referring to the sons of perdition who were to be cast into outer darkness for eternity. It is applicable to both, but the difference is the length of time.

General Authority Quotes

—President Marion G. Romney • D&C 133:5

Now other "words of eternal life" that have preceded "forth from the mouth of God" to which we must give more "diligent heed" if we would "have glory added upon [our] heads for ever and ever" are these: [quotes 133:5]. . . .

Certainly we priesthood bearers who would so magnify our callings in the priesthood as to obtain eternal life and "have glory added upon [our] heads for ever and ever" will diligently strive to keep the commandments [quotes D&C 133:5]. [CR, April 1974, 117–18]

—President Ezra Taft Benson • D&C 133:10–12; 26–35

The preparation must consist of more than just causal membership in the Church. We must be guided by personal revelation and the counsel of the living prophet so we will not be deceived. [*The Teachings of Ezra Taft Benson,* 106]

In the scriptures there are set forth three phases of the gathering of Israel. One, the gathering of Israel to the land of Zion which is America, this land. That is underway and has been underway since the Church was established and our missions abroad were inaugurated. Then two, the return of the lost tribes, the ten lost tribes from the land of the North (see D&C 133 [vv. 11–12, 26; and following]). And the third phase is the reestablishment of the Jews in Palestine as one of the events to precede the second coming of the master. [*The Teachings of Ezra Taft Benson,* 106, 91]

—*The Prophet Joseph Smith* • D&C 133:13

> [Orson Hyde] requested to know if converted Jews should go to Jerusalem or to come to Zion. I therefore wish you to inform him that converted Jews must come here. [*HC,* 2:232]

—*Elder James E. Talmage* • D&C 133:16

> [Concerning the] bringing forth of the Lost Tribes from their hiding place, which is known to God, but unknown to man. Nevertheless, I have found elders in Israel who would tell me that the predictions relating to the Lost Tribes are to be explained in the figurative manner—that the gathering of those tribes is already well advanced and that there is no hiding place whereunto God has led them, from which they shall come forth, led by their prophets to receive their blessings here at the hands of gathered Ephraim, the gathered portions that have been scattered among the nations. Yea, let God be true, and doubt we not his word, though it makes the opinions of men appear to be lies. The tribes shall come; they are not lost unto the Lord; they shall be brought forth as have been predicted. [CR, October 1960, as quoted in Daniel H. Ludlow, *A Companion to Your Study of the Doctrine and Covenants* (1978), 1:674–75]

—*President Joseph Fielding Smith* • D&C 133:26

> When the Savior taught the Nephites, he informed them that he had "other sheep" that are not of the Nephites, neither of the land of Jerusalem, and these also were to hear his voice and be ministered to by him. It is reasonable for us to conclude that among these others, who were hidden from the rest of the world, he likewise chose disciples—perhaps twelve—to perform like functions and minister unto their people with the same fulness of divine authority. [*Doctrines of Salvation,* 3:159]

—*President Gordon B. Hinckley* • D&C 133:36–37

> Since its [Book of Mormon] first publication in a rural print shop in Palmyra, New York, there have been more than 133 million copies produced. It has been translated into 105 languages. Not long ago it was named one of the 20 most influential books ever published in North America. [*Ensign,* November 2007, 85; CR, October 2007]

Chapter Twenty-Seven

Praise to the Man

D&C 113; 135

DOCTRINE AND COVENANTS 113

Historical Setting: "[March 1838] The Prophet's answers to questions on Scripture [Isaiah]" (*HC,* 3:9).

Introduction

"You don't know me; you never knew my heart. No man knows my history. I cannot tell it: I shall never undertake it. I don't blame anyone for believing my history. If I had not experienced what I have, I could not have believed it myself. I never did harm any man since I was born into the world. My voice is also for peace" (*TPJS,* 361)

We may not know his history, but we do know much about him from men who knew him. We will review just some of those men, and will start with the prophet Isaiah, who at least knew of him, and Joseph knew Isaiah's writings. The Lord also knew Joseph Smith, and is the source of the answers below.

D&C 113:1–6 • The Rod from the Stem of Jesse

1 WHO is the stem of Jesse spoken of in the 1st, 2d, 3d, 4th, and 5th verses of the 11th chapter of Isaiah?

2 Verily thus saith the Lord: It is Christ.

Jesse was the father of David, king of Israel. David was promised that "thine house and thy kingdom shall be established for ever before thee: thy throne shall be established for ever" (2 Samuel 7:16). Christ was of the seed of David (see Matthew 1:1–17), and as such will sit on the throne of David eternally. When the angel Moroni appeared to Joseph Smith, "he quoted the eleventh chapter of Isaiah, saying that it was about to be fulfilled" (JS—H 1:40). It was to be fulfilled through Joseph Smith, as the following verses will show:

> 3 What is the rod spoken of in the first verse of the 11th chapter of Isaiah, that should come of the Stem of Jesse?
>
> 4 Behold, thus saith the Lord: It is a servant in the hands of Christ, who is partly a descendant of Jesse as well as of Ephraim, or of the house of Joseph, on whom there is laid much power.
>
> 5 What is the root of Jesse spoken of in the 10th verse of the 11th chapter?
>
> 6 Behold, thus saith the Lord, it is a descendant of Jesse, as well as of Joseph, unto whom rightly belongs the priesthood, and the keys of the kingdom, for an ensign, and for the gathering of my people in the last days.

The servant in the hands of Christ, is Joseph Smith, a literal seed of Abraham, Isaac, and Jacob, to whom covenants for eternity were made (see Abraham 2:8–11; D&C 124:58; 132:30–31). As a descendant of the sons of Jacob, Joseph, and Judah, he was given great responsibilities. Ephraim was given the birthright, the responsibility for all of the twelve tribes (see 1 Chronicles 5:1; Jeremiah 31:9). On the rod was laid much power. The "power from on high, by the means which were before prepared [the Urim and Thummim], to translate the Book of Mormon" (D&C 20:8). He was given the power of the Holy Ghost to receive revelation from God (see D&C 20:35). He received the power of the Aaronic Priesthood to have angels minister to him and function in the preparatory gospel (D&C 13; 84:26–27). He received also the power of the Melchizedek Priesthood, and the power to know the mysteries and of godliness being manifest, even to see the face of God and live (see D&C 84:19–22).

As a descendant of Judah (vv. 4, 6), he had the political power to organize the political arm of the kingdom of God. This was known as the Council of Fifty and was organized on April 6, 1842. While it functioned in Nauvoo and Utah, it was disbanded—and is considered by many as the government that will function in the Millennium. We only mention it here to show the rationale for Joseph being partly of the blood of Judah, but will wait for further knowledge to come as the Millennium is ushered in.[109]

The priesthood rightly belonged to Joseph Smith (v. 6) because it was to continue "through the lineage of the fathers," and he was the "rightful heir" as discussed in D&C 86:8–10. The keys of the kingdom were delivered unto him, along with a second witness, Oliver Cowdery, in the Kirtland Temple. An ensign is a flag or banner identifying the kingdom. Joseph, along with the people of the Church, is part of that ensign. "By their fruits ye shall know them" (3 Nephi 14:20; Matthew 7:20). "Therefore, let your light so shine before this people, that they may see your good works and glorify your Father who is in heaven" (3 Nephi 12:16; Matthew 5:16). The gathering of the Lord's people (v. 6) was begun by Joseph and will continue until the Second Coming. Joseph, as the head of the dispensation of the fulness of times (D&C 112:31) is still involved with that gathering in the last days.

D&C 113:7–10 • Put On the Power of the Priesthood

7 Questions by Elias Higbee: What is meant by the command in Isaiah, 52d chapter, 1st verse, which saith: Put on thy strength, O Zion—and what people had Isaiah reference to?

8 He had reference to those whom God should call in the last days, who should hold the power of priesthood to bring again Zion, and the redemption of Israel; and to put on her strength is to put on the authority of the priesthood, which she, Zion, has a right to by lineage; also to return to that power which she had lost.

9 What are we to understand by Zion loosing herself from the bands of her neck; 2d verse?

10 We are to understand that the scattered remnants are exhorted to return to the Lord from whence they have fallen; which if they do, the promise of the Lord is that he will speak to them, or give them revelation. See the 6th, 7th, and 8th verses. The bands of her neck are

---

[109] See Andrew F. Ehat, "It seems Like Heaven on Earth: Joseph Smith and the Constitution of the Kingdom of God," *BYU Studies,* Spring 1980, 3:253–280.

the curses of God upon her, or the remnants of Israel in their scattered condition among the Gentiles.

Since the city of Zion will be a holy city, the inhabitants of the city will be holy. Therefore, they are entitled to the power of the priesthood (vv. 7–8), as well as from their lineage or adoption into that lineage (see Abraham 2:10–11). Furthermore, those who receive the priesthood were entitled to it from their faith and good works in the first place [premortal existence] (see Alma 13:3–5). "My sheep hear my voice, and I know them, and they follow me" (John 10:27) is as applicable in this day as it was in Christ's day. The words "right to" (v. 8) indicates, and was discussed in Doctrine and Covenants 85 and 86, that many who were to hold the priesthood were gathered out from the Gentiles where they had been scattered (see Amos 9:8–9, 14).

"The bands on the neck" is the culture the scattered remnant has lived under "in their scattered condition among the Gentiles" (vv. 9–10). Many have accepted it because of the traditions of their fathers (see D&C 93:39), and are having a hard time changing their ways. It is the scourge upon the children of Zion as identified in Doctrine and Covenants 84:58. Through the power of the priesthood they may receive revelation and overcome it.

DOCTRINE AND COVENANTS 135

*H*istorical Setting: "This document was written by Elder John Taylor of the Council of the Twelve, who was a witness of the events" (*HC,* 6:629; section heading).

TEXT AND COMMENTARY

D&C 135:1–2 • The Martyrdom

1 To seal the testimony of this book and the Book of Mormon, we announce the martyrdom of Joseph Smith the Prophet, and Hyrum Smith the Patriarch. They were shot in Carthage jail, on the 27th of June, 1844, about five o'clock P.M., by an armed mob—painted black—of from 150 to 200 persons. Hyrum was shot first and fell calmly, exclaiming: I am a dead man! Joseph leaped from the window, and was shot dead

in the attempt, exclaiming: O Lord my God! They were both shot after they were dead, in a brutal manner, and both received four balls.

2 John Taylor and Willard Richards, two of the Twelve, were the only persons in the room at the time; the former was wounded in a savage manner with four balls, but has since recovered; the latter, through the providence of God, escaped, without even a hole in his robe.

It was necessary for Joseph to seal his testimony as the head of the dispensation of the fulness of times (see D&C 112:30; Ephesians 1:10). Although said of Jesus Christ, it is also applicable to the Prophet Joseph: "For where a testament is, there must also of necessity be the death of the testator. For a testament is of force after men are dead: otherwise it is of no strength at all while the testator liveth (Hebrews 9:16–17). Many Old Testament prophets sealed their testimony with their blood as acknowledged by Jesus:

> Wherefore, behold, I send unto you prophets, and wise men, and scribes: and [some] of them ye shall kill and crucify; and [some] of them shall ye scourge in your synagogues, and persecute them from city to city: that upon you may come all the righteous blood shed upon the earth, from the blood of righteous Abel unto the blood of Zacharias son of Barachias, whom ye slew between the temple and the altar. [Matthew 23:34–35]

New Testament leaders were likewise martyrs: John the Baptist (Mark 6:18–28); Stephen (Acts 7:58–60); the Apostle James (Acts 12:2); and others not recorded in the Bible.

Two of the Apostles, John Taylor and Willard Richards (v. 2) stood as witnesses of Joseph and Hyrum's brutal deaths: "in the mouth of two or three every word may be established" (Matthew 18:16; Deuteronomy 17:6; 19:15).

D&C 135:3 • Joseph Has Done More Save Jesus Only

> 3 Joseph Smith, the Prophet and Seer of the Lord, has done more, save Jesus only, for the salvation of men in this world, than any other man that ever lived in it. In the short space of twenty years, he has brought forth the Book of Mormon, which he translated by the gift and power of God, and has been the means of publishing it on two continents; has sent the fulness of the everlasting gospel, which it contained, to the four quarters of the earth; has brought forth the revelations and

commandments which compose this book of Doctrine and Covenants, and many other wise documents and instructions for the benefit of the children of men; gathered many thousands of the Latter-day Saints, founded a great city, and left a fame and name that cannot be slain. He lived great, and he died great in the eyes of God and his people; and like most of the Lord's anointed in ancient time, has sealed his mission and his works with his own blood; and so has his brother Hyrum. In life they were not divided, and in death they were not separated!

Critics and inquirers of Joseph Smith may ask, "If Joseph Smith was such an important figure in the religious history of the world, why was he not mentioned in the Bible?" The answer to that question is: "He was mentioned, but to protect his agency, and to be a test to those living in the last dispensation, he was concealed in the language of the scriptures so that only those who were spiritually attuned would recognize the correct interpretation of the passages." Joseph, who was sold into Egypt, foretold of a choice seer in the latter days. He described the mission the seer was to perform by giving nine characteristics of him, or his accomplishments. Sadly, this prophecy of Joseph of Egypt was among the plain and precious parts lost from the Bible (see 1 Nephi 13:24–26), but is retained through the Book of Mormon when Lehi quoted it to his son Joseph (2 Nephi 3).

Isaiah, of whom Nephi said his words were plain unto "all those who are filled with the spirit of prophecy" (2 Nephi 25:4), foretold of Joseph Smith in his writings. And when the angel Moroni appeared to Joseph on September 22, 1823, "he quoted the eleventh chapter of Isaiah, saying that it was about to be fulfilled" (JS—H 1:40).[110] There are also over twenty pronouns in the original text of Isaiah chapter 29 that mention Joseph by pronoun instead of his name. This chapter has also lost many plain and precious parts, but was quoted by Nephi from the plates of brass in 2 Nephi 27. An interesting experience can be had reading 2 Nephi 27 aloud, and substituting the name of the person referred to instead of the pronoun. There are a few other people of Church history who fit into other pronouns, clearly showing the foreknowledge of God in the Restoration.

---

[110] For details of Joseph of Egypt's and Isaiah's prophecies, see Monte S. Nyman, *An Ensign to All People* [1987], chapter 2, "A Choice Seer Brings Forth the Ensign."

The things that Joseph Smith accomplished, enumerated by Elder John Taylor in this verse, are a testimony of Joseph's foreordained mission and his accomplishments. We will comment on Hyrum as a martyr later.

D&C 135:4–5 • I Shall Die Innocent

4 When Joseph went to Carthage to deliver himself up to the pretended requirements of the law, two or three days previous to his assassination, he said: "I am going like a lamb to the slaughter; but I am calm as a summer's morning; I have a conscience void of offense towards God, and towards all men. I SHALL DIE INNOCENT, AND IT SHALL YET BE SAID OF ME—HE WAS MURDERED IN COLD BLOOD—[see the rest of verse 4 in the next quotation].

5 And it came to pass that I prayed unto the Lord that he would give unto the Gentiles grace, that they might have charity. And it came to pass that the Lord said unto me: If they have not charity it mattereth not unto thee, thou hast been faithful; wherefore thy garments shall be made clean. And because thou hast seen thy weakness, thou shalt be made strong, even unto the sitting down in the place which I have prepared in the mansions of my Father. And now I . . . bid farewell unto the Gentiles; yea, and also unto my brethren whom I love, until we shall meet before the judgment-seat of Christ, where all men shall know that my garments are not spotted with your blood [Ether 12:36–38]. The testators are now dead, and their testament is in force.

Joseph knew he would die, but naturally did not want to. He had it implied to him in several revelations he had been given. As an example: "And that you be firm in keeping the commandments wherewith I have commanded you; and if you do this, behold I grant unto you eternal life, even if you should be slain" (D&C 5:22).[111] He also made statements, in the last few years of his life, of his death after his mission was accomplished:

My feelings at the present time are that, inasmuch as the Lord Almighty has preserved me until today, He will continue to preserve me, by the united faith and prayers of the Saints, until I have accomplished my mission in this life, and so firmly established the dispensation of the fullness of the priesthood in the last days, that all the powers of earth

---

[111] See also D&C 10:5, 34–35; 5:32–33; 6:29–30, 37; 17:4; 38:12–14, 28–29; 63:28; 98:13–14; 101:35–37; 103:27; 122:7–9; 132:57. Some of these references refer to more than one death.

and hell can never prevail against it. [*TPJS*, 258; August 31, 1842]

I know what I say; I understand my mission and business. God Almighty is my shield; what can man do if God is my friend? I shall not be sacrificed until my time comes; then I shall be offered freely. [*TPJS*, 274; January 22, 1843]

I prophecy, in the name of the Lord God of Israel, anguish and wrath and tribulation and the withdrawing of the Spirit of God from the earth await this generation, until they are visited with utter desolation. This generation is as corrupt as the generation of the Jews that crucified Christ; and if He were here today, and should preach the same doctrine He did then, they would put Him to death. I defy all the world to destroy the work of God; and I prophesy they never will have power to kill me till my work is accomplished, and I am ready to die. [*TPJS*, 328; October 15, 1843]

I cannot lie down until my work is finished. I never think any evil, nor do anything to the harm of my fellow-man. When I am weighed in the balances, you will all know me then. [*TPJS*, 361; April 6, 1844]

He had probably learned the principal of not dying until his mission was completed as he had translated the Book of Mormon, and learned of Abinadi: "Ye see that ye have not power to slay me, therefore I finish my message. Yea, and I perceive that it cuts you to your hearts because I tell you the truth concerning your iniquities. Yea, and my words fill you with wonder and amazement, and with anger. But I finish my message; and then it matters not whither I go, if it so be that I am saved" (Mosiah 13:7–9). Joseph did not know when would die, but he obviously sensed it as he went to Carthage.

D&C 135:4, 6 • The Best Blood of the Century

4. . . . The same morning, after Hyrum had made ready to go—shall it be said to the slaughter? yes, for so it was—he read the following paragraph, near the close of the twelfth chapter of Ether, in the Book of Mormon, and turned down the leaf upon it: . . . .

6 Hyrum Smith was forty-four years old in February, 1844, and Joseph Smith was thirty-eight in December, 1843; and henceforward their names will be classed among the martyrs of religion; and the reader in every nation will be reminded that the Book of Mormon, and this

book of Doctrine and Covenants of the church, cost the best blood of the nineteenth century to bring them forth for the salvation of a ruined world; and that if the fire can scathe a green tree for the glory of God, how easy it will burn up the dry trees to purify the vineyard of corruption. They lived for glory; they died for glory; and glory is their eternal reward. From age to age shall their names go down to posterity as gems for the sanctified.

Hyrum Smith was a man like unto Moroni, the final prophet among the Nephites and guardian of the plates, who he was quoting out of the Book of Mormon (Ether 12:36–38, quoted in v. 4 above). Hyrum was indirectly asking for charity for those Gentiles who were about to take his life. Nephi, son of Lehi, had made the same request of the Lord as he closed his recordings upon the small plates of Nephi (2 Nephi 33:9). Charity is the pure love of Christ, and as Hyrum was "found possessed of it at the last day, it shall be [was] well with him" (Moroni 7:47).

Why was Hyrum the second witness with Joseph to seal their blood? He had replaced Oliver Cowdery as the Assistant President of the Church (see D&C 124:95–96). Had Oliver remained faithful, it would have undoubtedly been Oliver instead of him. Joseph and Oliver had been given a revelation that told of their jointly holding the keys of translation, two witnesses, and Oliver had been promised the opportunity to translate other records. Both men were then warned that what had happened to the Savior may happen to them (see D&C 6:25–37). Hyrum, always supportive and faithful to Joseph and the Lord, was the second testator with Joseph, both were "now dead, and their testament is in force" (D&C 135:5). Their work of the Restoration of the gospel of Jesus Christ had "cost the best blood of the nineteenth century." "They lived for glory; they died for glory; and glory is their eternal reward" (v. 6). The office of Assistant President was no longer needed.

D&C 135:7 • Innocent Blood

7 They were innocent of any crime, as they had often been proved before, and were only confined in jail by the conspiracy of traitors and wicked men; and their *innocent blood* on the floor of Carthage jail is a broad seal affixed to "Mormonism" that cannot be rejected by any court on earth, and their *innocent blood* on the escutcheon of the State of Illinois, with the broken faith of the State as pledged by the governor, is a witness to the truth of the everlasting gospel that all the world cannot

impeach; and their *innocent blood* on the banner of liberty, and on the *magna charta* of the United States, is an ambassador for the religion of Jesus Christ, that will touch the hearts of honest men among all nations; and their innocent blood, with the *innocent blood* of all the martyrs under the altar that John saw, will cry unto the Lord of Hosts till he avenges that blood on the earth. Amen.

This last verse is a fitting tribute to two of the greatest men of this dispensation, and of every dispensation. The accusations made against them will be exonerated before all men in the eternities, and they will be honored as prophets of the living God who still stands at the head of this final dispensation.

General Authority Quotes

—Prophet Joseph Smith • D&C 135:3

. . . Would to God that I had forty days and forty nights in which to tell you all! I would let you know that I am not a "fallen prophet." [*TPJS,* 355]

—President Brigham Young • D&C 135:3

. . . It is [Joseph Smith's] mission to see that all the children of men in this last dispensation are saved, that can be, through the redemption. You will be thankful, every one of you, that Joseph Smith, junior, was ordained to this great calling before the world were. . . . It was decreed in the councils of eternity, long before the foundations of the earth were laid, that he should be the man, in the last dispensation of this world, to bring forth the word of God to the people, and receive the fulness of the keys and power of the priesthood of the Son of God. The Lord had his eye upon him, and upon his father, and upon his father's father, and upon their progenitors clear back to Abraham, and from Abraham to the flood, and from the flood to Enoch, and from Enoch to Adam. He has watched that family and that blood as it has circulated from its fountain to the blood of that man. [*Journal of Discourses,* 7:28]

—President Joseph Fielding Smith • D&C 135:4–5

It was Oliver Cowdery who was appointed to stand with Joseph Smith to hold the keys of this dispensation. . . .

I am convinced that if we had the full record, we would discover that Oliver Cowdery was associated with Joseph Smith the Prophet when the keys of all the other dispensations were revealed and restored in this dispensation. In this manner Oliver Cowdery was appointed and ordained to stand with the Prophet Joseph as an associate and witness, holding all the authority and keys of this most glorious of all dispensations—the dispensation of the fullness of times. [*Doctrines of Salvation,* 1:217]

. . . I am firmly of the opinion that had Oliver Cowdery remained true to his covenants and obligations as a witness with Joseph Smith, and retained his authority and place, he, not Hyrum Smith, would have gone with Joseph Smith as a prisoner and to martyrdom at Carthage.

The sealing of the testimony through the shedding of blood would not have been complete in the death of the prophet alone; it required the death of Hyrum Smith who jointly held the keys of this dispensation. It was needful that these martyrs seal their testimony with their blood, that they "might be honored and the wicked might be condemned. [*Doctrines of Salvation,* 1:219]

On another occasion the Prophet said: "I could pray in my heart that all my brethren were like unto my beloved brother Hyrum, who possess the mildness of a lamb, and the integrity of a Job, and in short, the meekness and humility of Christ; and I love him with that love that is stronger than death, for I never had occasion to rebuke him, nor he me, which he declared when he left me today. [*Doctrines of Salvation,* 1:219–220]

. . . Why do we not have today in the Church the same order of things, and an assistant President as well as two counselors in the First Presidency?

The answer to this is a simple one. It is because the peculiar condition requiring two witnesses to establish this work, is not required after the work is established. Joseph and Hyrum stand at the head of this dispensation jointly holding the keys, as the two necessary fulfilling the law as it is set down by our Lord in his answer to the Jews. Since the gospel will never again be restored there will be no occasion for this condition to arise again. We all look back to the two special witnesses, called to bear witness in full accord with the divine law. [*Doctrines of Salvation,* 1:222]

—*President Gordon B. Hinckley* • D&C 135:4–5

[Joseph Smith] and his brother were murdered June 27, 1844. Their enemies thought that this would end the cause for which they had given their lives. Little did they realize that the blood of the martyrs would give nurture to the young roots of the Church. [*Discourses of President Gordon B. Hinckley*, 1995–99 (2004), 1:66]

Chapter Twenty-Eight

Brigham Young—Colonizer

D&C 136; Official Declarations—1 & 2

DOCTRINE AND COVENANTS 136

Historical Setting: "The word and will of the Lord, given through President Young at the Winter Quarters of the Camp of Israel, Omaha Nation, West Bank of the Missouri River, near Council Bluffs, Iowa. Journal History of the Church, January 14, 1847" (section heading).

SECTION 136 • OUTLINE

➤ 136:1–17   The will of the Lord for the Camp Israel in journeying to the West.

    a.   All organize into companies and covenant to keep the commandments (v. 2).

    b.   Companies into hundreds, fifties, and tens, under the Twelve Apostles (vv. 3–4).

    c.   Provide teams, wagons, provisions, and prepare for those who tarry (vv. 5–6).

    d.   Each company decide the number to go and plant spring crops (v. 7).

    e.   Each company bear equal proportions of poor, widows, and fatherless (v. 8).

    f.   Provide houses and fields for those remaining, and do all to remove all people and establish a stake of Zion where the Lord locates them (vv. 9–11).

    g.   Leaders are appointed, and are to go and teach the people (vv. 12–17).

➤ 136:18–30   Zion shall be redeemed in the Lord's due time.

    a.   Any man who seeks to build up himself shall have no power (v. 19).

    b.   Keep all your pledges and do not covet that which is thy brothers (v. 20).

    c.   Do not take the name of the god of Abraham, Isaac, and Jacob in vain (v. 21).

    d.   I led Israel out of Egypt, and in the last days will save Israel (v. 22).

    e.   Cease to contend, speak evil, drunkenness, and edify one another (vv. 23–24).

    f.   Return the borrowed or found that which was lost to thy neighbor (vv. 25–26).

    g.   Preserve what you have and be a wise steward of the Lord (v. 26).

    h.   If merry praise the Lord, if sorrowful call on the Lord (vv. 28–29).

    I.   Fear not the enemy, for I will do my pleasure on them (v. 30).

➤ 136:31–36   My people shall be tried and prepared for the glory of Zion.

    a.   The ignorant shall learn by calling on the Lord, and the Spirit (vv. 32–33).

    b.   The nation has rejected you and driven you out (v. 34).

    c.   The day of their calamity shall be great if they do not repent (v. 35).

    d.   They killed the prophets, and shed innocent blood which cries out (v. 26).

➤ 136:37–42   Ye shall behold my glory if you obey my word from Adam to Joseph Smith.

    a.   Joseph laid the foundation, and I took him unto myself (v. 38).

    b.   It was necessary to seal his testimony with his blood (vv. 39–49).

    c.   You received my kingdom, be diligent, keep my commandments (vv. 41–42).

Introduction

Saturday Aug. 6, 1842—Passed over the river to Montrose, Iowa.... I had a conversation with a number of the brethren in the shade of the building on the subject of our persecutions in Missouri and the constant annoyance which has followed us since we were driven from that state. I prophesied that the Saints would continue to suffer much affliction and would be driven to the Rocky Mountains, many would apostatize, others would be put to death by our persecutors or lose their lives in consequence of exposure or disease, and some of you will live to go and assist in making settlements and build cities and see the Saints become a mighty people in the midst of the Rocky Mountains.... (*DHC*, 5:85). [*TPJS*, 255][112]

Did others also see this movement of the Saints? Yes, the prophet Jeremiah prophesied of the day when the remnant of Israel would come to the height [mountains] of Zion:

6 For there shall be a day, that the watchmen upon the mount Ephraim shall cry, Arise ye, and let us go up to Zion unto the LORD our God.

7 For thus saith the LORD; Sing with gladness for Jacob, and shout among the chief of the nations: publish ye, praise ye, and say, O LORD, save thy people, the remnant of Israel.

8 Behold, I will bring them from the north country, and gather them from the coasts of the earth, and with them the blind and the lame, the woman with child and her that travaileth with child together: a great company shall return thither.

9 They shall come with weeping, and with supplications will I lead them: I will cause them to walk by the rivers of waters in a straight way, wherein they shall not stumble: for I am a father to Israel, and Ephraim is my firstborn.

10 Hear the word of the LORD, O ye nations, and declare it in the isles afar off, and say, He that scattered Israel will gather him, and keep him, as a shepherd doth his flock.

---

[112] Hyrum Smith also prophesied of the Saints going to the Rocky Mountains, and Joseph did again on another occasion. See Karl Ricks Anderson, *Joseph Smith's Kirtland* [1989], 59, 73.

11 For the LORD hath redeemed Jacob, and ransomed him from the hand of him that was stronger than he.

12 Therefore they shall come and sing in the height of Zion, and shall flow together to the goodness of the LORD, for wheat, and for wine, and for oil, and for the young of the flock and of the herd: and their soul shall be as a watered garden; and they shall not sorrow any more at all.

13 Then shall the virgin rejoice in the dance, both young men and old together: for I will turn their mourning into joy, and will comfort them, and make them rejoice from their sorrow.

14 And I will satiate the soul of the priests with fatness, and my people shall be satisfied with my goodness, saith the LORD. [Jeremiah 31:6–14][113]

According to Oliver Cowdery, some of the above verses were quoted by the angel Moroni to Joseph Smith as soon to be fulfilled (see JS—H 1:41).[114] We will not analyze the prophecy here, but merely cite it as evidence of the movement west being known even in Old Testament times.

TEXT AND COMMENTARY

D&C 136:1–17 • Walk in All the Ordinances

1 THE Word and Will of the Lord concerning the Camp of Israel in their journeyings to the West:

2 Let all the people of the Church of Jesus Christ of Latter-day Saints, and those who journey with them, be organized into companies, with a covenant and promise to keep all the commandments and statutes of the Lord our God.

3 Let the companies be organized with captains of hundreds, captains of fifties, and captains of tens, with a president and his two counselors at their head, under the direction of the Twelve Apostles.

4 And this shall be our covenant—that we will walk in all the ordinances of the Lord.

---

[113] For an interpretation of these verses being about the Saints going west, see Monte S. Nyman, *The Words of Jeremiah* [1982]. A very detailed analysis was given by Elder LeGrand Richards in his *Marvelous Work and a Wonder*, and is included in this interpretation.

[114] Jeremiah 31:6, 8–9, *Messenger and Advocate* April 1835, 111.

5 Let each company provide themselves with all the teams, wagons, provisions, clothing, and other necessaries for the journey, that they can.

6 When the companies are organized let them go to with their might, to prepare for those who are to tarry.

7 Let each company, with their captains and presidents, decide how many can go next spring; then choose out a sufficient number of able-bodied and expert men, to take teams, seeds, and farming utensils, to go as pioneers to prepare for putting in spring crops.

8 Let each company bear an equal proportion, according to the dividend of their property, in taking the poor, the widows, the fatherless, and the families of those who have gone into the army, that the cries of the widow and the fatherless come not up into the ears of the Lord against this people.

9 Let each company prepare houses, and fields for raising grain, for those who are to remain behind this season; and this is the will of the Lord concerning his people.

10 Let every man use all his influence and property to remove this people to the place where the Lord shall locate a stake of Zion.

11 And if ye do this with a pure heart, in all faithfulness, ye shall be blessed; you shall be blessed in your flocks, and in your herds, and in your fields, and in your houses, and in your families.

12 Let my servants Ezra T. Benson and Erastus Snow organize a company.

13 And let my servants Orson Pratt and Wilford Woodruff organize a company.

14 Also, let my servants Amasa Lyman and George A. Smith organize a company.

15 And appoint presidents, and captains of hundreds, and of fifties, and of tens.

16 And let my servants that have been appointed go and teach this, my will, to the saints, that they may be ready to go to a land of peace.

17 Go thy way and do as I have told you, and fear not thine enemies; for they shall not have power to stop my work.

The covenant and promise to keep all the commandments (v. 2) is a form of "doing all things in the name of Christ" (D&C 46:31). The companies being organized into captains of hundreds, fifties, and tens (D&C 132:3) is similar to how Moses organized the children of Israel in their journeying in the wilderness, as suggested by Jethro, his Father-in-law: "And Moses chose able men out of all Israel, and made them heads over the people, rulers of thousands, rulers of hundreds, rulers of fifties, and rulers of tens. And they judged the people at all seasons: the hard causes they brought unto Moses, but every small matter they judged themselves" (Exodus 18:26). The preparation for those that were to tarry (D&C 136:6, 9) was done by establishing welfare stations at places that they named Garden Grove and Mt. Pisgah. They built log cabins, fenced land, and planted crops, and those who came later had places to stay and harvest the crops. They were great assets to the weary travelers. The commandment to love their neighbors was illustrated by their taking equal burden for the poor, the widows and fatherless (v. 8). They were blessed as promised (v. 11), and their enemies did not stop the Lord's work of moving His people westward (v. 17).

D&C 136:18–30 • The God Who Led Israel

18 Zion shall be redeemed in mine own due time.

19 And if any man shall seek to build up himself, and seeketh not my counsel, he shall have no power, and his folly shall be made manifest.

20 Seek ye; and keep all your pledges one with another; and covet not that which is thy brother's.

21 Keep yourselves from evil to take the name of the Lord in vain, for I am the Lord your God, even the God of your fathers, the God of Abraham and of Isaac and of Jacob.

22 I am he who led the children of Israel out of the land of Egypt; and my arm is stretched out in the last days, to save my people Israel.

23 Cease to contend one with another; cease to speak evil one of another.

24 Cease drunkenness; and let your words tend to edifying one another.

25 If thou borrowest of thy neighbor, thou shalt restore that which thou hast borrowed; and if thou canst not repay then go straightway and tell thy neighbor, lest he condemn thee.

26 If thou shalt find that which thy neighbor has lost, thou shalt make diligent search till thou shalt deliver it to him again.

27 Thou shalt be diligent in preserving what thou hast, that thou

mayest be a wise steward; for it is the free gift of the Lord thy God, and thou art his steward.

28 If thou art merry, praise the Lord with singing, with music, with dancing, and with a prayer of praise and thanksgiving.

29 If thou art sorrowful, call on the Lord thy God with supplication, that your souls may be joyful.

30 Fear not thine enemies, for they are in mine hands and I will do my pleasure with them.

The goal of the pioneers was to locate where the Lord wanted to establish a stake of Zion (v. 10 above). The establishing of the center place of Zion (D&C 57:3) was to come in the Lord's own due time (D&C 136:18). The requirements for a Zion people, whether in a stake or the city of Zion was to be "of one heart and one mind, and [dwell] in righteousness; and there was [to be] no poor among them" (Moses 7:18). To attain these attributes, they were to begin now. They were not to build themselves up (D&C 136:19), covet what was their brother's (v. 20), or take the name of the Lord in vain (v. 21). The same God of Abraham, Isaac, and Jacob, who had led the children of Israel out of Egypt was leading these people now. He was experienced, and had saved Israel then, and was there to save Israel in these last days (v. 22). They were not to contend, speak evil, but edify one another in words. They were to cease drunkenness, implying it was happening then (vv. 23–24). As he had warned those coming out of Egypt, they were to not borrow without returning it, and help search for what the neighbor had lost (vv. 25–26; see Exodus 3:22; Leviticus 6:3). They were to be wise stewards, turn to the Lord in praise and thanksgiving as well as in sorrow (D&C 136:27–29). Again He promises to take care of their enemies (v. 30; see v. 17).

D&C 136:31–36 • Innocent Blood Cries from the Ground

31 My people must be tried in all things, that they may be prepared to receive the glory that I have for them, even the glory of Zion; and he that will not bear chastisement is not worthy of my kingdom.

32 Let him that is ignorant learn wisdom by humbling himself and calling upon the Lord his God, that his eyes may be opened that he may see, and his ears opened that he may hear;

33 For my Spirit is sent forth into the world to enlighten the humble and contrite, and to the condemnation of the ungodly.

34 Thy brethren have rejected you and your testimony, even the nation that has driven you out;

35 And now cometh the day of their calamity, even the days of sorrow, like a woman that is taken in travail; and their sorrow shall be great unless they speedily repent, yea, very speedily.

36 For they killed the prophets, and them that were sent unto them; and they have shed innocent blood, which crieth from the ground against them.

The Lord warns them that it would not be easy. As he had warned them before, they must be tried even as Abraham was tried (v. 31; see D&C 101:4). In order to grow through their trials, they must learn wisdom by calling on His name, and His Spirit would enlighten them (D&C 136:32–33). The nation, the United States people, had driven them out (v. 34). The day of calamity, of which the Lord warns (v. 35), was probably the Civil War, when the nation divided and fought each other. It had been prophesied—along with other wars, fifteen years earlier (see D&C 87). They had cast out the righteous, and were left to war among themselves (see Helaman 13:12–14). "The blood of the saints," the innocent prophets, whom they had slain, cried for the justice of God to come upon the wicked (see 2 Nephi 26:3; 28:10; Mormon 8:41; Genesis 4:10; Revelation 19:2).

D&C 136:37–42 • Testimony Sealed with Blood

37 Therefore, marvel not at these things, for ye are not yet pure; ye can not yet bear my glory; but ye shall behold it if ye are faithful in keeping all my words that I have given you, from the days of Adam to Abraham, from Abraham to Moses, from Moses to Jesus and his apostles, and from Jesus and his apostles to Joseph Smith, whom I did call upon by mine angels, my ministering servants, and by mine own voice out of the heavens, to bring forth my work;

38 Which foundation he did lay, and was faithful; and I took him to myself.

39 Many have marveled because of his death; but it was needful that he should seal his testimony with his blood, that he might be honored and the wicked might be condemned.

40 Have I not delivered you from your enemies, only in that I have left a witness of my name?

41 Now, therefore, hearken, O ye people of my church; and ye elders listen together; you have received my kingdom.

42 Be diligent in keeping all my commandments, lest judgments come upon you, and your faith fail you, and your enemies triumph over you. So no more at present. Amen and Amen.

The Church members still had to work to prepare themselves for the Second Coming. The formula was to search the scriptures (v. 37), and live by them: "not only to say, but to do according to that which I have written" (D&C 84:57). The words of Adam to Jesus Christ were in the Old Testament. The words of Jesus Christ and His Apostles were in the New Testament. Joseph's work had been to bring forth the Book of Mormon and the Doctrine and Covenants, the Lord's "own voice out of the heavens" (v. 37). He also had restored much of the Bible through the Joseph Smith Translation, and the Pearl of Great Price. He had laid the foundation for building Zion, and his mission was complete. The Lord had taken "him to myself" (v. 38). The sealing of his testimony with his blood (v. 39) was discussed in the previous chapter. The Saints, whom he gathered and their posterity, will always honor his name. His words, his life, and his sealed testimony would condemn the wicked (v. 39). The Lord had delivered the Saints from their enemies in Missouri, and in Illinois, and left Joseph's witness of Jesus Christ to them (v. 40). The remaining Saints had received the kingdom of God, and it was their responsibility to carry on in diligence and faith (v. 41–42).

Each of the prophets who have carried on since Joseph was taken have fulfilled their mission, and built upon the foundation that Joseph laid. This revelation to Brigham Young illustrates that the Lord gave him revelation and led the Church through him. Each of the fourteen Presidents [2–15] of the Church have fulfilled their mission, and built upon the foundation that Joseph laid. Each one accomplished many things, but as an example of the Lord directing their work, one thing that they may be remembered by is listed below:

2. Brigham Young: The leading to and colonizing of the West.
3. John Taylor: The organizing and functioning of the priesthood.
4. Wilford Woodruff: The Manifesto, Official Declaration—1.

5. Lorenzo Snow: Freeing the Church from debt through the law of tithing.
6. Joseph F. Smith: Establishing the doctrine of the Church.
7. Heber J. Grant: The welfare program and the Word of Wisdom.
8. George Albert Smith: The love of all mankind.
9. David O. McKay: The importance of the family.
10. Joseph Fielding Smith: The doctrine of the Church.
11. Harold B. Lee: The correlation of the Church programs.
12. Spencer W. Kimball: Missionary work, Official Declaration—2.
13. Ezra Taft Benson: Proper use of the Book of Mormon.
14. Howard W. Hunter: Every member temple worthy.
15. Gordon B. Hinckley: Temple building and being acknowledged by the world.

While many more things could be listed for each of these great men, they will be long remembered and honored for their work of the Lord that they did. Since Official Declaration 1 and 2 are a part of the Doctrine of Covenants, we will comment on them before closing this chapter.

OFFICIAL DECLARATION—1

To Whom it may concern:

Press dispatches having been sent for political purposes, from Salt Lake City, which have been widely published, to the effect that the Utah Commission, in their recent report to the Secretary of the Interior, allege that plural marriages are still being solemnized and that forty or more such marriages have been contracted in Utah since last June or during the past year, also that in public discourses the leaders of the Church have taught, encouraged and urged the continuance of the practice of polygamy—

I, therefore, as President of the Church of Jesus Christ of Latter-day Saints, do hereby, in the most solemn manner, declare that these charges are false. We are not teaching polygamy or plural marriage, nor permitting any person to enter into its practice, and I deny that either forty or any other number of plural marriages have during that period been solemnized in our Temples or in any other place in the Territory.

One case has been reported, in which the parties allege that the marriage was performed in the Endowment House, in Salt Lake City, in the Spring of 1889, but I have not been able to learn who performed the ceremony; whatever was done in this matter was without my knowledge. In consequence of this alleged occurrence the Endowment House was, by my instructions, taken down without delay.

Inasmuch as laws have been enacted by Congress forbidding plural marriages, which laws have been pronounced constitutional by the court of last resort, I hereby declare my intentions to submit to those laws, and to use my influence with the members of the Church over which I preside to have them do likewise.

There is nothing in my teachings to the Church or in those of my associates, during the time specified, which can be reasonably construed to inculcate or encourage polygamy; and when any Elder of the Church has used language which appeared to convey any such teaching, he has been promptly reproved. And I now publicly declare that my advice to the Latter-day Saints is to refrain from contracting any marriage forbidden by the law of the land.

> WILFORD WOODRUFF
> President of the Church of Jesus Christ of
> Latter-day Saints.

The purpose of the Manifesto was discussed briefly at the end of chapter 25, Doctrine and Covenants 132. We invite you to also read the excerpts from President Woodruff on pages 292 and 293 of the Doctrine and Covenants further explaining the purpose of the declaration.

OFFICIAL DECLARATION—2

To Whom it May Concern:

On September 30, 1978, at the 148th Semiannual General Conference of The Church of Jesus Christ of Latter-day Saints, the following was presented by President N. Eldon Tanner, First Counselor in the First Presidency of the Church:

In early June of this year, the First Presidency announced that a revelation had been received by President Spencer W. Kimball extending priesthood and temple blessings to all worthy male members of the Church. President Kimball has asked that I advise the conference that after he had received this revelation, which came to him after extended meditation and prayer in the sacred rooms of the holy temple, he presented it to his counselors, who accepted it and approved it. It was then presented to the Quorum of the Twelve Apostles, who unanimously approved it, and was subsequently presented to all other General Authorities, who likewise approved it unanimously.

One of the purposes of the Restoration was: "That every man might speak in the name of God the Lord, even the Savior of the world" (D&C 1:20). During the time of Moses, the Lord chose only those who were of Levi, a tribe of Israel, to have the priesthood (see Exodus 32:26; Numbers 3:1–2). Jesus called his Apostles from Galilee, and only one was from Judah. We do not have the lineage of the others who were called, but Northern Israel was originally the home of the other tribes. One of them was Simon the Canaanite (Matthew 10:4). Therefore, Jesus extended the priesthood to more than the Levites. Peter also received a revelation to take the gospel to the Gentiles, which extended the opportunity for non-Israelites to hold the priesthood. The revelation to President Kimball extended the opportunity to all worthy members without regard to "race or color." The purpose of the Restoration, for all to speak in the name of the Lord, was therefore in place. We invite you to read the letter from the First Presidency on page 294 of the Doctrine and Covenants for a further explanation of the declaration.

General Authority Quotes
—President J. Reuben Clark • D&C 136:10

The fourth day—July 24, 1847—there came into the valley the great chief—Brigham Young.

As his carriage struggled out of the canyon, the leader, rising from his sick bed, got his first view of the full valley, which he had already seen in vision. And now, in renewed vision he "saw the future glory of Zion and of Israel as they would be, planted in the valleys of these mountains. When the vision had passed, he said, 'it is enough. This is the right place. Drive on.'". . . .

The pioneers were here. They had come to the place toward which their Prophet had looked, and to reach which he had one time made start. A whole people was now on the move.

Thus had come to the journey's end a great religious trek—one the greatest in all history—one thousand miles by ox team. Thus was made the beginning of a great commonwealth. [*J. Reuben Clark Selected Papers*, ed. David H. Yarn Jr. (1984), 28]

When in the evening the last wagon creaked slowly into its place in the circle corral and the brethren came to inquire how the day had been with the mother, then joy leaped in their hearts, for had not the brethren remembered them? New hope was born, weariness fled, fresh will to do was enkindled; gratitude to God was poured out for their knowledge of the truth, for their testimony that God lived, that Jesus was the Christ, that Joseph was a Prophet, that Brigham was his ordained successor, and that for the righteous a crown of glory awaited that should be theirs during the eternities of life to come. Then they would join in the songs and dancing in the camp, making the camp's gaiety their own—as much as mother's condition would permit.

Then the morning came when from out that wagon floated the la-la of the newborn babe, and mother love made a shrine and father bowed in reverence before it. But the train must move on. So out into the dust and dirt the last wagon moved again, swaying and jolting, while a mother eased as best she could each pain-giving jolt so no harm might be done her, that she might be strong to feed the little one, bone of her bone, flesh of her flesh. Who will dare to say that angels did not cluster around and guard her and ease her rude bed, for she had given another choice spirit its mortal body that it might work out its God-given destiny.

My mother was one of those babes so born in 1848, ninety-nine years ago. [*J. Reuben Clark Selected Papers*, 70–71]

—President Ezra Taft Benson • D&C 136

As the nation developed, out of this same mold came a special group, who, in a dramatic exodus, pushed the frontier of America from the banks of the Mississippi to the valleys of these magnificent mountains. They were the Mormon pioneers and we, who today enjoy the good life in the Intermountain West, are the beneficiaries of their noble efforts. The world knows that the Mormon pioneers were led here by Brigham Young; but the Mormon Pioneers knew that they were led here by the hand of Almighty God. They came here as a religious group—as a persecuted people—and they came here as American citizens.

They were a unique people, for they had been expelled from what was then the borders of the United States, by citizens and government leaders of their own America, and yet they continued firm in their allegiance to the United States and its great, inspired Constitution. [*The Teachings of Ezra Taft Benson*, 416]

—*President Gordon B. Hinckley* • D&C 136

The pioneers regarded their coming west as a blessing divinely given. Said Brigham Young on one occasion: "I do not wish men to understand I had anything to do with our being moved here, that was the providence of the Almighty; it was the power of God that wrought out the salvation for this people, I never could have devised such a plan." [*Discourses of Brigham Young*, 480]

The power that moved our forebears was the power of faith in God. It was the same power which made possible the exodus from Egypt, the passage through the Red Sea, the long journey through the wilderness, and the establishment of Israel in the Promised Land. [*Teachings of Gordon B. Hinckley*, 439]

Chapter Twenty-Nine

The Life Beyond

D&C 137–138

DOCTRINE AND COVENANTS 137

*H*istorical Setting: Elder Joseph Fielding Smith summarized the account given in the *History of the Church* 2:380–381 (Doctrine and Covenants 137):

> On the twenty-first day of January, 1836, the First Presidency, and a number of the presiding brethren in the Church, assembled in the Kirtland Temple where they engaged in the ordinances of the endowment, as far as it had at that time been revealed. After this was done the Prophet states that "All of the Presidency laid their hands upon me, and pronounced upon my head many prophecies and blessings, many of which I shall not notice at this time."
>
> "All of the Presidency" included Oliver Cowdery and Father Joseph Smith as well as the two counselors, Sidney Rigdon and Frederick G. Williams. Following this ordinance the following vision and revelation were given to the Prophet, making known to him and through him to the Church one of the most important principles pertaining to the salvation of men. [*TPJS,* 106–07]

In the April 1976 General Conference of the Church, the Prophet Joseph Smith's vision of the celestial kingdom which he saw on January 21, 1836, and President Joseph F. Smith's vision of the redemption of the dead which he saw on October 3, 1918, were accepted as scripture by the vote of the Church. The two revelations were then added to the Pearl of Great Price. When a new edition of the Doctrine and Covenants was published in 1981, the above two revelations were published as sections 137 and 138, respectively, in the new edition, and no longer published in the Pearl of Great Price. Because of their both shedding much light on life beyond the grave, they are considered here together.

Introduction

There are many differences of belief concerning life after death. Even those who believe in a life beyond are troubled over why some people are taken suddenly into the eternal realm, and others are required to suffer afflictions, pain, and misery for which there seems to be no explanatory reasoning of justice and mercy. One of the most troubling of these types of questions is concerning the suffering and death of little children. While these questions are universal and have been asked since the beginning of this earth's existence, the answers to at least many of these questions were revealed to the prophets of this dispensation.

TEXT AND COMMENTARY

D&C 137:1–6 • The Celestial Kingdom

1 THE heavens were opened upon us, and I beheld the celestial kingdom of God, and the glory thereof, whether in the body or out I cannot tell.

2 I saw the transcendent beauty of the gate through which the heirs of that kingdom will enter, which was like unto circling flames of fire;

3 Also the blazing throne of God, whereon was seated the Father and the Son.

4 I saw the beautiful streets of that kingdom, which had the appearance of being paved with gold.

5 I saw Father Adam and Abraham; and my father and my mother; my brother Alvin, that has long since slept;

6 And marveled how it was that he had obtained an inheritance in that kingdom, seeing that he had departed this life before the Lord had set his hand to gather Israel the second time, and had not been baptized for the remission of sins.

The Prophet Joseph's vision was given two months before the Kirtland Temple was dedicated (March 27, 1836), possibly in preparation for that glorious event. Just how many of the First Presidency saw the vision is not stated. The Prophet merely states, "The heavens were opened unto *us*, and *I* beheld the celestial kingdom of God (v. 1; italics added). That Joseph was not aware of the state of his body is consistent with others who have had similar experiences. The three Nephites who "were caught into heaven, and saw and heard unspeakable things" made the same statement (3 Nephi 27:12–15), as did the Apostle Paul when "caught up to the third heaven" (2 Corinthians 12:1–3). The boy Joseph, following "The First Vision," may have likewise been out of his body. Said he, "When I came to myself again, I found myself lying on my back, looking up into heaven" (JS—H 1:20). All of the above people experienced things too glorious to be written. What the Prophet was able to write of the visions of the celestial kingdom (D&C 137:2–4) was brief and inadequate. However, his description is comparable to that of Moses, Aaron, Nadab, Abihu, and seventy of the elders of Israel:

> 10 And they saw the God of Israel: and there was under his feet as it were a paved work of a sapphire stone, and as it were the body of heaven in his clearness.
>
> 11 And upon the nobles of the children of Israel he laid not his hand: also they saw God, and did eat and drink (Exodus 24:10–11).

The Prophet Ezekiel (1:26–28); John the Revelator (Revelation 4:1–3); and the appearance of the Lord later at the dedication of the Kirtland Temple (D&C 110:1–3) are also comparable.

The Prophet names five people that he saw in the vision: Adam, Abraham, his own father and mother, and his brother Alvin who had passed away (D&C 137:5). It was appropriate for him to mention Adam since he was the father of "the family of all the earth" (2 Nephi 2:20); and Abraham, since he was the father of the covenant people that Joseph was responsible for fulfilling the promises regarding his seed. The vision shown to Joseph was of the future since both his father and his mother were still alive, and his father was present when the vision was shown. Alvin had died about thirteen years earlier (1823, JS—H 1:56). Seeing him in the celestial kingdom was amazing to Joseph since Alvin's death had occurred before he had heard the restored gospel and been baptized (D&C 137:6). This line of reasoning brought a revelation to Joseph.

D&C 137:7–9 • Heirs of the Celestial Kingdom

7 Thus came the voice of the Lord unto me, saying: All who have died without a knowledge of this gospel, who would have received it if they had been permitted to tarry, shall be heirs of the celestial kingdom of God;

8 Also all that shall die henceforth without a knowledge of it, who would have received it with all their hearts, shall be heirs of that kingdom.

9 For I, the Lord, will judge all men according to their works, according to the desire of their hearts.

An heir is someone who is entitled to a gift, property, an endowment, or a blessing when they meet the requirements or conditions of the inheritance. For entrance into the celestial kingdom, a knowledge of the restored gospel was a requirement. This would be met by the gospel being preached in the spirit world as will be discussed in section 138 (see also 2 Peter 4:5–6). A second requirement is to perform ordinances for the dead vicariously. This concept was to be revealed to the Prophet in the near future (see *TPJS*, 179).

D&C 137:10 • Little Children Who Die?

10 And I also beheld that all children who die before they arrive at the years of accountability are saved in the celestial kingdom of heaven.

Joseph had learned from translating the Book of Mormon that "all little children are alive in Christ, and also all they that are without the law" (Moroni 8:22). He had also learned by revelation that children were not accountable for their sins until they were eight years old (see D&C 68:25). What he observed in the vision of the celestial kingdom was confirming this previous knowledge and adding to it. He learned that the eternal destiny of unaccountable children was to obtain the celestial kingdom. It should be noted that all little children are saved without regard to race, color, or culture.

The Prophet Joseph continued to reflect upon why innocent children die. About six years later, he preached a sermon and commented upon the reasons that had come to him concerning the death of children:

President Smith read the 14th chapter of Revelation, and said—We have again the warning voice sounded in our midst, which shows the uncertainty of human life; and in my leisure moments I have meditated upon the subject, and asked the question, why it is that infants, innocent children, are taken away from us, especially those that seem to be the most intelligent and interesting. The strongest reasons that present themselves to my mind are these: This world is a very wicked world; and it is a proverb that the "world grows weaker and wiser;" if that is the case, the world grows more wicked and corrupt. In the earlier ages of the world a righteous man, and a man of God and of intelligence, had a better chance to do good, to be believed and received than at the present day; but in these days such a man is much opposed and persecuted by most of the inhabitants of the earth, and he has much sorrow to pass through here. The Lord takes many away even in infancy, that they may escape the envy of man, and the sorrows and evils of this present world; they were too pure, too lovely, to live on earth; therefore, if rightly considered, instead of mourning we have reason to rejoice as they are delivered from evil, and we shall soon have them again.

What chance is there for infidelity when we are parting with our friends almost daily? None at all. The infidel will grasp at every straw for help until death stares him in the face, and then his infidelity takes its flight, for the realities of the eternal world are resting upon him in mighty power; and when every earthly support and prop fails him, he then sensibly feels the eternal truths of the immortality of the soul. We should take warning and not wait for the death-bed to repent, as we see the infant taken away by death, so may the youth and middle-aged, as well as the infant be suddenly called into eternity. Let this, then, prove as a warning to all not to procrastinate repentance, or wait till a death-bed, for it is the will of God that man should repent and serve Him in health, and in the strength and power of his mind, in order to secure his blessing, and not wait until he is called to die.

The doctrine of baptizing children, or sprinkling them, or they must welter in hell, is a doctrine not true, not supported in Holy Writ, and is not consistent with the character of God. All children are redeemed by the blood of Jesus Christ, and the moment that children leave this world, they are taken to the bosom of Abraham. The only difference between the old and the young dying is, one lives longer in heaven and eternal light and glory than the other, and is freed a little sooner from this miserable wicked world. Notwithstanding all this glory, we for a moment lose sight of it, and mourn the loss, but we do not mourn as those without hope. [*TPJS*, 196–97]

In summary of the above reasoning, the children who die needed to come to earth for the primary purpose of obtaining a body (see *TPJS*, 181). Their development in the premortal life was such that they were qualified to be celestial beings. In God's foreknowledge, he sent that choice spirit to a body that he knew would not live long, but did not cause the death. As Mormon taught, our challenge is to so live that we "shall all be saved with [the] little children" (Moroni 8:10).

DOCTRINE AND COVENANTS 138

H istorical Setting:

    A vision, given to President Joseph F. Smith in Salt Lake City, Utah, on October 3, 1918. In his opening address at the eighty-ninth Semi-annual General Conference of the Church, on October 4, 1918, President Smith declared that he had received several divine communications during the previous months. One of these, concerning the Savior's visit to the spirits of the dead while his body was in the tomb, he had received the previous day. It was written immediately following the close of the conference; on October 31, 1918, it was submitted to the counselors in the First Presidency, the Council of the Twelve, and the Patriarch, and it was unanimously accepted by them. [section heading]

SECTION 138 • OUTLINE

➤ 138:1–10   President Smith ponders over the scriptures on the atoning sacrifice of Christ.

    a.   By obedience to the gospel man could be saved (v. 4).

    b.   The third and fourth chapters of the first epistle of Peter (vv. 5–10).

➤ 138:11–17   President Smith saw the hosts of the dead both small and great.

    a.   The spirits of the just were gathered in one place (vv. 12–13).

    b.   They had departed mortal life in hopes of a glorious resurrection (vv. 24–15).

    c.   They awaited the advent of the Son of God into the spirit world (vv. 16–17).

➤ 138:18–28   The Son of God appeared and preached the everlasting gospel to them.

    a.   He did not go among the wicked where darkness reigned (vv. 20–22).

    b.   The Saints rejoiced in their redemption and sang praises (vv. 23–24).

    c.   President Smith marveled that His ministry was such a brief time (vv. 25–28).

➤ 138:29–37   President Smith saw that He organized forces to declare the gospel.

    a.   The gospel was preached to all who died without knowledge of the truth (v. 32).

    b.   They were taught all the principles necessary to be judged (vv. 33–34).

    c.   The sacrifice of the Son of God was made known among the unrighteous and the faithful (vv. 35–37).

➤ 138:38–52   Those who were assembled in the congregation of the righteous.

    a.   Adam through Malachi who prophesied of Elijah and temple work (vv. 38–48).

    b.   The prophets among the Nephites who waited for deliverance (vv. 49–52).

➤ 138:53–60   The Prophet Joseph and others who laid the foundation of the latter-day work.

    a.   They were among the noble and great chosen in the beginning (vv. 55–56).

    b.   The faithful elders of this dispensation continue to preach the gospel (v. 57).

    c.   The dead who repent are redeemed by ordinances in the temple (vv. 58–59).

TEXT AND COMMENTARY

D&C 138:1–10 • The Redemption of the Dead

1 ON the third of October, in the year nineteen hundred and eighteen, I sat in my room pondering over the scriptures;

2 And reflecting upon the great atoning sacrifice that was made by the Son of God, for the redemption of the world;

3 And the great and wonderful love made manifest by the Father and the Son in the coming of the Redeemer into the world;

4 That through his atonement, and by obedience to the principles of the gospel, mankind might be saved.

5 While I was thus engaged, my mind reverted to the writings of the apostle Peter, to the primitive saints scattered abroad throughout Pontus, Galatia, Cappadocia, and other parts of Asia, where the gospel had been preached after the crucifixion of the Lord.

6 I opened the Bible and read the third and fourth chapters of the first epistle of Peter, and as I read I was greatly impressed, more than I had ever been before, with the following passages:

7 "For Christ also hath once suffered for sins, the just for the unjust, that he might bring us to God, being put to death in the flesh, but quickened by the Spirit:

8 "By which also he went and preached unto the spirits in prison;

9 "Which sometime were disobedient, when once the longsuffering of God waited in the days of Noah, while the ark was a preparing, wherein few, that is, eight souls were saved by water." (1 Peter 3:18–20.)

10 "For for this cause was the gospel preached also to them that are dead, that they might be judged according to men in the flesh, but live according to God in the spirit." (1 Peter 4:6.)

The written account begins with how the revelation came. He was reflecting upon the atoning sacrifice of the Son of God and pondered over the writings of "the third and fourth chapters of the first epistle of Peter" (vv. 2–10). These well-known scriptures, among the Church members, verify that work for the dead was well known in New Testament times, and needs no commentary.

D&C 138:11–17 • Awaiting the Visit in the Spirit World

11 As I pondered over these things which are written, the eyes of my understanding were opened, and the Spirit of the Lord rested upon me, and I saw the hosts of the dead, both small and great.

12 And there were gathered together in one place an innumerable company of the spirits of the just, who had been faithful in the testimony of Jesus while they lived in mortality;

13 And who had offered sacrifice in the similitude of the great

sacrifice of the Son of God, and had suffered tribulation in their Redeemer's name.

14 All these had departed the mortal life, firm in the hope of a glorious resurrection, through the grace of God the Father and his Only Begotten Son, Jesus Christ.

15 I beheld that they were filled with joy and gladness, and were rejoicing together because the day of their deliverance was at hand.

16 They were assembled awaiting the advent of the Son of God into the spirit world, to declare their redemption from the bands of death.

17 Their sleeping dust was to be restored unto its perfect frame, bone to his bone, and the sinews and the flesh upon them, the spirit and the body to be united never again to be divided, that they might receive a fulness of joy.

He saw, through the Spirit of the Lord, "the hosts of the dead, both small and great" (v. 11). Those gathered together were the righteous spirits in paradise described by Alma in the Book of Mormon:

11 Now, concerning the state of the soul between death and the resurrection—Behold, it has been made known unto me by an angel, that the spirits of all men, as soon as they are departed from this mortal body, yea, the spirits of all men, whether they be good or evil, are taken home to that God who gave them life.

12 And then shall it come to pass, that the spirits of those who are righteous are received into a state of happiness, which is called paradise, a state of rest, a state of peace, where they shall rest from all their troubles and from all care, and sorrow. [Alma 40:11–12]

Having been faithful in their testimony of Jesus (D&C 138:12) suggests that they had accepted the principles and ordinances of the gospel (see D&C 76:51), the ordinances being in the similitude of Christ (see Romans 6:3–6). They had also endured the trials and tribulations of following Christ (D&C 138:13).

The faithful spirits were rejoicing over the long-awaited visit of the Son of God to "declare their redemption from the bands of death" (v. 15–16), and bring about their resurrection unto eternal life. Their bodies that slept in the dust were "to be restored unto its perfect frame," the bones and flesh, or "the spirit and the body to be united never again to be divided," and "receive a fulness of joy" (v. 17). The coming of the

Redeemer had obviously been preached to them while in the spirit world. They also knew that only through the resurrection could they attain a fulness of joy (see D&C 93:33).

D&C 138:18–19 • Liberty to the Captives

18 While this vast multitude waited and conversed, rejoicing in the hour of their deliverance from the chains of death, the Son of God appeared, declaring liberty to the captives who had been faithful;

19 And there he preached to them the everlasting gospel, the doctrine of the resurrection and the redemption of mankind from the fall, and from individual sins on conditions of repentance.

A "vast multitude" were assembled, and "the Son of God appeared, declaring liberty to the captives who had been faithful" (v. 18). The wording of His declaration is from Isaiah 61:1, which Jesus quoted in the synagogue in Nazareth: "The Spirit of the Lord is upon me, because he hath anointed me to preach the gospel to the poor; he hath sent me to heal the brokenhearted, to preach deliverance to the captives, and recovering of sight to the blind, to set at liberty them that are bruised, to preach the acceptable year of the Lord" (Luke 4:18–19). He then preached "the everlasting gospel, the doctrine of the resurrection" and redemption from the fall, and individual sins, on the "condition of repentance" (D&C 138:19).

D&C 138:20–24 • Unto the Wicked He Did Not Go

20 But unto the wicked he did not go, and among the ungodly and the unrepentant who had defiled themselves while in the flesh, his voice was not raised;

21 Neither did the rebellious who rejected the testimonies and the warnings of the ancient prophets behold his presence, nor look upon his face.

22 Where these were, darkness reigned, but among the righteous there was peace;

23 And the saints rejoiced in their redemption, and bowed the knee and acknowledged the Son of God as their Redeemer and Deliverer from death and the chains of hell.

24 Their countenances shone, and the radiance from the presence

of the Lord rested upon them, and they sang praises unto his holy name.

One of the contributions of President Smith's vision, unto our understanding of the work done in the spirit world, was His not going unto the wicked. The wicked included the "ungodly and the unrepentant who had defiled themselves while in the flesh" (v. 20). It also included "the rebellious who rejected the testimonies and the warnings of the ancient prophets" (v. 21). The above insight may cause some to wonder about the Savior's words to the thief on the cross: "Today thou shalt be with me in paradise" (Luke 23:43). Paradise was a place for the righteous where peace was felt. The wicked went to a place of darkness where the wicked were assigned (D&C 138:22; see also Alma 40:13–14; Luke 16:19–26). The Prophet Joseph Smith made the following observation concerning the thief on the cross:

> I will say something about the spirits in prison. There has been much said by modern divines about the words of Jesus (when on the cross) to the thief, saying, "This day shalt thou be with me in paradise." King James' translators make it out to say paradise. But what is paradise? It is a modern word: it does not answer at all the original word that Jesus made use of. Find the original of the word paradise. You may as easily find a needle in a haymow. Here is a chance for battle, ye learned men. There is nothing in the original word in Greek from which this was taken that signifies paradise; but it was—This day thou shalt be with me in the world of spirits: then I will teach you all about it and answer your inquiries. And Peter says he went and preached to the world of spirits (spirits in prison, 1 Peter, 3rd chapter 19th verse), so that they who would receive it could have it answered by proxy by those who live on earth, etc.
>
> . . . Hades, the Greek, or Sheol, the Hebrew, these two significations mean a world of spirits. Hades, Sheol, paradise, spirits in prison, are all one: it is a world of spirits.
>
> The righteous and the wicked all go to the same world of spirits until the resurrection. "I do not think so," says one. If you will go to my house any time, I will take my lexicon and prove it to you.
>
> The great misery of departed spirits in the world of spirits, where they go after death, is to know that they come short of the glory that others enjoy and that they might have enjoyed themselves, and they are their own accusers. "But," says one, "I believe in one universal heaven and hell, where all go, and are all alike, and equally miserable or equally happy." [*TPJS*, 309–11]

While all go to the same world of spirits upon death, there is a separation of the righteous from the wicked. This is probably a natural separation, but the gate that prevails against the wicked is baptism.

In earlier revelations, the Lord called His servants to preach the gospel to the congregations of the wicked, or the inhabitants of the earth (D&C 60:13; 61:33; 62:5). The wicked upon the earth are later described by the Lord as those who "are under the bondage of sin, because they come not unto me" (D&C 84:49–53). To come unto Christ is to be baptized (3 Nephi 21:6; 27:20). The same division between the righteous baptized and the wicked, or those not baptized, obviously existed in the spirit world. Through vicarious work for the dead, "the gates of hell shall not prevail" (Matthew 16:18; D&C 10:69; 17:8; 18:5; 21:6; 33:13). Hell or the spirit world has an exit as well as an entrance. With the advent of the Savior into the spirit world, the righteous who had been baptized and were awaiting His coming, were redeemed. However, He did not go among the wicked.

The reaction of the faithful saints in the spirit world was joyous: they "bowed the knee and acknowledged the Son of God as their Redeemer and Deliverer from death and the chains of hell" (D&C 138:23). Their countenances shone, as they apparently absorbed "the radiance from the presence of the Lord," bringing forth spontaneous songs of praise "unto his holy name" (v. 24).

D&C 138:25–28 • Limited Time of His Ministry?

25 I marveled, for I understood that the Savior spent about three years in his ministry among the Jews and those of the house of Israel, endeavoring to teach them the everlasting gospel and call them unto repentance;

26 And yet, notwithstanding his mighty works, and miracles, and proclamation of the truth, in great power and authority, there were but few who hearkened to his voice, and rejoiced in his presence, and received salvation at his hands.

27 But his ministry among those who were dead was limited to the brief time intervening between the crucifixion and his resurrection;

28 And I wondered at the words of Peter—wherein he said that the Son of God preached unto the spirits in prison, who sometime were disobedient, when once the long-suffering of God waited in the days of

Noah—and how it was possible for him to preach to those spirits and perform the necessary labor among them in so short a time.

Jesus' spirit world ministry of three days compared to his three-year mortal ministry on earth does seem short. There were undoubtedly millions of spirits in the spirit world, many more than in the confines of Jesus' earthly ministry. How could He teach so effectively? The miracles and mighty works performed on earth would not be probable there (vv. 25–26). It caused more wondering when Peter speaks of the disobedience of Old Testament times (1 Peter 3:18–19). How could Jesus' labor in so short a time be so effective upon so many (D&C 138:27–28)? As he wondered, the answer came; both in vision and in his understanding.

D&C 138:29–35 • Chosen Messengers Proclaim the Gospel

29 And as I wondered, my eyes were opened, and my understanding quickened, and I perceived that the Lord went not in person among the wicked and the disobedient who had rejected the truth, to teach them;

30 But behold, from among the righteous, he organized his forces and appointed messengers, clothed with power and authority, and commissioned them to go forth and carry the light of the gospel to them that were in darkness, even to all the spirits of men; and thus was the gospel preached to the dead

31 And the chosen messengers went forth to declare the acceptable day of the Lord and proclaim liberty to the captives who were bound, even unto all who would repent of their sins and receive the gospel.

32 Thus was the gospel preached to those who had died in their sins, without a knowledge of the truth, or in transgression, having rejected the prophets.

33 These were taught faith in God, repentance from sin, vicarious baptism for the remission of sins, the gift of the Holy Ghost by the laying on of hands,

34 And all other principles of the gospel that were necessary for them to know in order to qualify themselves that they might be judged according to men in the flesh, but live according to God in the spirit.

35 And so it was made known among the dead, both small and great, the unrighteous as well as the faithful, that redemption had been wrought through the sacrifice of the Son of God upon the cross.

The gospel was preached by these messengers throughout the spirit world (v. 31), as Isaiah had foretold (Isaiah 61:2). Those who had not been baptized because they had not been given the opportunity, or had rejected the prophets while upon the earth, were now given an opportunity, or their full opportunity to accept or reject the gospel (D&C 138:32). All the principles necessary to qualify for a just judgment before God, as Peter had declared (1 Peter 4:6) were taught to them (D&C 138:33–34). All of "the dead, both small and great (see Revelation 20:12), "the unrighteous as well as the faithful" were taught of the redemptions by the Son of God (D&C 138:35). As President Smith understood these things, the answer to his question was realized:

D&C 138:36–37 • The Faithful Spirits of the Prophets

36 Thus was it made known that our Redeemer spent his time during his sojourn in the world of spirits, instructing and preparing the faithful spirits of the prophets who had testified of him in the flesh;

37 That they might carry the message of redemption unto all the dead, unto whom he could not go personally, because of their rebellion and transgression, that they through the ministration of his servants might also hear his words.

Therefore, as was seen by Joseph Smith in his vision of the celestial kingdom, those heirs of the celestial kingdom of God were judged according to the desire of their hearts (see D&C 137:7–9 above).

D&C 138:38–52 • The Mighty and Great Ones

38 Among the great and mighty ones who were assembled in this vast congregation of the righteous were Father Adam, the Ancient of Days and father of all,

39 And our glorious Mother Eve, with many of her faithful daughters who had lived through the ages and worshiped the true and living God.

40 Abel, the first martyr, was there, and his brother Seth, one of the mighty ones, who was in the express image of his father, Adam.

41 Noah, who gave warning of the flood; Shem, the great high priest; Abraham, the father of the faithful; Isaac, Jacob, and Moses, the great law-giver of Israel;

42 And Isaiah, who declared by prophecy that the Redeemer was

anointed to bind up the broken-hearted, to proclaim liberty to the captives, and the opening of the prison to them that were bound, were also there.

43 Moreover, Ezekiel, who was shown in vision the great valley of dry bones, which were to be clothed upon with flesh, to come forth again in the resurrection of the dead, living souls;

44 Daniel, who foresaw and foretold the establishment of the kingdom of God in the latter days, never again to be destroyed nor given to other people;

45 Elias, who was with Moses on the Mount of Transfiguration;

46 And Malachi, the prophet who testified of the coming of Elijah—of whom also Moroni spake to the Prophet Joseph Smith, declaring that he should come before the ushering in of the great and dreadful day of the Lord—were also there.

47 The Prophet Elijah was to plant in the hearts of the children the promises made to their fathers,

48 Foreshadowing the great work to be done in the temples of the Lord in the dispensation of the fulness of times, for the redemption of the dead, and the sealing of the children to their parents, lest the whole earth be smitten with a curse and utterly wasted at his coming.

49 All these and many more, even the prophets who dwelt among the Nephites and testified of the coming of the Son of God, mingled in the vast assembly and waited for their deliverance,

50 For the dead had looked upon the long absence of their spirits from their bodies as a bondage.

51 These the Lord taught, and gave them power to come forth, after his resurrection from the dead, to enter into his Father's kingdom, there to be crowned with immortality and eternal life,

52 And continue thenceforth their labor as had been promised by the Lord, and be partakers of all blessings which were held in reserve for them that love him.

The revelation names some, but there were many others, of "the great and mighty ones who were assembled in this vast congregation of the righteous" (vv. 38–49). We will not enumerate all of those whom President Smith did, but will comment on some of the things we learn, or have confirmed about them in his revelation.

It is appropriate that President Smith begins with Adam, "the father of all" (see 2 Nephi 9:21), but significant that he also included simultaneously "our glorious Mother Eve, with many of her faithful daughters" (D&C 138:38–39). "Neither is the man without the woman. . . in the Lord" (1 Corinthians 11:11).

A second witness of "Seth, one of the mighty ones, [being] in the express image of his father, Adam" was given by President Smith. In Doctrine and Covenants 107:42 he was called "a perfect man." The reality of the flood is also confirmed by mentioning Noah, and Shem's designation as "the great high priest" strongly implies that he was also known as Melchizedek (D&C 138:41; compare D&C 107:2; Alma 13:14–19). Abraham and his successors, whose covenant is now being fulfilled through Joseph Smith (D&C 124:57–58); Isaiah, whose prophesies were quoted earlier and throughout the Doctrine and Covenants; Ezekiel and his vision of the resurrection of Israel as recorded in the same chapter as the prophecy of the two sticks—the Bible and the Book of Mormon (Ezekiel 37:1–20); and Daniel, who foretold the setting up of the latter-day kingdom of God, and that kingdom would never be destroyed (Daniel 2:44) are all significant to the theology of the Church (D&C 138:42–44). For example, the kingdom prophesied by Daniel is still rolling forward to fill the earth, and has not been destroyed, nor will it be.

"Elias, who was with Moses on the Mount of Transfiguration" (D&C 138:45; Matthew 17:1–13) may have reference to Elijah as translated in the New Testament; or his being mentioned along with Malachi's prophecy of Elijah (D&C 138:47) may confirm that others were upon the mount besides Moses and Elijah, and that a full account has not yet been given of that restoration of keys in the New Testament times (see D&C 63:20–21). The identity of the personage Elias as being different than the office of Elias, that many, including Christ, have fulfilled (see D&C 77:14; 110:12; JST, John 1:21–28 is also an important doctrinal point.

The Nephite prophets and many others, along with the ones named in the revelation, mingled and waited, "For the dead had looked upon the long absence of their spirits from their bodies as a bondage" (D&C 138:50; see also 45:17). As well as being taught by the Lord, Christ gave them power to come forth after His Resurrection to "be crowned with immortality and eternal life" (D&C 138:51). This crowning was the

Lord's work and glory (Moses 1:39). Having attained their eternal status, they were to continue their labors (D&C 138:52).

D&C 138:53–56 • Modern Leaders Among the Noble and Great

53 The Prophet Joseph Smith, and my father, Hyrum Smith, Brigham Young, John Taylor, Wilford Woodruff, and other choice spirits who were reserved to come forth in the fulness of times to take part in laying the foundations of the great latter-day work,

54 Including the building of the temples and the performance of ordinances therein for the redemption of the dead, were also in the spirit world.

55 I observed that they were also among the noble and great ones who were chosen in the beginning to be rulers in the Church of God.

56 Even before they were born, they, with many others, received their first lessons in the world of spirits and were prepared to come forth in the due time of the Lord to labor in his vineyard for the salvation of the souls of men.

The written account of President Smith's vision had concentrated on the noble and great ones in the premortal life who came to earth during Old Testament times. He now turns to modern times, naming many who were also noble and great in the premortal life (v. 55). The ones mentioned were the first four Presidents of the Church plus Hyrum Smith, who was the Assistant President that sealed his testimony in blood, with his Prophet brother Joseph, of the latter-day Restoration (D&C 124:91–96; 136:36–39). While these great leaders accomplished many things, the mention of their building of temples for the redemptive ordinances of the dead (D&C 138:54) was in correlation with the subject of the vision. Their preparation for their work on earth being given in the premortal life is also significant (v. 56). As the Apostle Paul preached on Mars Hill: "And hath made of one blood all nations of men for to dwell on all the face of the earth, and hath determined the times before appointed, and the bounds of their habitation" (Acts 17:26). These latter-day prophets were appointed to come when they did and where they did to fulfill this great work of the dispensation of the fulness of times. There were undoubtedly many others that President Smith saw.

D&C 138:57–59 • The Faithful Elders of
This Dispensation

57 I beheld that the faithful elders of this dispensation, when they departed from mortal life, continue their labors in the preaching of the gospel of repentance and redemption, through the sacrifice of the Only Begotten Son of God, among those who are in darkness and under the bondage of sin in the great world of the spirits of the dead.

58 The dead who repent will be redeemed, through obedience to the ordinances of the house of God,

59 And after they have paid the penalty of their transgressions, and are washed clean, shall receive a reward according to their works, for they are heirs of salvation.

The work of God continues in the spirit world (v. 57). This doctrine is particularly comforting to family and friends of those who may have their mission in life cut short due to accident or health problems, whether as full time missionaries or other positions in the Church. It answers such questions as: "Why would the Lord allow this to happen?" The Lord does not cause the accident or bring on the illness, but in His foreknowledge has full knowledge of the situation, and provides a transfer to another field of labor.

All are heirs of salvation. Every member of the family of Adam will be given a full and equal opportunity to accept the gospel and receive the necessary ordinances of the house of God (v. 58). Though some may have to suffer for their sins, they are heirs of salvation, and will get their reward when their conditions are met (v. 59). Those who do not receive these opportunities will know that justice and mercy have been properly balanced; justice cannot rob mercy (see Alma 42:21–25).

D&C 138:60 • I Know This Record Is True

60 Thus was the vision of the redemption of the dead revealed to me, and I bear record, and I know that this record is true, through the blessing of our Lord and Savior, Jesus Christ, even so. Amen.

President Smith's concluding verse is certainly a fitting conclusion for this revelation.

General Authority Quotes

—*Elder Boyd K. Packer* • D&C 137–138

As a very direct outgrowth of the scripture project, two new revelations were added to the Doctrine and Covenants, an event that had not occurred in over a hundred years. And before the books were closed, there came the glorious revelation on the priesthood, just in time for the declaration about it to be bound with the other revelations the Lord had given His Saints in this dispensation of the fullness of times. [*Let Not Your Heart Be Troubled* (1991), 9]

—*President Joseph Fielding Smith* • D&C 137:10

We were all mature spirits before we were born, and the bodies of little children will grow after the resurrection to the full stature of the spirit, and all the blessings will be theirs through their obedience, the same as if they had lived to maturity and received them on the earth.

The Lord is just and will not deprive anyone of a blessing, simply because he dies before that blessing can be received. It would be manifestly unfair to deprive a little child of the privilege of receiving all the blessings of exaltation in the world to come simply because it died in infancy. The same thing is true of the young men who were deprived of these blessings and laid down their lives during the war. The Lord judges every soul by the intent of the heart.

All we need to do for children is have them sealed to their parents. They need no baptism and never will, for our Lord has performed all the work necessary for them. . . .

The revelations of the Lord to the Prophet Joseph Smith declare that little children who die are heirs of the celestial kingdom. This would mean the children of every race. All the spirits that come to this world come from the presence of God and, therefore, must have been in his kingdom. [*Doctrines of Salvation*, 2:54–55]

—*Elder Harold B. Lee* • D&C 137:7; 138:1

. . . President [David O.] McKay related to the Twelve an interesting experience, and I asked him yesterday if I might repeat it to you this morning.

He said it is a great thing to be responsive to the whisperings of the Spirit, and we know that when these whisperings come it is a gift and our privilege to have them. They come when we are relaxed and not under pressure of appointments. (I want you to mark that.) The President then took occasion to relate an experience in the life of Bishop John Wells, former member of the Presiding Bishopric.

A son of Bishop Wells was killed in Emigration Canyon on a railroad track. Brother John Wells was a detail man and prepared many of the reports we are following up now. His boy was run over by a freight train. Sister Wells was inconsolable. She mourned during the three days prior to the funeral, received no comfort at the funeral, and was in a rather serious state of mind.

One day soon after the funeral services while she was lying on her bed relaxed, still mourning, she said her son appeared to her, and said, "Mother, do not mourn, do not cry. I am all right." He told her that she did not understand how the accident happened and explained that he had given the signal to move on, and then made the usual effort to catch the railing on the freight train; but as he attempted to do so his foot caught on a root and he failed to catch the handrail, and his body fell under the train. It was clearly an accident.

Now listen. He said that as soon as he realized he was in another environment he tried to see his father, but couldn't reach him. His father was so busy with the duties in his office he could not respond to his call. Therefore he had come to his mother. He said to her, "You tell Father that all is well with me, and I want you not to mourn anymore.

Then the President made the statement that the point he had in mind was that when we are relaxed in a private room we are more susceptible to those things; and that so far as he was concerned, his best thoughts come after he gets up in the morning and is relaxed and thinking about the duties of the day; that impressions come more clearly, as it were to hear a voice. Those impressions are right. If we are worried about something and upset in our feelings, the inspirations do not come. If we so live that are minds are free from worry and our conscience is clear and our feelings are right toward one another, the operation of the Spirit of the Lord upon our spirit is as real as when we pick up the telephone; but when they come, we must be brave enough to take the suggested action [This account was included for two purposes; the boy whose life was cut short was okay, and how to better ourselves to receive the inspiration of the Spirit]. [*The Teachings of Harold B. Lee*, 414–15]

—*The Prophet Joseph Smith* • D&C 138:52

. . . God has created man with a mind capable of instruction, and a faculty which may be enlarged in proportion to the heed and diligence given to the light communicated from heaven to the intellect; and that the nearer man approaches perfection, the clearer are his views, and the greater his enjoyments, till he has overcome the evils of his life and lost every desire for sin; and like the ancients, arrives at that point of faith where he is wrapped in the power and glory of his Maker and is caught up to dwell with him. But we consider that this is a station to which no man ever arrived in a moment: he must have been instructed in the government and laws of that kingdom by proper degrees, until his mind is capable in some measure of comprehending the propriety, justice, equality, and consistency of the same. [*TPJS*, 51]

—*Elder Bruce R. McConkie* • D&C 138:52

There is no equivocation, no doubt, no uncertainty in our minds. Those who have been true and faithful in this life will not fall by the wayside in the life to come. If they keep their covenants here and now and depart this life firm and true in the testimony of our blessed Lord, they shall come forth with an inheritance of eternal life.

We do not mean to say that those who die in the Lord, and who are true and faithful in this life, must be perfect in all things when they go into the next sphere of existence. There was only one perfect man—the Lord Jesus Christ. . . .

But what we are saying is that when the saints of God chart a course of righteousness, when they gain sure testimonies of the truth and divinity of the Lord's work, when they keep the commandments, when they overcome the world, when they put first in their lives the things of God's kingdom: when they do all of these things, and then depart this life—though they have not yet become perfect—they shall nonetheless gain eternal life in our Father's kingdom: and eventually they shall be perfect as God their Father and Christ His Son are perfect. [CR, October 1976, 159]

Epilogue

J oseph Smith, the Prophet and Seer of the Lord, has done more, save Jesus only, for the salvation of men in this world, than any other man that ever lived in it. In the short space of twenty years, he has brought forth the Book of Mormon, which he translated by the gift and power of God, and has been the means of publishing it on two continents; has sent the fulness of the everlasting gospel, which it contained, to the four quarters of the earth; has brought forth the revelations and commandments which compose this book of Doctrine and Covenants, and many other wise documents and instructions for the benefit of the children of men; gathered many thousands of the Latter-day Saints, founded a great city, and left a fame and name that cannot be slain. He lived great, and he died great in the eyes of God and his people; and like most of the Lord's anointed in ancient time, has sealed his mission and his works with his own blood; and so has his brother Hyrum. In life they were not divided, and in death they were not separated! . . . The testators are now dead, and their testament is in force. [D&C 135:3, 5]

. . . Joseph Smith, whom I did call upon by mine angels, my ministering servants, and by mine own voice out of the heavens, to bring forth my work; which foundation he did lay, and was faithful; and I took him to myself.

Many have marveled because of his death; but it was needful that he should seal his testimony with his blood, that he might be honored and the wicked might be condemned. [D&C 136:37–39]

The Prophet Joseph Smith, and my father, Hyrum Smith, Brigham Young, John Taylor, Wilford Woodruff, and other choice spirits who were reserved to come forth in the fulness of times to take part in laying the foundations of the great latter-day work, including the building of the temples and the performance of ordinances therein for the redemption of the dead, were also in the spirit world.

I observed that they were also among the noble and great ones who were chosen in the beginning to be rulers in the Church of God. [D&C 138:53–55]

Now, what do we hear in the gospel which we have received? A voice of gladness! A voice of mercy from heaven; and a voice of truth out of the earth; glad tidings for the dead; a voice of gladness for the living and the dead; glad tidings of great joy. How beautiful upon the mountains are the feet of those that bring glad tidings of good things, and that say unto Zion: Behold, thy God reigneth! As the dews of Carmel, so shall the knowledge of God descend upon them!

And again, what do we hear? Glad tidings from Cumorah! Moroni, an angel from heaven, declaring the fulfilment of the prophets—the book to be revealed. A voice of the Lord in the wilderness of Fayette, Seneca county, declaring the three witnesses to bear record of the book! The voice of Michael on the banks of the Susquehanna, detecting the devil when he appeared as an angel of light! The voice of Peter, James, and John in the wilderness between Harmony, Susquehanna county, and Colesville, Broome county, on the Susquehanna river, declaring themselves as possessing the keys of the kingdom, and of the dispensation of the fulness of times!

And again, the voice of God in the chamber of old Father Whitmer, in Fayette, Seneca county, and at sundry times, and in divers places through all the travels and tribulations of this Church of Jesus Christ of Latter-day Saints! And the voice of Michael, the archangel; the voice of Gabriel, and of Raphael, and of divers angels, from Michael or Adam down to the present time, all declaring their dispensation, their rights, their keys, their honors, their majesty and glory, and the power of their priesthood; giving line upon line, precept upon precept; here a little, and there a little; giving us consolation by holding forth that which is to come, confirming our hope!

Brethren, shall we not go on in so great a cause? Go forward and not backward. Courage, brethren; and on, on to the victory! Let your hearts rejoice, and be exceedingly glad. Let the earth break forth into singing. Let the dead speak forth anthems of eternal praise to the King Immanuel, who hath ordained, before the world was, that which would enable us to redeem them out of their prison; for the prisoners shall go free.

Let the mountains shout for joy, and all ye valleys cry aloud; and all ye seas and dry lands tell the wonders of your Eternal King! And ye rivers, and brooks, and rills, flow down with gladness. Let the woods and all the trees of the field praise the Lord; and ye solid rocks weep for joy! And let the sun, moon, and the morning stars sing together, and let all the sons of God shout for joy! And let the eternal creations declare his name forever and ever! And again I say, how glorious is the voice we hear from heaven, proclaiming in our ears, glory, and salvation, and honor, and immortality, and eternal life; kingdoms, principalities, and powers! [D&C 128:19–23]

Abbreviations used in this Book

CHC	–	*A Comprehensive History of the Church*
CR	–	Conference Report
DBY	–	*Discourses of Brigham Young*
DHC	–	*Doctrinal History of the Church*
DNTC	–	Doctrinal New Testament Commentary
DS	–	*Doctrines of Salvation*
DPGBH	–	*Discourses of President Gordon B. Hinckley*
GD	–	*Gospel Doctrine*
GI	–	*Gospel Ideals*
GS	–	*Gospel Standards*
HC	–	*History of the Church*
HJSM	–	*History of Joseph Smith, by His Mother*
JD	–	*Journal of Discourses*
LDPDC	–	*The Latter-day Prophets and the Doctrine and Covenants*
MFP	–	*Messages of the First Presidency*
TABE	–	*That all May be Edified*
TETB	–	*The Teachings of Ezra Taft Benson*
TGBH	–	*Teachings of Gordon B. Hinckley*
THBL	–	*The Teachings of Harold B. Lee*
THWH	–	*The Teachings of Howard W. Hunter*
TPJS	–	*Teachings of the Prophet Joseph Smith*
TSWK	–	*The Teachings of Spencer W. Kimball*

Scripture Index

OLD TESTAMENT

Genesis — PAGE

1:3, 6, 9	167
1:26	26
1:28	356
4:3–5	491
4:10	602
5:1–2	101
7	429
10:25	569
12:3	545
14:20	366
15:16	273
15:18	489
17:10–12	22
18:18–19	545
19:17–26	566
25:1–6	548
28:10–12	38
28:12	39
28:22	366
49:22–26	413

Exodus

2:16–17	548
3:22	601
12:21–23	199
17:8–12	215
18:26	600
20:5	271, 458
20:6	458
24:5	233
24:10–11	611

Exodus (cont.) — PAGE

25:8–9; 40	487
25:22	392
32:26	606
33:1–4	332
36:10	392
39:43	487

Leviticus

6:3	601
11	193
20:10	550

Numbers

1:51	130
3:1–2	606
4:15	130
12	332
12:1	548
12:8	395
13:6	100
25:5	268
31:17	268

Deuteronomy

17:6	587
18:18–19	578
18:21–22	140
19:15	101, 510, 587
20:10	269
22:22	550
25:5–10	539

Deuteronomy (cont.) **PAGE**
32:7–8   231
33:17   572

Joshua
1:2–5   269
8   269

1 Samuel
5 & 6   131
17:45   164

2 Samuel
6:6–7   131
7:16   584
12:7–12   548

1 Kings
11:1–8   548
15:5   548
18:17–46   522
18:40   268
19:12   130, 178
19:8   130

1 Chronicles
5:1   136, 572, 584
28:2–3   344

Ezra
2:61–62   128, 130, 131

Job
2–26   458
32:2   100
38:1–7   228
38:7   521
38–41   521
39:1–6   227
40:6–10   228

Psalms
24   360

Proverbs
13:24   241

Proverbs (cont.) **PAGE**
24:13–14   241
29:2   262

Ecclesiastes
3:4   185
7:20   88

Isaiah
1:2   40
2:3   261, 308, 412
2:8   219
4:5   99
4:5–6   252
7:14   521
8:16   182
11   583, 584, 588
11:9   296
11:6–8   294
13:10   576
14:1–2   148
14:7, 15–19   295
14:12   45
14:13–14   45
18   414
24:20   147
24:20–22   527
24:23   576
26:1–2   414
28:10   520
28:13   397, 465
28:19   252
28:21   242, 305
29   28, 265, 588
35:3   207
37:35   269
40:3   178
40:3–5   567
40:6–7   480
40:31   481
41:8   545
41:15   577
42:7   526
45:17   292
46:10   468
49:2   136

Isaiah (cont.) PAGE
50   579
50:1   579
50:2–3, 7   564
50:2–11   579
51:11   293
51:19–20   34
52:1   89, 238, 242, 585
52:7   520
52:7–8   121
52:11   565
52:12   302
52:15   305
53:2   228
53:12   82
54:2   89, 238, 328, 566
54:1–2   293
54:17   8, 407
55:6   177
60:1–2   480
60:1–3   252
60:2–5   441
60:3   345
60:5   480
60:7   480
60:22   577
61:1   618
61:1–2   234
61:2   621
62:2   575
63:1–9   563, 574, 575
64:1–4   563, 574
65:21   306
65:24   294
65:25   294

Jeremiah
12:1   456
30:11   143
31:6, 8–9   598
31:6–14   136, 598
31:9   584

Ezekiel PAGE
1:26–28   408, 611
33:1–9   113

Ezekiel (cont.) PAGE
37   265
37:1–20   624
47:13   210

Daniel
2:44   624
2:44–45   417
7   451
7:9–10   445
7:10   445
7:13–14   445
7:21–22   446

Joel
2:28–32   243
3:18   568

Amos
4:6–10   459
9:8–9   135, 242, 413
9:8–9, 14   586
9:11–15   331
9:14–15   136

Micah
4:2   261, 308

Habakkuk
1:2   456

Zechariah
4:14   34
14:4–11   568

Malachi
3:1   294, 408
3:1–3   521
3:8–19   366
3:16–18   282
4:1   129, 578
4:5   388
4:5–6   387, 388, 511
4:6   264

NEW TESTAMENT

Matthew	PAGE
1:1–17	584
3:10	249
5:5	169
5–7	209
5:8	329
5:12	509
5:13	297
5:16	585
5:26	84
5:44	412
5:48	416
6:11	87
6:14–15	553
6:22–23	178
7:6	79, 485
7:7	177
7:20	585
10:4	606
10:5–39	119
10:9–10	119
10:11	16
10:14–15	16
10:19–20	284
10:40	428
10:40–41	119
12:32	49
13:9	298
13:24–30	301
13:34–43	128
13:36	132
13:36–43	301
13:37	133
13:37–39	137
13:38	133
13:39	134
13:39–40	134
13:40	136
13:41–42	134
13:41–43	137
16:18	620

Matthew (cont.)	PAGE
16:18–19	511, 515
16:19	510
17:1–5	208
17:1–13	624
18:6	459
18:7	456
18:16	80, 101, 510, 587
18:15–17	312
18:21–22	271
20:16	243
21:33–41	298
22:14	243
22:23	539
22:29	113
22:39	426
22:24–30	539
22:31–32	540
22:36–40	90
23	464
23:23	448
23:25–26	349
23:34–35	587
24:22	120
25:21	552
25:1–13	566
25:14–30	552
26:24	49
26:39	360

Mark	
6:18–28	587
10:28–30	553
16:14–19	118
16:15–16	276
16:15	428
16:16	429

Luke	
1:17, 19	30
1:39–41	106

Luke	(cont.)	PAGE
2:46–50		228
3:11		122
4:16–20		101
4:18		526
4:18–19		618
8:1		16
9:24		263
10:1		16
10:7		16
10:30–37		426
12:48		87
12:52		198
13:28–30		385
14:2		10
14:11		297
16:19–26		619
18:1–8		304
20:34–36		540
21:25–32		292
22:29		82
22:35–36		119
23:43		619
24:49		244

John		
1:1		222
1:3, 10		44
1:4, 10		223
1:9		114, 167, 220
1:14		221, 223, 224
1:35–40		224
2:1–11		193
5:22		91, 221
5:27		221
5:29		172
5:36		221
10:27		586
10:30		220
13		188
13:10–17		188
14:2		41
14:6		167
14:10		220, 221
14:12		27, 164
14:16		111

John	(cont.)	PAGE
14:16–17, 26		165, 189
14:16–18		164
14:18, 21, 23		189
14:21, 23		111
14:21, 27		164
14:23		524
14:26		167
14:27		165
14:30		511
15:13		177
15:13–14		119
15:14		545
15:16		177, 294
16:12		508
17:3		103, 220
17:11		220
17:11, 20–22		220
17:15–19		91
18:38		227

Acts		
1:3		508
1:20		431
2:1–4		410
2:17		243
3:22–23		578
7:58–60		587
12:2		587
17:26		231, 625
17:28		168
20:20		16
24:15		172

Romans		
1:1		431
3:23		88
6:3–6		516, 617
8:15		260
8:26		461
8:28		468
9:6		110
9:6–8		131

1 Corinthians		
1:1		431

1 Corinthians (cont.) PAGE

1:27	577
3:2	181
3:16	230
3:17	230
7:14	21
8:7–13	193
9:5–6	431
11:11	537, 559, 624
12:14–16	122
13:4–7	464
15	39
15:4–8	517
15:21–22	172
15:29	511, 517
15:30–31	517
15:40–41	53–54
15:40–42	152
15:45	101
15:46–48	511, 515

2 Corinthians

5:10	274, 430
6:4–6	463
12:1–3	611
12:1–7	38
12:3–4	39

Galatians

1:20	431
3:19	366

Ephesians

1:9–10	520
1:10	207, 548, 587
1:20	209
2:20	424

Colossians

1:16–17	44

1 Timothy

6:10	497

Hebrews

1:1–2	44

Hebrews (cont.) PAGE

4:2	366
4:15	173
5:12–14	181
6:6	49
7:1–21	376
9:4–5	131
9:7, 25	392
9:16–17	587
10:26	84, 112, 544
11:4	491
11:40	516, 517
12	85
12:5–8	241
12:6	15, 297
12:9	227
12:23	53, 85
13:2	523

James

2:10	114
4:3	177
5:4	164
5:16	291

1 Peter

2:2	181
3, 4	616
3:7	536
3:18–19	621
3:18–20	616
3:19	619
3:19–20	526
4:6	616, 622

2 Peter

2:4	296
3:8	32, 150, 457
3:15–16, 21	516
4:5–6	612

1 John

3:1–2	524
4:16–19	482

Revelation	PAGE	Revelation (cont.)	PAGE
2:6, 15	449	11:7	33
2:17	24	12:6	133
4:1–3	611	12:7	417
4:6	24	12:7–9	45
4:7	26	13:7	446
4:8	26	14	612
4:10	27	14:6	29
5:1	27	14:6–7	152, 573
5:2	28	14:7	153, 563, 573
5:5	28	14:8	133, 150, 153
5:13	36	14:20	153, 576
6:14	150	17:2–5	133
7:1	28, 29	17:5	153
7:2	29, 30	19:2	602
7:3	31	19:13	576
7:4	31	19:15	576
7:4–8	568	19:20	49
8:1	28, 150	19:7–8	251
8:2	31	19:7–9	149
9	32	20:12	513, 622
10	32	22:16	28
10:8	32	29:12	511
10:11	33	4–11	24
11:3	34	8–10	32
11:4	34		

JOSEPH SMITH TRANSLATION

JST, Genesis	PAGE	JST, Isaiah (cont.)	PAGE
14:25–40	376	51:19–20	34
17	23	62:1–4	569
17:1–9	22	65:20	151, 295
17:11	106		
17:11–12	22	**JST, Amos**	
		3:7	110
JST, Exodus			
34:1–2	194	**JST, Matthew**	
		7:2	17
JST, Isaiah		10:16	438
29	28	16:26	427
35:10	571	17:14	30
40:3–5	567		

JST, Luke	PAGE
3:4–8	567
3:38	101
12:57	87
21:24–32	99

JST, John	
1:1	222
1:20–30	415
1:21–28	624

JST, Hebrews	PAGE
7:3	102, 376

JST, 1 Peter	
4:8	186

JST, Revelation	
11:5	133
12:5	133
12:7	251

BOOK OF MORMON

1 Nephi	PAGE
1:12–13	184
3	268
3:12–13	268
3:13, 25	268
3:24–25	268
3:26	268
4:1–18	267
4:11	268
4:13	268
5:11	101
5:18–19	296
10:12–19	181
13:24–26	588
13:24–29	44, 223, 242
14:3	407, 458
14:25, 27	38
14:26	38
17:35	273
17:36	169, 356
17:37	273
17:38	448
17:40	481–482
19:14	572
19:23	265, 517
22:14	407, 458
22:15–17	144
22:20–21	578
22:26	154

2 Nephi	PAGE
1:7	278
1:26	464
2:1	195
2:7–8	173
2:17–18	172
2:19–20	101
2:18	263
2:20	611
2:25	25, 101, 230
3	588
3:18–19	286
4:11	449
4:15–35	296
6:4–5	227
7	579
8:11	293
8:19	34
8:24	89
9:9	523
9:18	230
9:21	101, 389, 623
9:41	16
9:44	113, 430
13:24–29	548
14:5–6	252
25	101
25:4	588
25:7	33, 123, 147, 344, 568, 571

2 Nephi	(cont.)	PAGE
24:1–2		148
26:3		602
27:6–11		39
27:7–8; 10–11		28
27:8, 10–11		7
27, 28		588
27:10–11		28
27:11–12		153
28:9		559
28:10		602
28:30		465, 520
28:30–31		397
29:8		572
29:12–13		572
30:4		413
30:7		414
30:9		148
30:4–6		414
31:17		105
32:4, 7		177
33:1		285
33:8		413
33:9		591
33:15		29

Jacob

1:4	375
1:19	113, 181, 430
2:27	547
2:30	547, 555
4:5	291, 547
4:13	29, 227, 234
5	242, 478
5:20–25	210
5:54–63	136, 572
5:63	210, 414
5:67–73	242

Jarom

1:2	478

Words of Mormon

1:16–18	263

Mosiah	PAGE
2:21	168
3:16, 19	232
3:19	349
4:9–10	116
5:7	226
8:13	131
13:7–9	590
13:33–35	265
15:1–4	221
15:13–18	346, 520
16:3–4	232
26:36	321
29	279
29:25	273
29:26	273, 314

Alma

1:4	503
1:30	83
5:39	321
5:54	109
6:2–4	349
10:3	413
11:45	59, 171, 230
11:40–42	172
12:24	169
13:1–5	231
13:3–5	586
13:3	227
13:7	102
13:7–19	376
13:11–12	109
13:14–10	109
13:14–19	624
13:15	366
15:3, 5	355
26:21–22	181
34:35	196
36:14	544
36:15–21	544
36:24	226
37:11	181
40:11	268
40:11–12	617
40:13–14	619

Alma (cont.) PAGE

41:10	503
42:18–26	91
42:21–25	626
42:22–25	174
42:24–25	322
43:28–29	143
43:45–46	274
43:45–47	269
43–44	269
43–62	269
44:3	269
45:14	143
46:10	274
46:12	274
46:17	327, 569
48:16	269
51:6	143
58:40	143
60:12–13	260
60:13	8, 263
60:33	269
61:21	143

Helaman

1:8	143
3:35	109, 179
5:21–30	130
12:7–17	167
12:8–19	569
13:8–11	99
13:12–14	602
15:4	481

3 Nephi

2:12	143
9:18	168
11:3	130
11:29	244
12:3	114, 167
12:5	169
12:8	329
12–14	209
12:20	503
12:26	84
12:44	412

3 Nephi (cont.) PAGE

12:48	416
13:11	87
14:6	485
14:7	177
14:13–14	544
14:20	585
16:6–7	209
16:7–10	99
16:10–11	385
16:11	99
17:4	576
18:20	177
18:31	321
19:18	409
20:10–19	211
20:12	99
20:27	168
20:29–42	414
21:4	262, 278
21:6	103, 114, 167, 220, 620
21:11	578
21:22–23	99, 252
21:23	412, 488
21:24–26	571
22:2	89
22:1–2	293
22:17	8
23:1–6	211, 265
23:9–13	576
24:1	294
24:8–10	366
24:16–18	282
25:1	578
26:9	8, 444
26:9–11	296
26:13	440
27:3–8	441
27:12–15	611
27:17	59
27:20	103, 114, 167, 220, 620
27:21–22, 27	223
27:28	294

4 Nephi	PAGE
1:2–18	93
1:14	431
1:20–46	154
1:24–25	349

Mormon	
1:16–18	263
3:16–22	29
3:18–20	430
3:18–21	16
3:20	274, 389
8:41	602
9:4–5	170, 482

Ether	
2:9, 12	278
3:14	226
3:16	26
3:21–4:7	154
4:16	8, 24

Ether	(cont.) PAGE
7:23–27	263
12	590
12:36–38	589, 591
13:8–11	566

Moroni	
6:4	105
6:7	276, 313
6:7–8	313
7:5	464
7:16	114, 167
7:45	464
7:47	186, 591
7:48	524
8	23
8:10	614
8:22	612
9:24	143
19:34	29

DOCTRINE AND COVENANTS

D&C	PAGE
1	564
1:1–2	2
1:20	459, 565, 606
1:30	115, 133, 417, 450
1:31	263
1:37–38	110
1:38	116, 293
2	518
2:1	387, 388
5:1–5	127
5:9	296
5:8–10	99
5:14	133
5:22	589
5:32–33	589
6:6	329
6:25–37	591
6:29–30, 37	589

D&C	(cont.) PAGE
6:36–37	495
7:7	381
8:1	296
9:2	296
10:5	589
10:34–35	589
10:69	620
13	378-381, 567, 584
17:4	589
17:8	620
18:5	620
18:9	377
18:9, 37	423
18:16	425
18:26–27	381
18:27–28	382
18:32	385
18:34–36	382

D&C	(cont.) PAGE	D&C	(cont.) PAGE
18:37	371	38:12–14	589
18:37–38	242	38:28–29	589
19:16	174	39:15	403
19:27	210	41:3	120
20:2	395	41:9	501
20:2–3	242, 424	42	403, 549, 550
20:8	584	42:16–21	319
20:18–19	219	42:20–21	276
20:31–34	166	42:24–26	549, 557
20:35	584	42:29	114
20:38	377	42:29–73	75
20:84	79	42:30	84, 88, 89
21:4–5	395	42:32	89
21:5	208	42:34	78
21:6	620	42:57	493
25:14–15	552	42:61	230
27:1–14	444	42:72	497
27:6–7	30	42:31–35	77
27:7	36	42:71–73	77, 78
27:11	389	42:79–82	313
27:12	424	42:79–86	275
27:12–13	208, 381	42:80–83	549
28:2	208, 332, 395	42:82	77
28:3	286	42:88–92	312
28:5	23, 184	43:3, 5	395
29:12	17	43:4	208
29:26	389	43:25	148
29:27–28	59	43:30–31	295
29:29	59	45	149, 536
29:34	195	45:17	624
31:3	14	45:28–30	99
33:2	99	45:47–53	294
33:5	133	45:48	568
33:9	14	45:54	151
33:13	620	45:64–71	345
34:6	99	46:31	599
35:13–14	577	48	75
35:20–23	286	48:6	77
37	75	49:4	14
37:3	403	49:23	147
38:12	134	49:15–17	534
38:27	221	49:16	536
38:32	75, 243, 339, 404, 407	49:18–21	197
		51	75
38:11–12	150	51:3	90

D&C (cont.)	PAGE	**D&C** (cont.)	PAGE
51:5	77	66	5
51:10–11	360	67:1–9	5
51:12–13	77	67:10–12	103
52:9	184	67:10–14	333
53	75	67:13–14	105
53:4	77	68:7	15
55	75, 79	68:14	10
56:3–4	487	68:15–21	379
56:4	15	68:16–18	392
57	212	68:19	379
57:1–2	328	68:25	23, 106, 612
57:3	98, 287, 293, 328, 500, 601	69	5
		70	75
58	346	70:1–4	5
58:4	331	70:12	17
58:19–22	261	71	5, 9-11
58:26	197	71:1	8
58:31	98	71:1–6	5
58:34	98	71:3	7
58:42	88	71:7–11	6, 18, 19
58:45	572	71:10	8
59:2	10	72	9, 76, 346
59:15	185	72:1–8	5, 9
59:16	197	72:2	10
59:23	163, 273	72:3	10
60:13	14, 620	72:6	10
61:33	620	72:8	501
62:5	620	72:8–10	213
63:16	550	72:9–16	76
63:20–21	624	72:9–26	9, 75
63:27	302	72:17–19	76, 78
63:27–31	344	72:20	79
63:28	589	72:20–23	76, 79
63:29–31	299	72:24–26	77, 79
63:37–41	344	73	5, 11, 21
63:47–48	344	73:1–6	11
63:51	295	74	21
64:8–13	271	74:1	21
64:9–10	553	74:3–4	22
64:10	87	74:5	23
64:21	80	74:6	23
64:23	129	74:6–7	23
64:27	364	75	5, 12, 206, 377
64:35–36	138	75:1–5	12, 14
65:6	347	75:3	15

D&C	(cont.)	PAGE
75:6–12		13
75:12		14
75:13–17		13
75:13–22		15
75:18–22		13
75:19–20		16
75:20–21		120
75:21		16
75:23–29		17
75:23–36		13
75:24		17
75:27–28		18
75:28		20
75:30–36		18
76		1, 37, 40, 61, 577
76:1		62
76:1–10		39
76:2–4		62
76:5		63
76:6–7		63
76:8		63
76:9–10		63
76:11–18		40
76:11–19		184
76:12		64
76:13		64
76:14		64
76:15		64
76:21		64
76:22–24		65
76:24		223
76:25–27		65
76:25–29		44
76:28–29		65
76:30		65
76:30–49		46
76:31–33		66
76:34–35		66
76:36–39		66
76:38		172
76:40		67
76:41		67
76:42		67
76:43		67
76:43–48		172

D&C	(cont.)	PAGE
76:44		67
76:45–46		152
76:46–48		67
76:46–49		49
76:49		68
76:50		68
76:50–53		55
76:50–70		50
76:51–52		68
76:51		617
76:52		61
76:53–56		68
76:54		165
76:54–55		227
76:57–58		68
76:59–60		69
76:61		69
76:62–63		69
76:64		69
76:65–66		69
76:67		85
76:67–68		69
76:69–70		69
76:71		70
76:71–79		151
76:71–80, 91, 97		54
76:72–74		70
76:74		55
76:75		70
76:75–76		174
76:76–79		70
76:81		70
76:81–84		309
76:81–90		56
76:82		55, 70, 174
76:82–85		152
76:83–85		71
76:86–87		71
76:89		174
76:89–90		71
76:91		71
76:91, 97		56
76:92–93		71
76:92–96		53
76:94–95		72

D&C	(cont.)	**PAGE**	**D&C**	(cont.)	**PAGE**
76:96–97		152	82:13		89, 293
76:96–98		95, 72	82:13–14		238
76:98–113		56, 57	82:14–19		94
76:99–100		72	82:15–21		86, 89
76:101		72, 174	82:21		112
76:102		72	82:22		103
76:103		174	82:22–24		87, 91
76:105, 107–108		73	82:23–24		91
76:107		153	83		75, 91-93
76:111		174	83:1–6		92
76:112		61, 62, 75	84		95, 297
76:103–104		72	84:1–5		95, 97
76:109–110		73	84:2		99
76:111–112		73	84:4–5		99, 252, 488
76:114–117		73	84:5		99
76:114–119		60	84:6–16		100, 388
77		21, 23, 24, 149	84:6–18		95, 99
77:1		524, 525	84:7		100
77:3–4		36	84:8		100
77:9, 14		36	84:12		100
77:11		568	84:14		101
77:14		33, 415, 624	84:16		101
78		75, 80, 93	84:18		105
78:1–7		80, 81	84:19–22		251, 584
78:5–7		82, 90	84:19–25		96, 101, 107
78:7		94	84:19–26		333
78:8–16		80, 83	84:20–22		107, 111, 392
78:12		84, 91, 112, 544	84:21		544
78:13–14		84	84:23–24		109
78:14		94	84:25		102
78:15		443	84:26–27		584
78:17–22		81, 84	84:27		105, 106
79		5, 18, 272, 371	84:28		106
80		5, 18, 272, 371	84:29		392
81		203	84:32		108
81:1–7		203, 206	84:33		124
81:2		214, 381	84:34		109, 124
81:5		215	84:35		110
82		75, 85, 92, 93	84:36		116
82:1–4		85, 87	84:37		111
82:5–10		86, 88, 525	84:38		111, 124
82:9		88	84:39		108
82:10		226, 291, 481	84:41		125
82:11		93	84:46		167
82:11–14		86, 89	84:47		114, 167

D&C	(cont.)	PAGE		D&C	(cont.)	PAGE
84:48		114		85:10		131
84:57		603		86		131, 132, 301, 586
84:58		586		86:1–7		132
84:64		114		86:2		133
84:97		120		86:7		134, 137
84:98		120		86:8–9		109, 137, 138
84:23–25		104		86:8–10		413, 585
84:23–26		194		86:8–11		132
84:26–27		379		86:9		136
84:26–32		96, 104		86:10		136
84:31–32		107		86:11		136
84:33–34, 38		124		87		139, 157, 602
84:33–39		107, 122		87:1–2, 6		155
84:33–40		124		87:1–3		139-141, 525
84:33–62		96, 124		87:1–4		155
84:40–42		112		87:4		143
84:43–44		113		87:4–8		140, 142
84:43–48		112		87:5		143, 155
84:45–46		220		87:6		143
84:49–51		120		87:8		144, 146, 155, 156
84:49–53		114, 620		88		144, 157, 163, 165
84:54–59		115		88:1–5		158, 163, 530
84:60–76		116		88:1–86		157, 158
84:62–74		118		88:3–5		189
84:63–98		96		88:4		176, 189
84:77–86		118		88:5		165
84:78–86		119		88:6–13		158, 166, 220, 222
84:87–98		119		88:11		525
84:96–97		412		88:12		189
84:99–102		96, 121		88:13		168
84:103–105		122		88:14–20		159, 168
84:103–108		96		88:15		169, 230, 531
84:106–108		108, 394		88:17–20		24
84:109–110		122		88:19		170
84:109–111		122		88:20–24		190
84:109–120		96		88:21–24		159, 169, 230
84:112–116		122		88:25–32		49
84:113		213		88:25–33		159, 170
84:117–120		123		88:27		230
84:118–120		123		88:32		172
85		127, 586		88:33		172
85–86		127		88:34–35		223
85:1–5		128		88:34–41		160, 172
85:6		136, 178		88:37		44
85:6–12		127, 129		88:37–38		174

D&C (cont.)	PAGE	D&C (cont.)	PAGE
88:40	174	88:112	153
88:42–50	160, 174	88:117	565
88:48–50	175	88:117–120	182, 184, 401, 405
88:51–61	161, 175	88:117–141	157, 182, 190
88:62–66	161, 177	88:118	211
88:63	177	88:119	251, 403
88:64	177	88:121	185
88:65	177	88:121–126	182, 185
88:67–68	329	88:122	185
88:67–73	161, 178	88:124	198
88:68	219	88:127–131	183
88:69	179, 185	88:127–137	186
88:74–75	162	88:132–137	183
88:74–76	179	88:138–141	184, 187
88:75	99	89	191, 201
88:76	162	89:1–3	192, 193
88:77–80	190	89:2	199
88:77–82	162, 180	89:4	199
88:79	181	89:4–9	192, 194
88:83–86	163, 181	89:5–7	201
88:87	147	89:7–9	201
88:87–91	144, 146	89:9	201
88:87–116	139, 144	89:10–17	197
88:88	147	89:15	198
88:89–90	148	89:17	202
88:92	149	89:18–21	193, 198
88:92–95	144, 148	89:19–17	192
88:92–98	149	90	203, 377
88:92–107	32	90:1–5	204, 207
88:93	150	90:2–4	430
88:94	150	90:3	215, 265
88:95	150	90:5	381
88:96–98	145, 150	90:6	377
88:99–101	156	90:6–11	204, 209
88:99–102	145, 151	90:9	264, 276
88:100–101	152	90:9–11	216, 224
88:102	152	90:11	211, 216
88:103–107	145, 152	90:12–18	204, 210
88:104	153	90:13–15	234
88:105	153	90:19–21	205
88:106	153	90:19–27	212
88:107	153	90:22–24	205
88:108–110	28, 145, 153	90:23	364
88:110	154, 174	90:24	468
88:111–116	146, 154	90:25–27	205

D&C	(cont.) PAGE	D&C	(cont.) PAGE
90:28–31	205, 213	93:53	234
90:32–37	205, 213	94	237
91	21, 34, 217, 571	94–97	237
92	75, 93	94:1	293, 302, 385
92:1–2	93	94:1–9	237
93	217, 221, 224	94:8–9	253, 254
93:1	103, 251	94:10–12	238
93:1–4	220	94:13–17	239
93:1–5	219	95	239, 240
93:1–19	217	95:1	15, 297
93:2	220, 222	95:1–7	240, 241
93:3	220	95:3	403
93:4	221	95:4	249
93:5	221	95:5	462
93:6	224	95:8–12	240, 243
93:6–10	221	95:12	482
93:7–17	224	95:13–17	240, 244
93:9–10	222	95:17	85, 525
93:12–14	223, 234	95:22	525
93:15–17	223	96	245
93:18	224	96:1–9	245
93:19–28	225	96:7	246
93:20	233, 296	97	246, 254
93:20–32	218	97:1–9	247, 248
93:21–22	226	97:2–3	249
93:22	53, 226	97:7–9	249
93:23	222, 227	97:8–17	329
93:23–24	234	97:10–17	247, 249
93:24	227, 234, 235	97:12–16	339
93:25	228, 230	97:13–14	416
93:26	228	97:15	251, 253
93:27–28	228	97:15–16	410
93:29–30	235	97:15–18	255
93:29–32	228	97:16	251
93:30	235	97:17	251
93:33–39	218, 229	97:18–24	247, 251
93:33, 59	169, 617	97:21	252, 253, 328
93:35	230	97:22–24	252
93:36	230, 531	97:25–26	255
93:37	231	97:25–28	248, 253
93:39	232, 271, 586	98	257, 259, 272
93:40–50	232	98:1–3	257, 259
93:40–53	218	98:4–18	257, 260
93:41–51	233, 302	98:5	143, 412
93:51–53	233	98:5–6	277, 303

D&C (cont.)	**PAGE**	**D&C** (cont.)	**PAGE**
98:6	262, 278	101:17–21	288, 292
98:7	262	101:19	293, 342
98:9	262	101:20–21	293
98:10	262, 263, 273, 278, 314	101:21	342
		101:22–31	293
98:12	397	101:22–38	288
98:13	263	101:27	294
98:13–14	589	101:28	295
98:14–15	263	101:31	151
98:16	263, 279	101:32–38	295
98:19–22	258, 265	101:35–37	589
98:23–32	258, 266	101:35–38	296
98:25–26	267	101:36	230
98:27–28	267	101:39–40	330
98:28	268	101:39–42	289, 297
98:32	268	101:41–42	297
98:33	269	101:43–45	298
98:33–38	258, 268	101:43–62	289, 298, 333
98:33–39	274	101:44–62	298
98:34	269	101:46–51	298
98:36	333	101:47–50	299, 308
98:37	269, 335, 340	101:52–54	299
98:38	269	101:55–62	300
98:39–48	259, 270	101:63–66	301
98:44–45	271	101:63–75	289
98:46	271	101:64–66	136
99	257, 271	101:67–75	301
100	281	101:68	302
100:1–2	281, 283	101:69	302
100:3–8	281, 283	101:70–73	302
100:9–12	281, 286	101:76–80	289, 303
100:13	287	101:77	262
100:13–17	282, 286	101:77–80	307
100:15	260, 468	101:81–88	303
100:16–17	287	101:81–95	289
101	281, 287, 308	101:89–95	304
101:1–10	287, 290	101:96–101	289, 305
101:1–11	116	102	309
101:3	287	102:1–2	386
101:4	306, 307, 602	102:1–5	309, 311
101:5	291	102:2	313, 314
101:6	341	102:4	314
101:8	291	102:6–8	309, 314
101:11–16	288, 291	102:9–11	310, 314
101:17	342	102:12–18	310, 315

D&C	(cont.)	PAGE
102:19–23		310, 316
102:24–29		310, 317
102:26		203
102:30–32		318
102:30–33		311
102:34		311, 318
103		301, 325
103:6		341
103:10		330
103:1–10		325, 329
103:9–10		297
103:11–14		326, 331
103:15–17		339
103:15–20		326, 331
103:16		332
103:17		109, 413
103:19–20		332
103:21–28		301
103:21–29		326, 333
103:27		589
103:30–40		326, 334
104		351, 361
104:1–13		351, 354
104:4		448
104:14–18		351, 355, 367
104:15–16		123
104:16		356
104:17		356, 367
104:19–23		356
104:19–46		352
104:24–26		357
104:27–33		357
104:34–38		358
104:39–42		358
104:43–46		359
104:47–53		352, 359
104:54–59		352, 360
104:56–57		360
104:58		361
104:58–59		357
104:60–66		352, 361
104:67–77		353, 362
104:78		364
104:78–86		353, 363, 368
105		325, 335, 343

D&C	(cont.)	PAGE
105:1–8		335, 337
105:1–9		116
105:2		340
105:5		89, 348
105:6–8		348
105:9		348
105:9–13		336, 338
105:10–11		339, 407
105:14–19		336, 340
105:15		341
105:19		341
105:20–26		336, 341
105:23–24		302, 342
105:26		343
105:27–30		336, 343
105:28		349
105:28–29		344
105:29		346, 348
105:31		349
105:31–32		336, 344, 417
105:33–37		337, 345
105:38–41		337, 346
106		371
106:5–6		371
107		102, 371, 372, 397, 498
107:1–6		376
107:1–12		372
107:2		624
107:3–4		498
107:5		398
107:7–12		376
107:8		398
107:8–9		377
107:9		377
107:10		398
107:13–14		378
107:13–20		373, 378
107:17		379
107:20		379
107:21		399
107:21–26		373, 380
107:22		399
107:23		381, 382, 423
107:23, 33		433

D&C	(cont.)	PAGE
107:24		318
107:25		396
107:26		383
107:27–32		373, 383
107:30–33		393
107:33–38		373, 384
107:34		383
107:35		385, 400
107:36		386
107:39–52		386
107:39–57		374
107:42		624
107:51–52		388
107:52–57		400
107:53–57		388, 389, 400, 444
107:56		389
107:57		389
107:58–67		374, 390
107:59–100		379
107:68–76		374, 391
107:69–70		392
107:71–72		393
107:76		309, 318
107:77–84		374, 393
107:81–84		318
107:85–90		375, 394
107:91		332, 395
107:92		395, 538
107:99		113
107:91–92		332, 394
107:93–94		383
107:93–97		395
107:95–96		396
107:91–100		375
107:98–100		396
107:99–199		400, 409
108		371, 397
109–110		401
109:1–21		404
109:1–33		401
109:4		409
109:6–9		184
109:10		409
109:10–21		405
109:22		409

D&C	(cont.)	PAGE
109:22–33		406
109:24		409
109:24–28		407
109:29		409
109:34–37		410
109:34–46		401, 408
109:35		410
109:36		419
109:38–46		410
109:47–53		412
109:47–59		411
109:47–67		401
109:54–55		412
109:54–59		412
109:60–67		412
109:61		413
109:62–64		413
109:68–70		415
109:68–71		402, 415
109:71		416
109:72–73		420
109:72–76		402, 416, 417
109:73		133
109:77–80		402, 418
110		430
110:1–3		611
110:1–10		402, 407, 564
110:8–10		420
110:11		33, 413
110:11–15		403
110:12		30, 415, 416, 624
110:13–15		388, 417, 418
110:16		403, 418-420
111		435
111:1–5		436
111:6–11		436, 437
112		421, 424
112:1–9		422, 424
112:7		425
112:10–13		422, 425
112:11		426
112:14		427
112:14–15		422, 427
112:14–21		433
112:14–34		433

D&C (cont.)	PAGE		D&C (cont.)	PAGE
112:16	428		121	453, 455
112:16–20	385		121:1–6	453, 456
112:16–22	422, 427		121:7–15	457
112:20	428		121:7–25	453
112:21	499		121:8	468
112:23	433, 441, 446, 480		121:16–25	458
112:23–29	423, 428		121:26–32	454, 460
112:24	441		121:33	454, 461
112:30	430, 587		121:34	471
112:30–31	208		121:34–40	462
112:30–34	423, 429		121:34–44	471
112:31	585		121:34–46	454
112:34	430		121:35	462, 471
113	583		121:35–38	471
113:1–6	583		121 36–37	472
113:7–8	242		121:36–37	472
113:7–10	585		121:37	465
113:10	116		121:41–43	472
114	421, 430		121:41–46	463
114:1–2	430		121:43–44	464
115–117	435		121:43, 39–40	472
115	439		121:45	464
115:1–7	439, 440		121:46	465
115:4–6	450		121:45–46	472
115:5	450		122	455
115:5–6	252		122:1–9	454, 465
115:6	441, 566		122:6	509
115:8–16	439, 441		122:7	437
115:17–19	439, 442		122:7–9	589
115:18	566		122:9	468
116	443, 451		123	455
117	446		123:1–10	454, 468
117:1–11	446, 447		123:6	473
117:4–5	448		123:11–17	455, 470
117:6	273, 292, 436		124–126	475
117:8	448		124	475, 478
117:12–16	447, 449		124:1–11	475, 478
118	421, 431		124:2, 23	500
118:1–6	432		124:7	480
119–120	351		124:10	480
119	364		124:11	480
119:1–7	365		124:12–21	475, 480
119:3–4	368		124:15	503
120	364, 366		124:16	517
121–123	453		124:19	481

D&C (cont.)	PAGE	D&C (cont.)	PAGE
124:20	501	124:143–145	502
124:22–24	476, 482	125	502
124:25–28	483	126	499
124:25–55	476	127–130	507
124:28–32	504	127	507, 513
124:29–36	483	127:1–4	507, 508
124:31	484, 545	127:5–8	507, 510
124:37–41	485	127:9–12	507, 510
124:42–43	487	128	510, 511
124:42–55	486	128:1–5	511
124:45	505	128:2	509
124:49–50	98, 488, 555	128:5	526
124:54	488	128:6–9	511, 513
124:55	98	128:7	131
124:56–61	488	128:10–13	511, 515
124:56–71	476	128:13–15	511
124:57–58	489, 545, 624	128:14–15	516
124:58	415, 584	128:16	511, 517
124:62–71	489	128:17	418
124:72–83	490	128:17–18	388, 512, 518
124:72–90	476	128:18	418
124:84	219, 233, 505	128:19–21	511, 519
124:84–90	492	128:19–23	633
124:89	184	128:21	523
124:91–96	625	128:22–23	511, 520
124:91–102	476, 493	128:24	521, 527
124:94	495	128:24–25	512, 521
124:94–95	504	129	522
124:94–96	505	129:1–8	526
124:95–96	591	129:1–9	522
124:97–100	495	130	524
124:103–110	477, 495	130:1–3	524
124:111–118	496	130:4–8	25, 524
124:119–122	477, 497	130:4–11	21
124:123	395	130:5	29
124:123–126	497	130:5–7	153
124:123–145	477	130:9–11	25, 525
124:126	380	130:12–13	139, 141, 305, 525
124:127–28	385	130:14–17	525
124:127–130	498	130:18–19	525, 531
124:128	499	130:20–21	89, 226, 481
124:131–132	499	130:22–23	245, 526
124:133–142	500	130:23	167, 465
124:139	396	130:29–21	525
124:140	396	131–132	529

D&C	(cont.)	PAGE
131:1–4		52, 529, 530, 555, 556
131:5		53
131:5–6		31, 551
131:5–8		530
131:6		556-558
131:7–8		171, 525
132		531, 549, 558, 559, 605
132:1		536
132:3		599
132:5		557
132:7		391, 538, 558
132:7		41, 557
132:16		540
132:1–6		531, 535
132:3–5		537
132:6–7		558
132:7–11		537
132:7–20		532
132:12–14		538
132:15–17		538
132:18		540
132:19–20		541
132:21–27		532, 542
132:24		104, 544
132:26		558
132:28–33		532, 544
132:30		545
132:30–31		584
132:31		82, 545
132:32–33		546
132:34–40		532, 546
132:36		547
132:37		548
132:40		548
132:41		550
132:41–45		533, 549
132:44		550
132:46–50		533, 550
132:51–57		533, 551
132:50		551
132:54		552
132:55		552
132:56		553

D&C	(cont.)	PAGE
132:57		589
132:58–59		554
132:58–65		534, 553
132:60		554
132:63		555
132:66		534, 555
133		561, 564, 580
133:1–3		561, 564
133:4–11		561, 565
133:5		580
133:6		565
133:10–12		580
133:12–15		562, 566
133:13		566, 581
133:16		581
133:16–20		562, 567
133:21–24		562, 568
133:23		569
133:25–35		562, 569
133:26		581
133:26–29		571
133:26–34		414
133:26–35		580
133:30, 32		572
133:33		571
133:34		572
133:36		152
133:36–37		581
133:36–39		572
133:36–56		563
133:40–45		574
133:46–53		153, 574
133:48		196
133:49		575
133:54–56		576
133:56		577
133:57–62		577
133:57–74		563
133:58		577
133:63–64		578
133:65–71		579
133:67–70		579
133:72–74		579
134		257, 271, 272, 275, 279

D&C (cont.)	PAGE		D&C (cont.)	PAGE
134:1	278		138:1	627
134:1–2	277		138:1–10	614, 615
134:1–3	272		138:1–11	184
134:3	279		138:11–17	614, 616
134:4–6	273		138:12	617
134:5	274		138:12–13	56
134:6	274		138:13	617
134:7–9	275		138:18–19	618
134:10	313, 321		138:18–28	614
134:10–12	275		138:19	618
134:30	280		138:20–24	618
135	583, 586		138:22	619
135:1–2	586		138:23	620
135:3	587, 592		138:25–28	620
135:3, 5	631		138:27–28	621
135:4–5	589, 592, 593		138:29–35	621
135:4, 6	590		138:29–37	615
135:5	591		138:32	622
135:7	591		138:33–34	622
136	595, 608		138:35	622
136:1–17	595, 598		138:36–37	622
136:6, 9	600		138:38–39	624
136:10	606		138:38–52	615, 622
136:18	601		138:41	624
136:18–30	596, 600		138:42–44	624
136:19	601		138:45	624
136:27–29	601		138:47	624
136:31–36	596, 601		138:48	418
136:32–33	602		138:50	624
136:36–39	495, 625		138:51	624
136:37–39	631		138:52	624, 628, 629
136:37–42	596, 602		138:53–55	632
137–138	609, 627		138:53–56	625
137	609		138:53–60	615
137:1–6	610		138:54	625
137:2–4	611		138:57–59	626
137:5	611		138:60	626
137:6	611		Official Declarations— 1 & 2	595
137:7	627		Official Declaration—1	555
137:7–8	513			
137:7–9	611, 622			
137:10	612, 627			
138	614			

PEARL OF GREAT PRICE

Moses   PAGE

1:13–14	523
1:26–27	26
1:33	44
1:34	101
1:39	82, 155, 545, 578, 624
2:29–30	193
4:1–4	45
4:3	143
4:22	399
6:21–8:2	390
6:32	292
6:48–49, 55–56	232
7:18	93, 601
7:62	252, 412, 488

Abraham

1:22–23	307
1:26–27	26
2:3–4	100
2:8	468
2:8–11	584
2:9, 11	110
2:9–11	416, 488
2:10	110
2:10–11	586
2:11	135, 545
3	175, 461
3:4	150
3:4–9	154
3:13	448

Abraham (cont.) PAGE

3:22–23	231
3:23–26	263
3:24–27	168
3:25–26	229
3:26	174, 227
3:27–28	45
4	245
5	245
5:3	32

JS—Matthew

1:21–23	110
1:38–39	292

JS—History

1:20	611
1:33	466, 509
1:36–37	578
1:40	578, 584, 588
1:41	147, 243, 598
1:56	611
1:69–71	104

Articles of Faith

1:1	245
1:8	115
1:9	75, 85, 116, 263
1:10	136, 171
1:11	274, 275
1:12	259

Topical Index

—A—

Aaron, 96, 105, 106, 108, 392, 553, 554, 611
    and his seed, 100, 106, 378
    and his sons, 105
    and his sons forever, 106
    and the seed of Abraham, 107, 109
    called by God as was, 554
    descendant of, 393, 501
    family of, 392
    house of, 104
    lineage of the firstborn, 379
    lineal descendant of, 319, 374, 378,
        379, 391, 392
    literal first-born son of, 393
    literal sons of, 392
    of old, 52, 68, 130
    priesthood of, 33, 378, 394
    sons of, 105, 130, 379
    to officiate in the temple, 107
    were promised several blessings, 108
Aaronic Priesthood, 102, 104, 108, 319,
        332, 372, 373, 376, 378, 379, 392,
        394, 504, 584
    bishop who holds the keys of, 392
    holds the keys of ministering of
        angels, 373
    John held the keys of, 106
    keys of, 107
    presiding officers of, 391
    restoration of, 107
    the lesser priesthood, 379
Abel, 587
    the first martyr, 622

who was slain by the conspiracy of
    his brother, 100
Abihu, 611
Abinadi, 221, 590
Abraham, 22, 100, 101, 106, 109, 110, 135,
        137, 246, 267, 290, 291, 306, 307,
        412, 413, 460, 476, 481, 488, 532,
        533, 536, 539, 544-548, 550-554,
        576, 584, 592, 602, 610, 611, 624
    dated around 2000 B.C., 101
    background information on, 545
    blood of, 138
    book of, 448, 461
    bosom of, 613
    commanded to circumcise every male
        child when eight days old, 22
    covenant made to, 488
    covenant posterity of, 387
    covenant with, 167
    covenanted with, 415
    days of, 99
    descendants of, 135
    father, 135
    father of the faithful, 622
    friend of God, 545
    fulfills the law, 546
    God of, 540, 596, 600, 601
    gospel of, 30, 36, 403, 415, 416
    great grandfather of the twelve tribes,
        30
    land of, 402
    land promised to, 488
    law of the priesthood, 545
    left the land of the Chaldeans, 100
    lineage of, 109

literal descendant of, 416
literal seed of, 416
obedience of, 547
offering up of Isaac, 291
promise of, 545
promise to, 545
received all things by revelation, 532
received the priesthood from
    Melchizedek, 95, 100
revelation to, 22
seed of, 109, 131, 137, 138, 331, 339,
    387
tested as, 290
o marry Hagar, 532
trial of offering up his son Isaac, 291
was commanded to offer his son, 288
Abraham fulfills the law, 546
Abraham, Isaac, and Jacob, 135, 175, 246,
    536, 539, 548, 576, 584, 596, 601
    priesthood covenant holders of past
        generations, 135
accept the work of our hands, 404
Adam, 30, 36, 95, 231, 374, 386–390, 400,
    416, 443–445, 448, 451, 452,
    518–520, 592, 596, 602, 611, 615,
    623, 632
    Ancient of Days, 444
    and Eve, 451
    bestows his last blessing, 388
    blessing his posterity, 389
    death of, 444, 451
    death of, 388
    delivers up his stewardship to Christ,
        445
    family of, 626
    father, 100, 388, 610, 622, 624
    father of all the human family, 445
    first man, 101
    language of, 448
    Michael, the prince, the archangel,
        154, 374, 389, 444, 445
    the seventh angel, 153
    stood up in the midst of the
        congregation, 444
    was a vegetarian, 193

was first an earthly man, 516
was the first man, 100
words of, 603
Adam-ondi-Ahman, 81, 83, 84, 388, 389,
    400, 443, 444, 446, 448, 451, 452
    Ahman signifies God, 443
    place where Adam dwelt, 443
    Valley of God where Adam dwelt, 443
Adams, John, 278
Administrator God, 221
admonished, 212
afflictions, 458, 576
    and persecutions, 415
    bear your afflictions three times and
        you will be rewarded, 258
    because of man's sins, 458
    in all their, he was afflicted, 575
    Job had many, 458
    pain, and misery, 610
    shall be but a small moment, 453, 457
    shall work together for your good,
        257, 259
    small moment of adversity, 457
    suffered, because of transgression,
        287
    turn their afflictions to His good, 287
African-American, 142
after tribulation comes blessings, 331
after your testimony comes wrath, 146
agency and condemnation of man, 228
agency of man, 218, 228
    to destroy is the plan of Satan, 143
alcohol does have positive uses, 196
alcoholism is one of the major plagues of
    the last days, 195
Almighty God, 57, 139, 142, 152, 153, 607
Almighty will pour down knowledge, 461
Alpha and Omega, 12, 14, 123, 204, 206,
    430, 555
Alvin, 513, 610, 611
Amherst conference, 12
Amherst, Lorain County, Ohio, 12, 85
Amos
    prophecy, 135
    prophesied, 135

prophet, 242, 331
an honest mistake, 436
an imperative duty to God and angels, 468
Ancient of Days, 389, 443–446, 451, 622
angel
    fifth, Angel Moroni, 152
    fourth, 145, 152
    second, 145, 151, 153
    third, 145
Angel Moroni, 147, 243, 466, 504, 518, 573,
      578, 584, 588, 598
    angel of light, 65, 519, 522, 523, 527,
      632
another Comforter, 163
Another Testament of Jesus Christ, 115
    Book of Mormon, 29
answers to prayer, 103, 136, 291
Apocrypha, 34, 35, 217, 571
    sacred books of the Jewish people, 35
    secret or hidden, 35
apostasy, 19, 22, 27, 88, 100, 114, 321, 425,
      429, 578
    gross darkness of, 480
    high road to, 321
apostasy refers to Church members who:
    (1) repeatedly act in clear, open and
        deliberate public opposition to
        the Church or its leaders, 321
    (2)persist in teaching as Church
        doctrine information that is not
        Church doctrine after being
        corrected by their bishops or
        higher authority, 321
    (3) continue to follow the teachings of
        apostate cults, 321
Apostle
    Paul, 21, 23, 260, 424, 463, 467, 515,
      517, 611, 625
    Peter, 21, 510, 616
Apostles
    Jerusalem Twelve, 16, 119, 428
    Twelve, 23, 109, 156, 175, 208, 209,
      214, 221, 242, 264, 309, 311, 318,
      320, 371, 373
    and prophets, 42, 184, 211, 424

from Galilee, 606
appendix, 561
appearing of the Father and the Son, 524
appointed to go up to Zion, 79
archives of the Holy Temple, 510
Army of Israel becomes great, 341
arrogant
    high-minded, 212
Ashley, Major, 13, 15
ask and receive, 13, 161, 493
assemble and organize yourselves, 179
Atonement, 44, 84, 112, 173, 176, 291, 547,
      575, 576
    day of, 392
    full benefit of, 291, 360
    in Gethsemane, 220
    little children are holy through the, 21
authority of the priesthood, 100, 102, 111,
      242, 530, 585
    is eternal, 101
awaiting the visit in the Spirit World, 616

—B—

Babbitt, Almon, 476, 492
Babylon, 133, 566
    as spiritual wickedness, 566
    go from the nations of, 562
    go out from, 562, 565
    go ye out from, 565
    the symbolic term of wickedness, 153
Bailey, Thomas A.
    The American Pageant (book), 141
Baker, Jesse, 500
Ballard, Melvin J., 556
    Sermons and Missionary Services of
      Melvin J, Ballard (book), 556
banner of Zion, 345
banners to the world, 344, 345
baptism, 92, 106, 429, 509, 515, 517, 620,
      621, 627
    by immersion, 378
    covenant of, 114, 167
    for the dead, 483, 484, 485, 507, 509,
      511, 512, 517, 518, 526

for the dead resumed, 512
gospel of repentance and of, 104, 105
infant, 106
of repentance, 378, 379
ordinance of, 23, 103
ordinance of water, 105
waters of, 114, 415
baptismal font, 307, 476, 483, 504, 515, 516
baptized, 423, 429, 483, 515, 517, 611, 620, 622
after the manner of his burial, 50
by proxy, 526
by water for the remission of sins, 117
for all these men, 308
for every President of the United States except three, 307
for the dead, if the dead rise not at all, 517
for the remission of sins, 164, 610
for the remission of their sins, 117
for their relatives who are dead, 526
for your dead, 31, 510, 527
in his childhood does not refer to infant baptism, 106
Jesus was, 224
planet was baptized with the waters of the flood, 170
Savior was baptized with water, 224
while he was yet in his childhood, 104
why are they then baptized for the dead, 517
will be baptized by fire at the beginning of the Millennium, 170
with fire and the Holy Ghost are spiritually begotten sons and daughters, 226
Barzillai
children of, 131
the Gileadite, 131
be not partial of thy brethren in love, and to all men, 422
be still and know that I Am God, 291
bear record of my name unto the ends of

the earth, 424
bear testimony, 116, 120, 308, 411, 422, 424
all the world, 116
become
a great mountain and fill the whole earth, 417
as little children, 460
perfected and sanctified, 172
Bennett, John C., 476, 480, 481
Benson, Ezra T., 599
Benson, Ezra Taft, 6, 94, 116, 202, 278, 349, 367, 375, 400, 479, 491, 580, 607
proper use of the Book of Mormon, 604
The Teachings of Ezra Taft Benson (book), 94, 202, 279, 367, 400, 580, 607
Secretary of Agriculture for United States, 202
Bent, Samuel, 499
Bible, 12, 22, 41, 45, 115, 119, 147, 211, 217, 242, 252, 269, 327, 364, 376, 390, 471, 493, 548, 569, 587, 588, 603, 616
Hebrew, 35
Joseph Smith Translation, 360, 517
King James Version, 35, 222, 295, 388, 579
scholars, 100
two sticks, 624
Bible Dictionary, 22, 35, 135, 164, 243, 571
binding power on earth, 510
birthright holder, 136, 572
bishop
judge in Israel, 313, 319, 374, 391–393
bishop's council, 312
blaspheming, 434
blasting the reputation of neighbors, 434
blessings, 40, 52, 53, 61, 71, 84, 85, 87–89, 91, 108
and gifts of the spirit abound, 69
and riches of the earth are yours, 81

of exaltation, 627
of God, 139
of heaven, 157
of liberty, 278
of my church, 497
of my people, 448, 449
of salvation, 110, 135
of the building of the temple, 249
of the Church, 373, 378, 477
of the elements, 459
of the fulness of the priesthood, 108
of the Gospel, 110, 135
of the Lord, 266
of the promise, 246
of the temple, 243, 557
of the Word of Wisdom, 198
or punishments for what we have
    chosen to do, 91
promised, 14, 292, 405, 407, 464
the Father has for you, 81
blindness of heart, 433
blood
    best of the century, 590
    of Israel, 136, 138
    of the lamb, 466
    of the saints, 140, 142, 143, 602
Boggs, Lilburn W.
    Missouri Governor, 304, 473, 475
Bond, Christopher S., 473
    governor of the state of Missouri, 473
Book of Mormon and the Church
    must be waved for the world to see,
        345
    the ensign, 345
book of remembrance, 128, 129, 131, 282
book of Revelation
    be unfolded in the eyes of all people,
        24
    John told exactly what he saw in
        heaven, 23
    one of the plainest books God ever
        caused to be written, 23
Book of the Law of God, 128
Boothe, Ezra, 7, 11
    apostatized, 5

Methodist minister, 7
bound in heaven, 493, 507, 510, 514, 515
Boynton, John F., 432
Brewster Jr., Hoyt W.
    Doctrine and Covenants Encyclopedia
        (book), 203, 213, 449
Bridegroom, 144, 148, 149, 251, 434, 562,
        565, 567
    coming of the, 566
Brigham Young University, 115
    1977 Devotional Speeches of the Year,
        235
    BYU Studies, 585
Broome County, 519, 632
Brother of Jared, 26, 38, 154
Brown, Hugh B., 472
Brown, Victor L., 216
Brunson, Seymour, 499
building
    a temple, 97
    committee, 239, 240, 244
    up of Zion, 79, 329
Burgess, 435
Burnett, Stephen, 18
burning, 128, 444
    at the end of the world, 134
    at the Second Coming, 129, 480
    by fire, 429
    day of, 137, 409, 410, 428
    in the last days, 543
    rays of the rising sun, 457, 471
    with fire and brimstone, 50
bushwhackers, 341
Butterfield, Josiah, 500

—C—

Cahoon, Reynolds, 239
Cainan, 387, 388, 444
Caleb, 99, 100
    the spy was a descendant, 100
    was ordained by Elihu, 100
    who ordained Moses, 100
Camp of Israel, 585, 598
    Omaha Nation, 595

Canaan, land of, 100
Cannon, George Q., 220, 307, 320, 323
    Journal of Discourses, 320
cannot be saved in ignorance, 530
Carter, Jared, 18, 239, 312, 318
Carter, John S., 312, 318
Carthage Jail, 306, 586, 591
cast out devils, 117, 494
cast pearls before swine, 79
casting lots, 315, 318
celestial, 28
    glories or kingdoms, 38
    glory, 52, 53, 59, 159, 160, 168–170,
        173, 190, 301, 529, 530, 537, 556
    goal, 50
    kingdom, 47
    law, 41
    whose glory is that of the sun, 51
    world, 80, 82–84, 90, 94, 124, 158,
        163, 540
celestial
    degree, 339
    earth, 24, 25, 154, 169–171
    glory—three heavens, 529
    home, 229
    kingdom, 24, 47, 49, 50, 52, 55, 56, 59,
        61, 62, 89, 91, 94, 158, 159, 163,
        165, 168–170, 173, 176, 182, 216,
        230, 306, 335, 337, 338, 346, 397,
        513, 537, 540, 556, 558, 609–612,
        622
    marriage, 535
    nature, 39, 230
    saints, 150–152
center place of Zion, 90, 287, 293, 302, 328,
    340, 346, 500, 601
certificate of acceptability, 78
CES Religious Educators Symposium, 19
Chaldeans
    land of, 100
charity, 185, 240, 373, 383, 384, 463, 496,
    589, 591
    a mantle of perfectness and peace,
        183
    fourth principle for priesthood use is,
        464
    is the pure love of Christ, 186, 591
    preventeth a multitude of sins, 186
chasten, 14
    all those who will not endure
        chastening, but deny me, cannot
        be, 290
    because of His love for them, 214
    bishop of my church, hath need to be
        chastened, 232
    Brother McLellin is chastened, 13
    he must needs be chastened and
        stand rebuked before my face,
        241
    He chastened them because He loved
        them, 241
    He will chasten them if they do not
        repent, 258
    my people must needs be chastened
        until they learn obedience, 337
    Newel K. Whitney needs be
        chastened, 218
    others would not endure their
        chastening, and unless they
        repent, 291
    that I, the Lord, will chasten them
        and will do whatsoever I list, 265
    the chastening of the Lord came
        because their personal reactions
        to each other, and wrongful
        desires, had polluted their
        inheritances, 291
    the Lord chastened His people for a
        very grievous sin, 403
    the Lord chastens those He loves, and
        priesthood holders should do
        likewise, 464
    the Lord chastens whom he loves that
        they be forgiven of their sins,
        240
    the Lord did chasten him because He
        loved him, 15
    there are those that must needs be
        chastened, 248
    therefore they must be chastened, 297

therefore they must needs be chastened, 297

they must be chastened as Abraham was commanded to offer his son, 288

they must be chastened until they learn obedience, 335

they must needs be chastened and tried, 290

those who call themselves by my name will be chastened a little, 325

until she is clean, 205

until she overcomes and is clean before me, 214

whom I love I also chasten, 241

why the Lord chastens His people, 241

will be merciful to the residue of the school, some must be chastened, 247

Zion shall be redeemed, although she is chastened for a little season, 282, 286, 287

chastening hand

of an Almighty God, 142

chastised the leaders, 233

chastisements

are self-explanatory, 233

as needed to help the individual, 482

children

bring up in light and truth, 218, 233

bring up in truth, 232

Christ

Firstborn, 218

gospel of, 22, 50, 55, 56, 70, 72, 526

is the Lion of the tribe Judah, 28

root of David, 28

was the Father and the Son, 221

Church and kingdom, 107, 109, 110, 124, 137, 209, 211, 238, 345, 360, 361, 417, 433, 472, 573

to come forth out of the wilderness, 417

Church discipline, 311, 312

among the Nephites, 312

General Authorities do not direct the decisions of local discipline, 321

understanding of, 319

Church in Kirtland, 265

Church membership, 343

continues to grow, 343

loss of, 320

church of God, 100, 102, 274, 393, 625, 632

church of the Firstborn, 31, 51, 53, 54, 57, 81, 84, 85, 111, 156, 158, 163, 165, 218, 225, 226, 378

Church shine forth, 416

Church stands independent, 83

circumcision, 22, 23

is not baptism, 23

law of, 21

ordinance of baptism replaced, 23

Civil War, 140–143, 155, 305, 341, 602

claims of widows and children, 92

Clark Jr., J. Reuben, 93, 471

Clark, J. Reuben, 368, 381, 606

J. Reuben Clark, Selected Papers (book), 94, 381, 389, 606, 607

Clay County, 287

Colesville, 92, 519, 632

Coltrin, Zebedee, 351

Columbus, 307, 573

come unto Christ, 103, 114, 620

Comforter, 13, 15, 17, 71, 111, 158, 163–165, 176, 177, 180, 209–211, 493

Holy Ghost, 138, 165, 167, 189

Holy Spirit of Promise, 158, 189

Son of God, 189

commandments, 6, 10, 12, 14, 18, 22, 50, 83, 88, 90, 93, 98, 100, 103–105, 110, 111, 114–116, 118, 124, 125, 156, 157, 164, 176, 180, 181, 192, 193, 198, 199, 217–219, 225, 228, 232, 235, 240, 243, 244, 246, 248, 253, 258, 271, 286, 287, 299, 300, 330, 332–334, 337, 345, 358, 361, 363, 375, 377–379, 390, 395, 407, 412, 415, 427, 481, 486, 487, 492,

502, 503, 545, 547, 552, 553, 556,
561, 577, 578, 580, 587, 589, 595,
596, 598, 599, 603, 629, 631
if we continue to keep the, 18
keep my, 8
keeping the, 55, 61
prepare for the, 5
prepare the way for the, 7
search the, 110
seeks knowledge and gives heed to
the, 50
thou shalt keep the, 22
walk in all the, 186
commit acts of the foulest kind, 434
concerning adultery, 549
concerning the laws of the land, 257
condemnation of man, 228, 229
conditions of the law, 537
consecration and stewardship
principle of, 497
consequences
of adultery under the law unto the
Church, 549
of wickedness, 487
conspiring men in the last days, 194
constitution, 277
a glorious standard, 262
amendments, 262
basic laws of a nation, 464
befriend the, 258, 262, 278, 303
continuance of, 278
drafted the, 264
established by wise men, 289
God-inspired, 278
high council of the Church of Christ,
309
law of the land, 257
made only for a moral and religious
people, 278
nature, and use of man, 196
of our land, 411
of the Church, 1
of the High Council, 309
of the people, 262, 303
of the priesthood, 463, 464

of the United States, 261, 262, 264,
271, 276, 277, 304, 412, 461, 470,
471, 607
of this land, 303
principles of, 262
read and ponder it, 278
understand and abide the principles
of, 279
very verge of destruction, 279
will be saved, 278
constitutional
befriend the, 303
form of government, 308
law maketh you free, 262
law of the land, 260, 262
system of government, 261
contention, 21, 48, 244
avoid disputation and, 19
contentions, 290, 341
arose in the School of the Prophets,
240, 243
in the School of the Prophets were
caused by the devil, 243
Cook, Lyndon W.
*The Revelations of the Prophet Joseph
Smith* (book), 158, 187, 203, 237,
362, 372, 449, 450
corner stake of a tent, 500
cornerstone of Zion, 478, 500
council and Mine Own Voice, 366
Council Bluffs, Iowa 595
Council of the Eternal God, 454, 460, 461
councilors nominated by the President,
314
covenant
broken, 354
made to Abraham fulfilled, 488
of the Priesthood holder, 112
Cowdery, Oliver, 5, 30, 33, 89, 104, 147,
242, 272, 279, 286, 309, 312, 318,
351, 352, 357, 358, 371, 377, 378,
381, 382, 408, 423, 424, 435, 477,
493, 494, 504, 505, 585, 591–593,
598, 609
Cowdery, Warren, 371

crooked and perverse, 99
crown of eternal life, 27
Cullimore, James A., 322
Cumorah, 519, 520, 632
Cutler, Alpheus, 500

—D—

darkness
    covereth the earth, 428, 433
    covers the earth, 423, 428
David, seed of, 584
Davies County, 451
Davies, Amos, 477, 496
day of
    be not moved until, 142
    calamity, 602
    choosing, 337, 345, 346
    Pentecost, 243, 401, 408, 410, 419
    stand in holy places until, 140
    the Lord, 146, 403, 417, 419, 434, 518,
        562, 621, 623
    vengeance, 11, 128, 234, 575
decision made by the President, 316
decisions of these Quorums, 383
Declaration of Independence, 264, 277,
    307, 308
dedicatory prayer, 405, 409, 412, 415, 416
    of the Kirtland Temple, 184
deeds of the blackest dye, 434
defrauding, 434
degrees of glory, 1, 38, 39, 41, 42, 60
descendant of Joseph, 245, 246
Deseret News
    The Council of the First Presidency
        and the Quorum of the Twelve,
        321
designs of the world, 341
desolation, 34, 123, 327
    and abomination, 182
    and destruction, 147
    day of, 428
    day of burning and, 423
    of abomination in the last days, 123
    of abominations, 163, 181

utter, 590
destinies of all nations, 435, 447
devil
    who is the father of contention, 244
Dibble, Philo, 37
diligence and faith, 603
diligent
    be, in all things, 14, 17
disciplinary action, 321, 322
disobedience, 230
    attitude of many of the Church
        members, 338
    children of, 458
    of Old Testament times, 621
    to the word of wisdom, 194
    willful, 48
dispensation of the fullness of times, 207,
    526, 593, 627
do not sell lands in Jackson County, 305
Dodds, Asa, 13, 15
Dort, David, 499
dove
    sign of the, 223
Doxey, Roy W.
    compiler of "Messages of the First
        Presidency," as quoted in *The
        Latter-day Prophets and the
        Doctrine and Covenants,*
        (pamphlet) 201
    "Zion in the Last Days," *Deseret News,*
        341
Dunn, Loren C., 20
Durham, G. Homer
    compiled, *Evidences and
        Reconciliations*, 112, 201, 332
dusting off of the feet, 13, 16
duties of
    the bishop, 77
    the First Presidency, 209
    the Twelve and Seventy, 384
duty of
    the bishop, 10, 77
    the Bishop in Kirtland, 77
    the church, 13, 17

—E—

earth life
    second stage, 229
earthquake, 140, 142–144, 146, 148, 155,
    446
    in divers places, 149
Egypt, 33, 199, 234, 246, 302, 488, 588, 596,
    601
    exodus from, 608
    land of, 600
Egyptian manuscript
    Coptic, 508
Ehat, Andrew F.
    *It Seems Like Heaven on Earth: Joseph
        Smith and the Constitution*
        (book), 585
eight years old, 22, 612
    not accountable before, 22, 106, 612
elect of God, 107, 109, 110, 124
Elias, 29, 57, 403, 420
    doctrine of, 33
    Gabriel, 36, 416
    gospel of Abraham, 415
    in the Kirtland Temple, 430
    Noah, 29, 30, 36, 415, 416
    office of, 624
    Priesthood of, 33
    restored the gospel of Abraham, 36
    spirit of, 33
    who was, 36
    with Moses, 623, 624
Elias, Noah, and Gabriel
    appeared to Zacharias, 30
    are all the same person, 30
    brought keys of gospel to Joseph
        Smith, 30
    spirit and power of, 30
    would restore all things, 30
Elihu, 99, 100
Elijah, 130, 417, 418, 420, 527, 576, 623,
    624
    and temple work, 615
    and the keys of the Patriarchal
        Priesthood, 417

    appears with the keys of turning the
        hearts, 403
    in the Kirtland Temple, 430
    Malachi's prophecy of, 624
    Spirit of, 264
    the Prophet, 387, 417, 518, 526, 543,
        623
Elijah's mission
    provide a welding link between the
        fathers and the children, 418
Elohim
    spirit children of, 45
    usually the name we use for the
        Father, 245
Emma's commandment, 551
endow the chosen with power, 243
endowment, 345, 382, 408, 419, 485, 504,
    558
    an endowment, or a blessing, 338,
        612
    blessed with this, 403
    blessing and an, 340
    blessing of, 336
    later revealed, 504
    of power, 406, 407
    of spiritual power, 339
    ordinances and endowments,
        washings and anointings, 485
    ordinances of the, 609
    ordinances which were later revealed,
        504
    personal, 339
    promise of the, 340
    receive the ordinances and, 521
    receiving of their temple, 571
    saints received their, 504
    spiritual, 381
    temple, 339, 347
Endowment House, 307, 604
    in Salt Lake City, 604
Enoch, 52, 57, 69, 72, 93, 100, 387, 388,
    444, 563, 576, 592
    book of, 374, 388–390, 444
    church of, 51
    order of, 51

record of, 292
Enos, 386, 388, 444
ensign of peace, 346
envyings, 290, 341
Ephraim, 136, 138, 210, 563, 570, 572, 581,
    584, 597
    children of, 570, 571
    head of, 572
    is my firstborn, 597
    mixed with the blood of all the earth,
        137
    must be gathered first to prepare the
        way, 138
    richer blessing on the head of, 563
    servants of the Lord, 569
    should be plucked out, 138
    should not be rebellious, 138
    stand in his place at the head, 138
    the birthright holder, 136
    was given the birthright, 584
Ephraim, servants of the Lord, 569
equal in earthly things, 81
equality
    principle of, 275
Esaias, 57, 95, 99
    is the New Testament translation of
        the prophet Isaiah, 101
    received the priesthood under the
        hand of God, 100
eternal glory, 215, 229, 524, 556
eternal marriage, 103, 104, 125, 536, 549
    principle of, 536
eternal principle
    age of eight is an, 106
    Prophet Joseph taught an, 321
    right to have freedom was an, 229
eternal realm, 610
eternity of the marriage covenant, 531, 556
European
    gentile, 143
    wars, 141
Evangelic Ministers—Patriarchs, 386
evangelical order of the priesthood, 374
even a great revelation, 371
evening and morning star, 158

everlasting
    dominion, 445, 463, 465
    gospel, 29, 30, 122, 145, 152, 288, 289,
        293, 297, 406, 413, 492, 518, 563,
        572, 587, 591, 614, 618, 620, 631
everlasting gospel to all, 572
    power, 465
every man in his own office, 122
every man may improve his talents, 89
excommunicate, 275, 276, 313
excommunicated, 320, 425
    member of the Church, 322
excommunication, 322, 323
    of Frederick G. Williams, 494
exhort the church, 11
expound the scriptures, 6, 281
extermination order
    issued by former Governor Lilburn
        W. Boggs, 344
extravagance, 433
eye single to the glory of God, 86, 90, 178
excerpts from Three Addresses by
                President Wilford Woodruff
                Regarding the Manifesto,
                Doctrine and Covenants, 555
    Official Declarations—1 & 2, 595
    Official Declaration—1, 555
Ezekiel
    glorious visions, 111

—F—

face of God
    see the, 219, 251, 392, 584
faith
    and repentance, 23
    of Christ, 179
faithful
    and wise steward, 10, 84, 85, 300
    elders of this dispensation, 626
    spirits of the prophets, 622
fall of Satan, 44, 47
false doctrine, 22
Family History Library, 527
famine, 34, 140, 142, 143, 192, 197, 367
    wild animals in case of famine and

excess hunger, 197

Far West, 364, 430–432, 439–443, 447–449
city of, shall be built, 442

Father
and the Son, 47, 111, 221, 503, 524,
610, 615
cannot break, 112
in Heaven, 82, 227, 230, 278
spirit children of our, 230

Federalist Papers, 278

few there be that find it, 542

Fielding, Rev. James, 421

fifth
angel, 32, 145, 152
scriptural evidence, 518
trump, 152

fifth vision, 56
the Terrestrial Kingdom, 54

first
angel, 145, 150, 153
casting of lots, 318
Comforter, 138, 164, 165, 167, 189
key to discern an angel, 523
scripture as evidence, 513

First Epistle to the Corinthians
explanation of, 21

First Presidency, 93, 109, 130, 156, 175,
200, 203, 207, 208, 211, 212, 214,
215, 233, 234, 279, 308, 311, 317,
318, 320, 345, 366, 380–385, 394,
397, 400, 419, 423, 428, 429, 433,
447, 449, 477, 479, 496, 555, 593,
605, 606, 609, 610, 614
are prophets of the living God, 156
divine investiture of authority, 221
duties of, 209
Frederick G. Williams appointed a
counselor in, 93
given the power of the priesthood for
the dispensation of the fulness
of times, 423
hasten to translate and to fulfill other
duties, 234
lifetime appointments to administer
the business and mission of the

Church, 211
Lord chastised the leaders of the
Church in, 233
have had assigned to them a special
calling, 381
have power to determine whether a
case may have a rehearing, 311
holds the oracles, the infallible
authority, or the keys for the,
498
is dissolved upon the death of the
President, 382
must be the forerunner in preparing
the gospel to be taught, 211
of the New Testament Dispensation,
208
other duties of, 210
personal needs of the counselors were
to, 212
political leaders and dignitaries who
come to Utah visit, 345
possess a special gift, 381
Presidency of the High Priesthood,
203
pruning of the vineyard would refer
to, 242
receive the oracles for the whole
church, 380
responsible for the weekly meetings
with all of the General
Authorities, 209
sent out a message to the Church on
the *Origin of Man*, 231
should only be called upon difficult
cases, 311
sustained as prophets, seers, and
revelators, 399
this talk was later approved by, 323
two counselors are accounted equal
with, 209
well beyond the normal retirement
age of our day, 109
what is the position of the Church
with respect to war, 279

First Vision, 43, 504, 611
the Throne of God, 42

five blessings promised to those who
follow the five principles,
464–465
(1) confidence, 464
(2) doctrine of the priesthood, 465
(3) Holy Ghost shall be thy constant
companion, 465
(4) mantle of righteousness and
truth, 465
(5) everlasting dominion of the
priesthood, 465
five prerequisites in the formula for seeing
God, 219–220
(1) forsaking of sin is repentance, 219
(2) to come unto Christ is to be
baptized, 220
(3) calling on the Lord's name is a
manner of prayer, 220
(4) to obey His voice is to receive and
accept revelation, 220
(5) keep the commandments, those
recorded in the scriptures, 220
five principles for using the priesthood,
463–464
(1) quiet dignity, 463
(2) by revelation, 463
(3) be sharp, 464
(4) charity, 464
(5) virtue, 464
Floyd, John B., 284, 285
forgive all men, 87
forgiveness
principle of, 271
form of a dove, 223, 224
former sins return, 88
Foster, James, 500
Foster, Robert D., 477, 496
Founding Fathers
drafted the constitution, 264
learn the principles of the, 278
of our great nation, 438
of the nation who established the U.S.
Constitution, 460
fourth
angel, 145, 152

scriptural evidence, 517
trump, 151
vision, 53
Celestial Kingdom, 50
Franklin, Benjamin, 264
Frederick and Oliver, 357
free enterprise
principle of, 277
free exercise
of belief, 274
of conscience, 273
freedom
principle of, 143, 260
from bondage, 143
friends of the Mammon of
Unrighteousness, 91
from grace to grace—a fulness, 223
fulfill Moses and Malachi, 578
full end of all nations, 142
Fullmer, David, 500
fulness of
all truth, 218
divine authority, 581
glory, 72, 223
glory and holy applause, 43, 64
glory and light, 68
God on his throne, 70
his glory, 102, 296
his gospel, 577
his wrath must come, 143
John's record, 221, 224
joy, 218, 617
knowledge, 224
light, 71
my glory, 221, 532, 536
my gospel, 148
my scriptures, 360
the everlasting gospel, 413, 587, 631
the Father, 54, 85, 221, 225–227, 229,
232–234
the glory, 223
the gospel, 7, 41, 209, 216, 577
the gospel of Jesus Christ, 339
the Holy Ghost, 405
the keys and power of the priesthood

of the Son of God, 592
the Lord's glory, 104, 296
the priesthood, 108, 433, 476, 483
the priesthood ordinances, 483
the record of John, 224
the same glory, 172
the truth, 227
the wrath of God, 143
their glory, 460
time, 73, 418, 423
times, 57, 208, 429, 430, 460, 485,
    505, 518–520, 548, 555, 567, 585,
    587, 623, 625, 631, 632
truth, 225, 228
truth (from grace to grace), 228
truth, yea, even of all truth, 228
fulness
joy, 218, 229, 230, 617
of John's record, 221, 224
of the Father, 225
of truth, 225, 228
no man can receive unless he keeps
    the commandments, 228
the Celestial Home, 229
funding for the benefit of the Church, 79

—G—

Gabriel, 30, 36, 416, 519, 632
appeared to Zacharias, 36
stands next in authority to Adam, 416
Gad, 99
Garden Grove, 600
Garden of Eden, 400
in Missouri, 444
located where the city Zion, or the
    New Jerusalem will be built, 451
gather warriors for Zion, 333
gathering
key to, of Israel, 32
of former years [to build the
    kingdom], 450
of his saints, 97
of Israel, 136, 413, 414, 580
of my people in the last days, 584

of my Saints, 289, 292, 302, 442
of my Saints to worship, 439
of the dispensation, 327
of the Literal Seed, 246
of the Lord's people, 585
of the people in every age of the
    world, 485
of the saints, 97, 328
of the Saints to Far West, 443
of the wheat, 134
of those among the Gentiles, 414
of those tribes, 581
of those who had been scattered back
    into the fold of the restoration,
    242
of thy people, 412
Gause, Jesse, 203
genealogy
and temple work for their ancestors,
    264
not to be found on the records of the
    Church, 127
of the apostates not being kept, 129
reckoned by, 131
General Authorities, 3, 8, 109, 187, 311,
    318, 320, 321, 380, 381, 396, 398,
    501, 605
General Handbook of Instructions (book),
    321
General Moroni, 260, 269, 327
General Washington, 264, 308
Gentiles, 38, 99, 106, 135, 136, 140, 142,
    147, 148, 155, 168, 181, 182, 204,
    209, 211, 252, 261, 264, 345, 346,
    380, 384, 385, 395, 396, 402, 412,
    413, 422, 424, 441, 479, 562, 565,
    566, 578, 585, 586, 589, 591
a light to the, 136
a light unto the, 135
coming to the light of truth, 480
continue to be a light to the, 132
flee unto Zion, 566
identified with the, 413
in their scattered condition among
    the, 586

ministry among, 163
preaching the gospel to, 373
scattered upon the mountains, 414
send the elders to the nations of the, 562
shall come to thy light, 441
take the gospel to the, 606
taking of the gospel to, 271
traveling ministers, unto the, 396
vex the, 143
gift
of the Holy Ghost, 107, 167
of the spirit of truth, 68
of tongues, 408, 410
the Holy Ghost, 460, 621
gifts
of God, 375, 395
of God unto men, 385
of the priesthood, 493, 505
of the spirit abound, 69
the Holy Spirit, 254
Gilbert, A. Sidney, 89, 212, 214, 305
gird
thy loins, 422
up your loins, 12, 16, 371, 422, 427
glory
of God is intelligence, 218, 229, 230, 531
of the Lord, 42, 60, 95, 97, 99, 105, 107, 131, 204, 238, 252, 294, 295, 408, 480, 541, 567
of Zion, 475, 479, 488, 489, 596, 601, 606
Gnostic or of the Egyptian Church, 508
go
forward and not backward, 520
from house to house, 15, 21
ye into all the world, and preach the gospel to every creature, 428
God
children of, 45, 131, 540
it came from, 1, 2, 61, 194
order of, 30, 72, 100
spirit children of, 322
the Lord, 606

things not of, are destroyed, 538
who led Israel, 600
Godfrey, Kenneth W.
Hearken O Ye People (book), 437
golden calves, 233
images of wood and stone and metal, 505
gospel
principle of the, 518
spread the, 330
Gospel of John, 220, 222, 224
governments and laws in general, 272
grace to grace, 223, 224, 226, 228, 233, 296
Granger, Oliver, 447, 449
Grant, Heber J., 201
Gospel Standards (book), 201
welfare program and the Word of Wisdom, 604
Grant, Jedediah M., 284
Great Britain, 139, 141, 142
great day of the Lord, 512, 521, 565
Grover, Thomas, 499

—H—

Habaiah
children of, 131
habits
slothfulness, 212
Hancock County, 531
Hancock, Levi, 500
happiness
principle of, 25, 230
Harmony, 519, 632
Harris, George W., 499
Harris, Martin
stewardship, 357
Haws, Peter, 489
Hayden's History of the Disciples (a Campbellite work), 7
heal the sick, 117, 493
hear our plea, answer us from heaven, 418
Hearken
altogether unto the precepts and

commandments which I gave
    unto, 330
and hear, O ye inhabitants of the
    earth, 567
and listen to the voice of the Lord, 10
not to observe all my words, 330
O ye people of my church, 564, 603
O ye who have given your names to
    go forth to proclaim my gospel,
    14
those who hearken not shall be cut off
    as Moses said, 564
to my counsel, 325
to my voice, 486
to my voice to throw down the
    towers, 336
to the calling wherewith you are
    called, 206
to the counsel of Joseph Smith, 492
to the counsel of my servant Joseph,
    492
to the Lord, 289, 553
to the Lord's commandments to give
    them the records, 268
to the voice of my Spirit, 428
to the voice of the Spirit cometh unto
    God, even the Father, 167
to your counsel, 480
unto God, 288
unto His counsel, 330
unto me, saith the Lord your God, 81
unto my voice, 486, 495, 505
unto the commandments of the Lord,
    268
unto the counsel of my servant
    Joseph, 496
unto the voice of the Lord their God,
    290
unto this counsel, 302
upon them that hearken not to the
    voice of the Lord, 578
hearkened
    not unto the commandments of their
       lord, 299
    to his voice, 620

to the Lord, 340
unto my words, 340
to the voice of the Spirit, 113
to the voice of the Spirit cometh unto
    God, 114
hearkening
    to observe all the words which I, the
       Lord their God, shall speak unto
       them, 330
hearts of the children of men, 143, 245, 285
heavenly Church, 53, 85, 165, 227
heirs of the Celestial Kingdom, 611
Herod, 234
Herriman, Henry, 500
Hicks, John A., 500
Higbee, Elias, 585
High Council, 314, 315, 317, 318, 366, 385,
    386, 440, 499
    as organized by the Prophet Joseph
       Smith, 313
    assembly of, 194
    constitution of, 309
    describing an excommunication by a
       high council, 322
    distinction between the high council
       or traveling high priests, 318
    for the corner stone of Zion, 477
    form a quorum equal in authority in
       the affairs of the church, 384
    hand of the Lord must be recognized
       in, 315
    is one form of doing the [Church]
       business by the voice of the, 314
    may appeal to, 317
    may have a different function, 500
    of the church of Christ, 311
    of Zion, 374, 385, 499, 500
    organization of, 309, 311
    stake, 500
    to officiate in the name of the Lord,
       384
    traveling high council composed of
       the twelve apostles, 318
    Twelve are a Traveling Presiding

High Council under direction of, 373

was appointed by revelation, 312

High Priesthood, 12, 80, 81, 85, 96, 102, 105, 109, 128, 130, 203, 206, 319, 332, 373–377, 380, 390–395, 398, 538, 555

high-mindedness, 211, 461

Hinckley, Bryant S.

Sermons and Missionary Services of Melvin J. Ballard (book), 556

Hinckley, Gordon B., 1, 201, 420, 472, 527, 581, 593, 604, 607

Discourses of President Gordon B. Hinckley (book), 593

Teachings of Gordon B. Hinckley (book), 2, 201, 420, 528, 608

temple building, 604

Hiram, Ohio, 7, 37

History of the Church, 93, 191, 203, 237, 278

History of the Church (book), 1, 2, 5, 7, 9, 11, 12, 21, 23, 31, 33, 34, 37, 42, 61, 80, 85, 92, 94, 95, 107, 127, 132, 139, 144, 150, 157, 171, 194, 217, 240, 242, 245, 246, 257, 272, 276, 281, 287, 309, 319, 325, 335, 339, 351, 364, 371, 372, 381, 382, 397, 401, 410, 414, 419, 421, 430, 431, 439, 443, 456, 457, 460–462, 468, 471, 475, 486, 499, 502, 507, 511, 522, 524, 529, 531, 535, 561, 568, 570, 581, 583, 586

Holy Ghost, 2, 50, 52, 104, 106, 107, 109, 114, 117, 137, 138, 164, 167, 168, 172, 189, 223, 224, 226, 245, 283, 285, 388, 405, 420, 444, 460, 478, 526, 532, 556

blasphemy against the, 542

by the power of the, 478

cleansing power of, 105

comes through Christ, 167

comes through the Light of Christ, 168

first Comforter, 138, 165, 167

gift of the, 621

given the gift of the, 167

God's messenger to administer in all [the] priesthoods, 114

has no other effect than pure intelligence, 138

Holy Spirit of Promise, 189, 557

moved upon by the, 521

must receive the, 48

part of the light of truth, 167

personage of Spirit, 245

power and inspiration of the, 420

power of the, 285, 385, 584

sealing of the Holy Spirit of Promise is the, 538

shall be given you by the, 478

shall be thy constant companion, 463, 465

shall bear record, 281

sin against the, 48

sinned against, 48

sins against the, 49

the Comforter, 167

when moved upon by the, 463

will benefit the whole world by revealing truths, 114

will teach those who have come unto Christ, 114

written by the power of the, 475

Holy Priesthood, 53, 95, 96, 99, 102, 104, 246, 484, 498, 515, 530, 532, 544, 545, 549, 556

after the Order of the Son of God, 376, 498

power and authority of, 530

power to seal on earth and in heaven, 550

Holy Spirit, 42, 46, 50, 51, 53, 56, 60, 77, 79, 80, 158, 163, 187, 189, 254, 454, 460, 461, 497, 498, 532, 537, 538, 540–542, 544, 557

honest

and good, 262

men and wise men, 260, 262

honorable and wise men, 302

Horeb

the mount of God, 130
house for
    the Most High, 483
    the Presidency, 237
    printing, 238
house of God, 129, 130, 182–184, 186–188,
    264, 308, 403, 404, 626
humble
    be, and the Lord will lead you and
        answer your prayers, 422
    be, before me, 356, 493
humility
    and long-suffering, 432
    and the prayer of faith, 364
    by the prayer of faith, 317
Hunter, Howard W., 189, 201, 255, 399,
    420, 505, 557
    every member temple worthy, 604
    The Teachings of Howard W. Hunter
        (book), 190, 201, 255, 399, 420,
        557
Huntington, William, 500
Hyde, Orson, 13, 15, 157, 286, 309, 312,
    318, 334, 372, 414, 421, 425, 499,
    523, 524, 581

—I—

idolatry, 433, 505
imagery, 459, 575
    Babylon as spiritual wickedness, 566
    eagle wings, 481
    fruitful tree which is planted in a
        goodly land, 249
    key to understanding, 24
    mountains used to depict temples,
        566
    of a man flexing his muscles, 564
    of the parable, 298
    of the tree, 249
    parable of the nobleman, 333
    pruning of the vineyard, 249
    reference to the allegory of the house
        of Israel, 249
    wise servants, 438
immorality, 433

immortality
    and eternal life, 13, 82, 155, 204, 397,
        515, 545, 578, 623
    be crowned with, and eternal life, 624
indifference toward the things of eternity
    increasing, 434
individual instructions, 212
individuals who may buy stock, 490
infant baptism, 22
    apostate condition, 22
infidelity, 434, 613
innocent blood, 591
    cries from the ground, 601
instructions
    on the process of laboring with
        members, 313
intelligence, 174, 218, 228, 230, 613
    all that really has ever been revealed
        about, 231
    cleaves to intelligence, 160
    cleaveth unto intelligence, 173
    combined with the spirit constitutes a
        spiritual identity, 231
    from which the spirit children of our
        Father in Heaven were
        organized, 230
    glory of God, 229
    glory of God is, 230, 531
    if a person gains more knowledge
        and, 531
    light here refers to intelligence or
        intellect, 167
    or the light of truth, 228
    principle of, 531
    pure, 138, 167
    spirit of, 138
    the light of truth, 230
    was not created, 218
    was organized from an eternal matter
        called intelligence, 229
    whatever principle of intelligence we
        attain unto in this life, 531
    which always existed, 231
    yet not blessed with the intelligence
        necessary to govern, 263

intemperance, 433
intense light of the Lord, 293
Isaiah, 269, 527, 545, 563, 565, 569, 571, 576, 588
    final prophecy of, 295
    glorious visions, 111
    language of, 40
    prophecies, 147
    prophecies of, 33, 123, 147, 480, 571
    prophecy of, 34, 99, 147, 178, 261, 293, 306, 308
    prophet, 8, 33, 45, 57, 89, 101, 121, 123, 136, 143, 146, 165, 177, 182, 207, 218, 227, 228, 234, 242, 252, 328, 441, 480, 569, 583
Isaiah 63:1–9 & 64:1–4 fulfilled, 574
islands become one land, 568
Isles of Patmos, 111
Israel
    children of, 102, 104, 106, 194, 198, 297, 331, 332, 339, 366, 392, 599–601, 611
    ye are of, 127

—J—

Jackson County, 98, 99, 257, 287, 289, 302, 305, 306, 325, 328, 330, 341, 343, 346, 349, 401
    Missouri, 5, 98, 262, 302, 328, 349, 353, 411, 412, 487
Jacob, 58, 72, 135, 266–268, 546, 548, 597, 600
    brother of Nephi, 113, 227, 242, 375
    children of, 412, 413
    father of the twelve tribes of Israel, 246
    God of, 540
    house of, 135
    Jacob, the father of the twelve tribes of Israel, 99
    Lehi taught, 173
    Lehi's son, 173
    major writer, 29
    mighty God of, 415
    prediction of, 155

    remnants of, 402, 412
    saw a vision of the degrees of glory, 39
    son of Lehi, 579
    sons of, 402, 412, 584
    the father of the twelve tribes of Israel, 38
Jacob's ladder, 38
Jacques, Vienna
    convert to the Church, 213
    handmaid, 213
Jared, 387, 388, 444
Jaredites, 400
jarrings, 290, 341
Jayhawkers, 341
Jefferson, Thomas, 278
Jehovah, 25, 73, 164, 401, 408–411, 514, 515
    anointing of His ministers, 410
    covenant with, 402
    covenanted with, 415
    description of, 408
    knows the end from the beginning, 468
    voice of, 407
Jeremy, 99
Jerusalem, 118, 149, 243, 252, 269, 284, 308, 327, 414, 484, 508, 562, 566, 568, 569, 571, 581
    city of, 34
    day of Pentecost in, 410
    Elder Hyde had a glorious vision of his mission to, 414
    land of, 414, 581
    mount of Olives, 568
    redemption of, 414
    temple, 484
Jerusalem Twelve, 431
Jesse, 583
    father of David, king of Israel, 583
Jesus Christ
    atoned for other worlds as well, 44
    atonement of, 22, 112, 173, 291, 547
    call on me while I am near, 177
    gospel of, 21, 41, 42, 137, 163, 174,

234, 339, 385, 403, 412, 460, 534, 558, 591

Prince of Peace, 434
  Son of Man, 41, 133, 134, 137, 141, 147, 149, 156, 221, 404, 405, 408, 445, 454, 466, 468, 525
  the great Jehovah, 25

Jesus the Christ
  spirit body of, 26

Jethro, 95, 99
  Moses' father-in-law, 95, 99, 100, 599
  received the priesthood, 100
  Reuel, 548

jewel is a precious stone, 282

jewels, 281–283, 286, 287, 290, 296
  celestial, 291
  commanded to speak in the name of the Lord, 285
  is the fulness of the Lord's glory, 296
  Lord's, 295
  Lord's jewels in eternity, 297
  Lord's polishing of His, 296
  natural, 294
  polishing our souls, 297
  reflect His light, 283

Jews, 22, 137, 175, 204, 209, 210, 237, 258, 261, 264, 265, 294, 384, 385, 395, 396, 413, 424, 425, 562, 565, 566, 571, 572, 581, 590, 593, 620
  are scattered, 414
  as a nation, 106
  gathering the, 237
  gospel to the, 264
  hearts of the, 264, 265
  in Palestine, 580
  Jesus had been rejected by the, 579
  kingdom of the, 104, 106
  physically gather, 414
  preaching the gospel to, 373
  prophesy to the, 34
  prophets to the, 265
  prophets unto, 265

John
  bore record, 218, 222, 225, 228
  glorious visions, 111

  testimony of, 158, 163–167, 217, 220, 221

John the Baptist, 30, 106, 224, 379
  admonition of, 122
  appeared to Joseph Smith and Oliver Cowdery, 378
  bore record of him, 218
  conferred the Aaronic Priesthood, 104
  kept a record, 224
  martyr, 587
  mission of, 178, 567
  ordination of, 106

John the Beloved, 8
  revelation of, 8

John the Revelator, 31, 33, 38, 133, 224, 449, 513, 570, 573, 611
  writings of, 23

Johnson, Aaron, 500

Johnson, Father, 37

Johnson, John, 7, 245, 246, 312, 318, 351, 352, 357, 358
  stewardship, 358

Johnson, Lisa
  lame arm, 7
  wife of John Johnson, 7

Johnson, Luke, 13, 14, 318

Johnson, Luke S., 432

Johnson, Lyman, 13, 15

Johnson, Lyman E., 432

Joseph of Egypt
  prophecy of, 588

Journal History of the Church, 595

Judah
  children of, 402, 412, 413

judgment
  bar of Christ, 29, 268, 274, 430
  day of, 13, 16, 59, 247, 303, 451, 481

justice
  and judgement, 8
  and judgments, 86, 87
  of the Father, 59

justice and mercy, 610, 626
  are not fully realized until the day the Lord comes, 292

reasoning of, 610
will be properly balanced, 91
Juvenile Instructor, 38

—K—

keep the whole law, 114
Kennedy, David M.
    editor, 141
key
    to history, 27
    to the Gathering of Israel, 32
    to the Millennial Reign, 31
    to the Second Coming, 28
    to understanding the imagery, 24
keys
    and power of the priesthood, 538,
        549, 550, 592
    never taken from Joseph, 207
    to detect angels, 522
keys of
    all the other dispensations were
        revealed, 592
    all the spiritual blessings of the
        church, 378
    authority, 373, 504
    Gathering Israel, 413
    his priesthood, 215
    ministering of angels and outward
        ordinances, 373
    my kingdom, 427
    preaching the gospel to Gentiles and
        Jews, 373
    salvation, 81, 83, 452
    salvation and exaltation, 504
    salvation over all the earth for all
        ages, 452
    that ministry, 389
    that particular labor, 214
    that priesthood, 391
    the Aaronic priesthood, 106, 107, 379,
        392
    the dispensation of the fulness of
        times, 429
    the dispensation, which ye have
        received, 430

the gathering, 403
the gathering of Israel, 414
the gospel, 30
the gospel of Abraham, 30, 403
the holy priesthood ordained, 484
the kingdom, 204, 206, 207, 215, 380,
    383, 439, 443, 516, 519, 584, 585,
    632
the kingdom in their days, 451
the kingdom of an endless life, 291
the kingdom of God on the earth, 433
the kingdom of heaven, 52, 68, 515
the kingdom of the Twelve among the
    nations, 422
the last dispensation, 419
the leading of the ten tribes, 33
the Melchizedek Priesthood, 377
the ministering of angels, 96, 378, 379
the mysteries of God, 96
the patriarchal blessings upon the
    heads of all my people, 493
the patriarchal Priesthood, 389, 417
the power of Elias, 33
the power of this priesthood, 553
the priesthood, 209, 214, 502, 534,
    558
the priesthood held, 497
the school of the prophets, 209
the spiritual blessings of the Church,
    373
the universe, 167, 445
this authority are held by the
    President of the Church, 391
this dispensation, 401, 418, 504, 592,
    593
this dispensation are committed
    before the day of the Lord, 403
this glorious of all dispensations, 505
this kingdom and ministry, 442
this last kingdom, 209
this ministry, 319, 385, 392
this most glorious of all
    dispensations, 592
this power, 547, 554
this priesthood, 378, 537, 541

this priesthood are conferred, 391, 558
this priesthood have the right to be ministered to by the angels, 105
translation, 591
turning the hearts of the fathers to the children, 403
which kingdom, 250
which kingdom have been conferred upon you, 416
Kimball, Edward L.
  editor, *The Teachings of Spencer W. Kimball* (book), 62
Kimball, Heber C., 341, 498
Kimball, Spencer W., 62, 125, 207, 235, 242, 277, 319, 323, 348, 398, 421, 473, 479, 492, 505, 559, 605, 606
  Missionary Work, 604
  Official Declaration—2, 604
  The Teachings of Spencer W. Kimball (book), 62, 125, 277, 348, 398, 559
King Benjamin, 116
King David
  king of Israel, 583
King Hezekiah, 269
King Mosiah, 279
King William the Fourth, 421
kingdom
  children of the, 133, 235
  of God, 46, 75, 106, 111, 124, 137, 165, 180, 181, 230, 235, 250, 254, 306, 330, 344, 347, 380, 389, 397, 416, 419, 433, 472, 499, 508, 556, 558, 573, 584, 603, 610–612, 622–624
  of Zion, 336, 344, 345, 347, 417
  order of, 60
Kirtland Council Minute Book, 158, 372
Kirtland Temple, 30, 33, 107, 184, 246, 339, 401, 403, 408, 414, 417, 420, 430, 504, 564, 585, 609–611
Kirtland, Ohio, 9, 10, 75–78, 80, 82, 86, 89, 157, 179, 187, 191, 193, 212, 213, 238, 240, 243, 244, 246, 257, 258, 265, 272, 293, 317, 325, 337, 345,

352, 358, 359, 364, 372, 385, 404, 421, 429, 435, 437, 446–449, 483, 491, 501, 522
  Church in, 428
  land of, 89, 356, 358
  Order, 358
  Stake, 90
  United Order of, 352, 353
Knight, Newel, 499
Knight, Vinson, 501
know how and what you worship, 217
know my disciples, 119
knowledge
  principle of, 557
Kohath, 130
Koz
  children of, 131

—L—

Laban, 268, 296
  about to be brought before the judgment bar of Christ, 268
  guilty of these offenses against him, 267
  had sought to take Nephi's life, 268
  had taken away their property, 268
  Nephi slaying, 267
  three of the offenses by, 268
Lamech, 387, 388
land of liberty, 327
Last Supper, 111, 508
last time to the Gentiles, 181
Latter-day prophets and the Doctrine and Covenants (pamphlet), 201
life
  after death, 609
  beyond death, 609
Lord accepts the house, 407
law of
  Christ's Holy Priesthood, 544
  consecration, 75, 78, 82, 83, 85, 88, 89, 93, 94, 129, 212, 213, 345–348, 353, 355, 356, 360, 365, 366
  forgiveness, 269

God, 106, 127–129, 131, 262, 514
retaliation, 258, 266–268, 270
Sarah, 553
the Church, 75, 275, 276, 313, 514
the kingdom, 79
the land, 92, 257, 260, 272, 313
   of United States of America, 261
   the priesthood, 534, 545, 553, 554
tithing, 348, 351, 364–366
War, 268
witnesses, 80
Law, William, 476, 477, 491–496, 498
lawful heirs of the priesthood, 134
Lectures on Faith (book), 371
Lee, Harold B., 18, 52, 94, 155, 190, 215, 216, 253, 279, 296, 308, 367, 368, 397, 399, 400, 426, 450, 471, 558, 627
   Stand Ye in Holy Places (book), 397
   the correlation of the Church programs, 604
   The Teachings of Harold B. Lee (book), 94, 155, 156, 190, 216, 253, 254, 279, 280, 308, 367, 369, 398–400, 427, 450, 471–472, 558–559, 628
Levites, 130, 606
Levitical Priesthood, 106, 108, 376
Lewis, T. B.
   A String of Pearls, Anecdotes of Elder Grant (book), 285
Liberty Jail, 453
Liberty to the captives, 618
life after death, 610
lift up your voices, 14, 283
lifted up at the last day, 13, 15, 16
light
   and truth, 218, 229–233, 531
   children of, 371
   light to the world, 326, 330
Light of Christ, 114, 158, 166–168, 176, 222, 305
   of the World, 222
   of truth, 137, 158, 163, 166, 167, 176,

   228–230, 479, 480
light-mindedness, 183, 185
lightnings, 144, 146, 148
lively member of the Order, 93
limited time of His Ministry?, 620
lineage, 135, 242, 379, 386, 388, 390, 585, 586, 606
   blessing, 110
   inherit their lineage blessing, 110
   legal heir must prove his, 379
   of Abraham, 109
   of his fathers, 100, 101
   of the first-generation Church members, 136
   of their fathers, 100, 135
   of your fathers, 134
   traced in the revelation to the twelve, 388
little children, 22, 81, 84, 459, 614
   are alive in Christ, 612
   are holy, 22
   are holy through the atonement, 21
   are not to be baptized, 23
   are saved without regard to race, color, or culture, 612
   become as, 460
   bodies of little children will grow after the resurrection to the full stature of the spirit, 627
   death of, 610
   were alive in Christ, 23
   who die, 612
   who die are heirs of the celestial kingdom, 627
Liverpool, 421
Lorain County, 12
Lord
   of Hosts, 129, 164, 243, 282, 390, 459, 509, 510, 578, 592
   of Sabaoth, 142, 163, 164, 240, 241, 243, 259
   shall lead thee by the hand, 425
   will fight your battles, 340
Lord's
   friends, 118

jewels, 281
oath to the priesthood, 107
prayer, 87
servants, 89, 116, 120, 148, 285, 287
loss of natural affection, 433
love
    of the world, 433
    thy neighbors as thyself, 426
lowliness of heart, 432
Ludlow, Daniel H.
    *A Companion to Your Study of the
    Doctrine and Covenants* (book),
    432, 581
lustful and covetous desires, 290, 341
Lyman, Amasa, 500, 599

—M—

magnifying, 107
    of the priesthood, 98
    the priesthood, 113
    their calling, 109, 113
Mahalaleel, 387, 388, 444
Malachi, 263, 408, 417, 521, 564, 578
    Old Testament prophet, 129, 387
    prophecy of Elijah, 624
    referring to the Spirit of Elijah, 264
    testified of the coming of Elijah, 623
    the prophet, 418
    who prophesied of Elijah, 615
    words of Malachi as quoted by the
    Angel Moroni, 518
man like unto Moses, 331, 394
Manasseh, 210, 413, 572
many are called, but few are chosen
    is also a New Testament phrase, 243
    was used by Christ in the New
    Testament, 462
marriage
    that is of God, 541
    that is not of God, 538
Marsh, Thomas B., 385, 421, 422, 424–426
    did not live up to his calling, 425
    excommunicated from the Church in
    1839, 425

marshaled and disciplined for war, 143
martyrdom, 493, 494, 586
    at Carthage, 593
    of Joseph Smith the Prophet, 586
    of the Prophet, 499
martyrs seal their testimony with their
    blood, 593
Matthews, Robert J.
    *A Plainer Translation, Joseph Smith's
    Translation of the Bible*, 217
Maxwell, Neal A., 234
McCleary, Sophronia, 524
McConkie, Bruce R., 56, 124, 189, 348, 433,
    445, 451, 629
    A New Witness for the Articles of Faith
    (book), 125
    compiler of *Doctrines of Salvation*
    (book), 138
    *Doctrinal New Testament
    Commentary* (book), 189, 530
    Doctrine and Covenants Compendium
    (book), 224
    The Millennial Messiah (book), 451
    The Mortal Messiah (book), 224
McKay, David O., 199, 277, 327, 627
    Gospel Ideals (book), 200
    the importance of the family, 604
    Zion shall flourish, 327
McLellin, William E., 13–15, 214, 372, 432
meekness, 432
    and humility of Christ, 593
Melchizedek, 51, 52, 68, 95, 100–102, 319,
    376, 383, 391–393, 624
    after the order of, 393, 497
    an example of one who magnified his
    priesthood, 109
    because he was such a great high
    priest, 372
    order of, 68
    the eternal priesthood, 101
    the great high priest, 376, 624
Melchizedek Priesthood, 102–105,
    107–109, 112, 117, 119, 124, 251,
    313, 332, 372, 373, 376–380, 387,

388, 392, 394, 398, 433, 498, 504,
584
principle of, 104
Messages of the First Presidency, 201
*The Latter-day Prophets and the
Doctrine and Covenants* (book),
201
Messages of the First Presidency
(book), 130, 221, 231
Messenger and Advocate, 147, 598
messengers
chosen to proclaim the gospel, 621
Methuselah, 387, 388, 444
Michael, 81, 83, 84, 154, 389, 445, 451, 519
Adam, 36, 154, 374, 388, 416, 632
mine archangel, 389
shall fight and overcome him who
seeks the Lamb's throne, 146
shall fight their battles, 154
the prince, the archangel, 374, 388,
389, 444
the seventh angel, 146, 154
voice of, 519, 520, 632
Mighty and Great Ones, 622
Miles, Daniel, 500
Millennial Reign, 156, 228, 361
key to, 31
Millennium, 28, 32, 39, 151, 154, 171,
292–296, 347, 524, 525, 570, 580,
585
beginning of the, 147
the earth will become a terrestrial
planet, 27
Miller, George, 476, 481, 482, 489, 501
minds and bodies invigorated, 198
cease to be idle, 183, 198
missionaries
to work, 14
missionary companions, 123
Missouri, 89, 127, 243, 246, 252, 255, 259,
291, 317, 325, 344, 366, 371, 473,
508
1978, the governor of, 344
Church in, 264, 360
compelled to leave, 475

driven from, 355
driven out of, 293
driving of the Saints from, 443
early Saints called to move to, 346
estimates of the number of people
driven out of, 343
Far West, 431
Garden of Eden in, 444
Independence, 257, 328, 566
jail, 467
jail at Liberty, 453
land in, 344
land of Zion, 82
land will be purchased, not
conquered, 344
opposing factions battled in, 341
people in, 265, 283
persecutions in Missouri, 597
purchased land in, 344
return to, 339
river, 461, 595
Saints, 262
Saints from, 303
Saints in, 257, 306
Saints to, 341
seriousness of the situation in, 257
some have believed that all the
members of the Church would
leave their homes and go to
Missouri, 346
state of, 473
sweeping clean of, 341
the destruction of Missouri fulfilled a
prophecy of Joseph Smith, 341
the Lord had delivered the Saints
from their enemies in, 603
the place for the temple was
designated by revelation, 98
those who were pure in heart, but had
been slain in, 488
today, many members live happily in,
341
western boundaries of the State of, 97
modern leaders among the noble and
great, 625

money consecrated to building Zion, 122
more
    duties of the Twelve and Seventy, 384
    revealed later, 555
    treasures than one, 437
Mormon
    major writer and abridger, 29
Moroni
    general, 260, 269, 327
    major writer, 29
    missionary son of Mormon, 23
    the fifth angel, 153
mortal life, 166, 227, 229, 614, 616, 626
    purpose of, 230
    second stage, 229
mortality, 56, 190, 225, 227, 231, 234, 295,
    471, 503, 616
    laws of, 151
Moses, 57, 72, 96, 100, 102, 104, 109, 130,
    193, 215, 326, 328, 332, 339, 342,
    347, 375, 395, 403, 413, 414, 420,
    441, 484, 487, 523, 533, 546, 564,
    572, 576, 578, 599, 600, 602, 606,
    611, 624
    a man like unto, 331, 332, 394, 395
    and the Keys of Gathering Israel, 413
    authority of the priesthood given to,
    100
    in the Kirtland Temple, 414, 420, 430
    law of, 22, 23, 182, 193, 194, 366, 392,
    539, 540, 549
    married to Zipporah, 548
    on the Mount of Transfiguration, 623,
    624
    organized the children of Israel, 599
    prophet, 578
    received the holy priesthood from
    Jethro, 95
    sons of, 99, 105, 107–109
    tabernacle built by, 485
    the great law-giver of Israel, 622
why Moses built a tabernacle, 484
Mother Eve
    faithful daughters, 622
Mount Sinai, 194

Mt. Pisgah, 600
much given—much required, 87
murdering, 434, 525
Murdock, John, 157, 271
murmurings
    of the heart, 13–15
Myers, Brother, 351
mysteries
    of the Kingdom, 60, 101, 205, 210,
211, 378
    of the Kingdom of God, 111, 165

—N—

Nadab, 611
name of the Church, 440
narrow-mindedness
    of men, 1, 61
Nauvoo, 502–504, 507, 535, 584
    a corner stone of the glory of Zion,
    489
    house, 476, 477, 482, 488–490, 496,
    497
        stock for the, 489
    Stake of Zion, 500
    Temple, 403, 484, 487, 488, 504
Nauvoo, Hancock County, Illinois, 62, 73,
    98, 196, 208, 414, 449, 475, 483,
    495, 522, 531
Nelson, Russell M., 482, 503
Nephi
    and Lehi
        were imprisoned, 130
        major writer of the Book of Mormon,
        29
    son of Lehi, 375, 591
Nephites, 93, 136, 154, 169, 223, 276, 296,
    312, 313, 349, 400, 409, 438, 440,
    571, 572, 576, 578, 581, 591, 615,
    623
    after Christ's visit to them, 93
    Jesus taught the, 59, 167
    Savior taught the, 99, 261, 581
    Savior to the, 147
    three, 611
    wars, 143

new and everlasting covenant of marriage,
529, 540, 549, 550
New Jerusalem, 95, 97–99, 252, 293,
327–329, 332, 342, 344–346,
348, 349, 412, 437, 451, 500, 568,
570, 576, 577
New Testament Apostles, 22, 96, 243, 536
Newel K. Whitney's Stewardship, 358
Newquist, Jerreld L.
*Gospel Truth, Discourses and Writings
of President George Q. Cannon*
(book), 220
Nickerson, Freeman, 281
Noah, 29, 30, 100, 101, 193, 387, 388, 415,
416, 429, 576, 624
came and restored his keys, 36
days of, 616, 620
father of all living, 30, 416
is the Elias spoken of, 30
stands next to Michael or Adam, 36
warning of the flood, 622
who is Gabriel, 30
noble
and great, 206, 471, 615, 625
and great ones, 625, 632
nobleman and the choice land, 298
none exempted from justice, 318
Northern States, 139, 141, 142
not after the manner of the world, 244
not confident
confounded, 212
Nyman, Monte S.
An Ensign to All People (book), 588
Great are the Words of Isaiah (book),
261, 566, 574
More Precious Than Gold (book), 1,
75
*The Pearl of Great Price: Revelations
from God* (book), 488
*The Record of Alma: Book of Mormon
Commentary* (book), 517
The Second Gathering of the Literal
Seed, *Doctrines for Exaltation,
1989 Sperry Symposium* 246
The Words of Jeremiah (book), 598

—O—

Oaks, Dallin H., 8, 19, 115
CES Fireside, 115
oath
and covenant, 96, 108, 112, 119, 124
and covenant of the Priesthood, 95
obtain the Spirit
basic formula for missionaries, 15
Official Declaration—1, 604
Official Declaration—2, 605
Ohio Star, 11
Old Testament, 88, 131, 164, 241, 521
evidence of the movement west being
known even in, 598
four thousand years of, 27
has suffered the loss of many plain
and precious parts, 548
Malachi in the, 387
noble and great ones in the premortal
life who came to earth during
Old Testament times, 625
Peter speaks of the disobedience of,
621
plural marriage being practiced in,
536
practice in question, 536
principle of speaking through the
prophets, 110
prophecy, 437
prophet Amos, 242, 331
prophet Habakkuk, 456
prophet had also foretold this great
movement of the Restoration,
574
prophet Isaiah, 8, 101
prophet Malachi, 129
prophet, Zenos, 242
prophets, 265
prophets and the writings of John the
Revelator, 23
prophets sealed their testimony with
their blood, 587
times, 219
translation of the, 217, 536

used by the Lord in this revelation, 130

words of Adam to Jesus Christ were in the, 603

Olive Leaf, 157, 166, 169, 173, 176, 189, 222

omnipotent
all powerful, 220

omnipresent
in all presence, 220

omniscient
all knowing, 220

one mighty and strong, 129, 130

Only Begotten, 43, 64–66, 223, 224, 307, 523
Son, 41, 44, 46, 51, 52, 219, 220, 497, 547, 617, 626

open the door of my kingdom, 427

open the eyes of the blind, 117

ordained in the Council of the Eternal God, 460

ordinance of
baptism, 23, 103
baptism by water, 515
baptism for the dead, 515
baptizing for the dead, 484
my holy house, 485
the baptism by water, 515
the gospel of Jesus Christ, 534
washing of the feet, 158, 184, 187, 188
water baptism, 105

organization of the High Council, 311

origin of man, 231

other councils, 500

other duties of the First Presidency, 210

other kingdoms, 169

other officers of the Church, 396

others planted in their stead, 430

—P—

Packard, Noah, 500

Packer, Boyd K., 19, 136, 307, 544, 627
That All May Be Edified (book), 307

Page, John E., 414, 432, 499

Pahoran, 260

Palestine, 425

parable
concerning the redemption of Zion, 298
gathering was to be done according to the, 301

let the wheat and tares grow together, 132
like all these kingdoms according to the decree of God, 161
of scattered Israel, 303
of the fig tree, 292
of the gathering of my Saints, 289
of gathering—the Wheat and the Tares, 301
parable of scattered Israel, 303
of the good Samaritan, 426
of the Kingdoms, 175, 176
of the nobleman and the choice land, 298, 333
of the redemption of Zion, 289
of the talents, 552
of the tares of the field, 133
of the ten virgins, 149, 566
of the wheat and the tares, 128, 132, 135, 136, 150, 289, 301
of the woman and the unjust judge, 289, 303, 304
spoken in, 137
to gather warriors to go to the Zion, 326
who hath ears to hear, 298

Parliament, 421

Partridge, Edward
Bishop, 85, 89, 130, 440, 456, 476, 481, 501

patriarchal
authority, 418
blessing, 572
blessings, 389, 493, 494
families are, 517
line, 388
order of the priesthood, 387
order of the priesthood was revealed, 387
power, 494

Priesthood, 389, 390, 417
the second Priesthood is patriarchal
authority, 387
Patten, David, 431, 432, 481, 499
Patten, David W., 410, 430
Paul, 21, 23, 38, 39, 58, 69, 73, 92, 102, 122,
131, 230, 241, 431, 433, 463, 502,
507, 509, 515–517, 523, 536, 577
ascended into the third heavens, 38
forbidden to reveal his revelation, 39
mentions a third heaven, 39
of Apollos, 57, 58, 72
of Cephas, 57, 58
reference to the baptisms for the
dead, 517
taught the Romans, 110
the Apostle to the Gentiles, 38
treatise of the three different types of
resurrection, 39
pay all your debts, 363
penalty
affixed to my law, 86
for adultery under the law of Moses
was death, 549
for adultery under the new and
everlasting covenant, may mean
spiritual destruction, 550
for our sins, 559
for such a crime, 558
given in section 132, 549
is much more severe for those under
the covenant, 549
of excommunication, 323
of their transgressions, 626
which is affixed unto my law, 87
Perrysburg, New York, 281
personal living
revelation, 184, 291, 332, 580
uncleanness, 212
Peter, James, and John, 208, 380, 519, 520
at the Susquehanna river
commemorates the restoration
of the priesthood, 520
in the wilderness between Harmony,
Susquehanna County, 519, 632

Phelps, W. W., 42, 49, 62, 79, 89, 157
Philip, 221
Philistines, 131
philosophers, 215, 220
Pilgrim Fathers of New England, 435
place of governments, 272
plague, 131, 140, 142, 143, 200, 253
shall go forth, 120
that will go forth, 120
plain and precious, 28, 44, 223, 224, 242,
548, 588
things, 44
plan—gather and sanctify, 565
pleas for mercy, 411
plural marriage, 321, 535–537, 547, 548,
604
congress forbidding, 605
law of, 548
practice of, 555
poison of a serpent
shall not have power to harm them,
117
polished stones—all things revealed, 295
polishing effort
for the Lord's jewels, 296
polluted their inheritance, 288, 290, 291
polygamy, 605
practice of, 604
we are not teaching, 604
poor and the rich, 122
postmortal
era, 228
life, 227
power
of attorney, 221
of the priesthood, 398, 423, 430, 464,
472, 498, 504, 514, 530, 538, 549,
550, 585, 586, 592
praise to the man, 583
Pratt, Orson, 13, 15, 44, 171, 244, 334, 420,
443, 498, 599
Journal of Discourses (book), 244, 444
Pratt, Parley P., 247–249, 254, 325, 334,
467, 498
Autobiography of Parley P. Pratt

(book), 255, 467
Pratt, Parley P.
    his son, the editor, 255, 467
pray always, 15, 166, 185, 212, 232, 289
    and faint not (persistence), 304
prayer
    and prophecies, 453
    dedicatory prayer of the Kirtland
        Temple, 184
    great intercessory prayer, 103
    high priestly prayer, 103
    of a righteous man availeth much,
        291
    of faith, 233, 363, 364
    of praise and thanksgiving, 601
    of the church, 380, 399
    of the First Presidency, 308
    of the temple dedication, 414
pre-existence, 231
premortal life, 166, 222, 227–229, 231, 613,
    625
    the first stage, 229
prerequisites outlined by the Lord for the
        redemption of Zion, 338, 347
    (1) a man will be raised up like unto
        Moses to lead the people out of
        bondage, 347
    (2) the people have been prepared
        and taught more perfectly, and
        have experience, and know more
        perfectly concerning their duty
        through the temple endowment,
        347
    (3) the Lord will fight the battle for
        Zion, 347
    (4) faithful and prayerful and humble
        before the Lord, 347
    (5) the army of Israel has become
        very great, 347
    (6) Lord has softened the hearts of
        the people, 347
    (7) many of the army of Israel have
        become sanctified, 347
    (8) many are worthy, and when
        manifest to the Lord's servant ll

        return and live the celestial law
        of Zion (law of consecration),
        347
    (9) the members of the Church are
        proclaiming peace many people
        by lifting up an ensign of peace,
        and making a proclamation of
        peace unto the ends of the earth,
        347
presidency of the High Priesthood, 206
president
    of the Church, 187, 214, 215, 310, 314,
        319, 320, 332, 381, 382, 391, 399,
        427, 433, 505, 591, 604, 605
    of the High Priesthood, 390
        presides over the Church like
        Moses, 375
    of the Twelve, 385, 399, 425, 499
President Van Buren, 304
presiding
    councils, 380
    officers of the Aaronic Priesthood,
        391
pressure of the world, 283
Preston, England, 421
pride, 182, 185, 205, 211, 265, 349, 462,
    552
    and arrogance, 433
    and joy to success in the
        accomplishment, 367
    beware of, 460, 552
    conquering, 349
is the great stumbling block to Zion, 349
    of their hearts above all nations, 148
    sin of, 349
    to lift up with pride and joy to
        success, 367
prideful
    arrogant, 212
    or high-minded, 212
priesthood, 36
    authority, 99, 445, 463, 541
    board meeting, 322
    covenant holders, 135

inseparably connected with heaven, 462

new appointments in the, 493

of Aaron, 378, 394

of Elias, 33

of Melchizedek, 376, 377

of the Son of God, 592

ordinances of the, 97

Priesthood courts of the Church

are courts of love, 323

are not courts of retribution, 323

proclaim the gospel, 17

proclamation, 475, 476, 479

first of five proclamations that has been sent since the Church was organized, 479

first proclamation to all the nations of the world, 479

fourth proclamation is printed in the Conference Report of October 1980, 479

he commands them to write, on the prophecies of Isaiah, 480

lift up an ensign of peace, and make a proclamation of peace unto the ends of the earth, 346

made to the human family, 61

of my gospel, 478

of peace to the ends of the earth, 337, 346, 347

of the gospel of Jesus Christ, 384, 385

of the greatness and glory of the Lord, 60

of the truth, 620

President Jackson issued his proclamation against this rebellion, 139

shall be made to all the kings of the world, 478

that was commanded to be written, 479

that will cover a broader ground, 327

The Family: A Proclamation to the World, 479, 556

to the leaders of the nations of the world, 475

to the world, 475, 478

to the world from the First Presidency and the Quorum of the Twelve, 479

to the world, and not move to the east, 496

unto the kings of the earth, 495

promise

children of the, 131

properties of the order, 352, 356

Prophet

and Seer, 372, 510, 587, 631

Ezekiel, 611

Nephi, 285, 296

Prophets Might Be Fulfilled, 292

Prophet's plea, 456

prosper

no weapon shall, 8

proverb

nevertheless, when the wicked rule the people mourn, 262

world grows weaker and wiser, 613

pruning of the vineyard, 242, 246, 249

public debates, 8

Pulsipher, Zera, 500

pure in heart, 107, 147, 247, 249–254, 288, 292, 293, 328, 329, 339, 342, 348, 410, 450, 454, 455, 465, 470, 488

shall see god, 249

purpose

of keys, 502

of life, 330

put on the power of the priesthood, 585

—Q—

Queen Victoria, 421

Quorum of the Twelve, 208, 209, 242, 264, 311, 318, 320, 371, 381–383, 385, 386, 399, 414, 424, 426, 427, 430, 433, 479, 491, 555, 605

Apostles, 109, 175

I say unto all the, 427

—R—

raise up a pure people, 282
Ramus, Illinois, 524, 529, 530
Raphael, 519, 632
Ravenna, 11
record of John, 218, 222, 224, 225
records
    kept in heaven, 131
    kept on earth, 131
redemption
    of the dead, 615
    of Zion, 289, 298, 325–327, 329, 331,
        333, 338, 339, 347, 407
    nine prerequisites outlined by the
        Lord, 347
religion and man, 273
religious societies rights, 275
remnant of Israel, 135, 597
repentance, 48, 49, 66, 105, 112, 196, 311,
        322, 411, 425, 477, 620
    baptism of, 378, 379
    conditions of, 618
    declare, 567
    forsaking of sin is, 265
    from sin, 621
    gospel of, 378, 379, 626
    principle of, 103
    steps of, 196
replacements for the Twelve, 432
reproof
    if used with principle number one,
        will be used in kindness, and
        patience, 464
    means to rebuke, to chastise, to
        reprimand, with intent to
        correct, 464
requirement
    for every steward to render an
        account, 10
    for the celestial kingdom, 82
        (1) receiving the testimony of
            Jesus and following the
            principles of the gospel, 52
        (2) give diligent heed to the

words of eternal life, 113
        (3) bear testimony to all the
            world, 117
requirements
    for exaltation, 47
    for people who will be in the celestial
        kingdom, 52
    for the various heavens or degrees, 52
    for stock holders, 497
    of the new covenant, 157
        (1) keep the commandments,
            226
        (2) to attain a fulness of the
            Father, 226
        (3) receive a fulness of truth, 227
        (4) proclaiming of the
            acceptable year of the Lord,
            233
        (5) translation of the scriptures,
            234
    bring up your children in light and
        truth, 233
restoration, 482, 579, 588
    a fulfillment of prophecy, 565
    day of, 182
    first portion of, 577
    foretelling the, 265
    great movement of, 574
    latter-day, 625
    message of, 16
    of the gospel, 242, 305
    of the gospel of Jesus Christ, 403, 591
    prominent tribe of, 572
    purposes of the, 459, 565, 606
    revelations of, 6
    second purpose of, 577
    second witness of the, 494
    strange to the ways of the world, 305
    testimony of, 182
    third purpose of, 577
    vital part of, 493
resurrection, 41, 46, 49, 59, 130
    and eternal life, 517
    celestial, 151
    children of the, 540

Christ gave them power to come forth after His resurrection, 624
doctrine of, 618
Ezekiel and his vision of, 624
first, 51, 156, 541, 542, 576, 577
first fruits of, 151
for the earth's inhabitants, 59
from the dead, 168, 169, 537, 540, 623
glorious, 614, 617
if we are worthy, 61
in the first resurrection of Christ, 52
last, 56
of the dead, 41, 46, 49, 159, 163, 168, 173, 176, 515, 540, 623
of the just, 41, 50–52
of the mortal body, 171
of the unjust, 41
only through the resurrection could they attain a fulness of joy, 617
state of the soul between death and, 617
terrestrial, 151
the spirit and the body become one body, 230
three different types of, 39
unto eternal life, 617
revelation, 97
by, not commandment, 193
principle of, 315
Rich, Charles C., 499
Richards, LeGrand, 445
Marvelous Work and a Wonder (book), 598
Richards, Willard, 432, 499, 587
riches of eternity, 85
are yours, 84
Richmond, Missouri
jail, 467
Rigdon, Sidney, 5–9, 11, 37, 38, 40–43, 45, 47, 49, 52, 54, 57, 81, 83, 85, 89, 157, 204, 205, 209, 212, 218, 232, 233, 260, 281, 283, 286, 312, 326, 333, 334, 351, 352, 356, 377, 422, 427, 435, 439, 440, 442, 443, 477, 495, 496, 498, 609

Sidney Rigdon's
properties, 356
repent, 495
spokesman unto Joseph, 281, 286
Riggs, Burr, 13, 15
robbing, 434
Roberts, B. H.
A Comprehensive History of The Church of Jesus Christ of Latter-day Saints (book), 341, 435
Robinson, George W., 443
Rocky Mountains, 597
Romans, 467
Apostle Paul to the Roman Saints, 260
ordinance of baptism taught by the Apostle Paul to the Romans, 515
Paul taught the, 110
principle given to the Romans by the Apostle Paul, 467
Rome, 141
Romney, Marion G., 124, 155, 580
root of David, 28
Roundy, Shadrach, 501

—S—

sacred
remembrance of Oliver Granger, 449
treasury, 353, 361
sacrifice
principle of, 250
Saints
at Ephesus, 502
in Missouri, 257, 259, 260, 291, 306
Salem, Massachusetts, 435
salt
has lost its savor, 326, 330
of the earth, 289, 297
savor of men, 289, 297
symbolism of, 297
used as a seasoning, 330
Salt Lake City, 279, 483, 527, 604, 614
salvation
principle of, 557
and redemption of Zion, 325, 329

exaltation for both the living and the dead, 504

exaltation of all his children, 546

Satan

all people living in a fallen world, and are subject to, 88

be delivered over to the buffetings of, 112

buffetings are the mental anguish that comes after the, 355

buffetings of, 137, 354, 532, 542, 544, 558

buffetings of Satan until the day of redemption, 84, 87

cannot escape the buffetings of Satan until the day of redemption, 354

choosing to follow, 47

destroy the agency of man is the plan of, 143

fall of, 44, 47

First Presidency hold off the storm, wind, and rains that Satan sends against the Church, 208

guilty would not escape the buffetings of Satan except they repent, 355

has spread the false rumor that confidences are rarely kept, 323

is behind all of them as a way of winning souls, 195

is bound and time is no longer, 121

loosed for a season, 154

loosing of, 154

many additional insights about Satan and the fall revealed in section 76, 45

nor have any power over us here, 188

objective is to take away knowledge of these three stages of man, 228

power of, 66

prince of this world, 510

probably works harder on the Quorum of the Twelve than he does us, 426

righteousness of the people binds, 154

seeketh to destroy, 552

seeketh to turn their hearts away from the truth, 83

seeking to destroy him, 553

seeks the misery of all mankind, 195, 263

seeks to destroy Joseph, 533

seeks to destroy the children, 232

seeks to turn their hearts from the truth, 81

shall be bound, 294

shall be bound and not loosed for a thousand years, 146

shall be bound, that old serpent, who is called the devil, 153

shall be delivered over to the buffetings of, 83, 90

shall be loosed for a little season to gather his armies, 146

shall have no more power over the hearts of the children of men, 143

shall have no power to tempt man, 288

shall not have power to tempt any man, 294

some men can't repent until they are turned over to the buffeting of Satan by the loss of the Spirit of the Lord, 322

sons of perdition, 48

sows the tares, 132

that old serpent, 45

the Twelve must battle Satan and his evil ways that come against the Saints, 427

the whore, even Babylon, 133

transgressors are cut off and delivered to the buffetings of, 351

turned over to the buffetings of, 91

will lay waste the enemies of, 336

witchcraft of Salem, 437

would be there to turn their hearts from the truth, 83

Savior, 39, 43, 44, 50, 52, 58, 62, 64, 111,
124, 137, 151, 187, 188, 198, 208,
225, 261, 284, 321, 412, 414, 419,
459, 464, 504, 510, 524, 526, 553,
562, 566, 569, 570, 576, 581, 591,
620
   advent of the Savior into the spirit
world, 620
   Ascension, 118
   Jesus Christ, 166, 177, 626
   of the world, 606
   received the Holy Ghost, 224
   taught the Nephites, 99
   those who came with the, 576
   used symbolism of salt in the Sermon
on the Mount, 297
   words to the thief on the cross, 619
saviors
   of men, 297, 326, 330
   on Mount Zion, 31, 526
savor of men
   the gospel brings seasoning, or
understanding to the purpose of
life, 330
School
   of the Elders, 187, 254, 371
   of the Prophets, 183, 186, 187, 191,
204, 209, 211, 240, 243
Scott, Richard G., 557
scriptural evidence, 60, 513
   first, 513
   second, 515
   third, 516
   fourth, 517
   fifth, 518
scriptures, 5, 9, 313
   expound the, 6
   know and understand the, 50
   purity of, 60
   translation of, 21, 23, 41
sealed testimony
   would condemn the wicked, 603
Sealing Power, 550
Second
   Comforter, 189, 498, 530, 557

Coming, 30, 32, 97, 99, 129, 142, 144,
149, 150, 218, 251, 265, 282, 292,
294, 330, 343, 410, 412, 444, 451,
470, 480, 525, 564, 575, 578–580,
585, 603
   key to second coming, 28
second
   example not of god, 540
   key to discern an angel, 523
   scriptural evidence, 515
   trump, 151
   Vision
      the Fall of Satan, 44
secret acts of men, 153
seek
   first the kingdom of God, 235
   the guidance of the Lord, 103
Seneca County, 519, 632
separate United Orders, 359
servants testimony sealed, 579
set in order
   all the affairs, 205
   all the affairs of this church, 211
   all the affairs of this church and
kingdom, 211
   all the other officers of the church,
374, 390
   and direct the affairs of the Church,
433
   by the Twelve agreeable, 390
   his family, 232
   the churches, 205, 210
   the house of God, 127, 129, 130
   thy house, 232
your homes, 205
   your houses, 211
   your own house, 232
Seth, 386–388, 444, 622, 624
settle differences
   where stakes were not organized, 317
seven
   angels, 31, 32, 149, 150
      fly through heaven, 148
      sounding their trumpets, 149
      will disclose all things, 154

seals, 27, 28
 trumps, 32
seventh angel, 32, 145, 146, 152–154
Seventy, 382
shake off the dust of your feet, 13, 16
Shalersville, 11
Shalmaneser
 king of Assyria, 33, 570
shedding of blood, 303, 344, 593
Shem, 101, 624
 son of Noah, 101
 the great high priest, 622
Sherman, Lyman, 397
Sherwood, Henry G., 491, 499
shout for joy, 512, 520, 632, 633
shy
 ashamed, 212
Simon the Canaanite, 606
Simpson, Robert L., 322
sixth
 angel, 32, 145, 152, 153
 seal, 30
 vision, 57
  the Telestial Kingdom, 56
slaves, 142
Smith Jr., Joseph Fielding, 49
Smith, Don C., 456, 477, 500
Smith, Eden, 18
Smith, Emma, 533, 551
Smith, George A., 410, 499, 599
Smith, George Albert, 61, 261
 the love of all mankind, 604
Smith, Hyrum, 157, 196, 239, 334, 422,
  427, 428, 435, 439, 440, 442, 476,
  477, 480, 481, 490, 491, 493–498,
  505, 535, 586–591, 593, 597, 625,
  631
Smith, Joseph, 2, 5–8, 11, 21, 24, 30, 33, 37,
  38, 40–43, 45, 47, 49, 50, 52, 54,
  57, 60, 81, 83, 89, 97, 99, 102,
  104, 105, 119, 131, 147, 157, 167,
  177, 179, 180, 189, 196, 197, 203,
  206–208, 218, 220, 224, 226,
  232–234, 242, 243, 246, 257, 260,
  276, 278, 279, 283, 287, 300, 306,
  309, 311, 312, 326, 332–334, 340,
  343, 352, 357, 359, 372, 377, 378,
  382, 388, 389, 400, 402, 408,
  414–416, 424, 431, 437, 439, 440,
  442, 444, 461, 466, 469, 475, 477,
  478, 480, 487, 488, 491, 492, 494,
  504, 505, 508, 516, 518, 521, 523,
  526, 532, 533, 535, 536, 538, 545,
  547, 554, 555, 568, 571, 573, 578,
  583–585, 587, 588, 590–593,
  596, 598, 602, 624, 631
 and all the presidents, 415
 every angel who held any keys in
  previous dispensations from
  Adam, 523
 had the qualifications to speak about
  angels, 523
 has done more save Jesus only, 587
 History of the Church, 2
 "I shall die innocent," 589
 my name should be had for good and
  evil, 466
 prophecy of, 341
 said Song of Solomon not inspired,
  345
silence, ye fiends of the infernal pit, 467
 takes leave, 508
 Teachings of the Prophet Joseph Smith
  (book), 23–25, 30, 33, 36, 38, 41,
  42, 46, 49, 50, 82, 83, 97, 102,
  104, 106–108, 111, 114, 137, 138,
  144, 147, 165, 167, 171, 177, 179,
  188, 190, 206–208, 224, 226,
  228–231, 235, 237, 252, 262, 277,
  285, 291, 313, 317, 321, 327, 329,
  348, 366, 382, 385–387, 389, 392,
  397–399, 403, 419, 434, 441, 445,
  446, 456–458, 460–462, 468,
  471, 482–484, 491, 503, 511, 517,
  523, 526, 527, 530, 531, 543,
  546–548, 551, 554, 557, 566, 569,
  577, 583, 589, 590, 592, 597, 609,
  612, 613, 619, 629
 the Prophet, 1, 10, 12, 23–25, 30, 31,
  33, 36, 38, 39, 41, 42, 46, 48, 82,
  88, 94, 104, 106, 108, 111, 114,

130, 134, 136–138, 144,
147–149, 153, 164, 165, 167, 171,
179, 187, 190, 191, 207, 208, 214,
217, 225, 226, 228–230, 235, 237,
252, 262, 276, 278, 291, 306, 313,
319, 321, 329, 348, 349, 366, 379,
382, 384, 386, 387, 389, 392, 397,
398, 403, 410, 414, 415, 419, 433,
438, 441, 444–446, 449, 451, 453,
461, 482–485, 492, 499, 504, 505,
511, 517, 518, 526, 529, 530, 534,
543, 545, 547, 548, 556, 558, 566,
568, 581, 586, 587, 592, 609, 610,
612, 615, 619, 623, 625, 627, 628,
631

the Prophet and Seer, 587
the Prophet and Seer of the Lord, 631
Translation, 184, 239, 511, 603
translation of the Bible, 360
vision, 62, 609, 622
when Joseph was 85 years old, 525
when the lord requires no more, 486
Smith, Joseph F., 136, 194, 209, 214, 270,
398, 418
establishing the doctrine of the
Church, 604
Gospel Doctrine (book), 136, 214, 270,
398
I know this record is true, 626
letter of the First Presidency, 130
vision concerning the Savior's visit to
the spirits of the dead, 614
vision of the redemption of the dead,
609
vision of the spirit world, 55
Smith, Joseph Fielding, 18, 36, 45, 124,
138, 155, 156, 189, 199, 214, 230,
255, 349, 391, 415, 433, 451, 455,
494, 498, 504, 557, 581, 592, 609,
627
Answers to Gospel Questions (book),
49
*Church History and Modern
Revelation* (book), 18, 45, 155,
199, 455
Doctrines of Salvation (book), 138,

156, 165, 189, 255, 349, 391, 433,
451, 498, 504, 505, 538, 549, 557,
558, 581, 593, 627
the doctrine of the Church, 604
The Progress of Man (book), 231
Smith, Joseph Sen., 205, 212, 213, 312, 318,
352, 359, 389, 481, 494
Smith, Lucy Mack
*History of Joseph Smith, By His
Mother, Lucy Mack Smith*
(book), 494
Smith, Samuel, 13
Smith, Samuel H., 15, 157, 312, 318, 501
Smith, Sylvester, 319
Smith, William, 499
Snider, John, 482, 489
Snow, Erastus, 437, 599
Snow, Lorenzo, 234, 368
freeing the Church from debt through
the law of tithing, 603
The Teachings of Lorenzo Snow
(book), 368
solemn
assembly, 162, 178–180, 182, 184,
188, 241, 404
covenant, 558
Son of Ahman, 84, 85, 244
Son of God, 36, 56, 102, 189, 223, 234, 244,
376, 416, 420, 451, 498, 523, 592,
614–618, 621–623
King Immanuel, 521
Only Begotten, 626
preached unto the spirits in prison,
620
redeemer and deliverer, 618, 620
Song in Zion, 121
Song of Solomon, 345
sons of perdition, 46–50, 65–67, 151, 152,
170, 172, 173, 580
Sorokin, Pitirum, 142
soul of man, 159, 168, 230, 531
sound of the trump, 14, 495
sources of the words of eternal life
(1) the Light of Christ, 114
(2) the Holy Ghost, 114

(3) the scriptures, 115
(4) words of the Lord's servants, 116
South Carolina, 139–141
Southern States, 139, 141, 142, 155, 284
speculations and false claims, 130
Spirit
    of Christ, 114
    of God, 66, 71, 103, 226, 230, 308, 320,
        590
    of Truth, 63, 65, 68, 164, 178, 189,
        218, 222, 223, 225, 228, 391
spirit of man, 25
    existed from eternity, 235
    is a combination of the intelligence
        and the spirit which is an entity
        begotten of God, 231
    is not a created being, 235
    was innocent in the beginning, 218,
        229
    will exist into eternity, 235
spirit of meekness, 283, 478, 480, 552
spirit speaketh the truth, 227
spirit world, 55, 151, 174, 339, 519, 578,
        580, 612, 614, 616–618, 620, 621,
        625, 626, 632
spirits
    can only be revealed in flaming fire
        and glory, 523
    of the dead, 307, 614, 626
St. George Temple, 264
St. Paul, 111, 165
stake
    high council, 318, 374, 386, 500
    of Zion, 238, 293, 329, 352, 359, 368,
        391, 441, 500, 595, 599, 601
standard works, 42, 101, 115, 184
standing high council, 384, 386
steady the ark, 128–130
stealing, 434
stem of Jesse, 583, 584
    rod from the, 583
stewardships and love, 480
still many are kept from the truth, 470
still small voice, 127, 129, 130, 136, 178
    pierceth all things, 130

storehouse, 76, 78–80, 82, 90, 92, 93, 205,
        212, 213, 289, 305, 363
    bishops, 79, 82
    for the poor of my people, 82
    in Jackson County, 306
    major purpose of, 78
    of the Lord, 364
    supplement wants, 78
    surplus commodities, 78
    to benefit the whole church, 86
    to receive the funds of the church, 77
strength
    of mine house, 300, 340
    of my house, 333, 334, 336, 340, 343
    of our God, 61
    of these stakes, 293
    of Zion, 342
strifes, 290, 341
surplus property, 365
sun, moon, and stars, 147
Susquehanna
    County, 519, 632
    River, 519, 520, 632
sword, 143, 253, 260, 288, 456, 466
    and bloodshed, 143
    and by bloodshed, 142
    of mine indignation, 290
symbolism
    of His clothing color, 575
    of salt in the Sermon on the Mount,
        297
    of the Lord polishing of His jewels,
        296
    of the winepress, 153

—T—

tabernacle of God, 218, 229, 230
Talmage, James E., 581
Tanner, N. Eldon, 215, 322
    Official Declaration—2, 605
Taylor, John, 44, 61, 306, 319, 323, 332,
        432, 499, 501, 555, 586–588, 625,
        631
    in *Messages of the First Presidency*
        (book), 61

in *Journal of Discourses* (book), 306, 501

the organizing and functioning of the priesthood, 603

Tazewell County, 284

teachings of
any others who come before them as revelations or commandments, 395

Jesus as He ministered in Palestine, 537

Jesus Christ during His forty-day ministry, 508

Moroni, 520

the Book of Mormon, 116

the gospel of Jesus Christ, 163

the Lord Jesus Christ, 556

the modern prophets and Apostles, 233

the Prophet Joseph Smith, 451

the Shakers, 534

telestial, 56, 59, 62, 70–72, 151, 154, 577
beings, 54, 580

earth, 25, 27

glory, 56, 71, 160, 169, 170, 530, 537

inheritance, 56

kingdom, 38, 47, 55–58, 61, 62, 156, 169, 170, 174

law, 159, 190

men, 58

people, 25, 48, 291

spirits, 152

wickedness, 153

world, 38, 54, 57, 58, 73

tempests, 144, 146, 148

temple
building, 504

cornerstone, 299

endowment, 190, 339, 340, 549

in Far West, 441

in the New Jerusalem, 97

is the Lord's university, 339

must be built in Zion, 97

of God, 230

temple ordinances, 339, 437, 510

are absolutely crucial, 420

culminating blessing of the gospel, 416

for the living, 416

temporal and spiritual welfare, 9

temporal salvation
is different than a temporal law, 194

of all saints in the last days, 193

of the children of men, 199

of the Saints in the last days, 192

terrestrial, 54, 56, 71, 72, 151
creations, 294

glory, 54, 59, 160, 169, 170, 190, 530, 537, 577

terrestrial kingdom, 38, 47, 54, 61, 62, 159, 169, 170, 174

law, 159

laws, 190

nature, 39

order, 156

peoples, 48

planet, 27, 154

requirements, 291

resurrection, 151

world, 54, 58, 70

testimony sealed, 579
with blood, 602

Thayer, Ezra, 157

third and final stage of man
the resurrected state, 230

third
angel, 145

key is to discern the devil, 523

scriptural evidence, 516

trump, 151, 152

vision—Sons of Perdition, 46

Thompson, Robert D., 475, 480, 481, 496

three grand orders of priesthood
(1) Melchizedek, 387

(2) patriarchal authority, 387

(3) Levitical or Aaronic, 387

witnesses
three, to the Book of Mormon, 371

three-fold mission of the Church
(1) proclaim the gospel of the Lord

Jesus Christ to every nation, kindred, tongue, and people, 419
(2) perfect the Saints, 416, 419
(3) redemption of the dead, 418
thunderings, 148
thy friends do still stand by thee, 457
thy people shall never be turned against thee, 465
Times and Seasons (publication), 44, 62, 73, 160, 174, 196, 332, 435, 454, 457, 458
times of the Gentiles, 99
tithing, 52, 129, 364, 366, 367
    and sacrifice, 247, 249
    law of, 364–366
    lesser law of, 348
    of labor and time, 250
    of my people, 249, 250, 365
    one-tenth of all their interest, 368
    part of the law, 129
    pay a full, 368, 369
    pay tithing in full, 368
    promised blessing of, 129
tongue of the dumb shall speak, 117
translate
    hasten to, and obtain knowledge, 233
translating the Apocrypha, 217
translation of
    glad tidings is the Hebrew translation of gospel, 519
    my holy word, 492
    my scriptures, 238
    New Testament, 101
    of the Scriptures, 5
    the Bible, 211, 217, 360, 517
    the Bible to His Saints, 12
    the Old Testament, 217, 536
    the prophets, 204, 210
    the scriptures, 21, 23, 41, 234, 362
traveling
    high council, 318, 374, 384, 385, 499, 500
    high priests abroad, 317
    presiding high council, 373, 384
treasury, 352, 353, 361–363, 527

another prepared, 362
tribulation(s)
    after much, 331
    and perils, 467
    comparing the Son of Man's, with Joseph's, 468
    great and grievous, 200
    of your brethren, 331
    temptations and, 422, 426
    that the Lord knew would come, 84
    travels and, 519, 632
    trials and, 283, 617
trump of an angel
    first, 150
second, 151
    third, 152
    fourth, 152
truth will prevail, 421
twelve tribes, 30, 31, 584
twelve tribes of Israel, 29, 38, 99, 175, 210, 246
two more stewardships, 496
two priesthoods in the Church, 376

—U—

under the covenant, 117, 549
unfaithful and an unwise steward, 362, 363
united order, 93, 348, 351–354, 359, 363, 369
    is an individualistic system, not a communal system, 94
    separate, 359
    was not a communal life, 94
unity, harmony, and charity, 240
unstop the ears of the deaf, 117
unto the wicked he did not go, 618
Urim and Thummim, 24, 25, 535, 584
    white stone, 24
Utah Genealogical Society, 527, 528
Uzzah
    anger of the Lord was kindled against, 131
    God smote him for his error, 131
    put forth his hand to steady the ark of God, 130

—V—

Van Buren County, 287
vanity and unbelief, 115
various tribes of Israel gathered, 412
vicarious
    work, 55
    work for the dead, 540, 620
vision, 1, 37, 38, 42, 43, 45, 47, 48, 54, 58,
        59, 62, 64, 65, 68, 71, 395, 606,
        610–612, 625, 626
    of the Seventy, 395
    of the Almighty, 389, 420
voice(s)
    of the people, 273, 314
    from Heaven, 519

—W—

walk in all the ordinances, 598
war upon all nations, 139, 140
war would begin
    in South Carolina, 141
warning voice to keep the inhabitants from
        sleeping, 425
washings and anointings, 485
Washington, George, 264
    camp of, 573
    General, 264, 308
waves of the sea heaving, 146, 148
weak confound the wise, 577
weakest of all saints, 191
Wells, John, 628
Wesley, John, 307
what
    it shall be given, to say 283
    the Lord said, 299
    the Lord said to do, 300
    the servants did, 298
Whitmer, David, 377, 381, 410, 423
Whitmer, Father, 519, 632
Whitmer, John, 5, 89
    History of the Church (book), 33, 570
Whitmer, Peter, 479
Whitney, Newel K., 9, 10, 81, 83, 89, 122,
        157, 218, 245, 246, 319, 351, 352,
        358, 446–448, 501
    Bishop, 10, 123, 191, 213, 232, 449
Whitney, Orson F., 544
whole church under condemnation, 115
whole world lies in sin, 114
whom and what you worship, 219
why pray and persist, 304
wicked generation, 99, 162
Widtsoe, John A., 138, 332
    Evidences and Reconciliation (book),
        332
Wight, Lyman, 325, 334, 476, 480–482, 489
    Colonel, 443
Williams, Clyde J.
    compiler, 368
    editor, 94
    editor of *The Teachings of Howard W.
        Hunter* (book), 190
Williams, Frederick G., 93, 157, 203–206,
        209, 212, 218, 232, 233, 312, 334,
        351, 352, 357, 377, 410, 428, 494,
        609
Williams, Samuel, 500
Wilson, Calves, 13, 15
Wilson, Dunbar, 499
Winter Quarters
    Camp of Israel, 595
Wirthlin, Joseph L., 155
wise steward, 77–79, 596, 600, 601
witnesses, 16, 23, 34, 65, 188, 227, 380,
        426, 512, 514, 520, 558, 587, 591,
        593
    especial, 396
    faithful, 17
    in the mouth of two or three, 101,
        312, 512
    law of, 80
    special, 381, 423, 426
    special witnesses or Apostles, 380
    three, 23, 312, 371, 519, 520, 632
    two special, 593
Woodruff, Wilford, 61, 111, 208, 264, 307,
        382, 432, 499, 555, 599, 605, 625,
        631

in *Journal of Discourses* (book), 61, 308

The Discourses of Wilford Woodruff, 112

The Manifesto, Official Declaration—1, 603

Word of Wisdom, 191, 193–195, 197–202, 471, 604

   a principal with a promise adapted to the weakest of Saints, 192

   adapted to the capacity of the weak and the weakest of all saints, 193

   all grain is made for the use of man and beasts for the staff of life, 192

   all grain, fruits of the vine, above and in the ground, is for man's use, 192

   all wholesome herbs God made for the constitution, nature, and use of man, 192

   each dispensation had its own word of wisdom, 193

   each herb and fruit in their season, 192

   flesh of beasts and fowls are made to use sparingly, 192

   for the benefit of the council of high priests, 193

   given for a principle with promise, 193

   given by revelation, 194

   hot drinks are not for the body or belly, 192

   Moses was given detailed instructions—many due to their being in the wilderness for forty years where sanitation and disease control were major considerations, 193

   shall find wisdom and great treasures of knowledge, hidden treasures, 192

   strong drinks are not for the body, 192

   the reason why the Word of Wisdom

   was given, 194

   tobacco is not good for man, 192

   wheat for man, 192

   wild animals are for man's use in times of famine and excess hunger, 192

   wine and strong drinks are not good, 192

word on baptism for your dead, 509

worship the golden calf, 492

—Y—

Yarn Jr., David H.

   editor, 94, 368, 606

yellow dog prophecy, 341

Young, Brigham, 47, 137, 190, 191, 194, 215, 329, 364, 477, 498, 499, 555, 592, 595, 603, 606, 607, 625, 631

   colonizer, 595

   Discourses of Brigham Young (book), 138, 190, 194, 216, 608

   gave a short address in tongues, 410

   in *Journal of Discourses* (book), 48, 191, 329, 364, 592

   President of the Quorum of the Twelve, 385

   President of the Twelve, 499

   the leading to and colonizing of the West, 603

Young, Joseph, 500

—Z—

Zacharias, 106, 107, 416

   a priest of God, 106

   father of John the Baptist, 30, 106

   son of Barachias, 587

   will attend the great sacrament meeting, 30

Zenos

   Old Testament prophet, 242, 249

Zion

   a specific place of gathering, 328

   arise and put on her garments, 89

   as the land of America, 327

build up the waste places of, 292
building of the waste places of, 331
built by the Law of the Celestial
    Kingdom, 337
children of, 115, 297, 303, 304, 334,
    586
eight things that must be
    accomplished before Zion will
    be redeemed
eight more things that must be
    accomplished before that
    redemption will come to pass,
    338–339
establish a center place of, 329
in the Lord's own due time, 213
is the pure in heart, 251
means, literally, a sunny place, or
    sunny mountain, 327
must become a fruitful tree, 248
reinstitution of the law of
    consecration in, 345
salvation and redemption of, 329
seek to bring forth and establish the
    cause of, 329
shall be great and terrible, 237
shall be redeemed, 286

shall escape if?, 253
strength of, 245, 292, 293
the curtains or the strength of, 293
the pure in heart, 328
two gathering places, 566
when will it be redeemed?, 325, 326
whole of North and South America,
    327
will be redeemed, 306, 327, 338
Zion has three designations, 327
    (1) the land of America, 327
    (2) a specific place of gathering, 327
    (3) the pure in heart, 327
Zion's Camp, 300, 301, 334, 339, 340, 343,
    371
    failed collectively to qualify for the
        Lord to fight their battles, 341
    individually the Lord had brought
        them thus far for a trial of their
        faith, 341
    journey to Zion, 326
    mission to redeem Zion, 301
    organized to redeem Zion, 338
    was no easy task, 335